CENTURY'S

END

Első évfolyam.

2. szám.

HILLEL SCHWARTZ

DOUBLEDAY

FOUNDED JANUARY 1900

NEW YORK LONDON TORONTO SYDNEY AUCKLAND

CENTURY'S END

A CULTURAL HISTORY OF THE FIN DE SIÈCLE FROM THE 990s THROUGH THE 1990s

PUBLISHED BY DOUBLEDAY
a division of Bantam Doubleday Dell Publishing Group, Inc.

666 Fifth Avenue, New York, New York 10103

DOUBLEDAY and the portrayal of an anchor with a dolphin are
trademarks of Doubleday, a division of Bantam Doubleday
Dell Publishing Group, Inc.

Library of Congress Cataloging-in-Publication Data

Schwartz, Hillel, 1948–
    Century's end : a cultural history of the fin de siècle from
the 990s through the 1990s / Hillel Schwartz.—1st ed.
      p. cm.
    Bibliography: p.
    Includes index.
    1. Civilization, Modern—1950– 2. Millennium.
    3. One thousand, A.D. 4. Civilization—History. I. Title.
    II. Title: Fin-de-siècle from the 990s through the 1990s.
    CB428.S39 1990
    909—dc20   89-35097
    ISBN 0-385-24379-0   CIP

Frontispiece is from the masthead of the Budapest magazine
A Század Vége (January 10, 1892). Courtesy of the Széchényi
National Library, Budapest.

To the memory of
those born near last century's end

Minnie Levin, 1881–1980
Hyman Levin, 1882–1967
Ben Schwartz, 1895–1976
Gussie Schwartz, 1896–1976
Roger Dagan, 1897–1988
Sandra Dagan, 1904–1987

PREFACE

Drawing adapted from a Greek coin by Sir Edward J. Poynter for the title page of *The Nineteenth Century and After*, January 1901.

WHAT TO EXPECT

The future is empty and is filled by our imagination. Our imagination can only picture a perfection on our scale. It is just as imperfect as we are; it does not surpass us by a single hair's breadth.

Simone Weil

FOREGONE CONCLUSIONS

CONCLUSIONS

THE

LEGEND

OF THE

YEAR

1000

—

Fire descending from the sky, and a huge dragon seen through a fissure in the heavens, depicted in Stanislaus Lubienietzki's *Theatrum cometicum* (Amsterdam, 1666–68), based on the 12th-century annals of Sigebert of Gembloux, one of the earliest to describe the celestial wonders of the year 1000 A.D. (or A.C., Anno Christi).

ONCE UPON A TIME, ON THE EVE OF THE YEAR 1000, the people of Europe were stricken with panic. The end of the millennium, so it is thought, had long been anticipated by prophets, prelates, monks, mathematicians, soothsayers, and surveyors of stars. None of them had anything good to say about Anno Domini 1000, for the world that year was to be drawn to its catastrophic conclusion. Throughout the 10th Christian century, men wrote nervously pious prologues into their last testaments, acknowledging not only the brevity and jeopardy of their charitable lives but also the precariousness of the world itself in this the last age. Royal charters began with allusions to "the wanton fortune of this deceiving world, not lovely with the milk-white radiance of unfading lilies, but odious with the gall-steeped bitterness of lamentable corruption, raging with venomous wide-stretched jaws." Those jaws would soon swallow whole villages in earthquakes, devour the countryside with plagues, drought, and famine. Portents of apocalypse appeared in the somber eyes of two-headed calves out by the barn and in the terribly bright tails of comets overhead. The skies were as crowded with unaccountable marvels as shrines were with newly uncovered relics. In the clouds, armies of ghosts fought battles between claps of thunder while serpents twined themselves into halos of light. Sun and moon were obscured so often by eclipse that the earth was constantly dark with foreboding.

No wonder that knights and ladies donated their lands to the Church, gave their belongings to beggars, and headed for Jerusalem; nor that merchants left off trading in the ephemeral goods of this aged world and made for monasteries; nor that peasants abandoned their livestock and crops to make pilgrimage to the nearest sacred relic. Shopkeepers in December of 999, it is written, closed up shop and distributed their money to the poor. At home, wives forgave adulterous husbands, and husbands forgave adulterous wives. Children were released from their school benches by masters who saw no point in *trivium* or *quadrivium* so close unto the world's end.

The terror accelerated. There came monstrous downpours of rain, raging once-in-a-blue-moon floods, epidemics as rampant as the crosses painted hastily on shields. Double suns and strange flying objects moved through the heavens in blithe disregard of scholastic subtleties and philosophical conventions. Buildings left to decay across the penultimate years began to topple; churches themselves were in states of such perilous ruin that the pious at their prayers must have been almost as frightened of walls collapsing immediately upon them as of the imminent collapse of civilization entire. Where there was not prayerfulness amidst ruins, there was public flagellation and lamentation, private resort to suicide, double suicide. Wandering hermits delivered impromptu, impassioned sermons urging repentance in the few days remaining before Judgment.

In Rome, a city as decayed as the empire at whose center it sat, the new Pope was a necromancer, astrologer, and wizard who consorted with Arabic numerals, mechanical clocks, and other powers of darkness. Whether he was the Antichrist was uncertain, but surely the learned monk Gerbert had taken the name of Sylvester II in order that he might stand in relation to the young Emperor Otto III as the first Pope Sylvester had stood in relation to Constantine, who established Christianity as the religion of the late Roman Empire. Otto III himself was hoping that the onset of the millennial year would confirm his ambitions at once for the holy and the imperial, if just for an atom of an instant before the End.

New Year's Eve, December 31, 999, found Christians everywhere in decrepit churches and chapels, awaiting with utmost anxiety whatever the pregnant darkness would bring forth on the stroke of midnight. The suspense of that hour united Christendom in a single community of faith and fear. From Gibraltar to the Baltic, from the English Channel to the Bosporus, from Rome to Constantinople to Jerusalem, the fearful and the faithful gathered their loved ones about them and looked up expectantly toward the celestial vault of the medieval heavens.

When nothing remarkable happened, when the world entered intact upon the year 1000, Sylvester II at his special midnight mass in Rome turned to the astonished congregation, who lifted up their voices to the Lord in the *Te Deum* and hallelujah choruses while clocktowers chimed in the second Christian millennium and bells rang out from all the steeples. Grand sighs of relief became even grander breaths of fresh air as people turned to the rebuilding of dilapidated chapels, the foundation of monasteries, the creation of Romanesque cathedrals, until the landscape was cloaked in a "white mantle" of churches. Hungary, Poland, Russia converted to the True Faith in one miraculous gasp. European society, redeemed and transformed, expanded outward under full sails, soon unfurling crusader flags to reclaim Jerusalem from the heathens. Viking raiders vanished into thin (northern) air, the international climate softened, and sweet winds blew across the wilderness where serfs energetically cleared away first growth for a surging population bound now for that series of renaissances which would propel them into modernity. If ostensibly anticlimactic, the calendrical millennium turned out to have been (and still to be) extraordinarily convenient, a supernally notable year in which the West, after the doldrums of the Dark Ages, at last shook off the reins of barbarians who had not so much succeeded the classical world as ridden roughshod over it. The year 1000 was, if not the ultimate *annus terribilis*, certainly an *annus mirabilis*. A year of miracles. A year to remember.

Of such violet prose and violent anachronism has the legend of the year 1000 been constituted.[1] Lest I be accused of wantonness in my reconstruction of the legend, allow 18th-century Scottish historian William Robertson his say concerning the "panic terror" around and about the year 1000: "A general consternation seized mankind; many relinquished their possessions, and abandoning their friends and families, hurried with precipitation to the Holy Land, where they imagined that Christ would quickly appear to judge the world." Or Robertson's compatriot, Charles Mackay, writing in 1852 of *Extraordinary Popular Delusions and the Madness of Crowds*: "In the year 999, the number of pilgrims proceeding eastward, to await the coming of the Lord in that city, was so great that they were compared to a desolating army. . . . Buildings of every sort were suffered to fall into ruins. It was thought useless to repair them, when the end of the world was so near. . . . Knights, citizens, and serfs travelled eastwards in company, taking with them their wives and children, singing psalms as they went, and looking with fearful eyes upon the sky, which they expected each minute to open, to let the Son of God descend in his glory." Or the French poet Eugène Mordret, Mackay's contemporary, situating us near midnight of the fateful year:

> *Brothers, do you hear the roaring tempest,*
> *Do you hear the woods moan as they twist*
> *Beneath the winds unloosed by God's strong arms,*
> *Do you hear the foundations of the world split apart?*

"It is impossible at this late day," wrote an American commentator in 1857, "to imagine the terror which reigned throughout Christendom as the thousandth year from the birth of Christ approached," but even later in the day, one hundred years later, a German analyst of prophecies and predictions would indeed imagine that terror, calling attention to the very number itself, the number 1000, "which oppressed Europe like a nightmare. A wave of fatalism seized the people. . . . Whole towns repaired to church as one man, or assembled round crucifixes under the open sky." And now, at this latest of hours, twilight of the 20th century, Charles F. Berlitz in *Doomsday, 1999 A.D.* has written of that earlier doomsday, "As the year 999 neared its end a sort of mass hysteria took hold of Europe." Debts were forgiven, convicts released from prison, men and women absolved of their infidelities. Pilgrims whipped themselves along the road to Jerusalem while others, beset by visions of flaming swords and arrows shooting through the sky, took another avenue toward apocalypse: there came "a wave of suicides," writes Berlitz, "as people sought to punish themselves in advance of Doomsday or simply could not stand the pressure of waiting for Judgment Day."[2]

None of this is true. Not the suicides, not the flaming swords, not the whips. Not the absolution, nor the parole, nor the forgiveness of debts. Not the mass hysteria, the fatalism, the nightmare, the terror of the number itself. Not the families abandoned (or swept up) by an army of pilgrims, nor the wealth divested (or spent on saddlebag supplies) by pilgrim knights, pilgrim serfs. No, not the buildings left to decay, not the churches in ruins. Not even the panic itself, unless all accounts of general consternation have been suppressed. And no mechanical clocks to strike the midnight hour at millennium's end, no hallelujah choruses at a minute past twelve.

None of it—at least according to the last hundred years of scholarship. A score of medievalists have published books and articles in Italian, French, English, and German,[3] demolishing the evidence for a "panic terror" at the approach of the year 1000. They have traced the modern origins of the legend back to the end of the 16th century, to seven lines on the first page of the eleventh volume of the *Annales ecclesiastici* of Cardinal Cesare Baronio, Vatican librarian twice nearly elected pope. Thence, after an equally brief 1633 French Catholic notice of churches in ruins around the turn of the millennium, to the second edition of the *Annales Hirsaugienses* of the German abbot Johannes Tritheim (d. 1516), who in his original edition had presumed an earthquake and a horrible comet for the year 1000 but had neglected to mention any millennial fears, which fears were introduced posthumously by his editors, the monks of St. Gall, in 1690. Thence through a few further notices of

architectural decay and the pages of William Robertson to the French bourgeois republicans of 1830, who saw in the July Revolution an end to the
ancien régime as final as the year 1000 must have been an end to the Dark
Ages. Thence into the mainstream of 19th-century encyclopedias, dictionaries, literary annals, novels, and comic operas, prompted by the excited
narratives of that most popular of historians, Jules Michelet. Michelet's year
1000 was a mélange of marvels and monitions scraped from all corners of
the 10th and 11th centuries, with reference as well to the Etruscans, who
had set a prophetic term of ten centuries to their own civilization and had
found it, sadly, to be too true.[4]

Leaving the Etruscans aside for the nonce, what remains true of the
legend of the millennial panic, in the wake of the conventional demolition,
is as follows. Centuries of medieval charters and wills had conventional
prologues or epilogues alluding to the last age of the world, drawn from
assorted rhetorical formulas and never specific as to the date of the End. A
small book about the Antichrist, filling out his *vita* but making no claims
as to his dates, was written around 954 by the Abbot Adso for Queen
Gerberge of France, then sent with a new preface to the Archbishop of
Cologne in 999. Two prophecies of impending judgment may have circulated
after 960, one from a hermit speaking with chronologically vague urgency
to a council of princes in Worms, the other delivered in Paris without
repercussion, though specific as to the advent of the Antichrist in the year
1000. Fears about a comet were expressed in 975, as also fears that decade
about Annunciation Day falling on Good Friday in 973, 981, or 992. A
comet did appear on December 4, 1000 (or 999, or 1001). The earth probably
did quake in 999 or 1000, and there must have been storms, as usual, and
perhaps half a dozen celestial wonders—as in many other medieval years for
which we have annals. In 1000, Holy Roman Emperor Otto III left Ravenna
for Ratisbon, then for Poland and the coronation of Bołeslaw the Mighty.
Near the close of the millennial year, a French peasant claimed to have been
possessed by a swarm of bees, who inspired him to chase away his wife,
trample crucifixes, and repudiate church tithes. With a large entourage of
other peasants, Leutard debated the local bishop, then (wrote hostile chroniclers) drowned himself in a well.[5]

It might have been far wiser, as we shall see, to construct a legend around
the year 1033, yet the legend of the year 1000 reappears today in allusions
so constant and casual that there must be—mustn't there?—much more to
it than an obscure prophecy, a comet, a quake, and a swarm of bees. Despite
our conservative medievalists with their scrutiny of sources, the millennial

"panic terror" surfaces again and again in the works of prominent modern historians, literary analysts, cultural critics, political commentators, university presidents, novelists, journalists, and futurologists.[6] Even those who have become resigned to the legend as fiction have tended to exalt the year 1000 as a turning point in Western Civilization. The famous Belgian historian Henri Pirenne said in 1922, "It is doubtless untrue that men expected the end of the world in the year 1000. Yet the century which came in at that date is characterized, in contrast with the preceding one, by a recrudescence of activity so marked that it could pass for the vigorous and joyful awakening of a society long oppressed by a nightmare of anguish."[7] Austrian historian Franz Borkenau wrote in the 1950s, "Modern research has added many qualifications to the statement of the chronicler Raoul Glaber, who reported that the West expected the end of the world in 1000 A.D. But Glaber's statement, even if historically incorrect, must yet reflect the mood of his age," which soon shifted to accomplish the "final break with the aboriginal Germanic tradition of lonely prowess."[8] More recently, the eminent French historian Georges Duby has acknowledged, "One would be wrong to believe in the terrors of the Year One Thousand." But, he goes on, "one must admit in return, that the best Christians of that time lived with a latent anxiety and that, meditating upon the Gospel, they made of their anxiety a virtue."[9]

The legend too has had its virtue bespoken, *as* legend, by more than one authority eyeing a new (calendrical) millennium. "Of old," wrote medievalist and theologian Etienne Gilson in 1949, "children were taught to hold as certain that around the year One Thousand a great terror took possession of people. We were told so, at any rate, and we believed it, and the really amazing thing is that all was not completely false in this story. . . . [I]f the terrors of the year One Thousand are not a certainty for today's historians, those of the year Two Thousand will surely be so for future historians. . . . On the threshold of a new millennium, man has the proud conviction that the day is perhaps not far off when he himself will be able to explode the planet." Writing for a different generation of children in 1973, popular chronicler Daniel Cohen explains, "Perhaps the year 1000 meant little to men of the Middle Ages, but the year 2000 means a great deal to modern numerologists who believe that there is an overpowering significance to certain numbers and dates. Already there have been numerous predictions that 'something,' a great war, a great religious revival, perhaps something as catastrophic as the end of the world will take place in that year."[10]

Something, surely, is going on here, something which demolition expert George L. Burr caught wind of in 1901: "But, I hear you exclaim, you who have felt how awesome, even in these rational days, is the ending of a century, how could there help being terror, in that age, at the close of a millennium?"[11] As usual, we come to our end of century as others have come to theirs—convinced of exhaustion, extreme peril, exorbitant risk, explosive transformation. This *fin de siècle*, like those before it, is the last gasp, the critical moment, the overture to a new age. Everything we love is falling apart around us and we can only hope for a good death; everything we deplore is falling away and the pangs of a great birth are upon us. At century's end we are inevitably host to an oxymoronic time: the best and the worst, the most desperate and the most exultant; the most constrained and the most chaotic.

And, somehow, we mean it to be this way. Although each generation may speak of itself as uniquely cursed, uniquely blessed, at century's end the calendar and our own cultural clocks encourage us toward extremes. Whether we be devoted to holding ourselves remote or prepared to thrust ourselves into the amazing flux, the turn of the century is remarkable and unavoidable. The cat must be let out of the bag, the rabbit pulled from the hat.

In a sense, of course, the century's end is a trick, a little razzle-dazzle with nines and zeros. The end of a millennium—*our* century's end, with three nines, then three zeroes, then a Stanley Kubrick film—is more theatrical an illusion, so more compelling, and it too has more than a little of the confidence game about it. We lead ourselves, as in any confidence game, to the belief that it is now or never. According to our dispositions, we will invest in futures, the 2, or divest ourselves just before the 000.

If the *fin de siècle* is a trick, it is a trick that in the West has been played at least seven times before, a trick that works because we are time-minded enough to prospect for ends, numerate but visionary enough to be impressed by imaginary numbers, punctual enough to attend to a common calendar of years. This book is dedicated to tracking the Western tradition of the *fin de siècle* and to determining how the trick may be next played out on our final approach to the third millennium.

The Millennium, if it too is a trick, is a much older trick, the trump of jubilee. Never put into effect, the jubilee of the Hebrew Bible was meant by post-exilic authorities as the climax to a series of seven sabbatical years, a fiftieth year of festival restitution—the release of Jewish slaves, the restoration of property bought from fellow Jews. Inaugurated by the blowing of the great ram's horn trumpet (or jubal), the jubilee was in theory the sabbath of sabbaths, modelled perhaps on the old pentecontal calendar which had yielded a festival each fiftieth day after seven seven-day weeks. The seventh day of the week had originally been considered so unlucky that work was to be avoided at all costs. In Jewish post-exilic times, this seventh day, the sabbath, gradually assumed an ephod of holiness, becoming not only, as in Babylonia, a private "day of quieting of the heart," but also a day of public worship. Similarly, the seventh or sabbatical year, which began as a year of fields and vineyards lying fallow, became identified with ideas of purification and the cancellation of Jewish debts. During the time of the Maccabees, in the late 2nd century B.C., was composed the apocalyptic *Book of Jubilees*, which extended the significance of the jubilee cycle to world history, each historical period the span of a jubilee. Elevating a ritual jubilation into a messianic age required but this new world-historical frame of reference and the Psalmist's magniloquent claim (Psalms 90.4) that a thousand years appeared as a single day in the sight of the Lord. Prompted as well by Zoroastrian (Mazdean) cosmology and the emphasis on the Psalmist's thousand-year days in 2 Peter 3.8, Christian theologians of the 2nd century A.D. transformed world history into a world-week, and the seventh day thereof into the world-sabbath, a jubilee of sweetness, peace, and earthly delight after six thousand-year days of human labor. Such was the "Chiliad" (Greek) or "Millennium" (Latin, for "1000") which early Christians awaited in the nearest of futures. Although St. Augustine at the end of the 4th century repudiated the doctrine of an imminent, paradisiacal Millennium in favor of a last world age coterminous with the inestimable tenure of the Church itself, millenarian calculations and expectations would survive his sophisticated conservatism and continue on as a vital motif in Catholicism, then in Lutheranism and sectarian Protestantism, down to the present, across such pregnant years as 1260, 1492, 1588, 1666, 1789, 1844, . . . toward 1999 and the year 2000.[12]

Endtime prophecies have not always or necessarily been focused on the calendrical ends of centuries. Millenarians labor to larger purposes, bent on genealogies of creation and destruction, symmetries of exile and redemption. But, at the end of each century, the rest of us come to share with millenarians a sense of suspense, a held breath. Our cultural inheritance of *fin de siècle* experiences has set us up to expect the end of a century to be the end of an era, the new century to initiate a new age. We may not hurry into white gowns or gather on hilltops, but at each century's end, the X's on the calendar do seem darker, do seem to be leading us beyond the run-of-the-mill toward apocalypse.

"Apocalypse," at root, is bravely neutral: the drawing back of a veil. The word, however, has taken on the Christian stigmata of John of Patmos's bloody prospectus for the End, as depicted in his *Apocalypse* or *Book of Revelation*, whence come the seven trumpets, the seven devastating vials, the predatory beasts, the Gog, Magog, and Armageddon which enter with us, willy-nilly, into the 1990s. So Roberto Vacca, envisioning *The Coming Dark Age* in 1971, posted the essential epigraph from Revelation 20.1–5, where the Millennium is introduced after eleven harrowing chapters of *Sturm und Drang*: "And I saw an angel come down from heaven, having the key of the bottomless pit and a great chain in his hand. And he laid hold on the dragon, that old serpent, which is the Devil, and Satan, and bound him a thousand years, And cast him into the bottomless pit, and shut him up, and set a seal upon him, that he should deceive the nations no more, till the thousand years should be fulfilled. . . ." Then Vacca himself began, "I am writing when the second millennium of our era is less than thirty years from completion and when, for reasons different from those of a thousand years ago, many people expect that before long there will be a tragic and total catastrophe." So President Ronald Reagan often told friends in the 1980s, "We may be the generation that sees Armageddon."[13]

Each century's end since the year 1300 has borne ever more vivid witness to the ambivalence inherent in Western millennial visions of decay and disaster aforehand, re-creation and regeneration "in the sweet bye and bye." Nightmares unconfirmed, utopian dreams unfulfilled, these do not fade forever from memory as a new century goes resolutely on. Prophecies unachieved in past '99s, '00s, '01s tend to accumulate toward successive centuries' ends. However disturbing it may seem to the historian accustomed to careful alignment of events in patient sequence, the jumps from one *fin de siècle* to the next have become cumulative, wherefore this book too must needs be at once saltatory and progressive, moving by leaps and bounds from century's end to century's end, and nonetheless building—as the prophecies themselves have built—toward the end of the 20th century, not far from which, at the latest, wrote American architect Ralph Cram in the winter of 1907–08, "the new era will begin."[14]

That we have been preparing for the end of our century further in advance than people in any other century means that those manichaean tensions common to the *fin de siècle* experience will be exaggerated in the 1990s.

Indeed, we can already observe such exaggeration in the 1982 rhetoric of University of Michigan economist Thomas G. Gies: "Revolutionary changes in technology and human values have pushed us to either the brink of doom or the threshold of the greatest Golden Age the world has ever known."[15] *Fin de siècle* sentiments are rarely so polite as to make their entry on the dot of the tenth decade; the phrase *"fin de siècle,"* for example, had its debut in 1886, from which we can date, at least, the French experience of one century's end. Whatever starting date we may assign to our *fin de siècle* (a question I shall address nearer the conclusion), it should become evident in the course of these pages that the 1990s will present a particularly florid episode in the Western tradition of centuries' ends.

Such a prediction, of course, inclines toward precisely that hyperbole of which this book is both a warning and an advertisement. Talk at century's end is always of critical moments and irrevocable decisions, but in these times the choices are etched most starkly as good will or holocaust, ecology or extinction, higher consciousness or the end of (Western) civilization. The millennial pivots seem more razor-edged than ever. Does terrorism take us over the brink into "nuclear Armageddon," or compel us once and for all to overlook national boundaries and work toward world peace? Does the indebtedness of "developing" nations threaten the collapse of the world economy or force upon us global interdependence? Does our pollution of rivers, lakes, oceans, forests, and jungles threaten the suffocation of humanity or confront us with a last, most blatant chance to redeem ourselves by redeeming our planet? Writes Dutch diplomat Jacobus Gijsbertus de Beus in his 1982 book, *Shall We Make the Year 2000? The Decisive Challenge to Western Civilization*, "People went literally mad with fear [on the approach of the year 1000], believing the end of the world was at hand. Today we know that the end of the millennium does not mean the end of the world, at least not through outside, supernatural forces. . . . Our sense of impending doom is growing; it is stronger now than at any point in man's memory."[16]

Yet, thus far, each century's end has been a comedy: we have always made it through, and we have regularly been surprised at just how we did it. Bombast of the "New Age" on one side, bomb blasts of desperation on the other, the century's end has typically made fools of us even as we have made terrible fools of ourselves. Certain cultural constellations come to the fore at the ends of centuries, time and again, for the very reason that we feel it to be the end of a century, feel torn between the sweet distress of endings and the uncertain promises of starting anew. These constellations, increasingly visible over the ends of the last five centuries, have to do with limits and extremes: frontiers, poles, exhaustion, loss, dissociation, disappearance, death, and the realm beyond. Other *fin de siècle* constellations, revolving upon the Janus face of the *turn* of the century, have to do with amnesia and anamnesis, with dichotomy and doubling. Each constellation comes into view at century's end according to contemporary rules of discourse, such that the Double, for instance, appears as incubus at the ends of the 16th and 17th centuries, as Doppelgänger at the end of the 18th, as secondary or competing consciousness at the end of the 19th, and as multiple personality at the end of the 20th.

We may appreciate the influence of these constellations by returning to the legend of the year 1000 and more specifically to the axial position of Pope Sylvester II within that legend. Revered during his lifetime and his brief career as pope (999–1003), he has since become the archetypally ambivalent figure of century's end, century's turn. He has perforce been portrayed as a man of extremes, contracting with demons in order to gain access to the darkest secrets of the natural (and unnatural) worlds of mathematics and astronomy. He has been split down the middle, looking back toward an earlier, imperial Sylvester, and looking forward to crusades while his student Otto III mourns, "The last year of the thousand years is here, and now I go out in the desert to await, with fasting, prayer, and penance, the day of the Lord, and the coming of my Redeemer." It was Sylvester's (supposed) invention of the chiming wheel-clock that split history down the middle, between medieval and modern, or between the binding and the loosing of Satan. For 13th-century Dominicans and 17th-century Protestants, Sylvester became the double-faced antichristian image of imperial (papal) holiness which must reveal at last its evil visage, so Sylvester was "that infamous Sodomite, Necromancer, and Conjuror, under whom the filthinesse and Idolatry of the Romish Church was brought to the height." He was, for playwright August Strindberg at the start of the 20th century, the hero of the middle age, proud of the sudden rise of Christianity on the frontiers of Europe (Poland, Russia, Hungary, Scandinavia), but looking forward at his death to the next millennium: "Those who are alive at the end of another thousand years will perhaps see the ripe fruits, while we have only seen the blossoms." And in 1977, those thousand years nearly up, Frank de Graaf in his *Anno Domini 1000, Anno Domini 2000,* has compared Sylvester to Caiaphas, instrumental in the ritual murder of (the son of) God, Otto III. This objective, scientific pope then sacrificed himself in 1003 in order to save Christianity for the year of reckoning in A.D. 2000, a year we could have reached only through Sylvester's Arabic numerals, mechanical clocks, and astrolabes.[17]

We should not be entirely surprised that the Sylvester legend has still such power, nor that the riotous New Year's Eve of omens and deviltry is still called, in Central Europe, *Silvesternacht*—for our Fausts are preeminently *fin de siècle* figures who must live up to the worst and best of humanity, just as we at century's end feel most strongly torn between enthusiasm and alarm. Is it any relief to learn that, despite his pact with demons, Sylvester (at least in some Catholic versions of his story) confessed to all and was forgiven at the eleventh hour?[18]

One may object here that centuries-old legends do not the centuries make; that it is one thing to remark anxieties at centuries' ends, quite another to give causal prominence to the arbitrary numbers of our calendars; that to move through 1100 years of Western history by setting the tabs for 90 might well be the height of foolishness. Our lives, however, are lived in good measure according to legends (guardedly phrased *vitae*, anecdotes retailed through generations, family histories, grammar-school fables of virtue and good fortune, *National Enquirer* parables of vengeance and saving grace, dogmatic tales of rags-to-riches and riches-to-rags). We also take more seriously than we care to admit a host of arbitrary years (birthdays at 13, 16, 21, 30, and especially 40; "golden" anniversaries; living to be—as I am convinced my mother's mother lived to be—99 or 100). And we do, for reasons I shall later make clear, tend toward prospects and retrospects of exactly one hundred years, from whenever we are, but particularly at centuries' ends.[19]

Agreed, nothing would be so foolish as to claim that all events of import occur at century's end. Natural disasters do not cluster naturally around the '90s. Nor do wars. Economies do not crash because it is the *fin de siècle*, nor do empires have the presence of mind to collapse in '99. Obversely, great inventions are not constrained to the first months of a new century, nor are the greatest poems composed, the greatest ballgowns sewn, the greatest houses designed, the greatest recipes concocted, the greatest symphonies inevitably given their premieres at the turn of the '99 into the '00 or the '00 into the '01. What does happen must be anticlimactic—unless there arrive a Peaceable Kingdom on the kicking heels of Chaos & Consternation. So much are centuries' ends foregone conclusions that when they have passed, we look back upon them with sadness and relief: sadness for moments unseized as well as for dreams momentarily unbounded; relief that the apocalypses (the disasters *and* the revelations) were, if any, minor and manageable. Then, generations down the road, we come upon another century's end, and such is the might of the numbers looming on the horizon that we seem to have learned nothing from the last *fin de siècle* except to enlarge upon the troublesome problem of when, exactly, the hundred years will be over.

Sarcastic, bitter, sometimes passionate debates *in re* a terminus on New Year's Eve, '99, vis-à-vis New Year's Eve, '00, have been prosecuted since the 1690s, and confusion has spread to the mathematics of the millennial year. For Baronio and his (sparse) medieval sources, the excitements of the millennium were centered upon the end of the year 1000, while the end of 999 has since figured more prominently in the legend of the panic terror.[20] Furious debates between precisians, sticklers, country philosophers, plain-spoken engineers, and no-nonsense newspaper editors will doubtless make headlines again this coming decade. Already the crafty ex-President Richard Nixon and the luminous astronomer Carl Sagan have put in their bids for 1999 as symbolic finale to the 20th century and the second Christian millennium.[21] All the heat, and smoke, of these debates, which flame up like prairie fires at the turns of centuries, must belie any postures of indifference we may assume toward the "arbitrary" numbers in the arbitrary squares of our *fin de siècle* calendars.

'Twould be possible to set historical tabs for other decades (the '40s, say, for millenarianism) or by cycles of drought, sunspots, and solar flares.[22] More than any other decade, however, and most unlike climatic cycles, the cultural construct that is the end of a century has been fashioned over seven hundred years of Western history as a cooperative, ecumenical, increasingly international venture. Just in these few introductory pages I have implicated Americans, Austrians, Belgians, Canadians, Dutchmen, Englishmen, Frenchmen, Germans, Italians, Scots, and Swedes in the legend of the year 1000 and the *fin de siècle* cast of mind. Although these have all been men, before long there will be women; although these have all been Christians, before long there will be Jews, Muslims, Marxists, Immortalists, and Buddhists; although these have all been persons of repute, before long there will be more anonymous folk, next-door neighbors. The sexes, the faiths, the classes may each differently express or deflect their anxieties, but the experiences of the *fin de siècle* can be as intense for one as for another.

Should this book appear too intent on claims for the exceptional character of the ends of centuries, lay its obsession to the present epoch, which has been relentlessly represented as exceptional[23] and from whose "unparalleled" dilemmas this author cannot pretend to have escaped. If I take the tools of the cultural historian to our own times, it is not to pose as a prophet but to furnish somewhat of a star chart to the recurrent constellations at centuries' ends and, in consequence, something of a prospective *guide bleu* to the nature of our century's end, and the onset of a new millennium.

The work of this book is threefold. First, I must show how centuries themselves, then their ends and turns, have become so salient to the Western sense of the passage of time. Next, I must explain how and why certain cultural concerns have been the recurrent focal points of those exaggerated hopes and fears that come into play at each century's end. Last, I must trace the historical burdens of our century's end and account for those tensions likely to be most painful, or most evocative, as we pass through the 1990s and the year 2000 into the 21st century, if one there be.

We live in an era more poignant than pleasant. I offer in these pages neither opiate nor elixir but perhaps some red maple, some eyebright, for clearer vision.

THE CENTURIES LAID END TO END

999

TO

1901

———

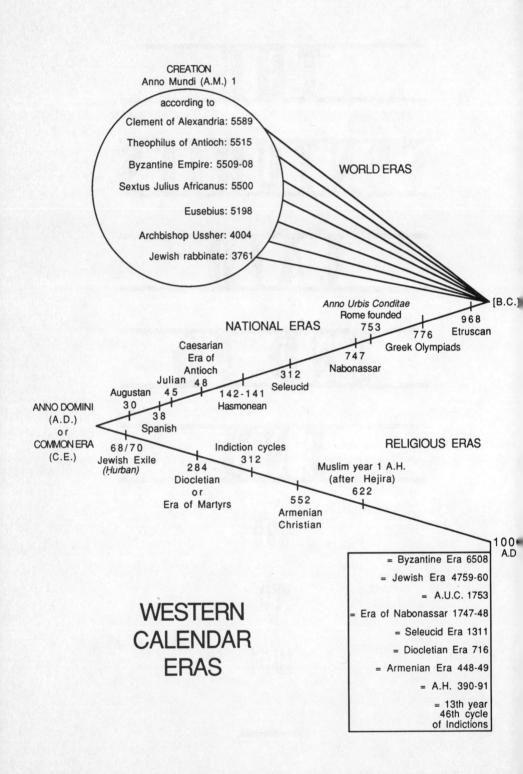

CREATION
Anno Mundi (A.M.) 1

according to

Clement of Alexandria: 5589

Theophilus of Antioch: 5515

Byzantine Empire: 5509-08

Sextus Julius Africanus: 5500

Eusebius: 5198

Archbishop Ussher: 4004

Jewish rabbinate: 3761

WORLD ERAS

[B.C.]

Anno Urbis Conditae
Rome founded
753

968
Etruscan

776
Greek Olympiads

NATIONAL ERAS

747
Nabonassar

Caesarian
Era of
Antioch
48

312
Seleucid

Julian
45

142-141
Hasmonean

Augustan
30

38
Spanish

ANNO DOMINI
(A.D.)
or
COMMON ERA
(C.E.)

68/70
Jewish Exile
(Ḥurban)

284
Diocletian
or
Era of Martyrs

Indiction cycles
312

RELIGIOUS ERAS

Muslim year 1 A.H.
(after Hejira)
622

552
Armenian
Christian

100
A.D

= Byzantine Era 6508

= Jewish Era 4759-60

= A.U.C. 1753

= Era of Nabonassar 1747-48

= Seleucid Era 1311

= Diocletian Era 716

= Armenian Era 448-49

= A.H. 390-91

= 13th year
46th cycle
of Indictions

WESTERN
CALENDAR
ERAS

ARITHMETICS OF TIME

IN THE BEGINNING WERE THE ETRUSCANS, WHOSE WEEK WAS eight days long and whose allotted time was eight centuries. These centuries were not as we know them, spans of one hundred years apiece, but *saecula*, ages which came to term upon the death of the oldest surviving member of a generation. Each year that passed was given its quietus with a nail driven into the temple wall at Volsinii; each generation that passed had as epitaph a sky full of thunderbolts, read by Etruscan diviners, masters at entrails and lightning.

The sibyl Begoia, who had revealed the art of interpreting and invoking flashes of lightning, had also established rules for the marking of boundaries, upon which Etruscans placed great significance. As their territorial boundaries in northern Italy were overrun by Romans during the 5th and 4th centuries B.C., Etruscans appear to have begun a countdown to the last of their temporal boundaries, the eighth generation. They who had crafted sarcophagi and burial chambers of a reflective, even joyous calm now painted into their tombs underworld demons and deities with violent, threatening faces. Diviners fixed Etruscan civilization within the stern divisions of a world-week, in the course of whose last day/year cunning men would uproot the boundary stones that kept men and women mindful of place and fate. By the 2nd century B.C., the countdown of the *saecula* had been made explicit and prophetic: since the founding of Etruria in the (legendary) year 968 B.C., there had lived, end to end, four generations of 100 years each, one generation of 123 years, and two generations of 119 years. If the last of the current (eighth) generation should also succumb at the age of 119, then the Etruscan world-week would be up in 88 B.C. "A strange elusive race whose language and whose origins are still problematic," the Etruscans were at just this time vanishing into the Roman population of Umbria and Tuscany, but as late as 44 B.C., impressed by a flaming (Halley's) comet, the diviner Vulcatius announced in Rome the end of a ninth, penultimate, *saeculum*.

He anticipated a tenth, conclusive *saeculum* which no Etruscan would survive but the diviners themselves, who outlived their fallen civilization long enough to call down lightning upon the Visigoths centuries hence at the fall of Rome.[1]

Vulcatius with his ninth and tenth *saecula* had been working at a small instance of that vanishing act by which Etruscans became indistinguishable from Romans—that is, he had been transforming Etruscan octaves into Roman decimals. The Romans, for their part, had both centuries and *saecula*, neither of which were arithmetically as precise as we might expect. Their centuries, ostensibly aggregates of 100 (*centum*), were rarely exact. The centurion commanded a company of round about 100 men, later one sixtieth of a legion, whatever that might amount to. The *centuriae*, political assemblies based originally on the military unit, had little to do with 100s. The *centumviri*, a select panel of Roman jurors, counted 105 members during the Republic, 180 during the Empire.[2]

Years, accumulating as nails hammered into the portal of the temple of Jupiter Capitolinus, were grouped by *saecula* almost as irregular as the various and variable Roman centuries. Graced with poetic valence by Virgil's *Fourth Eclogue* during the latter days of the Republic, Roman *saecula* of something like a hundred years may earlier have served in determinations of the periodic Tarentine Games, held first to ward off catastrophe during the First Punic War (249 B.C.), next at the end of the Third Punic War (146 B.C.), and deferred under the duress of the civil wars of 49–31 B.C. *Saecula* came into their own with Augustus, whose Secular Games (*Ludi Saeculares*) thoroughly recast tradition. Whereas the Tarentine Games had been dedicated to underworld deities, either as prophylactic to disaster or thanksgiving for escape therefrom, the Augustan festival was dedicated to the Fates, to the goddesses of childbirth, and to the appearance of a New Age. It was the opening of an era of peace that Augustus meant to celebrate with his *saeculum*: not an Etruscan funeral but a Roman inaugural. For this, in May of 17 B.C., Augustus sent out heralds inviting citizens to an event no one alive had ever seen before nor would ever see again. On the evening of May 31st began three days of offerings, sacrifices, prayers, and praises, culminating with the poet Horace's *Carmen Saeculare*, an ode performed by a chorus of twenty-seven boys and twenty-seven girls, asking that the Gods "inspire . . . our toward youth with pure and upright morals; grant a calm tranquility to those in years, and crown our empire with prosperity, honor, and a numerous progeny."[3]

Because new ages are retrodictive as well as prospective, Augustus had hierarchs consult the sibylline books in order to discover (*post hoc*) that his were the fifth Secular Games since the founding of Rome, and that a *saeculum* was historically a period of 110 years. This number, 110, represented a neat compromise between the Etruscan sense of ages bounded by the uncertainties of human life and the Roman inclination toward symbolically certain tens and hundreds. Despite such imperial neatness, the next Secular Games were held not 110 years later in 93–94 A.D. but in 47 A.D. by the Emperor Claudius, whose heralds (of an event none living had ever seen nor would see again) drew laughter from those over seventy who remembered well the Augustan fanfares. Claudius, however, was calculating *saecula* by exact hundreds from the (legendary) year 753 B.C.; his games, like his passions, were retrospective, intended to commemorate the eight hundredth anniversary of the founding of Rome. Notwithstanding Augustus or Claudius, the succeeding Secular Games were sponsored by Domitian in 88 A.D., cheating ahead on the Augustan *saeculum* for reasons of state—the glory of commandeering a new age taking precedence over mere arithmetic. A single unsubstantiated reference returns us to the Claudian *saecula* for games in 146 A.D. under Antoninus Pius, but we are confident of the games hosted by Septimius Severus in 204 A.D. as the seventh in the series of Augustan *Ludi Saeculares*. Septimius had reason to be pleased with this sequence, for it confirmed the magic of the fateful seven of his name. Fresh from victories in Africa, the Emperor in 203 built himself a triumphal arch diagonally across from the Arch of Augustus, "on account of the restoration of the republic," and took seriously the Augustan coincidence of a new *saeculum* with a new political age. He arranged for the next year's games "so that the immortal gods may pass on to future generations what our ancestors have built up and the things which, after previously conferring them on our ancestors, they have granted to our own times as well." Future generations would witness the games just once more, and these in the Claudian manner, as Rome's 1000th anniversary in 248 A.D. Under Julius Verus Philippus the Arabian, three days of ritual were followed, as customary, by a week of theater, gladiatorial combats, circus races, processions, and exhibitions, commemorated by coins circumscribed "*milliarium saeculum*" and stamped with images of a victory column or the profile of a hippopotamus. The Secular Games, unlike the hippo yet true to the age-old invitations of the heralds, would not be seen again.[4]

Three competing traditions of the *saeculum* had been bespoken in the Classical West. These we will see again and again as century and *saeculum* slowly converge. The Etruscan *saeculum* ran the full natural length of a generation; it was less a fixed number of years than a recognizance of mortality. The Claudian *saeculum* was an anniversary running in fixed hundreds from an act of creation, the founding of Rome. The Augustan *saeculum*, fixed by thoughtful fiat to a run of 110 years that hinted at the natural limit to a human life, was in practice modulated by politic desires to herald a new order. In mnemonic brief, the Etruscan tradition was most attentive to ends, the Claudian to recurrence and critical moments, the Augustan to the advent of new ages. Over the years, we have embraced all three, abandoned none. The Etruscan *saeculum* is our inexact "end of the century" or *fin de siècle*, taken also as the end of a generation. The Claudian *saeculum* is our "turn of the century," a more specific calendrical moment when we tend to look back and forth by hundreds. The Augustan *saeculum* is our "dawn of a new age," allied to but not bound by the strict arithmetic of centuries.

Of this arithmetic there is more to be written, for all the centuries indicated on these pages have been, of course, anachronisms. Etruscans and Romans did not code their dates B.C. or A.D., did not center their ritual calendars on the conception, birth, life, death, or (legendary) resurrection of an obscure Galilean who led a brief career as a wandering miracle worker on one of the dustier fringes of the Empire. We must take a look at the Roman calendars, then at the calendars which superseded them in the Christian West, to appreciate the historical development of the modern sense of an end to a (standard) century.

Simply put, the immediate predicament of any annual calendar is that the obvious monthly changes in the phases of the nighttime moon are incommensurable with the equally obvious if more gradual seasonal changes in the overhead angle of the daytime sun. Babylonian astronomer-priests patiently observed that a span of 19 solar years came within two hours of matching 235 (mean synodal) lunar months. Their observations led them to a lunisolar calendar cycle of 19 years of 12 lunar months (29 or 30 days each), with an extra thirteenth month intercalated in the third, fifth, eighth, eleventh, thirteenth, sixteenth, and nineteenth years. Adopted by the Seleucid successors to the empire of Alexander the Great, then by the Romans, this lunisolar system had suffered such abuse through the political intrusion of unwarranted intercalated months that the reforms of Julius Caesar had to correct a calendar whose designated dates for solstice and equinox were almost three months wide of their celestial marks. Working from an Egyptian model, the reforms introduced a strictly solar year of 365 days, which entailed a wholesale supplement of 80 days during the year 708 A.U.C. (*Anno Urbis Conditae*, from the year that Rome was founded). A new year began on January 1, 709 A.U.C., with a 366th day to be intercalated every fourth year, to account for the discrepancy between the Julian year and the actual solar year of approximately 365¼ days.

The Julian reforms solved, for the time being, the problem of a regular year, though it was Augustus who, arranging for a long namesake month, August, gave us the present standard lengths for each of our twelve months. What the reforms did not settle was the confusion of eras. For example, the Julian Era began with the first 365-day year of the Julian calendar, equivalent to 709 A.U.C., another new style of reckoning, and to the year 3–4 of the Caesarian Era of Antioch, instituted to commemorate the battle of Pharsalia. The same year, 1 Julian, 709 A.U.C., 3–4 Caesarian, was for Greeks the middle of the third to the middle of the fourth year of the 183rd Olympiad; for those on the eastern shores of the Mediterranean, it was the year 266–67 of the Seleucid Era. Jews went by the Seleucid Era, but for a while they used as well a Maccabean epoch which put the year 1 Julian at 97–98 of the Hasmonean Era. Augustus, not to be outshone by his great-uncle Julius, instituted his own eras, one in honor of his victory at Actium, another in honor of his reform of the Egyptian calendar. Hellenistic astronomer Ptolemy, whose writings would be consulted closely for some fifteen hundred years, referred his detailed calendrical computations back to the reign of the Babylonian king who had installed the vernal equinox under the astrological/astronomical sign of the Ram. Thus, year 1 of the Julian Era, 709 A.U.C., 3–4 Caesarian, 183rd Olympiad 3–4, 266–67 Seleucid, 97–98 Hasmonean, was 701–02 of the Era of Nabonassar.

My worried set of chronological correspondences bewrays a way of thinking hardly antique. The careful alignment of eras would become desirable only when it seemed important to braid the affairs of diverse peoples into one long plait—when, that is, world events were thought to be heading toward a single moment. For the Roman historian Polybius, that climax was the Roman conquest of the Mediterranean, upon which, in the third year of the 140th Olympiad, all chronologies had to converge. Most people within the Roman imperium, however, continued to live season by season, year by year, reign by reign, and did not trouble themselves about eras. Even the annalists Livy and Tacitus, who worked through Roman history consulship by consulship, wrote so that series and sequence were independent of the epochal date for the founding of Rome.[5]

Among early Christians, it was a different story. With the apparent delay of the Second Coming, the faithful had to begin to concern themselves with the longer haul of history. They needed to straighten out their calculations of the Millennium, which through the Book of Daniel and the

Apocalypse of John had been fitted to the age of the world and to the world-week of seven (sometimes eight) thousand years. They needed to establish a distinct, distinguished place for Jesus within both sacred (testamental) and profane (annalistic) history, since he had not yet brought Time to a close and they themselves had still to live as best they could in the quotidian world. They needed, therefore, to determine the chronological correspondence between events in Scripture and events in more pedestrian chronicles, especially around the time of their Christ. And they needed—as, literally, *followers* of that Christ—to position themselves securely with regard to the implacable heavens; if their rituals were geared to pivotal events in the gospel narratives, they could scarcely ignore the rising and setting of the sun, the waxing and waning of the moon, the annual return of equinox and solstice as celestial events of symbolic moment for the celebration of the birth, death, and resurrection of Jesus.

Necessity, then, was the midwife of invention. A new, all-encompassing era was brought to light: the *Anno Mundi*, year (from the Creation) of the world. Dating the Creation was an ambitious project, calling for difficult calculations from none too coherent Biblical lists of lifespans and generations from Adam to the Flood, the Flood to Abraham, Abraham to Moses, Moses to David, David to the Babylonian Captivity, Captivity to Joseph and Mary, and thenceforward by gospel and chronicle into more recent history. For Theophilus of Antioch, there had been 5695 years from Adam to the death of Emperor Marcus Aurelius. For Clement of Alexandria, 5784 years, 2 months, 12 days had passed from Adam to the death of the succeeding Emperor, Commodus, which put the birth of Christ in the year 5590 A.M. For Sextus Julius Africanus, composing the first extensive Christian history of the world, there had been 5000 years from Adam to the end of the Babylonian Captivity, and another 500 years in preparation for Jesus of Nazareth. That left a waiting room of 500 years from his birth in 5500 A.M. to the millennial world-sabbath and the Second Coming at the end of the 6000 years of Creation.[6]

Unfortunately, such an exquisite figure for the Incarnation as the year 5500 A.M., which situated the infant Jesus at the midpoint of the final thousand years of human history, was difficult to square with gospel accounts of his death thirty-some years later. Whenever Christ was born (a still-disputed issue), he had to be nailed to the cross during (Matthew 26.17, Luke 2.7) or just before (John 19.31) the Passover, whose date, the 14th day of the month of Nisan when the moon is full, bore a shifting annual relationship to the intercalations of the complicated, sometimes locally arbitrary, Jewish lunisolar calendar. Also, as Christians distanced themselves from the Jewish milieu by embracing as their sabbath not the seventh but the first day of the week, the Easter ritual recalling the Resurrection three days after the Crucifixion had to be held (according to most Christian communities) on the Lord's Day, a Sunday. Christian chronologists, juggling sacred and profane time, lunar and solar calendar cycles, Roman imperial annals and the gospel lives of Jesus, had then to make complex aesthetic choices between impressively balanced world-historical epochs and ritually centered calendar days. Church historian Eusebius, member of the Council of Nicaea which decreed that Easter must be celebrated on the first Sunday after the full moon following the vernal equinox (March 21st), worked backward from those years in the paschal tables that would admit the appropriate Sunday, and forward from the patriarch Abraham, determining that Jesus had to have been born in 5199 A.M. The symbological demands of Christian worship and his own distaste for a millennial 6000th year that would otherwise be looming on the near horizon led Eusebius to sacrifice the world-historical balance of an Incarnational year 5500 A.M.[7]

Chronologists of the Eastern Church struggled to maintain a calendrical era that had as its Christian pivot a year as near as possible to 5500 A.M. while still synchronous with a Passover Last Supper and an Easter Sunday. Inspired too by mythopoetic appeals for symmetry between the day of the week of the Passion or the Resurrection and the day of the week in Genesis during which either the Sun or Man was created, Alexandrian and Byzantine historians arrived at such Incarnational years as 5494, 5501, 5505, 5506, 5507, and 5508 A.M. When the latter date was officially endorsed (around 6200 A.M.) as the point of departure for the Byzantine Era, debates over the dating of Christ's birth continued to circle the year 5500.[8]

Meanwhile, a decisive Roman emperor had inadvertently set in motion a new era with his violent attacks on the Church. Known in civil terms as the Diocletian Era for the conversion of Egypt to the Roman calendar year (January through December), it became known to Christians as the "Era of the Martyrs" for the Great Persecutions directed by Diocletian. This "Era of the Martyrs" was the first calendrical epoch to take its cue from a specifically Christian circumstance.[9] The next such epoch, invented 241 years later, would be the one we have been waiting for, the one to which we in the West are accustomed, the one without which most readers may have been at sea during the last seven paragraphs.

If in this narrative I have temporarily abandoned the comforting charms of centuries, if I have left off the familiar A.D. bracelets from the lives of

Sextus Julius Africanus, Eusebius, and Diocletian, it has been to demonstrate how dependent we are upon centuries and a common era for making sense of history. Although Romans used *lustra* (five-year intervals), and Eusebius mustered events by decades, and popes began counting across fifteen-year tax periods called indictions, many *lustra*, decades, and indictions would elapse before people took to reckoning their past by centuries. Nor did people in the Christian West have *Anno Domini* as their historical anchor before Dennis the Diminutive dealt with the problem of the date of Easter for the year that he would be the first to identify as 526 A.D.

By this time, according to calendars prevailing in the Eastern Church, the millennial year 6000 A.M. had come and gone without much trace of panic terror or sabbath rest, and the Latin West, surmounting apocalyptic tensions during the late 4th and 5th centuries (A.D.), had switched allegiance to the Eusebian Incarnational year 5199 A.M., such that the 6000th year A.M. lay safely distant, in 800 (A.D.). By this time, Alaric the Goth, undeterred by the thunderbolts of the last Etruscan diviners, had sacked the imperial city, Franks and Visigoths had succeeded to the Western Roman Empire, and a Scythian monk had been elected abbot of a monastery in Rome. For Dionysius Exiguus or Dennis the Small, the Humble, the Diminutive, the way was therefore open to a system of dating that had as incipit neither the Law of the *Old* Testament nor the games and twins of fallen empires but the birth of a child whose words had overtaken the one and outlived the others.[10]

The Scythian monk, father of canon law, was not too humble to have aspired to a universally acceptable Christian Era as another means of reconciling Eastern and Western Churches. Their divergent, troublesome paschal tables, both soon to lapse, were in urgent need of revision. Negotiating 19-year and 84-year Easter cycles, imprecise gospel accounts of the public ministry and Passion of Christ, Julian epochs, and years A.U.C., Dennis the Diminutive extended the paschal tables another ninety-five years on the basis of a calendar whose first year, 754 A.U.C., corresponded to the first year in the life of Jesus, hence 1 A.D. (*Anno Domini*, Year of Our Lord).[11]

This *Anno Domini* began neither with the Conception (March 25th) nor with the Incarnation (December 25th). It began with the circumcision, January 1st, New Year's Day in Roman and Latin Christian calendars. So, figured Dennis, Jesus was born December 25, 753 A.U.C., in the year *before* 1 A.D. That year was not, has never been, the year 0, and a millennium would pass before that year would be known as 1 "B.C." As we shall discover, people at the ends of centuries will have no end of perplexity with this quirk of the Western calendar, so it is best that we address our own farewells to that exiguous year. Since there never has been an A.D. 0, our ages, distances, and dollars do not add up in quite the same fashion as do the years in a standard century. Someone babbling through her first birthday party has a full twelve months under her bib, while year 1 of Dennis the Diminutive's calendar entered entirely naive. Wherefore the 1st century—the first full and exact one hundred years—was completed with the last moment of December 31, 100 A.D.; each successive century must culminate on New Year's Eve, '00–'01. When a centenarian is asked for advice on how to live a long life, now that she has made it past 99 to 100, she has enjoyed, or endured, a full one hundred years. When our 20th century reaches midnight, December 31, 1999, it will have yet the 366 days of (leap) year 2000 to close out its hundredth year. The second millennium A.D. will disappear with the fireworks of New Year's Eve, December 31, 2000. This should settle matters once and for all, but it won't.

Nor did our abbot's *Anno Domini* era settle matters once and for all. After months of computations, Dennis got the prime number wrong: Jesus was likely born four, six, or seven years before 1 A.D. This oxymoronic error, a topic of letters to editors at the end of the 19th century and sure to be featured again at this century's end, can be of no practical consequence to the value or arithmetic of the A.D. system itself, for a calendar era gains its authority less from the accuracy of its beginning date (often a fiction) than from the religious or political usefulness of its mode of arranging time.

The good abbot never dated his own letters in years A.D.; he used indictions and "epacts," the number of days since the new moon at the start of the year. His calendar was accepted at first solely for its paschal tables. Only later, as the Eusebian (and now obnoxiously millennial) 6000 A.M. hove into view, did "A.D." displace other epochal moorings in the Latin West. Adopted by the Synod of Whitby in 664, the A.D. system spread slowly from Anglo-Saxon territories through the Carolingian domains into the rest of Western Europe. Most reluctant were the Spanish, who long remained loyal to an era of their own harking back to the Roman conquest, and whose apocalypticism in the years before 6000 A.M. was not as effectively suppressed as was the apocalyptic element in the timing of the imperial coronation of Charlemagne, which conservative Church annalists took care to assign to Christmas Day of the innocuous year 800 A.D. (In silence they passed over the fact that it was also the end of the sixth day-age of the world-week and the sixth millennium A.M.) Clerics and countries farther east were under the sway of a Byzantine calendar moored to a 1 A.M. equivalent to

5509/08 B.C. Armenians lived according to an era that commenced with their schism from Eastern Orthodoxy (in our A.D. year 522).[12]

So, as we make a second approach to the first *Anno Domini* millennium, we find ourselves shorn of a uniform calendar, bereft of standard centuries, and unimpressed by the status of an A.D. for counting up to the year 1000. We may also be at a loss for a unanimous New Year's Day. The legendary midnight mass led by the Pope would have been held in Rome on the eve of the Nativity, December 25th, but in Florence the New Year fell on March 25th, Annunciation Day; in Venice on March 1st; in France on Easter; in England intermittently on Lady Day (March 25th), on Christmas, and on the Feast of the Circumcision, January 1st; in Spain and Portugal, always on January 1st; in the Byzantine world on September 1st or 24th; and in Armenia on July 9th.

No uniform calendar for Christendom, no standard centuries counted *either* from '00 through '99 or from '01 through '00, no exclusive embrace of Dennis the Diminutive's *Anno Domini*, no unanimous month for the New Year—what can possibly remain of the legend of the panic terror on the verge of the millennium? Even the start of a new day was in question: did the day begin at midnight (with the hour and service called matins), at dawn (with the hour and service called prime, and work in the fields), or at sundown (a Greek and Jewish custom retained in parts of the Eastern Church)?[13] When common folk went their ways by sun and moon, when local bigwigs heeded somewhat regular intervals for taxes and tithes, when monarchs ruled by regnal years (dated here from accession, there from coronation, elsewhere from the first New Year's Day thereof), and when few anywhere were numerate enough to handle (in Roman I, V, X, L, C, D, and M) the number of days in each month, let alone the labyrinth of indictions, Julian leap years, years *Anno Mundi*, years *Anno Domini*—how then could a singular year M (or sometimes ∞, or ↄ, or ↄ, or ↑) have blazed on everyone's horizon?

THE YEAR 1000,
SECOND TIME AROUND

WE CONFRONT THE SAME DILEMMAS WITH THE LATIN Christian year 1000 as we do with that Roman god of beginnings, Janus.[14] Neither appears to us full-bodied; both face in two directions. Neither has an ancestry entirely clear or a realm entirely unclouded; both come down to us as more tremendous figures than perhaps they ever were. Indeed, the

Miniature depicting the general resurrection at the Last Judgment, from fol. 201ᵛ of Emperor Henry II's *Pericope* or *Book of Extracts*, dated 1007–12 A.D. Courtesy of the Bayerische Staatsbibliothek, Munich.

companionate relations of Janus and the millennium, a relationship I mean to pursue, may be an artifact of the 20th century. Wrote the archeologist and Egyptologist W. M. Flinders Petrie in 1907, "Janus, who looked to the past and to the future, was the god whose temple stood always open during war, that he might bring peace on earth. And in our day it is only the view of the past and the future which can warn us of evils to come, and save us from violence and confusion."[15] For polemicist and litterateur Arthur Koestler in 1978, Janus takes us to *A Summing Up*. Our "schizophysiology" seems to condemn us to living on borrowed time "in the post-Hiroshima era." What can save us, maybe, is the Janus principle at work in biological holons, those "self-regulating entities which manifest both the independent properties of wholes and the dependent properties of parts." Our two-faced selves have one last chance during this possibly final *fin de siècle*, and that chance rests with Janus.[16]

We may be pardoned if we now most urgently invoke Janus (as *janitor* mopping up our messes, as *Janissary* defending us from ourselves), for the end of a century—or the end of a millennium, or The End—is the end of a year, writ large. New Year's Eve has traditionally stood between a world in chaos and a world reclaimed. New Year's rituals have everywhere been radical, *bifrons*, and extreme: abstinence then orgy, grief and atonement then joy and abandon. The old year, a blind man in the hide of a he-goat, is driven with whips or sticks into the House of the Dead or out beyond the walls of the city: farewell to regret and remorse, bad debts and worse recriminations. Enter assurance and clear intent: the Big Man, the Mayor, the Hierophant, the King, or the Queen, who circles the realm to inscribe a new year within clean perimeters. After the fasting, the trance, and the revels, time must be back in its place, not just restored but revived, rededicated, and raring to go. The first days of the year prefigure the rest. New Year's gifts are, literally, omens (in Rome, *strenia* < *strenae*, omens); the first person to step across the threshold sets us up for a year of good fortune or ill; the first animal we see, the first clothes we wear, the first food we eat, the first voice we hear, all tell us something of the year to come. From nostalgia to prophecy, from recklessness to vigilance, from chaos to clarity is the path of the New Year.[17]

Given this trajectory, it is more than reasonable that Janus, presiding spirit of the New Year, should make his presences keenly felt at the end of a second thousand years A.D. And there is reason enough that the legend of the year 1000 should still wax strong, for we have often honored the turn of the first millennium as a New Year writ most large. New Year's Eve became, in parts of Europe, the reenactment of that legendary New Year's Eve, a *Silvesternacht* alluding to that pope whom playwrights and novelists have drawn as janiform. At midnight of the millennium, the Dark Ages departed like barbarian ghosts; at dawn the sun rose brilliant on a new age. New Year's Eve . . . New Year's Day (the first of *January* in Rome and Iberia, later in England, later in Germany, Italy, and France, much later in Russia) . . . new year . . . new century . . . new millennium . . . new age.

Writing as I am within the portico of the already legendary precincts of the 1990s, I would be foolish to presume that we are free to set the record forever straight about the 990s. Too many centuries' worth of prophecies hang in the balance; too many grand retrospections require the footing of an earlier, momentous millennium. Indeed, medievalists of the late 20th century, looking afresh at the documents, are finding proof that apocalypticism *was* rife during the late 10th century. The best historians of this new generation may soon be making us a *fin de siècle* gift—as well they should, around the year 2000—of decades of genuinely millenarian excitement around the year 1000.[18]

While awaiting the judgment of the ages upon this most current scholarly legerdemain, let the turn of that millennium pass in review under the various aspects of Janus himself. Through such an unfashionable rhetorical device we can best appreciate the extent to which historically sophisticated images of the (actual) years around *Anno Domini* 1000 have been shaped by a modern janiform sense of transfiguration at century's end.

Among the earliest of Roman gods, Janus had no cult of his own until late in the Empire. Invoked before all other gods at rituals on the first day or kalends of each month, Janus had no cogent place within the Etruscan, Greek, or Roman pantheons. His faces, impressed on the first bronze coins and standard silver didrachms, were public and familiar, yet he held aloof from folktale, epic, and myth. He remains therefore an enigma, a god of uncertain origin whose well-known name is of uncertain etymology. Neither occult nor reclusive, Janus over the years assumed a series of guises, and we are left to guess at the original.

He comes perhaps from an Indo-European matrix, as the wind god of beginnings. In fact, a new wind was blowing around the year 1000: Western Europe was entering upon a climatic optimum. Arctic ice was melting, so that Vikings could explore the North Atlantic, settle (and farm) Greenland, and touch upon Vineland on the northeastern edge of North America. The warmer weather opened up previously forbidding ranges of cold plain and dense forest to new settlements. Good weather overlay the sudden spurt of growth in the European population early in the 11th century, and a concomitant resurgence of cities and commerce.

"[T]he dawn of Europe [was] now beginning to gleam," wrote an Italian economic historian in 1962, quoting a verse from the 10th century: "Dawn on the somber sea brings on the sun—Then passes the hill: look, darkness is lifting." Annalist Thietmar of Merseberg in 1018 had dated this aurora more precisely: "When the thousandth and fourth year since the salvific birth of the Immaculate Virgin had come, a radiant dawn rose over the world." Here smiled Matuta, Roman goddess of the early morn, and behind her bright Diana of the crescent moon, auspicious for all commencements. Were the two faces of Janus drawn from the two lunar crescents set back to back, the fading old moon and the rising new? Wrote French cultural historians in 1964, "900–1100, those were the years of the collapse of the old Orders and the triumph of new blood." St. Adalbert of Prague in Poland, St. Bruno of Augsburg in Hungary and Russia, and Pope Sylvester II in letters flung far from Rome sought out that new blood with a revival of missionary purpose. Whole nations (Poland, Hungary, Russia) seemed to shed old skins and accept new, Christian, identities at the turn of the 10th century, though none so instantly as Iceland, where Olaf Tryggvessøn ordered the country to convert exactly in that matutinal year, 1000 A.D. "From about the year 1000," wrote an American social historian in 1968, "profound changes became evident on virtually all levels of medieval social and cultural life." If there was any panic or fear, it was the fear of change, fear of the new, against which we today still carry lucky charms, still nail an iron crescent moon (the horseshoe) over our doorways.[19]

Not just any doorways, but gates, arches, and bridgeheads were under the watchful eyes of Janus, who was much less concerned with peace at home than with success abroad. He was the god of setting out and returning safely—which meant to Romans the crossing of rivers and streams, those living waters that protect, avenge, redeem, and restore. Ideal then for the wandering holy men, hermits and preachers, who strode onto the European scene around the year 1000; for the noble lords who took to visiting holy places with all of their retainers; and for common pilgrims who had suddenly stronger desires to go farther afield in their devotions. Ideal too for the monastic reformers who played so vibrant a part in spiritual life from the very start of the 11th century, setting the Church in motion again across the living waters of Europe. If heretics made unusually dramatic appearances at this time, they too could be countenanced by Janus, for they were as obsessed with restoration (safe return) as were the monastic reformers, and as was Emperor Otto III himself, obedient disciple of St. Nilus the Ascetic. The heretics—in Vertus, Toulouse, Orléans, Liège, Monforte, Milan—were responding to a new lay enthusiasm for more inspiring models of religious life; they demanded Christian rigor and priestly purity, denouncing concubinage and simony. The bees that drove Leutard in the year 1000 to speak against ecclesiastical privilege would within the century drive crusaders east across the Mediterranean to do battle with the greater threat of Islam.[20]

Crusade, an idea first broached at midcentury but often and mistakenly attributed to Pope Sylvester II, takes us to the steps of the Temple of Janus. When the Temple was open, Romans were doing battle somewhere in the world. When on rare occasions the Temple was closed, Romans understood that peace had come to the imperium: Janus had no longer to cast kind eyes upon soldiers crossing over into strange lands beyond the living waters of Rome. Each closure was a gala, commemorating not simply a safe but a triumphant return of the legions. Celebrated on imperial coins and in distant military colonies, Janus was the god of martial beginnings and pacific conclusions. Facing two times (old and new, past and future), two directions (east and west), Janus now took on the two moods of anxious farewell and victorious reunion or, as those of the year 1000 would have it, of apocalyptic threat and millennial truce.

Among the innovations at the turn of the 11th century, two of the most remarkable were most janiform: the appearance of a new social order of *chevaliers* or knights, men dedicated to the fine arts of war, and the simultaneous coalition of a Peace Movement dedicated to limiting the rampage of axe and sword. While European artists and poets put the finishing touches to some of their most powerful apocalyptic visions, churchmen met in councils to set godly bounds to the otherwise random violence of medieval warfare, and town folk sought to protect civilians from the brutalities of battle. If Satan was emerging as a nearly independent potentate; if the Antichrist had just acquired a lengthy *vita* and a lucid *modus vivendi*; if Fimbulwinter, the doom of man, and Ragnarok, the twilight of the gods, were taking on their penultimate shadows in eddic poetry and scaldic verse—then the pious could at least establish a Peace of God: rules of refuge for women, children, and *pauperes* (the unarmed); rights of safe passage for pilgrims, monks, holy men, peasants, and the very poor. Here, in Reichenau, Germany, soon after the year 1000, Janus pored through an exquisitely illuminated manuscript of the *Apocalypse*; there, in Le Puy in south–central France in 975, Janus assembled with knights and peasants to talk with Bishop Guy (and his sister Adelaide), who wanted to "hear from them what advice they had to give about keeping the peace." Here, in Irish domains late in the 10th century, Janus watched as the Fifteen Signs for the fifteen days before Doomsday were written down in good order, complete with quaking seas and burning waters, bloody dew and battling stones, falling stars and rising dead; there, in France, he met with councils at Charroux (989/90), Narbonne (990), Limoges and Le Puy (994), and Poitiers (1000), to assert the Peace of God under the motto, "A delicious name indeed is that of peace," while (at Limoges) "the huge crowd of people filling all the places to twelve miles around the city [was] rejoicing under open brilliant skies." Here, Janus saw the Last World Emperor, conquering hero and herald of the eschaton, grow from an obscure 7th-century Syriac legend into a towering 11th-century European figure of redemption and apocalypse; there, Janus observed the Truce of God as it grew from a simple desire in 1027 for quiet on the Lord's Day to bolder demands that the clash of arms be forsworn during Easter, Pentecost, Advent, Christmas, Epiphany, and, in theory, from every Wednesday vespers to every Monday prime.[21]

Those crowds of common people "crying out with hands uplifted, 'Peace! Peace! Peace!' " had been stirred by the recent and fortuitous recovery of an amazing number of relics identified with earliest Christianity. Recovery of such relics became central to a larger excitement that an Age of Peace might recover the faith of the Apostolic Age, hence the shift of devotional emphasis from God the Father to the Son of God, the historical Jesus who had walked the earth and suffered on the cross. Given the new enthusiasms for the Passion of Christ and for pilgrimage to the shrines of apostolic relics, it would seem that those past and those present were not immeasurably distant from one another, that a supple human bond might exist between the living and the dead. Whence the Day of the Dead, or All Souls' Day, instituted by Odilo, Abbot of Cluny, on November 2nd, around the year 1000, as a new feast confirming that the dead needed the public prayers of the living. Holy relics, the tombs of the saintly, images of the suffering Christ were focal points for contact between the ages, between generations, between those who had departed and those who yet remained. Janus must have been pleased with the Day of the Dead, for as (ancient) god of the *interlunium*, he had been positioned in that prayerful darkness between crescent moons; as god of water crossings, he had been guardian of ferrymen and cousin to Charon, classical ferryman for departing souls; later, as (sometimes *quadrifons*, four-faced) god of crossroads, he had been centered in space and in time between the paths of the living and the paths of the dead.[22]

The only official representation of Janus Quadrifons appeared on coins issued by the Emperor Hadrian, whose mystique of a *Renovatio temporum* (a Renewal of Time) and a new Golden Age had been aligned in 128 A.D. with the 880th anniversary of the city of Rome. The four faces of Janus looked out over the end of a cycle of four 110-year (Augustan) *saecula*, toward the start of another cycle. Agent or overseer of epochal renovation, Janus would be enlisted again by Commodus in 186 A.D. and by Gallienus, who issued the last Janus (*bifrons*) coin in 260 A.D. at a moment charged with desires for a new imperial beginning.[23]

When Otto III was crowned emperor in Rome in the year 996, almost exactly two centuries after the Roman coronation of Charlemagne, dreams of restoration and renovation were at the forefront of the ceremony. Like Charlemagne in 799, Otto in 998 had also to suppress a Roman insurrection and punish a counter-pope before he could sit comfortably on an imperial Roman throne. Like Charlemagne, Otto had grand visions of holy empire. Son of a Byzantine princess, disciple of a Greek monk, Otto could aspire as well to the ultimate reunion of East and West. God of crossroads, god of the new moon, month, year, *saeculum*, and age, Janus must surely have been looking over the shoulder of Otto III on Pentecost Monday in the year 1000 as the young Emperor studied the newly unearthed sarcophagus of Charlemagne, who lay in perfect state and full piety with a cross of gold around his neck. The apostle Paul had visited Otto, had spoken in spirit for the expulsion of unworthy men from the ranks of an ailing Church, and here was Otto in Aachen, or Aix-la-Chapelle, known to Janus and the Romans as the healing spa of Aquae Grani. Its sulphur springs, fed by the underworld, had convened the living and the dead; now could this great relic, the body of Charlemagne, be the source of that infusion of grace necessary to a *Renovatio temporum*, last resort of the millennium?[24]

Howsoever skeptical of the legend of the panic terror, modern historians draw portraits of the late 10th century that bear the janiform imprints of a crossroads in time, a bridge between two ages. My argument need not be that the 990s were experienced by contemporaries as we today experience a *fin de siècle*, nor that the years 1000/1001 were celebrated with any of the clamor or glamour we anticipate for the millennial fêtes of the years 2000/2001. Rather, I suggest that the Western temptation to depict the turn of the first Christian calendrical millennium as the end of one epoch and the start of another has become well-nigh irresistible.[25] With or without the panic terror, *Anno Domini* 1000 survives in 20th-century culture as an inescapably seductive year.

For the anti–apocalyptic English monk Byrhtferth, who composed a manual on timekeeping just after the millennium, M or *millesimus* or one thousand (for which he had no Hindu-Arabic zeros) was "a perfect number," alluding to the six ages of the world, each of a thousand years. "But," wrote Byrhtferth, undisturbed by the imperfection of the perfect number, "these same ages did not consist of equal numbers. The first thousand years, that is to say, the first age of this life [from Adam to Noah], consisted of MDCLVI years, according to Hebrew verity. According to the Septuagint, it lasted MMDCCXLII years." And so on, in very ragged "thousands," from Noah to Abraham, Abraham to David, David to the Babylonian Exile, the Exile to Jesus. As for the sixth and current age, from the Advent of Christ, it "is not fixed by any series of generations or times, but as the age is decrepit it must be consummated by the death, that is to say the end, of the whole world." The number M was symbolically perfect, but in practice it was conveniently elastic, as were other numbers in Byrhtferth's day—the land-holdings called "hundreds," the great or long hundreds (six score) of fish, and the hundredweights of grain, which ranged in pounds from C to CXII to CXX.[26]

We too, despite the exactness of our quartz crystal watches and electronic scales, often use numbers—hundreds, thousands, millions, billions—for their incantatory precision. In a sense the year 1000 is more our experience than it was ever the experience of those who lived through the year M, for the year 1000 has taken historical shape over the last five centuries, and the nearer we come to the year 2000, the more vital it is that the year 1000 be symbolically perfect. While Byrhtferth furnished arithmetical rules for computing the ecclesiastical calendar, while he extolled the *millesimus* and dated the sixth age from the Advent of Christ, he made no mention of the millennium which had passed some eleven years before.

The first annalist to be seduced by the year M was Radulphus Glaber, Ralph the Bald, who wrote from Saint-Benigne of Dijon between MXXV and MXXX, "According to our promise, we begin the third book of this present work [his *History*] with the thousandth year of the birth of the Word. As we have already said, on the approach of this year one could see throughout almost the whole world the disappearance of great and notable men from among the Church and the nobility." One generation of leaders was dying away with the year 1000, but Glaber seemed far more aroused by the transit of generations on the anniversary of another millennium. As the Easter Crucifixion and Resurrection were of greater moment in the 11th century than the Christmas Nativity, so the height of pilgrimage and popular agitation may have arrived not with the Incarnational year 1000 but with the year of the Passion 1000. That year, 1033 A.D., was afflicted by a saffron sun and a solar eclipse which bathed the earth in a sapphire mist, turning the faces of men pale as death, and by a famine so severe that "Men believed that the orderly procession of the seasons and the laws of nature, which until then had ruled the world, had relapsed into the eternal chaos and they feared that mankind would end." Such fears had been in evidence since the year 1009, when Saracen infidels had laid waste the Church of the Holy Sepulchre in Jerusalem. A French chronicler recorded for 1010 ominous signs in the stars, terrible storms, horrible plagues, grave famines, and the highest floods in memory. The chronicler, Adémar of Chabannes, was one of the chief propagandists for the Peace of God, which movement he understood as prelude to the Last Judgment. He would die on pilgrimage to Jerusalem in 1034, not long after the death of the principal lay patron of the Peace Movement, Duke William the Great of Aquitaine. If at the end of the 20th century we must have a prepotent end to the 10th century, that earlier millennium might in good faith be shunted from the year 1000 to the year 1033, when an earthquake shook the Holy Land "from the sea to Fort Dan, in all cities of the Negev and the Mount to Jerusalem, to Shechem and her villages, Tiberias and her villages, the Galilean mountains and the whole of Palestine."[27]

So much for the beginnings of ends. The year 1000 may haunt the rest of this book, pale rider on a pale horse, but we are free now to move on toward other ends, forewarned and mindful of our own apocalyptic moods. The centuries will appear in due course and in different lights, as Etruscan generations, Claudian anniversaries, Augustan ages. Nine centuries will pass before the Christian West reaches a final consensus on one calendar (Dennis the Diminutive's *Anno Domini*), one calendar reform (the Gregorian), and one New Year's Eve. Always Janus will be there at the crossroads, glancing behind, gazing forward: the *Renovatio temporum*, perhaps; war or peace; twilight or dawn; two crescent moons; a wind at our backs.

CALENDARS OF THE DEAD:
THE 1090s

"IN THE YEAR FOUR THOUSAND EIGHT HUNDRED FIFTY-SIX, THE year one thousand twenty-eight of our exile, in the eleventh year of the cycle *Ranu* [=sing], the year in which we anticipated salvation and solace, in accordance with the prophecy of Jeremiah [31.7]: 'Sing with gladness for

God Willeth It—romantic illustration of Peter the Hermit preaching the First Crusade, from François Pierre Guillaume Guizot and Mme. Guizot de Witt, *The History of France from the Earliest Times to 1848* (New York, 1880?).

Jacob, and shout at the head of the nations,'—this year turned instead to sorrow and groaning, weeping and outcry." So opens a Jewish chronicle of the First Crusade, which began in the 4856th year after Creation, in the 1028th year after the destruction of the Second Temple, in the middle of the 256th lunar cycle of the 19-year ritual calendar, in the year 1096 of the Common Era (a more accurate and ecumenical term than *Anno Domini*). "At this time arrogant people, a people of strange speech, a nation bitter and impetuous, Frenchmen and Germans, set out for the Holy City," and since this time, as bands of bastard crusaders turned upon communities of Jews in their path, the year 4856 has borne an historical burden of no less weight in the Jewish world than the year 1000 has borne in the Christian West. Indeed, that year 4856 may have had greater significance to contemporary Jews than did the year 1000 to contemporary Christians; within decades of the crusader violence, the terrors of 4856 came to stand in relation to Jewish history as the "terror" of 1000 would come to stand, centuries later, in relation to the annals of Western Christianity: epilogue to one age and prologue to another. Time has intemperately strengthened these relations. As the first Christian millennium stands now at the indelible center between the momentous birth of the infant Jesus and the apocalyptic end of the second millennium, so the martyrdom of the year 1028 of the exile stands at the emblematic midpoint between *Ḥurban habayit*, the destruction of the Second Temple in 70 C.E., and the Holocaust of World War II.[28]

When, on the verge of the 12th Christian century, the crusading knights of Count Emicho of Leiningen attacked the Rhineland Jewish communities of Speyer, Worms, and Mainz; when his more zealous captains went after the Jews of Metz, Neuss, Wevelinghofen, Eller, and Xanten; when Volkmar's pious forces assaulted the Jews of Prague and Gottschalk's inspired soldiers assailed the Jews of Ratisbon—in those drear days Jews were working desperately with four calendars of their own. They had an astronomical calendar by which to position themselves in regard to the celestial round: the nineteen-year liturgical cycle. They had a political calendar by which to position themselves in the flux of empires rising and falling: the Seleucid Era, dating from the conquest of Babylonia by Seleucus Nicator (312 B.C.E.). They had a national calendar by which to position themselves in regard to a moment of archetypal trauma: years in exile from the Holy Land, commencing with *Ḥurban habayit*, which took place according to medieval Jews in the equivalent of 68 C.E. They had, finally, a cosmogonic calendar by which to position themselves in regard to the origin of the universe: the Era of Creation, its year 1 given variously as the equivalent of 3762, 3761, 3760, or 3758 B.C.E.

Retreating the furthest in time, this Jewish *Anno Mundi* calendar was paradoxically the least ancient, widely adopted only around or after the middle of the 251st cycle, 1311 of the Seleucid Era, 932 *Hurban*, 4760 A.M., or, if you will, the year 1000 C.E.[29]

With so many runs of time, with so ready a set of prophetic periods as those in the Book of Daniel, with so rehearsed a habit of converting letters into numbers and years into words by means of the ciphering techniques known as *gematria*, medieval Jews had a wide ambit for messianic mathematics. The Messiah might appear after five thousand years of Creation to reign over a sixth millennium before a concluding thousand years of chaos (4 Ezra 14.48; Sanhedrin 97a), or at the end of six thousand-year days of the world-week (2 Enoch 33), or at the tag end of the wars of Gog and Magog (Ezekiel 38), or 1290 or 1335 day-years "from the moment that the perpetual sacrifice is abolished and the disastrous abomination erected" (Daniel 12.11), or "two thousand three hundred evenings and mornings" after the sanctuary has been trampled underfoot (Daniel 8.14), or upon the completion of "a time and [two] times and half a time" (Daniel 12.7, 7.25). If the interpretation of such numbers made for a redemptive schedule too slack or too slow, the rabbis had recourse to historical symmetries: the four hundred years of bondage in Egypt would be matched by four hundred years of Roman persecution, from the *Ḥurban habayit* to a final exodus, the messianic age, in the not impossibly distant future. At hand as placemarkers toward that messianic age were the four, later five, great empires—Assyrian/Babylonian, Persian, Greek, Roman, later Islamic—under whom Israel had suffered, and after whose successive rise and fall the Messiah would be sure to come (Daniel 7).[30]

The more compelling the interpretation of a prophetic vision, the more impressive had to be its historical coordinates. Approaching 500 C.E., for example, Jewish apocalyptic expectations ran high because of the imposing coincidence of the fall of Rome, the expiration of the six thousand years of the (Byzantine) world-week, and the end of the four hundred years beyond *Ḥurban*. When the dramatic onslaught of Islamic armies changed the conditions of Jewish life on the eastern and southern shores of the Mediterranean, Jews staked their messianic calculations to Islam as Gog or Magog, then to successive caliphates as the last of the world empires. Some looked to an instant redemption, others further ahead, allowing the world more rope by which to hang itself. In the original *Book of Zerubabel*, composed shortly before or after Muhammad's death, the messianic age was imminent, but as dynasty followed dynasty, editors entrusted the angel Metatron with a more circumspect prediction: the Messiah would arrive nine hundred ninety years after the destruction of the Second Temple, or in 1058 C.E. Messianic speculations also converged upon an earlier year, 968 C.E., while the *Book of Zerubabel* remained a well-read apocalyptic text, provoking the usually phlegmatic, present-minded sages of the Rhineland to wonder whether the Messiah was indeed on his way.[31]

Once the millennial years 990 and 1000 Ḥurban had passed without commotion, the messianic impulse was, it seems, translated by way of *gematria* into the music of the 256th lunar cycle: the number 256 when set out in Hebrew characters yielded *Ranu*, the first word of the prophetic promise of Jeremiah 31.7, "Sing"—with gladness for Jacob, etc., as we have already heard. Composing within earshot of weeping and outcry, Solomon bar Simson and other Jewish chroniclers of the First Crusade made careful allusion to an era of messianic hopes just before, a singing time during which the harmonies of Redemption had been alive in the air.[32]

These hopes were a pious fiction, contrived more promptly than the "panic terror" of 1000 A.D. but toward the same rhetorical effect, to heighten the contrast between what had been and what would be. In temper and tenor, however, the Christian millennial legend and the Jewish memorial records were retrograde. The Janus faces of 1000 A.D. turn from terror to relief, from darkness to light; the Talmudic double-faced Adam of 4856 A.M. turns from a passive attendance upon the Messiah to an active, vehement martyrdom.[33]

What had to be absolutely clear, what Jewish chroniclers had to *make* absolutely clear, was not suspense but shock. Jewish communities had earlier been subject to sporadic attacks and expulsions, but they had customarily fended off disaster by bribing their enemies and appealing for protection to the highest authorities, bishops and kings who relied upon their services as translators, physicians, commercial brokers and bankers. In 1096 neither gold nor Peace of God nor royal guarantee sufficed. Nor were Jews, rarely trained in combat or granted the privilege of wearing a sword, better able to protect themselves when they donned armor and fought on the parapets at Mainz. Nor could they trust to the sanctuary of holy places, Jewish or Christian. Nor could caves, cellars, or catacombs keep them long from the gangs of Count Emicho, "may his bones be ground to dust between iron millstones." There was no refuge from the slaughter. Five thousand European Jews—children, women, men—died in the first months of the First Crusade.[34]

If such extreme violence was unanticipated, equally unanticipated was the extreme response of the Jews under siege, for many of the five thousand martyrs died by their own hands or at the hands of their loved ones, "each man his kin, his wife and children; bridegrooms slew their betrothed and merciful women their only children." These ritual suicides were, for medieval Jews, entirely without precedent. "Let the ears hearing this . . . be seared, for who has heard or seen the likes of it? Inquire and seek: was there ever such a mass sacrificial offering since the time of Adam? Did it ever occur that there were one thousand and one hundred offerings on one single day— all of them comparable to the sacrifice of Isaac, the son of Abraham?" Yet, at the last, Isaac was not sacrificed by Abraham on Mount Moriah. In the heat of the rhetorical moment, Solomon bar Simson took to a merciless extreme one of the very few parallels he could summon from Scripture. The closest Biblical parallel lay in the Book of Daniel, where the Jews Hananiah, Mishael, and Azariah (Shadrach, Meshach, and Abednego) refused to disavow their God and were thrown into Nebuchadnezzar's fiery furnace. Yet they too were delivered from death; after praising the name of the Lord, they emerged unscathed from the flames. Jews in 1096 did not emerge unscathed, were not delivered by a merciful God. "[T]heir Father did not answer them; He obstructed their prayers, concealing Himself in a cloud through which their prayers could not pass . . . [for] this was the generation that had been chosen by Him to be His portion," the burnt offering that had lapsed with the destruction of the Second Temple.[35]

What became clear, what chroniclers, rabbis, and poets *made* clear, was that nothing but the Temple sacrifice itself could be sufficient analogue to the martyrdoms of 1096. Those who killed themselves and their children rather than betray their faith had reenacted the Temple cult as both high priests and sacrificial victims. They had spilled their own blood for *Kiddush haShem*, to Sanctify the Name of the Lord. Their suicides were aspersive enough to cleanse the Holy of Holies even as they invoked *Ḥurban*.[36]

Through these janiform deaths, the year 4856 A.M./1028 *Ḥurban*/11 *Ranu*/1407 of the Seleucid Era was fixed at the crossroads of four calendars. In the cosmogonic calendar, 4856 testified to an event without precedent since Creation. The event was fashioned into a second Week of Creation, moving from the chaos of crusader violence, past the first day of martyrdom as the slain faithful entered the "World-that-is-All-Light," to a day of rec-ollection—the sabbath before Shavuot, "the very day on which the Children of Israel arrived at Mount Sinai to receive the Torah," and the very day on which Jews would soon commemorate the martyrs. In the national calendar, 1028 stood witness to the recapitulation of *Ḥurban*, end and renewal of sacred time. That year was also claimed as the end of a generation: "The majority of the rabbis in all the communities and many distinguished personalities passed away a year before the advent of the day of the Lord, the time of the enactment of the decree" proclaiming the Crusade. The new generation had then to be, through holy suicide, a re-generation. In the astronomical cycle of the liturgical calendar, 11 *Ranu* gave rise to an epicycle, a calendar of the dead. Annually, on the new moon of the month of Sivan (the sabbath before Shavuot), Jews in synagogue would now read out the individual names of the martyrs. This was a startling innovation for a culture whose ritual focus had been always on the group as a whole, and it would lead to the introduction of a Mourner's Kaddish which extended the formal, vocal act of remembrance beyond the circle of the martyred to all Jews who had died, and to each by name. In the political calendar, 1407 bore the marks of the first important Jewish acknowledgment of Christendom as another empire in the sequence of world empires, for not since the fall of Rome (or, in the East, the rise of Islam) had Jews set their historical clocks by an event whose political momentum came so completely from without. We may suspect too that such an allusion as Solomon bar Simson's to "one thousand and one hundred offerings on a single day" depended less on a count of the bodies of the martyred than on a caustic numerology meant to implicate the Christian year 1100 A.D. in the massacre of Jews.[37]

As 4856 A.M. or 1028 *Ḥurban* or 11 *Ranu* or 1407 of the Seleucid Era, the year was most clearly a New Year, party at once to chaos and creation, to defilement and sanctification, to the wandering in Sinai and the giving of the Law, to exile and return. Even though the remorselessness of the crusaders and the stubbornness of the martyrs left little if any lasting scar on the body politic of European Jewry, this year of shock and suicide became *the* liturgical and historical heartstead for all the martyrdoms that would follow in the wake of Inquisition, expulsion, and pogrom, through 1492, 1648, 1881, 1905, 1919, to the devastation of the Holocaust. This selfsame janiform year, Jews in France, Sicily, Salonika, and the Khazar Kingdom met the news of the First Crusade with messianic excitement, with desert marches to recover the Ten Lost Tribes, and with visions of Elijah, precursor to the arrival of the Messiah. In the immediate wake of the Crusade, messianic pretenders appeared in Spain, northern Palestine, and Khazaria. Centuries later, mystics would yet flag 4856 A.M. as putatively redemptive, the year when the Messiah should have come. And today, for Jewish literary scholars, the year is still heralded as "a true turning point" in the "image-making capacity of the [Jewish] religious mentality."[38]

The other prey of the crusaders, the Muslim "infidels," found themselves around the year 489 A.H. (after the Hejira) locked in a conflict over two images already fashioned by the (Islamic) religious mentality. That comparative ease with which Christian armies conquered the Holy Land was due in good measure to ongoing hostilities between two İslamic empires—the first North African (Fatimid), the second Turkish (Seljuq)—and between two opposed images of Islamic leadership, Shicite and Sunni. Shicites had split from Sunni orthodoxy over the nature of the succession to the robes of the Prophet, whose assumption of the magistracy of Medina in 622 A.D. became year 1 A.H. of the Islamic calendar. The Sunni/Shicite split went far beyond a simple if mortal feud between those (the Sunni) who adhered to the line from Muhammad's father-in-law and those (the Shicites) who hewed to the line from son-in-law cAli. What most deeply divided the two parties were their guiding images of Islam. In both Sunni and Shica tradition the law of the Qurcan was the single inviolable standard, but the Sunni state allowed for a diplomatic distinction between religious and political life, whereas the Shicite state was intensely theocratic, centered upon an inspired man, or *imam*, of the same prophetic mold as Muhammad. For uncompromising Shicites, Muslim leadership had to bespeak more than cunning intimidation and power play; it had to be numinous and charismatic.

This severely foreshortened explanation of Islamic schism has not been meant solely as a ruse to introduce one more calendar into the Western scheme of things, nor is a single paragraph meant to stand as surety of fairness to a complex culture which has always been at the elbows of the West and often its master intelligence. Rather, I mean here to take us directly to another calendar of the dead and to the earliest chronic anticipation of the ends of centuries.

For some Shicites, the murder of cAli's son and the violent deaths of succeeding imams led to the notion that the fate of all but the last imam was to be martyred. The last, the twelfth imam, who disappeared as a child in the middle of the 3rd century A.H., was in hiding. So arose the Twelver Shicites, constantly alert for signs that the times were ripe for the twelfth imam to reveal himself and restore to Islam a justly ordered state. A more radical group, splitting once again over the issue of succession, built up a profoundly esoteric theosophy around the image of the imam "in occultation." Secret, fervid, and strictly organized by grades of initiates, Ismacili Shicites were the motive force behind the Fatimid dynasty. The first of the Fatimid caliphs, arising in Tunisia at the very end of the 3rd century A.H., implied that he was the last imam, revealing himself for the good of Islam.[39]

In lieu of, if not in conjunction with, the (hidden) imam, another redemptive figure had become central to Islamic eschatology: the *Mahdi* or "rightly guided one," a political leader whose commanding virtues were frequently (con)fused with the spiritual and prophetic authority of the Awaited One, the last imam. By the end of the 4th century A.H., Islamic lore—Shiᶜite and sometimes also Sunni—had it that the beginning of each century A.H. would be graced with the emergence of a Mahdi to reform the faith and lead Muslims into a new age. Thus the positive excitement over the otherwise disturbing extremism of Fatimid caliph al-Ḥakim, who resumed a policy of Muslim exclusivism exactly in the year 400 A.H. (written with zeros, using Hindu-Arabic numerals). The revival of intolerance for Jews and Christians, both subject to humiliation and persecution under al-Ḥakim, was meant as manifesto that the Islamic world was about to be purified by the Mahdi. Before his death or disappearance in 412 A.H., al-Ḥakim had gone much further than the appropriation of the role of Mahdi; he had declared that he was not only inaugurating a new age but was himself an aspect of the godhead. It was as deity incarnate that al-Ḥakim in 400 A.H. (1009 A.D.) could without qualm demolish the Church of the Holy Sepulchre in Jerusalem.[40]

While the knights and bishops of the First Crusade were envisioning a Christian kingdom in Jerusalem and the reconstruction of the Church of the Holy Sepulchre, images of Mahdi, imam, and martyrdom had come together in an end-of-century movement led by the Persian Ismaᶜili Shiᶜite Ḥasan i Ṣabbaḥ. Quarreling with the moral and institutional decay of the Fatimids, and yet again with the succession to the caliphate in 487 A.H. (1094 A.D.), Ḥasan established within eastern (Seljuq) territories the "New Preaching," an Islamic reform campaign that became increasingly deadly over the course of the next century, when the sect would enter the annals of the Christian West as the Assassins. Fiercely loyal to their Grand Master, called the Old Man of the Mountain, who ruled from the fortress of Alamut in the mountains south of the Caspian Sea, these Ismaᶜili zealots murdered their political rivals in the name of the hidden imam, whose place in time was complicated now by an extraordinarily elaborate theory of vast historical cycles of chaos and redemption. Most Assassins, neither philosophers nor theologians, positioned themselves within those cycles by appending to the Twelver calendar of the martyred imams their own individual martyrdoms, for the cause of Islam and at the behest of the Old Man of the Mountain. If on their wayward road to the Holy Land, marauding crusaders had caused European Jews to recast their images of martyrdom, notions of redemptive time, and rituals of mourning, crusaders closer to Jerusalem would ride through rival and fragmenting Muslim domains, Fatimid Shiʿite and Seljuq Sunni both threatened by the upsurge of New Preaching which recast Islamic images of martyrdom, notions of redemptive time, and manners of attendance upon a hidden imam who lay in suspended animation at the end of a calendar of imams long dead.[41]

The crusaders themselves came armed with a papal assurance that each crusading death would be tallied as the death of a Christian martyr. An indulgence, or partial remission of penalties for sins, had first been granted in 1063 to Christians fighting against infidels in Spain. Holy warfare appealed not only to knights chafing at the bit of the Truce of God, but also to the papacy in its bid for political supremacy in Europe. When Pope Urban II campaigned in 1095 for a holy war to liberate Jerusalem, he began with an address to the nobles and clerics of the Council of Clermont, who had been hard at work on the details of the Truce of God. By centering the crusade upon Jerusalem, and by offering crusaders indulgences, including a full remission of sins should they die "on the road or the sea or fighting against the pagan," Urban II transformed a military expedition into a massive pilgrimage. While shrines were inundated with the sloughed-off crutches of those who had been miraculously healed of their paralysis, prospective warriors were moved by visions of dead friends exhorting them to take up the cross. A papal bull, dated 1010 but forged around 1096, gave historical momentum to the crusade, calling for a fleet of one thousand ships to avenge the (recent) destruction of the Church of the Holy Sepulchre.[42]

Shoved from behind by a forceful bull and the friendly dead, taken arm in arm by papal warrants of immediate sanctity and clear sailing after death, crusaders were drawn toward Jerusalem by highly colored visions of the Holy City as Heavenly City at the end of time. Although the eschatological images of Urban II's crusade orations may have been fabricated by subsequent chroniclers, the Millennium clearly beckoned in the crusade preaching of Peter the Hermit, who shared with the Pope an intense admiration for the "apostolic life," a slogan referring at once to Church reform and the approach of the Last Judgment. In 1096, according to the influential *Rosenfeld Annals*, "balls of fire . . . shone forth in different places and reconstituted themselves in another part of the sky." These were nought but "angelic powers which, by their migration, were signifying the movement and foreshadowing the departure of people from their places, which later seized nearly all the western world." Then did Peter emerge, "carrying around a *cartula*, which he claimed to have fallen from heaven, which said that all Christendom from all parts of the world must migrate in arms to Jerusalem, drive the pagans out from there and take possession of it with its region forever." Peter was preaching from Luke 21.24: "And Jerusalem shall be trodden down by the gentiles, until the times of the gentiles are fulfilled."[43]

If the times were fulfilling, if the urban poor who swarmed to the side of Peter the Hermit were to enter the millennial city, then the Last World Emperor had also to wake and make his way to Jerusalem, where he must be crowned. The First Crusade opened with men measuring their leaders against this mythic figure, arisen from a sibylline sleep to do battle with a newly articulate and articulated Antichrist. Some recognized the Last Emperor in the person of Count Raymond of Toulouse, others in Count Emicho of Leiningen, who did indeed have messianic pretensions and who sped to the apocalyptic task of scouring Christendom of those betrayers of Christ, the Jews.[44]

We have come to one of the full circles in this book, from the Jewish 4856 A.M. through the Islamic 489 A.H. to the Christian 1096 A.D., and back to the Jews. In each case, and at approximately the same time, issues of martyrdom and of mourning, calendars of the dead and of redemption, elliptical figures of prophetic succession and historical climax became vitally important. I have tailored the narrative of this convergence of critical concerns among Jews, Muslims, and Christians so that it appears as more than mere coincidence at the end of the 11th century (A.D.). But coincidence it is, and one that need not be attributed to end-of-*century* expectations. Neither Jews nor Christians in 1096 were necessarily counting by centuries, and I have presumed mightily upon Muslim tradition, whose 5th century A.H. came to its end a full decade after the launching of the First Crusade. Everything written here about the 1090s has been a prime example of special pleading toward that special effect, the *fin de siècle*.[45]

And yet, at the close of centuries we feed upon coincidence. We speak often of serendipity, synchronicity, conjunctions. The janiform calendar of the '90s conjures up "Auld Lang Syne" and Armageddon, future conditional and future perfect. Martyrs and messiahs, mourning and morning *should* converge in the fullness of time each hundred years. We are therefore inclined to be persuaded of grand convergences at other centuries' ends, and inclined to assume that people have always remarked those convergences, always understood them as the natural inclination of History. We have however a few historical hills to climb before we can survey a *fin de siècle* which is not a figment of our own.

Abbas Joachim magnus propheta.

Hec subiecta in hoc continentur libello.
Expositio magni ppbete Joachim: in libruz beati Ci-
rilli de magnis tribulationib⁹ z statu sancte mfis ecclesie: ab hiis nostris tcporib⁹ vscz in funem seculi: vna cuz
copilatione et diuersis ppbetz noui ac veterz testameti
Theolosphori de Cusentia: presbyteri z heremite.
Item explanatio figurata z pulchra in Apochalypsiz
de residuo statu ecclesie: z de trib⁹ veh vcturis debitis
semper adiectis terrib⁹sacrc scripture ac prophetar.
Item tractatus de antechristo magistri Joanis pari-
siensis ordinis predicatorum.
Item tractatus de septem statib⁹ ecclesic deuoti do-
ctoris fratris Abertini de Casali ordinis minorum.
Cum gratia vt patet infra.

Portrait of Abbot Joachim of Fiore, "the great prophet," from the title page of *De Magnis Tribulationibus* . . . (Venice, 1516), reproduced in Marjorie Reeves and Warwick Gould, *Joachim of Fiore and the Myth of the Eternal Evangel in the Nineteenth Century* (Clarendon Press, 1987). Courtesy of Oxford University Press.

A THIRD AGE:
THE 1190s

NIGH UNTO THE END OF THE 12TH CENTURY, A GRAND CON-
vergence did occur: all the known planets came together under the sign of
Libra, the Scales of Justice. This conjunction boded so ill that a pseudonymous Spanish astrologer wrote to warn of the high winds and harsh quakes
that would level the earth in September of 1186. John of Toledo's warnings
did not go unheeded: "In Germany, people began to dig shelters, in Persia
and Mesopotamia they repaired their cellars, in Constantinople the Byzantine
Emperor caused the windows of his palace to be walled up, in England the
Archbishop of Canterbury proclaimed a national fast of atonement." I am
quoting from a modern, dubiously inflated account of responses to John's
revelations, but his Toledo Letter was without doubt one of the most popular
and evocative of short medieval prophecies. Its conjunction rescheduled, its
warnings revised, it would circulate from one end of Europe to another for
some three hundred years.[46]

The wide reach of the Toledo Letter, starting in the late 12th century,
signalled the adoption by the Christian West of a sophisticated Islamic
astrological tradition which granted planetary motions a fateful power over
terrestrial events. Judicial astrology was distinct from the typical European
chronicler's regard for celestial phenomena. Hail, lightning storms, blood-
red suns, or a moon and stars circling four other moons in the evening sky
around Christmas of the year 1200—these were taken as unique insignia
of disaster or prodigy, special to the moment and uncomplicated by physical law. The movements of the planets, on the contrary, were lawful and
recurrent, seeming to align, cluster, conjoin, and oppose each other in
compelling historical cycles which allowed astrologers the luxury of prediction.[47]

To be sure, the skies had been closely monitored by astrologers in Rome,
and medieval Christian doctors had kept up the old Stoic associations between
the balance of humors in the human body and the dynamics of the seven
determinate heavenly bodies (sun, moon, Mercury, Venus, Mars, Jupiter,
and Saturn). European concern with systematic astrology, however, was new
to the 12th century, preparing the way for the analogous idea of periodic
convergences of pivotal human events. The cast of mind which could be
impressed by astrological conjunctions occurring at rare but regular intervals

was similar to the cast of mind which could anticipate the end of each hundred calendar years as inevitably the end of an epoch.

Barely escaped from the Jupiter Effect, wading in the shallows of the Aquarian Age, we who consult the astrological columns of daily newspapers, or who wear bracelets identifying ourselves by birth signs, or who work for world peace under the aegis of the Harmonic Convergence, we more than any others may appreciate the appeal of the Toledo Letter. Systematic astrology during the 12th century was a timely and rational approach to the increasingly urgent problem of accommodating change and novelty within a conservative world of divine law. Not everything new could be claimed either as miracle or as evidence of human ignorance; astrology with its long celestial cycles and charts of benign and malign influences could account at once for regularity and for what seemed to come completely unannounced.

Well, not completely unannounced. The comet of 1196/97, like other comets before and after, was still a puzzle. Neither astrology nor astronomy nor physics nor theology afforded convincing explanations for swashes of celestial fire and light which appeared then disappeared in the course of weeks or months. Comets posed problems overhead which during the 12th century were also being posed on terra firma in the first debates between Ancients and Moderns: What philosophical and aesthetic value should we assign to the new as against the old? Does novelty have any moral standing? What can it teach the pious who have in Scripture a fund of eternal truths? The answer to these questions was never easy for Christians, who had of course to accommodate history to a *New* Testament. The stock answer in the past had been that the old was the enduring and the true; that the new was untrustworthy unless certified by (as) miracle, and that novelty was (excepting always the novelty of Christ) a temporary suspension of natural law. Late in the 12th century there was a recognizable shift away from the stock answer. While the Church in the 1170s began to map out Purgatory, a place of radical tensions between the temporal and the eternal; while merchants in the 1190s began to shape insurance instruments through which daily risks and long-term investments could be counterpoised; while exchequers began to work with a new set of (Hindu-Arabic) figures and a new symbol, the zero, theologians and historians began to think in terms of change.[48]

Some changes seemed to call attention to themselves. Prompted by the winter comet of 1196/97, English prelate Robert Grosseteste wrote *De Cometis*, mulling over the consistently awkward position of comets (hybrids between heaven and earth, not unlike Purgatory). At the same time he was disturbed about the position of the Christian festivals, which were pulling uncomfortably ahead of the seasons to which they were apt. Since the Julian/ Dionysian year of 365 days (even with its leap year of 366 days) was fractionally longer than the solar year, the Western Christian calendar was gradually withdrawing its major rituals from the equinoxes and solstices which punctuate the seasons. The ecclesiastical round in 1200 A.D. would be a full ten days in advance of the sun. This deviation was more distressing to Grosseteste and his contemporaries than to learned men of earlier periods, who had lived calmly with eight and nine days' deviation; in addition to their estimate of the cumulative deviation, it was their new respect for the conjunction of time and event which made calendar reform so salient a concern of scholars in the late 12th and 13th centuries.[49]

Similarly, chroniclers were beginning to occupy themselves with the cumulative effects of history as a progression of human events from ancient to modern times. The progression, it now seemed, had not come to its practical end with the foundation of the Christian Church; indeed, there were in the 12th century earnest discussions of the fixedness of "futurity" itself, whose events were perhaps necessary, perhaps contingent. As men (and at least one woman, Hildegard of Bingen) began to entertain the prospect of continuous historical development through to the end of time at the Last Judgment, they sapped the formal structure of Augustinian chronodoxy, which had imposed a solemn historical perfection upon the sixth age, the (indefinite) millennial reign of the Church. If the passage of the soul involved a new, purgatorial stage, and if the mundane world passed under the successive influences of newly potent planetary conjunctions, then the moment was ripe for rethinking the nature and sequence of historical ages.[50]

He who most persuasively reconceived the ages was also he who gave most thought to futurity, and who acted as seer to popes and kings alike: the abbot Joachim of Fiore. In 1183, wrote Joachim, "about the middle of the night's silence, as I think, the hour when it is thought that our Lion of the tribe of Judah rose from the dead, as I was meditating [upon the *Apocalypse*], suddenly something of the fullness of this book and of the entire harmony of the Old and New Testaments was perceived with clarity of understanding in my mind's eye." The midnight harmony led the Calabrian abbot from the past through the present into the future, for in the concordance between the Testaments Joachim saw an historical progression which was not yet complete. There had been, for example, seven persecutions of Jews in the Old Testament, so there must be seven trials of the Church under the New Testament; four trials had passed, three lay (just) ahead. In

1184, Joachim was reading the *Apocalypse* as a prophetic book, much as it had been read by early Christians until St. Augustine transmuted it into an exclusively spiritual text dedicated to issues of faith and ecclesia. Applying the *Apocalypse* narrative to events in Christian history, Joachim found that his were the times of the opening of the sixth seal (Revelation 6.12–17) with its earthquake, its sun black as sackcloth, its moon red as blood, its stars falling to earth like figs dropping from a fig tree in high winds—all forecast that same year by the Toledo Letter, which had conjoined 12th-century translations of Islamic astrology to 12th-century intoxication with the symbols of the *Apocalypse*. These were also, it turned out, the times of the vigorous Muslim commander Saladin, sixth head of the seven-headed dragon of Revelation 12.3, who crushed the Crusader Kingdom of Jerusalem in 1187. And these were the times of Antichrist himself, young and restless, waiting impatiently to suborn the faithful. Expect therefore and soon a double trouble, trials five and six of the Church, assailed by infidels without and betrayed from within, wrote Joachim, who was not loath to speak of such imminent tribulations in the presence of Pope Lucius III, Richard Lion-Heart of England, or Emperor Henry VI of Germany.[51]

Joachim took one further, radical, boldly prophetic step. Intent on figures and analogies of historical and spiritual progress, Joachim posited a third age (or *status*) which was neither a heavenly kingdom nor a millennial sabbath. Rather, the third age lay entirely within history, apotheosis to a trinitarian historical series: the Age of God the Father, under the authority of the Old Testament and the Jewish family; the Age of Christ the Son, under the New Testament and Christian clergy; the Age of the Holy Spirit, under the same gospels but guided by a reformed Church, a truly devout Pope, and a "new people of God." These *viri spirituales* would be of two sorts, preachers and contemplatives, modelled upon the best of monastics. Together they would have the spiritual stamina to overcome the threats from Islam and Antichrist, the spiritual intelligence to comprehend the prophetic fullness of Scripture, and the spiritual force to convert the Jews and Eastern Christians to the Universal Church of St. Peter.[52]

The Age of the Holy Spirit had already begun in Joachim's day, and the year 1200 appealed to him as a dramatic vantage point from which its first stages might be reviewed. But Joachim never established a specific inaugural date for the peaceable world which was implicit in his vision of a third *status*; only later, after his death in 1202, would his most fervent (Franciscan) admirers look toward 1260 A.D. for the spiritual and political transformation enjoined by the Joachimite Age of the Holy Spirit. Nor did Joachim ever suppose a third testament to supersede the other two; his trinitarian logic was taken to this extreme by Gerard of Borgo San Donnino, who declared in 1254 that scriptural authority was now passing to the Everlasting Gospel (of Revelation 14.6), an Eternal Evangel of a deepening, progressive revelation. Nor did Joachim, avid though he was for Church reform and peace between kings and pontiffs, foresee a supremely spiritual, virtually celestial avatar of the third age; the image of an Angel Pope would be cut in high relief over the portals of the next generations as holy twin to the Last World Emperor, about whom Joachim never spoke. Mistaken, misappropriated, Joachim's wonderfully schematic trees of salvation history would bear misshapen fruit for hundreds of years, down to the New Age sweetsops of the 1980s.[53]

We ourselves may be excused from a strict construction of Joachim's canon. What matters here is that his works—or, more often than not, extravagances palmed off on Joachim by his Epigoni—are called into active service so frequently at the ends of centuries, when the spiritual reform and Everlasting Gospel of a new historical age are most welcome. In this context, Joachim's legacy has been threefold: the emphasis upon a metamorphosis (1) still to come *within* history, promising (2) profound new revelations of world harmonies, and (3) charged to a new breed of men.

At the end of the 12th century there were several distinct candidates for this new breed of man. First, the Cathars, heterodox Christians who claimed explicitly to be new men and new women sanctified by a class of *perfecti*, an unblemished elite whose ascetic lives stood absolutely on the side of good in the precarious conflict between God's pure realm of the spirit and Satan's foul realm of matter. So inviting was such heretical dualism in the 1190s that the Church had to enlist Inquisition (from 1199) and Crusade (from 1209) against Cathar strongholds in Italy, Aragon, and southern France. Next, the monks of a new mendicant order (approved in 1209), an order whose founder, St. Francis of Assisi, was regularly depicted as the prototype of Joachim's *viri spirituales*. Last, an apostolic complement of knights and their singular wizard, Merlin, whose prophecies were studied at midcentury in university cloisters, chanceries, and cathedrals while the earliest of Grail romances made the rounds of courts and castle gardens. The bones of Arthur himself, "a renowned king of Britain," were found "in a very old sarcophagus" at Glastonbury in 1191.[54]

Three very different avant-gardes for the new age: one which meant to keep clear of the degenerate, incarnate, historical world, cleaving instead to the irrefrangible world of the spirit; another which waded into the morass of the material world, free of affection for its dubious goods but all heart for the poorest of its people, through whom (with the help of the Holy Spirit) all might be redeemed; a third, romantic, which recalled the heroism and magical finesse of a lost world, inspiring ladies and their knights toward a Christian, almost pentecostal, chivalry. Three opposing avant-gardes who will put themselves forward again and again at centuries' ends: the Manichaeans, hardliners who spurn any compromise with *fin de siècle* decadence and who seem partial to those disasters attendant upon the cleansing of the world; the Redeemers, selfless campaigners sacrificing themselves in the straits between the awfully probable and the woefully unthinkable; the Fantasticks, who envision a world dramatically restored in the name of infinite possibility. We meet them at our *fin de siècle* as, in turn, fundamentalists, ecologists, technobrats. All have their roots, as avant-gardes, in Joachim of Fiore's "new people of God."[55]

Despite the Cathars, the Franciscans, the Round-Table Knights, despite the astrology of John of Toledo and the prophecies of Merlin, there was little public thought given in the last days of Joachim to the 1190s as the closing of one age and the years 1200/1201 as the opening of another. The end of the 12th century was not quite, in our terms, a century's end. True, around 1200 St. Abraham of Smolensk was preaching an imminent Last Judgment, but this was in the Russian context of a Byzantine world-era of 6708 A.M. True, Fulk of Neuilly in 1200 was preaching a crusade to the poor, but this was more evangelical than millenarian, and the "Unholy" Fourth Crusade of 1204 would conquer not the antichristian Turks but the Eastern Christians of Constantinople. True, Pope Innocent III around 1200 had expectations of the Second Coming, but these were for the year 1284 A.D., 666 years after the rise of Islam, the Beast of the *Apocalypse*. True, Jews in 1200 were counting toward their own messianic kingdom, but even after the first blood libels accusing Jews of the ritual murder of Christian children (1144, 1147, 1168, 1171, 1182), the first burnings of Jews at the stake (1171, 1191), massacres of Rhineland Jews during the Second and Third Crusades (1146, 1183), and renewed acts of suicidal martyrdom in the midst of anti-Jewish riots (1190), deliverance of the Chosen People was generally held at arm's length, forty years off, in that promised land of the Jewish calendar, 5000 A.M.[56]

With the advent of the Mongols, those demon "Tartars" from the depths of hell or Tartarus, the end of the fifth Jewish millennium had something to recommend it as an epochal year in world history.[57] Mongol horsemen had swept across Russia between 1237 and 1240; the next year, 1241/5001,

Central Europe lay open to them upon their defeat of an Hungarian army, but the Golden Horde paused, distracted by events elsewhere in Asia, and Mongol cavalry did not ride, as well they might have, through to the North Sea or the Atlantic. This fortuitous pause was the janiform relief (war/peace) of the first year of the sixth Jewish millennium. We ourselves cannot rest content with mere relief, for within our sights is jubilee.

JUBILEE: THE 1290s

THERE IS CAUSE FOR JUBILATION. WE HAVE ARRIVED AT THE first end of a Christian century that was publicly celebrated by Christians as a century's end. Finally in place were the desiderata of any *fin de siècle*:

a standard (*Anno Domini*) calendar;

an additive, arithmetical sense of the passage of time;

an especial concern with ages and periods;

a habit of looking for historically meaningful conjunctions of events;

despair over the decay of institutions and the lapse of moral courage in these, the last days;

prophetic hopes of a new, vigorous, spiritually reformed (third) age *within* history;

the image of an avant-garde.

These are the barest rudiments of a century's end, and some were barely present at the end of the 13th century. Over subsequent centuries, the standard calendar would become more uniform and more universal, common folk would become more numerate and time more numerical, ages would be more demanding, historical conjunctions more transfixing, despair perhaps more despondent, hope perhaps more delirious, avant-gardes more forward and offensive. We are however on reasonably secure ground to salute the 1290s as the first, primitive, European *fin de siècle*.

We have come to this ground by courtesy of the abbots Dennis the Diminutive and Joachim of Fiore, and it is to monks that we owe the mechanisms not only of an *Anno Domini* calendar and a third historical age but also of that new timepiece, the weight-driven clock, an invention of the late 13th century. Monastic obsession with punctuality had its origins in the early Christian desire for prayer day and night—a desire rooted in apocalypse: prayer must be constant when the end is near. Such constancy was impractical for the vast majority of the faithful, who found that in the lingering meanwhile before the Second Coming they had to pursue their

Pope Boniface VIII on the Gallery of the Lateran Palace, announcing the Jubilee of
1300. Reproduction of the fresco, attributed to Giotto, formerly in San Giovanni
Lateran in Rome, from MS. F227 inf., in the Biblioteca Ambrosiana, Milan. Courtesy
of the Biblioteca Ambrosiana.

livelihoods in the same old world. Monks then took upon themselves the eschatological burden; their fidelity to a tight, rigorous schedule of worship became one of the cardinal points of monastic discipline. Monasteries had therefore to maintain systems for alerting their religious to the hours of communal prayer, which were spaced closely and with increasing regularity throughout the morning, noon, and night. Monastic custodians used burning tapers that melted at a steady rate down through the divisions of the ritual day, but these demanded tedious attention from monks who would rush to ring the bells for matins (lauds), prime, tierce, sext, none, vespers, compline, and sometimes vigils. During the 11th century, when religious exactness had parsed the day into 541,440 (theoretical) atoms of time, monasteries developed water clocks which through ingenious design automatically rang bells for each of the canonical hours. Gearing and ingenuity were no match for the freezing of water in winter or its evaporation at the height of summer, but they could—and eventually did—contribute to the creation of a time-keeping device genuinely independent of the sun, the seasons, and the obsessive monks.[58]

Engineers of a mechanical, weight-driven clock were confronted with the technical problem of acceleration. Falling weights on strong cords furnished the motive force for the turning of a wheel through one full rotation each full day. As the wheel turned, it set in motion a train connected to a pointer or dial and to other gears for ringing bells. If the descent of the falling weights were not controlled, intervals from hour to hour would be uneven, and time would run more furiously at the end of the day than at the beginning. What European clockmakers had to invent was an escapement, something that would so control the descent of the weights as to apportion their energy in even increments or pulses. This they had done, by the remarkable means of verge and foliot, in the decades just before Pope Boniface VIII proclaimed a Jubilee.[59]

That the first (monastic) mechanical clocks and the first (papal) Jubilee should have been conjunct was more than fortuitous, for the church bells that rang out the Jubilee of 1300 were in a sense the monastic bells raised to a higher power. While the prayerful day was first being marked out by clockwork in discrete, even, precisely equal hourly intervals, Church-historical periods were for the first time being marked off exactly at the end of each one hundred years. Pilgrims, it was said, had been crying out to the Pope, "Give us your blessing before we die. We have heard it from those of old that every hundredth year every Christian who shall visit the bodies of the Blessed Apostles Peter and Paul is freed from the stain of sin and from its punishment." So, according to promoters of the Jubilee, in response to popular demand Boniface issued the bull *Antiquorum* on February 22, 1300 (retroactive to the Roman start of the year, Christmas), alluding to an ancient tradition of jubilee indulgences at centuries' ends. The indulgence would be granted to all Roman inhabitants who visited the designated basilicas thirty times, and to all pilgrims who made the holy rounds fifteen times. "And it was the most marvellous thing that was ever seen, for through-out the year, without break, there were in Rome . . . 200,000 pilgrims, not counting those who were coming and going on their journeys . . . and I can bear witness to this," wrote the Florentine historian Giovanni Villani, "for I was present and saw it." Cardinal Giacomo Stefaneschi, who was also present and saw it, recorded the story of a Savoyard, 107 years old, who had been carried to and through Rome on a litter in order to gain the Jubilee indulgence just as he remembered from his childhood his father had done a century ago.[60]

In truth, there had been no earlier Christian jubilee, neither in ancient days nor in the year 1200. Boniface's Jubilee was an invention almost as unparalleled as the verge and foliot escapement of the first weight-driven clocks. He had transformed the Levitical jubilee of forty-nine or fifty years into a centennial celebration of a new age that would begin with the clean slate of a year of absolution. There were no appreciable precedents. Late medieval chroniclers had on occasion noted "a year of jubilee," but they were referring to jubilation over victories against Muslim infidels and Cathar heretics or to the joy of a spell of peace in Europe. Since a partial remission of sins was promised to all crusaders, any year of crusade was in effect a year of indulgences, but the institution of a regular, calendrical jubilee was nowhere to be found.[61]

Those modern historians who, impressed by the *fin de siècle* spirit of the 1890s, assume that an astute pope was exploiting the inevitable fascination with a "mysterious change of century"[62] have missed the essential novelty of the event. Regardless of its nod toward antiquity, the bull *Antiquorum* did not build on custom. It established custom. For the Church: a Jubilee anchored to the '00 of the *Anno Domini* calendar, exclusive of paschal tables and all other gauges of ritual time. For Christian Europe: an expectation of momentous, once-in-a-lifetime opportunities at century's turn.

This is scarcely to claim that Boniface's Jubilee came as a bolt out of the blue. Rather, it was something of a flying buttress against the millenarian thrust of a powerfully theatrical penitential movement and dramatic proph-ecies of a third age soon to erupt from incubation. Processions of Flagellants had wound through Italy and then southern Germany in 1260–62, scourging themselves with whips, crying out for peace and mercy in years during which Spiritual Franciscans were intent on the coming to majority of the Age of the Holy Spirit under the aegis of a new breed of spiritual men and a new, Everlasting Gospel. That third historical age was apparently deferred, but new scriptures were shortly under way, conceived not by spiritual men but by spiritual women. The women were devoted to Guglielma of Milan, born on Pentecost and blazed in the 1270s with the stigmata of the crucified Christ. At her death and ascension to heaven in 1282, followers (female and male) identified her as the third person of the Trinity, who would return in 1300 to supervise a worldwide pentecostal conversion to the Church of the Holy Spirit. In the interim, her disciple Mayfreda di Piravano would stand as her earthly vicar, a new pope to usher in the new age with a new gospel, a new set of sacramental rites, and a college of female cardinals. Alarmed, inquisitors in 1300 subjected Guglielmites to cross-examination and torture, put three to death in 1302, then exhumed and burned the body of the Paraclete Guglielma so that she could not come around again. Making the rounds about the same time, however, were other radical resurrectees, Last World Emperors returned from the grave of the charismatic Emperor Frederick II, who had died (or disappeared) in 1250 before he could complete the world-historical mission many had imagined for him.[63]

Images of a final redemption shone with meteoric brilliance in 1294, when hermit and ascetic Pietro di Murrone was elevated to the papacy. At prayer in his cave in the mountains, the recluse protested his election, only to be routed from his wilderness retreat by a multitude of celebratory monks who saw in him the churchly avatar of the third age. Taking the name Celestine V, Pietro was (inadvertently?) encouraging visions of himself as Angel Pope at the head of the Joachimite *viri spirituales*. His resignation after five inept months convinced the most fervent reformers that if the holiest of men could do no good on St. Peter's throne, then Antichrist had to be close by. Indeed he was, according to the Spiritual Franciscans Peter John Olivi and Fra Dolcino, both of whom saw the end of the 13th century as the end of the age of a corrupt Church, with Celestine V's successor Boniface VIII as the false pope or Antichrist whose downfall must immediately precede the age of a reformed Church and the Holy Spirit. Boniface it was who, after the surprising abdication, ordered the imprisonment of Pietro in a cell in the castle of Fumone, where the unfortunate holy man died in 1296. That year bands of Flagellants once again made cruelly penitent tours of Europe, and a new Frederick, actual and actively opposed to the interests of Pope Boniface, was crowned king in Sicily. At the turn of the century, Fra Dolcino went so far as to predict that the Antichristian Boniface would die very soon, in 1303, to be followed by the true Angel Pope and the third age.[64]

Boniface did die in 1303, but not before proclaiming the Jubilee, which was meant in part to turn the millenarian tide at century's end to the advantage of the Papal See. Since the remaining Christian outposts in the Holy Land had been surrendered by 1291; since 13th-century crusades had in the long run exalted lay princes at the expense of the pontificate; and since European sovereigns were now less moved by the high adventure of crusade than by the high finance of statecraft, Boniface strategically dissolved the nearly exclusive bond between indulgence and crusade. In 1297 he offered one year and forty days' remission of sins to those who made Lenten pilgrimage to the "stations" or basilicas of Rome, in imitation of the stations of the cross in Jerusalem. The Jubilee of 1300 symbolically translated Jerusalem to Rome; the reward of a plenary indulgence for the Jubilee pilgrimage to Rome was as great as that granted pilgrims to Jerusalem and crusaders who died in battle with the Turk. Reorienting penitential and millennial enthusiasms toward the Holy City of Rome, refocusing Christian anticipation upon the powers of the head of the Church to draw tight the strings of ritual and purgatorial time, Boniface was laboring to strengthen the prestige of his position as earthly vicar of the Lord.[65]

The Jubilee of 1300 was therefore flying buttress as well against the dangerous political thrust of the secular state, whose monarchs were increasingly hostile to the privileges and prerogatives assumed by the Church in lands far from Rome. Boniface excluded from the benefits of the Jubilee his political opponents Frederick of Sicily, the Italian family of the Colonnas, their friends and allies (who would later take Boniface prisoner). And he attracted to Rome thousands of pilgrims who crossed the disputed borders of one secular state after another in their eagerness for the insuperable gift of plenary indulgence from that "Magnanimus Pontifex," great and charitable ruler, the Pope. In this respect the Jubilee was a shrewd demonstration of papal authority and an instructive prelude to the famous *Unam Sanctum* bull of 1302, in which Boniface asserted the ultimate supremacy of the Church over emperors, kings, and lesser potentates.[66]

It must have seemed to Boniface, as it did to the Flagellants, to pseudo-Fredericks, to Spiritual Franciscans, to Mayfreda di Piravano and her Guglielmite cardinals, to Fra Dolcino and his Apostolic Brethren, and to all those enthralled by the comet of 1299, that things were coming quickly to a head. Clearly, Boniface was reacting to inchoate *fin de siècle* sensations of the onrush of events when he invented the papal Jubilee, whose novelty he would have understood from the start, expert canon lawyer that he was. However, even as he used the Jubilee to re-center the Church in time and to dictate for the new century his own sort of new age, Boniface was looking over his shoulder. If he had taken up the jubal horn with his bulls, it was to sound the defense of a medieval Church under mounting pressure from radical reformers and rambunctious kings. Boniface's other jubilant innovation was also meant to keep the Church in control of the falling weights of its times. At the end of the Jubilee year, on Christmas Day, 1300/1301, Boniface issued a bull granting full indulgences to pilgrims who had died en route to Rome and—something new—to "certain souls in Purgatory." This unprecedented mandate over the purgatorial calendar was, like the Jubilee, a kind of escapement, a pontifical device for assuring command of time in an era when all the world seemed to be speeding up.[67]

Between the vignette of the old Savoyard, the Giotto fresco of Boniface blessing Jubilee pilgrims, and the prophetic portraits of an Angel Pope, European Christians had their choice of those three competing pictures of the *saeculum* which had earlier been painted by the Classical West. With the Savoyard at the visible end of his life borne to the Holy City like his father long before, the Etruscan *saeculum* was dominant: a century as the full natural length of a generation.[68] With Boniface's bulls and other propaganda for the Jubilee, the Claudian *saeculum* reappeared: a century as a centennial anniversary. With the pseudo-Joachimite prophecies, the visions of Fra Dolcino, the Guglielmite dedication to a female pope, the Augustan *saeculum* had taken hold: a century as the dawn of a new age—a third age, an Age of the Holy Spirit, a redemptive age of holy women.

Those with less prodigal *fin de siècle* dreams still took 1300 as their inspiration. Struck by the contrast between the thrill of the Jubilee crowds and the ruins of Rome, Giovanni Villani explained how he had decided to begin his history of Florence: "And I, finding myself on that blessed pilgrimage in the holy city of Rome, beholding the great and ancient things therein, . . . [b]ut considering that our city of Florence, the daughter and creature of Rome, was rising, and had great things before her, whilst Rome was declining, it seemed to me fitting to collect in this volume and new chronicle all the deeds and beginnings of the city of Florence . . . and thus in the year 1300, having returned from Rome, I began to compile this book." Villani's was a mild version of the Augustan *saeculum*, but he would not have composed his chronicle if he had not seen in 1300 that a new age was coming, and that Florence was its rising star.[69]

Another Florentine, banished from his beloved city by the Jubilee Pope, would set his *Divine Comedy* at Eastertide of the Jubilee year, during which many a pilgrim could envision himself standing atop Mount Purgatory on the way to the Empyrean. It was no mistake that Boniface VIII appears in the eighth circle of Hell, dangling the keys of salvation before Dante, intolerably proud of his power as Pope to "close and unclose" the gates of Heaven, while the geared mechanical clock appears in the eighth circle of Paradise, joyful image of spiritual acceleration under complete control.

> *As wheels in the smooth workings of a clock*
> *Turn so that the first seems motionless to him*
> *Who watches it, and the last seems to fly,*

so do happy spirits among the company of the blessed dance in spinning circles. For Dante, seduced in 1299 by the Pope's promises of divine forgiveness, Boniface VIII was a figure of fraud, of time misappropriated and faith misled. The mechanical clock, on the other hand, was a figure of time well heeded, of the true quickening of the soul through the appropriate circles of Purgatory, on to Paradise itself.[70]

Set in contraposition to the Jubilee, the *Divine Comedy* was a book of passage through the species of time, one *saeculum* after another. Dante begins "Halfway along the journey of our life," beset by the parabolic beasts who have put in question the thirty-five years of his middle age: the nimble leopard of his youth, the savage lion of his maturity, the famished she-wolf, ever gaunt, who devours those in their decline. She more than the leopard and the lion terrifies the poet, halts his ascent. She is the dark Etruscan symbol of the *saeculum* as a generation terminated by old age,

> *Who step by step was slowly drawing close,*
> *Kept pushing me to where the sun is silent.*

Rescued by Virgil, Dante tours an interminable Hell where the ages are drear, unmoving, and indistinct—no greater torment than to be frozen in place and flayed. Then up through a Purgatory of Claudian time, efficient and accountable. Only in Purgatory does time seem as precious as clockwork: "My son," Virgil says to Dante only once, in canto 23 of *Purgatorio*,

*"Let us move on, for the time apportioned us
Should be divided up more usefully."*

Atop Mount Purgatory, the two men approach the Augustan *saeculum*, transformed now into an eternally vibrant Christian new age. Alive for the imperial
renovations of Augustus but not for the Secular Games, reputed to have
foreseen the advent of Jesus but dust and bones years before his birth, pagan
Virgil can go no further. He must yield to Beatrice, beloved woman of the
Vita Nuova and glorious woman of the new age, who will guide Dante
through Paradise, past blessed spirits whirling as smoothly as the workings
of a clock, to the last lines of the last, the hundredth, canto:

> *The strength for this high fantasy was gone now.
> But at last my will and my desire—
> Like a wheel moving evenly—were revolving
> From the love that moves the sun and all the stars.*

So comedy's end is, literally and figuratively, century's end. Etruscan, Claudian, and Augustan *saecula* have come to a celestial conjunction, and Dante's
century of cantos ends with the evenly moving wheel of the weight-driven
clock, whose escapement has proved to be, like the escarpments of Purgatory
and the ten heavens of Paradise, the resolution to the crisis of accelerating
time during the first true *fin de siècle*.[71]

Afterwards, each century's end more and more clearly in view, time will
always be seen hurrying toward the Jubilee '00 of the *Anno Domini* calendar.
Over the long term, neither the tempered beat of clocks nor the *terza rima*
of a poet's cantos could damp the feverish rhythms of a *fin de siècle*. What
could damp them, for a spell, was a Gram-negative, bipolar-staining, fac-
ultative anaerobic, non-lactose-fermenting, non-spore-forming bacterium.[72]

DECADENCE AND
DECOMPOSITION: THE 1390s

PESTILENCE MUST DISRUPT THE GATHERING MOMENTUM OF THIS
book as it did, most violently, the surging population of Europe. Whether
it was bubonic plague or, perhaps, anthrax, the Black Death established the
years 1348–52 as a countervailing historical moment, a century's end at
midcentury. The 1300s had opened traumatically: an ambitious pope taken

St. John shielding his face from the heat of the fire falling from heaven (Revelation 8.8–9). One of a series of tapestry panels commissioned for the private chapel of Louis I of Anjou, brother of Charles V, and woven in Paris by Nicolas Bataille, 1375–81, from designs by Jean de Bandol. Inventaire N° 18, Tapisserie de l'Apocalypse, Trésor de la Cathédrale d'Angers, at the Château et Galerie de l'Apocalypse.

captive by minions of a French king who would brook no bulls asserting the supremacy of the pontiff. Released within three days but terribly shaken, Boniface VIII soon died, whereupon Philip the Fair's own candidate was elected to the papal throne, which by 1309 had been transferred closer to France, from Rome to Avignon. While one pope after another reigned from this "Babylonian Captivity," raising money through the sale of church offices to the highest bidders, farmers and merchants suffered from a new, harsh climatic regime of short wet summers and bitterly long winters. Corruption and treachery in the palaces of Avignon, famine and bank failures almost everywhere else—disease and death could not be far behind. The desperate people, it is said, begged Pope Clement VI to proclaim a Jubilee for his generation, afflicted by bad weather and worse politics. Nine years old in 1300, Clement at the age of fifty-one assented to another, properly Levitical celebration; he issued a bull announcing a Jubilee year for 1350.[73]

Rome was in a sad state at midcentury, its basilicas in ruins from the neglect of absent popes and the shock waves of a 1348 earthquake so strong that it had been felt from Greece to Germany. But the pilgrims too were in a sad state, overwhelmed by the "Great Mortality" that was taking the lives of one quarter to one half of all Europeans. Rumors in 1346 had led Clement to calculate that 23,840,000 had already died of the plague in China, India, Persia, Egypt, and Asia Minor. Now the pestilence was moving across Europe from Sicily to Wales, where a Welsh poet wrote in 1349, "We see death coming into our midst like black smoke, a plague which cuts off the young, a rootless phantom which has no mercy for fair countenance. Woe is me of the shilling in the armpit; it is seething, terrible, wherever it may come. . . ." In the Irish convent of Kilkenny, Brother John Clyn wrote an account of the plague so that it would not be forgotten: "I, seeing so many evils and the whole world, as it were, placed within the grasp of the evil one, being myself as if among the dead, waiting for death to visit me, have put into writing truthfully all the things that I have heard. And, lest the writing should perish with the writer and the work fail with the labourer, I leave parchment to continue this work, if perchance any man survive and any of the race of Adam escape this pestilence." Agnolo di Tura of Siena, who during the plague had buried five of his children with his own hands, wrote into his chronicle for 1348/49, "And no bells tolled and nobody wept no matter what his loss because almost everyone expected death. . . . And people said and believed, 'This is the end of the world.' "[74]

It was not quite the end of the world, but those of Adam's race who did survive were doomed to meet up with the "rootless phantom" again and again—in 1361–63, 1374, 1383, and, if their luck had held out, at century's end. The "painful angry knob" of the plague would not let loose. Deserted villages and desolate towns bore mute testimony to the virulence of the Black Death. The Christ of frescoes and altarpieces became more majestic, a frontal presence staring the damned down into a crueler hell than ever they had known before. The Virgin Mary herself often withdrew from her congregations, a celestial rather than compassionate madonna drawing the penitent away from things of the flesh. In his mandate for the annual dissection of a corpse by the medical school at Montpellier, the Duc d'Anjou was stirred by this *memento mori* to refer to the wars and epidemics which had stricken Europe, whose population "may be diminished to ever greater extent and the world brought to nothing." Dances of Death would not be painted on cemetery walls until the 1420s, but the *Danse Macabre* had writhed its way into verse by the 1370s, drama by the 1390s.[75]

The 1390s were as grim a *fin de siècle* as any nihilist might wish for, any moralist shake a bony finger at. When historian Barbara Tuchman in the 1970s chose to consort with the 1300s, "a violent, tormented, bewildered, suffering and disintegrating age, a time, as many thought, of Satan triumphant," it was because the 14th century was "consoling in a period of similar disarray. If our last decade or two of collapsing assumptions has been a period of unusual discomfort, it is reassuring to know that the human species has lived through worse before." Even as she brought *A Distant Mirror* to focus upon the Dark Wood and *Danse Macabre* of the end of the 14th century, she knew that, toward the middle of the next century, "by some mysterious chemistry, energies were refreshed, ideas broke out of the mold of the Middle Ages into new realms, and humanity found itself redirected." There could be, however, little consoling the women and men of the 1390s, who might look beyond apocalypse to the Millennium but could not divine the "mysterious chemistry" of the Renaissance.[76]

The corrupt Jubilee of 1390 set the tone for the decade. In 1377 Gregory XI had returned the papacy to Rome from Avignon, but upon his death in 1378 a new Babylonian Captivity was subsumed by the Great Schism, during which pope and antipope reigned from opposing thrones in Rome and Avignon. Boniface IX's Jubilee of 1390 may have been the delayed celebration of the Jubilee proclaimed by the returning Gregory XI (and scheduled for 1383, thirty-three years after the previous Jubilee, alluding to Christ's age at resurrection), or it may have been a cunning interpolation by a pope desirous of restoring the wealth and prestige of the Papal See at Rome. In either case, it could not be taken as the inaugural event of a new era; it was, rather, the symbol of a Church falling apart and an age that was failing.[77]

Ahead lay ten years of fury, madness, and collapse. Attacks upon Jews, epidemic at midcentury during the Black Death, became at century's end massive pogroms in Prague, Toledo, Valencia, Barcelona, Lérida; there were expulsions from France, Strasbourg, the Palatinate, and forced conversions throughout Aragon and Castile. All European projects for peace and unity failed of their least objectives. The crusader assault upon the infidel Barbary coast in 1390 was held to the frustration of three months' unsuccessful siege of the fortress town of Mahdia. The chivalric rush to defend the eastern flank of Christian Europe from the forces of the Turkish Sultan Bajazet resulted in the trampling of knighthood-in-flower at Nicopolis in 1396. Schemes for resolving the Great Schism were perpetually undercut by obstinate popes and feuding princes. Negotiations for peace between France and England (dawdling through what would come to be called the Hundred Years' War) were broken off, resumed, abandoned, delayed, renewed—culminating in brief, tumid truces for which the healing balm of such diplomats as Philippe de Mézières could be only visionary. When the King of France, Charles VI, met with the Holy Roman Emperor Wenceslas IV in 1398 to reconcile their differences and so put an end to the Great Schism, the King was insane, the Emperor was drunk, and nothing came of their fuming tête-à-tête. In 1399 Richard II of England, high on astrology and supposedly mad with his own power, was dethroned by Henry of Bolingbroke; across the Channel the King of France was hiding in corners, convinced that he was made of glass. The next year, 1400, Richard II was murdered, Wenceslas was deposed as Emperor, Charles was being treated by magicians, and the Black Death had returned with its scythe for another generation of Europeans. In despair or disgust, Jean Froissart cut short his famous chronicles of the history of England, France, and Spain, begun long before "To encourage all valorous hearts." The Antichrist was born in 1403, claimed Vincent Ferrer, the popular Dominican preacher who continued to incite the torture and forced conversion of Jews, and who spoke passionately of an imminent Last Judgment.[78]

It was, wrote the poet Eustache Deschamps near the turn of the century, a

Time of mourning and temptation,
Age of tears, longing, and torment,
Time of languishing and damnation,
Age of decline close to the end,

during which

> *All hearts have been taken by storm*
> *By sadness and melancholy.*

Although hearts may have risen with the uprisings of peasants and artisans in Paris, Florence, Catalonia, the Auvergne, and East Anglia between 1358 and 1381, the dominant mood of the 1390s was depressed. Deschamps's ballads ran the gamut from despair to gloom, his despair stylish, his gloom fashionable. A new word, "decadence," had just begun its travels through the Romance languages. It was applied to people, families, buildings in decay but not yet to an epoch of moral collapse or a society in ruins. The metaphor of cultural decadence would come later. Meanwhile Petrarch, first to name the "Middle Ages" (which stood between him and the glory of Rome), was composing a treatise, "Of Senile Things," on the atrophy of institutions during these years of war and plague. Poet John Gower in 1393 would write in Middle English,

> *What schal befalle hierafterward*
> *God wot, for now upon this tyde*
> *men se the world on every syde*
> *In sondry wyse so dyversed*
> *That it welnyh stant all reversed,*
> *As forto speke of tyme ago.*[79]

A new word, a young metaphor, but as a manner, as an attitude, decadence was maturing in this *fin de siècle*. If the 1290s presented us with the archetypal visions of a new age at century's turn, the 1390s present us with the archetypal disillusionment at century's end. The pessimism of the 1390s manifested itself in a decadent style which was, then as now, an embrace of extremes—of the brutal and the sentimental, the stark and the ornate, the ascetic and the sensual, the wild and the refined, the obscene and the mystical, the demonic and the devout.[80]

THE BRUTAL. In England, which had to some degree held out against those judicial tortures common on the Continent, a statute of 1400 declared burning alive a legal punishment for heresy. In Spain, many hundreds of Jews who refused to convert were murdered, their synagogues demolished. In Italy, St. Sebastian's martyred body became ever more gruesome as artists painted in seven, twelve, fifteen deadly arrows. Across Europe the crucified

Christ took on a crown of thorns. THE SENTIMENTAL. The pietà appeared near century's end, first in German-speaking lands and then in France in 1390, sculpted for the Duke of Burgundy by Claus Sluter, whose final masterpiece (1404–05) would be the forty Weepers, their faces often hidden in grief, around the tomb of his patron, Philip the Bold. The Virgin everywhere now had Seven Sorrows.[81]

THE STARK. Transi tombs appeared, their stone figures swathed in shrouds or decomposing like the bodies within. Guillaume de Harsigny, French physician born in 1300, dead in 1392, left behind instructions that the effigy on his tomb be cut to the image of his corpse itself, a thin, naked man with hands crossed over his genitals. In Switzerland, frogs crouched on the stone face of bailiff François de la Sarra, whose chest was a maze of snakes. Cardinal Jean de la Grange, dead in 1402, had inscribed above the effigy of his emaciated corpse,

So, miserable one, why are you proud?
You are only ash and will revert,
as we have done, to a stinking cadaver,
food and tidbits for worms, and ashes.

THE ORNATE. Isabeau of Bavaria, making her royal entry into Paris in 1389, passed beneath firmaments of cloth, was refreshed at fountains of red and white wine, then crowned by a pair of angels descending through blue taffeta and golden fleurs-de-lis. Noblemen on lesser occasions were announced by the long points on the toes of their shoes; aristocratic ladies had as their entourage enormous braided shells spiralling up from their ears. Both sexes, when blessed by wealth, walked within a profusion of jewels, emblems, fringes, sleeves, and hanging balls of perfume. The cathedral under construction in Milan at century's end was likewise an expression of a deathly horror of emptiness, every inch ornamented with stone tracery and arabesque. Throughout Europe the mullions of cathedral windows twisted like flames in that Flamboyant or International Gothic style which favored a world of fable, intricate fragments, and fantastic stone vegetation.[82]

THE ASCETIC. Late 14th-century and early 15th-century women—Catherine of Siena, Lidwina of Schiedam, Jane Mary of Maille, Colette of Corbie, and others less extreme or less public—took to heart a devotion to the Eucharist which had intensified since the first ritual elevations of the host (in 1200) and the first Corpus Christi festivals (1264, repromulgated 1311, 1317). Identifying themselves body and soul with the suffering Christ, these women were deemed to have survived for months or years exclusively on communion wine and wafers while committed day in day out to the care and feeding of the poor. Their own hunger, the women explained, was for Christ, whose blood and flesh were all that could truly satisfy them. Through determined fasting they re-created the gaunt figure on the cross and made of themselves eucharistic miracles, capable of nourishing hundreds of others as Christ alone was nourishing them. In their abstinence they became saintly and vital, holy and passionate, inspired and fertile. Such close identification with the thin, broken body of the Son of God was as erotic as it was elevated. The Savior, who first appeared to Englishwoman Margery Kempe around 1395, spoke to her explicitly of a spiritual carnal love. She recorded Christ's invitation in the chapter on fasting in her autobiography: "Daughter, thou desirest greatly to see Me, and thou mayest boldly, when thou art in thy bed, take Me to thee as thy wedded husband, as thy dearworthy darling. . . . Therefore thou mayest boldly take Me in the arms of thy soul and kiss My mouth, my Head, and My feet, as sweetly as thou will." Where there was the most persuasive, painstaking asceticism of the 1390s there was also and insistently THE SENSUAL.[83]

THE WILDman, giant and rude, loped at the head of Candlemas processions, his face a forest of leaves, his body matted with fur. Like the Christ child, he had been born among animals: he was the son or foundling raised by Ursus the bear, who would wake from hibernation this day, February 2nd, to pronounce upon the severity of the winter and the balance of the seasons. Long the symbol of animal lust, of desire unquenchable, of quest unending, late in the 14th century the wildman took on as well the features of the Noble Savage who leads a simple life uncorrupted by civilization, and his father the bear was blazoned on noble shields as chivalric emblem of quest and resurrection. Still obnoxious at carnivals, headed for ruckus and shambles, the wildman in full costume was, paradoxically, a representation of humanity unmasked as brute or as innocent. In the spirit of this paradox, one week before Candlemas, on January 28, 1393, Charles VI of France and five friends put on masks, sewed themselves into linen costumes, applied pitch to the linen and tufts of hair to the pitch, to become "wood savages" for the masquerade at the remarriage of one of the Queen's ladies-in-waiting. The six noble wildmen ran howling into the wedding hall, where they played at rudeness and wilderness until a spark from a torch ignited these sons of bears. The King and another managed to escape the flaming pitch and flax; four were burnt alive. This savage dance of death was macabre evidence of the coupling of THE WILD and THE REFINED at century's end, for in the court of Charles VI, as at other European courts, a mannered chivalry absorbed both men and women. Jean le Maingre, imprisoned in Damascus in 1388 with three other knights, whiled away the hours composing ballads in defense of a romantic, honorable love from afar; back home in France, the tough Christian soldier was reputed to have spoken of little but virtue and the saints, and to have forbidden his servants to swear. In 1400 Christine de Pizan concealed an allegory about French politics behind a series of chivalric letters to the Trojan hero, Hector; soon she would write of the "City of Ladies," a decorous utopia for women, including the Queen of Heaven. In 1400, Jean Gerson, rector of the University of Paris, certain that the Antichrist was skulking around the corner of the century, launched a personal crusade against the riotous disorder of those "impious and insane rites," the Feast of Fools.[84]

THE OBSCENE. Obscenity was everywhere—anal intercourse, anal offerings, and enemas carved by journeyman masons beneath choir stall seats in churches; stone figures farting from the corbels of cathedral roofs; illustrations of heretics kissing each other's asses in ritual greeting, as rumors said they did; priapic stone men with huge penises atop their heads and between their legs, advertising the diuretic waters of Lacaune at the "Fountain of Pissers" built in 1399. During the Feast of Fools, celebrated on one or another of the twelve days of Christmas, priests conducted services from behind monstrous masks, ate black puddings at the altar, burned shit or old shoes instead of incense. Townspeople selected an Abbot of Misrule, sometimes a King or Pope, whom they led backwards on a donkey into cathedrals, where they read scatological parodies of the mass. Undercut by the effects of the Great Schism, challenged by radical attacks from John Wyclif and his continental successors, the Church became increasingly sensitive to, and intolerant of, such rituals of inversion as the Feast of Fools, which clerics thought to be the pagan survival of ancient Janus worship. Neither mummery nor obscenity, of course, was an innovation of the 1390s, but days of carnival may have been more obscene and more violent after the Black Death than before. When loyalists to the deposed King of England, Richard II, sought to carry off the usurper, Henry IV, they made their attempt during the bawdiness and riot of Twelfth Night in the year 1400. THE MYSTICAL. From the Low Countries in the last half of the century came the "modern devotion" of Geert Groote of Deventer and his disciples, the Brethren of the Common Life, with their concern for an interior experience of the lovingkindness of God and an active social conscience. Thomas à Kempis, born in 1380 near Deventer and schooled by the Brethren, would put together at his monastic desk the movement's most influential tract, *Of the Imitation of Christ*, around 1425, but the work most reflects the phobic times during which he was out in the world, before the turn of the century. He counsels against too much familiarity with strangers, warns that "perfect security and full peace cannot be had in this world," where "we cannot be without tribulation and temptation." The profit of adversity is to teach us to trust to an inward sensation of Christ and to work to serve God in acts of charity and good will. Much of this advice was proverbial, yet the emphatic reliance upon the self (in frequent contemplative and eucharistic communion with the Lord) and the equally emphatic distrust of the fractious world were in keeping with other mystical texts completed during the late 14th century. It was by no mistake that Geoffrey Chaucer, destined to die in the fall of 1400, played the wild against the refined and the mystical against the obscene in so many of the tales told by his thirty pilgrims on their way to the shrine of the martyred Thomas à Becket in Canterbury.[85]

THE DEMONIC. "[C]ertain invokers of demons," noted Nicholas Eymeric, Inquisitor to the Kingdom of Aragon, "willingly celebrate the praises of the demon or sing songs in his honor and genuflect or prostrate themselves before him. They observe chastity out of reverence for the demon or abstain upon his instructions or they lacerate their own flesh. Out of reverence for the demon or by his instructions they wear white or black vestments. They worship him by signs and characters and unknown names. They burn candles or incense to him or aromatic spices. They sacrifice animals and birds, catching their blood as a curative agent, or they burn them, throwing salt in the fire and making a holocaust in this manner." Eymeric in 1369 was resuming what was known of ritual magic, the practice of which the Knights Templar had been accused near century's start. Ritual magic was sorcery, but it was not yet witchcraft, not yet a malevolent conspiracy under the command of Satan. Legal and popular stereotypes of the witch were taking final shape at century's end through the confessions of such as the Swiss peasant, Stedelen of Boltigen, from whom a torturing inquisitor drew out what he had in mind to hear. Like other sorcerers, Stedelen had worked black magic: he had caused a woman to suffer seven miscarriages, cattle to become infertile, children to drown. More to the purpose of the inquisition, he described conventions of witches meeting in fields to beg the Prince of Darkness to send up an emissary, who duly snatched the flesh of a black cock sacrificed at a crossroads, and who thereupon manufactured hailstorms to strike Stedelen's enemies. From the forced confessions of women on trial for sorcery in Milan and Paris in 1390 came further tales of heretical conspiracy, of satanic burlesques of the mass, of nightflying, kidnap, and cannibalism. Within European high culture, no little impressed by new romances of Melusine the alluring serpent–woman and of Merlin the magician sired by an incubus, the profile of the witch would be refined and stylized until inquisitors and storytellers knew precisely what to look for: a woman or man bound to the Devil and bent on harm, who flew at midnight to desolate places where groups of the Devil's devotees held black sabbats and enjoyed the orgiastic favors of Beelzebub. Trials of sorcerers would escalate into witch hunts as torturers (inquisitors) sought proof not only of ritual magic but also of conspiracy against the true religion. The earliest witch hunts began less than a generation after the conclave at the University of Paris, whose dignitaries in 1398 declared that any summoning of spirits was tantamount to a pact with the Devil and sufficient evidence for prosecution as a heretic. THE DEVOUT. Visions in 1399 in Spain and 1400 in France of processions of men and women all in white, led by the celestial brightness of the Virgin Mary, may have been pious frauds toward the building of shrines, but in Italy these processions were fact. The solid citizen, a merchant of Prato, Francesco di Marco Datini, on August 18, 1399, "resolved to go on a pilgrimage, clothed entirely in white linen and barefoot, as was the custom then for many people of the city and territory of Florence, and also of the surrounding region." Francesco went in the company of thirty thousand others, "all barefoot, and scourging ourselves with a rod and accusing ourselves to Our Lord Jesus Christ of our sins, devoutly and with good will." The pilgrims, called *I Bianchi* after their white linen robes and cowls, were engaged in something of a peace movement and something of a jubilee. A peace movement, because they tried to settle on a local level, family to family, town to town, the feuds between papal and imperial parties that had split Italy into murderous factions for a hundred years. A jubilee, because Pope Boniface IX issued no bull for a Jubilee in 1400. Some pilgrims proceeded to Rome anyway during the centurial year, but the century's end of these decadent days was cloaked by penitents in white, trailing behind huge crucifixes, bearing lighted tapers, chanting for peace and mercy during—once again—a pestilential year.[86]

Here and there in the 1390s one might come across predictions of good times hard on the heels of bad, prophecies of the downfall of the Turk or the election of an Angel Pope or the prompt defeat of Antichrist on the dot in 1400. Merchants might prosper, and even, like Datini, make their fortunes insuring cargoes "against all risks." No matter how bleak, the hours came and went, sometimes as fancifully as in the clocktower of the Strasbourg

Cathedral, where a mechanical cock a meter tall flapped its wings, lowered its tail, and crowed at the stroke of twelve. In a letter of August 30, 1400, the Florentine humanist Coluccio Salutati would make one of the earliest references to a century by its ordinal number; he wanted (as quiet retrospect for a passing century, it seems) to single out two writers whose eloquent poetry and fiction had brightened the *"quartodecimo seculo,"* the *fourteenth* century.[87]

Unlike the 13th century, the 14th century did not appear to come to a head in '99 or '00. Brutal and sentimental, stark and ornate, ascetic and sensual, wild and refined, obscene and mystical, demonic and devout, its *fin de siècle* was finally as pointless as years of war and schism had been fruitless. Midcentury plague had taken the wind out of the sails of any drama at century's end. We must leave chastened by the 1390s, for although they have given us a model for the extremity and pessimism we shall find at other centuries' ends, they are also proof positive that Janus must share his power with Chaos in the run of history.

WORLDS ENOUGH AND
TIME: THE 1490s

IN 1492 TIME RAN OUT. THAT THE BYZANTINE EMPIRE AFTER more than a thousand years of splendor had fallen in 1453 was only fitting: the world itself was due to lapse with Anno Mundi 7000 of the Byzantine calendar, or 1492 A.D. The year had been anticipated in Russia for at least three centuries, ever since the preaching of St. Abraham of Smolensk and his disciple Ephrem, whose apocalyptic sermons took 7000 A.M. as the flaming End, when the earth by heavenly arson would be burned to a newness, flat and whiter than snow, then golden and luxuriant. The Metropolitans of Moscow, heirs to the patriarchate of the Eastern Church, were still courting this apocalypse in the decades after Constantinople had been taken by the Turks. Archbishop Gennadii of Novgorod in 1485 began his campaign to convince his superiors in Moscow, not only the capital of Ivan the Great's imperial Russia but soon aspirant to the title of the "Third Rome," to burn the Motherland clean of heretics in these last days before the judgments of the world-fire. As late as 1487, and perhaps later, none of the paschal calendars went beyond 7000 A.M. Zosima, the Metropolitan of Moscow to whom fell the responsibility for propelling the Church past the fateful year, had to reconstitute the calendar for an eighth (and, surely, final) millennium.

The Four Horsemen of the Apocalypse by Albrecht Dürer, woodcut from a series of fifteen on the Apocalypse, issued in 1498.

He consulted men learned in astronomy and mathematics, men familiar with the languages and sciences of Islam and Western Europe. Were these men those same heretical rationalists known in Novgorod as Judaizers? Gennadii thought so, and in his zeal to purge the realm of such antitrinitarian, iconoclastic Christian heretics, he accused them of keeping Jewish time and "concealing years" from Eastern Orthodoxy. Zosima's renewed calendar, which presumed to set time in motion beyond the end of the Byzantine world-week, was therefore embroiled in the ecclesiastical politics of a Church representing itself as the New Zion, in the cultural politics which opposed Russian purity and faith to Western corruption and skepticism, and in the millenarian politics which held out for apocalypse and redemption as against another uninspiring thousand years of humdrum history. Whether the Judaizers were secretly Jews or had embraced select Jewish practices and beliefs associated with early Christian life, whether Zosima himself was an admirer or devotee, we cannot be certain, but certain it is that Zosima was removed from office in 1494, by which year the Russian quarantine and persecution of Jews had begun, in earnest imitation of the inquisitorial purges in Spain.[88]

Where time had indeed run out for the Jews. There too, they were caught on the *fin de siècle* knife-edge between one age and the next. While Ivan the Great had by force of arms united Russia and convinced the Mongols to withdraw at last from territories held for nearly three hundred years, Ferdinand and Isabella had married Aragon and Castile into one Kingdom of Spain and, with the surrender of Granada, taken the last Moorish stronghold. Their triumph, in January of 1492, put a conclusion to nearly eight hundred years of Islamic caliphates on the Iberian Peninsula. Less than three months later, impelled by the crusading enthusiasms of this Christian Reconquest, the joint sovereigns decreed the expulsion of all Jews who did not convert by July. Already, in the 1480s, a uniquely Spanish form of the Inquisition, "its body, an amalgam of hard iron and deadly poison . . . [rising] . . . on a thousand wings with black and poisonous pinions," had been terrorizing the families of Jews who had converted at the end of the last century, during or after the pogroms of 1391. These *conversos* or Marranos were suspected by the Inquisition of having remained Jews, secretly observant. Suffering from venomous accusations of ritual murder and from the black fumes of autos-da-fé at which two thousand *conversos* were burned to death, some fifteen thousand Spanish Jews and Marranos had departed for less hostile lands in the decade before the expulsion. If the Jewish year 5250 A.M. (1490 C.E.) came up frequently—and mistakenly—in Jewish speculation as to the date for messianic deliverance, the year 5252 presented itself as climax to a long era of persecutions, and the fifty thousand Jews fleeing Spain would carry with them a Sephardic legacy of messianic arithmetic pointing first to 5263/64 and then to the end of the Jewish century, the 5290s (the 1530s C.E.). Those Jews who remained in Spain as ancient or recent *conversos* would play a significant role among the Alumbrados, Spanish millenarians who built on Spiritual Franciscan and Joachimite beliefs at the turn of the (Christian) century. Whether intended rather to convert than to expel, whether initiated by or imposed politically upon Ferdinand and Isabella, the expulsion decree of 1492 was clearly a *fin de siècle* statement of time run out for the people of the Old Testament, and time reset for those of the New.[89]

The end of the 15th century A.D. was the end of the 9th and start of the 10th century A.H. In Iran the dilapidated Timurid dynasty was overthrown at century's turn by Turkoman chiefs and nomadic tribes who drew their inspiration from Shiᶜite mahdism and Sufi mysticism. Ismaᶜil I, founder of what would be the Safavid Empire, had risen to the occasion in 905 A.H./ 1499 A.D. amidst leaflets describing him as precursor to the Lord of the Age; during his reign, stables of superb horses were kept at the ready to welcome the Mahdi whenever and wherever he should appear. Within a decade, however, his regime secure, Ismaᶜil turned upon the more extreme, activist Sufi orders and Shiᶜite tribes whose faith in the imminent arrival of the Lord of the Age could undermine his dynastic authority as he, touting his precursorship, had undermined the legitimacy of the Persian Timurids. Whether the mahdism of Ismaᶜil had been politic or sincere, he had drawn great profit from Shiᶜite expectations of a new leader for a new century and from Sufi mystics who had intuited the historical cycles through which Islam might be renewed.[90]

We have been circling Europe counterclockwise, from Russia to Spain to Iran, but *fin de siècle* feelings that time had to be reset were equally strong at the heart of the Renaissance, in Florence, where Lorenzo the Magnificent had just died in 1492. With him had passed the splendid age of the Medicis, or so the Florentines feared: "As from his death the greatest devastation would shortly ensue, the heavens gave many evident tokens of its approach; among other signs, the highest pinnacle of the Church of Santa Reparata was struck with lightning, and great part of it thrown down, to the terror and amazement of everyone." Wolves howled, wind blew, hail fell, thunder roared, and another lightning bolt tore open one side of the cupola of the cathedral. These were signs of the divine scourge soon to come, declared the Dominican friar Girolamo Savonarola, who would claim to have predicted

Lorenzo's death as he did the invasion of Italy by another divine instrument, a second Cyrus, Charles VIII of France. When Charles came south, as truly he did come in 1494, with forty thousand troops and a hundred cannon at his side, he believed himself to be not a Cyrus but a second Charlemagne, driven by divine purpose toward the reclamation of Italy, the regeneration of Europe, the conquest of the infidel East, and, God willing, an angelic monarchy over a universal Christendom. And so he was, and so He was, agreed Fra Savonarola after negotiating with Charles a treaty of reconciliation which left Florence unscathed. Savonarola's back-to-front reversal of the figure of Charles VIII was in keeping with the reversal of the fortunes of Florence itself, once headed for hellish catastrophe and now, it seemed, toward a New Day. Five years Savonarola had dedicated to preaching apocalypse and repentance; on December 10, 1494, he announced "this good news to the city, that Florence will be more glorious, richer, more powerful than she has ever been. First, glorious in the sight of God as well as of men: and you, O Florence, will be the reformation of all Italy, and from here the renewal will begin and spread everywhere." Purified of its dross through bonfires of vanities and pious processions, Florence would be the New Jerusalem, reformer to the world, city of the Millennium. Savonarola's career spiralled from preacher to prophet to prelate (in practice) of what he called the second Rome, whereupon in June of 1497 he was excommunicated. He commanded the loyalty of many a Florentine despite the excommunication, the summer food shortages, the recurrence of plague, but did not long survive an opponent's challenge to an ordeal by fire to confirm the source of his inspirations. Issued on New Year's Day, March 25, 1498, the challenge was to be met by a pair of friars intent on walking unscathed through flames on behalf of their saintly compatriot Savonarola. Saturday, April 7th, the fire was lit. A restive crowd prayed then muttered in the Piazza della Signoria as Savonarola's two champions fiddled and quibbled with the terms of the ordeal until night fell and, with it, an ambiguous rain. Next morning, Palm Sunday, all three friars were arrested by armed guards, imprisoned, subjected to torture, then hanged and burned on May 23rd, the day before Ascension Day.[91]

If he had not been a godsend, then Savonarola must have been the emissary of Another. In the aftermath of the public burning, visions of a New Day and a New Jerusalem turned to the smoke and ashes of the Last Days and Armageddon. Savonarola was represented in sermons, frescoes, and later histories as a species of Antichrist, he who deludes the faithful with a potent masquerade of holiness. The *fin de siècle* oscillation between ends and beginnings, catastrophe and redemption, time unravelled and time rewound, was particularly fierce in the 1490s. People found themselves living in two times at once: a new golden age and the end of the world. The conjunction of Jupiter and Saturn in 1484, understood as the completion of an astronomical Great Year (the 25,800 years over which the sun finally returns to its original equinoctial position), was also understood to herald an era of religious renovation; the conjunction of Saturn, Jupiter, and Mars in the water sign of Pisces in 1524 was (according to astrologer Johann Stoeffler in 1499) the harbinger of universal flood. Courtesy of that new-golden-age invention, the printing press, Europe was swamped with tracts warning of the Deluge of 1524 while Leonardo da Vinci was obsessing over thunderclouds, sudden inundations in Armenia, the roil of waters that could return the earth to its primitive chaos—a chaos prominent in his sketchbooks and painted on the horizons behind his *Madonna of the Rocks, Madonna with St. Anne and St. John,* and the *Mona Lisa.* Hieronymus Bosch's *Garden of Earthly Delights* (c. 1500) was as much about judgment as paradise, a millennial state at odds with itself. And in 1498 Albrecht Dürer issued his fifteen woodcuts of the Apocalypse, as persuasive then as they are now in imagining the phantasmagoria of the Book of Revelation. Dürer's Four Horsemen, riding toward century's end with bow, sword, scales of justice, and pitchfork of death, would reappear on tapestries, enamels, engravings, and reliefs, even as John Skelton was writing around 1500 of "The Manner of the World Nowadays,"

> *So many gay swordes,*
> *So many altered wordes,*
> *And so few covered boardes,*
>   *Saw I never:*
> *So many empty purses,*
> *So few good horses,*
> *And so many curses,*
>   *Saw I never. . . .*
> *Amendment*
> *Were convenient,*
> *But it may not be;*
> *We have exiled veritie.*
> *God is neither dead nor sick;*
> *He may amend all yet,*
> *And trow ye so indeed,*
> *As ye believe ye shall have mede.*

After better I hope ever,
For worse was it never.[92]

Skelton's jeremiad may have been the clumsy-footed exercise of a poetic convention, Dürer's woodcuts may have masterfully reworked blockbook motifs, but late-15th-century Europe was cursed with an alarming number of almanacs and *Prognostica* of doom, and Europeans were decidedly mindful of closure. Although the bleakest of prophecies fell short, although the world never came to a full stop, time did run out for each woman and man. The exact moment of death, circumscribed earlier in the century by the first popular guides to the Art of Dying Well, had become by century's end the Last Judgment in miniature. The *Ars moriendi* began as a treatise of ten thousand words and as a book of eleven woodcuts depicting the deathbed ordeal of Moriens, the terminal Everyman, who must learn to make "a good death." A good death, like a good will, was both testament and inventory, a declaration of faith and a catalogue of sins. Like a will, a good death had as preamble humility and prayer, as text patience, surrender, and charity in imitation of Christ on the cross, and as farewell a self-consuming hope and faith: "put all thy trust in [Christ's] passion and in his death only, having trust in no other things; to this death commit thee fully, with this death cover thee fully, in this death wrap all thyself fully."[93]

Death itself was all bones by the 1490s, not merely a corpse but a skeleton leading knight and lady, merchant and beggar, housewife and whore in Dances of Death. Woodcut imps tempting Moriens with earthly delights had become foul fiends, his deathbed a battleground between heaven and hell for the eternal soul. Judgment had traditionally been reserved for the Last Days, at which the myriad dead would learn their fate; now something akin to Judgment was also felt to be taking place at the instant of death. Amidst a new plague, syphilis, spread ironically by the soldiers of the messianic Charles VIII, dying became a personal apocalypse during which one's life passed swiftly before one's eyes as a summary Judgment. Popular prints and expositions of the Fifteen Last Things—storms, floods, cataclysms, conflagrations, monstrosities—were syncopated with the Last Four Things of the *Ars moriendi*. The ever impending but elusive End of the World became, at the end of the 15th century, a disputed codicil to that increasingly sudden but unavoidable end, one's own death.[94]

The *Arte and Crafte to Knowe Well to Dye* of the 1490s followed implicitly the Etruscan sense of a century's close as the close of a generation at the close of a single (long) life. At just this period, Giovanni Nanni was rediscovering and reinventing the Etruscans. Native of Viterbo, one of the four Etruscan sacred cities, Nanni stuffed his *Antiquities* with a tangle of fabrications that made of ancient Etruria a golden world. In this ball of historical wool, authoritative throughout the High Renaissance and Reformation, source for artists designing gardens, cavalcades, and theatrical backdrops, Janus stood front, sideways, and center. He was "most ancient father of gods and men," patriarch of the Roman pantheon; he was a giant from the age before the Flood; he was Noah, founder-priest-king of a theocratic golden age in Etruria after the Flood; he was the celestial master of the revolving heavens; and he was Vertumnus, deity of the four seasons. Where Janus was free of Nanni, he was conflated with the triune Prudence, whose old face looks back at the past over the head of a ravening wolf; whose mature face regards us upon the head of a lion, violent and sudden as the present; and whose youthful face looks out toward the future above the head of a dog beguiling us with hope. As primeval giant, as god of gods, as the seasons, as first king of the golden age, as Prudence, Janus appeared around the turn of the century on terra-cotta reliefs, in paintings and processions. At the Florentine celebration of the accession of Lorenzo the Magnificent's second son to the papal throne in 1513, Janus arrived with his "son" Saturn in the first triumphal chariot. In the seventh chariot was a globe on which lay a man of the last, the iron age, his armor rusting and split; from his back emerged a little boy, naked and gilded: the new golden age.[95]

Son of a baker who made ten crowns on the deal, the boy would die of this intemperate allegory, gold leaf his poisoned wrap, but the rediscovery of Janus and the Etruscans was one means by which the educated classes at century's end hoped to live on in a time reset. They reached back for a golden age and brought it forward, claiming, as did Lorenzo the Magnificent's pennant, that "*le tems revient*," time returns, or the great times are come, or Happy Days Are Here Again. The philosopher Marsilio Ficino, who had advised his friend Lorenzo never to put off till tomorrow what he could do today, wrote of the golden age to another friend, Paul of Middelburg, author of the most popular of contemporary *Prognostica*. "If . . . we are to call any age golden," he suggested to Paul in 1492, "it is beyond doubt that age which brings forth golden talents in different places. That such is true of this our age he who wishes to consider the illustrious discoveries of this century [*seculum*] will hardly doubt." For this century, "like a golden age," Ficino continued, "has restored to light the liberal arts, . . . joined wisdom with eloquence, and prudence with the military art," witnessed the invention of printing and "appears to have mastered astronomy," with ingenious astronomical clocks and tables "in which in a single hour (if I may speak thus) the whole face of the heavens for an entire century is revealed."[96]

To be so bold with time and the ages, to take in a century at a glance and turn iron into gold, demanded a kind of magic with which Ficino was quite familiar. In 1463 he had translated from Greek into Latin the *Pimander* or *Corpus Hermeticum*, fifteen dialogues reputed to have come down through the ages from the wisest of Egyptians, near contemporary of Moses, founder of a City of the Sun, giver of laws, expositor of the ancient theology (*prisca theologia*), priest, king, and philosopher, therefore thrice-great, Hermes, Hermes Termaximus, Hermes Trismegistus. As a sage, Hermes had explained the path and process for the regeneration of the soul and the cosmos. As a prophet, he had foreseen Christ and Christianity. As a holy magician, a magus, he had been the master of animation, invoking angelic spirits to enliven statues shaped from herbs, spices, and stone. Guided by the *Corpus Hermeticum*, by a complementary work, *The Perfect Word* or the *Asclepius*, and by a manual of astral magic, the *Picatrix*, a Renaissance magus would so clearly apprehend the sign languages of the universe that he might construct an effective image of the universe at that hour when "a certain destiny of the world as though being born again returns." In other words—and the more perfect the word, the more perfect the image, the more effective the magus—through contemplation of harmonies of life from the celestial spheres to the lower terrestrial spheres of human beings, animals, plants, and rocks, a philosopher committed to the *concordia mundi* could actively participate in the renovation of the world.[97]

Like the hermetic texts, actually composed in the 2nd and 3rd centuries A.D. but esteemed as Mosaic in age, wisdom, and temperament, kabbalistic texts were also attributed a magisterial antiquity and seen as another avenue back to the pristine theology of the ancients. A system of Jewish mystical thought and magical practice, kabbalah had taken root in Spain no earlier than the end of the 13th century and would flower into a gorgeous messianism only after the expulsions at the end of the 15th century. Meanwhile, the young Florentine polymath Pico della Mirandola, with many of his humanist colleagues in France and southern Germany, found that the kabbalah offered what astrology did not, a means for transforming historical and cosmological insight into dynamic intelligence. Through devout diagrams, alphanumeric word combinations, occult insignia, and clement prayers, the Renaissance magus might become the vehicle for the transformation of dark into light, iron into gold. For Christian kabbalists such as Pico, for neoplatonic philosophers such as Ficino, for mystical painters such as Sandro Botticelli, the first golden age had been an age of pure magic, and in this new golden age magic must once again prevail. At century's end these men and others less gifted sought to divorce themselves from the fatalism of judicial astrology by embracing a creative, spiritual, sympathetic magic through which the mind's eye shaped images so real they could act upon human affairs. When Botticelli painted his *Primavera* in 1477–78, he was, according to historian Frances Yates, creating a "figure of the world" by which to ensure its (and our: the viewers') rejuvenation. Later, the painter became a partisan of Savonarola's New Jerusalem, and after the friar had gone up in flames, Botticelli would paint a *Nativity* at the top of which he inscribed, "I Sandro painted this picture at the end of the year 1500 in the troubles of Italy in the half time after the time according to the eleventh chapter of Saint John in the second woe of the Apocalypse in the loosing of the devil for three and a half years. Then he will be chained in the twelfth chapter and we shall see him trodden down as in this picture." Here was painting as prophecy—of the rebirth of Florence after final tribulations—and as millenarian instrument, the artist verily the avant-garde of the New Jerusalem.[98]

In Renaissance high culture, a true picture was not merely accurate. It was evidence of the virtue of its maker, for none could see this world as it truly was who dismissed the divine spirit. A correct picture had also a force of its own: it could *do* things. The construction of a correct picture of the world—the entire world—was hence an art of revelation and an act of restoration, at once revealing and restoring universal harmony. Just such a map of the world was in the mind's eye of a forty-year-old mariner invited to Santa Fe, the royal encampment among the Spanish troops besieging Granada in December 1491.

The mariner had before him the *Imago mundi* of Cardinal Pierre d'Ailly, who in 1410 had compiled geographical lore and cosmological speculation into a textbook on the "figure" or "image" of the world. Making some nine hundred annotations on the margins of this textbook, the mariner was most impressed by d'Ailly's chapter on the extent of habitable land over the (yes) globe. It seemed that most of the globe was land, which agreed with a passage from an apocryphal book dear to the mariner, 2 Esdras 6.42: "Upon the third day thou didst command that the waters should be gathered in the seventh part of the earth: six parts hast thou dried up, and kept them, to the intent that of these some being planted of God and tilled might serve thee." East and West, then, Spain and Japan (Marco Polo's Chipangu), Europe and the Indies might not be separated by so impossibly wide an Ocean Sea. Bound with the printed edition of the *Imago mundi* (1480–83) were other of d'Ailly's compendia, which concerned not territory but time. At the end of the 14th century and into the 15th, d'Ailly had been as anxious about time as he was about the world, an eloquent advocate of calendar reform and a participant in the planning of the great astronomical clock of Cambrai (completed 1397), which represented the days, the months, the Zodiac, the phases of the moon, and at the hour of the carillon sent forth an angel to sound the Last Trump to each of the four cardinal points of the (new) compass. What the mariner found in d'Ailly's other works was the age of the world. It was old. The time remaining before the End was short: less than two hundred years. But the six ages prior to the millennial seventh could not conclude until the gospel had been preached to all people on the six-sevenths of the globe that was habitable land. Was not this the promise of John 10.16: "And other sheep I have, which are not of this fold; them also I must bring, and they shall hear my voice; and there shall be one fold, and one shepherd"? The Good Lord had to have designed the world so that it was small enough for Christians to complete the missionary enterprise. There *had* to be a shorter, more direct route to the Orient than the long and perilous journey overland. The ends of the world could not otherwise be brought together in these few years before the End of the World.[99]

Cristoforo Colombo (the "Christ-bearer" or *Christoferens*, as he signed himself from 1493 on) had come to plead with Ferdinand and Isabella at a genuinely opportune moment. He would begin the logbook of his first voyage by describing this moment: "On 2 January in the year 1492, when your Highnesses had concluded their war with the Moors who reigned in Europe, I saw your Highnesses' banner victoriously raised on the towers of the Alhambra, the citadel of that city," Granada. Weeks later, Their Highnesses granted his petition for ships for a westerly expedition across the Ocean Sea to the Indies. It was the mightiest of symbolic conjunctions that this voyage should be given its earnest during the very month of the Christian triumph, for Columbus thought that he and Spain were from this moment forth set upon a joint millennial venture. With the conquest of Moorish Granada and, quickly, the expulsion of the Jews, Spanish forces should head east toward the reconquest of the Ark of Zion, as Spain was chosen by God to do, according to Joachimite prophecies prevalent in Franciscan circles near century's end. Columbus on his part would head west toward the mass conversion of those no-longer-so-distant nations of the Far East, and of all those simple island savages innocent of gospel truths. In tandem, the Admiral of the Ocean Sea and the Most Christian and Mighty King and Queen of

Spain would imprint upon the globe a map of the world which was equally a revelation and a restoration.[100]

If Columbus in 1492 had not already privately confirmed himself in his messianic role, by 1500 he was publicly certain, writing to Juan de la Torres at the Spanish court, "God made me the messenger of the new heaven and the new earth of which he spoke in the Apocalypse of St. John after having spoken of it through the mouth of Isaiah: and he showed me the spot where to find it." The spot? The new heaven and new earth were surely not a single spot, but what Columbus had in his mind's eye was the Mount of Zion *he* had reached, on the opposite side of the world from the Mount Zion which Spain had not yet reclaimed. Wrote Columbus to the King and Queen in 1502, "In this voyage to the Indies Our Lord wished to perform a very evident miracle in order to console me and the others in the matter of this other voyage to the Holy Sepulchre." The spot Columbus had reached was another Zion, the mount of Paradise or very close thereto (as he intimated and then insisted in his logbooks). The spot represented both the moment and the place at which the conversion of the world had been made practicable by the devotion of one *colombo*, "dove" of the Holy Spirit, dove of Noah's Ark bearing olive branch and baptismal oil to the "Indians," who should be, noted Columbus upon his earliest encounters with them, "good and intelligent servants, for I see that they say very quickly everything that is said to them, and I believe that they would become Christians very easily, for it seemed to me that they had no religion." So Cristoforo Colombo, the Christ-bearing dove, had been divinely led to the one spot at which the potential for a fully Christian cosmos was absolutely clear, and he would stubbornly believe in this spot despite all evidence to the contrary that his voyages were taking him not along the coast of Asia but to continents entirely unexpected and a world entirely too large.[101]

After all, he had returned from his first voyage in 1493, publication date for Sebastian Brandt's extremely popular *Nuremberg Chronicles*, which had left blank but six pages at the end for any events leading up to Judgment Day, and at century's end the Admiral was still immersed in apocalyptic prophecies that left but 155 years for evangelical missions to convert the peoples of the earth. The Americas were ultimately a stupendous disappointment to Columbus, not solely because these "Indies" during his lifetime refused to yield up oriental treasureholds of jewels, spices, and gold to finance a Spanish crusade to the Holy Land, but also and especially because they disrupted a *fin de siècle* vision of the ageing world made whole, holy, and harmonious. Beset by storms on his last voyage, 1502–04, Columbus, "completely alone outside on this dangerous [Veragua] coast in a high fever and a state of great exhaustion," had to be reassured by a stately inner voice, perhaps the voice of God, that he had indeed been blessed, had been given "the keys of the barriers of the ocean seas which were closed with such mighty chains . . . and gained an honourable fame throughout Christendom." Columbus "heard all this as if in a swoon," and wept for his transgressions as the voice concluded, "Fear not, have trust, all these tribulations are inscribed on marble and are not purposeless." When Christopher Columbus died in 1506, he died looking not toward Amerigo Vespucci's *Mundus Novus* but toward the heart of the Old World. In his will he directed that his son establish a fund for the reconquest of Jerusalem.[102]

As Vespucci's *New World*, with thirty editions in six languages between 1503 and 1515, the Americas were of course something of a success. Although Europeans paid far more attention to the seamanship of Vasco da Gama, whose celebrated return from India in 1499 had completed the conversion of the Cape of Storms into the Cape of Good Hope, the real Indies around the southern tip of Africa and east across the Indian Ocean were iconologically no match for the mythic zones of the New World. From the beginning, from the letter written by Columbus on his way home after his first landfalls, the New World's "Indies" were an exotic composite of Biblical Eden, Greek Atlantis, Roman Arcadia, medieval Isles of the Blessed, late medieval romantic wilderness, and the Renaissance image of the earth in its primitive state, inhabited by noble savages, naked, friendly, generous, living (unawares) in their own golden age. Columbus heard, as he could not have heard, nightingales singing in Hispaniola among "tall trees of different kinds which seem to reach the sky," from which sky the natives believed that he and his men had descended. And it was almost always from above that Europeans surveyed the "new golden land," as if they could not emotionally afford to be dwarfed by this *terra* so suddenly *cognita*. Soon the most influential of Renaissance cartomancers, Sir Thomas More, would take as his starting point the property evidently held in common by the "Indians" of America, and assume as his framing fiction the last voyage of Amerigo Vespucci, from whose farthest fort a certain Raphael Hythloday (= Nonsense) would depart with a double order of apostles toward the island of Utopia (= Nowhere).[103]

Nowhere had not been forever an idyllic island. It was originally Abraxa, a peninsula of rude and uncivilized people. King Utopus had conquered these barbarians, reshaping their lives and their land. He educated them into the highest of civilizations, then isolated them from all others by cutting a fifteen-mile-wide channel between his dominion and the continent. Though properly beyond the reach of this book, as it was beyond the reach of explorers in 1516, More's Utopia took to its furthest latitude the strongest therapeutic response to the feeling at the end of the 15th century that time was running out. There was, it seemed, between the Indies to the east and the "Indies" to the west, between the Florentine New Jerusalem and the incredibly distant Utopia, world enough for another run at redeeming time. From here on out we will observe at centuries' ends a tremendous fascination with frontiers and antipodes as locales where time can be reset, where a person or a society can start anew. [104]

If some printed calendars after 1475 were no longer perpetual but specific as to the year; if merchants now were cautioned "to keep always with you a small notebook in which you shall note day by day and hour by hour even the minute [detail] of your transactions"; if clocks in town squares might now strike every quarter hour and minute hands (grossly inaccurate) race across the faces of tower clocks and chamber clocks, then time might be heard and seen as well as thought to be running out more quickly than ever before, minute by minute, bell by bell. Thus at century's end (and at centuries' ends) a straitened sensitivity to chance, luck, fortune. Kept by poverty, family, or gender from sailing out to seize new worlds, one could at the very least seize the time, catch Opportunity by the forelock when it came along. Earlier, Petrarch in his *Trionfi* had arranged six triumphal chariots in their Renaissance order: Love, conquered by Chastity, conquered by Death, conquered by Fame, conquered by Time, overcome only and at last by Eternity. Once depicted either as Kairos, winged figure of Opportunity balancing a pair of scales on a knife edge, or as Aion, snake-wound figure of the inexhaustible, Time in Petrarch's archetypal procession was a destroyer, consuming all vestiges of the human. Across the 15th century, Time became further confused with Death, a confusion bred by two Greek homonyms—*chronos*, the word for time, and *Kronos*, the Greek name for Saturn, oldest of the gods, who had devoured his children. The sickle in his right arm no longer a symbol of fertility but of mortality, his other arm now burdened with an enormous hourglass, Aion/chronos/Kronos/Father Time was invested with the cannibal insignia of the grim reaper around the same *fin de siècle* that Kairos was transformed from a young winged man into Fortuna, a young nude woman on a sphere floating in the sea. Time at the end of the century had become deadlier, Opportunity more precarious and more willful. Wrote Niccolò Machiavelli, with respect to the Romans but thinking back to the tumble of events in Savonarola's Florence in which he too had been swept along, "I repeat, then, as an incontrovertible truth, proved by all history, that men may second Fortune but cannot overcome her; they may develop her designs, but cannot defeat them." At a chivalric tournament in Bologna on October 4, 1490, Fortune won the field over Reason, and Massimiliano Sforza's victories for Milan in 1512 were celebrated with a triumphal arch upon which Fortune towered over Fame, Penitence, Courage, and Hope.[105]

"But men should never despair on that account," continued Machiavelli; "for, not knowing the aims of Fortune, which she pursues by dark and devious ways, men should always be hopeful, and never yield to despair, whatever troubles or ill fortune may befall them." The moral was to seize the moment; impetuosity and audacity might well be rewarded. Act with the moment, advised Florence's other turn-of-the-century historian, Francesco Guicciardini: "Future events are so chancy and subject to so many accidents that most times even those who are really wise are deceived in them. . . . Hence, to abandon present good for fear of future evil is usually madness." So, while painters and playwrights began to worry about anachronism, Machiavelli and Guicciardini in Italy, Philippe de Commynes and Guillaume Budé in France wrote of history as flux, of moments grasped or lost, and they worried over each year, to which they gave a clear beginning and end, as if each year had its own life, its own bearing.[106]

This novel concern with the historical biography of a year was reflected in the Jubilee of 1500, for which Pope Alexander VI devised a new ritual, unblocking the Porta Sancta of St. Peter's basilica at the start of the Jubilee year and bricking it up again at the close. There had been other 15th-century Jubilees—in 1423, thirty-three years after the last one, and sparsely attended; in 1450, a wild success, the rush of pilgrims compared to a flight of starlings or the march of ants, two hundred of whom were trampled to death in a battle for right of way on the bridge of Santo Angelo; in 1475, according to the decree of Paul II that every generation of Christians, every twenty-five years, should have the benefit of a Jubilee (as has been the pattern ever since). The Jubilee of 1500 was however the true pageant demarcating the century which Ficino in 1492 had self-consciously nominated as a new golden age. Alexander VI in 1493, taking the globe in hand, had drawn a line down the middle of the New World, the Line of Demarcation between Spanish and Portuguese dominion. Now, in 1500, he took a hammer to the wall of time, in much the same manner as the Etruscan priests at the temple wall at Volsinii, and opened the Holy Way into St. Peter's for a year of indulgences. The Jubilee had been proclaimed not once but thrice, on April

12, 1498, on March 28, 1499, and, restoring the jubal to the Jubilee, with a blast of trumpets on December 22nd. Christmas Day, the Pope had been carried, triumphator in a triumphal procession, to St. Peter's, holding a burning golden taper in one hand and blessing pilgrims with the other. All the bells of Rome had been ringing for three days solid as Alexander VI walked barefoot up to the Porta Sancta and hammered politely through the door of bricks into the Jubilee year and the prospects of a new century. [107]

Among the "Men and women, widows and maidens, monks and nuns . . . flocking to Rome to gain the Indulgence" was the astronomer Copernicus, who came at Easter and stayed to lecture privately to such as Michelangelo, he who had just finished (and, just this once, signed) a sculpture for St. Peter's. His neoclassical *Pietà*, self-possessed Virgin deeply but calmly mourning the beautiful Christ stretched across her knees, was as fitting a conclusion to the lost-and-found-and-lost-again golden age of the old century as his next commission, the young, defiant, messianic David, would be a fitting inaugural to the hopes for a new century. [108]

But the "golden year" of 1500 had its own bearings. It was rather a morality play than a triumph. On June 19th, feast day of Saints Peter and Paul, Rome was assaulted by a hailstorm and winds so strong that ceilings in the papal palace collapsed, killing a dozen and wounding the Pope. Was this a warning to him whose concupiscence had led to four illegitimate children and whose nepotism would culminate in the seizure of the Jubilee income by his son, the violent Caesar Borgia? From this outrage and the pervasive sale of indulgences, it would be a few short years to the Ninety-Five Theses and the Reformers' break with a Roman Church that stood accused of intractable corruption. [109]

"God give you time and space!" Knowledge wishes Everyman in the English version of the Flemish morality play printed in 1495. "God give you time and space!" is the prayer of the *fin de siècle*. It is the prayer that lies between remorse and repentance, between the Summons of Death and the Welcome of Heaven for Everyman, who must "Look well, and take good heed to the ending, / Be you never so gay." It is the prayer that lies between seven millennia on a completed calendar and the next thousand years; between a dark age and a golden age; between an old world and a new. It is the navigator's prayer as he squints past his astrolabe and considers his maps. It is the prayer which lies in the suspense of long division and the confrontation between minus and plus, two symbols and an operation first published in 1489 and 1491. It is the prayer for the spiritual magic of picturing the cosmos in all its dimensions and for the spiritual artistry of dying well. It is the Utopian's prayer, howsoever little comfort it was to those men and women imported from Africa in 1501 as the first of the Black slaves to work the Americas into a new golden land. And it was the most apt of prayers for European prophets at century's turn, who knew that the stars were poised between the Great Renovation of 1484 and the Final Deluge of 1524.[110]

CENTURIATORS: THE 1590S

MARTIN LUTHER WAS BORN NOVEMBER 10, 1483, ON THE CUSP, as it were, of the 1484 conjunction of Jupiter and Saturn. Though he bore with him the faith of a Reformer and the momentum of the Reformation, he lived ever in a personal suspense ("No one is sure of the integrity of his own contrition") and a world-historical crisis ("It is not to be expected that mankind will still see two or three thousand years after the birth of Christ. The end will come sooner than we think"). When came the actual Deluge of 1524—the Peasants' War in Germany and Austria, with the millenarianism of Thomas Müntzer and omens of a truly radical reformation—Luther was for a while persuaded toward a more discreet apocalypse, but through to his death in 1546 he maintained a strong, often intense, conviction of having been born into the "time of the end" of Daniel 12. Only the promise of a proximate Second Coming could possibly sustain Christians in these sour, senile years. In 1540 the world had worn out 5500 years of its welcome, Luther figured, and since Jesus had been born not on the round number 4000 A.M. but in 3960, so the End too would come in advance of the year 6000. The calendar instant of the Last Judgment might be uncertain, but, wrote Luther, "For my part I am sure that the Day of Judgment is just around the corner. It doesn't matter that we don't know the precise day . . . perhaps someone else can figure it out. But it is certain that time is now at an end."[111]

After his death, Luther's diverse calculations and considerations of the Last Days were collected in a single popular volume while his successors warmed to the preaching of an approaching End. Stirred by the amazing energies of their Reformation but staggered by the vitriol of Protestant schism, the bitterness of Catholic counterattack, the cruelties of persecution, and the meanness of religious war, Lutherans on the Continent and Calvinists in England had to strike an eschatological balance between glory and gloom. Lutheran theologian and educator Philipp Melanchthon, addressing some hundreds of students in a 1559 lecture hall, was reputed to have warned

Title page illustration from the 1668 Amsterdam edition of Nostradamus's *Centuries*, first published in their entirety in 1558.

them that "there will occur in times to come great and terrible changes and disorders. You young people are now yet living in the golden time, but there will soon hereafter follow much more horrible, more afflicted times" when the Turks might conquer Europe. Melanchthon then cited the prophecies of a 15th-century monk who had put Gog and Magog in command of Germany in the year 1600, and "there sit right here in this auditorium many among you who will experience it; may God then give you mercy." English Protestants also looked toward apocalypse at century's end, to 1588 "as a Climacterical, Criticall, or Decretoriall yeere of the world," or beyond, to 1600 itself. We will attend further to these prophecies, these "blind unreasonable whimwhams" (as one skeptic called them), but an issue of greater import to the central whimwham of this book is pleading for our attention.[112]

Essential to the Reformed sense of time, with its emphasis in the present tense upon the immediacy of faith and in the future tense upon the redemption of the faithful, was an equally emphatic claim to historical priority in the past perfect and imperfect. Reformers had to show that they, and not the hierophants of the Roman Church, were the sole legitimate heirs of true, apostolic Christianity. Luther, moving the Reformation beyond the apocalyptic critiques of late medieval reformers who had cast one or another pope as the satanic figure of the endtimes, convicted instead the very institution of the papacy as the embodiment of Antichrist. What remained to complete the Protestant historical polemic was to trace systematically and irrefutably the path by which the Roman Church had diverged further and further from Scripture and the spirit of the apostles, and to link in an unbroken chain from Resurrection to Reformation those Christians in every era who had maintained the apostolic spirit.

The latter half of this job was in good measure and to great effect carried out by the English Calvinist John Foxe, whose *Actes and Monuments of These Latter and Perillous Dayes* followed the blood, bones, and ashes of Christian martyrs from the first persecution under Nero through the persecutions under the (Arian) Vandals to the persecutions of Waldensians, Albigensians, Lollards, and more recent reformers by Inquisitors under the direction of the Church at Rome. Thus the popes were aligned with Roman atrocity and barbarian savagery while English Protestants who were tortured and burned at the stake under the Marian persecutions of the 1550s were allied with apostolic faith. The martyrs were the long-suffering Christian remnant, a Chosen People with a mission to redeem the world against well-nigh overwhelming odds. Foxe's *Book of Martyrs*, as it was known almost from the start (with the English translation in 1563 from the Latin original of 1559), would inform all subsequent Protestant millenarianism, especially that messianic image of a redeemer nation so dear to the English after their defeat of the Spanish Armada in 1588, as later to the Puritans in New England, and later still and dearest to the manifestly enterprising citizens of an upstart country, the United States of America.[113]

Once again we have gotten ahead of ourselves. It is to the achievement of the first half of the Reformers' historical program, to the thorough account of the Roman Church's deviation from Christian truth, that we must look for the real news. When the Polish Lutheran scholar Matthias Flacius Illyricus set to work with a committee of five and with the help of nine or ten other "studious and pious men in the city of Magdeburg" to detail the historical, irremediable corruption of the Roman Church, they meant to produce sixteen volumes, one for each century from the birth of Christ to the start of the Reformation. The first volume of the *Ecclesiastica historia integram ecclesiae Christi ideam* was published in 1559, year of Foxe's *Book of Martyrs*; the thirteenth volume, covering the 13th century, appeared in 1574, as elegantly printed, annotated, and indexed as each previous volume. The ambitious project came to a halt the next year at the death of Flacius, and the last three volumes were not written up. Nonetheless, the scholars of Magdeburg had erected a formidable monument to Protestant polemic and, more to our point, had inaugurated a new way of dividing history into ages: by century, each hundred-year period with its own beginning and end and its own character. Although the individual volumes of this masterwork proceeded by theme rather than by the chronological momentum of the century itself, never before in the Christian West had the long span of history been conceived in terms of centuries laid end to end. The set of thirteen volumes was known therefore by its most remarkable feature as the *Magdeburg Centuries*, and its authors were called the Centuriators.[114]

Absent the dedication of the Centuriators, we would have neither the English word "century" denoting a period of one hundred years nor the more modern notion of a century's end as the end of a hundred years all their own, from '01 to '00. Nor would we have, likely, so long-lived a legend of the year 1000. In 1558, under the discipline of the saintly Filippo de' Neri, a twenty-year-old boy from a small town near Naples had begun lecturing on Church history in Rome. Cesare Baronio aspired to the life of a contemplative, but he was pressured by Neri, by the foremen of the Catholic Renaissance (or Counter-Reformation), and then by celestial voices to shape his career and his research toward the publication of an august history of the Holy Church. In 1577, assiduously revising and editing his first volume,

Baronio finally read the Centuriators and was persuaded to construct his *Annales ecclesiastici* as a counterpunch to the *Magdeburg Centuries*. He did not, as did a German Catholic polemicist refuting the Centuriators, organize his *Annals* entirely by hundred-year intervals from the birth of Christ, but he did take unusual care to comment on the beginnings and ends of now-standard Anno Domini centuries. Baronio closed his tenth volume (published at the turn of the century) upon the notable silence of the records with regard to any celebration of that millennial year, the Anno periodi graeco-romane 6493, Ottonis III Reg. 18. Imp. 5, Silvestrii II Papae 2, Jesu Christi 1000, and (as we may recall) he opened his eleventh volume with seven lines about certain beliefs that this world would cease before the year 1001. So it was in the context of Catholic polemic, in defense of a Roman Church which had outlasted medieval fears of apocalyptic endings and would surely outlast Protestant histories of corruption and prophecies of doom, that the legend of the year 1000 made its formal modern debut. From the start, the legend was enmeshed in the mythos of the century's end, not only because it appeared in a set of volumes directed against the Centuriators, but also because of Baronio's initial twelve-year plan for the completion of that set by 1599, just in time for the opening ceremonies of the Jubilee of 1600.[115]

Baronio in 1600 did visit the four main Roman basilicas thirty times, gaining the Jubilee indulgence. The *Annals*, however, would not be finished until 1607. His labors—on what would be the most influential Catholic Church history of the next hundred years, printed in fifty-seven editions— had been interrupted too often to make practicable the conclusion of the *Annals* at the conclusion of the century. Instead, as he had foreseen in a vision, his life would end in 1607 at the age of sixty-nine with the end of his account of the life of the Church.[116]

Among the interruptions to Baronio's labors on the *Annals* had been his appointment to a commission to review the Roman Martyrology, a liturgical book listing the feasts of martyrs and other saints for each day of the year. The commission was to examine the thousands of names on the list and expunge those without historical footing. Such an assignment was partly in response to Protestant attacks upon Catholic "idolatry," but it was especially pressing as the Roman Church prepared for and carried through a dramatic revision of the yearly calendar itself. By the bull of February 24, 1582, Pope Gregory XIII proclaimed that October 4, 1582, would be succeeded by October 15, 1582, a ten-day correction demanded by the mounting discrepancy between the mean Julian year of 365.25 days and the slightly shorter solar year of 365.242 days. Since 325 A.D. and the Council of Nicaea, at which March 21st had been established as the date of the vernal equinox, the annual eleven-minute discrepancy had resulted in a liturgical calendar a bit more than ten days ahead of itself. That is, the pivot of the Christian calendar, Easter, designated by the Council of Nicaea as the first Sunday after the full moon following the vernal equinox, had over the centuries drifted some ten days away from spring toward summer as the Julian date March 21st had pulled ahead of the actual equinox by eleven minutes each year. In 1581, the vernal equinox occurred March 11th while Easter was celebrated as if the equinox had occurred on March 21st. Gregory XIII's calendar reform of 1582 restored Easter's proper relation with the heavens and the seasons. In order to adjust for the surplus fraction of the day un-corrected by the bold New Style jump from the night of October 4th to the morning of October 15th, Church mathematicians chose to concentrate spe-cifically upon the ends of standard Anno Domini centuries. Pursuant to their advice, Gregory declared in his bull that three of every four centurial years would not be (as previously all had been) leap years. Only those centurial years evenly divisible by 400 would henceforth be leap years: the year 1600, the year 2000.[117]

As the Gregorian calendar was taking effect in Rome, Joseph Justus Scaliger in Paris published his *Opus novum de emendatione temporum*, the first new comprehensive and critical (or "scientific") chronology of the world to appear in Western Europe since the chronologies of the Venerable Bede nine hundred years before. That Scaliger, a French Protestant, should also be critical of the New Style calendar was to be expected, for few self-respecting Reformers then had any desire to live according to a calendar "reformed" by the papal Antichrist. The fury over Gregory XIII's bull and his October Revolution was so clearly the fury of religious warfare that Protestant coun-tries would for centuries adhere dogmatically to the Old Style, their Julian calendars ten, then eleven, then twelve, eventually thirteen full days behind the New Style calendar embraced by Roman Catholics.[118]

Yet Scaliger's criticism of the Gregorian reform came also from a man insistent upon chronometric detail in an era during which finger-ring watches and astronomical clocks were all the rage at Western courts, and when even Turkish sultans and Chinese emperors were being impressed by the me-chanical flare of European clocks and planetary automata. Timepieces accurate to the second, with second hands, were being devised for the star-mapping operations of such astronomers as Christoph Rothmann at the court of Wil-liam IV of Hesse and, possibly, for the great man himself, Tycho Brahe, who spoke in terms of seconds as early as 1581 and whose patient timing of transits for his new astronomical tables would lead his exacting assistant Johannes Kepler to worry over some very small eccentricities in the orbit of Mars and so arrive at some very large laws of planetary motion. Scaliger, then, in the prestigious company of Europe's foremost mathematician, Fran-çois Viète, who published a table of trigonometric functions to ten decimal places for every degree, protested Gregory's reform on the grounds of im-precision. The New Style calendar would require further emendations in the future, to the tune of one full day over the course of the next three or four millennia.[119]

The battle over the calendar was won, as every nation now knows, by the Roman Catholics, whose experts had opted for simplicity of rule rather than absolute chronologic. Joseph Scaliger, finishing his recalculation of the age of the world, which had reached 5531 A.M. in September 1581 A.D., would write unabashedly to a friend, "Please remember what I'm telling you: I have changed the times," but it was Gregory XIII in February 1582 who changed the time, for his world and for ours. The new world chronology and the new annual calendar were both expressions of a new anxiety over the passage of time—time, which was crucial to the Reformation critique of the sale of indulgences and the escape from purgatory; time, which was at the center of Calvinist and protocapitalist notions of thrift, economy, and efficiency; time, whose autonomy and worth were at the breaking point between usury and fair profit in the late 16th-century reconsideration of interest and value; Time, whose daughter in late 16th-century paintings was suddenly Truth; Time the Destroyer, his scythe overtaking the skull and chaste bones of theatrical Death at century's end; Time as the foulest of Opportunities in *The Faerie Queene*, Edmund Spenser's "wicked hag" of the 1590s, "her face ill favored, full of wrinkles old"; and Time as Mutabilitie, Spenser's Titaness who

> . . . the face of earthly things so changed
> That all which Nature had established first
> In good estate, and in meet order ranged,
> She did pervert, and all their statutes burst.

Robert Grosseteste around 1200, Pierre d'Ailly around 1400, Paul of Mid-delburg around 1500 had seriously proposed calendar reform, but only under the pressures of a culture inordinately anxious about time would a new calendar at last be instituted, new world chronologies be put forward, and the century as a new historical standard be given its European blessing.[120]

Prior to the Centuriators, a "century" (as distinct from a *saeculum* or age) had referred broadly to collections of one hundred: one hundred poems, one hundred letters, one hundred stories. This sense of a "century" was heightened and then transformed in 1558 with the publication of *Les vraies centuries et prophéties de Maistre Michel Nostradamus*. We should be quite familiar with that name, Nostradamus, and with his reputation as *The Man Who Saw Tomorrow*, for both the 16th-century man and the 1981 pseudo-documentary on videocassette have made our headlines. A great quake would shake the West Coast in May 1988, announced Orson Welles in his on-screen narration of the life of Nostradamus, and up-to-date astrologers late that April noted with alarm certain fateful alignments for May 10th. Calls to talk shows and to the Griffith Observatory in Los Angeles were "almost hysterical." A comic weatherman designed a bumper sticker, "Honk If You Believe Nostradamus," just as the press revealed that Nancy Reagan had been consulting an astrologer before determining the President's schedule. California psychics booked flights out of state while common folk stocked bottled water. . . . This was not the first time that Welles had been responsible for a public panic. In 1938 his radio dramatization of *The War of the Worlds* (by namesake H. G. Wells) had jammed the phone lines with news of an alien invasion, thousands fleeing New Jersey homes to escape Martian death rays. And the mistaken quake of '88 was not the first time that one four-line verse from among the ten centuries of quatrains composed by Nostradamus had been (mis)interpreted. Nostradamus was a prophet scorned neither in his own age nor in his own country.[121]

Elder son of a Provençal Jewish notary who had converted to Catholicism in 1501 under threat of expropriation, grandson perhaps of physician-astrologers to "King" René of Anjou, Michel de Nostredame had begun his career as a physician, cosmetician, and chef. His fame as a healer during plague epidemics was achieved by means of clean water, fresh air, and rose-petal pills concocted of 1 oz. green cyprus sawdust, 6 oz. iris of Florence, 3 oz. cloves, 3 drams calamus, 6 drams purgative aloe, and rose-petal powder. As a cosmetician his renown was due to the beauty creams described in his *Treatise on Make-Up* of 1552, which included the recipe for a rejuvenating pomade compounded of coral, leaf gold, and lapis lazuli. Sweets were his forte as a chef, in particular a "quince jelly, of a sovereign beauty, goodness, taste, and excellence proper to be presented to a king."[122]

The quince jelly would indeed be presented to a king, Francis I, and his beauty creams would be in vogue with the court of Queen and then Regent Catherine de' Medici, who may also have known of Nostradamus through the popular almanacs he had been publishing since 1550. But his celebrity would not have endured had Nostradamus not mounted the steps to his study on the evening of Good Friday, 1554, "in a prophetical mood" in his fifty-first year, and begun his "Books of Prophecies, each containing a hundred Astronomical Stanzas, which I have joined obscurely, and are perpetual prophecies from this year to the year 3797." In 1555 the first three centuries were published; by 1558, when all ten centuries were in print, Nostradamus had become a European celebrity, reigning over all other astrologers in France "like a tyrant with his sooth sayings."[123]

Most of the "Astronomical" (i.e., astrological) quatrains were directed toward events much nearer than 3797, since Nostradamus believed that he was living in the middle of "the seventh millenary, which ends all," and most of them were undated, allusive, ambiguous, occulted. Consider:

> *That which shall live shall leave no direction,*
> *Its destruction and death will come by stratagem,*
> *Autun, Chalons, Langres, and from both sides,*
> *The war and ice shall do great harm.*

Such tempting prophecies borrowed their enigmatic style from a number of traditions very much alive in the 16th century: the cleverly equivocal pseudo-Sibylline oracles, imitated by many an almanac writer then and now; the coded mystical language of kabbalah, to which Nostradamus in his youth may have been exposed by his grandfathers; the widely admired anagrams and double meanings in Latin epigraphic wordplay, well known to the classicist Julius Caesar Scaliger, father of the world chronologer and friend to physician Nostradamus in the 1530s; the symbols of the alchemist, whose procedures and materials were identified macrocosmically as well as micro-cosmically and whose universe was expanded (while Nostradamus was creating pills and pomades) by the high-flying rhetoric of one Theophrastus Bombastus von Hohenheim, otherwise known as Paracelsus, to whom was also attributed a series of crude but prophetic woodblocks; the complex allegories of Neoplatonism, epitomized in Francesco Colonna's *Hypneroto-machia Poliphili* of 1499, a book so elegant that it has never been excelled in the annals of printing either for its graphic beauty or for its inexhaustible mystery; the hermetic Renaissance version of Egyptian hieroglyphs, understood to be profound illustrations invented by Hermes Trismegistus, explained in prose by the ancient magus Horapollo, and translated into verse by Nostradamus in the 1530s; emblems, highly figured moral verses published by Italian jurist Andrea Alciati in his *Emblemata* of 1531; finally, the banners, shields, and insignia of heraldry, by which poet, prophet, or pamphleteer might conceal the illustrious and the notorious behind the names and shapes of fish, fowl, or beast.[124]

This last tradition was certainly not least, for one heraldic quatrain of 1555 would bring a royal summons in 1556 and, three years later, a fearful royal reverence:

> *The young lion shall overcome the old,*
> *In warlike field in single duel:*
> *In a cage of gold he will pierce his eyes,*
> *Two wounds one, then die, a death cruel.*

That old lion, Catherine de' Medici suspected, might be her husband, King Henri II, for whom another astrologer had already predicted his death by duel. In 1559, on the third and final day of the tournament honoring the marriage of his younger daughter, the King, sporting a golden helmet, entered the lists against the captain of his Scottish guard, who (it is said) knew of the dark quatrain and was uncomfortable with his role as the climactic opponent. These chivalric combats were meant to be festive, and the King, of course, was meant to win, so after an undramatic, inconclusive round the King insisted (to the captain's despair) upon a rematch. During this bout the two knights duly and nobly splintered their lances, but the jagged point of Montgomery's broken lance pierced Henri's gilded visor and impaled one eye as a splinter went through his throat.[125]

In 1560, a second fatal quatrain, concerning Henri's son and successor, Francis II, proved correct. By July 1, 1566, the date of his own death, Nostradamus had been named Counselor and Physician in Ordinary to King Charles IX, another of Catherine de' Medici's ill-fated royal children, and a new complete edition of the *Centuries* was in press. Befitting a seer, and at his request, Michel de Nostredame was buried erect, his coffin upright along one wall of the Franciscan church of Salon in southern France. The marble slab was engraved in Latin, "Here rest the bones of the illustrious Michael Nostradamus, alone of all mortals judged worthy to record with his near divine pen, under the influence of the stars, the future events of the entire world."[126]

We seem now to have gotten behind ourselves, fixed at midcentury, but, like the apparent motion of the stars, there has been more going on here than meets the eye. For Nostradamus himself had a penchant toward the ends of centuries whenever he dared to specify a year—1585, 1606, 1607, 1609, 1700, 1727, 1792, and the most specific of them all,

> *The year 1999, seven months,*
> *From the sky will come a great King of terror,*
> *To resuscitate the great King of Angoulmois;*
> *Before, after, Mars will reign by good luck.*

Clearly, the Kings of terror and of Angoulmois, whoever or whatever they may be, must command our attention when we come to terms with our own *fin de siècle*, but until then I mean to use this infamous quatrain simply as evidence for the especial interest Nostradamus had in ends of centuries and ends of millennia. He was himself represented as no less than a Janus figure. His disciple Jean Aimé de Chavigny, writing the first full-scale commentary on the *Centuries*, would nominate his master as the "French Janus" who, through a diligent "conference" with events past and present, could "collect" (*collige*) the future. Like every later exegete of the quatrains, Chavigny had an agenda and thereby a magic glass for reading the messages Nostradamus had hidden behind his elliptical, polyglot verses, and in this case too Nostradamus had been prophetically committed to the century's end, to the crowning of Henry of Navarre in 1594 as Henry IV, King of France and Joachimite candidate (implied Chavigny) for Last World Emperor. Whenever others since have envisioned a new imperial era, someone has unearthed a telling quatrain from the *Centuries*, most particularly in regard to ends of centuries, to 1792 or 1999. [127]

The prophecies of Nostradamus have enjoyed such popularity that it seems almost natural that the use of the English noun "prediction" dates back to a 1561 invective against Nostradamus, and that the first book after the primer to be given to Théophilus de Garancières as a child was the *Centuries*. Could young Théophilus in the 1600s have avoided making a connection between centuries and predictions? Although in French *"centurie"* rarely referred to a period of one hundred years, I am willing to propose that the enduring celebrity of Nostradamus and his *Centuries* has contributed to a prevalent Western confusion between the chronological act of dividing years into standard hundreds and the divinatory act of making sense of the "momentum" of History "across the centuries." While the Protestant Centuriators of Magdeburg laid centuries end to end, leading the century (with the English "century") to the forefront of historical thought, and while the Bolognese Pope Gregory XIII made the ends of centuries focal moments for the adjustment of calendar time, a Catholic son of converted French Jews in Provence, crafting a thousand mysterious quatrains "joined obscurely" by hundreds, gave the century and the century's end an immeasurable *élan vital*.[128]

If Nostradamus, the Centuriators, their counterpart Baronio, Gregory XIII, and his critic Scaliger must be warmly acknowledged as having in the long run made this book possible, in the short run their concern with time and the times was as much a result as a cause of those desperate hopes for the world which climaxed in the 1590s with a vivid display of what a *fin de siècle* is all about. We can see the most dynamic of tensions, the most dramatic of contrasts between ends and beginnings, in Tintoretto's penultimate painting, the *Last Supper* of 1592–94. Here the Italian Baroque bursts from its Mannerist frame—the roughhewn table of the apostles slants diagonally up the center of the canvas from left to right, forcing us to search out Jesus by the brilliance of his halo, while flames from a hanging oil lamp cast a raking light across each face and figure during this Passover of sharp reliefs and shadowy uneasiness. We can see the tensions and contrasts, as well as the most exaggerated of emotions, in Caravaggio's *The Calling of St. Matthew* (1597–98) or in the mature work of El Greco, but at century's turn we may do even better with our ears than with our eyes. Listen.

"The dawn of the seventeenth century was breaking as Signor Luca left his house and proceeded toward the monastery . . . where dwelt Signor Vario . . . who indeed was momentarily expecting him." Yesterday, after leaving his lordship, Luca had been invited to hear some madrigals composed in the style called New Music. The texture of the madrigals had not been unpleasing, but, Luca now complained to Vario, "insofar as [the madrigals] introduced new rules, new modes, and new turns of phrase, these were harsh and little pleasing to the ear." Modern men that they were, Luca and Vario agreed that "discovering new things is not merely good but necessary." However, these New Musicians were entirely irrational: "if you would know what they say, they are content to know how to string their notes together after their fashion and to teach the singers to sing their compositions, accompanying themselves with many movements of the body, and in the end they let themselves go to such an extent that they seem to be actually dying—this is the perfection of their music."[129]

The Bolognese churchman who contrived this dialogue for his tract *Delle imperfezioni della moderna musica* in 1600 did not appreciate the innovations of such as Gesualdo and the young Monteverdi, but his ears had not deceived him concerning the emotionality of the New Musicians, who were often at their most inspired when composing grief-stricken laments. Madrigals and masques had already begun to take on the Baroque obligation to arouse the affections, to generate and sustain the purest states of fear, love, anger, sorrow, and joy, a few years before the New Music was theoretically defined by Vincenzo Galilei. One of the louder voices of the Florentine Camerata, Galilei in 1581 published a treatise critical of the "old music" of complex polyphony which overwhelmed the vocal line, reducing the words to gibberish and muffling all emotion. Galilei called instead for a New Music obedient to the moods of the text, sung with tremendous feeling to a series of simple chords above a continuous bass line. Impressed by the antiquarian news that ancient Greek drama had been sung throughout, Camerata composers during the next decades produced the first arias and, in 1598 and 1600, the first operas, or "tragedies represented in music."[130]

Although the *Dafne* of 1598 appears to have been rather a tame pastoral drama than a tragedy represented in music, the *Euridice* of 1600 was singularly appropriate to the extremes of the centurial year. Presented at the Florentine festivities for the wedding of Henry IV of France to Maria de' Medici, Jacopo Peri's version of the Greek myth followed the supernal musician Orpheus from his anguish at the death of his newlywed Eurydice, stung by a viper, through the journey down to the Underworld, where the Orphic music so charms Pluto that he consents to release the young bride. The myth not only afforded a fine opportunity for the musical expression of the extremes of pure love (for Eurydice), pure anger (at her untimely death), pure sorrow (at the loss), pure fear (at the entrance to Hades), and pure joy (at her release); it was also exemplary of the janiform vision of rebirth at century's turn. The librettist, Ottavio Rinuccini, apologized for omitting the last and tragic half of the story: the unique condition set by Pluto, that Orpheus should not look back at his beloved until they are both out of the cavern of Death; Orpheus looking back too soon, losing his beloved, then his mind, then his life, torn apart by a furious band of maenads. "To some I may seem to have been too bold in altering the conclusion of the fable of Orpheus," wrote Rinuccini in his dedication, "but so it seemed fitting to me at a time of such great rejoicing" as the wedding of Maria de' Medici (and the year of Jubilee). In 1607 Monteverdi's *Orfeo* would enlist the other half of the myth in a move toward an even more evocative score, but Orpheus still could not be the victim of the Furies. Apollo to the rescue, Orpheus is taken aloft in a cloud, where he may gaze upon Eurydice in the heavens.[131]

Ever since Pythagoras and his "harmony of the spheres," music and beauty had belonged in the heavens, and they belonged there yet in 1603, according to the Dutch composer Jan Pieterszoon Sweelinck, who was to lay the groundwork for the Baroque fugue. At work on musical settings for the Psalms, Sweelinck wrote to the burgomasters of Amsterdam: "All nature itself, to speak the truth, is nothing but a perfect music that the Creator causes to resound in the ears of man, to give him pleasure and to draw him gently to Himself. This we recognize at a glance in the excellent arrangement, the splendid proportions, and the orderly movements and revolutions of the celestial bodies." That cosmic harmony by which the heavens moved could also "move and moderate the emotions of the soul," wherefore the sages of ancient times "appropriated [music] for their oracles in order to gently instil yet firmly incorporate their doctrine into our minds, and thus, having awakened them, could raise them more easily to the contemplation and admiration of the divine. Orpheus among the pagans and David among the Hebrews made studies of these matters," and now Sweelinck was moved to clothe fifty of David's Psalms in new music. [132]

Johannes Kepler was also moving toward a new astronomy by way of the old oracles, the geometric philosophy of Pythagoras and the rediscovered geometric practices of Euclid. In 1596 Kepler proposed to solve the *Cosmographical Mystery* as if it were a musical puzzle, a question of celestial harmonies, and in the following years he would draw out the planetary orbits using musical notation. His Third Law, announced in 1619 as part of the *Harmonies of the World*, was as close to the Pythagorean ideal as a mathematician of Kepler's caliber might honestly come: the ratio of the squares of the orbital periods of the planets is equal to the ratio of the cubes of their average distances from the sun. Kepler's sun was not only at the center (or rather, at one focus) of the planetary system; it was also the Neoplatonic source of stability, unity, proportion, and beauty in the cosmos. Explaining his heliocentric theory, Copernicus half a century earlier had composed a solar rhapsody: "In the middle of all sits Sun enthroned. In this most beautiful temple [of the heavens] could we place this luminary in any better position from which he can illuminate the whole at once? He is rightly called the Lamp, the Mind, the Ruler of the Universe; Hermes Trismegistus names him the Visible God, Sophocles' Electra calls him the All-seeing. So the Sun sits as upon a royal throne ruling his children the planets, which circle round him." This was sun as triumphator, and this was Kepler's sun too, no matter that mathematical scruples had forced Kepler away from the planetary perfection of perfectly circular orbits. [133]

In the most perfect of worlds, in the City of the Sun, everything was neatly concentric. Writing in 1602 from his prison cell in the Castel Nuovo in Naples, Tommaso Campanella imagined a city of seven (planetary) circuits ascending toward an inmost summit and a sacred plain. Ancient Egyptian magus Hermes Trismegistus would have been at home in this reconstruction of Hermopolis, the walls around each circuit carved or painted with glyphs of all nature and all knowledge. Copernicus too could have been happy here, at least at the very center, entering a "perfectly circular" domed temple to find an altar with nothing "but a huge celestial globe, upon which all the heavens are described, with a terrestrial globe beside it." And how Kepler might have enjoyed a conversation about ratio and proportion with the city's spiritual and temporal governor, Prince Prelate and Metaphysician, known to the citizens as the Sun.[134]

Campanella's utopians may be supremely well educated, may live by a reformed calendar and a new (heliocentric) astronomy, may speak every human language, hold all things in common, copulate according to astrologically auspicious hours, and know a "secret, marvelous art by which they can renew their bodies painlessly every seven years," but even they "await the renewal of the world and perhaps its end." They admit, given the great corruption abroad, "that the ages of the world succeed one another according to the order of the planets, and they believe that changes in the apsides every thousand years or every thousand six hundred years produce great changes in the world." And "Oh, if you only knew," says the Genoese sailor, one of the men originally under Columbus and now back from a voyage round the globe and a forced landing on Taprobana or Ceylon, from which he had been led to the City of the Sun, "if you only knew what they deduce from astrology and from the prophets . . . about our present century, which has produced more history in a hundred years than the whole world did in the preceding four thousand!" The compass, the printing press, the harquebus are "mighty signs of the imminent union of the world," but first "the world will be uprooted and cleansed, and then it will be replanted and rebuilt." There's goodness knows how much more to tell, but the sailor hasn't the time. "Wait, wait!" implores his interlocutor, a Knight Hospitaler. "I can't," says the sailor, abruptly ending the dialogue, "I can't."[135]

Campanella himself had been unwilling to wait patiently upon the great changes in store for the world in 1600 after a century—a standard Anno Domini hundred years—so full of history. Since 1593 this Calabrian son of a shoemaker had been espousing a root-and-branch Catholic reformation, a new papacy, and a new universal order. In 1599, believing himself a prophet and rumored to be a magician, Campanella joined in a plot with monks and bandits to throw over the Spanish oppressors of southern Italy. On September

6, 1599, the many conspirators were arrested, among them Campanella, who at the age of thirty-one had already been tortured twice on suspicion of heresy, and who would spend the larger part of the rest of his life in prison cells, feigning madness or pleading contrition. Whether or not he identified with that most famous Calabrian visionary, Joachim of Fiore, and whether or not he had preached a new age and a new law, Campanella under torture again steadfastly denied that he was either a heretic or a rebel. What he did confess to, and what he would have the citizens of the City of the Sun confirm, was a highly specific turn-of-the-century excitement. Prophecies old and new, stars older and newer (the nova of 1572), all heralded tremendous upheavals and a universal rebirth in the centurial, Jubilee year.[136]

The hammer blow to the Porta Sancta was deferred from Christmas to the last day of December 1599, owing to Pope Clement VIII's gout, but the Jubilee was still a smashing success. By the end of 1600, some six hundred confraternity processions had wound through the narrow streets of Rome with crosses, banners, statues, and floats of men enacting the Passion. Half a million pilgrims visited the Holy City to obtain the indulgences or, like the Protestant Duke of Wittenberg, just from curiosity. The Pope heard Cardinal Baronio preach, and in February the Fugger Newsletters reported that Clement had determined "to lead a monastic life as an example to the whole world." He cleared his rooms of carpets and ornaments until his bedchamber had been stripped to a bare bedstead, a table, and several skulls. The high drama in Rome that month, however, was to be found neither within the walls of the papal palace nor alongside the Jubilee processions. It was in the Campo de' Fiore, where, on February 17, an extraordinary man named Giordano Bruno was being burnt alive.[137]

We cannot hope in these pages to take the measure of Bruno, "doctor of a more abstruse theology," as he called himself, "professor of a purer and more innocuous wisdom, noted in the best academies of Europe, an approved and honourably received philosopher, . . . the waker of sleeping souls, tamer of presumptuous and recalcitrant ignorance, proclaimer of a general philanthropy . . . who has pierced the air and penetrated the sky, wended his way amongst the stars and overpassed the margins of the world." Gnostic, poet, magus, mnemotechnician, and peripatetic master of philosophy; enemy of pedants, strict mathematicians, and Aristotelian logicians; advocate at once of Copernican Neoplatonism, hermetic Egyptian religion, and a refined, irenic Catholicism, Bruno had the temperamental brilliance and arrogance of Christopher Marlowe's 1588 *Doctor Faustus* but made pacts only with himself. Born in Nola on the foothills of Mount Vesuvius, he entered the

Dominican Order in 1563 at the age of fifteen, then fled Italy in 1576 amidst accusations of heresy. After years in exile, lecturing and writing in Geneva, Paris, London, Oxford, Wittenberg, Prague, Helmstedt, Frankfurt, and Elgg, Bruno chose to return to his native Italy in 1591, at the age of forty-three, intent at last on actively exercising his magical powers toward a worldwide religious reform. He had reason to be unreasonably optimistic. With the wondrous defeat of the Spanish Armada, Queen Elizabeth now ruled in England as securely as she must if she were to be Astraea, divine figure of justice for a new age; Henry of Navarre, victorious in France, could now assume the French crown on his way to world majesty; and Bruno, he of the heroic mind, was shining with self-confidence now that he had finely focused his own powers as a cosmic mnemonist. Able to recall to their proper places the archetypal images of the cosmos, by dint of astral magic Bruno might reform the human microcosm as he (re)conceived the macrocosm. He would expel the Triumphant Beast, that monstrous composite of all our vices, and work a goodly magic throughout this truly infinite universe. What could stop him from swaying the Pope and the Catholic Church in the direction of the incorrupt, hieroglyphic, Egyptian truths?[138]

The Inquisition. Bruno had meant to dedicate his newest work to the new Pope and so command an audience with Clement VIII, but Inquisitors in Venice and Rome were far more interested in a conference or two with this swaggering Neapolitan. Was Bruno an agent of the Protestant Henry of Navarre? Was Bruno's idea of reform the idea of Reform? Was his Triumphant Beast the Holy Church, whom heretics sometimes called the Antichrist? Or, to take other tacks, had Bruno written, as would a pantheist, of an earth alive and ensouled? Had he said, as would a black magician, that Christ was a magus? And what did he mean, exactly, by his talk of manifold worlds in an infinite universe?

Alternately obsequious, obstreperous, penitent, impenitent, tearful, taunting, Bruno was kept under lock and key for eight years by the Inquisition in Venice and Rome. From April to August 1599 he was confessing to everything, recanting all, and begging forgiveness, then suddenly he refused to abjure a single word. When the Holy Office decided to have him burnt alive in the middle of Rome on the Monday after the Ember Days of Lent in the year 1600, the Inquisition was making of Giordano Bruno a Jubilee martyr to the century's end. Had he not been inspired to return to Italy in 1591 to take action on his program for universal redemption, he would have been safe. Led to the Campo de' Fiore, a few steps from the Piazza Paradiso, was he sorry? "A heroic mind will prefer falling or missing the mark nobly in a lofty enterprise, whereby he manifests the dignity of his mind, to obtaining perfection in things less noble," Bruno had once written. ". . . Fear not noble destruction, burst boldly through the clouds, and die content, if heaven destines us to so illustrious a death."[139]

Such was the "heroic death" of the enthusiast, as described (or urged) by Bruno in 1588 in his *De gli eroici furori (Of Heroic Frenzy)*. Bruno had lived in a fury, had been the enthusiast, had embraced with a whole heart the extremes of an infinite, infinitely various, infinitely renewable universe. He was belligerently critical of every religious party yet devoted to tolerance and peace. He raged against many men, made love (it was said) to many women. He had descended into a likely Hell in order to redeem what he claimed on and off to be his Beloved Humanity or his Beloved Church, planning to charm the Roman pontiff with a book on the Seven Liberal Arts of grammar, dialectics, rhetoric, arithmetic, geometry, astronomy, and music. With Orpheus, he deserved an opera.

Giordano Bruno was too outlandish a man to stand easily as the model for a portrait of the 1590s, but the "heroic frenzy" of his life and the extremes of his "purer and more innocuous wisdom" were consonant with a *fin de siècle* caught between the two images of apocalypse—an old world closing in upon itself, new worlds unveiled. So, while the vagrant Pappenheimer family was being tortured in Munich in 1600 to disclose the names of four hundred accomplices in witchcraft, then burnt alive during these Last Days when magistrates were most zealously hunting down the "rampant, rabid, diabolical host of crazily furious witches and sorcerers," the telescope was being invented in Holland and, soon, Galileo Galilei, son of the New Musician Vincenzo, was staring up through one of those popular toys at our pitted moon and beyond, at the moons of Jupiter, and beyond, at more new stars than any but Bruno knew what to do with. So, while possessed children were pointing to witches in Northamptonshire, Lancashire, and Nottinghamshire; while the young Frenchwoman Marthe Brossier was in Rome being publicly exorcised of her demon in the weeks after Easter of the Jubilee year; while Ophelia was going mad and the gloomy Dane was mourning, "O God, I could be bounded in a nutshell and count myself a king of infinite space, were it not that I have bad dreams," the first Mercator world atlases were just being printed, the principles of the Mercator projection just being explained, and *The Tragedy of Hamlet* just having its premiere in 1600 on the stage of the new, octagonal Globe, a Brunonian architecture for imagining the expansive universe. So, while Spanish noblemen, monastics, and missionaries were despondent over an empire that seemed to be losing its wealth, its spiritual drive, and its sense of direction, and while some among the English nobility were turning their armigerous backs on the 1590s, preferring an archaic knight-errantry and the nostalgic melancholy of monastic ruins, those "bare ruin'd choirs where late the sweet birds sang," William Gilbert was discerning the properties of magnets, Queen Elizabeth was granting a charter to the East India Company, and Miguel de Cervantes Saavedra was mapping out the comedy of *The Ingenious Gentleman, Don Quixote de la Mancha*, a true if foolish adventurer, one of the "real knights-errant [who] take the measure of the entire globe with our feet, beneath the sun of day and in the cold of night, out in the open and exposed to all the inclemencies of the weather."[140]

The weather was terrible, and quixotic. Glaciers were moving south, blocking valleys, crashing into rivers, advancing farthest (to their historical maximum during this Little Ice Age) in 1599–1600. The sky was brimming with portents: from 1577 to 1596, eight comets crossed the English sky; from 1590 to 1600, eight eclipses. Storms, famines, plague seemed more furious after the astrological conjunction of 1583 known as the Fiery Trigon. Titania, Queen of the Fairies in *Midsummer Night's Dream* (acted in 1594, printed in 1600), accuses King Oberon of infidelity and impiety, wherefore

> *The spring, the summer,*
> *The childing autumn, angry winter, change*
> *Their wonted liveries, and the mazèd world,*
> *By their increase, now knows not which is which.*[141]

The political climate was also topsy-turvy. "I foresee in all countries wars, domestic and foreign," Louis Le Roy had written in 1577 in *De la vicissitude ou variété des choses en l'univers*, "factions and heresies which will profane all things human and divine; . . . the universe approaching an end, worldwide confusion, and the return of things to their original chaos." And so it might have seemed at the end of the century with the appearance of peasant pretenders to the throne during Russia's Time of Troubles, workers' revolts in Flanders and France, slave uprisings near Zaragoza in Nueva Granada (Colombia), and the 1600 revolt of the Maroons. A new genre of engravings showed the poor taking their revenge upon the rich, women upon men, animals upon human beings. The earliest book pointedly devoted to the study of political decadence was published by Claude Duret in France in 1595; in 1600 Martín Gonzalez de Cellorigo was among the first to discuss the "decline" (*declinación*) of Imperial Spain. Scottish Protestant Robert Pont in *A Newe Treatise of the Right Reckoning of Yeares* (1599) refused to consider 1600 a Jubilee. It was rather "the 60 yeare of the blast of the seaventh & last trumpet . . . a year of the decaying and fading age of the world."[142]

As usual at century's end—as at most any epoch—there was evidence aplenty that "time is changed, it was golden, it was good; it is wooden, it is evill." As usual—as at most any epoch—there was strikingly contrary evidence that the world was on the verge of a new golden age. Englishman Edward Topsell, who had written of the wooden and the evil in the dedication to his *Time's Lamentation* of 1599, in his text celebrated the defeat of the Spanish Armada, the long peace under Elizabeth, and the godliness of many of her subjects. What distinguished the *fin de siècle* from other epochs was the desperate intensity of the ambivalence between apocalypse as ruin and apocalypse as revelation. Was the Fiery Trigon, through which the Christian world had passed only twice before, during the lives of Christ and of Charlemagne, now driving the Christian world toward cataclysm or cities of the sun? What did the sum of the magical numbers 7 + 9 add up to for the year 1600?[143]

The tally for Queen Elizabeth on January 2, 1600 (Old Style), was about £750 in New Year's gifts of money and gold, and a boodle of jewels, kirtles, petticoats, perfumed gloves, marzipan, and pots of green ginger. Across the Channel, French courtiers on January 1st received a single coin impressed with the device of a rainbow, alluding to the end of the Biblical Flood and God's promise to Noah that there should never be another. In Germany, in the town of Görlitz just east of Dresden, a cobbler named Jacob Boehme in 1600 received another species of coin, one minted by Divine Wisdom: a mystical vision of the relatedness of the soul and the cosmos, from which would stem his influential theosophy and his inspirational treatise, *The Way of Christ*. Directly south, in Prague, at the hermetic, kabbalistic, alchemical capital of the Holy Roman Empire, Emperor Rudolf II, despondent in his search for a "sacred harmony," was succumbing to a fit of madness amidst his "wonder rooms" of automata and planetary clocks. Would the world after so many conflicts, the Turks battling on the Hungarian borders yet again, ever be peaceful and whole?[144]

At the end of a century which bequeathed to us our custom of counting years by centuries, our predilection for arranging history by centuries laid end to end, our modern (Gregorian) calendar with its pivotal corrections in centurial years, our legend of the year 1000, our fears for the year 1999, and some of our earliest specific millennial hopes for the year 2000—at the end of this 16th century, years were often preternatural numbers, and the deft manipulation of numbers was an inspired enterprise for engaging the whole, or the wholeness, of the universe. This was the enterprise driving that arch-magus of century's end, John Dee, from Euclidean geometry to the kabbalistic, alchemical, mathematical science of the *Monas hieroglyphica*, whose master might move at will throughout the cosmic spheres from the lowest of the low to the supercelestial abode of angelic spirits. A similar enterprise around 1594 drove the Eighth Laird of Merchiston, John Napier, toward the construction of the general principles of logarithms in order that he might more quickly calculate the age of the world and the advent of the Millennium. In 1595, when Edmund Spenser composed the *Epithalamion*, his 365 stanzas reproduced the yearly astronomical round in its numerological and astrological complexity, a technically accomplished hymn of praise for the marriage of a man and a woman and the union of the human with the cosmic or celestial. Another union, a *Chemical Wedding*, written in 1602 or 1603 as a playful little fiction by a sixteen-year-old student at the University of Württemberg, satirized the alchemical metaphor of the marriage of the elements, but in 1616 Johann Valentin Andreae's next version would be a serious attempt at perpetuating the mythos of a secret band of men empowered by alchemy, mathematics, and ancient spiritual truths to reconstitute the world. Andreae's second *Chemical Wedding* was issued pseudonymously under the name of "Christian Rosencreutz," alleged founder of the Fraternity of the Rosy Cross, or Rosicrucians. Entombed (so the stories went) in 1484 at the age of 106, Rosencreutz and his secrets had been rediscovered in his vault, lit by an inner sun, in the year of the nova, 1604. The Rosicrucian renovation of the dismal world, "both of divine and human things," could now proceed.[145]

"But is it credible that the extreme dismal state of the world, or any utter casualty of so mighty consequence should in very deed depend upon the fickle state of numbers and figures?" asked English physician John Harvey in the year 1588, which was also by common accounts 5550 A.M., whence "some see a deep mystery, a high secret in the very number 5550 it selfe." The answer is yes, it is credible. Or rather, yes, it had become credible, thanks to astromusicians, almaniacs, pansophisticates, Christorians, mathemagicians, kabbalanthropists, a calendaring pope, and a hybrid host of other centuriators. Out of the well-remembered excitement surrounding the year 1600 Francis Bacon would draft his *New Atlantis* in 1614, and Andreae, disenchanted with the fiction of the Rosy Cross, would envision *Christianapolis*, both of these utopian communities overseen by wisely spiritual scientist-philosophers. To the news of such adepts and virtuosi, partisans of mathematics as the language of truth, we may now proceed.[146]

PLAIN STYLE:
THE 1690s

AN ENGLISH MERCHANT GLANCING THROUGH THE PAPERS IN Lloyd's coffeehouse on Wednesday, January 2, 1701, would have read on the front page of one of the newssheets drifting from table to table with the smoke from Virginia tobaccos, "This Year, which closes this Age, and which we may now count among those Elaps'd, will be remarkable in History, not only by the great Events, but also by Singularities very surprising and extraordinary, which excites more than ever the attention of Spirits."

The *Post Boy* was waxing extravagant. Editor Bearshaw's language was the language of century's end, conclusive and hyperbolic. The year 1700 had not been especially remarkable in History, nor were the Spirits more than ever excited by such Singularities as the tempest in Scandinavia or by such great Events as a new doge in Venice, a new King of Spain, and a new Pope "young enough to see a new Jubilee." Venice was no longer a world power, the succession of Philip of Anjou to the Spanish throne was likely to mean yet another European war, and the Jubilee was treated more as tragicomic opera than as a work of redemption.[147]

The old Pope, Innocent XII, took the Jubilee with particular seriousness as a great personal event, for he was a tottering eighty-four in 1699 when he issued his Jubilee bull, which made much of the parallel between the approach of the last moments of the old century and the approach of the last moments of the longest of human lives, one hundred years. So sickly that Cardinal de Bouillon was obliged to stand proxy for him at the Porta Sancta, Innocent XII had put the emphasis of his bull (or last testament) upon the Jubilee as a recalling to mind of the gift of life eternal, "which must surpass all the centuries."[148]

A thousand miles away, the merchant in his coffeehouse would have heard much talk of the Jubilee, "which makes so great a noise through all the Christian world," and which was raising the roof of the Theatre Royal in Drury Lane, whose audiences were laughing at the new hit play, *The Constant Couple, or A Trip to the Jubilee.* George Farquhar's comedy opened in November 1699 and ran for an amazing fifty-three performances during

Title page illustration from an anonymous work of 1701 mocking the Jubilee of 1700. Courtesy of the General Research Division, New York Public Library, Astor, Lenox and Tilden Foundations.

its first season. Nightly, "a pert London Prentice" named Clincher, upon the death of his father now "a young powder'd extravagant English Heir," must prate "of nothing but Wines, Intreagues, Plays, Fashions, and going to the Jubilee," whatever that is, where "there will be Pageants, and Squibs, and Rary Shows," and where he designs to shoot seven jealous Italians a week. Coming closer to the Newgate gallows than to the Holy City, Clincher never quite advances to the slaughter of jealous Italian beaus with his case of Jubilee pistols, but in Rome the comedy proceeded apace. While Cardinal de Bouillon was proclaiming the Jubilee, "accompanied with so great a Worldly Pomp, that it may be taken rather for a Triumph of the Pagan Emperors than for an Act of Religion," above him in the balconies the Imperial, French, and Venetian ambassadors struggled noisily for pride of place, insulted at having been seated lower than the Queen Dowager of Poland. There were other entertainments throughout the Jubilee year, with music each night of the week, "and the best worth it, as our judges say, of any that ever was heard in Italy, or perhaps will be again till the next 100th year," wrote the young Englishman John Jackson from Rome, as it were in lieu of the pistol-packing Clincher. If the older devout were congratulating themselves for having reached the end of a century and the Porta Sancta of a centennial Jubilee, the younger sought out concerts in Rome, carnivals in Naples and Venice. Perhaps the "prodigious concourse of strangers" was to be laid at the unholiest of doors? In January of 1700 Elisabeth Charlotte of Bavaria, who had formally abjured her Protestant faith to become the Duchess of Orléans at the Catholic court of Louis XIV, wrote informally to her stepsister Amelia Elisabeth in Hanover, "That people go to Rome to see the antiquities, as did my uncle the Landgrave of Cassell, I can understand, but not that they want to see all that to-do of priests; nothing is more boring. Many probably also went to take a look at the thirty thousand ladies of easy virtue; but anyone who is curious about this sort of thing might just as well come to France, where he will find quite as much of it."[149]

John Jackson, rest assured, had gone to Rome with nobler motives, awaiting an opportunity to kiss the Pope's slipper of crimson velvet, which he managed to do at an audience that spring. "The poor old man lookt very thin and pale and weak," Jackson wrote to his uncle, and indeed Innocent XII would expire in September. These intimations and convictions of mortality, always sharper at century's end, do not however make Mr. Jackson any more deserving of our attention than, say, observers of the death in 1700 of the eleven-year-old Duke of Gloucester, only surviving child of the seventeen to whom Princess Anne of England had given birth. Gloucester's death put in question the Protestant succession to the throne, and Parliament would have to pass an Act of Settlement transferring the English crown from the Stuarts to the Hanoverians upon the death of Anne, but we stick by the side of the plebeian Mr. Jackson because he took the liberty, on January 1, 1700 (New Style), of wishing his uncle Samuel Pepys a prosperous new century. Jackson got the number of the century wrong, and Pepys, an inveterate diarist who was habitually up on his dates, wrote back, "Whatever you intended, you make . . . New Year's Day last the first of the 17th century." Jackson twice apologized, " 'Twas the 18th century I meant, whatever I might write."[150]

This was a new banter, proof of the awareness of standard centuries and centuries' ends at the end of a century whose true apocalypses of ruin and of revelation had taken place forty, fifty, sixty years before. Even in the briefest historical retrospect, regarding the 1600s from the Jubilee year of 1700, it should have been apparent that the century had climaxed near midcentury with the traumas of the Thirty Years' War that devastated Germany (1618–48), the Fronde or French insurrections that would not quit (1648–53–58), the Abyss of Despair or decade of repeated massacres of Jews in the Ukraine (1648–58), the English Civil War and Cromwellian Protectorate (1642–60). The crises had come somewhat later for Russian Old Believers, as Princess Sophia by imperial ukaz of 1684 ordered that government agents hunt down all who refused to comply with the Nikonian religious reforms; for French Protestants, as Louis XIV in 1685 revoked the Edict of Nantes, his dragoons compelling Huguenot families to convert or emigrate; for Irish Catholics, as their rebellion was crushed in 1691 and their lives oppressed by English Protestant administrators. Few were the "turning points" that had not already been turned by 1690: the Restoration of the English monarchy in 1660, the assumption of power by the Sun King in 1661, Jan Sobieski's election as King of Poland in 1674, the routing of the Turks at Mohacs in 1687, the Glorious Revolution in Britain in 1688, the taking of the reins of Russian government by Peter I (the Great) in 1685. The 1690s had been practically eviscerated of dramatic potential by events earlier in the century.

The end of the world had also come and gone years before century's end. The English Civil War had launched the millenarianism of Ranters, Muggletonians, Quakers, and Fifth Monarchists. After the Restoration, prophetic eyes were cast upon the calendrical collision of the number of the Beast of the Apocalypse, 666, with the millennial number, 1000. In that fantastic year 1000 + 666, London was not transformed into the New Jerusalem but razed by a great fire while shiploads of Jews from Amsterdam headed toward Smyrna to join the Messiah, who had arrived at last in the figure of Sabbatai Ṣevi. Throughout the Jewish world, from Holland to Italy to Morocco to Palestine and Turkey, from Russia to Poland to Germany to Hungary and Turkey, the messianic fervor had been building toward 1668, exactly 1600 years after the destruction of the Second Temple, as Nathan of Gaza for years had been building up the messianic status of his master, a moody mystic born (it was said) on the Ninth of Av, the date of the ritual commemoration of the destruction of both the First and the Second Temples. Mining a rich new vein of Jewish mystical thought, Lurianic kabbalism, Nathan had moved the often unpredictable, occasionally antinomian Sabbatai to the center stage of Jewish history by 1665. Arrested by the Turkish sultanate in 1666 for fomenting rebellion (so many and exuberant were his followers), Sabbatai was brought before a council of the Sultan's highest advisers and asked to choose between a tortured death or apostasy. The Messiah chose to convert. He took the name Mehemed Kapici Bashi, was given the honorary title of keeper of the palace gates, and was awarded a royal pension of 150 aspers per day. The shock was enormous. The majority of Jews, disbelieving, then mortified, forswore (for themselves, their children, and their children's children) all things actively messianic, and they obliterated, in so far as was possible after the storm of printed pamphlets announcing or condemning Sabbatai Ṣevi, all mention and memory of the cursed impostor. A significant minority of Jews, however, especially in Turkey and Salonika, wondered at the mystical meaning and divine purpose of the apostasy. Was Sabbatai, akin to the hidden imam, going into a brief but necessary occultation before his truly splendid manifestation in, perhaps, 1674? Was he, with his loyal "courtiers" who had also apostasized, intending to subvert Islam from within as the final preliminary to the rebuilding of the Temple in Jerusalem? Was he following the Lurianic kabbalistic model for the Messiah, gathering in all the shards of light belonging to the Godhead, even those shards that glinted amidst the cruel darkness of Islam, so that the Messianic Kingdom could emerge most brilliant and complete? Was he—but enough. What Sabbatai *was* doing, within two years of his apostasy, was practicing his idiosyncratic Jewish faith, attended on the night of Passover, 1668, by "twenty-four thousand angels, all saying: Thou art our Lord, thou art our King, thou art our Redeemer." In 1672 Mehemed Kapici Bashi was arrested, accused of conducting a Jewish prayer service in a synagogue, reviling Islam, and converting Muslims to Judaism. Mehemed/Sabbatai was exiled to the prison-castle of Dolcigno in Albania (now Ulcinj, Yugoslavia), where he died on the Day of Atonement, 1676, at the age of fifty.[151]

Like the secretive Dönmeh sect, convinced for decades after Sabbatai's death that he was the Messiah and would reappear in glory, those Christian millenarian groups surviving into the 1690s survived in occultation. Either they were secluded (the Old Believers, who would immolate themselves rather than surrender to Russian government forces), or private (Dutch and German pietists, French and Scottish quietists, who sought an inner New Jerusalem), or subdued (the Muggletonians, reading from their founder's *Transcendent Spiritual Treatise*, and the Quakers, stepping into the plain clothes of financially respectable, socially responsible Friends). Of the new millenarians at century's end—the men and women dancing on rector John Mason's holy ground in Water Stratford, Buckinghamshire, in 1694; the "true Rosicrucians" who followed Johannes Kelpius from Germany to the shores of the Wissahickon in Pennsylvania that same year; the Camisards in the mountains of the Cévennes whose Huguenot *inspirés* led a guerrilla war from 1702 to 1704 against twenty thousand royal troops; their offshoot, the French Prophets, prophesying from 1706 to 1714 across the length and breadth of Europe to warn of impending judgments; the French Catholic Company of Missionaries of Mary, inspired by Louis-Marie Grignion de Montfort early in the 1700s—of all these new groups, not one ever insisted upon the end of the 17th century as the end of an age or the end of the world.[152]

And yet, despite the noticeable European fatigue with the entire experience of great expectations, despite the *fin de siècle* definition of an "enthusiast" as a knave, a fool, a light-minded woman, or a madman, people around 1700 nonetheless spoke and acted as if the change of centuries from the 17th to the 18th really did matter. Almanac predictions and anonymous vaticinations, exegeses of the books of Daniel and Nostradamus, the prophecies of chronogrammisters, alchemical adepts, pseudo-medieval monks, and "Eclectical Chiliasts," all scheduled the most momentous of events for 1699: "and suddenly after [famine, tempests, battles at sea, swarms of fowl and flies] unexpectedly appears a great Conqueror, the World being filled with the Fame of this Man, who suddenly, like Augustus, gives Peace unto the whole Earth." Then for 1700, when the Jews would convert, the Turks too, and "Now old men live their full years, and our Youth grow up to Men's Estates."[153]

Neither the Turks nor the Jews obliged, but in 1699 the Protestant provinces of Germany did convert—from the Old Style (Julian) to the New Style (Gregorian) calendar, followed in 1700 by Denmark, Norway, and parts of Holland. Influenced by the drama of these national conversions, which meant skipping eleven days from the old into the new calendar, the very first of the centurial wars broke out. Two dozen Latin, German, and French treatises issued from the presses in 1699 and 1700, arguing belligerently for the start of the 18th century with the first day of 1700 or the first day of 1701, as if this transition were so important that it had to be accurately and unanimously blessed.[154]

In England, whose Protestant Parliament would resist the Catholic Gregorian calendar until 1752, the old Augustan tradition of an Horation ode to celebrate the new century was revived by the poets Matthew Prior and John Dryden. Prior's "Carmen Seculare, For the Year 1700," was an encomium to King William III, hero of the Glorious Revolution. Though the poet must

> *To all the list'ning World relate,*
> *(As Thou dost His Story read)*
> *That nothing went before so Great,*
> *And nothing Greater can succeed,*

Prior also prays that Janus

> *Be kind, and with a milder Hand,*
> *Closing the Volume of the finish'd Age*
> *(Tho' Noble, 'twas an Iron Page)*
> *A more delightful leaf expand,*
> *Free from Alarms, and fierce Bellona's Rage.*

No longer beleaguered by the goddess of war,

> *Our Pray'rs heard, our Master's Fleet shall go,*
> *As far as Winds can bear, or Waters flow,*
> *New Lands to make, new INDIES to explore,*
> *In Worlds unknown to plant BRITANNIA'S Power;*
> *Nations yet wild by Precept to reclaim,*
> *And teach 'em Arms, and Arts, in WILLIAM'S Name.*

So the new century, like this new English king, was for Prior at the age of thirty-five at once an escape and a release; the century's turn was as usual janiform.[155]

Enter Janus, in Dryden's "Secular Masque":

> CHRONOS, Chronos, *mend thy Pace,*
> *An hundred times the rowling Sun*
> *Around the Radiant Belt has run*
> *In his revolving Race.*

Enter Chronos with his scythe, on his back a globe which he sets down.

> WEARY, *weary of my Weight,*
> *Let me, let me drop my Freight,*
>   *And leave the World behind.*
> *I could not bear*
> *Another Year*
> *The Load of Human-Kind.*

Enter laughing Momus, god of ridicule:

> HA! *ha! ha! Ha! ha! ha! well hast thou done,*
>   *To lay down thy Pack,*
>   *And lighten thy Back,*
> *The World was a Fool, e'er since it begun,*
> *And since neither* Janus, *nor* Chronos, *nor I*
>   *Can hinder the Crimes,*
>   *Or mend the Bad Times,*
> *'Tis better to Laugh than to Cry.*

The ages have declined from the halcyon, "unthinking" times under the aegis of the goddess Diana. Momus points to the more recent rulers, Mars and Venus:

> THY *Wars brought nothing about;*
> *Thy Lovers were all untrue.*
> *'Tis well an Old Age is out,*
> *And time to begin a New.*

At this final pun, all dance: on Dryden's grave, as it happened, for the "Secular Masque" was the last of the poet's works, written at the age of sixty-eight in the year of his death, 1700.[156]

Weak and bedridden, "a fluid in his legs," John Locke at sixty-eight received new century's greetings from Paris, from his friend Nicolas Toinard, who had sided with those for whom the 18th century began in 1701. Locke shared Toinard's concern with rational calendar reform, and both prided themselves on their dispassionate approach to philosophical and historical problems, Locke the author of *An Essay Concerning Human Understanding*, Toinard a scholar of emblems, languages, and world chronology. Neither man, however, could restrain himself when it came to the century's turn. "Here, sir," wrote Toinard to Locke on January 1, 1701 (New Style), "is my first letter of this new century, and my first wishes are for your prosperity and perfect health. As for myself, the most that I hope for is to be able to embrace you, and not to be denied at the beginning of one century what the injustice of men denied me at the end of another." Toinard was referring to a lawsuit that had gone badly, and perhaps to the personal recognition that was his due, but in fact he had far grander hopes than these for the new century. He dreamed, as Locke did, of the publication of a work that would demonstrate incontrovertibly the logical coherence of the New Testament, and in this first letter of 1701 Toinard seemed to promise that "That work [the Harmony of the Gospels] to which you are so strongly committed and whose achievement was delayed by the circumstances of the seventeenth century, will be able to appear before the end of the eighteenth century." Locke, who had also received new century's greetings from correspondents in Holland, replied politely that he could have had no more agreeable a beginning to the century than the well-wishes of Toinard. He went on, more warmly: "In truth, sir, there is nothing that touches me more, and if I were to live yet another century, my paramount wishes would be to spend that time happily with you." Then, most warmly and most revealing of the new centurial passions: "It is not enough that the work to which I am so strongly committed [that Harmony of the Gospels] should be published before the end of the eighteenth century. If I had my way, it would appear at the beginning of this very first year."[157]

What did appear, in a London newspaper advertisement of January 1–3, 1701, was the "Parents New-Years-Gift," a Holy Bible in Verse, for those of weak memories, with woodcuts useful for the instruction of children, and complemented by "A Choice Collection of God's Judgments & Mercies." Across the Atlantic that year, in Boston, was one Samuel Sewall, who as a justice of the Massachusetts Supreme Court had been in constant close quarters with Judgments & Mercies, and who as a Puritan had struggled at length to understand God's will. In 1697 he publicly, voluntarily confessed to error as one of the convicting judges at the Salem witch trials; in 1700, just after the slave trade had been legally opened to New England merchants, Sewall published *The Selling of Joseph*, among the earliest of colonial antislavery tracts. Now, upon the "Entrance of the 18th Century," on January 1, 1701, he paid to have four trumpeters at break of day give a blast on Boston Common to herald the new century. He also printed up his "Verses upon the New Century," which he had the town crier read out:

> *Once more! Our God vouchsafe to shine:*
> *Correct the Coldness of our Clime.*
> *Make haste with thy Impartial light,*
> *And terminate this long dark night.*

> *Give the Indians Eyes to see*
> *The Light of Life, and set them free.*
> *So Men shall God in Christ adore,*
> *And worship Idols vain, no more.*

> *So Asia and Africa,*
> *Eurôpa, with America;*
> *All Four, in Consort join'd, shall Sing*
> *New Songs of Praise to Christ our King.*

Sewall's first two stanzas fell well within the tradition of the American jeremiad, that stern warning of the consequences of the decline of a heartfelt faith among the Elect chosen to settle, civilize, and redeem the New World and its savage inhabitants. The last stanza, however, with its image of continents in concert, belonged to the renascent tradition of the secular ode celebrating a new, peaceful, praiseworthy age. Writing his verses upon the change of centuries, Sewall had been puzzling over a verse from Scripture, Hebrews 8.11 (rescript of Jeremiah 31.34): "And they shall not teach every man his neighbour, and every man his brother, saying, Know the Lord: for all shall know me, from the least to the greatest." The passage was perplexing. "I read it over and over one time and another and could not be satisfied," he noted in his diary. "At last this came in my mind—know the Lord, i.e., know the Messiah, to whom the word Lord is very much appropriated. . . . Now my mind was quiet, and all seem'd to run smooth. As I hope this is Truth, so I bless God for this New-Years Gift." Like the almanac writers, the calendar controversialists, the poets Prior and Dryden, the philosophers Locke and Toinard, the devout justice Samuel Sewall had high and immediate expectations for the new century, which had already borne fruit. His New Year's Gift of 1701 was the centurial, millennial promise of a world so thoroughly evangelized that all knew Christ.[158]

Notwithstanding the relative plainness of the 1690s, a decade neither spectacular nor tragic nor frightening nor mysterious,[159] the years 1699, 1700, 1701 were still tantalizing. If the *fin de siècle* had fallen short of its historical obligations to anxiety and extremity, the turn of the 17th century held to its end of the tale.

This was possible because of the growing independence of the mythos of the century. During the 1600s the French were narrowing the *siècle* from "an age" to more or less one hundred years, Germans were starting to live by *Jahrhunderts*, Britons were speaking of the "judgment of the centuries." Students memorizing the Latin of that most influential trot, *Universal History, Briefly and Clearly Expounded, Divided into Antiquity, the Middle Ages, and the New Times* (1702), found that Professor Christoph Cellarius had not only established (forever?) the tripartition of European history but had also defined the last two of the three ages, and all years between, by the beginnings and ends of standard Anno Domini centuries. In less rarefied surroundings than lecture halls, the century made its appearance on "perpetual" almanacs good for one hundred years, very popular in 1700.[160]

As centuries became entities unto themselves, they no longer depended for their existence upon what actually took place from year to year. There were, of course, boundary events such as Jubilees and calendar conversions, but centuries were becoming their own creatures. "This century," wrote the Huguenot soldier-poet Agrippa d'Aubigné in 1616, "different in its ways, demands of us a different style." In 1688 the French Catholic moralist Jean de La Bruyère would make his fame with witty, satirical descriptions of *The Characters and Manners of This Century* as distinct from any other. Centuries had individual personalities, customs, lifecourses (start, first half, middle, second half, end), and nicknames: "the Apostolic Century," "the Reformation Century," "the Century of Louis the Great."[161]

Louis the Great was Louis XIV, and "Le siècle de Louis le Grand" was the title of a poem by Charles Perrault, whose inflammatory claim in 1687 that

Without fear of injustice one can compare
Louis' great century to Augustus' so fair

set off an explosion of essays in one more *fin de siècle* dispute between Ancients and Moderns. Youngest of five brothers, Perrault stood pen in hand with the Moderns. Perhaps for this reason, the youngest children were the heroes and heroines of his *Tales of Mother Goose*, published in 1697. The fairy tale, with its threat of terrible endings and its love of new beginnings, was a literary genre quite apt to the century's turn. No loyalty to his sources, I should think, had Perrault making *la belle au bois dormant* sleep for exactly one hundred years upon pricking her finger; the curse of death laid upon Sleeping Beauty, transmuted by a good fairy to a century's somnolence, was rather an expression of the appeal of the mythos of the century, which ends, as we all know, with the young princess waking to embrace a young prince. Perrault in fact had restyled the tale in such a manner that the end of the hundred years was more cleanly the beginning of a new era; originally the princess woke only after having been raped by the prince *and* having given birth to a child or two. The tale as we have come to know it had been "civilized" and centuriated by Perrault—the same Perrault who, between 1696 and 1700, composed two volumes of short biographies of *Famous Men Who Have Appeared in France During This Century*, each volume exactly one hundred pages in length, both volumes together encompassing exactly one hundred illustrious men who had died within the confines of the 17th century. [162]

We can remark at this century's turn the corresponding inclinations to locate centenarians and to centuriate one's own age. The French wit Saint-Evremond, writing from his English exile in 1700/01, was about ninety when he explained, "If my new infirmities, or rather my old ones which are very much grown upon me, had not hindered me from going to Boughton, I should have been as happy as a man almost a hundred years of age can be." Samuel Sewall took care to record in his diary on January 15, 1700, the death of Lawrence Copeland, actually an octogenarian, but " 'tis counted that he liv'd to be at least one hundred and ten years old." London's *Post-Angel* reported the death of a 114-year-old man "who outliv'd 16 popes, 5 emperors, 4 kings of Spain, 4 of France, 6 kings and queens of England." [163]

This precisely imprecise accounting of ages was due in part to the transitional status of the birthday in Western European culture. Two hundred years before, only the birthdays of sovereigns had been important enough to warrant celebration. For the rest, who rarely knew their dates of birth and who fixed them, when called upon at law to furnish proofs of age, by approximation to other more personally memorable, historically meaningful events such as movable feasts, catastrophes, and burials—for lord, lady, and commoner, birthdays passed unobserved. One's singular spot on the annual calendar was marked by the X of the martyrdom of one's patron saint. Through various 16th-century acts and instructions, English parish priests, continental ministers and clerics were directed to keep regular registers of births as well as of marriages and deaths, but epidemics, civil wars, religious wars, sectarian camouflage, parish vacancies, and church-state controversies all disposed toward the neglect of registration. Among those who did know their birth dates, whose parents likely had made pertinent entries on the flyleaves of Bibles, there was a reluctance in later life to make much of the day lest one provoke the evil eye or seem to be imitating the birthday festivities of pagan Rome. By 1700, however, birthdays were on the ascendant, in keeping with the customary use of exact calendar dates in daily business and private life, and with the increasingly stiff demands for punctuality as a result of the diffusion of household clocks and necklace- and pocket-watches accurate (by virtue of the new spiral balance springs) to within five minutes each day. The New England Puritan minister, Cotton Mather, vehemently opposed as were most Puritans to such paganisms as Christmas (solstice) merrymaking, had to contend with very mixed feelings as he approached his own birthday at century's turn. "The XXXVIIIth Year of My Age," he wrote in his journal on March 12, 1699/1700 (Old Style). "Geilenus [Galen] in an old Calendar . . . did upon his Birth-day, write that Motto, *Dies Calamitatis*. Altho' I have seen much Calamity in the world, yett I will not write the least Syllable, that shall complain of my *Birth* as a *Calamity*." Otherwise Mather would be the worst of ingrates, reviling Christ's sacrificial act on the Cross. Still, he added, "I am not fond of keeping my Birth-day, lest I fall into a *Superstition*, and tho' I find some Examples indeed for keeping such a Day, yett some of them were not the most encouraging." Yett the next year, "The XXXIXth Year of my Life," March 12, 1700/1701, Mather was encouraged: "I happen to begin this *New Year* of my Life, with a very agreeable Employment," namely Scripture study, fasting, prayer, and the singing of psalms. He had made no mention of the advent of the new century, and when he came to March 25th, the traditional English New Year's Day, he wrote, "Nothing remarkable occurred in the Day." But the century had indeed gotten the better of him two weeks after his thirty-ninth birthday, for he continued: "Only I thought I felt upon my Mind a perswasion from Heaven, that the Lord will quickly appear, with wonderful Dispensations, to retrieve and revive the evangelical Interests, in the European Parts of the World."[164]

The accounting of ages at century's end was beginning to run in tandem with an account of the Age. For the first time, some people sought out a tacit symmetry between their own lives and the life of the century. Although in 1700 reaching the age of forty was well beyond the statistically mortal midpoint that it is now for the best-kept of Europeans and Americans, forty had long been regarded as the janiform age, the age of retrospect balanced evenly against prospect. Given the conventional wisdoms of their day, Cotton Mather at thirty-nine, Samuel Sewall at forty-eight could both (correctly) anticipate another epoch to their New England careers. Some might die with the old century—in symbolic particular, centenarians: Samuel Pepys had gone to see "a piece of clockwork made by an Englishman; endeed, very good, wherein all the several states of man's age, to 100 years old, is shown very pretty and solemne, and several other things more cheerful." Some might be born with the new century—the eventual physicist Daniel Bernoulli in 1700; the eventual mastermind of the Bible concordance, Alexander Cruden, in 1701; and, stretching the point, John Wesley in 1703, to die eighty-eight years later among his Methodists as a man truly bounded by his century. Some—Mather, Sewall, the inventor Thomas Newcomen—were so fortunate as to turn the century at the turn of their lives at the turn of the world from the darkness of witch hunts and King William's War to the gospel light of, maybe, the Millennium, or at least the steam engine.[165]

Wasn't this new desire for symmetry between the course of one's life and the course of a century equivalent to the old rhapsodies of numerologists smitten with beautiful figures such as 666, that "runs roundly and hath a comely proportion to it; wher ever ye look, ye have sixe, and it is pretty pleasing to the fancy, and easie to remember"? No, for by 1700 the language of numbers had acquired a higher status and new functions. From the 1540s through to the 1680s, European pedagogues, natural philosophers, theologians, and millenarians (not mutually exclusive, often one and the same) had been in pursuit of the universal language, by which they meant a language whose lexicon was exactly constitutive of the universe. The language must not only name all things and all states of things; each substantive word in the language must express and define the essence of the thing, or state, so named. Adam, knowing the proper names for all of God's creations in the Garden of Eden, must have known, for example, that the word "slug" was the *perfect* name for that creature, true to the heart of its being. At the Tower of Babel, humankind lost its hold on Adamic language, the recovery and mastery of whose lexicon would assure a mastery of the entire natural world. The universal language had therefore to be universal in four respects: its lexicon coextensive with the universe of things; each of its substantive words definitive of the universal essence of the thing named; all of its meanings universally simple and accessible; all of its symbols (letters, signs) universally comprehensible. [166]

Theoretically, the universal language was the key to the sciences, a taxonomy of the world, ordering things while listing them, in the manner of a thesaurus which defines each word by location within a hierarchy of other words. It was the key to teaching, since any student could understand and appreciate universally true and simple words (or signs). It was consequently the key to the evangelical conversion of the polyglot world in these times when the pentecostal gift of tongues was sorely missed. Nary a natural philosopher of note was absent from the ranks of those who argued the virtues of the hieroglyphs attributed to Hermes Trismegistus (were they the elemental signs of the universal language?) or who debated the success of new universal languages invented out of a thin but inebriating air. "This last Century of years," wrote an English linguist in 1657, "much hath been the discourse and expectation of learned men concerning the finding out of an *Universal Character.*" A decade later, John Wilkins published his famous *Essay Towards a Real Character and a Philosophical Language*, which presented the first modern thesaurus and drew the attention of most members of the new Royal Society. Dreams of a universal language influenced contemporary projects for dictionaries organized by the roots of word-groups, to get at the origins of meaning, or designed for encyclopedic coverage, to capture and complete the world of things. Also directly influenced was the development of gesture and sign systems for communicating with the deaf and dumb, who were the prime test cases for any language supposed to be universal. [167]

Around 1690, the search for a universal language was generally abandoned. Convinced either by the insuperable difficulties of contriving a rational language isomorphic to the world, or by the impressive arguments of John Locke's *Essay Concerning Human Understanding* (1690), European philosophers began seriously to doubt that language, any language, could perfectly represent nature. They began to claim, rather, that languages, all languages, had a grammar corresponding to the operational structures of all human thought. Thoughts themselves, like things, were probably infinite in variety, but the laws governing the relations between our words and between our thoughts were few, identical, and crucial. We could never be certain of the true names of things or, as the German polymath Gottfried

Wilhelm von Leibniz had hoped, of a cogent alphabet of thoughts, but we could uncover the operations by which we systematically arrange and rearrange those names, constitute and build upon those thoughts. There could be no universal language; there could be a universal syntax.[168]

An emphasis upon syntax meant an emphasis on verbs rather than nouns, on connectives (prepositions, conjunctions) rather than adjectives. In the practice of law, literature, philosophy, rhetoric, the science of preaching and experimental science, it meant the triumph of the Plain Style, a "self-satisfied" style of prose that made clear and evident the pattern of each sentence. It meant the consistent use of the paragraph to organize thoughts, and of standard punctuation to squire phrases and clauses from one thought to the next.[169]

The Plain Style promised "Propriety, Perspicuity, Elegance and Cadence"; it could not promise universal truth. The burden of that promise was being assumed, at century's end, by the language of mathematics. Born on Christmas morning, 1642 (Old Style), and baptized January 1, 1642/1643 (English Style), Isaac Newton was an advocate of the Plain Style in his life as in his equations. This however did not prevent him from laboring lifelong to decipher alchemical recipes and Biblical prophecies as well as the attractions of natural bodies at some distance from one another. The astrological symbols and hermetic allusions of alchemists, the political and poetic metaphors of Daniel and the Book of Revelation, these were for Newton a hieroglyphic avenue toward ancient and universal truths, neither contradictory nor inconsequential to his studies of optics, astronomy, and physics. Like John Wilkins, led to his universal language while computing the dimensions of Noah's Ark, Newton hoped to be led to the first, the rational, the universal religion by way of the measurements of Solomon's Temple, an architectural cryptogram for the "frame of the world." Newton's penchant for numbers took him further, into a prodigious chronology of the kingdoms of the ancient world, and to *Observations upon the Prophecies of Daniel, and the Apocalypse of St. John*, from which he calculated the fall of the apocalyptic Beast for 1867 A.D., the Millennium for the year 2000.[170]

Appointed Master of the Mint on his fifty-seventh birthday, Newton made no predictions for the 18th century, nor did he make any pronouncements upon the end of the 17th, although he did take care in 1699 to look back through his student papers in order to document the priority of his invention of calculus in 1665. Newton did not, as did the other claimant to priority, Leibniz, concoct a long "chronostichon" for the year 1700, using a playful string of Roman numerals, CVCCVVCVVVLVLIILVDCIIVDI, as the basis for a Latin sentence. Neither Newton nor Leibniz was dreadfully impressed by the numerological import of a 1699 or a 1700, and neither was inclined to accept the end of a standard Anno Domini century as, willy-nilly, the definitive end of an age. *"No transition is made through a leap,"* Leibniz underlined in a letter to a Dutch friend in 1699, referring to physical bodies but applicable also to the axioms of his calculus and to his sense of historical change; "the same thing applies not only in transitions from place to place but also in transitions from one form to another form or from one state to another." Neither Leibniz nor Newton saw in the new century with festivities or fond greetings.[171]

Both men do nonetheless belong to this history of the ends of centuries, for they had dedicated many of their waking hours to the problems of time and chronology—Leibniz working for years on a history of the House of Brunswick in which he noted the "superstitious," apocalyptic fears for the year 1000; Newton preoccupied with the relative time of prophetic calendars and the "absolute time" of the physical world. In their cosmologies as in their histories and their more "exact" sciences, both were confronting the issue of connectedness, a burning issue at every century's end (and all the hotter when succession was the political tinderbox of the day). Space and the variety of bodies in space were surely infinite, but there must be laws governing the relation between bodies. Leibniz found those laws in the demonstrable harmony of monads, independent immaterial centers of force "involved in a perpetual and most free progress, so that [the entire universe] is always advancing toward greater culture." Newton found connectedness in the laws of gravitational attraction, and in the ether sustaining the grav-itational force. Both used mathematics to express this universal syntax, making of the language of mathematics the vehicle for a global vision trans-ferable (by latitudinarians in England and republicans in Holland, for ex-ample) to policies of religious toleration or programs for universal peace through universal reason. If Newton and Leibniz were intelligences too great to be cornered by a *fin de siècle*, their lifeworks contributed immeasurably to the late-17th-century globalism so characteristic of a century's end and turn.[172]

I am tempted here to make too much of the analogy between philo-sophical, scientific concerns with universal syntax and autobiographical con-cerns with a correlation between the pattern of one's life and the pattern of one's century. Instead, I will belabor a darker calculus, another set of op-erations upon numbers critical to the 1690s: the calculus of human lives. *Fin de siècle* obsessions with death were expressed at the end of the 17th century not in the form of effigy tombs, dancing skeletons, or gaunt figures of Devouring Time, but as columns of devouring figures known as bills of mortality. The European collection of vital statistics had been slowly improving during the 17th century, and London's bills of mortality, published weekly since about 1600, were first subjected to an arithmetical analysis by John Graunt in his *Natural and Political Observations Made Upon the Bills of Mortality* (1662). Graunt's efforts to make larger sense of the patterns of death were not well known, but the questions he asked would be asked again in the following decades by more public, more mathematical men: How long before England's numbers recuperated from a bout with the plague? Was London too populous for its own good? Was a country with a dense population better off than a country thinly populated? Given the rate of doubling of population and the estimate for the present population of the world, when did Adam and Eve, or Noah and his family, start us all off? These questions of political (and chronological) arithmetic rose to prominence near century's end in the context of mercantilist debates over the balance of trade and population, which spurred widespread local and regional attempts at thorough censuses in the 1690s. Who was losing inhabitants, and who was gaining, and did a nation's wealth necessarily grow with a growing population? In the process of answering these questions, optimists and pessimists alike developed the statistical commonplace of a geometric progression of population (toward unlimited prosperity or demographic catastrophe) and the economic habit of the centurial comparison (to show, from the baseline of 1600, that England or France or Spain was more or less populous, more or less prosperous in 1700). The century was being enlisted as a noteworthy constant in equations of commercial success and failure, national life and death.[173]

Taking accurate stock of general mortality demanded an understanding of some new, probabilistic laws, the laws of large numbers. These too were conceived at century's end, the last work of Swiss mathematician Jacques Bernoulli, whose *Ars Conjectandi* or *Art of Estimation* was published posthumously in 1713. Bernoulli had died in 1705 at the age of fifty: had he "died young"? Probably, but no one had solid data for taking stock of individual mortality. Even so, French, English, Dutch, and Prussian investors were willing at century's end to gamble on the first tontines, funds that paid out annual dividends proportional to the number of surviving investors, and in 1699 a Mr. Stanfield founded the Society of Assurance for Widows and Orphans, the first association for the assuring of lives.[174]

Profits, let alone annuarial predictions, were out of the reach of annuitors and assurers until they had more complete vital statistics than were yet available. Life insurance, or the taking of financial care to protect one's life, was in 1700 but the weakest of countermeasures to the *fin de siècle* fascination with the taking of one's own life, whose melodrama drew London's *Post-Angel* to describe in detail six suicides in February 1701: one charged with sodomy, one an alcoholic, one who starved herself to death, one who set himself afire, one who cut his throat, and a Presbyterian minister who, supposing himself bewitched, tied his own noose. This fascination with suicide was due in part to the fearful belief (recurrent at centuries' ends) that more people than usual were taking their own lives, in part to the angry controversy provoked by new editions of John Donne's *Biothanatos* and the appearance of several contemporary works defending self-destruction. John Adams, chaplain to William III, wrote against "an Error of so much Reputation, and which is set off with all the pompous Boasts of Reason, Courage, Honour and Liberty," but he could not hold English juries to the condemnation of suicides, and attempted suicides, as criminals. From the 1680s on, juries tended to find in the act of suicide evidence of madness rather than criminality; suicides were increasingly declared *non compos mentis* rather than atheistic self-murderers. Here too the Plain Style of century's end had made itself felt. Plainly, a person intent on self-destruction was not thinking rationally, could not appreciate the pattern of events.[175]

Such moderation in the legal treatment of suicides belonged to a larger historical trend toward the embrace of medical models in social judgments about disconcerting, peculiar, shameless, or self-destructive behavior. I venture to suggest, however, that legal compassion for British suicides in the 1680s and 1690s may also have been conditioned by an implicit *fin de siècle* parallelism between a life in ruins and a cosmos in ruins. The most publicly heated scientific and theological debate in England during this period devolved upon the diverse editions of one book that described the earth as a world in decay—Thomas Burnet's *The Sacred Theory of the Earth: Containing an Account of the Original of the Earth and of All the General Changes Which It Hath Already Undergone or Is to Undergo, till the Consummation of All Things*, published in Latin in 1681 and then, by the King's orders, in English translation in 1684, with a second part in 1689/90 *On the Conflagration of the World and the Future State of Things*, and many subsequent revisions and additions through to Burnet's death in 1715.

Burnet, an Anglican clergyman, meant to write in the Plain Style, but he was overcome by his subject: "I always endeavour to express myself in a plain and perspicuous manner; that the Reader may not lose Time, nor wait too long to know my Meaning. . . . You must not think it strange, however, that the Author sometimes, in meditating upon this Subject, is warm in his Thoughts and Expressions. For to see a World perishing in Flames, Rocks melting, the Earth trembling, and an Host of Angels in the Clouds, one must be very much a Stoick, to be a cold and unconcern'd Spectator of all this." This, from the preface to his second part; in his first part his expressions had been just as warm, though there he was describing not a future conflagration but the past deluge, Noah's Flood, which had made of a smooth, uniform, golden-age Earth a wrinkled, scarred, fractured, and ailing planet, "the Ruins of a Broken World." So now we lived among "wild, vast and indigested Heaps of Stone and Earth" called mountains and would build our impermanent empires between cliff and chasm for another one or two centuries, until our corrupt globe were redeemed by fire. Burnet imagined then "The everlasting Hills, the Mountains and Rocks of the Earth . . . melted as Wax before the Sun. . . . All the Varieties of Nature, all the Works of Art, all the Labours of Men . . . reduc'd to nothing; . . . and another Form and Face of Things, plain, simple, and every where the same, overspreads the whole Earth."[176]

Defender of the Christian Religion, Keeper of the King's Library at Oxford, Richard Bentley in 1692 attacked Burnet: "Some men are out of love with the features and mien of our earth; they do not like this rugged and irregular surface, these precipices and valleys, and the gaping channel of the ocean. This with them is deformity, and rather carries the face of ruin, or a rude and indigested lump of atoms that casually convened so, than a work of divine artifice." Burnet, of course, had not intended to belittle divine artifice. He intended to defend Scripture and Divinity by recourse to scientific models of the geocosm. He intended to render the Biblical Flood real and intelligible as a legitimate natural phenomenon proceeding under divine guidance, and before publication of the *Sacred Theory* he wrote for an expert opinion from Isaac Newton. As scientist and as theologian, Newton was sympathetic. Both men were increasingly wary of any theory of the universe as a perpetual motion machine, for that could imply an eternal universe in no need of a Creation or a Creator. Like Burnet, although less haunted in the 1680s than he would be at the turn of the century, Newton was thinking about universal decay: friction robbed particles of their momentum, the sun and stars used up their fuel. For Burnet, the world in ruins after the Flood, ground down further by storm and ice, had no internal mechanisms for repair; it could only be divinely transformed, instantaneously, by millennial flames. For Newton, God's active providence guaranteed the physical continuity of a cosmos that would otherwise decline toward coldness and immobility. How propitious that his friend Edmund Halley should be demonstrating the periodicity of comets, whose fiery tails sweeping through the heavens at rare but regular intervals could serve equally well to explain the physical shock that caused the Flood and the physical source for the renewal of the stars. If our immediate world was winding down, on the distant horizon God kept comets in orbits provident enough to restore the earth at some future date to a pristine glory, whether that be Burnet's shining plain or the sweet lakes and pleasant valleys of a more arcadian paradise.[177]

In his best-selling refutation of Burnet, the *New Theory of the Earth* (1696), mathematician William Whiston exploited Halley's work to prove that Noah's Flood had resulted from the near-miss of a comet, and Whiston anticipated another near-miss around 1866, to clear the air and earth after the final defeat of Antichrist. Botanist and zoologist John Ray, also responding to Burnet, praised the plentiful variety of Nature and claimed that "there is nothing in Nature which doth necessarily demonstrate a future Dissolution," but he could not completely rule it out, given the possibilities of the earth's waters again overflowing, or the sun becoming extinct, or a fire erupting from the center of the globe, or a multiple explosion of volcanoes, or "daily Consenescence and Decay." Fossil collector John Woodward, writing ostensibly against the *Sacred Theory*, actually expanded upon Burnet's Flood and put modern society in the midst not only of ragged ruins but of the remnants of prediluvian animals long gone.[178]

We may recognize ourselves in the debate over the *Sacred Theory*. Our *fin de siècle* has already been deeply moved by impassioned disputes over the earth's decay and its renewal. We inherit from the 1690s the specific images of comets on collision courses, of a sun burnt out, of radical extinction, images more appalling now that they have been divorced from the 17th century's millennial visions of this our earth jubilantly reborn from flood, cataclysm, or conflagration. When the first fire insurance company was established in 1680, it soon took the name of the Phoenix; nowadays the powers of the phoenix are in doubt, circumscribed by acid rain, oil spills, toxic waste, fluorocarbons, Chernobyl, the Greenhouse Effect. Those truth-bearing universal languages of higher mathematics and statistics born at the end of the 17th century may have been reassuringly precise, but they have bequeathed to subsequent centuries' ends a legacy of probabilities and uncertainties, fears of overpopulation, alarm at suicide rates, anxious feelings of being always and everywhere at risk. Although in handbooks of historical chronology the end of the 17th century appears as a tired denouement to a frantic century, in this book it has a certain startling energy which will become more apparent as we move on past Burnet's Deluge to another.

THE NAPOLEOZOIC ERA:
REVOLUTION AND
THE 1790s

THERE WAS, AND IS, NO GETTING AROUND THE FRENCH REVO-lution. After all, it had been anticipated for nearly a millenium, since the 9th century, when Abu Ma'shar (Albumasar), prime mover of Islamic astrology, predicted vast social upheaval for 1789. Nostradamus, in his Epistle to Henri II, had written of "a greater persecution against the Christian Church than ever was in Africa, and this will continue up to 1792, which year will be thought a renovation of the age." Before he lost his head in the middle of the 17th century, the English Presbyterian minister Christopher Love had calculated the destruction of the papacy for 1790, then in 1795 "God will be known by many. This will produce a great man.—The stars will wander, and the moon turn as blood, in 1800.—Africa, Asia, and America will tremble in 1803.—A great earthquake over all the world in 1805.—God will be universally known by all: then a general reformation and peace for ever." Later in the 17th century, the Huguenot minister Pierre Jurieu, partisan of the rebellious Camisards of the Cévennes and the millenarian French Prophets, calculated the "last revolt" against the Pope for the year 1785, but cautioned that he should not be taken as a false prophet if, when the time came, he was found to have been off by a scant nine or ten years. Minister of the Scots Church in London, Robert Fleming in 1701 had calculated that the French monarchy would fall "towards the end of this century; as the Spanish monarchy did before towards the end of the sixteenth age," and the Judgment on the Roman See would begin around 1794, "So that there is ground to hope, that about the beginning of another such century, things may again alter for the better."[179]

During the 1790s the reputations of Nostradamus, Love, and Fleming soared as their predictions and others equally accurate were gathered into impressive compendia. "It is certain," wrote one compiler, "that the authors of the French revolution had nothing less in view than the accomplishment of prophecy; yet had this been their only design, they could not have done

Death on a Pale Horse, drawing by Benjamin West, 1783, retouched 1803. Courtesy of the Royal Academy of Arts, Burlington House, London.

it more effectually. It is the Lord's usual method to effect his purposes by undesigning, and even *refractory* agents." Divinely driven or not, there seemed then, and seems still, to be a rhythm to the modern centuries, with some unavoidable revolution at the end of each. In this conjunction of revolution and century's end, we can see the old, astronomical, cyclical sense of "revolution" being superseded by the new, political, punctual sense of "revolution" as a complete, irrevocable change. The conjunction had begun in England even before the Glorious Revolution of 1688. We find it in the *Strange and wonderful Prophecies and Predictions Taken from the Apparition of the late Dreadful Comet, the Last Wonderful Ecclips, and the great and signal Conjunction of Jupiter and Saturn in the Fiery Trigon, That will happen on the 23 October next*, in which the last world-age was dated from Charlemagne's shift of the focus of empire from the ancient centers of the eastern Mediterranean and the classical center in Rome westward to Carolingian Germany and France. Now, in 1682, all were living close to the end of the "7th Revolution since the beginning of the world . . . which has a singular Mystery of Sabbatism, and promises great things more than ordinary to the world. Its effects will last several years, and [it] will be about the year 1801 ere this triplicity has its full period: about which time we may expect the utter overthrow of the Hierarchy of Rome, if not before; and that about that time we may expect a Total Catastrophe of the world."[180]

Was this what occurred to Madame Jeanne de Pompadour upon hearing news of the defeat of the French and Austrian armies at the battle of Rossbach? "After us the deluge," she told Louis XV in 1757. A grim consolation, but had she also intuited the Revolution? And the Lisbon earthquake which shook up most of Europe in 1755 as North Africa had been shaken a year before by a quake in Cairo and as England had been shaken by two quakes in London in 1750—were these not omens of "great things more than ordinary" in store at century's end? Men and women after 1789 looked back toward midcentury for the signs and suspicions that *must* have foretokened the maelstrom and deluge of the French Revolution.[181]

Century's end was not forgot in the midst of such turbulence. Indeed, it was accented. The French Revolution through to the coronation of Napoleon as emperor fit exceedingly well the janiform schema of a *fin de siècle*, oscillating wildly between extremes: between the Great Fear (of plague that never spread, of brigands who never arrived) and "La Marseillaise" (whose tune was contagious and whose day of glory had duly arrived); between the Terror of the guillotine and the massive, joyous chorales of civic festivals; between demagoguery and plain truths; between tyranny and democracy.[182]

Prophets of universal regeneration or universal conflagration kept one eye upon the phases of the Revolution and the other eye upon the end of the century, looking for the most convincing symbolic conjunctions between calendar and crisis. The popular French Catholic prophet, Suzette Labrousse, believing the Revolution the herald of the Millennium, was reported to have prophesied that "in 1792 there will be in heaven a meteor that all the inhabitants of the earth will see, that it will remain visible for a year, that then justice will reign on earth; the Pope will renounce his temporal power. . . . If this does not happen, there will be great bloodshed in Europe." In 1792 she went on pilgrimage to Rome, where she was arrested for preaching and plotting against the Pope. Diplomatic efforts were made to free her, but she resisted them, telling friends that she must remain in the Holy City until 1800, destined "for great things." Liberated from prison by the French army occupying Rome in 1798, Labrousse stayed in the city to speak in the streets about the final age, which she expected for the centurial year 1800.[183]

That year, according to a member of the Irish House of Commons, the Messiah would come in time to thwart the Act of Union scheduled to unite the Parliaments of England and Ireland on January 1, 1801. Which day would lead to the unsealing of the prophecies of Joanna Southcott of Exeter, whose "visitations" about the future had begun in 1792, and whose writings (from 1794 on) had been sealed up for a sabbath of years by divine imperative. She was however "to wait no longer than New Year's Day (Old Style) 1801" to have her writings published. "So here the century ends with men," she wrote on January 5, 1801. "If those Ministers, that I have written to, do not go to Mr. . . . before the year ends to the old style [on March 24, 1801], and prove these writings are not from the Lord, their silence gives consent that it is of God, and they will be made public." Century's end had become an ultimatum.[184]

As it was for William Bryan of Bristol and his illuminist brethren in Avignon, who expected the destruction of the Turks and the restoration of the Jews to Zion before 1800. As sunrise in Jerusalem on November 19, 1794, had been for Nathaniel Brassey Halhed, learned expositor of the system of his master, the English prophet Richard Brothers, who himself anticipated *The Restoration of the Hebrews to Jerusalem, by the Year 1798.* Everywhere, it seemed, the revolutionary excitement was synchronous with the eschatological excitement of century's end: among Bavarian illuminati, Scandinavian Swedenborgians, Polish and Russian occultists in St. Petersburg, Spanish Jesuits, American Shakers, New England Congregationalists, Seneca Indians, Appalachian Methodists, Welsh Baptists, and the more excitable of Freemasons throughout Europe, some of whom had considerable parts to play early on in the French Revolution. "The present moment teems with these anticipations of futurity, beyond the example of every former period," wrote a Calvinist antagonist in 1796, upset at this *Age of Credulity*.[185]

Leaders of the Revolution, making their own attempt to dispel credulity and sweep away centuries of superstition, recast the French calendar as a decimal masterwork, ten days each week, three weeks each month, twelve months each year, all renamed and reoriented to a Year I retroactive to the autumnal equinox, September 22, 1792. To no avail: few Frenchmen and fewer Frenchwomen took to a week that had lost the sabbatical charm of sevens and the sabbatical rest of Sunday; as for the Roman-numeral years, the prestigious astronomer Joseph Lalande had to be called upon to settle the many heated disputes in France over the day on which the standard *Anno Domini* 18th century would end. Napoleon's troops in Rome might sweep aside all likelihood of a papal Jubilee in the year 1800, but that did not stop Napoleon himself from addressing an impetuous letter to his "brother" King George III of England on Christmas Day, 1799, in his new role as First Consul of what had been the revolutionary Republic of France. "Must the war," asked Napoleon on the very day that the Porta Sancta would have been opened had there been a Jubilee of 1800, "must the war, which for four years has ravaged every part of the world, be eternal? Are there no means of coming to an understanding?"[186]

None, if we are to trust Mrs. Hester Lynch Salisbury Thrale Piozzi, of Bath and the best society. Mrs. Piozzi had been busy at her diary throughout the 1790s, tracking the French Revolution from its infant promise to that monstrosity of century's end, Napoleon. "There *are* people," she noted in December 1799, the same month she was awaiting pestilence, war, and famine before the century was out, "who say [Napoleon] is the Devil Incarnate, the Apollyon mentioned in Scripture [Revelation 9.11]: His name is Apollonio pronounced according to the Corsican dialect *N'Apollione*: and he does come forwards followed by a Cloud of devouring locusts from the bottomless Pit—whose stings are in their *Tails*, The Tagrag of our World, *The Democrates*." But, as Hester Thrale and Charles Dickens would have agreed, 'twas "an Age of Contradictions, of Exultations, of Seditions," and in 1800 there was an Englishman or two who might have come to some understanding with Napoleon and who, like the First Consul, had something of a Jubilee in mind. I am thinking of a poor Newcastle schoolteacher, Thomas Spence, earlier arrested for selling that revolutionary pamphlet, Tom Paine's *Rights of Man*, and soon to be accused of insurrectional conspiracy for having denounced all aristocracy and intimated (urged?) "some very great commotion" among working people. Great Britain was in for serious trouble if it did not at this ominous moment restore society to its natural state of "pure Justice." That Justice in place, wrote Spence in his own radically revised alphabet on October 12, 1800, "let this incomparable Jubilee, this New Creation be celebrated with that universal Joy and Fraternity becoming so grand an occasion."[187]

Was Napoleon the Devil Incarnate or avatar of the Millennium? Were the flips and flops of the French Revolution the symptoms of final decay or chaotic rebirth? Was the Revolution the degenerate end to what had been a stately era, or was it a sublime escape from what Scottish essayist Thomas Carlyle would call "the putrid Eighteenth Century: such an ocean of sordid nothingness, shams and scandalous hypocrisies as never weltered in the world before"? To what century did the Revolution belong?[188]

These questions were not academic. They were personal and pressing. Enlightenment figures had identified themselves with their enlightened century in which they had "the honor" of living. It was a century "full of marvels," a century "which prided itself on its rationality, its philosophy, and above all its taste." Dramatist Pierre de Beaumarchais, a watchmaker's son born in Paris in 1732 and fated to die there in 1799, declared his loyalty to the 18th century: "I am unaware of any century in which I would rather have been born." For the first time, people were *born to* a century, and adults at midcentury began to think of themselves as living in the *middle* of a century, gauging their own and the world's position vis-à-vis 1700/01. "What a century is ours!" exclaimed one French author in 1759. "Had someone sixty years ago seen in its horoscope what we see today, would he not have been taken for a madman?" Poinsinct de Sivry went on, "Ages may repeat themselves, but can this century ever have a twin?" His century had an inimitable personality, a *genius saeculi*, that shaped the character of its native-born. The more closely one identified with one's natal century, the more personal and pressing would be questions about the meaning of a revolution at its end.[189]

Moreover, whether oblivious to the long counts of history or acutely conscious of years in their hundreds, no one now could avoid being shaped by the century. There was something new in the air, something known as *l'esprit du temps*, the spirit of the times, the *Zeitgeist*. That something had grown out of the Italian philosopher Giambattista Vico's notion of the integral completeness of historical periods: the arts, the sciences, the language, the customs, the dominant philosophies and faiths of an era were of one piece. Great men best understood this, as Friedrich Hegel and Thomas Carlyle would later argue, but great or small, all people were caught up in their century's *Zeitgeist*, a word that appeared in German around 1789.[190]

The unparalleled numbers of retrospectives printed in newspapers and delivered in sermons between 1799 and 1801 were not looking vaguely back but taking exact measure of a body of time that had somehow to seem coherent. "The good *Old Lady* known by the name of the EIGHTEENTH CENTURY, who resigned all sublunary cares on Wednesday night last, was quietly buried in the family vault of *Eternity*," reported the *London Chronicle* in its first issue for 1801. The Old Lady left behind 100 suns, 36,500 grand-days, 876,000 great-grandhours, 52,560,000 great-great-grandminutes, and 3,153,600,000 great-great-great-grandseconds. She had been a distinguished Old Lady, "unequalled, not only in the annals of Europe, but of the world," maintained a contributor to London's *Gentleman's Magazine*. In Newburyport, Massachusetts, the editor of the *Herald* found that "In reviewing the events of the last hundred years, the mind is wrapt in astonishment. The most important scenes of the old world require an encyclopedia to record them, those of our own country cannot be named." There had been glory, perfidy, virtue, and villainy; there had been Locke, Johnson, Handel, Wren, Reynolds, Hanway, and an aged Newton, to whom

> *a Cent'ry owes*
> *Half what it boasts, and half what it knows.*

How put all this together? A poet for Boston's *Columbian Centinel* struck the balance in his ode, "The Enlightened Eighteenth Century":

> *That the world has improved some sages declare,*
> *In manners, religions and sciences rare,*
> *That this wonderful age has afforded a birth*
> *To improvements more vast, than were known upon earth,*
> *From Noah so fam'd for constructing the ark,*
> *To NEWTON who taught us to grope in the dark. . . .*
> *If in short you believ'd these philosophers sage,*
> *You'd confess that we live in a wonderful age,*
> *When poets, historians and orators rise*
> *From the prolific soil, like snails or like flies,*

and yet

Though philosophists thus all nature have mov'd,
We find neither manners nor morals improved,
Vice still wears its horrors, and virtue its charms,
And ambition still rules by its arts and its arms;
To OLD MANNERS and PRINCIPLES then let's adhere,
And the virtue, religion, of our fathers revere.[191]

What was bothering the poet was the impiety and bloodshed of the French Revolution, impossible to square with a sage century. He (or she?) was no convert to the new, enlightened faith in "a perpetual and irresistible advancement towards a better and more perfect state of society" as were many others who stood on the promontory of century's turn, looking forward as intently as they looked back. John Evans, reflecting upon the commencement of the 19th century for London's *Monthly Visitor and Entertaining Pocket Companion*, began by "Standing as it were on an eminence and looking around," from which vista he found the 18th century "on the whole" favorable to progress, and suggested that "We should enter upon the new century with the pleasing idea that *the progressive series of events* tends to *human improvement*." Standing before the eminent Medical Society of South Carolina on January 1, 1801, physician David Ramsay read his *Review of the Improvements, Progress and State of Medicine in the XVIIIth Century*, concluding that "Poor was the stock, to which our forefathers succeeded at the commencement of the 18th century, compared with that which devolves on us, on this the first day of the 19th. Let those who follow us in the 20th, have as much reason to respect our memories, as we have to venerate those who have gone before us." In January 1801 the editor of the *New Haven Messenger*, closing an extensive enumeration of the principal events of the last hundred years, foresaw a retrospective of 1901 that would recount even greater changes in world affairs for the 19th century than he had just recounted for the 18th.[192]

This too was unparalleled, the prospective toward the end of the next century. Thinking oneself into the future by centuries, looking back upon one's own future from another century's end, this was a novel prophetic form; one launched oneself ahead in time not from the harbors of apocalyptic Scripture but from the pier at century's end across to the dock of the next. So began the fictions of "future histories" which were, often, exercises of a centurial imagination, as in perhaps the earliest, *A New prophecy of several strange and wonderful revolutions that shall happen to the Kingdom of England in or about an Hundred years hence.* The broadside, printed in or about 1714, warned the English to fend off the Devil, the Pope, and the Turk—or else a century hence autos-da-fé would blacken Smithfield and St. Paul's Cathedral would be rechristened St. Peter's. By the 1790s, French and German fictions worked further ahead, centuries hence, following the lead of Louis Sebastien Mercier, an olympic sleeper who woke to the year 2500. From this vantage point, Mercier had written his "memoirs," describing the 18th century as an age of project[ion]s, the 25th century as the age of execution. Traffic was orderly in the Paris of 2500; coquetry and credit had been banished, likewise cruel paintings and dangerous books. A universal language sustained the peace and concord of an unharried world. Citizens of the year 2500 had everything that optimists of the 18th century could imagine for the year 1800.[193]

The long and short of it was that neither optimists nor pessimists nor stoics in the first days of 1800 and 1801 could be nonchalant about the end of one century and the beginning of another. Centuries now amounted to much more than generic collections of a hundred things; much more than the naked arithmetic of perpetual calendars; much more than historical abstractions or pedagogical conveniences. Centuries were, so to speak, Doppelgängers, coherent cultural entities in whose person and personality men and women might recognize themselves. Each century had a name, a genius or character, a spirit, and an historical career or biography that redounded upon both public and private lives.

Whence the unparalleled fustian over that beriddled issue of when, exactly, the 18th century was to give up her ghost and the 19th century to take his first breath. "The idle controversy, which has of late convulsed so many brains, respecting the commencement of the current century, did not disgrace the common sense of our fathers," claimed an inaccurate London journalist in a retrospect dated January 11, 1801. He was, however, right to notice how prominent the idle controversy now was. He himself sided, again inaccurately, with the '00, since "The remotest writers, who endeavoured to support the cause of Christianity, though not very Conspicuous for intellectual refinement and critical discrimination, employed the cipher o, to design[ate] the first year of our Redeemer's aera; in which . . . they at least avoided the charge of absurdity, which attaches to those who wish to make the Eighteenth Century older than it is." This was also the position assumed by Peter Porcupine of Philadelphia as early as All Hallows' Eve, 1798. Between William Cobbett, conservative editor of *Peter Porcupine's Gazette*, and John Ward Fenno, Federalist editor of the *Gazette of the United States*, Philadelphia became the testing ground for most of the heated arguments of later centurial feuds. To wit: If the 18th century does end on

December 31, 1800, then one should raise a hue and cry, for the first twelve months before the year 1 of the Christian calendar must have been stolen by thieves. Or, in favor of the '01, a letter to Porcupine from Simpleton of Front Street, to wit: We do not say it is one o'clock until the minute hand has passed through the sixty minutes between twelve and one; ipso facto, we cannot enter the 19th century until the full one hundred years of the 18th century are behind us, including 1800. "It is somewhat singular," commented Cobbett, "that all those, whether grown persons or children, who happen to be *wrong* respecting the termination of the century, invariably set out with declaring the question to be the *plainest* in the world." Cobbett admitted to standing with the minority, but did not the majority protest too much over so trivial a matter? "I cannot agree with Mr. Cobbett," wrote John Ward Fenno, "that the matter in dispute is of a trifling nature; since, unless some decision can be had, some conviction worked in the minds of the [seventeen] ninety-nine men, the dispute threatens to result in very great confusion of dates and calculations." He hoped for some show of rationality from Porcupine, whose claims thus far had been like the "dreams of a distempered imagination, to support which nothing has hitherto been offered but misconception, noise, and fury."[194]

The noise and fury were unabated by Porcupine's offer that "If any man, having the least title to respect or attention, will come forward in his own name, and assert that the XVIIIth Century does not close with the last moment of 1799, I will, without the least asperity or attempt to ridicule, endeavour to convince him of his error." And evidently the Porcupine's quills had an effect. "December 31, 1799. They are ringing and firing out the old year, according to the old, ridiculous custom—and as some say, the old century," Elizabeth Drinker of Philadelphia wrote in her diary. "M. Penry tells me, in her letter, that she is of that opinion, and gives her reason for her belief." A Quaker and an invalid, Mrs. Drinker at the age of sixty-five disapproved of all the noise—"guns firing, bells ringing, carriages running"—for she thought New Year's Eve a solemn time, but she too had been taken by the fury of the centurial debate in the Philadelphia papers, and she had decided that if there must be an especial noise at century's end, let it be (*pace* Porcupine) on December 31, 1800. Yet . . . yet there *was* something about that number, 1799, as Mrs. Drinker confessed to her diary: "January 1, 1800. A new date, the figures of 7 we have been so long accustomed to, done with. Trifling as it seems, I am struck by it, as parting with something that I have been always used to."[195]

Mrs. Drinker's concerns with the really not-so-trifling problem of the century's end were reflected by others in Europe and America who, if they did not enter the public debate that continued in the pages of the *Kentucky Gazette, Quebec Gazette, Gentleman's Magazine, Schwäbische Chronik*, and *Allgemeine Zeitung*, acknowledged it in private—and, like the Somerset parson William Holland, felt obliged to make their positions known on the pages of their diaries: "The Year 1801, Thursday, January 1. . . . Many things have been written in the newspapers pro and con the commencement of the New Century but nothing can be clearer to me than that the last century was all the preceding year in concluding. We were indeed in the year 1800 but that was not compleated before yesterday about twelve at night." For the first time we hear tell of semi-private wagers on the exact date of the end of the century: the Whig politicians and dramatists Richard Brinsley Sheridan and Joseph Richardson appealing to their elder statesman, Charles James Fox, for the deciding opinion; two of Baron Alleyne Fitzherbert St. Helens's neighbors appealing through the baron to Dr. Richard Pulteney of Blandford in Dorsetshire; two Scottish gentlemen appealing to the professor of mathematics at the University of Edinburgh; two New York literary gentlemen appealing to Timothy Dwight, president of Yale, the winner to enjoy a pipe of wine.[196]

Without exception these referees decided, as had the French astronomer Lalande, that the new century began in 1801. Nonetheless, England's poet laureate Henry James Pye, agreeable to Prior's ode and Dryden's masque for the year 1700, wrote his *Carmen Seculare for the Year 1800*. The *London Review*, though "believing that the public are heartily tired of the controversy," saw Pye's poem as "one of the classics of the present age," perhaps because Pye's imperial patriotism was unremitting:

> *In every clime from pole to pole,*
> *Where wind can blow, or billow roll,*
> *Britannia's barks the coasts explore,*
> *Waft Science, Peace, and Plenty o'er. . . .*

But there was no Pax Britannica over the controversy about the century's end, no act of Parliament such as that of March 1751, which had established December 31st as the official year's end and had proclaimed that September 2, 1752, would be followed by September 14th in order to bring the English (and colonial) calendar into harmony with the Gregorian reform. The first part of the poet laureate's *Carmen Seculare* was performed at St. James's on January 18, 1800, while King George III received new-century greetings for 1800 from the Bishop of Worcester. The young poet Samuel Taylor Coleridge was very excited about 1800, writing on January 1st to his friend, the chemist Humphry Davy, with hopes for a "compact compressed History of the Human Mind for the last Century," and imagining himself, Davy, William Godwin, Shakespeare, and Milton marching together, their countenances lit by an athanasiophagus grin—"By the word athanasiophagus I mean devouring Immortality by anticipation—'Tis a sweet Word!" Then, to fellow radical Godwin, on January 8th: "P.S. How many Thousand Letter-writers will in the first fortnight of this month write a 7 first, & then transmogrify it into an 8—in the dates of their Letters! I like to catch myself doing that which involves any identity of [i.e., with] the human Race." On December 31, 1800, while George III received another set of new-century greetings, a young Knight, nine and three-quarters years old, later king of the penny press, went to bed in his house near Windsor Castle, "with a vague fear that I should be awakened by a terrific noise which would shake the house more than the loudest thunder-clap, and would produce such a concussion of the air as would break every window-pane in Windsor town." The King, also fearful, had proscribed the New Year's (and new century's) firing of the castle cannon lest Benjamin West's painted windows, just installed in St. George's Chapel, be shattered. Charles Knight woke instead to church bells ringing out "a merry peal—not so much to welcome the coming of the new year and the beginning of the new century . . . but to hail the legal commencement of the Union with Ireland." Shortly after, His Majesty, now styled "George the Third, by the grace of God, of the United Kingdom of Great Britain and Ireland, King, Defender of the Faith," was shut up in his rooms with a month-long spell of insanity.[197]

On 10 Nivôse Year IX, or January 1, 1801, Napoleon was mad, smashing chairs, arresting journalists. That spring he had crossed the Alps without incident and defeated the Austrians at Marengo, but that Christmas Eve, 1800, on the way to the Théâtre des Arts, he had narrowly escaped death from the explosion of an infernal machine hidden in a cart blocking the route. This attempted assassination infuriated Napoleon, although he and Josephine did proceed to the opera, where they listened determinedly to the French premiere of Haydn's oratorio *The Creation*. Completed by 1799, performed in front of large applauding audiences in 1799, 1800, and 1801, *The Creation* was paradigmatic of the century's end and turn, moving as it did from the dissonance of "Chaos" to the love duet of Adam and Eve and a hymn of thanksgiving in the Garden of Eden.[198]

In the German artistic paradise of Weimar, on January 1, 1801, the poet-philosophers Friedrich Schiller, Friedrich Wilhelm Schelling, Johann Gottfried Herder, and the great Goethe himself attended a New Century's Day performance of *The Creation*. Schiller took little pleasure from the oratorio, which he thought a "typical mishmash," but he had been in a sour mood since the night before. With Schelling, the Norwegian nature philosopher Heinrich Steffens, and physician Christoph Wilhelm Hufeland, Schiller had gone to a fancy-dress ball that featured one of Goethe's pageants. After midnight, the men retired to a side room to toast the 19th century with champagne and a debate over aesthetics, during which Schiller had grown very serious as Goethe had become "unrestrained in his mirth even to excess." Schiller later would finish a short poem on "The Commencement of the New Century," a poem full of *Sturm und Drang*. It began:

> *Where will a place of refuge, noble friend,*
> *For peace and freedom ever open lie!*
> *The century in tempests had its end,*
> *The new one now begins with murder's cry.*

Herder's wife Karoline took far greater pleasure in all the centurial festivities, and wrote to an old friend in Halberstadt, "Now we find ourselves in the remarkable 19th century! O it deserves the loveliest garland of roses—may it bring us Peace and Good Fortune! Understanding and Love! Wisdom and Health! Fine Children and Friends! Good Government and good Weather! [And may it] change enemies into friends! *Amen!*" A hundred miles northeast of Halberstadt, in Berlin, on December 31, 1800, the wife of the Swedish minister hosted a centurial ball. The next day was performed *A Highly Amusing Carnival Lay of Old and New Century* by August Wilhelm von Schlegel, whose little burlesque revealed that the 18th century, that old hag, was not the true mother of the 19th. The infant's parents were really Genius and Freedom.[199]

"Liberty and the Constitution" read the legend below an eighty-foot transparency stretched above and across the grounds of Franklin College in Lancaster, Pennsylvania, during its celebration of the new century on January 1, 1801. "The World, Our Country—Man, Our Fellow Citizen—Benevolence, Our Religion" was the principal toast that day at the Sign of the Green Trees, where some Philadelphians had gathered to bespeak a favorable commencement for the new century. At Ephraim Bateman's New Jersey debating club that day, the count was seven against five in favor of the proposition that "Love has more influence over man than Anger." And so love might: in Boston, Louisa Adams Park, wife of a Navy physician, "Rose early to breakfast—Wishing our friends a happy new year and century was the business; but *I* dispensed with it, and sat down to write to my beloved husband for the first time since he sailed."[200]

As European and American celebrations stood, the 19th century had had a noisy, disputatious first and a definitive if ambivalent second coming. So this stanza, dated Hartford, January 1, 1801, from a poem in the *Connecticut Courant*:

> *P*recisely twelve o'clock, last night,
> The Eighteenth Century took its flight.
> Full many a calculating head
> Has rack'd its brains, its ink has shed,
> To prove by metaphysics fine
> A Hundred means but Ninety-nine;
> While at their wisdom others wonder'd,
> But took one more to make a hundred.
> Thus, by an unexampled riddle,
> The world's divided in the middle.
> The Century, waking from its bed,
> Finds half mankind a year a-head.

The centurial feud had hinged on the apparently incongruent application of cardinal and ordinal numbers to the counting of human age and of Anno Domini ages. Ordinal numbers, "first, second, third, fourth," describe position within a series; cardinal numbers, "one, two, three, four," describe amount. A woman born on January 1, 1700, would have had her first (ordinal) year during the twelve months of 1700, and would have been one (cardinal) year old on January 1, 1701, one hundred (cardinal) years old on January 1, 1800. Standard centuries, however, lacking an initial Anno Domini year zero, had their first (ordinal) year in the twelve months *between* year one (cardinal) and year two (cardinal). The 18th century, then, despite the transmogrification of the 7 into the "pretzel-shaped" 8, would not be a full one hundred years old until midnight, December 31, 1800. Always perplexing, this apparent incongruity had become all the more disturbing as people began to identify themselves with their century: the two ages, personal and centurial, ought to agree.[201]

The year 1800 was therefore experienced, I suspect, as something of an interregnum, a transitional period between centuries, a pregnant pause between epochs. For William Wordsworth, returning at the age of twenty-nine to his ancestral Lake Country, the year 1800 was interlude and prelude. *Home in Grasmere*, he wrote himself toward a pastoral Millennium:

> *P*aradise, and groves
> *Elysian, Fortunate Fields—like those of old*
> *Sought in the Atlantic Main—why should they be*
> *A history only of departed things,*
> *Or a mere fiction of what never was?*
> *For the discerning intellect of Man,*
> *When wedded to this goodly universe*
> *In love and holy passion, shall find these*
> *A simple produce of the common day.*
> *—I, long before the blissful hour arrives,*
> *Would chant, in lonely peace, the spousal verse*
> *Of this great consummation. . . .*

He recalled also his childhood and school-time in the first books of *The Prelude*, from which remembrance of times past he might summon the "vital breeze" and "vernal promises" of "the holy life of music and of verse." For G. W. F. Hegel, he who would be so instrumental in defining "the spirit of the times," the year 1800 was an exordium. With a small inheritance upon his father's death in 1799, Hegel was free to finish a manuscript on the philosophy of religion and decide to go to the University of Jena. Thirty years old (and, although he could not have known it, exactly at the midpoint of his life), Hegel prepared himself for the new century with a poetic exhortation on New Year's Eve, 1800/01: "Break then, peace with thyself, break with the work of the world! / Strive, seek something more than today or yesterday! So wilt thou / Better not be than the time, but still be the time at its best!" For Rahel Levin, twenty-nine and near the midpoint of her life, 1800 was a year of convalescence for a broken heart, a year of resolve to maintain her wit, her wits, her Jewish origins, and her originality as the mistress of the most sparkling salon in Berlin. For an outrider of that attic salon, Baron Alexander von Humboldt, thirty and destined for a longer life than Hegel or Rahel Levin Varnhagen, 1800 was a year of astonishing displacement. With his friend, the botanist Aimé Bonpland, Humboldt was beginning five years and six thousand miles of exploration in the Spanish colonies of the New World, intent on discovering "how the forces of nature interreact upon one another and how the geographic environment influences plant and animal life. In other words, I must find out about the unity of nature." In Venezuela for eighteen months from the summer of 1799, they found nature instead bewildering, an extravaganza of "fantastic plants, electric eels, armadillos, monkeys, parrots." Wrote Humboldt to his brother back in Berlin, "We rush around like the demented; in the first three days we were quite unable to classify anything; we pick up one object to throw it away for the next. Bonpland keeps telling me that he will go mad if the wonders do not cease soon." Bonpland kept his head, but the wonders did not cease. In the spring of 1800, he and Humboldt watched a million tortoises come to lay their eggs four hundred miles down the Orinoco. Only later would Humboldt sort out the wonders into a scientific geography, a volcanic geology, and a *Kosmos* pulsing with inner life.[202]

I have of course been playing favorites here, implying in a mildly Hegelian manner that the liminal experiences of Wordsworth, Hegel, Varnhagen, and Humboldt in 1800 were, because of their extraordinary personalities, extraordinarily characteristic of their age. Might we not just as well assign their coincident experiences to their ages, twenty-nine or thirty, a time of (modern) life infamous for its suspense? What then of the less illustrious John Pintard, a struggling New York merchant? He was forty in January of 1800 when his cousin and his wife presented him with a gold seal, "the device a Palm tree, whose property it is to surmount every obstacle that impedes its growth—Motto *Depressor Resurgo*. Reclining against the foot of the tree is the anchor of Hope with a shield bearing my initials J. P. motto Never Despair." Now Pintard must wait out 1800 and (a phrase new to the era) be on the alert: "Time must discover whether the device will be characteristic of my fortunes." On December 31, 1800, he wrote in his diary, "Concluded this year and century in my native City—Have many mercies for which I thank God most heartily, especially that I have survived my long misfortunes and have seen a termination of my past adversity." The next day, "A delightful morn from Sunrise till 10 when it clouded over," Pintard was studying 2 Corinthians 5, in which he would have read: "Therefore if any man be in Christ, he is a new creature: old things are passed away; behold, all things are become new."[203]

Recently converted to a fervid Christianity, thirty-one years old in 1800, Vicomte François René de Chateaubriand returned to France from an English exile in time to applaud Napoleon's Concordat of 1801 which led to the reestablishment of the Gallican Church. His romances, *Atala* and *René*, and his defense of religion; *Génie du Christianisme*, attracted the favors of Napoleon himself, but Chateaubriand would be disenchanted with Bonaparte in 1804 and go into exile once again. "I found myself between two centuries, as at the confluence of two rivers," he would write forty years later in his memoirs; "I plunged into their troubled waters, regretfully distancing myself from the old shore on which I was born, swimming hopefully toward an unknown bank." The extended metaphor was apt to an era that saw the first lifeboats and the first societies to rescue drowning people, but for Chateaubriand the swimming became a seasickness, symptomatic of a dis-ease which he claimed to have been the first to name and the first to suffer from: *mal du siècle*.[204]

The *mal du siècle* was an affliction not just of the single year 1800 but of the revolutionary period from the Terror to Napoleon's Empire, and beyond. It made of all the years around century's end an anxious interregnum, an anguished limbo. During this limbo, the *mal du siècle* took three sorts of victims. (1) Political conservatives like Chateaubriand and the English orator Edmund Burke, who in 1795 was terrified "when I think how much all things are gone out of the ordinary principles of calculations. I am something worse than terrified, I am sunk into something like absolute despair, when I consider the state of things at home." (2) Continental republicans, British radicals, North American democrats severely disappointed by an impressive revolution that had turned ugly: "Bliss was it in that dawn to be alive"— and then, "What disappointment of elevated hopes! what heart-rending scenes of public and private calamity! what audacity of crime! what triumph of violence and injustice!" (3) Romantics with a "devouring need for action or, rather, . . . this ardent need for the infinite," inspired as much by the *Weltschmerz* of Goethe's *Sorrows of Young Werther* (1774) as they were depressed by a world constantly at war. Desperate for the improbable and the miraculous, yet always coming up against power politics and phlegmatic religion, they sought the infinite in the cosmic fluids of Franz Anton Mesmer, the magnetic universe of occult cosmologies, the sublime terror of gothic novels, the trances of the somnambulist, the visions of the mystic, the judgments of the fortuneteller, the astronomical odds of lotteries and games of chance, never to be satisfied: "What is this inexpressible desire, this melancholy that impels me toward new and unknown pleasures? At the very moment that I fully realize my happiness, when I rise to the very peak of enthusiasm, a species of indifference suddenly seizes me, a somber foreboding. . . . If it were to overmaster me, it would drive me forever empty-hearted, from pole to pole."[205]

The *mal du siècle* was a motion sickness. The French Revolution had so jarred and jolted "nearly the whole of the universe" that time had been sped up. This was how the *London Chronicle* reviewed the year 1799:

> Though every year since that in which the scourge of the French revolution first attacked the world, has appeared to furnish one of the most memorable pages in the history of the unfortunate conclusion of the 18th century; none of them will bear so distinguished a part in it as that which has just elapsed. Never perhaps did the three quarters of the old world see at once in so short a space of time so many events of every kind succeed one another: never perhaps was the destiny of their inhabitants subjected to so many changes, so many evils, and such vicissitudes.

As at earlier centuries' ends, it seemed once again that history had accelerated. To the eyes of such spiritually imaginative prophets as William Blake in London and Jung-Stilling in Marburg, the acceleration of the 1790s was steeply apocalyptic—an epic, illuminated apocalypse for Blake and his Sons of Los, a visionary apocalyptic progression for Jung-Stilling. To the eyes of historians and philosophers of history, the acceleration meant modernity, *die neue Zeit*, and modernity meant change so quick and continual that an understanding of the past was inadequate to any action of the present; one had to look to the future to act effectively, responsively, in the here and now. Shaken by the French Revolution, Time itself was going out of historical control: "Time is in flight. . . . Monstrous things have happened: the world has suffered great transformations silently and noisily, in the quiet pace of the day and in the storms and eruptions of revolution; monstrosities will occur, greater things will be transformed."[206]

Were there no limits? On time, perhaps not, despite the widespread use of alarm clocks and watches with accurate second hands; despite the general adoption of the standard B.C. (Before Christ) dating system to balance and anchor those A.D. years now galloping into the nineteenth of their centuries. On people, perhaps there were limits, despite the prodigious progress of an enlightened century. Let the question be framed for us by the Reverend Thomas Malthus, who had read mathematics at Jesus College, taken holy orders in 1788, and as a single man at the age of thirty-two published *An Essay on the Principle of Population as it affects the Future Improvement of Society* (1798): "the great question is now at issue, whether man shall henceforth start forwards with accelerated velocity towards illimitable and hitherto unconceived improvement; or be condemned to a perpetual oscillation between happiness and misery, and after every effort remain still at an immeasurable distance from the wished-for good." Malthus was hardly the first to argue that populations would tend to overreach their means of subsistence were it not for the limiting factors of poverty, vice, debility, disease, pestilence, natural disasters, war, and finally famine. But his *Essay*, particularly in its second, expanded edition of 1803, was the fullest expression of the pessimistic thesis that the rate of population growth tends to exceed the rate of increase in per capita production. Eventually there must be, as early 19th-century economists began to phrase it, diminishing returns, with greater poverty, greater immorality, greater mortality among the poor, and so on and on. Contrary to popular opinion, Malthus was not in the grandstands cheering the Four Horsemen of the Apocalypse; if only the lower classes would postpone marriage until they could provide for children, then a population might grow within reasonable bounds. It was the human capacity for forethought and "calculating distant consequences" that afforded some hope for the future improvement of society. Malthus in his *Essay* pitted the Enlightenment ideals of reason and prudence against the traumatic *fin de siècle* experience of mob passions (revolutionary crowds in France, food rioters in England, lynch mobs in the United States) and the *fin de siècle* fear of uncontrollable acceleration.[207]

Even with reason and prudence on our part, history might pass us by, all of us, as it had passed by innumerable species of animals who lay buried as fossils beneath our very feet. Or the Earth itself might cool to uninhabitability: in ninety-three thousand years, estimated the most widely read naturalist of the late 18th century, the Comte de Buffon. Or, through impiety and war, we might exhaust ourselves, dwindling to a last, infertile man, Omegarus, and a last woman, Syderia. So wrote the French pulpit orator Cousin de Grainville between 1798 and 1805 in *Le dernier homme* or *The Last Man*, who then drowned himself in a canal at Amiens, another victim of the *mal du siècle* described by Charles Nodier that year in *Les Tristes*, drawn from the fictive memoirs of a suicide. Or the plague would take a world grown decrepit, and the few survivors would stand "equal sharers of the last throes of time-worn nature," says Mary Shelley's last man, Lionel Verney, in the desert ruins of Rome at "the end of all—the single point in which, as a pyramid, the mighty fabric of society had ended, while I, on the giddy height, saw vacant space around me." Shelley, born in 1797, published *The Last Man* in 1826, but it was insistently a work of century's end, keyed back to Schiller's dramatic poem of 1798, *Wallenstein* ("Yet I would not call *them* / Voices of warning that announce to us / Only the inevitable") and keyed forward to the year 2099, during which Verney completes his memorial to an extinct species, mankind. "In the old out-worn age, the Sovereign Pontiff was used to go in solemn pomp and mark the renewal of the year by driving a nail in the gate of the temple of Janus. On that [New Year's] day I ascended St. Peter's, and carved on its topmost stone the aera 2100, last year of the world!"[208]

At the end of the 18th century, Rome's ruins already seemed worn out. The ruins of Egypt, Palestine, Syria, and Persia were rediscovered. New ruins were built for German grounds and English gardens. Poets wrote in and about country ruins. Gothic novelists encrusted their plots with mysterious castellated ruins. Painters set young girls to dancing around ruined obelisks. "All men have a secret attraction to ruins," Chateaubriand declared from among the Christian ruins of the Middle East. There too began the Comte de Volney with *The Ruins, or, Meditation on the Revolutions of Empires* in 1791. The Corinthian ruins of Palmyra in Syria posed the question, "Will the Human Race Improve?" To which Volney replied, yes, it will, given a new spirit of civilization, religious tolerance, and social progress toward the construction of a new political "pyramid of the legislators" to replace the decaying pyramids, literal and figurative, of past centuries.[209]

Ruins were admonitions against cupidity and ignorance, they were sensible reminders of hubris, but during the 1790s they were not a terminus, they did not represent an inviolable limit to human achievement. Rather, like the six volumes of Edward Gibbon's *Decline and Fall of the Roman Empire* (1776–88), they were monuments to an historically progressive cycle of decay and uplift, such that Gibbon could write as peroration, "the experience of four thousand years should enlarge our hopes, and diminish our apprehensions; we cannot determine to what height the human species may aspire in their advances towards perfection; but it may safely be presumed that no people, unless the face of nature is changed, will relapse into their original barbarism. . . . We may therefore acquiesce in the pleasing conclusion that every age of the world has increased, and still increases, the real wealth, the happiness, the knowledge, and perhaps the virtue, of the human race." This was also the conclusion reached by Antoine Nicolas de Condorcet in 1794 in his *Sketch for a Historical Picture of the Progress of the Human Mind*, though Condorcet was more strident in his belief "that nature has set no term to the perfection of human faculties; that the perfectibility of man is truly indefinite; and that the progress of this perfectibility . . . has no other limit than the duration of the globe upon which nature has cast us."[210]

Nay, that progress might continue beyond our globe to the many other inhabited planets, and our globe, "should it be entirely annihilated, would be no more missed, by an eye that could survey all creation, than a handful of sand taken from the sea shore, or a cup of water from the ocean." Thus Abraham Bradley of Pennsylvania, in his *New Theory of the Earth; or, the*

Present World Created in the Ruins of an Old World (1801). If the best remedy for the motion sickness of the *mal du siècle* was an unshakable faith in progress, then nowhere could the cure better be taken than in the New World, which had indeed been created out of (away from) the ruins of the Old. Or so thought many a citizen of the United States, to whom and to which the mantle of civilization was passing as westward the course of empire took its way. "This is probably the last peculiar people which [the Lord] means to form, and the last great empire which he means to erect, before the kingdoms of this world are absorbed in the Kingdom of Christ," claimed Nathanael Eamons, D.D., as president of the Massachusetts Missionary Society in 1800.[211]

At century's end in the United States there was in consequence relatively little of the *mal du siècle* endemic to Europe. The wayward course of the French Revolution had shocked and disappointed republicans in America, and spread "a cloud of gloomy uncertainty and apprehension" over the brilliant future, but the sun shone bright for most—even in the isolation of Marietta, Ohio, where the Reverend Manasseh Cutler in 1798 was giving his Charge to Daniel Story, the first regularly ordained and settled Congregationalist minister west of the Alleghenies. Cutler was inspired to behold "a country which was lately, very lately, a howling wilderness, the gloomy abode of numerous savage tribes," now "so rapidly changing into cultured fields, inhabited by civil and well-regulated societies . . . illumined by the pure and benevolent religion of the gospel." Howling wilderness tamed was an old trope of America's errand thereunto. Cutler however went further, impressed by Marietta's Indian mounds. "I can not forbear reminding you, my dear sir, that on the very ground where you are stately to dispense the gospel you behold those ancient ruins, those extended walls and elevated mounds, which were erected many years ago." Present natives might recall nothing of the manner of building these earthworks, but an evangelical Christian might well establish the gospel among these American ruins. Farther west, lifted by a squadron of seraphic warriors to a mountaintop in the middle of North America, a pseudonymous patriot saw on the western horizon a land of united nations, "a French, a Spanish, a Dutch, an Irish, an English, &c. yea, a Jewish State, here in process of time.—And all of them united in brotherly affection, will at last form the most potent empire on the face of the earth."[212]

Such millennial puffery did not obscure the drama of century's turn. In the United States too, the year 1800 was experienced as peculiarly interregnal, peculiarly critical. "With you, sir," the House of Representatives responded to President John Adams on December 9, 1799, "we deem the present period critical and momentous," and the period continued critical and momentous through to the spring of 1801. Momentous was the death of George Washington on December 14, 1799; critical was the presidential election in the fall and winter of 1800.[213]

Washington's death came with utmost convenience within cannonshot of the end of the century, as if he intended thereby a dignified finis to an epoch: "In the century past, a Washington was born (alas! that he should die in the same!)." His doctors, who had treated the General's bad sore throat with four copious bleedings, three doses of calomel (a strong emetic), two blisters, an enema, and a cataplasm of bran and vinegar, insisted immediately and publicly that "He was fully impressed at the beginning of his complaint . . . that its conclusion would be mortal," that he had "anticipated his approaching dissolution with every demonstration of that equanimity, for which his whole life has been so uniformly and singularly conspicuous," and that he had *"expired without a struggle!"* Elegists and hagiographers took up this image of the great man's calm death, in pain, but "not a sigh, not a groan escaped him; and with undisturbed serenity he closed his well spent life." His last words were reputed to have been, "I would take leave," and the 18th century would take leave with him. Thirty days of national mourning, black silk gowns, and crepe armbands entirely eclipsed the centurial celebrations scheduled by partisans of 1799 as the last year of the century, but with Washington's departure, 1800 began as a symbolic year of transition to a new era, and a new century. Diarists, correspondents, orators rarely commented on the passage of 1799 into 1800; they were too preoccupied with the news of the tranquil passage of George Washington, "the great Occidental political luminary" for whom a distinctly oriental mausoleum was proposed, a pyramid of American granite and marble, one hundred feet square at the base.[214]

Although this monumental masonry was deferred, slenderized, exalted, interrupted, and delayed for eighty years, a pyramid had already appeared on the Great Seal of the United States, with a Masonic all-seeing eye at its tip and beneath its base the motto (legible still on the back of the dollar bill), *NOVUS ORDO SECLORUM*, new order of the ages. Fisher Ames, writing to a fellow Federalist on January 26, 1801, after the Republican Thomas Jefferson had at length won the presidential election, conflated new century (*saeculum*) and new political order: "The *novus ordo seclorum* must not begin with an impression on the popular mind that we are a disgraced if we are a disappointed party." Electoral college votes had been tied between

Jefferson and Aaron Burr; it took thirty-six ballots in the House of Representatives for the tie to be broken in Jefferson's favor and the political tide
to turn from the party of Burr, John Adams, and Fisher Ames, the party
of the 1790s, to Jefferson and a party for the start of the 19th century. The
centurial phrasing here is my own, but I am keeping company with a column
in New York's *Spectator* of January 1, 1801: "At the close of the Eighteenth
Century, and near the close of the Third Presidency in the American Admin-
istration, events have taken place that have excited no small surprise among
men who are considered as possessing great political discernment. Men
wonder! and speculate! They are surprised at the issue of the election, and
look about them for the causes that have defeated their calculations." Some
Federalists were more than surprised; like Lewis Beebe at his Philadelphia
diary early in 1801, they were terrified—of that "infidel" Jefferson, of the
democrats he represented ("the legitimate offspring of the Devil"), and of
the likelihood of apocalypse: "I think it rational to suppose, by scripture
prophecy; that from this time, to the commencement of the Milennium,
there will be nothing but wars, revolutions, & overturnings amongst all the
nations of the earth." Jeffersonians, meanwhile, were exultant at the prospects for a true *novus ordo seclorum*: "Every [R]epublican will, undoubtedly,
behold with peculiar satisfaction in the opening of a new century, a new era
marked in the political annals of the United States."[215]

As the last days of 1799 and the first days of 1800 had been distinguished
by rituals commemorating the passage of the founding father, so the last
days of 1800 and the first days of 1801 were distinguished by private anxieties
and public suspense over a critical test of constitutional mechanisms for the
passage of political power from one party to another. The young nation
weathered this trial as successfully as the celebrated Don Pedro Cloris must
have negotiated the slack wire, performing "Graceful and manly Feats" in
Washington Hall, in Salem, Massachusetts, on New Year's Day, 1801.[216]

Of the dozens of century sermons delivered around the country that
Thursday or the following Sunday, not a few took as their subject the Etruscan
theme of generational mortality at century's end, citing Ecclesiastes 1.4:
"One generation passeth away, and another generation cometh: but the earth
abideth forever." Some were Claudian sticklers, reviewing the events of the
hundred years exactly past, in the custom of sermons upon a church centennial, or contrasting the howling wilderness of 1701 with the cultivated
society of 1801. Many were confidently Augustan, drawing upon civic millenarian motifs of America as the avant-garde of a new age. The Reverend
Benjamin Trumbull led his New Haven congregation through all three

"Portrait of a Calculating Gentleman (not at all a bad looking chap) who has solved the problem as to whether we are in the Nineteenth or Twentieth Century." From *Punch* (January 10, 1900).

traditions. The Etruscan: "Wonderful, tremendous mortality!!! What an astonishing current of souls is rapidly borne on the tide of time, incessantly shooting into the ocean of eternity, and appearing before GOD, in judgment!" The Claudian: "The improvements of the last century, in philosophy, astronomy, mathematics, language, physic, the fine arts, navigation, commerce, and manufacture have exceeded all former precedent." The Augustan: "We are now advanced to a new year and century. The events of it will be vast and momentous. . . . From past and present appearances, and from a general view of the prophecies [which tell us we are now under the pouring out of the last part of the sixth vial of the Apocalypse], the present century will be one of the most eventful and interesting periods in which GOD, in rapid succession, will be carrying into execution his judgments against his enemies." America, protected by a series of remarkable providences, blessed by a Great Awakening in the 1740s and a late awakening this two or three years past, would surely be at the forefront of the Christian conversion of the globe.[217]

One nation after another would claim the 19th century for its own: France, by reason of its Napoleozoic era; Germany, by the extent of its cultural hegemony, from Beethoven's First Symphony (1800) onward through the "Ode to Joy"; Great Britain, by courtesy of the imperial length of Queen Victoria's reign; and the United States, by virtue of its youth, its temper, its mission to the West and to the world. If the 19th century began with an emotional debate over its effective beginning, if the centurial year of 1800 was a year of profound uneasiness and suspense, this was in good measure because the stakes were so high. The century's turn had become a pivotal moment in the definition of national destinies.

R*PTURE: THE 1890s

ON THE FIRST DAY OF THE FIRST YEAR OF THE 19TH CENTURY, Giuseppe Piazzi, an Italian astronomer, caught sight of a small uncatalogued star which, he discovered, was in fact a planet. His discovery was confirmed on the last day of the year, December 31, 1801, and the planet was named Ceres. Ceres was just where it ought to have been. According to Bode's Law that "the distance of the successive planets from the orbit of Mercury increases in a twofold proportion," there ought to be a planet in the vast reaches between the orbits of Mars and Jupiter, twice as far from Mars as Mars was from Earth. And so, short by a decimal tenth, there it was.[218]

Ceres, it was soon determined, is an asteroid, and the German astronomer Johann Bode could not have known in 1766 that his Law would fail to account for the orbits of the outermost (and yet undiscovered) planets, Neptune and Pluto. Nevertheless, we may use Piazzi's planet and Bode's Law as keynotes to the end of the 19th century, whose citizens looked out toward Mars with a dreadful curiosity, and who found themselves caught up in the toils of many a geometric progression.

On the dot in 1801 appeared the first magazine explicitly of the new century: *Eumonia: eine Zeitschrift des neunzehnten Jahrhunderts*—"a Journal of the Nineteenth Century." The 18th century had entertained no *Eighteenth Century* periodical, no Eighteenth Century Club. The 19th century was far more self-conscious, with a New Century Fire Society in Boston in 1801, a Nineteenth Century Club in New York City, *La revue du XIXe siècle* in Paris in 1836, a quarterly miscellany, *The Nineteenth Century*, in Philadelphia in 1848, another, *The Nineteenth Century*, in Charleston, South Carolina, in 1869, and, starting in 1877, London's prestigious *The Nineteenth Century*, which journal became, on the stroke of midnight, December 31, 1900, *The Nineteenth Century . . . and After*, Janus facing back and forth on the title page of the first issue of the new century.

Other publishers were less reticent than those of *The Nineteenth Century . . . and After* to wave the banner of the next century, less hesitant to greet the year 1900 than an ailing Henry James ("This dreadful gruesome New Year, so monstrously numbered, makes me turn back to the warm and coloured past and away from the big black avenue that gapes in front of us") or a bitter Mark Twain ("The 20th Century is a stranger to me—I wish it well but my heart is all for my own century. I took 65 years of it, just on a risk, but if I had known as much about it as I know now I would have taken the whole of it"). During the 1890s the Rand McNally Company had already issued a Twentieth Century Series of popular fiction in 167 volumes, Humboldt Publishers a Twentieth Century Library in 60 volumes, W. Wood & Company a medical series on Twentieth Century Practice in 21 volumes, Appleton a Twentieth Century Text-Books series in 4 volumes. A Twentieth Century Club was founded in Boston as early as 1894; its leading lights were the philosopher and historian John Fiske, who would die on Independence Day, 1901, and the Unitarian minister and orator Edward Everett Hale, whose *Memories of a Hundred Years* would appear in 1902. Their Twentieth Century Club of the 1890s was so named "not because such a title was catchy and at that time unworn, but to give the club mission and character as progressive, in sympathy with the advancing spirit of brotherhood in the world." Men *and* women of the Twentieth Century Club, committed to public service and a better social order, beautified Boston, sponsored organ recitals, attended evening lectures, and "conceived and brought about the most remarkable end-of-the-century celebration . . . witnessed anywhere in Christendom."[219]

Later, we will hear from some eyewitnesses to that celebration. For the time being, we must do a little slide and backstep in order to appreciate the unusual extent to which the 20th century was anxiously anticipated by citizens of the 19th. Back past a *New Century Cookbook* published a bit prematurely in 1899 by Chicago's Wesley Hospital Cook Book Committee. Past a San Diego theosophical magazine, *The New Century*, first issued in 1897 by Katherine A. Tingley as part of a cosmic enterprise to "construct practically a new 'order of the ages,' " and past the *New Century Review* printed by the Unicorn Press of London, with its faith that "to be young at the beginning of the twentieth century, with all the marvels it must surely unfold, would be almost the greatest blessing and the highest privilege." Past some *Forecasts of the Coming Century* by a decade of English trade unionists, artists, dramatists, and feminists asked in 1896 by the Committee of the Labour Press to expostulate upon the future of socialism and shout goodbye "to the timid, shrinking, fragile, blushing miss of seventeen, who fainted more or less gracefully at least once in each volume of the [19th-century] novel." Back past Henry B. Brown's address on "The Twentieth Century" to the graduating class of Yale Law School, June 24, 1895, opposed to socialism and afraid that labor and capital were dangerously irreconcilable. Past an occasional journal, *Das 20. Jahrhundert*, edited in 1894 by the German novelist Heinrich Mann, older brother of Thomas (whose own first novel, *Buddenbrooks*, would appear at century's turn). Back past an 1890 reviewer for *The Literary World*, certain that "books on the 20th or 21st century are getting to be so numerous that the whole subject will soon be a deadly bore." Past *The Dawn of the Twentieth Century, 1st January, 1901* in 1888, from a series of rosy British government reports to the effect that "our vast Colonial Commonwealth [will be] consolidated and secure." Back past *The Great Crisis from 1890 to 1901, Comprising Fifteen Coming Events* and the *End of This Age about the End of This Century*, according to the editor of England's *Christian Herald* in 1887; "we are living in the rapids of the stream of Time," wrote Michael Paget Baxter, "and are fast approaching the downfall of the kingdoms of this world, and the consequent establishment of Christ's Millennial Kingdom." Past Mme. Helena Blavatsky, theosophist extraordinaire, unveiling Isis and the Secret Doctrine, who agreed: "We are in 1887 and the nineteenth century is close to its death. The twentieth century has strange developments in store for humanity, and may even be the last of its name." Back, back, back, to the prize oration of John R. Mott on the subject, "Our Debt to the Twentieth Century," delivered to the Methodist student body of Upper Iowa University, Fayette, June 1885. "Our debt to the twentieth century," speechified the future secretary of the International YMCA at the optimistic age of twenty, "consists in preserving unimpaired for it all the links in the chain of progress which have been entrusted to our care, and in the welding on a link of our own."[220]

Already, in 1885, it felt like the end of the century. Antichrist or the Beast of the Apocalypse had not perished in 1866/67, as had figured many a millenarian exegete since the days of Isaac Newton. Nor had Mother Shipton, a 16th-century sibyl, called the shot with her (new) couplet, insinuated by Charles Hindley into her collected doggerel in 1862,

The world to an end shall come
In eighteen hundred and eighty-one.

But the world of the 19th century did seem to have come to its end shortly after that. In 1883 in Paris, a scattering of anarchistic artists, the Incohérents, had seen the century to its sickbed with their parodic exposition of drawings by people who did not know how. In 1884 Joris-Karl Huysmans, a career clerk in the French Ministry of the Interior, published *A rebours (Against Nature)*, a novel whose central yet minor character had lost all hope in his own times, winging away from the cankered century "to the land of dreams, seeking refuge in extravagant illusions, living alone and apart, far from the present-day world, in an atmosphere suggestive of more cordial epochs and less odious surroundings." In 1885 the century lay on its deathbed, mourned under the Arc de Triomphe at the funeral, wake, elegy, and orgy for its most representative Frenchman, Victor Hugo, born almost at its start, eighty-three years before.[221]

Late in 1885 *fin de siècle* made its popular debut as a single phrase, a phrase at first descriptive of personal manner and carriage, then of the manners and carriage of the epoch itself. "To be *fin de siècle*," explained one French article in 1886, "is to be no longer responsible; it is to resign oneself in a nearly fatal fashion to the influence of the times and environs. . . . It is to languish with one's century, to decay along with it." A French play of 1888, *Fin de siècle*, began appropriately in a waiting room, made its desultory way through an exotic salon overseen by a statue of the Buddha above a circular divan, and climaxed with a murderer's sardonic laughter when accused of being insane. The moral was either that life is "a rather sick pleasantry" or that "Should Jesus Christ, Mahomet, Charlemagne or Napoleon reappear today, they wouldn't last a week." The most a *fin de siècle* (and faithless) individual could muster was *emballement*, flights of temper. Or suicide: Humbert de Gallier's 1889 novel, *Fin de siècle*, followed a rich young man from ennui through gambling to death at his own hands. The same for *fin de siècle* society: "*Fin de siècle*, end of the century, end of European culture," concluded a character in an 1891 German novel, *Müde Seelen (Weary Souls)*, while the influential German philosopher of history, Wilhelm Dilthey, wrote to a friend, "Our time has something about it of the end of an epoch. One sign thereof is the disappearance of an elemental joy in historical reality." Oscar Wilde's Dorian Gray, escaping that reality by transposing all age to his portrait so that he might keep his youth, has this dinner-table exchange with Lord Henry Wotton and Lady Narborough, who says,

> "Nowadays all the married men live like bachelors, and all the bachelors live like married men."
> "*Fin du siècle*," murmured Lord Henry.
> "*Fin du globe*," answered his hostess.
> "I wish it were *fin du globe*," said Dorian, with a sigh. "Life is a great disappointment."

On the last pages of the book, Dorian slashes at the portrait to kill the past of which it is such a grotesque reminder, only to die, as it were, of his own *fin de siècle*, a murderer and a suicide.[222]

Across the globe, in the United States, where life was not quite so great a disappointment, what with Horatio Alger's boys always rising to the honest occasion, and where the past was not nearly so grotesque a burden, despite the salted wounds of the Civil War, there too an editorialist for the *Atlantic Monthly* could find in 1891 that "Everywhere we are treated to dissertations on fin-de-siècle literature, fin-de-siècle statesmanship, fin-de-siècle morality. . . . People seem to take for granted that a moribund century implies, not to say excuses, disenchantment, languor, literary, artistic, and political weariness, and that in 1901 the world will make a fresh start." Even then, in 1901, the phrase was hard to lay aside. An editorialist for the *Century* wrote, "It is yet to be revealed whether the sentiment of a century's commencement will call forth a phrase as apt and catching as that which has expressed, in certain minds, the sentiment of the close of an era." *Fin de siècle* had stood proud and alone as the title of French plays, a French novel, a French financial weekly turned scandal sheet, a German ballet, a Hungarian newspaper, an American publisher's series of "Operettas, Exhibition Drills, Special Day Exercises, and Spectacular Entertainments" for grammar schools. How inconsiderately abrupt must be its departure: "The people who tell us that a century is merely an arbitrary division of time with no ethical significance are poor observers. Else would they have noticed a cataclysm of Nature which synchronised with the end of the year 1900. Suddenly, absolutely, the Woman with a Past disappeared from the stage. It is remarkable. We called her *fin-de-siècle*. The century finishes and she no longer exists."[223]

The editor of London's *Fun* magazine continued in an equally serious vein, "As the new century grows older, poisonous growths may again appear." This was not morbid wit; it was the lingering reflection of a new sense of century's end. There was something about the approach of the calendrical '00 that made for an epoch-in-waiting during the "Nineties," which were at once an endtime and a betweentime, years of nervousness, decadence, boredom and thrill-seeking, suicide and Ferris wheels, faithlessness and occult philosophies, anarchy and artificiality—all that behavior called by 1902 "manic-depressive." More than "a fashionable 'gag,' indicating the supposed moral, intellectual, and political disintegration attendant on a moribund century," the *fin de siècle* seemed now to be a distinct, recurrent, full-bodied historical period, half Etruscan, half Claudian. "We are living in the end not merely of a century . . . but of an era," wrote one essayist who dated the beginning of his era to the death of George IV in 1830 and the accession of Victoria to the British throne. "The close of the century must, alas!, just see out the generation which witnessed the beginning of this era." The Etruscan motif of the end of a generation as the end of a *saeculum* and the Claudian motif of centuries in sequences of exact hundreds of years would merge in 1900 upon the deaths of Oscar Wilde, John Ruskin, Arthur Sullivan, Friedrich Nietzsche, and be absolutely united upon the death of Queen Victoria in January 1901. Yet a decade before, at the start of the never-so-gay Nineties, it was already logical to suppose that every century had its *fin de siècle*, during which the old generation met its Maker and a younger generation waited impatiently or despondently upon the funeral and wake of '00 and '01.[224]

The new phrase, insisted Berlin journalist and philologist Fritz Mauthner in his 1890/91 essays on *fin de siècle* as adjective and presumptive noun, had begun as a rather empty reference to some vague anticipations of the century's end, but the very act of giving a name to those anticipations had made possible a way of thinking about one's time that had been unavailable before. Originally an allusion to indeterminate feelings, *fin de siècle* had become an active agent for historical thought. Mauthner was developing a philosophy of language, of which Ludwig Wittgenstein would soon be the peerless exponent, that knowledge and perception are tightly interlaced with language, and that their horizons expand only and conjointly with new acts of naming. Himself beset with inescapable feelings of culmination and threshold, Mauthner was impressed that *fin de siècle* had arrived a decade in advance of the next century. He was eager "to outfit for the twentieth century" by rethinking the common past, which meant reconsidering the language in which that past had been cast.[225]

Never before, according to such a functionalist philosophy of language, could anyone have conceived of earlier *fin de siècle* epochs, for only in the 1890s had such epochs become thinkable, courtesy of the new phrase. This was in fact the case. When Elhanan Winchester, preaching in London in 1788, exceeded the bounds of the century sermon by addressing himself to 1588 as well as 1688, he had in mind not a recurrent epoch but coincidental providences: the sinking of the Spanish Armada in 1588, the Glorious Revolution in 1688, and in 1788 a twelve-shot pistol. The time had come, however, in 1892, for the readers of *La nouvelle revue* and the *Chautauquan* to consider, with Charles Louis Stanislas, Count de Moüy, "if centenary periods have not often covered the natural duration of certain developments of civilization; . . . if they have not sometimes taken on the aspect of that plant which, having concentrated all its force during long years to one end, at last produces the one supreme flower, which is immediately followed by its death." At the end of the 16th century, religious faith had been overcome by wild superstition; at the end of the 17th century, a vigorous aristocracy had grown senile, a good king cruel; at the end of the 18th century, the grand dreams of the Enlightenment had been lost in the gutter of puerile utopias. And in this 19th-century *fin de siècle*, the world was "undergoing a decadence which is too marked to deny, which is slowly transforming its polity into confused hesitations and sterile agitations, which makes of literature a field of tares with poisonous plants scattered thickly through it; which dares to boast in painting of a false school of daubers without ideas, without design, and without color; which takes delight in pleasure, in luxury, in paradoxical theories, and in that studied unconsciousness which has brought ruin to all the great empires."[226]

We might dismiss the Count's castigation of the 1890s as aristocratic sour grapes were it not that he had raised "the old mechanical jeremiad that has been raised by every age almost," as a 1901 reviewer remarked and as another proceeded to demonstrate by quoting from like-sounding attacks on "the grievous habits of latter-day women" at the ends of the 19th, 18th, 17th, 16th centuries . . . back to Horace's "What has not cankering time made worse?" "This," noted the reviewer, "was written shortly before the year one and carries the *fin-de-siècle* degeneracy even beyond the Christian era." Others carried it forward again, less from personal grudge than from devout concern to make the years at each century's end as historically significant as the years leading up to 1900 must also turn out to be, from the first Christmas celebration in 98 A.D., to Diocletian's reorganization of the Roman Empire in 300, to the fall of Rome around 400, the imperial coronation of Charlemagne in 800, the death of Alfred the Great in 900, the crowning of Otto III around 1000, the Jubilee of 1300, the Bank of Genoa in 1401, the discovery of America around 1500, the golden age of Queen Elizabeth in 1600, the Bank of England in 1694, the first high silk hat in 1797 and Napoleon riding over the Alps in 1800, to Charles E. Tripler's liquid air perpetual motion machine of the 1890s.[227]

It would follow, and it did follow, from the janiform nature of century's turn, that a Cornelius B. Bradley, speaking before the Berkeley Club in California in 1901, would explain the obvious and expatiate upon the obverse. If the *fin de siècle* was a genuine, recurrent historical period, so the very first years of each century were also invariably of one piece. They were inspired years, making good on all the buried hopes of the naughty Nineties for a new era in Naught-One. "[O]ur centuries, as we know, are mere fortuitous units of measure," Bradley quabbled in deference to an old scholar or two at the club. "Yet how strange it is that, as we look back over the nineteen hundred years of our era, we find the events of real significance and moment somehow clustering about these milestones which we have set up to keep us from losing our way! There is the great defeat of the Roman legions under Varus at the very opening of the count—prophetic of long centuries of losing battle for the old world-order, and the passing of the sceptre to a new race." At the end of each century an old order passed; at the start of each century a new order dawned. "The Century is dead. Long live the Century!"[228]

Maurice Ravel's "Pavane for a Dead Infanta" (1899) behind them, Pablo Picasso's *La fin du numéro (End of the Number)* completed in 1900 in the style of Toulouse-Lautrec, who would die in 1901 in strange tandem with Queen Victoria and President McKinley, the Western world was free to enjoy the sousaphone, Peter Rabbit, Teddy Roosevelt, Marconi's wireless transmissions, Isadora Duncan's barefoot dancing, the Count von Zeppelin's dirigible balloons, and James Gordon Bennett's auto races. So swiftly had people shifted gears from the 19th century into the 20th that on January 2, 1901, *Puck*, the American counterpart to *Punch*, was moved to observe, "Centuries, nowadays, die younger than they used to. When it was first caught and harnessed to the calendar, Time was heavy-footed; so slow that the centuries died of senile old age. A century in its last days held but musty memories even of its middle life!" Came writing, and the printing press, almanacs, newspapers, and "the centuries took to diaries. So, here is this 19th century going off in its lusty prime," chock full of the freshest memories of its youth a brief hundred years before. In San Francisco, cyclists rode circles around the end of the 19th century. At the head of the pack, Fred West of the Bay City Wheelmen finished the first 20th-century century (of miles) in the first nine hours thirty-five minutes of 1901.[229]

As we have seen, in the precocious speech of John R. Mott and the preemptive strike of the *fin de siècle*, the new century (of years) had been widely anticipated since at least '85. During the Nineties, if something *au courant* was not already dubbed "twentieth-century," it was surely "modern" or "new": the New Woman, the new journalism, the new morality, Art Nouveau, the *Neuen Welt*. An abrupt, heartless dismissal of the 1800s and an instantaneous welcome to the 1900s was therefore to be expected.[230]

The old century had been further hurried to its conclusion by two world's fairs, Chicago's Columbian Exposition of 1892/93 and the Paris Exhibition of 1900. Both were promoted—and experienced—as midways toward a new era. The Columbian Exposition meant, indeed, to be something of its own Millennium, a howling wilderness tamed, a White City erected on 666(!) acres of swamp and marsh along the shore of Lake Michigan, a New Jerusalem in the New World discovered by Columbus four hundred years before. Theatrical visionary Steele MacKaye proposed a Spectatorium with twenty-five telescopic stages in full view of nine thousand people watching a six-act historical drama, *The Great Discovery, or the World Finder*, accompanied by full orchestra and an epic score. The Spectatorium was begun but never completed; the score, commissioned of Antonin Dvořák, became his *New World Symphony*. A welcoming address to the first World Parliament of Religions, held at the fair, promised that "If this Congress shall faithfully execute the duties with which it has been charged, it will become a joy of the whole earth, and will stand in human history like a new Mount Zion, crowned with glory and marking the actual beginning of a new epoch of brotherhood and peace." Taking a ride on George Washington Gale Ferris's gigantic revolving wheel, Hezekiah Butterworth figured that "We shall see the whole earth soon." It was, said another, "the beginning of an Olympian era," and even a dour Swede, socialist Fredrik Karlsson, looked for the Exposition to be "not only the most typical, but also the last of the bourgeoisie's great triumphal festivals."[231]

Despite labor agitation, anarchist dramas, and capital violence throughout Europe and the Americas; despite attempts upon the lives of the Prince of Wales, the German Emperor, and the Shah of Persia, and the assassination of King Umberto of Italy; despite the uproar over the Dreyfus trials, despite everything, fifty million of the bourgeoisie shared in another triumphal festival in 1900. The Paris Exhibition was centennial in its history, millennial in its horizon. The first national industrial exhibition anywhere had been mounted in Paris in 1798, its facades designed by the neoclassical painter Jacques Louis David; the exhibition a century later "probably was the largest and most ambitious international gathering for any purpose ever," and its Old Paris facades were designed by Albert Robida, who drew futuristic scenes of the 20th century after declaring that "nearly all centuries end badly, [and] ours appears to follow the common law." If not an aesthetic triumph, the Paris Exhibition was a triumph of electricity, from the moving sidewalk (too loud and shaky for seven-year-old Pauline de Broglie) to the immense dynamos of the German industrial hall (most impressive to young American physicist Robert Millikan) to the Spirit of Electricity danced by Loie Fuller, her silks, and her scarves. The fair and the year would be written of as the turning point from the dark, dirty world of coal to the bright, clean, magical world of electricity. Subterranean grottoes of dinosaurs frightened Pauline into the perils of measles, but for the young artist Paula Modersohn-Becker, in Paris for the first time at age twenty-four, visiting the pavilions was a singular event of her *fin de siècle*: "I was at the Exhibition yesterday and today. These days clearly form an epoch in my life."[232]

Monet, Degas, Renoir, Pisarro, Cézanne were ignored by the directors of the French galleries at the Exhibition. What must catch our eye is the archway to the United States pavilion, a sorry attempt at the Pantheon. There, above a modern, efficient linoleum floor, was sculpted the Goddess of Liberty in her Chariot of Progress. To be sure, visitors at every major fairground since London's Crystal Palace in 1851 had been escorted through national buildings by some Chariot of Progress or another, but at century's end a truly imprudent hyperbole of progress was making the rounds not only of the Paris Exhibition but in almost every retrospective in every newspaper and on every podium. The 19th century had been (of course) a century of progress—especially in the United States, grown from sixteen states in

1800 to forty-five in 1900, from nine hundred thousand square miles to almost four million, from a population of five million to seventy-six million, and from no gold medals in 1800 to six hundred (well, 597) at this Paris Exhibition, not counting those its athletes would win at the concurrent Olympics. Out of America had come the air brake, the phonograph, the bicycle, the torpedo, the cash register, and cottonseed oil. One hundred years ago there had been no savings banks, steamships, railroads, streetcars, telephones, telegraphs, harvesting machines, threshers, cotton gins, cooking ranges, sewing machines, typewriters, electric lights, illuminating gas, photographs, adhesive postage stamps . . . and the list went on. For Edward W. Byrn, reviewing *The Progress of Invention in the Nineteenth Century*, the comparison of the start of the century with the end of the century was "like the juxtaposition of a star with the noonday sun." Frank B. Parsons of the Boston University School of Law found that it was difficult "even to imagine the difference of conditions now and in the early years of the century." Wrote a columnist for the *Evening Star* of Washington, D.C., "Whatever the future may bring, the nineteenth century must be looked upon as a turning point in the history of the world. In material achievement it has surpassed every century that preceded it."[233]

This language was not confined to Americans at century's end, and we have heard the same sort of superlatives directed toward the "unparalleled" 18th century in retrospectives dated 1801. The truly imprudent hyperbole went a giant step beyond such centurial boosterism to claim that "not only is our century superior to any that have gone before it, but . . . it may be best compared with the whole preceding historical period," as the British naturalist Alfred Russel Wallace wrote before launching a socialist attack on the failures of the century. Popular historian Jane de Forest Shelton in 1892 was being timid when she noted that "There is said to be more difference between Napoleon's day and ours than between Napoleon's and Julius Caesar's. One century against eighteen!" More often it was one century against the rest: "In the actual gain made in the realm of science [and of ethics] the nineteenth century is really comparable, not with any one century preceding, but with all recorded history"; "the nineteenth century has achieved triumphs and accomplished wonders equal, if not superior, to all other centuries combined." "Take it all in all," wrote the English intellectual Frederic Harrison, who may have been the first to take the 19th century all in all, "the merely material, physical, mechanical change in human life in the hundred years, from the days of Watt and Arkwright to our own, is greater than occurred in the thousand years that preceded, perhaps even in the two thousand years or twenty thousand years."[234]

The runaway inflation of rhetoric was due to a feeling that the times were racing ahead faster than ever before. The four horses pulling the Chariot of Progress at the entrance to the American pavilion in 1900 were wild horses, scarcely restrained by four exuberant neoclassical nudes. Words failed David J. Brewer in his effort to contrast 1800 with 1900 because there had been a "geometrical progression" at which this Associate Justice of the United States Supreme Court stood dumbfounded. Premature ejaculations in the 1880s and 1890s concerning the 20th century had been symptomatic of the *fin de siècle* dis-ease, acceleration. Brewer himself was dizzy enough to rhapsodize, "Who can describe man as he will be when he writes 1999? Fancy forgets her cunning and imagination's wings are not strong enough to soar to a full conception of what he shall then be."[235]

Brewer's dithyramb was matched by a Max Beerbohm cartoon in the *Daily Mail* which showed goggled Time speeding across the last day of the 19th century. "Father Time Outdone" had been the 1890 headline of the New York *World* after Nellie Bly circled Jules Verne's world in less than eighty days. In 1901 her record of seventy-two days was cut to less than sixty-one days by Charles Fitzmorris, and Joseph Pulitzer gave over his *World* for one day, January 1, 1901, to English publisher Alfred Harmsworth, who demonstrated what the newspaper of the 20th or "Time-Saving" century must be, its pledge "All the News in Sixty Seconds." According to the editor of the *Peking and Tientsin Times*, "Brevity is the soul of wit" would be the motto for the new century, "and anything which tends to annihilate space and time will take precedence of all else." Frederick W. Taylor's stopwatches had already begun to override customary work methods, "improving" industrial efficiency; pocket watches and clocks had already begun to determine the length of social intercourse—"five-minute interviews, minute-long telephone conversations, and five-second exchanges on bicycles." In San Francisco, at the Concordia Club New Year's (and new century's) banquet, the Nineteenth Century, a boy on a bicycle, was overtaken by the Twentieth Century, a young woman riding in an automobile, an effect so pretty it had to be repeated. Again and again, delighted audiences were horrified as trolley cars descended directly upon them in their seats in the new motion picture houses, millions thrilled to the ragtime syncopations of roller coasters in the new amusement parks, thousands cheered the treadmill chariot race during the 1899 run of *Ben Hur* at the Broadway Theatre amidst the new electric brilliance of that famous boulevard, and in parlors from Valparaiso to Vienna, Rimsky-Korsakov's "Flight of the Bumble Bee" was one of the most popular instrumentals of 1900.[236]

Not the buzz of the bee but the almost inaudible drone of the dynamo and the supersensual silence of x-rays excited Henry Adams, who had toiled for many of his sixty-one years to arrange the historical sequence of human affairs by biographies, or societies, or ideas, in some tolerable relation of cause and effect. In vain, until "he turned at last to the sequence of force; and thus it happened that, after ten years' pursuit, he found himself lying in the Gallery of Machines at the Great Exposition of 1900, his historical neck broken by the sudden irruption of forces totally new." There, in Paris, and then, at century's turn, Adams was struck by the first phosphors of his Law of Acceleration. The dynamic of history was the dynamic of the lines of force, understood as the perfusion of science and spirit. Western society had gathered force as force had gathered society, slowly from 1400 to 1800, then with "stupendous acceleration after 1800" which "ended in 1900 with the appearance of the new class of supersensual forces, before which the man of science stood at first as bewildered and helpless, as in the fourth century, a priest of Isis before the Cross of Christ." Robert Millikan, also impressed by the dynamos, chose to date the 20th century from January 1, 1896, and the notion of "electronics," but Adams opted for the historical squareness of decades, each decade since 1800 doubling, perhaps even quadrupling, the effective force of the previous decade until, "in 1900, the continuity snapped." Adams explained: "Vaguely conscious of the cataclysm, the world sometimes dated it from 1893, by the Roentgen rays, or from 1898, by the Curies' radium; but in 1904, Arthur Balfour announced on the part of British science that the human race without exception had lived and died in a world of illusion until the last year of the century. The date was convenient, and convenience was truth." The truth was that Balfour had organized a Synthetic Society to make orderly sense of the physical, spiritual, and psychical phenomena at century's end, and that this cataclysm of which Adams wrote was as much rapture as rupture. The slightly improper Bostonian on the floor of the Gallery of Machines could see that the American born since 1900, "the new American—the child of incalculable coal-power, chemical power, electric power, and radiating energy, as well as new forces yet undetermined—must be a sort of God compared with any former creation of nature. At the rate of progress since 1800, every American who lived in the year 2000 would know how to control unlimited power."[237]

Such progressive acceleration, such unlimited power could conduce to a better fit between the individual and the universal, although Adams himself, "an elderly and timid single gentleman in Paris, who never drove down the Champs Elysées without expecting an accident, and commonly witnessing one," was in doubt. The faster things and people moved, the smaller if not safer the world was. Telegraphs, telephones, transatlantic cables, transcontinental railroads were, some said, bringing people closer together. President of Columbia University Seth Low identified *The Trend of the Century* in 1899 as the "unification of the world, and its reduction in size from the point of view of commerce." The world atlas whose many vague and shadowy patches had been governed by mythical kingdoms and compound beasts in 1600, 1700, even 1800, had become gazetteers, definitive and rational (with a few exceptions at the poles and in Joseph Conrad's "Heart of Darkness"). Herbert Spencer, he of the Social Gospel of irreproachable evolutionary progress, was asked to write a little something on the Parliament of Man and the Federation of the World in answer to the question, "To what extent do the Events of the year 1901 foreshadow the Realization of this Ideal in the Twentieth Century?" That century might at last be the Century of Humanity, suggested an English socialist at Nelson Town Hall in November 1900, "meaning that its mission will be the moral welfare of the whole human family." Swami Vivekananda had concluded his address to the World Parliament of Religions at the Columbian Exposition with a global blessing, "May He who is the Brahma of the Hindus, the Ahura Mazda of the Zoroastrians, the Buddha of the Buddhists, the Jehovah of the Jews, the Father in Heaven of the Christians, give strength to you to carry out your noble idea" of an ecumenical world, and

> Lo! now on the midnight of the soul of the century passing
>   And on midnight the voice of the Lord! . . .
> "In the years that have been I have bound man closer to man,
>   And closer woman to woman;
> And the stranger hath seen in a stranger his brother at last,
>   And a sister in eyes that were strange.
> In the years that shall be I will bind me nation to nation
>   And shore unto shore," saith our God.

Thus wrote an English dramatic poet, Stephen Phillips, distant descendant of Wordsworth, in what was called "the weightiest of all the poetical ventures that have speeded the parting and welcomed the coming century."[238]

A weightier venture was Esperanto, a universal language explicitly intended by Ludwig Lazarus Zamenhof to unite a divided world. Born in 1859, Zamenhof was a Jewish oculist in Bialystok, where Russians, Poles, Germans, and Jews were kept apart by language as well as by faith and politics. Zamenhof's Esperanto (from "one who hopes") was not the first universal language of the 19th century—Jean François Sudre's Solresol or Universal Musical Language had been endorsed by Victor Hugo and awarded a prize at the Paris Exhibition of 1855—but it would be the most successful of the many *fin de siècle* simplified languages (Balta, Bopal, Dil, Orba, Spelin, Volapük) proposed to make the world safer and friendlier as it grew smaller. Clubs dedicated to Monsignor Johann Martin Schleyer's Volapük converted in the 1890s to Zamenhof's "Lingro Internacia" even if they did not convert in 1901 to Zamenhof's simplified version of a universally tolerant Judaism called (after the revered rabbi of the 1st century B.C.E.) Hillelism. Zamenhof soon changed the name of this ecumenical persuasion to Homaranismo ("member of the human race") and by 1909 could point to an Esperanto membership among the human race of nearly fifteen hundred local societies publishing ninety journals and reading more than one hundred books in his language. The British diplomat Oscar Browning attended a number of Esperanto congresses around the turn of the century, including one at Dresden where the whole city, festive with the nine hundred roots and sixteen rules of grammar, made bold to present *Iphigenia* in the original Esperanto.[239]

Another sort of universal language, more successful as drama, far more successful as a world enterprise, made its debut (or rather, its comeback) exactly at century's turn. British and American Protestants, in particular those filling the pews and camp meetings of the Holiness Movement, had been anticipating a new Pentecost since at least the 1880s. When the Evangelical Alliance of the United States met in Washington, D.C., in 1887, the assembly began by singing the hymn, "Come Gracious Spirit, Heavenly Dove," then reading Acts 2 ("And they were filled with the Holy Ghost, and began to speak with other tongues, as the Spirit gave them utterance"). A major conference on the Holy Spirit convened in Baltimore in 1890, one speaker favorably comparing the pentecostal "cloven tongues, like as of fire" to electricity and the ever impressive energy of the dynamo. In 1899 the millenarian evangelist Cyrus I. Scofield would claim with characteristic *fin de siècle* panache, "Indeed, within the last twenty years more has been written and said upon the doctrine of the Holy Spirit than in the preceding eighteen hundred years." Shortly before his death in December 1899, the transatlantic revivalist Dwight L. Moody professed, "I think it is getting very dark but don't think for a moment I am a pessimist. . . . Pentecost isn't over yet."[240]

Right he was. On the evening of December 31, 1900, in Topeka, Kansas, the Holy Spirit descended upon the forty students of Charles F. Parham's Bethel College. Parham had felt the call to the ministry when he was nine, but after years of leading Sunday School classes and doing some preaching, he left the Methodist Church in 1895 at the age of twenty-one, seeking after a more charismatic persuasion. He found himself drawn to "the third experience" of the Fire-Baptized Holiness Church, whose congregations moved beyond salvation and sanctification to baptisms of fire, of holy lyddite, holy oxidite, and holy dynamite. He went to visit the prophetic healer John Alexander Dowie, a shoe salesman who had seen the light in Australia, announced his universal mission in 1888, come to the United States, healed a cousin of Abraham Lincoln, and founded a theocratic Zion north of Chicago at the time of the Columbian Exposition. Parham also sought out the "Holy Ghost and Us" Society of Shiloh, Maine, enrolling in its missionary training school. Then he returned to Topeka, to his own Divine Healing Home (estab. 1898), to open a college whose sole text was the Bible and whose prime directive was worldwide evangelism.[241]

There, in Bethel's one building, Stone's Folly, patterned after an English castle, and then, on New Year's Eve of 1900/01, just as Dowie was unveiling a painting of the future city of Zion and revealing himself to be Elijah the Restorer, Pentecostalism began. "I had felt for years that any missionary going to the foreign field should preach in the language of the natives," Parham had said, and so he had set his students to studying the Bible evidence for Holy Ghost baptism. By 10:00 A.M. of December 31st, the students were reporting indisputable Biblical proof of speech in tongues, and that night Sister Agnes N. Ozman asked that hands be laid upon her to receive the Spirit, "as she hoped to go to foreign fields." Soon "a glory fell upon her, a halo seemed to surround her head and face," and she began to speak in Chinese. Within a week, Bethel students were gifted with twenty dialects of Chinese and twenty other tongues, among them Bulgarian, Norwegian, and Lillian Thistlewaite's childlike version of "Jesus is mighty to save, Jesus is ready to hear, God is love," which became "Euossa, Euossa use, relia sema cala mala kanah leullia sage nalan. Ligle logle lazle logle. Ene mene mo, sah rah el me sah rah me."[242]

While the pentecostal tongues (strangely akin to the new jazz scat-singing) spread from the white Watch-Nighters of Topeka to the black Holy Rollers of Los Angeles and out to other foreign fields in enthusiastic Christian fellowship, and while Esperanto crossed from Europe to the Americas as part of an oculist's Jewish vision of global understanding, a third sort of universal language was being put to work to make an accelerating world, if not more fervent or friendly, at least more pellucid and predictable: statistics. National censuses had been taken regularly since the late 18th century, Sweden and the United States leading the way. By the mid-19th century, under the sway of the "law of large numbers," the "normal" (or Gaussian) distribution, and an idealized "average man," positivists and utopian planners often considered the figures of statistics to be "like the hieroglyphics of ancient Egypt, where the lessons of history, the precepts of wisdom, and the secrets of the future were concealed in mysterious characters. They reveal the increase in the power of empire, the progress of arts and of civilization, and the ascent or retrogression of the European societies."[243]

Such faith in the collection and manipulation of large numbers contributed substantially to the discovery of sociohistorical "geometric progressions" in the 1890s, but during that *fin de siècle* a more complex, less deterministic approach to statistical data was taking shape among the cognoscenti. Rather than focusing on averages, they focused on interconnectedness. The English geniuses Francis Galton and Karl Pearson devised mathematical strategies for establishing percentiles, standard deviations, coefficients of correlation, and tests for the goodness of fit. Galton, who also labored over the problem of designing an interstellar language for signalling between Earth and any civilization on Mars, considered statistical analysis a beautiful means toward closing the gap between the possible and the probable, between youthful promise and adult performance, between nature and nurture. When Karl Pearson founded the journal *Biometrika* in 1901, Galton was delighted, for he believed that the "primary object of Biometry is to afford material that shall be exact enough for the discovery of incipient changes in evolution which are too small to be otherwise apparent." The organic world as a whole was "a perpetual flux of changing types," but out of this seeming chaos scientists using the mathematical tools of statistics might locate a momentary order and (hoped Galton) some indications toward the improvement of humankind.[244]

As the volume of raw data multiplied under the advance of the Baldwin calculating machines, the Burroughs adding machines, and the Hollerith punched-card controlled computing machines, the abundance of commercial and social statistics was further stimulus to the *fin de siècle* desire that all things come together in apocalypse (revelation or catastrophe) at century's end. Elaborating upon apocalypse had in the past been the forte of religious communities who typically found another kind of numbers game most compelling, and these, to be sure, were not behind times during the 1890s.

International Prophetic Conferences met from 1878 to 1901, promoting the prophetic portions of the Bible as a "photographically exact forecasting of the future." Mormons, following the vision of Joseph Smith (b. 1805) that if he should live to be eighty-five he would see the face of the Son of Man, expected their Zion to be redeemed in 1890/91. American Adventists, tactful since the Millerite humiliations of the 1840s and 1850s, wrote out new prophetic invoices for 1900. In England, John Hugh Smyth-Pigott, moved by the death in 1899 of Henry James Prince, final messenger of the Holy Ghost, announced himself as Christ returned. Angels spoke to Mlle. Henriette Couédon in Paris, warning her in 1896 that the country would suffer conflagration and war until café singer Yvette Guilbert was converted to true Catholicism and the French monarchy was restored. English, French, and above all German Protestant scholars determined that Jewish apocalypticism had been integral to the message of Jesus and the spiritual lives of early Christians, opening up "respectable" Christianity to a new theological emphasis upon eschatology among those otherwise inclined to scoff at New Jerusalems—such as Antonio Conselheiro's Canudos in northeast Brazil, a refuge for the faithful at the end of the world in 1900. Yet farther afield, Dikran Terzian of Amasia, Turkey, who had mastered the *Mathematics of Religion* by 1898, estimated that the end of the persecutions of Armenian Christians would come in the millennial year 1902. Pathan mullahs on the Northwest Frontier led millenarian revolts in 1897 while in India (im)proper the young Birsa Munda, educated at a German Protestant mission, thrice announced the fire and brimstone of apocalypse before inspiring a rebellion on Christmas Day, 1899. Most shocking to the Victorian world was the resilience of Islamic messianism in the Sudan, the outcome of mahdist expectations in the years before the end of the 13th century A.H. (1881 A.D.) and of a mahdist movement powerful enough to defeat the English forces of Charles George Gordon at Khartoum, and still disturbing the British Empire in 1899.[245]

Even so, the shaping of images of the future was beginning to have as much to do with the statistical manipulation of social and demographic data as with the refinement of prophetic equations from Scripture. Progressives and reactionaries alike began to prognosticate in newspapers, literary magazines, academic journals, and popular books according to the relationships perceived between mortality rates, crime rates, suicide rates, urban growth rates, and whatever else was available. In the new "science" of sociology, as in the older science of the psychology of perception, there arose during the 1890s the theory of the *Gestaltqualität*, that a form (an organism, a crowd, a mob, a culture, a civilization, an optical illusion) has qualities as a *gestalt* over and above the qualities of its individual constitutive elements. If one were to extrapolate from the past into the future, an inescapable habit at centuries' ends, one would have to take into account a global set of correlations.[246]

This was a literal prescript in the case of the art or science of weather forecasting. Jane de Forest Shelton remarked that weather reports in 1800 had been annals of yesterday's weather; in 1892 they were predictions of tomorrow's weather. The method of weather forecasting most famous for its successes in the 1790s had been based upon observations of the behavior of spiders, who seemed supernaturally sensitive to incipient changes of temperature; in the 1890s, benefitting from weather balloons and telegraphically linked weather stations, Russian, German, French, Dutch, British, and North American meteorologists issued daily weather bulletins based on synoptic charts that tried to make hemispheric sense of barometric pressures, wind directions, cyclonic patterns, squall lines or fronts, and cloud sequences or systems. The first official storm warnings had been issued in the 1860s through the Netherlands Meteorological Institute; by the 1890s there were national weather bureaus dedicated to short- and long-term forecasting.[247]

Was the cycle of sunspot activity also an index to weather patterns, which affected crops, which affected national economies, which responded in turn with cycles of boom and bust? So speculated the English economist W. S. Jevons in 1878, as did an Ohio hog and corn farmer, Samuel Benner, whose *Prophecies of Future Ups and Downs in Prices* were published in successive editions from 1876 to 1907. His father the owner of an ironworks in Bloom Furnace, Ohio, Benner had been watching the yearly annual prices of pig iron, corn, and hogs for twenty years, correlating these with equinoctial disturbances on Jupiter, spots on the sun, and years of financial panic. He believed that "God is in prices, and the over and under production of every commodity is in accordance with his will," and that "man in his onward path of progress, with the aid of electric science, will ultimately grasp the future, and make plain all the ways of God; which, when accomplished in this world, will be the acme of human knowledge, the consummation of human perfection, and the end of human destiny." Toward this economists' Millennium, and with similarly global methods, Alfred de Foville in 1888 constructed an economic barometer based upon thirty-two (unrelated?) economic and social phenomena, and others at century's end refined Clement Juglar's 1860 theories of crises as phases in long business cycles. Charles Dow founded Dow Jones and Company in 1882, began to publish the *Wall*

Street Journal in 1889, and after the financial panic of May 13, 1899, upon the death of the stock manipulator Roscoe P. Flower, Dow proposed the day-to-day variations in the trading value of a cluster of rail and industrial stocks as a reliable index to trends not only in the stock market but in business in general.[248]

Studying this abundance of interrelated financial, commercial, meteorological, demographic, and social data with an eye to the future was the modern equivalent of an Etruscan fulguriator reading lightning, an Etruscan diviner examining the proportions or texture of the entrails of sacred animals. Either way, one meant to discover where one stood in the flux of time—in what part of what cycle, in what position vis-à-vis the gods. Between the newer, statistical approach to the future and the older approaches through significant viscera or prophetic Scripture, the difference was that the newer approach was slightly more probabilistic: the statistical future was not written in liver or stone. Since 1866 and the chronometrical Egyptology of Piazzi Smyth (godson of that other precise Piazzi who saw the first asteroid), many Christian eschatologians had been reading the Great Pyramid of Cheops as a magnificent prophetic calendar, 1 pyramid inch = 1 solar year, the full length of the royal passages ending around 2000 A.D. and the Millennium. The numbers correlated by statisticians were faster than they were hard, the future therefore a darker passage than Piazzi Smyth's pyramid would lead one to expect. Benner may have chosen another material and italicized his *Cast Iron Rule*—*one extreme invariably follows another*, but the future as God had ordained it for mankind was cast more completely in Daniel and the Book of Revelation than in the average prices of pig iron. Young people might read their overdetermined futures off Ouija boards (patented by a Maryland novelty company in 1892), but even the simplest statistical analyses implied that the future was in-process.[249]

Classical Liberals, Social Darwinists, Progressives, Syndicalists, Anarchists, Marxists, and Socialists of many stripes had sharp disagreements over present intimations of the future, what could be done to shape it or square oneself with it, and who must be its avant-garde; for none of them was the future a fixed affair. "Detailed prescriptions concerning the organization of the society of the future?" Friedrich Engels wrote to a *Le Figaro* correspondent in 1893. "You will find no trace of them among us. We shall be satisfied when we put the means of production in the hands of the community." Political disagreements over the future were sharpest at century's turn not because the future had been prearranged but because it was so much at issue and so much on the loose. "The future is one of the best advertised institutions in the world, and just now it is having an unusually vigorous boom," noted a columnist for the London magazine, *Pick-Me-Up*, on January 5, 1901. "The present condition of the human race has become so painfully third-rate that people are returning for relief to a surmise of what the world will be like in a few hundred years' time. There is no need to keep it a secret any longer. In a century or so remarkable changes will take place; and the earth is going to be under entire new management."[250]

All in all, the intense anticipation of the 20th century (and beyond) made for an experience of the 19th century's end that was more extreme in its janiformity than any before. The boom in speculations about the future gave rise to almost as many fictive dystopias as utopias. Coefficients of correlation, sociological and psychological gestalts, the *fin de siècle* insistence upon global interconnectedness led as easily to feelings of helplessness in the face of an overwhelming complexity as to pride in the approximate mastery of a universe of data. General sensations of a world growing smaller minute by telegraphic minute were as likely to become fears of resource depletion or planetary exhaustion as they were to engender hopes for global sisterhood, global brotherhood. And were the times accelerating out of control? Was the Chariot of Progress in 1900 hitched to horses so wild that ordinary mortals had not the strength to turn them toward good ends? Among the new words in English at century's turn were "time bomb," "emergency exit," "emergency brakes." At 3:52 A.M. on April 30, 1900, immortal locomotive engineer John Luther "Casey" Jones died at the throttle trying in vain to slow down the Cannon Ball Express before it slammed into the back of a tram near Canton, Mississippi. "The tremendous and highly complex industrial development which went on with ever accelerated rapidity during the latter half of the nineteenth century brings us face to face, at the beginning of the twentieth, with very serious social problems," declared the rough-riding Theodore Roosevelt in his first annual Presidential Message to Congress in December 1901. "The old laws, and the old customs which had almost the binding force of law, were once quite sufficient to regulate the accumulation and distribution of wealth. Since the industrial changes which have so enormously increased the productive power of mankind, they are no longer sufficient." Had the incomparable 19th century set civilization racing on a track toward rapture or rupture?[251]

The Janus displayed on the 1901 title page of *The Nineteenth Century and After* had the benign faces of a downcast but virile bearded man reflecting upon the old century and of an unblemished young woman with long locks gazing upward toward the new; the Janus displayed in the late 1890s on one of a new breed of swift naval craft was the figurehead of a destroyer. If the 19th century had been a century of inordinate progress, it had also progressed to torpedoes, machine guns, smokeless powder with nitrogly-cerine, mortars, and the four-mile range of 3.2-inch field guns, as Lieutenant Colonel Arthur L. Wagner, Assistant Adjutant General of the United States Army, was proud to inform the readers of *Triumphs and Wonders of the Nineteenth Century*. "Wars," he wrote, "have become shorter, sharper, more decisive and more terrible; and increased emphasis has been placed upon the warning, 'In time of peace prepare for war.' " Since 1871 and the crushing defeat of the French armies during the Franco-Prussian War, the growing number of European and American fictions of the future were split between pacific utopias and deadly wars, and too often the utopias could be gained only through devastating war. From Lieutenant Colonel George T. Chesney's *The Battle of Dorking* (1871), which projected a German invasion of England and sold eighty thousand copies as a sixpenny pamphlet, to the consortium of senior officers working under Rear Admiral Sir Philip Colomb on the 1892 serial "forecast," *The Great War of 189-*, to the sixteen editions of William Le Queux's *The Great War in England in 1897* (1894), to the most prophetic, Polish writer Jan Bloch's 1897 *The War of the Future in Its Technical, Economic and Political Relations*, which predicted that the next major war would be one of entrenchment, slaughter, attrition, and stalemate, all the technological advances of the 19th century and the brightest prospects for the 20th became war matériel: the Canadian Pacific Railway taking troops to India, night attacks under electric lights, bombardments from airships. The talk was of Armageddon, not as a plain, not as a place, but as an event, the "Great War," a "universal war that will shake the world to its foundations." Under a "heavy, soppy," descending August moon in 1898, Claude G. Bowers walked the streets of Indianapolis with his high school pal Abie Cronbach, discussing the hand of Divine Providence that had guided the French Revolution. "This led to the question of the impending crisis between the nations of the world, and Abie after calling my attention to the warfare of the past between the Occident and the Orient, suggested that the same spectre was hovering over the civilization of the future. He claimed that the Oriental forces would be led by Russia and Turkey and that the conflict would be the most horrible that the world had yet seen. This," wrote Bowers in his diary, "he thought was probably what people looked forward to as the end of the world. It would be the end of conditions existing at the time, but the dawn of a far more splendid era."[252]

Abie Cronbach was speaking in the wake of the brief Spanish-American

War, whose legacies to the triumphant United States were the Philippines and an insurrection in 1900. That centurial year American troops also joined European and Japanese forces in China to suppress the Boxer Rebellion. That year the Russians invaded Manchuria and slaughtered forty-five thousand Chinese soldiers. That year the British Empire was flailing in its battles with the ragtag army of South African Boers, at whose hands vastly "superior" British troops had just suffered three disastrous defeats, the loss of three thousand men, and a staggering blow to imperial prestige.[253]

The year had begun in a martial mode. Kaiser Wilhelm II of Germany mandated the start of the 20th century on New Year's Day, 1900, speaking to the officers of the Berlin garrison: "The first day of the new century sees our army—in other words, our people—in arms, gathered around their standards, kneeling before the Lord of Hosts." Now, promised the Kaiser, he would concentrate on making the German navy equal to its imperial task. "The days of political impotence and economic submissiveness are past, and shall not return." The 19th century had become very quickly a Never-Never Land, as quickly as Kaiser Wilhelm of the withered arm had become Captain Hook in *Peter Pan*, a tale J. M. Barrie had been telling his godsons since 1897, then a story printed in 1902, a play performed in 1904. From the mouth of the malevolent Hook would come the line, oft-excised in modern productions, "A holocaust of children, there is something grand in the idea!" (Barrie's godson George would die in the Great War; his godson Peter would be shellshocked. Better, perhaps, had they not grown up at all.) Events of 1900, wrote the Swedish social reformer Ellen Key, "caused the new century to be represented as a small naked child, descending upon the earth, but drawing himself back in terror at the sight of a world bristling with weapons." The centurial year said of itself, in a poem in the *London Times* on the last day of 1900,

> *I was born, as I died, amid wrath and smoke,*
> *When the war-wains rolled, and the cannons spoke,*
> *When the vulture's cry and the raven's croak*
> *Flapped hungrily over the dying shriek.*

That night, New Year's Eve, as Canon Gore told the crowd at Westminster Abbey that the 19th century was closing "with a certain widespread sense of disappointment and anxiety," Frederic Harrison of the Positivist Society was lecturing on "The Day of All the Dead," on fatality and war. In *Le Petit Parisien*, Jean Frollo wrote of the 1800s as a century that had been lavish with life only to multiply the works of death. A volcanic century, a century of flames, wrote Jacinto López for *El Cojo Illustrado* of Caracas; it had begun with lust, ended with tragedy. In Yokohama the American diplomat Jeremiah Curtin sat poring over Chinese books on December 31, 1900. He confided to his diary, "The century closes with a war [against the Boxers] as unprovoked, unjust, and merciless as any of which we have an account in history. . . . It will be interesting to know how the twentieth century will judge this most conspicuous and characteristic act of the last and preceding year of the nineteenth century." Mark Twain knew; his Nineteenth Century made a Salutation Speech to the Twentieth, saying, "I bring you the stately maiden named Christendom returning bedraggled and besmirched, dishonoured from pirate raids in Kiaochau, Manchuria, South Africa, and the Philippines, with her soul full of meanness, her pocket full of boodle, and her mouth full of pious hypocrisies."[254]

Had Czar Nicholas II's invitations to an international peace conference in 1898 been one of those pious hypocrisies? The World Peace Movement had been organized since the Baroness Bertha von Suttner's call to *Lay Down Your Arms* in 1889. The first Pan-American Congress for International Arbitration met that year, the first Anglo-American Arbitration Treaty was signed in 1897, and then in 1898 had come the Czar's circular letter, opposed to the crushing economic burden of war preparations and denouncing war itself as the destroyer of civilization. "This conference should be, by the help of God, a happy presage for the century which is about to open. It would converge in one powerful focus the efforts of all States which are sincerely seeking to make the great idea of universal peace triumph over the elements of trouble and discord."[255]

The conference opened on May 18, 1899, in The Hague's Summer Palace, the House in the Wood. At four rows of semicircular tables sat representatives from most European countries, the United States, China, Japan, Persia, Mexico, Russia, Turkey, and Siam, surrounded by the allegorical figures on the walls of the Orange Room, including that of Peace coming to close the Temple of Janus. The delegates passed a Convention with Respect to the Laws and Customs of War, prescribing the humane treatment of prisoners of war, establishing a permanent International Court of Arbitration, and proscribing pillage, poison, and any bombardment of undefended towns. The feeling at the conclusion of the conference was that it had inaugurated "a new era in the history of international relations between civilized peoples," although the delegates had refused to outlaw the use of high explosives, dumdum bullets, or the powerful new field guns. The next year, as high explosives and field guns demonstrated their destructiveness in Peking, Manchuria, the Philippines, and South Africa, the Pope melted down barrows of old swords and sold them as pig iron.[256]

In 1901 was awarded the first Nobel Peace Prize, itself endowed with a peculiar janiformity. Alfred Nobel had spent his life investigating the properties of nitroglycerine, inventing and manufacturing those high explosives known as dynamite, cordite, and gelignite. Before he died in 1896 (taking nitroglycerine by physician's prescription), Nobel left an annual bequest "to the person who shall have done the most or the best work for fraternity among the nations, for the abolition or reduction of standing armies, and for the holding and promotion of peace congresses." The Swedish millionaire early in the 1890s had claimed that "My factories may well put an end to war sooner than your congresses," given the demonstrably terrible and therefore deterrent power of the explosives he manufactured. If not he, then we must find an outrageous *fin de siècle* irony in the fact that the first Nobel Peace Prize was shared by Henri Dumont, founder of the International Red Cross, and the advocate Frédéric Passy, founder of the Ligue Internationale et Permanente de la Paix, who in 1895 had written that "the whole world feels that it only requires some unforeseen incident, some unpreventable accident, for the sparks to fall in a flash . . . on those heaps of inflammable material which are being foolishly piled up . . . and blow all Europe sky-high."[257]

Or higher. The doom of global war might become the doom of *The War of the Worlds*. H. G. Wells had already taken *The Time Machine* 802,000 years into the future, far beyond the traditional temporal bounds of science fiction in 1895. Now, in 1898, he was expanding the geographic frontier of civilization beyond Earth, to the poles, continents, and seas of Mars, recognized by Victorian astronomers as "the only object in the whole heavens which is known to exhibit features resembling those of our earth." The orb of the God of War had become the planet of choice for space fantasies after spectroscopy in 1867 had revealed a thin but possibly breathable atmosphere on the red planet; after its two moons, named Phobos (Fear) and Deimos (Panic), had been discovered in 1877; and especially after the Italian astronomer Giovanni Schiaparelli in 1887 published his first maps of the fine dark straight lines on its surface, which he called *canali* or channels, translated popularly as canals. Receiving what were thought to be projections, flashes, or cloud signals from Earth's nearest planetary neighbor as it came into opposition (closest proximity) in 1894, earthmen such as Galton, Edison, Marconi, and electrical engineer Nikola Tesla worked on schemes for signalling back to the Martians. Percival Lowell, scion of the wealthy Boston family, his brother A. Lawrence to become president of Harvard, his sister Amy to become the premiere spokeswoman for imagist poetry, promptly built an astronomical observatory near Flagstaff, Arizona, to observe a planet which could be no more or less mysterious than the Orient in which he had spent the last decade of his patrician life. From 1895 on, confirming the work of Schiaparelli, "The Columbus of a New Planetary World," he would write of Mars as a planet from whose system of canals could be inferred the state of its inhabitants. Martians must be at the last stages of their civilization, "eminently sagacious" but threatened with imminent ecological collapse. Their planet appeared unified by a network of canals of which Lowell was such an (impossibly keen) telescopic observer, and for which there could be no better explanation than that Mars was an ageing, desiccated world in the mortal grip of a planetary desert. The highly geometric canals were a last-ditch and necessarily global effort at Martian survival. By contrast, the Earth was young. Its oceans were not dried up; its smallish deserts had just begun to encroach upon fertile land; its separate nations were still divided by language and politics.[258]

With desperate reason, therefore, wrote H. G. Wells, and with "intelligences such as we have scarcely dreamed of," the Martians looked toward Earth, "a morning star of hope," warm, green, and wet. Then, in 1900, they came, projected by huge cannons (those were the flashes that had been mistaken as signals) in metallic capsules flaming as they crashed near Ottershaw (mistaken at first for another of the more than five hundred meteorites seen to fall or found during the 19th century). *The War of the Worlds* was one of some fifty *fin de siècle* book-length fictions featuring Martians at home or abroad, but what made it so popular was that Wells depicted Martian civilization as the expression of 19th-century mechanical progress taken to its most frightening extreme. Martians were primarily brains and tentacles. They had no messy digestive apparatus, no gender, no sex drive, little or no fatigue. They would be neither dyspeptic nor unruly nor exhaustible. Tied telepathically to each other and to their slave machines, they were the ideally efficient factory workers, the ideally imperturbable factory managers. BUT they were also vampires: they lived by sucking blood, transfusing it directly from human victims into their own veins. . . . They had mastered those technologies most exciting to earthlings in the 1890s. Their heat rays, intense and invisible, were as formidable as x-rays and radium. At their ease they could manufacture aluminum, the magic metal of the Nineties. They could build and control hundred-foot-tall walking metal tripods far more complex than the Eiffel Tower or the Ferris wheel. They knew the secret of mechanical heavier-than-air flight. BUT they violated every canon of the Hague Convention: they attacked and destroyed undefended towns, used poison gas against artillery positions, and sucked dry their prisoners of war. "Never before in the history of warfare had destruction been so indiscriminate and so universal." . . . And they were the epitome of the "panic terror" of acceleration. When their capsules landed, they unscrewed the tops from inside with such infinite patience, emerged so slowly, moved around so laboriously under the drag of Earth's greater gravity that everyone believed them to be physically confined to the crash site. Meanwhile the Martians set to work a-hammering, and more capsules landed, more tops were patiently unscrewed, until their juggernauts had been built. The invasion had begun with utmost deliberation, inch by inch, BUT the long strides of the Martian tripods and the instant brutality of their heat rays quickly reduced the English countryside to ruins, then overtook the great capital itself, six million Londoners stampeding in panic terror. "Never before in the history of the world had such a mass of human beings moved and suffered together. . . . It was the beginning of the rout of civilization, of the massacre of mankind."[259] One ancient, unified, technologically brilliant and desperate world was devouring a younger world that had lately taken to boasting of its own matchless technological progress BUT whose last weapon would turn out to be . . . putrefaction.

Marvelous *fin de siècle* paradox, England (= the Earth, the sun never setting on its imperium over one fourth of the inhabited globe) saved by an invisible army of bacteria growing at an exponential rate. For Western Civilization, whose stellar work of synthesis in the 1890s was Max Nordau's *Degeneration*, to be rescued from a death worse than fate by the most deconstructive of its own bodily attendants, this was a perversely *fin de siècle* triumph. There was in *The War of the Worlds* equally backhanded play with other motifs of the century's end—decadence, impotence, exhaustion, vampirism, pollution—and a reminder that human beings themselves had pursued certain animals and aborigines to extinction. As H. G. Wells drew them out, the insectile Martians were undeniably janiform: their glories lay in the past, on a more viable Mars; their present days, dry, humorless, and desperate, could be our future.[260]

Of this future Wells also wrote in less breathless though no less adventurous prose. His series of articles for the *North American Review* in 1901, collected the next year as *Anticipations of the Reaction of Mechanical and Scientific Progress Upon Human Life and Thought*, followed his precept that, unlike the hundred modern fictions of the future which one could name, "modern prophecy should be, one submits, a branch of speculation, and should follow with all decorum the scientific method." Orienting his modern prophecies to the length of the 20th century and to the year 2000, Wells expected that "this gray confusion that is democracy must pass away inevitably . . . into the higher organism, the world-state of the coming years." There would be world unity, world peace, a world language, and a reconstructed ethical system with no superstitions about death.[261]

In short, we would have achieved without the threat of global desiccation exactly what the Martians had achieved, as best the modern astronomer Lowell and the modern Fabian Socialist reformer Wells could tell. Mars at century's end was not only janiform in time; it was a geography of fictive extremes, of dystopia or, more often, utopia. The phlegmatic hero of Percy Greg's *Across the Zodiac* in 1880 discovered on Mars a society that had evolved through democracy, communism, and anarchy to scientocracy. *Mr. Stranger's Sealed Packet*, unwrapped in 1889, revealed a Mars enjoying socialism, electric lights, and tape recordings. Robert Cromie took *A Plunge into Space* in 1890 and found Mars one perfectly civilized nation, smart and electrified. William Simpson's *Man from Mars*, born to a civilization ten thousand years ahead of our own, teleported himself to California in 1891 to explain that earthmen were too greedy and that on Mars all religions had been reduced to a single spirituality, just as all elements were reducible to a single basic unit, even gold and silver. In 1893, Henry Olerich of Holstein, Iowa, met a Mr. Midith from *A Cityless and Countryless World* known as Mars, where folks spoke one language, lived to be 150 years old, and, as agnostics, neither mourned their dead nor built them memorials. On an excursion to Mars, reported via Malden, Massachusetts, by Professor Willis Mitchell, revivalist and "inventor of Modern Electrical Heating," Mr. Ego was pleased that no one was bald, women remained beautiful at seventy, chemical laboratories took the place of kitchens, hypnosis took the place of morphine, and theologians considered faith to be something like electricity. From England, George Du Maurier wrote in 1896 of *The Martian*, Martia by name, a highly reincarnated spirit ascended from the amphibious Martian race with its webbed fingers and toes, its sixth (magnetic) sense, its extrasensory perception, an advanced moral sense, and now near the end of its term as a civilization. From Germany, from the Kantian pen of Kurd Lasswitz, a professor of mathematics in Gotha, came the tremendously popular tale of *Two Planets*, Mars and Earth. In the spirit of the real but almost unbelievable Swede, Salomon August Andrée, who with two companions lifted off that same year, 1897, to reach the North Pole by balloon, Lasswitz's balloonists discover a ring of 144 pillars on an island at the center of the sea inside the mountains of ice surrounding the Pole. There, at this secret polar research station, and above, on the space station hovering 6356 kilometers over the pole, the balloonists learn of a society of three billion intellectually and morally superior Martians who speak one language, create proteins and carbohydrates from rocks and soil, and exploit solar energy to power huge electromagnets. Only after an attack upon the Martians by arrogant, foolish Englishmen do the omnicompetent outlanders, piloting airships with disintegrating rays, establish a protectorate over the whole of the globe, and only after forming a world federation to defend their skies do humans achieve independence and, as Immanuel Kant had been hoping since 1795, a perpetual world peace.[262]

We need not consult the Swiss-Hungarian spirit medium Hélène Smith, who began writing out moral and celestial messages in the Martian language during the 1890s, in order to appreciate how central to *fin de siècle* mythmaking was the Red Planet. Nor need we read through much of Edward Bellamy's story, "The Blindman's World," to realize that the writer of the most influential utopia of the 1890s, *Looking Backward, 2000–1887,* had first (in 1886) to engage a Mars where the unity of things was understood, where rational beings astutely let the dead past go, living in the present and comprehending the future. The finest of Martians were Americans seen through an optimist's crystal ball; the desert planet Mars was America in mothballs. While the young English girl Rebecca West in 1900 envisioned America "as a vast, unpolluted, underpopulated continent, with broad pure rivers, vast cornlands, clear mountains, the Pacific that met travellers on the further coast with its crystal breakers," Mars was small and parched. The often ascetic Martians contrived their entropic utopias by dint of a social intelligence and political grace as yet lacking in America, a land of such opportunity that Charles Dickens in 1865 believed that "the heaviest blow ever dealt at Liberty's Head, will be dealt by this nation in its ultimate failure of its example to the Earth." The presumption, shared by boosters and skeptics, was that America was for better or worse the land of the future, where the "modern" was free to be itself, unhampered by the past. "Of all our race, God has marked the American people as His chosen Nation to finally lead in the regeneration of the world," crowed Indiana Senator Albert J. Beveridge on January 9, 1900. "We are trustees of the world's progress, guardians of its peace." A failed America would be a mean, ancient, ruptured, and impoverished place like Mars; a successful America would have the global peace and wisdom of the Martians, the rapturous wealth of a younger, still bountiful planet. Mars at its two extremes was America at one or the other extreme of its—and Earth's—future. A confident breed, these Americans, agreed H. G. Wells in *The Future in America*, but "When one talks to an American of his national purpose, he seems a little at a loss." Which Mars was America to be?[263]

The question was of immediate concern. With the closing of the Western frontier, announced unofficially by the young historian Frederick Jackson Turner at the Columbian Exposition, space had a new premium for Americans. Frontier myths and frontier realities had conditioned American ideas about the (unlimited) future since the birth of the Republic. Suddenly, the free land on the "hither edge" of settlement had disappeared. Americans now had to reconceive their relationship to time as they reconsidered their place on the continent and in the world. "The great gates to the West have just been closed, and they are closed tightly and are impassable. The opportunities are gone there," insisted William Stanley Child in 1898, whereupon he called for city planning as an urgent social necessity. No longer an American gift, space was in demand as a human need for open air: painting out of doors; bicycling on "week-ends" in the countryside; playing in the sun beyond the dark walls of city slums; opening up the home to natural light and landscape. Space—the space between molecules and atoms, the space of physics—was so important that the young architect Frank Lloyd Wright would emphasize "the new reality that is *space* instead of matter." The loss of space meant the compression of time, felt no more keenly than by the Plains Indians late in the 1880s as they found themselves in a painful limbo, their hunting grounds lost to railroads and white settlers, their burial grounds violated, their ceremonial grounds desecrated. Another world was coming, believed the Ghost Dancers as they danced in white shirts; another world was coming, said the Paiute prophet Wovoka, and "it would come in a whirlwind out of the west and would crush everything on this world, which was old and dying."[264]

There was another frontier, an open space, a last chance. The sky. Dim and wonderful was the narrator's vision at the end of *The War of the Worlds*, a vision "of life spreading slowly from this little seedbed of the solar system throughout the inanimate vastness of sidereal space." That, he wrote, was a remote dream. In the meantime, however, an airship, its powerful lights beaming amidst the evening stars, was seen moving purposefully across the California heavens just before Thanksgiving, 1896.

This airship was in the long tradition of unusual celestial phenomena regularly chronicled at centuries' ends, but it was of a different league. It was distinct from the burning globe large as a carriage out of which supposedly came a person in a tight-fitting suit who spoke some incomprehensible words to two mayors and a doctor near Alençon, France, in 1790. It was distinct from the luminous flying ship seen over Baton Rouge on April 5, 1800, and the three-hundred-yard-long cruiser, the color of a red-hot stove, seen over Shreveport in 1860. It was distinct from the giant mechanical bird that flapped over Copiago, Chile, in 1868; distinct from the large Ezekiel wheels spinning over the Persian Gulf in 1879; distinct from a cigar-shaped greenish light discerned by a British astronomer in 1882. It more nearly resembled the navigable balloons sighted across Poland in March 1892, during a springtime of war tensions between Germany and Russia: soldiers and civilians in Russian Poland reported seeing balloons whose electric spotlights and steering mechanisms enabled German aerial navigators to sail against the wind and spy at will on military positions night and day. Like these completely maneuverable spy balloons, long desired but not yet (and not then) achieved, the American airship four years later was notable for its bright lights and its orderly, directed progress through the sky.[265]

Occasionally, observers imagined that the American airship was also on a military mission (usually to Cuba, in these months before the Spanish-American War). And occasionally they imagined that the airship was from Mars. Of greater import, even so, was the sheer popularity of the airship, which was seen, evidently, by thousands of people from Sacramento to Los Angeles, and then by thousands more in other western and midwestern states through to Milwaukee and Chicago, for a full six months from November 17, 1896, to May of 1897. Hoaxes—landings for rest stops or repairs, crash landings, airmail letters, patent claims, cownappings, cast-off aluminum wheels, warblings overheard from seven-foot-tall creatures with a "specific gravity" of less than an ounce—were sometimes obtruded upon the regular run of reports, but generally the sightings were content with the amazing fact of human command of powered flight.[266]

Such flight was no *fait accompli*. Neither in 1892 nor in 1897 were any German balloons or American lighter-than-air craft capable of performing as the newspaper accounts had them performing. Whether a simple trio of lights making radical changes of direction over San Francisco, or "a dark body outlined in the form of an egg," or two men pedalling on bicycle frames below a cigar-shaped upper body with wheels at the side "like the side wheels on Fulton's old steam boat," or a conical object thirty to forty feet long with two sets of wings and a large fan-shaped rudder witnessed over Invale, Nebraska, after a prayer meeting, or a night flyer "about seventy feet in length, of slender proportions and fragile construction" sailing with twenty-foot-long wings over Chicago—and whether silent or sounding "for all the world like the working of an air pump on a locomotive" or broadcasting the melody of the song "Just Tell Them That You Saw Me," the airship was a *fin de siècle* fantasy of celestial dynamos (for the brilliant electric searchlights), controlled acceleration (for swift changes of direction), and joyful release (from a bounded earth and a decadent epoch into open space and new opportunities).[267]

Glider pilots had had brief minutes of airborne glory, balloonists had had days of hopeful floating on the winds, cartoonists had had months of fun in the years before Zeppelin's dirigible of 1900 and the Wright brothers' biplane of 1903, and there had been many a pleasantly fictitious voyage to the moon in vehicles far more sophisticated than those reported in 1897. But the wave of sightings of an unidentified flying object, half arcadian, half industrial, entirely imaginary, travelling from utopian California, end of the American frontier, east to Chicago, rail nexus for the nation, was unprecedented, bearing extraordinary testimony to the imaginal importance of powered flight in the 1890s.[268]

Janus reigned here too. National and international tensions between global war and global peace at century's end were translatable into acutely personal tensions, fight or flight. These tensions appeared in the mix of pacific and bellicose purposes attributed to the airship. They were blatant in Cyrus Scofield's *Reference Bible* of 1909, which codified the late-19th-century Fundamentalist development of the images of Tribulation and Rapture: in this last historical era or Dispensation, ending as each must with a divine judgment, there will be a necessarily violent, purgative period of Tribulation across the face of the earth; the 144,000 living faithful, constantly expectant of the Lord's Second Coming, will be rescued or en-Raptured, lifted above the earth to a cerulean observation deck just before or during the Tribulation. In the pagan galleries of popular art, the *fin de siècle* tensions between fight and flight were less literal, but the suspended animation of the ubiquitous winged sphinxes, sirens, and sleeping beauties could turn at the twist of a brush into the deadliest flights of passion, the violence of the *femme fatale*, the vampire, Judith with sword in one hand, in her other the dripping head of the Assyrian general Holofernes.[269]

To dream of a fighting woman meant that "Scandal will ruin you," wrote a modern sibyl; to dream of flight (of running away) meant catastrophe. A certain forty-three-year-old Jewish physician in Austria, preoccupied with issues of fight and flight, would likely have agreed with the part about catastrophe. If Carlotta de Barsy of Chicago had seen *The Gates of the Future thrown open* in 1899, Sigmund Freud of Vienna meant that year to throw open the gates of the past with what he called in jest his "Egyptian dream book," the first full-length work "completely my own, my own dung heap, my seedling, and a *nova species mihi* on top of it," entitled *Traumdeutung*, a word usually referring to fairground fortunetellers' *Interpretation of Dreams*. Dreams, wrote Freud, felt forward but looked backward; like the symptoms of hysterics, they were the expression of desires repressed, the fulfillment of wishes denied. It was most fitting, then, that Freud's passions for archaeology and for ancient Rome should have led him to acquire in July a few ancient gods, among them "a stone Janus who looks at me with his two faces in a very superior manner" from atop the pages of his nearly completed manuscript. The book was published on November 4, 1899, but Freud's publisher chose to imprint it with the date 1900, a more significant year for such a significant book (or so the legend goes). Freud, who had been reading prehistory, seemed to approach the start of the 20th century (*ex parte* the Kaiser) in the Etruscan manner. "The new century, the most interesting thing about which for us may be that it contains the dates of our deaths, has brought me nothing but a stupid review in the *Zeit*," he wrote to his friend and fellow physician Wilhelm Fliess on January 8, 1900. Fliess, however, had been busy calculating biological rhythms, and although Freud was despairing of his small income and smaller reputation, he had not been loath to remind himself, in a letter to Fliess on October 11, 1899, "According to an earlier calculation of yours, a productive period, 1900–1901 (every seven and a half years), lies ahead of me." And although in November he had written that "I go on putting new layers of resignation over my yearning [to visit Rome, to achieve a professorship, to be recognized]," in February of 1900 he was mildly Augustan, explaining that "I am actually not at all a man of science, not an observer, not an experimenter, not a thinker. I am by temperament nothing but a conquistador—an adventurer, if you want it translated—with all the curiosity, daring, and tenacity characteristic of a man of this sort." In 1901 Freud went at last to visit Rome.[270]

The "Egyptian dream book" was not composed *because* it was 1899, nor did Freud go to Rome *because* it was 1901. Yet he who wrote of the revolt of the sons against the father and whose own trip to the Eternal City was possible only as he laid to rest the ghost of his dead father, he would have been the last to deny the influence of desires that the end of the century be the end of a generation and the beginning of a century the beginning of a new age. In that same centurial letter to Fliess, on January 8, 1900, Freud had started out with happy predictions for Fliess's new son Conrad, whom he had already identified with the new century, and then, for the first time, Freud insisted upon his own position among the avant-garde: "I do not count on recognition, at least not in my lifetime. . . . I have to deal in obscure matters with people I am ten to fifteen years ahead of and who will not catch up with me."[271]

Those who might catch up with him were in high school, like the schoolmates of another Austrian Jew, Stefan Zweig, whose zeal for the vanguard was the truest stuff of youth and who "found the new because we desired the new, because we hungered for something that belonged to us alone, and not to the world of our fathers, to the world around us. Youth, like certain animals, possess an excellent instinct for change of weather, and so our generation sensed, before our teachers and our universities knew it, that in the realm of the arts something had come to an end with the old century, and that a revolution, or at least a change of values, was in the offing." Then they graduated. "The long desired moment finally came with the last year of the old century, and we were able to slam the door of the hated *Gymnasium* behind us," to enter a new century and a new world.[272]

The revolution was felt everywhere, not just in Austria and not just in the arts or the art of dream interpretation. Wherever one looked, the year 1900 became a personal turning point, frequently marked by resolutions of the *fin de siècle* tension between fight and flight. In Vienna, the poet Hugo von Hofmannsthal had led a life of "melancholy passivity" through 1899, but in 1901 he married, became a father, and turned to writing lyrical comedies. In Paris, Maurice Barrès, partisan of the cult of the self in the 1890s, turned to the political right and published novels of *National Energy*. In Heidelberg, economist Max Weber had endured four years of deep depression precipitated by a battle with his father (epitome of the Spirit of Capitalism), but the disease, the fits of weeping and of rage, had its compensations—"It has opened to me the human side of life"—and by 1901 he was regaining his vitality and his sociological ambitions. In Berlin, Max Planck was undermining traditional physics with his studies of heat radiation and the development of quantum theory; "thus it happened, around the turn of the century," wrote Albert Einstein years later, that "a second fundamental crisis [in physics] set in," and it became "clear to me as long ago as shortly after 1900, i.e., shortly after Planck's trailblazing work, that neither mechanics nor thermodynamics could (except in limiting cases) claim exact validity." From the ensuing revolution in physics to a singular moment in

the history of the Russian Revolution, when Lenin met with the liberal
editors of the political magazine *Iskra* at the end of December 1900: "It was
a notable and 'historic' meeting of sorts," Lenin noted at 2 A.M. on December
30th, after the first day of negotiations; "at any rate, it was historic in my
life, a summing-up of a whole epoch, or at any rate, of a way of life; one
that will determine for a long time to come my conduct and life path," for
he had become convinced that further collaboration with bourgeois liberals
was pointless. In England the equally resolute socialist campaigner Beatrice
Webb confessed that during 1900 "I seem to have passed into an emotional
and imaginative phase, which, while it gives me a certain magnetic effect
on others, knocks me to pieces myself. Indeed, I feel [that I am] becoming
mediumistic." A similar rush of feelings was felt a bit later, in 1903, by
John Maynard Keynes and other young Cambridge intellectuals confronted
with Bertrand Russell's *Principia Mathematica* and G. E. Moore's *Principia
Ethica*. Moore's influence in particular, wrote Keynes, "was not only overwhelming; . . . it was exciting, exhilarating, the beginning of a new
renaissance, the opening of a new heaven on a new earth, we were the fore-
runners of a new dispensation, we were not afraid of any thing."[273]

All of the United States, of course, was in the avant-garde. "It would
seem as though no careful student of history at all in touch with our part
of the world to-day but must rejoice at the outlook for the new century,"
declared the editor of the *New Century Leader* in January 1900, in the first
issue of this Sunday School Teacher's Monthly, published out of Elgin,
Illinois. "Verily the dawn of heaven seems breaking." While Samuel Langley,
America's official hope in the race to construct a practicable flying machine,
was showing Henry Adams through the Great Hall of Dynamos in Paris,
Henry's cousin Evangeline, soon to be America's premier astrologer, was
drawing up the horoscopes of society ladies in New York City, and Henry's
brother Brooks was completing *The New Empire*, whose thesis was that "During the last decade the world has traversed one of those periodic crises which
attend an alteration in the social equilibrium. The seat of energy has migrated
from Europe to America."[274]

That energy was conspicuous on the evening of December 31, 1900. If
America was to be the darling and dynamo of what the French poet Paul
Valéry was already calling the *saecula saeculorum*, then the nation must enter
the "century of centuries" with the most brilliant of flourishes. "A new
century," after all, "is to a nation very much what a new year is to a man."
The celebration in Boston—but stay. Given a *fin de siècle* so anxious to
announce the end of a century, an era so convinced of the acceleration of

time, an epoch so ready to move on to the next century, there could be no escaping a furious centurial debate. It was not simply Kaiser Wilhelm's 1900 against the rest of the West's 1901. It was modern man, impatient and commonsensical, against the old guard, studied and traditional.[275]

We have heard the bulk of the arguments before, but, as we could have guessed, the debate got under way much earlier than in previous centuries. Thirty (or twenty-nine) years in advance, at a Century Dinner in Glasgow in 1870, the Lord Dean of Guild after a full discussion of the question decided that the next century would start on January 1, 1901. J. H. Tingley of Philadelphia, publishing in 1886 *The Nineteenth Century Almanac: A Complete Calendar from 1800 to 1900,* made sure to print in boldface that **The Calendars commence with 1800, although the century really begins with 1801,** and to identify the year 1900 as the last of the 19th century. Public controversy was anticipated (and stimulated) by the *London Times* and the *New York Times* in the fall of 1896: "As the present century draws to its close we see looming not very far ahead the venerable dispute which reappears every hundred years—viz.: When does the next century begin?" The dispute carried on, suggested the *New York Times,* because the issue appeared simple enough to require no expertise; each person had an opinion, and anyone of a contrary opinion must be a stubborn fool. Maintaining a diplomatic stance as august as it was ultimately provocative, the newspaper stated that "There can be no doubt that one person may hold that the next century begins on the 1st of January, 1900, and another that it begins on the 1st of January, 1901, and yet that both of them may be in full possession of their faculties." Promptly came one letter to the editor after another, then and again in 1899, when the *Boston Herald* presented the results of an academic survey. The presidents of Harvard, Yale, Princeton, Cornell, Columbia, Chicago, Vassar, Bowdoin, Dartmouth, Brown, and the University of Pennsylvania stood for 1901; Caroline Hazard of Wellesley and L. Clark Seelye of Smith stood for 1900, with William J. Witt and Anna Waddilove of New Jersey, who arranged to be married at 12:01 A.M. on January 1, 1900.[276]

Witt and Waddilove were young German Americans who had taken the Kaiser at his word. Back in Germany, however, centurial feuds had only been aggravated by the imperial decree. On December 31, 1899, Max Halbe got together in Munich with a circle of literary friends that included Frank Wedekind, editor of one of Freud's favorite satirical journals, *Simplicissimus,* to enjoy a boisterous wake for the 19th century. The rowdiness of their celebration would later pale in comparison with the vehemence of the centurial debate. "In my life I have seen many people do battle over many things, but over few things with such fanaticism as over the academic question [of when the century would end]. . . . Each of the two parties produced for its side the trickiest of calculations and maintained at the same time that it was the simplest matter in the world, one that any child should understand." Meanwhile, editors dueled with other editors, the King of Sweden came to the defense of the Kaiser, and Oscar Blumenthal in the *Berliner Tageblatt* made fun of them all, the pedant, the optimist, the confused newspaper reader, and the New Year's poet, blessed with two separate occasions calling for a centurial poem.[277]

The debate raged from Capetown, South Africa, to Palencia, Spain; from the official Bureau des Longitudes in Paris to the unofficial, irreverent pages of Alfred Jarry's *Almanach illustré du Père Ubu (XXᵉ Siècle)*; from Switzerland and the private declaration in favor of 1901 by the mathematical economist Léon Walras to Scotland and the public declaration in favor of 1900 by the physicist Sir William Thomson, Lord Kelvin. The *Levant Herald and Eastern Express*, taking a less blinkered view of the whole affair from its offices in Constantinople, accepted the '01 but reminded its English readers "that January 1, 1901, has no significance to the majority of people who inhabit this globe. The Gregorian calendar is only one among many. . . . To Turkey, the whole of Asia, and a large part of Africa, the year 1901 will mark no particular epoch." In England, nonetheless, they were "fighting like cats and dogs," wrote Henry James, "as to where in our speck of time we are." From the first to the sixth of January 1900, the *London Times* published more than sixty contentious letters on the subject of the century's end, one writer harking as far back as 4000 A.M. to establish precedent, another to an 18th-century edition of the Book of Common Prayer. Many attempted to second-guess Dennis the Diminutive. Of all correspondents Lord Medway was most in a muddle: "I cannot understand how people can be found to maintain that a century does not begin until the end of its first year."[278]

He should have gone to Rome. There, Pope Leo XIII struck the Porta Sancta with a golden mallet, intoned the *Jubilate Deo*, knelt to the *Te deum*, and proclaimed the Jubilee of 1900. Rome had its own Anno Santo Exhibition to entertain the Jubilee crowds, and then, on January 1, 1901, it had its second centurial celebration, anticipated by Leo's halfhearted encyclical on the New Century that had been issued on All Saints' Day: "The close of the century really seems in God's mercy to afford us some degree of consolation and hope."[279]

Two introductory passes to the new century, one for '00 and one for '01, this was a compromise whose time had come, beyond Rome and aside from New Year's poets. As Edward Alden of Brooklyn explained to the patrons of the *New York Times*, as E. J. Reed explained to the readers of the *London Times*, from the point of view of common sense and common usage the 20th century began on the first day of 1900, and from the perspective of astronomers, mathematicians, civil engineers, scientists, and official chronologers it began on the first day of 1901. An English government official, Sir Courtenay Boyle, was gracious enough to admit that "Inasmuch as those persons who desire to reach the 20th century are probably more numerous than those who care nothing for any such record, it seems to me that they should be gratified at the earliest moment. There is no reason why essayists, preachers, and paragraphists should have to postpone their eloquence on the subject till 1901." If K. B. Ferguson of Sussex would "defy the most bigoted precisian to work up any enthusiasm over the year 1901, when we will already have had twelve months' experience of the 1900's," Neal H. Ewing of New York City was hardly less conciliatory, for though he acknowledged the abstract logic of '01, he knew that "the centurial figures are the symbol, and the only symbol, of the centuries. Once every hundred years there is a change in the symbol, and this great secular event is of startling prominence. What more natural than to bring the century into harmony with its only visible mark? . . . No, we will not pass over the significant year 1900, which is stamped with the great secular change, but with cheers we will welcome it and the new century."[280]

Brave words. Outside Germany, however, and its colonial possessions, few were the festivities on the eve of January 1, 1900, which "appeals to the human imagination, seems to the eye, and sounds to the ear, more like the beginning of a century than does January 1, 1901." This time around, logicians and officialdom had their victory as, next time around, on January 1, 2000, they will not. The *Christian Science Journal*, whose editorship had supposed, "for reasons quite satisfactory to ourselves, that we had entered upon the Twentieth Century" on the first day of 1900, apologized on the first day of 1901, since "Our governmental authorities officially postponed the beginning of the new century until this year."[281]

The "postponement" made for celebrations on January 1, 1901, more extensive and elaborate than for any earlier century's turn. After all the Etruscan desires to put the old to rest, and after all the Claudian retrospectives of the last unparalleled hundred years, and after all the Augustan anticipations of a millennial new era of peace, Westerners across the planet welcomed the next century. Dennis the Diminutive's 20th century A.D. opened among the

Friendly Islanders, closest people to the International Date Line. Travelling west with the sun, the 20th century came to Sydney just as Australia became a British Commonwealth; a two-mile-long triumphal procession wound under and through a fleecy, pyramidal Wool Arch, a Wheat Arch, and a Coal Arch with miners standing like statues in the niches. It was, warm and bright, the first day of the 20th Christian century minutes later in Japan, which had converted to the Gregorian calendar in 1873; Jeremiah Curtin's Chinese teacher paid him a ceremonious call that morning in Yokohoma. The discharge of guns by Western soldiers in Peking (Beijing) at midnight was so loud that some suspected another Boxer uprising. There were reports of plague in Mysore and famine throughout India, and "Heaven knows where we are drifting, with the constant pressure of famine and pestilence," wrote the editors of *The Hindu* in Madras, but they published a poem which began,

> *Come, new year, come amidst our joy!*
> *The first of the coming century,*
> *May the war successful end,*
> *The famine cease and the plague mend.*

Poet Wilfrid Scawen Blunt bade goodbye to the old century from Egypt, with the pyramids watching "as they watched Joseph, when, as a young man four thousand years ago, perhaps in this very garden, he walked and gazed at the sunset behind them, wondering about the future just as I did this evening." In St. Petersburg, almost directly north, Russia's 20th century was coincident with preparations for the January 18th centenary of its union with Georgia. In Berlin, the Kaiser was having his centurial cake and eating it too, the capital festive for the two hundredth anniversary of the foundation of the Prussian monarchy. Marcel Proust, asthmatic, received a New Year's telegram, and the city of Paris under a siege of bad weather distributed to the poor the 100,000 francs that would have gone to fêtes. Leopold Rothschild sent a New Year's gift of a brace of pheasant to each omnibus driver in London, where Canon Mason of St. Paul's Cathedral preached from Revelation 21.6, "I am Alpha and Omega, the beginning and the end"; at the stroke of midnight a man in a hansom cab led a gloomy rendition of "Auld Lang Syne" while a woman with a baby in one hand, a pot of ale in the other, sang something like "They All Love Jack." Across the Atlantic, in Rio de Janeiro, the old century was given a grand funeral and a huge cross was erected on the Monte de la Providencia in honor of the new. There were firecrackers, floats, fiestas throughout Valparaiso, Chile: *un entusiasmo frenético.*

Louise Merritt Parker saw an all-star cast perform *Lohengrin* at the Metropolitan Opera House, then went down to City Hall, adorned with four thousand electric lights and two thousand flags, to find a crowd of one hundred thousand New Yorkers celebrating the new century with forty bombs, John Philip Sousa's Marching Band, and a People's Choral Union of more than a thousand singers. Philadelphia put lights in its pine trees, turned all the lights out at 11:55 P.M., turned them on again at midnight amidst pyrotechnics and a twenty-round gun salute, while John L. Smith, "demoralized, tired out," inserted in his diary a poem by Arthur Lewis Tubbs, "When the Century Comes In," which described

> *a rumpus an' a racket—*
> *Ev'rybuddy's out p'radin'—young an' old,*
> *an' youth and maiden,*
> *In the New Year jubilee t'have a share. . . .*
> *Why, t'set down an' be quiet seems a sin,*
> *Fer we can't stay here ferever, an' not one*
> *uv us will ever*
> *Live t'see another century come in.*

Army doctor Walter Reed was praying for the cure of yellow fever as he sat in barracks in Cuba; twenty-four buglers outside sounded "Taps" for the old century. Uncle Ezra had a "New Year Reverie" on the front page of *The Recorder*, the black newspaper of Indianapolis, listing the technological miracles of the 19th century and those probable in the 20th (a train through the earth from America to China, the moon divided amongst the nations, news telegraphed from Mars), but the editor of Chicago's *Broad-Ax* paid no attention to the century's turn, counting instead the number of blacks mobbed and lynched in the United States in the year gone by: 107. An anarchist attempted to blow up the La Salle Street tunnel at the height of New Year's Eve celebrations in the Windy City. Mexico City was bright with explosions, incandescent bulbs, beaming crowds, and an allegorical statue of Peace bearing light and an olive branch. The Latter-Day Saints of Salt Lake City held centennial services in their Tabernacle, where Brigham Young, Jr., heard Lorenzo Snow's son Leroy read the Mormon President's Greeting to the World. "Other songs and music followed, but I could think of nothing but the grandeur of Pres. Snow's epistle. God bless him. I wanted to throw my arms around him and shout Alleluia Glory to God on high for the inspiration given to His servant." The Greeting was certainly uplifting:

"Awake, ye monarchs of the earth and rulers among nations, and gaze upon the scene wherein the early rays of the rising Millennial day gild the morn of the twentieth century!" A cannon boomed from the roof of the Times Building in Los Angeles; sirens, bells, whistles, guns, and tin horns split the air outside the Church of the Unity, whose Century Party featured twenty men and women in the garb of 1800, and a spelling bee. The *Herald*'s electric sign followed the onset of the new century from Nova Scotia west to San Francisco and the fiery cross on the stage of Golden Gate Hall, where the Red Cross read greetings from Clara Barton, Thomas Hardy, and other world figures. Far to the north, in the Yukon Territory, the Kangaroo Boys of 24, 25, and 26 Eldorado (Avenue?) in Dawson threw a shindig for sixty people, pausing to listen for the midnight steam whistles up and down the creek, then dancing on until 2:30 A.M., "when everybody seemed to think they had done justice to the incoming of the twentieth century."[282]

And the Twentieth Century Club of Boston "conceived and brought about the most remarkable end-of-the-century celebration on the night of December 31, 1900, witnessed anywhere in Christendom," even if it did say so itself. Twenty thousand people gathered before the State House. Four trumpeters, following the custom established by Samuel Sewall, took their places with one hundred singers on the front balcony at 11:45 P.M. Edward Everett Hale read the Nineteenth Psalm ("Their line is gone out through all the earth, and their words to the end of the world. In them hath he set a tabernacle for the sun"). The trumpeters trumpeted, church bells pealed, chimes rang, the assembled thousands sang one of the national anthems, and "The question as to when the 20th century began is not even mentioned, the voices of the past who contended so loudly for last Jan. 1 are silent, [and] thus arguments adhered to so long are lost in the general acclamation." Up in Byfield, Susan E. Parsons Brown Forbes, seventy-six, sat alone in the library to watch the year out and the century in. "I thought of the many old years I had watched out with young comrades most of whom have passed the boundary of time—and long since entered upon the Eternal round. . . . I made no resolutions because of all previous failures to keep such. I hope, however, to accomplish something in the way of better living, and of making others happy—more than ever before." His family and servants out to midnight services, Robert Apthorp Boit, an insurance executive, president of the Boston Associated Board of Trade, stayed home by himself, prosperous but tired, to reflect upon his wealth and his mortality—after thirty-odd years of hard work he was worth enough, he hoped, to keep his family out of the gutter. Marian Lawrence, sixteen, got out of bed at 11 P.M. and went to the Watch Night service at Emmanuel Church. At the close of the service, "we all knelt and at the same time the lights went out all over the church and it was total darkness except for a ray of moonlight which streamed down directly on the altar! In the silence the bells rang twelve and then the organ pealed out, the lights sprang out brilliantly," and everyone sang "Praise God from Whom All Blessings Flow." Then Marian went in Aunt Hetty's carriage to see the crowd at the center of Boston. "It was the most curious sensation in the middle of a beautiful peaceful night to hear the jangling of the bells and the chimes pealing so that the air was full of sound and then this enormous crowd all looking so quietly happy. A few groups singing and all walking at a good pace *all over* the city. All the streets were full of people and yet the houses were mostly dark. Everybody was out. Beacon Hill was thronged, strings and strings of carriages and lines of automobiles slipping around in the mud and incessantly jangling their bells and the sidewalks thronged with jolly crowds and the bells rang through it all and above it all incessantly."[283]

The century of centuries had come. Back across the Atlantic, on an island at the edge of the European continent, a violent gale over the silent Salisbury Plain blew down one of the stones at Stonehenge.

Illustration to a story by William Juhre, "The End of the World: It Can Happen Tomorrow," from the back cover of *Amazing Stories* (May 1939). Courtesy of the Eaton Collection, University of California, Riverside.

CONSTELLATIONS

THE

1990s

—

THE TWENTIETH CENTURY LIMITED

WERE IT NOT FOR THE GRANDEUR OF THE YEAR 2000, THIS *fin de siècle* must seem about as hollow as that of the 1390s or 1690s. Holocaust, Hiroshima, H-bomb . . . our Nineties could only be aftermath. Instead, the millennial integers on everyone's horizon draw us toward a century's end denser and perhaps richer than any before. Although we have yet to make our peace with a long midcentury of racism and genocide, a new millennium holds out the promise of absolution or, at least, forgiveness or, at the very least, forgetfulness. The three zeros at the dead end of our century stand prefigured by the hearty 2 of regeneration. So, cursed by the minefields and mustard gas of a War to End All Wars, oppressed by the hunger and horror of the Thirties and Forties, scarred by the political violence of '68, relieved by the inconsequence of 1984, we approach the next thousand years beset by the most corrosive of tensions. Our *fin de siècle*, which began the moment that George Orwell's spell was broken, has become—as it was fated to be—a Now or Never time. Living it through, we will feel all middle ground slipping rapidly away toward one or the other pole of apocalypse, toward a glory revealed or a globe laid waste.

Since our century bears the same relation to the next millennium as the Nineties bear to a new century, that tenseness characteristic of the experience of any *fin de siècle* has already been ascribed to the 1900s in their entirety. "What the last decade is to a century the last century is to a millennium," argued a contributor to the *Atlantic Monthly* in 1891; "so far, therefore, from sighing for 1901, we ought to be positively dreading it, and 2001 ought to be as great a relief as was 1001." The century was heralded on May 28, 1900, by a total eclipse of the sun ("a solid disk of utter blackness . . . surpassingly solemn"); on September 8, 1900, by the hurricane devastation of Galveston, Texas; and on Ascension Day, May 8, 1902, by the eruption of Mount Pelée in the "earthly paradise" of Martinique, thirty thousand burned and smothered by a tidal wave of lava. NO SUCH FRIGHTFUL CA-

LAMITY, UNEQUALED FOR THE SUDDENNESS OF THE BLOW, THE NUMBER OF VICTIMS, THE COMPLETENESS OF THE DESOLATION HAS EVER COME UPON THE CIVILIZED WORLD WITH SUCH OVERWHELMING AND HARROWING FORCE, insisted two journalists, who counted the number of survivors on their fingers. Pope Pius X in an encyclical of 1903 found the world aquiver with such insane projects against the Creator that he had cause to fear the onset of those evils forerunning the end of time. Excommunicated in 1901 by the Russian Orthodox Church, the pacifist Leo Tolstoy, seventy-seven, wrote in 1905 of "The End of the Age," of armaments, cruelties, frauds, treacheries, the lawlessness of the rich and the despair of the poor. If the Christian nations were to survive, they must abandon the mean fictions of State and Fatherland for the true principles of cooperation and love.[1]

From the start, then, the 20th century has often been regarded as a century less to celebrate than to survive. "The twentieth century after the birth of Christ was the period of the last great wars, civil dissension and revolutions," prophesied the Russian mystic Vladimir Solov'ev before his death in 1900. The Great War that began in 1914 confirmed the millennial calendar of the American pastor, Charles Taze Russell: the Times of the Gentiles closed with the guns of August; Jehovah's Witnesses would endure despite the collapse of human government, for Jesus now had mounted his judgment throne, assuring the faithful that *Millions Now Living Will Never Die*. Struck by the discovery of King Tut's golden tomb amidst the crumbling pyramids of Egypt and by the excavations of the splendid palaces at Knossos amidst the rubble of Crete, an English evangelist wrote in 1924, "We moderns are compelled to read the lessons of these dead civilizations." Christabel Pankhurst continued: "Strange, uncanny, and menacing to the world-system of to-day is the doom of these older systems. Human society does not, we see, move onward and upward in a straight ascending line." The Dutch historian Johan Huizinga in 1935 admitted, "We are living in a demented world. And we know it." There was, however, hope: "In contrast with the naive expectations of earlier times which saw the approach of the end of all things or of a golden age, our thinking is founded in the steady conviction that the crisis through which we are passing is a phase in a progressive irreversible sequence . . . [W]e all know that there is no way back, that we must fight our way *through*." That year, 1935, an increasingly bitter H. G. Wells identified the period between 1919 and 2059 as the Age of Frustration, flailing toward world government and world peace.[2]

Under such duress, the human prospect was questionable enough that even the sanguine president of the New York World's Fair of 1939 would confess that the word "future" bothered him ("I kept thinking of fortune-telling"). The secretary of his planning committee declared, "The world is in chaos struggling to master its own inventions. We are in danger of being annihilated by forces which we ourselves set up." Whereupon the Westinghouse fathers brought forth a new device, conceived by industry and dedicated to the Fair proposition that all centuries are not created equal. Their eight-hundred-pound time capsule, first of its kind, contained a Bible, the Lord's Prayer in three hundred languages, an English dictionary, four spools of microfilm, a magnifying instrument, two motion picture reels, samples of medicines, chemicals, and cosmetics, a woman's hat, and a guidebook to these proud remnants of 20th-century civilization, secure within an "inner crypt" of Pyrex glass and nitrogen gas. *The Book of Record of the Time Capsule of Cupaloy Deemed Capable of Resisting the Effects of Time for Five Thousand Years* did not begin with a technological boast or a paean to progress, as one might have expected from an exposition whose theme was "The World of Tomorrow" and whose prime attractions were the "time machine" moving chairs of the General Motors Futurama and the curvilinear ramps of the Perisphere surmounting an electrified model of Democracity, "a perfectly planned community of 11,000 square miles and 1.5 million people" where a heavenly chorus sang at dusk,

> "*We're the rising tide*
> *Coming from far and wide,*
> *Marching side by side on our way*
> *For a brave new world,*
> *Tomorrow's world*
> *That we shall build today.*"

Rather, *The Book of Record* took as epigraph two verses from Job 14: "If a man die, shall he live again? all the days of my appointed time will I wait, till my change come. Thou shalt call, and I will answer thee: thou wilt have a desire to the work of thine hands." Absent but implicit were the next verses: "For now thou numberest my steps: dost thou not watch over my sin? My transgression is sealed up in a bag, and thou sewest up my iniquity." Sealed with molten asphalt, the time capsule was buried fifty feet deep in Flushing Meadows at the instant of the autumnal equinox, September 23, 1938. "History teaches us that every culture passes through definite cycles of development, climax, and decay," read the introduction to *The Book of Record*. "And so, we must recognize, ultimately may ours." The book concluded with Messages for the Future from such distinguished men as physicist Robert Millikan ("If the rational scientific, progressive principles win out in this struggle [against despotism], there is a possibility of a warless, golden age ahead for mankind"), Albert Einstein ("anyone who thinks about the future must live in fear and terror"), and the German novelist Thomas Mann, in American refuge—like Einstein—from Hitler's Third Reich. Wrote Mann, "We know now that the idea of the future as a 'better world' was a fallacy of the doctrine of progress. The hopes we center on you, citizens of the future, are in no way exaggerated." Yet in each generation there had to be a certain indwelling spirit, "the endeavor on the part of man to approximate to his idea of himself." This, maybe, would survive to the day of the opening of the capsule five thousand years up, or down, the road.[3]

One year down the road, almost to the day, saw the opening of World War II. By the Jewish calendar the 1st of September 1939 was the 17th of Elul 5699. In thirteen days would come the new year 5700 A.M. and, according to popular kabbalistic traditions, the end of days, the Messiah, and the Redemption. Neither the Messiah nor the Redemption came that year, we know now, and the "end of days" arrived with the boxcars at the crematoria of Auschwitz and Treblinka, or at the Eastern Front, on the banks of anonymous shooting pits slaked with lime. If the 20th century has been throughout a *fin de siècle* raised tenfold to the pitch of a millennium's end, it has abounded in the most malign of *fin de siècle* ironies, the most baneful of janiform oppositions, and the Jews who have so far outlasted them have particular reason to regard this as a century less to celebrate than to survive.[4]

A brief review of the "Jewish question" should, in fact, afford us a sharper perspective from which to appreciate the extremity and janiformity of our present *fin de siècle*. Christendom has long cast the Jew with a bifrons countenance: one, the rearguard, stiff-necked, nearsighted, secretive, tribal, vengeful, slave to the Old Law, antagonist to the New; the other, the avantgarde, agile, farsighted, brilliant, cosmopolitan, compassionate, whose return out of exile to the Holy Land is critical to the fulfillment of New Testament prophecies of the Second Coming. Since the Napoleozoic Era, the bifrons countenance of the Jew has been cut in ever higher relief. On the sinistral side, images borrowed from the new sciences of biology, sociology, and bacteriology have been used to depict the Jew as a racial degenerate, a cultural atavism, an insidious parasite. From these images (and the older image of the Jew as Christ-killer) it was a short distance to the Russian pogroms of the 1880s, of 1903, of 1919; to the *fin de siècle* anti-Semitism of the French right wing and the anti-Semitic riots of 1898 around the retrial of Captain Alfred Dreyfus, a Jewish officer falsely convicted of spying; and to Nazi Germany's Final Solution (the "Third Reich" itself a Joachimist image misbegotten at century's turn).[5]

On the dextral side, the Abbé Grégoire was imagining a millennial harmony of the peoples of the world as he advanced the civil rights of the Jews during the French Revolution. The 19th-century Christian sponsors of Jewish settlement in that region of the Ottoman Empire called Palestine were looking ahead to Christ's millennial reign; the emancipation of the Jews and their emigration to the Holy Land were "Foregleams of the Day." Anticipating the final return of the tribes of Judah and Israel for 1899, American fundamentalists on March 4, 1891, petitioned U.S. President Benjamin Harrison (as if it were in his power) to see that Palestine was given immediately to the Jews so that they could rebuild the Temple on the tight schedule of these Last Days. With similar though muted Christian millennial hopes, Arthur Balfour, British Foreign Minister, issued his Declaration in favor of a Jewish national home in Palestine in November 1917, one month before General Sir Edmund Allenby wrested Palestine from the Turks and dismounted (it is said) to enter Jerusalem on foot, lest he presume upon that One whose sovereign right it soon would be to make a triumphal entry on horseback into the holiest of cities.[6]

Within the Jewish world, a bifrons countenance had also been shaped by Jews themselves: one, the Eastern visage, orthodox, narrow-minded, superstitious, mean-spirited, unhealthy, conservative, slave to tradition and enemy of progress; the other, the Western visage, enlightened, intellectually limber, rational, humanitarian, robust, liberal, advocate of change and progress. This of course was the countenance as shaped by Western European Jews, but when anti-Semitic gangs and their impresarios struck at both visages at once, attacking "backward" Polish/Russian Jews for sacrificing Christian children, accusing "enlightened" Jews in Vienna, Paris, and New York of secretly conspiring to world dominion, there was no cheek left to turn. Ancient or modern, the Jew at the end of the 19th century had, it seemed, no safe face, no safe place.

A Jew could perhaps turn tail and assimilate to the society and religion of Christians, as a number of well-established German and Austrian Jews had done, beginning with the daughters of that eminent 18th-century philosopher, Moses Mendelssohn. He could declare his exclusive allegiance to suffering humanity at large and write *Das Kapital*. She or he could march with brazen socialist banners announcing a workers' international, as the young Russian Chaim Zhitlowsky did when he found "the Jewish question confronting me like a Sphinx: Solve my riddle or I will devour you." But these, decided Theodor Herzl, were acts of denial; they could not survive the Sphinx's riddles: Where is the place of the Jew *as* a Jew in contemporary life? What shall be done in the present by the bifrons Jew facing a long-endured exilic past and a long-deferred messianic future?[7]

Herzl's own strenuous efforts to leave his Jewishness behind for the cultivated aristocracy of Vienna had been only half-successful. Frustrated as a dandy and an aesthete, alarmed by French anti-Semitism to which he was witness as correspondent for a Viennese newspaper, Herzl in 1895 began "pounding away . . . at a work of tremendous magnitude. I don't know even now if I will be able to carry it through," he wrote on the first page of his diary, dated Shavuot, the Feast of Weeks, commemorating God's gift of the Torah. Like that revelation at Mount Sinai, this new revelation in Paris bore "the aspects of a mighty dream. . . . What will come of it is still too early to say. However, I have had experience enough to tell me that even as a dream it is remarkable and should be written down—if not as a memorial for mankind, then for my own pleasure and meditation in years to come. Or perhaps as something between these two possibilities—that is, as something for literature. If no action comes out of this romancing, a Romance at least will come out of this activity." The title of the mighty dream was *The Promised Land*, which became *The Jewish State*, a pamphlet of 1896, and *Altneuland* (*Oldnewland*), a utopian novel of 1900 with as explicitly janiform a title as any historian might desire for Herzl's reply to the Sphinx.[8]

The Zionist movement which Herzl made into his life's romance was exemplary of the century's end at which Herzl found himself. Max Nordau, who had so vehemently charged his generation with degeneration, delivered the opening address to the first Zionist Congress in 1897, arguing that a national home could regenerate "a race of accursed beggars" whose talents were repressed or repudiated by the gentile establishment. Jan Bloch, whose six volumes on *The Future War* (1898) were the most prophetic of the many *fin de siècle* works anticipating the Great War, would become the Zionist general secretary despite an early conversion to Calvinism. And Herzl, believing in 1895 that "for me life has ended and world history has begun," stepped to the podium of the Zionist Congress in Basel two years later fully aware of the mighty dream of redemption and rebirth at century's turn. "Before us rose a marvelous and exalted figure, kingly in bearing and stature, with deep eyes in which could be read quiet majesty and unuttered sorrow," reported one of the delegates. "It is no longer the elegant Dr. Herzl of

Vienna; it is a royal scion of the House of David, risen from among the dead, clothed in legend and fantasy and beauty." Herzl spoke in millennial, janiform clauses: "Zionism has already brought about something remarkable, heretofore regarded as impossible: a close union between the ultramodern and the ultraconservative elements of Jewry. . . . Should we not be stirred by a premonition of great events when we remember that at this moment the hopes of thousands upon thousands of our people depend upon our assemblage? . . . Let {our Congress} be worthy of our past, the renown of which, though remote, is eternal!" Wild applause. "For fifteen minutes the delegates clapped, shouted and waved their handkerchiefs. The dream of two thousand years was on the point of realization."[9]

The birth of a Jewish republic a jubilee later, on Friday, May 14, 1948, on the eve of the Christian Pentecost, was a rejoinder to the nightmare of the Holocaust, a defiant response to the Sphinx's riddle, and the waking of a "dream of two thousand years." From its conception, however, Israel has been an Oldnewland torn between antiquity and futurity, its present preoccupied with survival, and the country has become the primary janiform site of our *fin de siècle*. For most Christians, Israel lies in the sacred past, a poorly inked map at the back of the Bible, the territory of Jesus in whose footsteps thousands of pilgrims follow each spring. For many fundamentalist or "born-again" Christians, the existence of Israel is the pledge of an imminent Second Coming—for did not Jesus in Matthew 24 promise that upon the return of the Jews to their homeland all of the latter signs of the end of the world would be seen in short order, and then the Tribulation, and finally the "Son of man coming in the clouds of heaven, with power and great glory"? Those privileged to be alive at the creation of the State of Israel must therefore take to heart Christ's prophecy, "Verily I say unto you, This generation shall not pass till all these things be fulfilled." When Israeli troops occupied the Old City of Jerusalem during the Six-Day War of 1967, the millenarian evangelist Hal Lindsey was most delighted. As he explained in *The Late Great Planet Earth*, the single best-selling English-language book of the 1970s, he and the prophet Zechariah had been expecting such a miracle: their Armageddon timetable called for a prior "abomination of desolation" or defilement of the Jewish Temple, a Third Temple which the Jews must begin to build upon Mount Moriah, in the (Islamic) heart of the Old City. Soon, within *our* generation (of forty years? sixty years?), around this century's end, the perpetual Middle East crisis must explode into the Millennium.[10]

"You know," Ronald Reagan told Tom Dine, executive director of the American-Israel Public Affairs Committee, "I turn back to your ancient prophets in the Old Testament and the signs foretelling Armageddon, and I find myself wondering if—if we're the generation that's going to see that come about. I don't know if you've noted any of those prophecies lately but, believe me, they certainly describe the times we're going through." That an American President in 1983 should speak so casually of Israel in such less than casual terms (and of Russia as the Gog from the North who must attack Israel to initiate the battle of Armageddon) may be less than comforting, but it serves notice of the close and continuous identification American Protestants have made between themselves and Old Testament Jews ever since New England missionaries mistook Algonquian for Hebrew and the North American natives for the Ten Lost Tribes. If Puritan theocracy eventually gave way to Enlightenment democracy, American poets, preachers, and politicians have never abandoned the image of America as a New Jerusalem, home for exiles, light unto the nations, last best hope of humankind. From this perspective the State of Israel is an American state of mind, Israel's survival a testimonial to the spiritual integrity of the fifty (jubilee) United States. Reagan's fellow traveler, the Reverend Jerry Falwell, who at the President's behest attended National Security Council briefings, would assert that "God has raised up America in these last days for the cause of world evangelization and for the protection of his people, the Jews." America's "vital interests" in the Mideast may refer to energy and security, but those interests are far more complex than the immiscible oil and water of political economy and naval strategy. America has been the historical middle ground between once and future kingdoms, a provisional Zion, and now it must stand surety that what began in the Holy Land millennia ago will come to its prophetic conclusion near the town of Megiddo on the plain of Esdraelon in the Galilee.[11]

Defined in time by the extremes of a Holocaust past and a holocaust apparently to come, loosely but inextricably bound by Christian and American myth-historical agendas, Israel also finds itself split from within as it confronts a resurgent Arab world. This too, the Islamic revival, is a *fin de siècle* phenomenon whose mahdist excitement began with the elegant, eloquent, six-foot-six Shiʿite leader Sayyid Musa al Sadr, who emerged in Lebanon as (an) Imam in 1390 A.H. (1970) and disappeared mysteriously in 1398 A.H. (as had the twelfth imam a thousand years before). Shiʿite revolutionaries from Iran searched for Musa under the direct orders of the Ayatollah Ruhollah Khomeini, who saw Musa as his son and disciple. Musa could not be found, but Khomeini, assuming the title of Imam, could and did overturn the Shah's regime in, of all years, 1399/1400 A.H. The Shiʿite revolutionaries of 1978/80 prayed, "O God, keep Khomeini until the revolution of the Mahdi," a figure frequently sighted on the Iraqi front. One deputy to the Islamic Parliament in Teheran predicted an Iranian victory over Iraq as prelude to a march on Jerusalem "in order to acclaim the reappearance of the Hidden Imam as the Mahdi, and to witness the reappearance of Jesus Christ and his final conversion to Islam."[12]

Focus of powerful, competing, and increasingly impatient chiliastic expectations at this century's end, Israel as Oldnewland is being stretched from within to tremendous extremes. While some Jews press impatiently to extend the nation's borders to its Old Testament frontiers in anticipation of the Messiah or another Masada, others fearful of a final, obliterating violence press impatiently for the millennial reconciliation of Arab and Jew. It is scarcely a visionary act to foresee that tensions between the diverse political and religious parties and factions will not ease on the approach of the year 2000. The impatience in the air is a *fin de siècle* impatience and will not readily dissolve. Characteristic of such impatience (and exasperation), an American Jewish Sunday School text suggests that the only way toward lasting peace in the Middle East, now that all the older generations have fought themselves to bitter exhaustion, is to send the little children out to war. On their long march sometime before the year 2000, they shed their cumbersome belts of bullets, their heavy rifles, and reach the field of combat eager for lunch. Sharing the contents of their lunchbuckets and canteens with one another, Arab child-warriors and Jewish child-warriors are transformed into permanent ambassadors of peace to their anxious elders back home.[13]

Would that this generation not pass away till these things be fulfilled, but already the young children of Israel, Arab and Jew, are being raised as warriors. At our century's end, Israel presents the full and double aspect of apocalypse: New revelations from old scrolls / old rivalries rekindled. A land of lively pioneers / a land of burnt-out tanks and dry bones. A blooming desert in the Negev / a burning plain near Megiddo.

That we should so often trace world disorder through assassination and terrorism to conflicts in the Middle East; that we should conceive of Israel as the flashpoint for global nuclear war; that Israeli hunters and judges of Nazi war criminals should be represented forty years after World War II as keepers of the modern conscience; that the Millennium itself should hinge upon affairs in Jerusalem—all this makes it clear that from a Western prospect Israel stands (or falls) as *fin de siècle* synecdoche to the world. Its tensions between culturally disparate refugee-immigrants, between the old settlers from Europe and new settlers from North Africa and the Mideast, between socialist left and religious right, between Muslim and Jew, are, writ small but concentrated, the extreme global tensions we claim (or too vehemently disclaim) as our own at this century's end—tensions between "natives" and "aliens," between industrialized "North" and labor-intensive "South," between "First World" and "Third World," between the ravelins and unraveling of tradition, between methods of prophecy, modes of revelation, philosophies of time. If Israel seems always to be in a state of emergency, we are everyone, says Swiss historian Denis de Rougemont, in a state of emergency; if Israel's fate seems insusceptible to reason, our fate as a humane species has become "unthinkable," at the mercy of the irrational. "The civilization of the world today," warns the Japanese Buddhist leader Daisaku Ikeda on an April Fool's Day, "is swayed almost completely by the desires of the lesser selves of mankind."[14]

Flectere si nequeo superos, Acheronta movebo: "If I cannot bend the higher powers, I shall stir up [the river of] hell below." Thus the frustrated goddess Juno in Virgil's *Aeneid* as she summons Allecto, a demonic hermaphroditic Fury, to whip the camp of Aeneas's allies into a sexual and martial frenzy. Thus Sigmund Freud in a letter of July 17, 1899, as he chooses this motto for the *Interpretation of Dreams*, then refers to a sculpture on his desk, the stone Janus "who looks at me with his two faces in a very superior manner." Thus Theodor Herzl, in a letter of December 31, 1900, as he considers a creditable rumor that no amount of money can persuade the Sultan to part with Palestine, then vows to convince his financier friends to cut off funds to the Turkish government. Thus, by implication, the *fin de siècle* embrace of passion and violence, of the forbidden and the repressed, and the *fin de siècle* detour from diplomacy to blackmail, from Camp David to armed camps.[15]

If not heaven, then hell. This is the endemic ultimatum of centuries' ends, an ultimatum all the more ultimate at millennium's end. "I may live in a time in which no congruence can be established between the good things of the present and the necessary things of the future," wrote the American social economist Robert L. Heilbroner in 1980. The Eighties and the Nineties hold out such extremes that what we fear and what we desire threaten to tear us apart one from another and, like the medieval *psychomachia*, from within, a battle of the selves. "We are in search of a second naiveté," notes a Jesuit theologian, but the wholeness of innocence escapes us.[16] We come instead to speak of ourselves as

MULTIPLE PERSONALITIES

IT FOLLOWS FROM THE ESSENTIAL JANIFORMITY OF CENTURIES'
ends and from the extremity of our century's end that we should now most
acutely experience ourselves, like our times, as double: young *and* old,
rational *and* irrational, cruel *and* loving, masculine *and* feminine, deadly *and*
nurturing. While we talk of transcending these polarities, while our most
serious cultural debates concern the reconception of age, intelligence, emotion, gender, humanity itself, we commonly oppose right-brain to left-brain
talents, our artistic "side" to our prosaic "side," and complain of "splitting"
headaches, split personalities, schizophrenic lives. There is a looseness of
language and a confusion of diagnoses here, for technically the two halves
of the brain have as little to do with "split personality" as "split personality"
has to do with schizophrenia. But in a world of doubles, a world of instant
copiers, instant replays, voice synthesizers, female impersonators, surgical
transsexuals, "lovable" automata, industrial robots, genetic clones, double
agents, double binds, doubletalk, doublethink, doublespeak ("War Is
Peace," "Less Is More," a spluttering President is a "Great Communicator"),
the looseness and confusion are pervasive and persuasive.

Doubles, to be sure, are scarcely confined to appearances at ends of
centuries, yet their appearances are brushed with intimations of ending.
Young, cold, and beautiful Narcissus, punished for his indifference by the
goddess Nemesis, dies of an unrequitable love for his own reflection. The
obsessive doctor Henry Jekyll, M.D., D.C.L., LL.D., F.R.S., dies entrapped
in the noxious person of Edward Hyde. After death, the soul of a Central
Australian aborigine joins his Double in an ancestral cave, where he is reborn.
These are examples of the three archetypal encounters with a Double. An
encounter of the first (or Freudian) kind is with the Double as a haunting,
ghostlike or childlike self out of the past. An encounter of the second (or
Faustian) kind is with the Double as antitype, the worse but seductive half
of a self struggling to mature in the present. An encounter of the third (or
Jungian) kind is with the Double as the self's unearthly counterpart from
the dreamtime, the collective unconscious, or the future. Encounters of the
first kind concern amnesia, insatiable desire, and the exclusion of others; of
the second kind, ambition, obsession, and the extension of oneself; of the
third kind, amplitude, discontinuity, and the extension of one's time. In
each and every case, to meet up with one's Double is to meet up with one's
fate.[17]

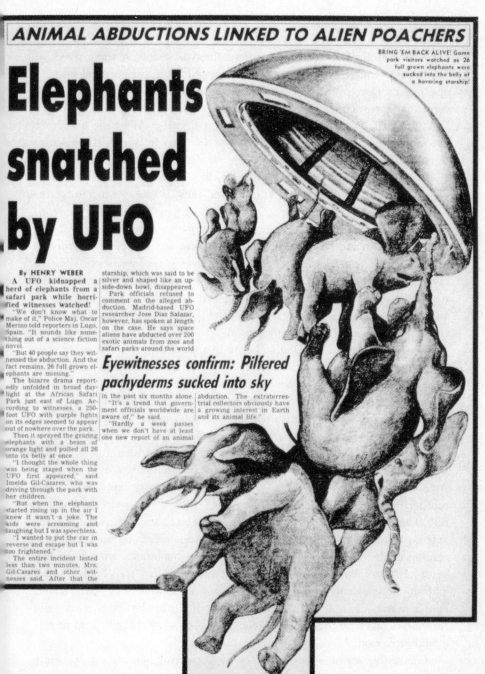

ANIMAL ABDUCTIONS LINKED TO ALIEN POACHERS

Elephants snatched by UFO

BRING 'EM BACK ALIVE! Game park visitors watched as 26 full grown elephants were sucked into the belly of a hovering starship!

By HENRY WEBER

A UFO kidnapped a herd of elephants from a safari park while horrified witnesses watched!

"We don't know what to make of it," Police Maj. Oscar Merino told reporters in Lugo, Spain. "It sounds like something out of a science fiction novel.

"But 40 people say they witnessed the abduction. And the fact remains, 26 full grown elephants are missing."

The bizarre drama reportedly unfolded in broad daylight at the African Safari Park just east of Lugo. According to witnesses, a 250-foot UFO with purple lights on its edges seemed to appear out of nowhere over the park.

Then it sprayed the grazing elephants with a beam of orange light and pulled all 26 into its belly at once.

"I thought the whole thing was being staged when the UFO first appeared," said Imelda Gil-Casares, who was driving through the park with her children.

"But when the elephants started rising up in the air I knew it wasn't a joke. The kids were screaming and laughing but I was speechless.

"I wanted to put the car in reverse and escape but I was too frightened."

The entire incident lasted less than two minutes, Mrs. Gil-Casares and other witnesses said. After that the starship, which was said to be silver and shaped like an upside-down bowl, disappeared.

Park officials refused to comment on the alleged abduction. Madrid-based UFO researcher Jose Diaz Salazar, however, has spoken at length on the case. He says space aliens have abducted over 200 exotic animals from zoos and safari parks around the world

Eyewitnesses confirm: Pilfered pachyderms sucked into sky

in the past six months alone.

"It's a trend that government officials worldwide are aware of," he said.

"Hardly a week passes when we don't have at least one new report of an animal abduction. The extraterrestrial collectors obviously have a growing interest in Earth and its animal life."

Fanciful illustration to an article concerning the UFO abduction of twenty-six elephants from a safari park in Spain, from the *Weekly World News*, July 26, 1988.

At the ends of centuries, when fatefulness is widely at stake, Doubles rise to the occasion. So we have observed the wildman, the heretical woman, and Faust's Devil making dramatic appearances at centuries' ends, in the company of Antichrist, paramount encounter of the second kind, Christ's Double in the years just before the Second Coming. We have noted the appeal of the Abbot Joachim's "men of a new breed," spiritual emissaries or radical avant-gardes of the Third Age expected or celebrated at centuries' ends in encounters of the third kind. Of the first kind we have seen men, women, and children possessed at centuries' ends (as late as 1692 in Salem, Massachusetts) by self-absorbed Doubles who act with demonic abandon, play merciless pranks, threaten pregnancy and parturition. Here belong that misogyny and witch-hunting, that anti-Semitism and Jew-baiting conformable to *fin de siècle* perceptions of women and Jews as the nemeses of Western civilization, for in these delusive encounters women appear as sensual, corrupt, spiteful, ageless Doubles violating the handsome innocence of men, and Jews appear as sensual, ghastly, spiteful, ancient Doubles subverting the new-found grace of the Holy Ghost.

During the 1790s the Double began to appear without disguise in novelistic encounters of the second kind. "Man is like those twin-births, that have two heads indeed, and four hands; but if you attempt to detach them from each other, they are inevitably subjected to miserable and lingering destruction," wrote the English radical William Godwin in 1794 in *Things as They Are, or The Adventures of Caleb Williams*, whose title character is "second conscience" to Falkland, an irresistibly attractive country gentleman whose act of murder Williams (despite himself) must expose. The monk Ambrosio's Double lies within, urging him on to lust, rape, incest, and murder throughout that tale of horror, *The Monk*, "a curst Book after all, full of every Thing that should not be anywhere," and, of course, all the rage in 1796. Matthew Gregory Lewis, the adolescent author, had been reading Godwin, but he had also an intimate acquaintance with a German genre of *Horrid Mysteries*, and it was a German novelist, Jean Paul Richter, who would repeatedly invoke the Doppelgänger (his word, in 1796), an alter ego, a nearly identical twin without whom the other has neither past nor future, yet in whose present and presence tragedy must ensue: a dead ringer, a fatal attraction.[18]

Gradually, across a 19th century of fascinating semblances, of Mary Shelley's *Frankenstein*, E. T. A. Hoffmann's "Sand-Man," Edgar Allan Poe's "William Wilson," of a moving waxwork Napoleon, of French magician

Robert-Houdin's mechanical conjuring man, of English magician John Nevil Maskelyne's mind-reading automaton Psycho, the Double became at once more familiar and more estranging. When Robert Louis Stevenson's *Strange Case of Dr. Jekyll and Mr. Hyde* was published in 1886, its immediate popularity was due in part to a *fin de siècle* suspicion that, as the American detective Allan Pinkerton already knew, many an evil man could be living a double life. Pinkerton in 1885 had written of the "strange career of a man, who for years moved in the best circles of society, who was universally respected, . . . and yet who was for years associated with hardened criminals, and actively engaged in criminal exploits." Stevenson's Dr. Jekyll, likewise, has not simply made an alchemical miscalculation; Mr. Hyde is a fundament of his being. Henry Jekyll long ago recognized in himself an "impatient gaiety of disposition" that was "incommensurate" with a desire for public honor. "Hence it came about that I concealed my pleasures; and that when I reached the years of reflection, and began to look round me and take stock of my progress and position in the world, I stood already committed to a profound duplicity of life." Jekyll's attraction to Hyde is at heart an addiction; the doctor must use ever stronger doses of his metamorphic drug to restore himself to propriety as Hyde becomes ever more insistent upon his own right to life. In the toils of what he calls a "moral weakness," Jekyll acknowledges "that truth, by whose partial discovery I have been doomed to such a dreadful shipwreck: that man is not truly one, but truly two. . . . I hazard the guess that man will be ultimately known for a mere polity of multifarious, incongruous, and independent denizens."[19]

Not man so much as woman, if the truth be known and trust be given to accounts bursting into public view during the late 19th century. Contemporary with late-18th-century gothic novels of Doppelgängers, necromancers, ghosts, and sleepwalkers, there had been many reports of mesmeric trances and prophetic somnambulism, which raised questions about a waking and a sleeping consciousness, and there had been two reports of Doubles of the second kind in 1791, one from Germany describing a twenty-year-old Stuttgart woman who suddenly "exchanged her personality"—language, manners, habits—for that of an aristocratic French lady, another from the United States describing a young man of Massachusetts who, some time past, "seemed to have two distinct minds." Between this *fin de siècle* and the next, accounts of actual cases of "double consciousness" or "divided consciousness" or "double personality" were rare, despite a growing genre of fiction that included Dostoyevsky's *The Double* (1846). Indeed, only a dozen cases were reported before 1880, preponderantly women, preponderantly Mary Reynolds, whose history was so variously recounted that her case was confused into three.[20]

According to a comprehensive review in 1888 by the famous American physician and novelist Silas Weir Mitchell, Mary Reynolds in the spring of 1811 began to have "two distinct lives antipodal from every mental and moral point of view." Her first self was sedate, melancholy, bookish, reserved; her second self charged joyfully through the Pennsylvania woods, grinned down a bear, seized rattlesnakes by the tail, and played inventive, acutely embarrassing tricks on her stick-in-the-mud other self. Sole competitor for fame in medical annals was Félida X., a young Frenchwoman whose first self was depressed, morose, uncommunicative, and whose second self (from 1858 on) was lively, gay, confident, and chatty.[21]

Then, abruptly, cases of "divided consciousness" quintupled; more than sixty were reported in Europe and America between 1880 and 1906. The reports fit a *fin de siècle* of "double vision" (1889) and "double exposure" (1892); of spirit photography and of ethereal beings speaking from astral planes or Edison phonographs; of new "double" agents and silent mimes; of androgynous lovers in occult fiction and the popular paintings of centaurs, sphinxes, mermaids; of the biostatistical study of monsters and twins; of a physiological, neurological, and philosophical fascination with the left and right sides of the brain; and of a medical and psychological fascination with hypnosis, a technique that seemed to lay bare the layers of consciousness. All this led to speculation that each of us might be host to another self. By 1897 the New York physician R. Osgood Mason was willing to dare the blatant question, "Is it not quite possible, then, that other normal, ordinary people, possess a second personality, deep-down beneath their ordinary, everyday self, and that under conditions which favor a readjustment, this hidden subliminal self may emerge . . . ?" English writer and wheelwright George Sturt, "at a loose end" after finishing his book on *Art and Evolution* in the fall of 1900, walked through an "uncomfortably sloppy fog" twelve days into the new century and had a vision of the artistic side of his life. "At the same moment there went through my mind a memory of that sense of *solidity*—of reality—which we derive from touching a thing with two fingers instead of one, or from seeing it with two eyes, so that, feeling it in two places, our sense of it is a combination of two impressions. And for just that moment, because I had seen my existence on two sides simultaneously instead of on only the one side, it seemed decidedly more real than before."[22]

In such context, "divided consciousness" was an eminently presentable experience and diagnosis, ripe for Broadway. Cases did not merely multiply; they became multiple. Alma Z. began with a "duplex personality" consisting of a dignified, bedridden "No. 1" who quoted flawlessly from Tennyson, and a childish, healthy "Twoey" whose limited vocabulary was further muddled by an Indian accent; soon there was a third person, "The Boy," to help out "No. 1" after marriage. French psychologist Pierre Janet's patient Léonie was sad, calm, slow, timid; as Léontine she was gay, noisy, restless, and pert; later, as Léonore, she was very grave. Mollie Fancher, "the Brooklyn enigma," a fasting girl, bedridden, educated, and clairvoyant, started off by defining the reflection of her first self as Sunbeam, who did fine knitting. Then came Idol, her jealous, mischievous enemy who unravelled the knitting; Pearl, a smooth, cultured letter writer; Rosebud, curled up, speaking as a child; and Ruby, bright, vivacious, witty, fond of making fun. Miss Beauchamp of Boston was a scrupulously conscientious bibliophile, neurasthenic, insomniac, often invalid. She was also Sally, "the spirit of mischief incarnate," fighting for her independence against the hypnotic entreaties of therapist Morton Prince, whose painstaking work eventually brought to light B.I (the saintly, suffering Miss Beauchamp, herself a faction); B.Ia (a substrate); B.II (a shadow); B.III (Sally, a robust, defiant, childish, selfish "devil"); B.IV (the Idiot, a good person but otherwise the antithesis of B.I), B.IVa and B.IVb (substrates). Prince marked the "real self" with an X, suggesting that the achievement of X would be a true resurrection, a perfect fusion of the lives of B.IV ("before," the Idiot [or the Innocent]) and B.I ("be one," the Saint [and the Martyr]). The resolution of this complex encounter with Doubles of the first and second kinds would be, it seemed, a Second Coming.[23]

When Miss Beauchamp arrived on Broadway in the persons of actress Frances Starr in *The Case of Becky* in 1912, Prince's *fin de siècle* apocalyptic imagery was muted. A reviewer noted that "one is as deeply moved to see 'wicked little Becky' going back into the darkness from whence she came as one is happy in seeing 'sweet Dorothy' relieved of her fears." By this time, too, cases of multiple personality had begun their dramatic decline, disbelieved by Freudian psychiatrists and/or subsumed under a new diagnostic category that did not allow each "self" the independence of "co-consciousness." In 1911 Swiss physician Eugen Bleuler had fully described and designated "schizophrenia," a misnomer referring not to a "split" personality, not to full and distinct selves doing battle with each other, but to psychic disorganization, to a malady of blunted affect, autistic behavior, delusions, hallucinations, voices not from within but, as it were, from beyond. Between 1911 and 1939, there were 36 reported cases of multiple personality, 3600 reported cases of schizophrenia. When C. H. Thigpen and H. M. Cleckley wrote up the case of Mrs. White in 1954 and again, with greater verve, as *The Three Faces of Eve*, in 1957, they believed that they were dealing with the only multiple personality alive, while schizophrenics occupied the majority of beds in mental hospitals in Europe and North America.[24]

At the approach of this century's end, multiple personalities have resurfaced. According to Dr. Bennett G. Braun, a partisan of the disorder, there were 500 legitimate cases reported in the 1970s, 1000 by 1983, 5000 by 1986—another of those *fin de siècle* statistical series pointing to a "geometric increase." Conservative estimates, however, are equally impressive: 15 cases published or recognized between 1945 and 1969, 50 cases identified during the 1970s, 150 cases treated since 1979 at the National Institute of Mental Health in Maryland alone, perhaps 1000 reports worldwide. In 1986, Dr. Eugene L. Bliss, another partisan, claimed personally to have seen more than a hundred multiple personality cases over the last five years. "There's a galaxy of them out there," said Bliss.[25]

It is a galaxy more multiple than ever. No longer the three faces of Eve but Sybil's sixteen (Sybil, Vicky, Marcia, Vanessa, Mary, Helen, Clara, Sybil Ann, The Blonde, Peggy Ann, Peggy Lou, Mike, Sid, Nancy Lou Ann, Marjorie, and Ruthie) making their public appearance in a 1973 bestseller and a two-part television movie. Or Billie Milligan with twenty-four, among them an escape artist, a con artist, a lesbian, a thug, a drug dealer, an Australian big-game hunter, a "Boston bitch," an Orthodox Jew, a comedian, a keeper of pain, a conservative Englishman fluent in Arabic, a brutal Yugoslav fluent in Serbo-Croatian, and "Billy all in one piece," the Teacher, appearing in another bestseller in 1981. Or Nancy Lynn Gooch's fifty-six, including Nancy/Regan, summoned hypnotherapeutically at the command words, "Zenith, Zero," according to her 1987 *Nightmare*. Or the Toby of *Through a Mind Divided* (1988), whose mere thirteen personalities consisted of five pairs of matched twins and three supernatural entities, the Dark Ones, sent by Archangel Michael to watch over the spiritual progress of them all.[26]

Whether or not an artifact of therapy, elicited through suggestion, manufactured under hypnosis, or fabricated by talented thespians, multiple personality is an especial artifact of this century's end. Skeptical inquirers may suspect the motives of therapists and clients alike, but the bestsellers are fact; the television movies and investigative reports on "20/20" and "Sixty Minutes" are fact; the recognition of a Multiple Personality Disorder by the

1980 edition of the standard psychiatric authority, *The Diagnostic and Statistical Manual of Mental Disorders* (*DSM-III*), is fact; the more than two hundred therapists, "each with one or more multiples in treatment," jamming the Georgian Ballroom of the Penta Hotel in New York City in 1986 for the First International Conference on Multiple Personality and Dissociative States, are fact; and the legal credence given to multiple personality as an exculpatory disorder in the acquittals of Billie Milligan (1978), Ester Minor (1979), and Paul Miskimen (1980) is fact. (That each of a multiple's personalities might have the right to independent legal counsel is, so far, supposition.)[27]

Noticing the sudden concern with Doubles and plural existences during the 1790s and again during the 1890s, Dutch historian J. H. van den Berg has called attention to Hegel's *fin de siècle* observations on estrangement and Durkheim's observations, a *fin de siècle* later, on anomie or normlessness. Van den Berg suggests that images of a divided existence—of the Double, the Doppelgänger, the "subconscious," the "unconscious," the multiple consciousness—become most compelling when relationships between people are most deranged, when communities are most disjointed, when labor is so subdivided that workers are estranged from their work. This is a mildly Marxist argument, and other critics have argued further that the incidence of schizophrenia in the modern West must be understood as a leading symptom of capitalism, a mortal disease which alienates us from our work, our desires, our human integrity, our very selves. Living as we are in the later phases of Late Capitalism, we should expect to see the disjointedness of our civilization reflected in the prominence of schizophrenia, one of whose common features is a distorted, frequently futureless or apocalyptic sense of time.[28]

The drift here is toward yet another confusion of schizophrenia with multiple personality, a confusion as rife on psychiatric wards as at cocktail parties.[29] That the schizophrenic's "apparent chaos of inconsistent visions, voices, and characters" should at this late date be confused with the multiple's apparent stage-management of the different personalities, "often in the form of a more or less sentimental drama,"[30] may be a revealing instance of the typical *fin de siècle* confusion of chaos with plurality, but I do not intend to pursue a thesis directly linking Doubles and multiple personalities with social disruption or industrial oppression. There have been too many crises of community and of capitalism to account for the periodic specificity of multiple personalities, who are embraced as extreme but natural expressions of all our lives only at centuries' ends. "Two souls live, alas, in my breast!"

cried Goethe's Faust around 1800. "Have we all within us such a second personality?" asked Morton Prince rhetorically in 1890, years before he had met Clara Norton Fowler (his "Miss Beauchamp"). "With co-consciousness now the norm," claims a contributor to the *Brain/Mind Bulletin* in 1983, "the multiple personality syndrome can no longer be seen as a freak of nature but rather as a paradigm of how a process common to each and all of us can go wrong."[31]

What has gone wrong, it seems to us now, is childhood. The amnesia, the missing periods of time, the fugue states of timeless wandering by which multiple personalities are usually identified, cover episodes of childhood trauma during which other selves took over in dissociative self-defense against physical isolation, beatings, emotional violence, seduction, rape, incest. Such an etiology for the *disorder* of multiple personality is apposite to our tremendous impromptu anxiety in the 1980s over child abuse and "the epidemic of missing and exploited children." Nearly two million American children are reported missing every year, fifty thousand of them abducted by strangers, twice as many by an estranged parent. The children are tracked down by Child Find, Inc., by Find Me, Inc., by SEARCH, by Family & Friends of Missing Persons, by the National Center for Missing & Exploited Children, and through an FBI computer network established under the 1982 Missing Children Act. Their faces appear on milk cartons next to nutritional data, on post office flyers next to the Ten Most Wanted, on public service television bulletins between commercials for war toys and cleanser, on supermarket notice boards between coupons for air fresheners and chocolate chip cereal, on neighborhood telephone poles, competing with yard sales and lost dogs. The Pied Piper of Hamelin has been everywhere, and if most of the children do return, the "multiple personality epidemic" is here to remind us that children, and childhood, may be lost in more ways than one.[32]

Like the related "epidemic" of adolescent suicides, the "epidemics" of missing children and of multiple personalities are "epidemics" of centuries' ends. My ostentatious quotation marks are meant as warnings, for we have no incontestable proof that, proportional to population, the numbers of adolescent suicides, missing children, or multiple personalities are greater now than in the past. Whether due to a change in diagnostic fashions, or to a renewed interest in hypnosis, or to the persuasive electricity of the media, or to more sophisticated methods of collecting and processing medical data, or to a verifiable explosion of child abuse during the Cold War, our heightened cultural sensitivity to multiple personalities—as also to missing children and adolescent suicides—is an artifact of our highly janiform epoch.[33]

Multiple personalities have been recurring with such virulence at this century's end because they are peculiarly vivid expressions of our *fin de siècle* fears of the loss of generational continuity. They represent a radical break between parents and child, whose other personalities often assume different family names. They represent the harsh distancing of childhood from maturity; each person (or persona) blocks out more of the life history of the collective self, until life is disconcertingly atemporal. They represent a succession of encounters with Doubles of the first kind, such that there is no person left for the future.

In their acts of dissociation, multiple personalities withdraw from history by redistributing the experience and memory of unutterable pain. They stand as the darkest shadows of what critic Christopher Lasch has called our "minimal selves." Like most of the rest of us who meet the terrors of this nuclear age with the "psychic numbing" described by Robert Jay Lifton in *The Broken Connection*, multiple personalities mean to be survivors, but their motions toward disengagement are far more elaborate and extensive. During the Orwellian year 1984, psychiatrist David Spiegel defined multiple personality "as a post-traumatic stress disorder," bringing multiple personalities into the ranks of all the survivors of our times, from Bergen-Belsen and Nagasaki to Vietnam, Northern Ireland, and Lebanon.[34]

Since the end of the last century, we have been accustomed to mark off past and present according to generations scarred in their youth by war, Depression, political upheaval, or violently stunted dreams. Worried as we are at this century's end about our bequest to future generations, the issue of childhood trauma must come to the fore. And so it has—not only with the "epidemics" of missing children and multiple personalities, but on the largest scale, with increasingly heated confrontations over what it is we are doing to the environment in which our children must live. Is Western civilization conducting a massive campaign of child abuse? While science and literature are converging once again upon *fin de siècle* images of extinction through instant apocalypse, aggravated assault, or sheer exhaustion, philosophy is finding of a sudden that the rights of future generations are cloudy. "What should we do about future people?" asked philosopher Trudy Govier in 1979. Contending that we can and should "give heavier weight to claims of those who do exist than those of the future," Govier was emphatically not denying an urgent need to consider the consequences of our choices upon later generations. Rather, she maintained that parents can without moral prejudice decide against having a child if they expect that the child will be unhappy, and better off not existing. Her clinching argument was that, since the likelihood of "world-wide catastrophe as a result of nuclear or germ warfare or accidents involving sophisticated weaponry . . . is not insignificant, it is unreasonable to claim that we *know* now that people not born yet will be born and develop into persons."[35]

Govier was addressing a question ever more central to contemporary controversies over abortion, nuclear waste disposal, environmental protection, national debts. Like the combatants on one side or another of those conflicts, her paper is haunted by the *fin de siècle* ghosts of battered infants, missing children, suicidal youth, lost generations, self-destructing societies. At this century's end, each of us seems to bear within a wounded child whose presence is epitomized by the multiple personality. If, as has been proposed, "We are bound by ties of justice to real future persons," we seem at present to be equally bound by memories of unspeakable injustice to those in our individual and collective past. It is this janiform torment, represented by the *disorder* of multiple personality, that attends the turn of our millennium.[36]

In fission lies dissolution, in fusion a solution, as nuclear engineers, peace activists, and psychotherapists might say. The healing of a multiple personality through fusion or "merger" is exemplary of the "despairwork" detailed in *Despair and Personal Power in the Nuclear Age*. "Until now," wrote Joanna Macy in 1983, "every generation throughout history lived with the tacit certainty that other generations would follow." Now, "to be conscious in our world today involves awareness of unprecedented peril." In the place of *apatheia*, the inability or refusal to express pain, and of *apatheia*'s concomitant "double life" of despair and denial, we must recognize our grief, anticipatory though it may be, and use it "to build compassion, community, and commitment to act." We must not deceive our children with nuclear submarines christened *Corpus Christi* or nuclear warheads dubbed "Peacekeepers." A numb, doubletalking species has no future.[37]

"Toby was sad after her last personality integrated and the Dark Ones destroyed the internal world," noted her therapist. "There was no longer a place for her to escape to." Should these chaotic times happen also to be the endtimes, what mercy could there have been in such unforgiving therapy? After all, those who fully intend to survive the coming cataclysms are reading Chameleon's article, "Confessions of a V.I.P. (Variable Identity Person)" in the Loompanics Unlimited *1988 Main Catalog*, and they are ordering books on *How to Hide Anything*, *Camouflage: U. S. Army Field Manual FM 5-20*,

New I.D. in America: How to Create a Foolproof New Identity by Anonymous, *Disguise Techniques: Fool All of the People Some of the Time, How to Disappear Completely and Never Be Found, How to Get Lost and Start All Over Again,* and *Vanish!*—"Learn how to 'die' through advertisement—how to do it fast and make it last. Die and live. *Vanish!*" The fugue states, the absences and metamorphoses of the multiple personality are—are they not?—the skills of a survivor watching the Western family disintegrate around her and finding no refuge beyond herself, her selves. While rights to individual privacy are violated by governments that go so far as to put what some call the Mark of the Beast (the Social Security number) on each newborn, survivalists (unbeknownst to themselves) take as their implicit model the ultimate *fin de siècle* survivor, the multiple personality. They train themselves to be part woodswoman, part gunslinger, part medic, part handyman, part philosopher, alternately practical, mean, compassionate, ingenious, speculative—and devious, for they must not draw undue attention to their stockpiles of emergency supplies, their rifle practice, their camps in the hills of southern Oregon safe from terrorists and thermonuclear winds.[38]

Not just from a Third World War do we need the refuge and skills of the survivalist in these precarious years. Survivor Industries, Inc., of Newbury Park, California, provides seventy-two-hour emergency preparedness units for families and individuals (including Ark III, "A Great Starter Pak!") with rations, medicines, and tools "For Peace of Mind in any Emergency: Natural or Man-Made," such as "Auto breakdowns * Freeway delays/accidents * Floods, earthquakes, hurricanes, fires * Chemical spills." We must every one be Noahs, learning *How to Prosper during the Coming Bad Years* and *How You Can Find Happiness during the Collapse of Western Civilization.* "The situations requiring a survival outlook are endless and varied," says R.V.: Three Mile Island, old age, nuclear war. More moderate than many, R.V. around 1980 became a survivalist "almost as though someone else was working through me." At forty-one he has "a strange feeling that something of immense impact is going to occur in our lifetimes and, although I really don't know what it is, I want to be prepared for any contingency."[39]

Whitley Strieber may know what that something is, and he wants us all to be prepared for *Communion.* Earlier, in the Orwellian year, Strieber collaborated with James W. Kunetka on *War Day and the Journey Onward,* an impressively sober account of the aftermath of a "trivial," aborted nuclear war on October 18, 1988, during which only seven million Americans are instantly vaporized. Another sixty million die later of its effects. Then comes the Cincinnati flu of 1990 which kills more than two hundred million worldwide. *War Day* is a survivor's tale, and "The survivor's tale is the essential document of our time," write the narrators at the beginning of their journey across a post-nuclear America. "All of us have them; even babies have them." Now, in *Communion: A True Story*, a 1987 "Number One Bestseller," Strieber discovers that he himself, from childhood, has been a survivor.[40]

Of abduction by aliens.

Since the "flying saucer" waves of midcentury, Unidentified Flying Objects have established a janiform presence at the nuclear crossroads of Western culture. With their obviously supreme technology, the UFO commanders mean either to warn us (against our worst natures), or destroy us (for our hubris), or transform us (into higher beings). Nearing the millennium, still dubious of our abilities to split atoms for our own or the galactic good, the aliens over the last two decades have felt increasingly compelled to manifest themselves to us in shapes we may recognize as more or less human. They have become, accordingly, Doubles of the first kind, short, thin, neuter, childlike sibyls, silent or enigmatic; or Doubles of the second kind, rapacious reptiles or demons enclosed in a deceptive costume of earthling skin and hair but intent on conquest; or Doubles of the third kind, beautiful giants, baldheaded master intelligences, maternal ancients, anthropomorphic figures of pure energy inspiring us toward a global consciousness. These last may also stroll among us in perfect disguise as "walk-ins" and "star people," or they may choose as messengers a pair of Houston humans in alligator cardigans, Herff Applewhite and Bonnie Lee Trousdale Nettles, rebaptized Bo and Peep, to lead the lost sheep of the Earth back to Jesus and the Kingdom of God in an unidentified flying cloud of light.[41]

Meanwhile, the Space Supreme Court has been convening to determine the fate of the Earth. Out of a "huge floating space egg" comes, evenings and matinees since 1987, the fifteen-foot hologram of Sir Laurence Olivier (AKA Akash) to mediate a hearing during which a British rock star must show that humanity deserves more than a swan song. Whatever the Court's decision in the musical *Time*, there are bound to be in our immediate future waves of UFO sightings like those 185 in the last decade over Moscow, 242 over Jakarta, 250 over Rio de Janeiro, 285 over Tunis, 364 over Lima, and 392 over Beijing, or like the 5000 sightings above New York's Hudson Valley in the mid-Eighties. We must expect further revelations of "cover-ups" of UFO chases and crashes, more controversial *Close Encounters of the Third Kind* (1977) with more than one *E.T. the Extra-Terrestrial* (1982), and a surfeit of space aliens killed by cheeseburgers from Spanish drive-ins. "In fact, as the end nears, we are 'lousy' with space people everywhere we turn. You can't even trust your own mother, these days," writes Laura Mundo of Detroit, sixty-eight years old in 1981 and a thirty-year veteran of flying saucer research who has just received her first telepathic messages from the Spacepeople, informing her that "the Dire Emergency to the Planet is AT HAND."[42]

The Spacepeople and their saucers are here for us in such great numbers as firebreaks for the new millennium. Representatives from sixty extraterrestrial civilizations plan to "arrive on Earth and openly talk with world leaders before the end of the century," claims Mark Bauer, a Swiss astronomer. More people (some ninety-five percent) have heard of UFOs than have heard of almost anything else for which George Gallup ever polled, and two thirds of adult Americans believe that the Earth is being visited by extraterrestrial craft right this moment. They are everywhere: in beer commercials, rock videos, toy stores, movie theaters, department store windows, the skies above soccer stadiums. Astronauts and cosmonauts have seen them too—a myth so modern and attractive it cannot be dispelled. A *Variety* show-business headline in 1987 reads, "UFO projects eye otherworldly B.O. Four-decade-old topic hot again."[43]

Among the projects being readied for the otherworldly Box Office is a $10,000,000 film adaptation of Whitley Strieber's *Communion*, a book that brings into focus all the distal points of the *fin de siècle* constellation which I have been calling multiple personality. On December 26, 1985, in the middle of the night, in a high-security log cabin in upstate New York, one of the double doors into Strieber's bedroom moved. Peering around the door was a figure "too small to be a person, unless a child." It was three and a half feet tall, with "two dark holes for eyes and a black down-turning line of a mouth that later became an O." The figure, in a rounded hat and a square breastplate, rushed into the room. Blackness. Paralysis. A depression in the woods. Small figures in gray-tan body suits doing things to his head, trying to explain, cradling him in a messy round room. Extreme dread. "I was in a mental state that separated me from myself so completely that I had no way to filter my emotions or most immediate reactions, nor could my personality initiate anything. . . . I was in my forebrain, locked away from the rest of myself." A squat figure proposing to insert a hair-thin needle into his brain. Argument, screaming. "What can we do to help you stop screaming?" "You could let me smell you." Cardboard and cinnamon. A bang and a flash. Operation under four kinds of alien eyes: robotic; dark holes; black slanted; buttonlike. Alien hands—"soft, even soothing, but there were so many of them that it felt a little as if I were being passed along by rows of insects." Legs drawn apart. Gray, scaly, narrow object a foot long with wires at end, inserted into rectum. Anger. Warning. Forefinger incision. . . . Morning.[44]

Such alien abductions and operations are a new phenomenon. The first few cases were "authenticated" in the mid-Sixties, elaborated in the Seventies with reports of UFOs kidnapping planeloads of people, then codified by the books of abstract artist Budd Hopkins early in the Eighties. Nearing century's end, estimates of the number of abductees have risen into the tens of thousands, although most cannot remember their abductions as anything more than bad dreams. They are not supposed to remember, but they have clues: unaccountable patches of missing time in their lives. Strieber, disturbed by his Christmas nightmare, went to Budd Hopkins and to a medical specialist in hypnosis to make sense of the episode; in so doing he reclaimed patch after patch of missing time. The abductions had begun in 1957, when he was twelve and beginning to read Kafka. The space visitors have experimented upon him some dozen times since. "You are our chosen one," he has been told by the alien crone who appears at each abduction, but Strieber's young son dreams dreams of being operated upon by futuristic strange-faced doctors, and many are the chosen: cosmetologists, scientists, business executives, dancers, musicians, museum curators.[45]

What does all this mean? "People who face the visitors report fierce little figures with eyes that seem to stare into the deepest core of being. And those eyes are asking for something, perhaps even demanding it." They want, it seems, "an act of mutual insight and courage." They must make us real; we must make them real: through communion to transformation. The aliens have shown Strieber and other abductees images of the world blowing up. Joan, a beautician, has also been shown a picture of a city the space visitors are building. "What we're doing now to our planet is killing it little by little, and it's going to come to a point where there's not going to be anything left," Joan tells a group of fellow abductees in 1986. "I think that they're getting ready to start another world. And there will be people who are a part of that. And it scares me, because I have trouble dealing with what's going on in my life now because I start thinking, *This isn't really what's happening*."[46]

What's really happening is that a book has become a bestseller by drawing together into one apocalyptic survivor's tale the *fin de siècle* motifs of child abuse, amnesia, missing children, mysterious disappearances, dissociation, encounters with doubles of the first and third kinds, and a heartsick fear for the continuity of generations. "If mine was not an uncommon experience," writes Strieber, "it might be that we live in a society that bears a secret bruise from it." So Eugene Bliss notes that "Many [multiple personality] patients display multiple lacerations and scars on their forearms" from forgotten, suppressed episodes of abuse; so Walker Percy's protagonists slip into fugue states in more than one of his apocalyptic novels; so the Mother Ship of Steven Spielberg's *Close Encounters of the Third Kind* returns unharmed many children and pilots who have mysteriously disappeared; so David Henry Hwang, Philip Glass, and Jerome Sirlin collaborate on the 1988 premiere of a sophisticated "music drama" about abductees, *One Thousand Airplanes on the Roof*, in which the main character is played simultaneously by an actor and an actress; so, on the opposite edge of the cultural spectrum, the supermarket tabloid *Weekly World News* reports in 1988 that not only do "Space aliens kidnap 10,000 humans a year for slave labor" but that an immense UFO with purple lights has snatched up a herd of elephants from a safari park in Spain. And so, waking one morning to find two little triangles inscribed on his left forearm, coming to grips with what would seem to have been a series of fugue states in his past, "amazed to think how much of a fugitive I have been" during a life on the run from the cardboard-and-cinnamon presence of the aliens, Whitley Strieber under hypnosis recalls alien-induced pictures of the world turning into "a whole red ball of fire" with "great horns made of smoke," sees his little boy sitting in a park, all wobbly, his eyes entirely black—"If I don't help him, he's gonna die"— and then, as the space visitor "puts that thing down on my head again," has images of his father's death: "I miss you, Daddy. Oh, God, Daddy, why did you die? Daddy, why . . . why—I just never got to know you, Dad."[47]

From the political left (the Movement for a New Society to which Joanna Macy belongs), the political right (Live Free, Inc., the Christian Patriots Defense League, and other survivalist groups), and from Strieber's New Age political center, there is at century's end a constant close configuration, more emotional than mathematical, between painful sensations of childhood lost, time out of mind, dislocation, dissociation, and our immeasurable desires for fusion, merger, communion, the resetting of time, the rebinding of the generations. "Nowadays men find themselves on examining tables in flying saucers with vacuum devices attached to their privates, while women must endure the very real agony of having their pregnancies disappear," says Strieber, making it crystal clear that the continuity of the generations is what is really at stake in these latter-day visitations.[48] The space visitors— our Doubles, our counterparts—may not be saints but they may be our avant-garde, needling us from an Etruscan generational break toward an Augustan new era and

FOURTH DIMENSIONS

THE ANTIPODES BECKON AT CENTURIES' ENDS. OH, NOT literally the antipodes, that place on the opposite side of the medieval globe where people stood with their feet turned "against" ours, but an imaginal antipodes, a place so strange and distant that our natural laws may not hold: the ends of the earth, *finis terrae*, no-one's-land, the poles. All the vertical lines on European maps began to radiate from the North Pole just after 1500; sophisticated north polar projections appeared in the 1590s. Ever since, the North Pole has been both our cosmographical *fons et origo*, our source and origin, and our mythographical *point de zéro*, first and last resort of *adynata* or impossible things. The more thoroughly we have plotted the rest of the world, the more we have populated the Arctic and its Double, Antarctica, with monsters and "wicked beasts," then with wildmen, cannibals, and hermaphrodites, then with passages to lost or forgotten civilizations. *Terra infirma*, not-so-solid land of speculation: the North Pole, a black and glistening rock of magnetic stone at the center of a huge whirlpool ringed by four great islands; *Terra Australis Incognita*, unknown southern land, the South Pole its volcanic capital, beneath which dwell classical Mayan or Egyptian kingdoms. *Terminus ad quem*: the limit beyond which one cannot go.[49]

Fine flurry of foreign phrases for floes still foreign, frozen fields as fascinating at this *fin de siècle* as at the last. "It may be only a waste of ice-covered sea," wrote Cyrus C. Adams in 1901, reviewing the storm of north (and south) polar expeditions around the century's turn; "but the truth, however dreary, will be golden treasure compared with the dross of Symmes' Hole [through the North Pole to the hollow inhabited center of the Earth], or the yarn evolved by Howgate from Eskimo legends of north-polar denizens living under a genial sun and making clocks and other New England knickknacks." In 1912, three years after the reputed success of Robert Edwin Peary and his black valet, a commentator observed, "We have reached the North Pole . . . and it has been proved that no one need go there again." Yet, one way and another, they must: in 1986 Dmitri Shparo and ten other Russian explorers ski toward the "relative inaccessibility pole." They hallucinate snow walls, log cabins, apartment buildings, a man becoming a

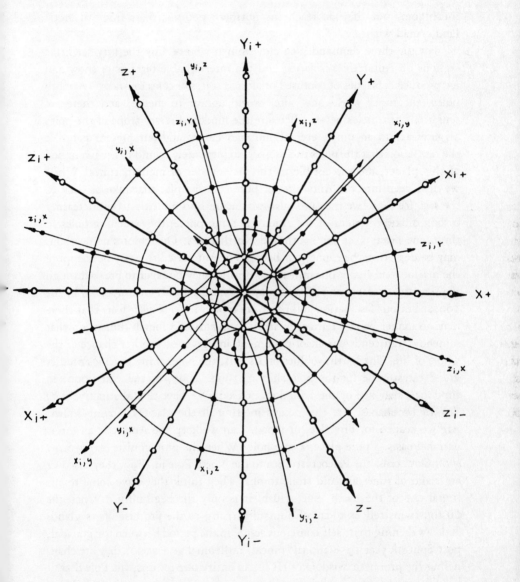

Diagram of a complex hypersolid as a space of constant negative curvature, requiring six dimensions. Arrived at by using the equation for a sphere with a radius of the square root of negative one. Figure 28 of David W. Brisson's essay on "Visual Comprehension of *n*-Dimensions," from David W. Brisson et al., *Hypergraphics* (1978). Courtesy of Harriet E. Brisson.

mushroom, but they do reach the northern point farthest from all arctic land, "mad with joy."[50]

For the three thousand men and women who occupy the fifty scientific stations on Antarctica, isolation and the interminable terrains of snow and ice produce "episodes of confused or altered states of consciousness." At both poles, the inner world and outer world appear to merge, and there are sensations of timelessness—wherefore the modern literary trope of the poles as gateways to an inner, eternal, utopian Earth, and our present panic at the revelation that the poles themselves, so intricately bound to the livelihood of this planet, are susceptible to the vicissitudes of modern times. While we drill deep into the Antarctic for pure core samples that take us back to the last Ice Age, we measure our own future by impurities: the increasing carbon dioxide content of the Antarctic atmosphere; the widening holes in the ozone layers over the South and North Poles. Our chlorofluorocarbons may be depleting the ozone, our harvests of Antarctic krill may be snapping the marine food chain, our mineral companies may be eager to break through the sensitive icecaps, and all this may be bearing down hard upon us in the 1990s, but our fascination and panic are rooted in *fin de siècle* fears that there may no longer be any refuge, *fin de siècle* dreams of a fourth dimension that somehow transcends our chaotic moment and gives us another chance at the whole of life. The Earth wobbles on its axis, the poles shift, psychics predict grand catastrophe for the pole shift of 1998, 1999, or the year 2000, in time for a new age or the Kingdom of God. We have now distinctively *fin de siècle* brouhahas: Are the icecaps melting or the glaciers moving south? Are we headed for Fire, Ice, or Flood? Can we keep the Antarctic an international oasis, a pure place, a true pole? When the protagonists of *The Secret of the Earth* cross the Paleocrystic Sea to the North Pole in 1899, they discover an island of runes and old stone tombs. They think they have come to the literal end of the Earth, but "Hush! it is only the beginning." When the Lusson twins tell us today of humanity rising to the promise of its glands and "awakening to its self-conscious state" in the period between the gonadal, post-Sputnik year 1958 and the pineal, millennial year 2000, they are channeling the prophetic wisdom of Hi Jo, an entity of Arcturus, the Pole Star.[51]

Sic i tur ad astra: such is the way to the stars, or immortality. Or Mars. The North Pole, we may recall, was the Terran conduit to Mars in Kurd Lasswitz's *Two Planets* of 1897; in the 1990s we look toward the Martian polar icecaps for signs of life and plan for a Martian colony. Lenin and Columbus whip us on. In 1992 the nation of the red star, long attracted to the Red Planet, may launch its cosmonauts toward Mars on the seventy-fifth anniversary of the Russian Revolution; in 1992 the Earth will be five hundred years ripe for a New World. Then, as it should, comes *Mars 1999:* "One Soviet cosmonaut and one U.S. astronaut make a sortie from [the moon] Phobos to the surface of Mars. The next giant leap for mankind in the quest for the high frontier." Then, as it must, comes "A Millennium Project: Mars 2000": international expeditions at millennium's turn prepare a permanent base, a Second Home for humankind, on Mars. "Why the hurry? Why a Millennium Project that stretches our reach to the limit? The answer," writes astronaut Harrison H. Schmitt, "is in the minds of young people who will carry us into the third millennium. . . . As with our ancestors, their freedom lies across a new ocean—the new ocean of space." It's "MARS OR BUST!" announces the Young Astronaut Council. No dithering at this late date. "Diplomatic justification for a Mars jaunt?" asks Jody D. Backer of Carthage, Missouri, winner of a 1988 Mars Letter Contest. "Deep down I think we all know the true reasons we must go into space—or sink back into the mud." And well we might sink back. The same Titans that can lift Viking modules toward Mars lie underground in concrete silos, aimed and armed.[52]

Once again Mars is a focal point of the *fin de siècle* obsession with limits. In the 1890s, Schiaparelli, Lowell, and science fiction writers saw networks of canals and extrapolated intellectually superior beings, a dying or exhausted civilization; in the 1980s we see ancient river valleys, giant extinct volcanos, "strange bright and dark markings on the surface, mountains shaped like pyramids," and we extrapolate a great stone face. According to Richard C. Hoagland, founder of the High Frontiers Foundation and quondam editor of *Star and Sky*, the face appears in frame 35A72 of the Viking Orbiter's 1976 photographs during its thirty-fifth orbit over the barren Martian region of Cydonia. The face is a mile long, vaguely Egyptian, pharaonic, sphinxlike. Because it bears our human features, it is even more enticing than the precise solid geometry of the monoliths that lead astronauts from the Moon to Jupiter to Rebirth in Arthur C. Clarke's (and Stanley Kubrick's) *2001: A Space Odyssey.* A monumental interplanetary Double stares back at us from what may be the ruins of "A City on the Edge of Forever"; now, in the nick of time, we may lead ourselves on, knowing we are not alone. A woman who all her life has lived with a dread of nuclear war writes after hearing of the face on Mars, "This is the first thing that has given me hope . . . the idea that someone would have gone through all that trouble to build this image of us on another planet." Hoagland too is hope-stricken: "the Face may well turn out to be a major precipitating factor in the history of consciousness itself."[53]

It (*fin de siècle* Mars, the face on Mars, the sphinxlike quality of that face) seems to be challenging us to move beyond ourselves. "Mars, in this grand sense," writes John Noble Wilford for the *New York Times*, "is not only a destination, it is a beginning," as Electric Blue Peggy Sue and the Revolutionions from Mars in their own Gaga Goodies punk rock fashion would quite probably agree. We could begin by colonizing the Red Planet and then depart an overcrowded "Spaceship Earth" for other planets, other solar systems, by means of "warp" drives, dilithium crystals, and similar Star Trekking doodads. We could begin by taking at his word Princeton physicist Edward Witten, called "The Martian" by his students, and engage a ten-dimensional universe of pointillistic vibrating closed strings. Or we could begin to fine-tune ourselves to vibrations cosmic and spiritual, n-dimensional worlds of ascended masters, etheric guides, Hi Jos.[54]

In *Flatland*, women are short straight lines, working-class men are isosceles triangles, professional men squares or pentagons, priests circles. On the last day of the 1999th year, A. Square of Flatland met a stranger from Spaceland and had a stupefying vision, "a dizzy, sickening sensation of sight that was not like seeing. I saw a Line that was no Line; Space that was not Space. I was myself, and not myself." This was neither madness nor Hell but the world of three dimensions—"a new world!" A. Square saw "a different order of Beings," and became as if a god, observing the entire plane of two-dimensional Flatland all at once. Solids stood fully revealed, "O divine ideal of consummate loveliness." It was morning, "the first hour of the first day of the two thousandth year." Flatlander circles met in solemn conclave, as they had met in the year 1000 and the year 0, to condemn as heretical the Gospel of Three Dimensions, a gospel which, according to secret archives, had surfaced twice before, at each turn of a millennium.

Thus Edwin A. Abbott in 1884 made *A Romance of Many Dimensions* into a romance peculiarly suited to our times. Edgar D. Mitchell, piloting the Apollo 14 lunar module in 1971, gained enough perspective on our "small spaceship" called Earth to achieve an *instant global consciousness*. "I suddenly experienced the universe as intelligent, loving and harmonious. . . . I realized that the next frontier of human exploration was the human mind and spirit. So in 1973 I founded the Institute of Noetic Sciences to foster the neglected science of consciousness." From California, ostensibly on the pedestrian surface of this Earth, Mitchell's Institute during the 1980s sponsors radio programs of meditative "Space Music," promotes studies of paranormal capacities, spiritual healing, and "the whole issue of mind/body plasticity," including the phenomenon of multiple personality. "Suddenly, multiples are here in numbers," says a New York City psychotherapist in 1986, "like messengers of the gods who can skip eons ahead of our scientific understanding of brain and body." Perhaps multiples make transits across inner space the way science fiction starships career through outer space. Perhaps multiples are not dissociated but fourth-dimensionally associated. Perhaps each of a multiple's selves inhabits a different realm, a different time. Perhaps each of us carries within as many woofs of space and warps of time as there are galaxies in the great beyond. Perhaps we need only contact our other selves in past lives to reach the antipodes.[55]

Enantiodromia is what Jungian therapist Roger J. Woolger has in mind: "the movement between opposites" by which his patients go from one past-life regression to the next, from victim to torturer, slave to despot, woman to man to woman to man; "from a Roman proconsul ruling all of Spain to a landless Dutch peasant; from an ostracized slave to a Chinese warlord; from a sexually abused child to a battlefield rapist and mutilator. These are the extremes of human nature that we all, it seems, contain within us in a state of uneasy equilibrium." While "channels" must disembarrass themselves of any human tampering with supercelestial truths by distancing themselves from or "disowning" the "discarnate entities" who speak through them, Woolger's clients must "reown" their other, historical selves. Only by embracing their personal fourth dimension can they "find reconciliation and meaning in these polarized personalities with their seemingly irrevocable karmic residues left by past actions." Past-life regression is for Woolger the work of healing secret bruises so that an individual (or a family, or a community, or the next generation) may no longer be bound to replay old grief.[56]

Like the psychology of past lives, the usually occult philosophies of metempsychosis and reincarnation enter into wider arenas of Western cultural discourse at centuries' ends because they turn the *fin de siècle* into *l'aube du siècle*, the dawn of a new age. They become, as it were, sets of differential gears for turning Etruscan finalities into Augustan festivities. In 1787 the Irish orator Francis Dobbs gave many reasons why the Second Coming of Christ was immediately to be expected for 1790, but the novelty of his exposition in *Millennium: A Poem* was the "great key" he had found to many parts of Scripture, that

> *all do live*
> *In different periods, to themselves unknown.*

Did not Jesus say in John 3.3, "Except a man be born again, he cannot see the kingdom of God"? "I apprehend," reasoned Dobbs, "that no man has lived since the Flood, who was not in existence before it." Was it not Jesus speaking in Luke 21.32 of the series of events leading up to the Millennium, and did he not conclude, "Verily I say unto you, This generation shall not pass away till all be fulfilled"? Therefore, the generation alive at Christ's crucifixion must be present again for his reappearance. "It may seem strange that men do not recollect their former stages of existence," Dobbs admitted, but doubtless "a consciousness of it will in the end be known."[57]

That consciousness was present to some at the end of the 19th century: to spirit mediums relishing past lives; to theosophists indulging the journeys of astral souls; to European artists from St. Petersburg to Paris who were working at sacred geometries and abstractions expressive of an other, a spiritual, a fourth dimension, a higher world of vibrations giving rise "to the most exquisite and constantly changing colours, waves of varying shades like the rainbow hues in mother-of-pearl."[58]

That consciousness is present to many at this century's end. To the many who have been *Dancing in the Light* with actress Shirley MacLaine, convinced as she is that "many happy returns" alludes to reincarnation and that "The world may seem to be in a polarized mess right now, but there are new human beings ready to make a breakthrough." To the many who have read Thea Alexander's "macro-philosophy bestseller," *2150 A.D.*, from which perspective the "soul matrix entity" Jon Lakes in his high-vibration astral body reviews an American micro society that "perished sometime around the year 2000, along with most other micro societies of the Earth, due to their inability to cooperate with one another." To the many (the one quarter of European and American adults) who have answered in the affirmative when asked by pollsters, "Do you believe in reincarnation?" Reincarnation, after all, is "A New Horizon in Science, Religion and Society," and "Thoughts of Reincarnation Can Prevent Self-Destruction."[59]

Nil desperandum: no cause for despair. It behooves a self-destructive civilization "Living on the Brink of Apocalypse" to foster an *ars moriendi* that allays apprehensions of total eclipse, complete cessation. It befits a Western civilization caught in the clutches of cycles of chaos and collapse to contrive an art of dying that makes light of the end so as to transcend it. The constellation of *fin de siècle* motifs that I have grouped under the rubric of

Fourth Dimensions is a constellation luminous with the prospects of release from the confines of our immediate geography, our present biography, our "post-modern" times, our impending mortality.[60]

In extremis, at the end (certainly) of a millennium, at the end (probably) of a civilization, at the end (possibly) of life-as-we-know-it, we have discovered (predictably) the Near-Death Experience (NDE). Unlike medieval visions, which were more likely to be descents into Hell than ascents into Heaven, the NDE nowadays is typically uplifting, even inspiring. Several millions of Americans—men in cardiac shock, women in the throes of a difficult childbirth, automobile accident victims—have temporarily left below their ponderous, painful, earthbound bodies and risen into lighter, more perfect bodies viable in a place or time of great light, great energy, true democracy, and true peace. There they may encounter guides, as in medieval otherworldly travels, but these contemporary Virgils rarely draw their Dantes through an Inferno or a Purgatorio, rarely flinch at glimpses of Paradiso. The NDE Heaven is not so much a timeless haven as an invigorating leaven, a liveliness beyond the body, a vibrant afterlife of *Far Journeys*, antipodean revelations, n-dimensional highs.[61]

It is a happy fact, then, that the seminal article on NDEs appeared in 1892 in the *Yearbook of the Swiss Alpine Club*, from which heights Albert Heim, a Swiss geology professor, described the "calm seriousness, profound acceptance, and . . . sense of surety" felt by mountain climbers in the moments before near-fatal falls. By 1975 one overeager author could entitle a chapter of his book on the *Afterlife* "The Thrill of Dying." In 1977 Sunn Classic Pictures could produce a documentary film, *Beyond and Back*, depicting the long spiral tunnel, the white light, and the gatherings of dead friends and relatives characteristic, toward this century's end, of the NDE. Philip José Farmer that year published the third in his (interminable?) series of novels about Riverworld, "Where everyone who ever died, from Karl Marx to Tom Mix to Joan of Arc, wakes up the day after death on the banks of a giant river, to take part in what many consider to be the greatest adventure in all Science Fiction." The next year the California Museum of Science and Industry mounted "Continuum," an exhibit suggesting that consciousness is energy and endures independent of the physical body after death. In 1979, reflecting upon a personal encounter with death, Sheldon Ruderman would argue that "A universe in which one becomes aware of consciousness after death has a far greater intuitive feeling of rightness to it than the more analytical egocentric belief that this life is 'where it's at.' " An Association for the Scientific Study of Near-Death Phenomena was founded in 1978, *Anabiosis* or *The Journal for Near-Death Studies* in 1979. In 1984, Orwell swept aside, civilization was *Heading Toward Omega*: NDEs, wrote Kenneth Ring, are experiences of a transcendental consciousness whose discharge of subtle biological energies might reconstitute the nervous system so as to activate latent spiritual potentials and generate a new type of human being with an understanding of the universe noetic enough to transform our planet.[62]

If enigmatic, invasive space visitors are the not-so-simple tricks of a *fin de siècle* imagination, if Project Ozma fails by the end of the century in its radiotelescopic sweeps of the heavens for electromagnetic signs of extraterrestrial intelligence, then we ourselves, it seems, must become the avant-garde for the new millennium. What better moment than the 1990s for humankind to pull itself up by its own bootstraps out of its *fin de siècle* grave into another dimension? A few, calling themselves Venturists or cryonauts, may freeze themselves toward physical immortality, repudiating a "slack-gutted submission to the decay and stench of death," but more alluring than Trans Time cryonic stasis is the metamorphic or incorporeal adventure, passages through time and space in utterly renovated bodies, glowing starships, or thoroughly transubstantial vehicles of light. Psychically adept, karmically balanced, whole-brained, multipersonal, ensouled and empowered, the avant-gardes proposed these days verge on the immortal. Whether sleeping the sleep of the just-in-time in suspended animation on their way to the next planetary system light-years ahead, or regressing from one past life to another across thousands of trance-years, or moving out-of-body through the many worlds of the Mark-Age masters, our new breed of *viri spirituales* must have ever greater powers over death the closer they come to the year 2000.[63]

In 1988, surveying two decades of research on death and dying, Richard Schulz and Janet Schlarb reported in the journal *Omega* that, thanks in part to the marvels of modern medicine, in part to the ageing of our society, sixty percent of those who die in the United States know of their deaths at least several weeks in advance. We will have, during our nineties and our Nineties, time aplenty to go through Elisabeth Kübler-Ross's stages of anger, denial, bargaining, grief, and acceptance. Death is but "The Final Stage of Growth," as Dr. Kübler-Ross wrote in 1975, and, as she has more recently discovered, it may not be so final a stage at that. Something else, nondenominational, awaits us all *in articulo mortis*, at the point of death: Omega, as Dr. Ring would say. "I think everyone realizes that the closing decades of this century already give us grave cause for uneasiness concerning the destiny of the human race on this planet," Ring wrote in 1980. "Could it be, then, that one reason why the study of death has emerged as one of the dominant concerns of our time is to help us to become globally sensitized to the experience of death precisely because the notion of death on a *planetary scale* now hangs, like the sword of Damocles, over our heads? Could this be the universe's way of 'inoculating' us against the fear of death?"[64]

Lately, however, we have taken to contemplating the death of the universe itself in round about one hundred billion years. This is a rather larger number, granted, than similar speculations during the 1890s, but it still gives pause to such as Harvard astrophysicist Steven Weinberg. Devoting most of a book to the spasms of *The First Three Minutes* of the universe, Weinberg concludes with an aerial view of Wyoming, "snow turning pink as the sun sets, roads stretching straight across the country from one town to another." He confesses that "It is very hard to realize that this all is just a tiny part of an overwhelmingly hostile universe. It is even harder to realize that this present universe has evolved from an unspeakably unfamiliar early condition, and faces a future extinction of endless cold or intolerable heat. The more the universe seems comprehensible, the more it also seems pointless."[65] *Respice finem.* Look to the end: white dwarf stars, black dwarf stars, neutron stars, and

BLACK HOLES

ROUNDING AFRICA'S CAPE OF GOOD HOPE IN NOVEMBER 1497, Vasco da Gama sailed across to the Indian subcontinent in the spring of 1498. Ashore, on his way to an audience with the King of Calicut, da Gama did obeisance to Mari, Hindu goddess of smallpox, mistaking her for the Virgin Mary. Mari was worthy of respect in her own right. She had been killing, blinding, or scarring one generation after another, from Asia to Africa to Europe, and had just begun her first harvest in the Americas. Many a face was still deeply pitted by Mari's handiwork two centuries later, in the 1690s, when the English at Calcutta built Fort William, and in 1756, when sixty-four young Englishmen, taken prisoner by a victorious Indian siege force, were locked by mistake into the fort's dark detention room for drunken soldiers. Thirty died of suffocation before someone thought to release them. Coaxed into a legend useful to the imperial agenda of the East India Company, the Black Hole of Calcutta was the only Black Hole aside from

Calvin and Hobbes   by Bill Watterson

Cartoon by Bill Watterson, copyright © March 21, 1987. Universal Press Syndicate.

the Devil's arse and the gaping mouth of Hell that would have been known in 1796 to Pierre Simon, Marquis de Laplace.[66]

The Marquis was mulling over Isaac Newton's gravitational laws and his theory of light. If light did indeed consist of streams of corpuscles, then celestial bodies of sufficiently great mass might have the gravitational pull to distrain all light. They would be *corps obscurs*, dark bodies. Who could tell, wondered Laplace, how many such great, dark, invisible bodies there might be in the universe?[67]

Laplace's *corps obscurs* were conjectures, not followed up, and the next set of black holes, arising at the next century's end, were literary figments. On November 9, 1878, "Charles Ashmore's Trail" stopped abruptly in the Illinois snow. One of the "Mysterious Disappearances" of Ambrose Bierce's *Can Such Things Be?* of 1893, young Charles Ashmore had taken a tin bucket and started off for the spring, never to return. Essaying an explanation, Bierce invokes a "Dr. Hern of Leipsic," who has speculated that the universe might be dangerously non-Euclidean and that the visible world might be deeply pitted with any number of cavities or voids into which the unsuspecting could fall, to be seen and heard no more. A decade later Simon Newcomb, America's leading mathematical astronomer, envisioned for the readers of *McClure's Magazine* a "dark star" bringing on "The End of the World." Three thousand years after the first exchange of signals between the inhabitants of Mars and Earth, Martian astronomers signal the impending collision of a dark celestial body with the sun. An ever-ready Professor of Physics descends into his well-stocked vault with a few others of the human race and emerges two years later to find no signs of civilization. "Such is the course of evolution," sighs the Professor in his finest Panglossian manner; it has been all for the best. The collision has revived the dying sun, created "a new earth and a new order of animated nature."[68]

Bierce's *vacua* in the universal medium at which parallel universes intersect, Newcomb's ultimately luciferous dark stars, these were holes less black than that other Black Hole of century's end, the "Heart of Darkness." Published in 1902, Joseph Conrad's story drew upon his own journey in 1890 up the Congo River, "an immense snake uncoiled, . . . its tail lost in the depths of the land." There, in the depths, Mr. Kurtz, chief of the Inner Station, is dying. Even in death Kurtz is "a soul that knew no restraint, no faith, and no fear, yet struggling blindly with itself." Marlow, philosopher-adventurer, fighting to save him, must "deal with a being to whom I could not appeal in the name of anything high or low. I had, even like the niggers, to invoke him—himself—his own exalted and incredible degradation. There was nothing either above or below him, and I knew it. He had kicked himself free of the earth. Confound the man! he had kicked the very earth to pieces. He was alone, and I before him did not know whether I stood on the ground or floated in the air." Marlow manages to get Kurtz aboard a riverboat heading back toward Western civilization, but Kurtz is delirious, and very dark. "His was an impenetrable darkness. I looked at him as you peer down at a man who is lying at the bottom of a precipice where the sun never shines." *In articulo mortis* Kurtz sees no tunnel of light. He shouts, "The horror! the horror!" then dies. His was a *horror vacui*, a horror of emptiness, and when, later, Marlow cannot shake the agent's ghost, he has a vision of Kurtz on his deathbed stretcher, "opening his mouth voraciously, as if to devour all the earth with all its mankind. He lived then before me; he lived as much as he had ever lived—a shadow insatiable of splendid appearances, of frightful realities, a shadow darker than the shadow of the night."[69]

Joseph Conrad in 1902 proved the frightful psychic and cultural reality of black holes; physicists Karl Schwarzschild in 1916 and J. Robert Oppenheimer with Hartland Snyder in 1939 proved the mathematical reality that a "cold and sufficiently massive star must collapse indefinitely, becoming a black hole." In 1965 a space rocket discovered x-ray source Cygnus X-1; in 1971 astronomers identified it with a radio source, HDE Star No. 226,868; by 1972 Cygnus X-1 was suspected of being a supergiant star circling an invisible companion—so far as we can tell, one of Laplace's *corps obscurs*, a "dark body," a true celestial Black Hole. In 1978 another newly discovered x-ray binary system, V861 Scorpii, became a good candidate for black stardom, and in 1979 the Walt Disney Studios took the deep space research vessel *Palamino*, with Maximilian Schell, Anthony Perkins, Yvette Mimieux, and Ernest Borgnine, to and through *The Black Hole* in 70mm Technovision.[70]

Since then, black holes have been invested with a powerfully antipodean presence. They are points of no return. They are the tombstones of massive stars that have collapsed upon themselves. They are the unseen Doppelgängers of supergiant stars, appearing in our microcosm on bumper stickers and T-shirts: "Black holes are outta sight." According to art historian Frederick R. Karl in 1985, black holes embody what modernism has been all about from the word go in the year 1900: an engulfing, invisible phenomenon whose pull is so strong that nothing can escape it, resulting from a compression in which space and time become distorted, yielding a world our reason cannot take full measure of. "Calling these things 'black holes' was a masterstroke by [American physicist] John Wheeler," says contemporary English cosmologist Stephen Hawking. "The name conjures up a lot of human neuroses. . . . It could be a good image for human fears of the universe."[71]

A constellation of black holes is a singularly fine if paradoxical image for *fin de siècle* fears about the universe, and I intend to illustrate a bit schematically the metaphorical pull of black holes upon us at this century's end. Each of my illustrations will begin with an astrophysical description of a black hole drawn from Harry L. Shipman's *Black Holes, Quasars, & the Universe*. Each will be followed by a poetic leap certainly no greater than that required of physicists themselves as they explore what Shipman calls these "outer limits of Einstein's theory of gravitation."[72]

PHYSICS. The gravitational forces, or tides, of a black hole would be felt long before a body entered its immediate neighborhood. These tides would increasingly distort any body as it approached the hole. THE LEAP. Considering a centurial year as a black hole, we have seen how its tides tug the preceding years into a *fin de siècle* epoch increasingly self-conscious of decadence and deformity. The millennial year 2000 has gravitational tides of maximal reach. Its entire preceding hundred years, our century, has come to be felt as a final epoch, a time of grotesque extremity, beginning perhaps with the deaths of one hundred thousand horses during the Boer War. By 1945, if not much earlier, the century had become an apocalyptic century: "now eschatology confounds us at the very center of consciousness." For Italian theologian Romano Guardini, lecturing at the University of Munich in 1947–49, the 20th century required of humankind "a naked bravery," a *ne plus ultra* faith, lest all that remain of us be ruins. "Centuries of the future," declaimed Franz in 1956 in Jean-Paul Sartre's play, *The Condemned of Altona*, "here is my century, solitary and deformed—the accused. . . . The century might have been a good one had not men been watched from time immemorial by the cruel enemy who had sworn to destroy him, that hairless, evil, flesh-eating beast—man himself. . . . This century is a woman in labor." It is also the "Great Transition" to a "post-civilized" world, an "accidental century" entailing an accidental but total revolution. "In the twentieth century," wrote social economist Michael Harrington in 1966, "something enormous is being born. And something enormous is dying."[73]

It has been a long-anticipated birth, a long-drawn-out death, a long fall toward the black hole of the millennium. "The world of the year 2000 has already arrived," announced sociologist Daniel Bell as early as 1968, "for in the decisions we make now, in the way we design our environment and thus sketch the lines of constraints, the future is committed." By 1974, the 20th century could boast of the most precocious *fin de siècle* on record, and that with a Parisian imprimatur. A new French journal, *Fin de siècle*, was published on the rails of a global oil crisis; Daniel Pommereulle's *"Fin de siècle"* series of found-object sculptures, a monumental collision of the last *fin de siècle* with this *fin de siècle*, was installed at the Centre Pompidou.[74]

"If there is one point on which both secular forecasters and inspired mystics agree, it is that during the brief two and a half decades separating us from the year 2000, the present world order will undergo a total change." I might have italicized those "brief two and a half decades" upon which Omar V. Garrison insisted in the 1978 preface to his *Encyclopedia of Prophecy*, were it not that Garrison's sense of the immediacy of the millennium was scarcely unusual. Columnist Flora Lewis of the *New York Times* wrote in 1982 of a "feeling of dangerous weakness" in the West due to "a deeper bewilderment as societies move into the third millennium and sense change coming without knowing how to direct it." "This, mind you, in 1982," remarked a columnist for the *New Republic*, "with eighteen years to go." Then the C's of the calendar parted for the supergiant MDCCCCLXXXIV. Although Eric Arthur Blair had merely reversed the 4 and the 8 of the year in which he was writing, *Nineteen Eighty-Four* had become Big Brother to the year 2000. Inner Party members newspoke, Outer Party members rectified, the proles were polled, and those Winstons and Julias with dreams of the Golden Country had to deal with Amnesty International reports of thousands of rooms 101, tens of thousands of unpersons. Doubleplusungood or not, the year 1984 once past, the turn of the century could no longer be held off. *Turn-of-the-Century Women*, a new historical periodical out of Charlottesville, Virginia, appeared in 1984 with this editorial *raison d'être*: "As we enter the turn of our own century, now is the time to examine the legacy left to us by an earlier period of transition." The next year, the French magazine *Traverses* devoted a double issue to the *fin de siècle*, Jean Baudrillard wondering whether we were at a vanishing point or could achieve a velocity sufficient to escape the terrorism of History. In December 1987 cadmium-yellow journalist Tom Wolfe composed "A Eulogy for the Twentieth Century"—a century, he wrote, that has been obsessed with the idea of starting, always and everywhere, from zero.[75]

PHYSICS. A black hole forms when a massive star, exhausting the hydrogen fuel at its core, is so overwhelmed by the force of its own gravity that it cannot keep from collapsing. THE LEAP. Our 20th century ended, Hungarian educator László Vörös has assured me, with the global energy crisis of 1973. An all-enveloping darkness then descended upon civilization in Poul Anderson's science fiction novel, *A Knight of Ghosts and Shadows*. Prevailing images of physical and psychological exhaustion, of collapse from within, of the spiritual decay and material corruption of the "First World," make of these interregnal years the years of Western collapse from great star into black hole. It is time to read, in alphabetical order, such popular nonfiction as *Crumbling Foundations: Death and Rebirth in an Age of Upheaval; The Eco-Spasm Report; The End of Affluence; The Great Depression of 1990; How to Prosper during the Coming Bad Years; Millennium Management: Last Chance for American Business; Mortal Splendor: The American Empire in Transition; New Rules: Searching for Self-Fulfillment in a World Turned Upside-Down; The Rise and Fall of the Great Powers: Economic Change and Military Conflict from 1500–2000*. It is time to browse through San Francisco's *Darknerve*, "A new [maga]zine that intends to look at the dark side of things as our civilization collapses into the muck." And Seattle's *Zero Hour*, "A new tabloid dedicated to covering the decline of our society for as long as they can." And the October 1987 issue of Boston's *Atlantic*, with Floyd C. Stuart's meditation on the passing of time in a salt marsh, Mark Crispin Miller's review of Russell Jacoby's *The Last Intellectuals*, G. W. Hawkes's story set "At the Walls of Jericho" where "there was no way, any longer in this world, to bring the besieged out if they didn't want to come," Guy Billout's "There Is No Safe Place" cartoon of a snake appearing and disappearing between city cobblestones, Donald A. Ranard's report on Hmong refugees on "The Last Bus," Pfizer Pharmaceuticals's advertisement about **Depression. It can affect you in ways you would never suspect** ("Over 30 million Americans today may suffer from some form of depressive illness"), CBS Video Library's promise of **Suspense. Terror. Obsession. Delivered to Your Door**, David Owen's article on the high failure rate of Multi-Level Marketing companies, the Nature Company's offer of the extinct but now "Giant Inflatable Pteranodon" at $21.95 postpaid, and the cover essay, Peter G. Peterson's "The Morning After," arguing that "America has let its infrastructure crumble, its foreign markets decline, its productivity dwindle, its savings evaporate, and its budget and borrowing burgeon. And now the day of reckoning is at hand."[76]

It is time for "an unparalleled international interest" in ancient gnostic and apocalyptic texts. It is time for doomsday carriers, clocks, contracts, cults, gangs, genes, ghosts, jobs, squads, and syndromes. "The apocalypse is part of our ideological baggage. It is aphrodisiac, nightmare, a commodity like any other," wrote German social theorist Hans Magnus Enzensberger in 1978. "[T]he element of surprise is missing, it seems only to be a question of time. The doom we picture for ourselves is insidious and torturingly slow in its approach, the apocalypse in slow motion." It is time to sit through horror films that expose the bankruptcy of culture and the "total unrecuperability of society without transcendence or renewal." It is time to debate with the Club of Rome concerning the collapse of the world economy under the inevitable pressures of population and South–North migration; time to recognize overwhelming fatigue as Chronic Epstein-Barr Virus, the "fear of fear" as Panic Disorder.[77]

It is time to acknowledge that "industrial civilization has borrowed on credit from nature, and now an enormous debt is due," that this is "an age where things seem to have gotten beyond control," that we live in a world "after virtue," a world "of impoverished social and moral possibilities." In 1982 historian Joel Colton speculated that "Future historians will probably record that from the mid-twentieth century on, it was difficult for anyone to retain faith in the idea of inevitable and continuing progress. People increasingly now use the word in quotation marks or with mocking sarcasm or speak not of progress in civilization but in barbarism. As Western dominance and self-confidence wane, so too does the idea of progress." "The world is unhappy," French politician Valéry Giscard d'Estaing tells us. "It is unhappy because it doesn't know where it is going and because it senses that, if it knew, it would discover that it was heading for disaster." Professor Warren Wagar, who has spent much of his academic life studying fictions of dystopia and apocalypse, wrote in 1982 (at the age of forty, "a good age for presentiments of extinction") that "we do indeed live in an endtime, an era in history marked by the collapse of the traditional civilizations of the non-Western world and by the senescence of the national-bourgeois social order of the West. There have been endtimes aplenty in the six thousand years of recorded history, but none so universal or so dangerous. Only the demon of relativism bars us from full consciousness of our predicament. Be not deceived. Our twentieth-century endtime does surpass, in scope and destructive potential, all others." And what could be more distinctive of our *fin de siècle* than that extraordinary invention, the countdown from ten to zero?[78]

PHYSICS. A collapsing star shrinks. If its core is massive enough, it keeps shrinking. The surface keeps collapsing until the entire star has shrunk to a point. THE LEAP. We are turning the Earth into a cesspool. Ecologists and environmentalists have acquired such current political capital because images of depletion and pollution refer, ultimately, to the dead star that is a black hole. Every minute of every day, an area of tropical forest larger than twenty soccer fields is logged or burned; every year, rain forest larger than Costa Rica is destroyed; worldwide, almost half of all rain forest has been lost during the last thirty years. At least a quarter of the world's land surface (three billion hectares) is at risk from desertification, acid rain, bad irrigation, or other human depredation. Tellurium, asbestos, peroxides, chlorates, selenium, radionucleides, trichloroethylene, isocycanates, organohalogens, mercury, cadmium, thallium, beryllium, lead, chromium, metal carbonyls, and PCBs are concentrating in the soil and groundwater supplies of the United States. Four of five child deaths in the Third World in 1980 resulted from diseases contracted due to dirty water. In excess of one billion pounds of radioactive waste had accumulated in the world as of 1985; some 100,000 years from now, the amount of plutonium we have already dumped into the North Sea could still be lethal to fifteen million people. A single chlorine atom can destroy ten thousand ozone molecules and remain in the atmosphere for a century, but every hour Britain alone produces fifty thousand aerosol cans releasing chlorofluorocarbons, and a hole the size of the United States has developed in the high-level ozone layer over Antarctica. Annually, through deforestation and the burning of fossil fuels, we add fourteen trillion pounds of carbon to the atmosphere, speeding up the Greenhouse Effect that may soon reduce our breadbaskets to dustbowls while fifteen million children each year die of hunger. In sum, according to the Canadian environmental group G.A.I.A. (Global Awareness in Action) in 1988, "The time passes and the point of no return approaches quickly, maybe in less than ten years."[79]

PHYSICS. The essence of a black hole is the event horizon, the point of no return. At the event horizon, you would have to travel at the speed of light to escape from the black hole. Since no material object can travel that fast, nothing can return to the outside world once it has stepped over this invisible boundary. THE LEAP. At centuries' ends we see ourselves in a double jeopardy, singly and collectively. Personal margins of safety seem even thinner, social margins of safety ever more frangible, at millennium's end. Conversations, exhortations, editorials often allude to the irreversible, the irrevocable. We look out of the corners of our eyes for the event horizon. Ours is "The Age of Living Dangerously," the age of the "thriller," the age of no-fault insurance. As individuals and as societies, we have fallen under the spell—the enchantment, the curse—of what we call risk. The phrase "at risk" dates back to 1901, "risk-taking" to 1921, "medical risk" to 1961, "risk analysis" to 1964, "risk-benefit analysis" to 1969/1975, "risk management" to 1978, the journal *Risk Analysis* to 1981, the First International

Risk Seminar to the Ides of March, 1983. Risk "assessors" have become the shamans for the Nervous Nineties. Behind our present "urgent, massive, collective concern to ward off risk" looms the *fin de siècle* essence of a black hole, the point of no return.[80]

A disquieting incongruence has arisen between cause and effect: from small missteps and technical miscues may ensue great tragedy. During the first thirteen seconds of the "transient" or accident at the Three Mile Island nuclear power plant, a false signal caused a condensation pump to fail, two valves for emergency cooling were out of position, the indicator thereof was obscured, another valve failed to reseat, the indicator thereof malfunctioned, and the TMI operators could not have been aware of a single one of these problems. "When we add complexity and coupling to catastrophe, we have something that is fairly new in the world," wrote Charles Perrow in 1984 in *Normal Accidents: Living with High-Risk Technologies*. In 1985, *The New Yorker* commented on the industrial accident at the American chemical plant in Bhopal, India: "What truly grips us in these accounts is not so much the numbers [of dead and wounded] as the spectacle of suddenly vanishing competence, of men utterly routed by technology, of fail-safe systems failing with a logic as inexorable as it was once—indeed, right up to that very moment—unforeseeable. And the spectacle haunts us because it seems to carry allegorical import, like the whispery omen of a hovering figure."[81]

That "whispery omen of a hovering figure," a figure itself so uncustomary of *New Yorker* rhetorical restraint, is the omen of hubris. The hovering figure is Cassandra: things will go wrong; "the probability of *something* very unlikely happening is very high"; some things will go very wrong. In a world which we tend to see at century's end as complex and coupled, chaotic and incontinent, we pretend to calculate and choose between "acceptable" and "unacceptable" risks. Willy-nilly, each of us at century's end is a risk-taker. "The truth," explains Robert P. Giovacchini, the Gillette Company's vice-president for corporate product integrity, "is that *nothing* is safe." For example, the danger inherent in having an annual x-ray is equivalent to the danger of flying 1000 miles in an airplane, driving 50 miles by car, riding 10 miles on a bicycle, eating 40 tablespoonsful of peanut butter, drinking 30 diet sodas, downing 20 cans of beer, spending 2 days in New York City, paddling 6 minutes in a canoe, or smoking 1.5 cigarettes. " 'Safety' (unmodified) is a word of primitive simplicity that has lost its utility in the face, not just of expanded technology, but of growing knowledge about the sometimes malignant complexities of nature," write the insurance-oriented authors of *Risk Watch*. "Safe," the United States Supreme Court decided in 1980, does not mean risk-free.[82]

At other epochs the call for such a decision would appear preposterous or silly, but in our janiform epoch "unsafe" can imply an uncontrollable chain reaction, a meltdown, a loose missile, the devastation of the Earth, and there must on this side of the event horizon be some reassuring consensus on what it means to be "safe." When individual lives these days are valued by the courts and insurance companies at a maximum of six million dollars apiece; when the U. S. Federal Emergency Management Agency has training courses for fallout shelter officers who must practice for acts of triage (shall we accept prisoners released from jail in nuclear emergency? would patients hurried out of hospitals strain shelter resources overmuch? are there too many people in here already?); when a *"calamity* is an actualized hazard," a *"harm* is an actualized danger," and *"insult probabilities* are *ex ante* estimates of each plausible type of harm" although "there is no equivalent in human experience for the destructiveness of multi-megaton hydrogen weapons," then notions of sanctity and sanctuary are themselves at radical risk.[83]

"How extraordinary!" exclaimed the optimistic social scientist Aaron Wildavsky in 1979. "The richest, longest lived, best protected, most resourceful civilization, with the highest degree of insight into its own technology, is on its way to becoming the most frightened." Years before, a more pessimistic social scientist predicted that the 1970s would see the Politics of Despair, the 1980s the Politics of Desperation, the 1990s the Politics of Catastrophe, and that the 21st century would be the Era of Annihilation. This picture of the world going downhill very fast, a staple at centuries' ends, makes every risk we identify in the 1980s that much riskier, every unknown peril that much more perilous. Fright comes of our *fin de siècle* sensitivity to risks of "unprecedented" magnitude and latitude compounded by our *fin de siècle* conviction that "history [is set] on a course of accelerating acceleration."[84]

The acceleration of population, of technology, of history, of time itself, is a 20th-century cliché so entrenched and credible that we have taken to the image of "future shock" as mechanical ducks to an electronic decoy. We are, it seems, being drawn ever more rapidly and automatically toward the point of no return. "In the last century," according to John Platt, "we have increased our speeds of communication by a factor of 10^7; our speeds of travel by 10^2; our speeds of data handling by 10^6; our energy resources by 10^3; our power of weapons by 10^6; our ability to control diseases by something like 10^2; and our rate of population growth to 10^3 times what it was a few thousand years ago." But, said G. R. Urban over Radio Free Europe, our moral and political strategies lag behind. "The sobering fact is . . . that there is (literally) a critical mass beyond which the clearest foresight and the wisest policy will founder on our inability to deal with large numbers." And founder again on the bewildering speed, "the incredible speed at which our innovations have brought us to the edge of doom." Suddenly, on what seems to be the edge of the event horizon, time activists arise among us to protest the compression and distortion of time. Jeremy Rifkin, author of *Time Wars*, proposes in 1987 to tilt at the "accelerated time frame of the modern age" by returning to biological rhythms and the periodicities of the Earth; not the computer nanosecond but nature's circadian way should guide our lives. Michael Young, Harvard sociologist, proposes in 1988 that the fisherman be our model for a new approach balancing linear and cyclical time; otherwise the "time famine" of modern civilization, its "fundamental shortage of time," may lead to hasty, possibly fatal decisions about the course of humankind at this critical juncture.[85]

Crisis is another cliché of the 20th century, so much so that it no longer strikes us as particularly oxymoronic to refer to a "perpetual crisis." The more grievous our feelings of being at risk and the more fevered our sense of acceleration, the more redoubtable the crisis. If there be any qualitative difference between the crises of past decades and the crises of our century's end, it is that now the crises are felt as compound fractures, breaks in the security of person, the certainty of place, the manageability of time. Perhaps, as physicist Freeman Dyson claims, "*We* are the risks. We're the ones who are destroying life on the planet." Drawn toward the point of no return, our world in all its dimensions becomes a painful blur.[86]

PHYSICS. Anything that falls into a black hole loses its identity. All we know is that a certain amount of mass fell down the hole. THE LEAP. While psychologists would here address the psychic numbing of victims of disaster and psychiatrists would address the end-of-the-world fantasies of schizo-phrenics, I wish to address the future of cockroaches. While Marxist critical theorists would here describe "how the agencies of capitalist modernization disintegrate the cohesive integrity of the self and thereby prevent individuals from making sense of their world," I wish to call attention to the fact that there are three quarters of a ton of termites for each human being on earth. Poet Betty Adcock's 1988 "Digression on the Nuclear Age" begins not with silos but with the work of a termite tribe in Africa. The tribe

builds elaborate tenements that might be called
cathedrals, were they for anything so terminal
as Milton's God. Who was it said
the perfect arch will always separate
the civilized from the not? Never mind.
These creatures are quite blind and soft
and hard at labor chemically induced.

So they go on, piling up pellets into towers, making towers meet in arches.
. . . "I've got this far," writes Adcock,

and don't know what
termites can be made to mean. Or this poem:
a joke, a play on arrogance, an exercise, nothing
but language? Untranslated, the world gets on
with dark, flawless constructions rising, rising
even where we think we are. Think
how we have to hope convergences will fail this time,
that whatever it is we're working on won't work.

Headed as we appear to be toward that final convergence, a black hole, our
cultural imaginations return persistently to scenes of masses of small, un-
individuated creatures milling inside dark underground tunnels. Insects are
the mound builders and gravediggers of the *fin de siècle*, index to decay and
putrefaction, and we have shaped them into the archetypal survivors of
holocaust. "The world after a nuclear war will be a mass of rotting and
burned plants and animals. Hundreds of thousands of insects and diseases
will spread across the land." The phytophagous species of insects, those that
feed directly on vegetation, might survive a "nuclear winter" as well as those
capable of prolonged hibernation. We may poison and exterminate ourselves
through our pesticidal follies, but insects in their quadrillions will march
blindly on. Crickets at a point of no return in the growth of their populations
begin to react as a whole, with synchronized reflexes, and they start moving
in straight lines. "They go forward like a battalion of sleepwalkers." Should
the regiments of crickets die off, flies, mosquitoes, midges, earthworms,
cockroaches, and termite ants will remain to represent this planet—to visitors
or invaders from other planets whom we also imagine, more often than not,
as insectile.[87]

Our Doubles, our competitors, our survivors, our antitypes, insects were formally prosecuted for pestilence in ecclesiastical courts from the late 15th century until 1733. Naturalists have felt signally called at centuries' ends to the anatomy and census of insects. Ulysse Aldrovandi's 1602 volume, *De Animalibus Insectis*, established entomology as a science; Francesco Redi around 1688 proved that insects are not spontaneously generated from decaying matter, and Anton van Leeuwenhoek used his microscope in 1692 to work out the life course of a flea; *Entomologia Systematica*, four volumes published by J. C. Fabricius in 1792–94, became the first textbook, while larger works during the same period took stock of the genera and families of insects—G. A. Olivier's six volumes on *Entomologie*, E. Donovan's sixteen volumes on *The Natural History of British Insects*. By the end of the 19th century, insects had become coldhearted, alien invaders: they were the Martians of *The War of the Worlds*, insectile figures commanding huge insectoid fighting machines, their last words ("ulla, ulla, ulla") an inversion of "hallelujah"; they were Amazonian ants advancing inexorably upon humanity in "Empire of the Ants," another story by H. G. Wells. Baal Zebul, "Lord of Princes," in 1898–1900 once again became Beelzebub, prince of devils and "Lord of the Flies," as the anopheles and *Aedes aegypti* mosquitoes were shown to be the carriers, respectively, of malaria and of the black vomit or yellow fever.[88]

But the insect distinctively bound up with 20th-century civilization has been the cockroach. "No insects are more abundant as fossils, and none so widely distributed through the various formations, as are the cockroaches . . . , a remarkably conservative group, having retained throughout their long existence, as compared with other insects, a relatively generalized structure," wrote an admiring University of Florida professor in 1906. Cockroaches appeared on Earth during the Carboniferous Age, some 320,000,000 years ago, and they may be the final denizens of a planet carbonized by nuclear explosions. Relics of a prehuman past, relicts of a post-human future, cockroaches have also borne close witness to an inhuman present—ever since the publication of a certain waking nightmare in November 1915, in amongst a series of literary fictions entitled *Der Jüngste Tag* (*Judgment Day*). Although "Gregor Samsa awoke one morning from uneasy dreams" to find himself "transformed in his bed into a gigantic insect" never further named, that insect has been commonly considered a cockroach. Gregor does not survive Franz Kafka's "Metamorphosis" precisely because the plating of his hard shell and the segments of his stiff arched body are too forthright an evolutionary response to the ballistic, segmented world around him. Conversely, the romantic, poetic, typewriter-dancing cockroach "archy" created in 1927 by American satirist Don Marquis cannot quite accommodate the callousness of cats and human beings. Early in the 1980s, musical comedian Alan Williams was performing a Cockroach Trilogy still celebrating that "horrible, little, indestructible insect." In "The Cockroach That Ate Cincinnati," "The Return of the Cockroach," and "The Cockroach Has Landed," a cockroach who has set out to destroy rock music is locked away in an asylum, then turns into a roadie for a dadaist rockabilly band called "Trevor and the Golden Gates of Despair." A roach for this generation, hoping to lose itself in the music.[89]

PHYSICS. At the center of a black hole is a singularity. A singularity is an absurdity. It is a point containing all the mass of the hole. A singularity has no volume, but the density of its matter is infinite. THE LEAP. As the French savant Jacques Derrida pointed up in his "deconstruction" of the nuclear age, our age is not a simple epoch but an absolute *épochè*, from the Greek (ἐποχή) for the suspension of judgment before the last, irrevocable decision. We stand on the edge of that event horizon called thermonuclear war, a war that would be the first of its kind and the last of any kind, a war to end all wars and our world, therefore absolutely inventive: nonesuch before, and only one, and ultimately unnameable, for we the namers would be gone. "The name of nuclear war is the name of the first war which can be fought in the name of the name alone, that is, of everything and of nothing." Ontology would recapitulate oncology. Just as the critical technique of deconstruction exposes the "radical precariousness" of literature, so the deconstruction of nuclear rhetoric must expose the radical precariousness, the singularity, the irreducible absurdity of life at this millennium's end.[90]

The first atomic bomb was exploded in that area of Alamogordo Air Force Base called *Jornade del Muerto* or The Death Tract, south of La Luz or The Light, in the desert lands of New Mexico or New Place of the God of War (Mexico < *Mexitli*, name for the Aztec war god Huitzilopochtli). From there and then, 1945 or the Year One (from the traditional casting out of nines, $1 + 9 + 4 + 5 = 19 = 1 + 9 = 1$), singularity, terror, and absurdity have been at the center of our lives. By 1978, the art critic Peter Schjeldahl could write of "the present widespread disarray and morbidity of the arts in Western Civilization" as "a long-term toxic effect of the atom-bomb terror of the last three decades. . . . What makes the '70s so eerie is the sneaking conviction we all have that this decade *wasn't supposed to happen*. In a civilization living as if there were no tomorrow, we are the tomorrow. We are inhabiting, in effect, the no-future of the '50s and '60s." Hence the fascination of the avant-garde of the '70s (and the '80s) with ruins—old tablets, crumbling megaliths, cave paintings—and with the no-past of Pop, the no-future of minimalism. The arts had come to the end of modernism, itself an expression of "an upheaval of the third and cataclysmic order"; now, in "crisis," the avant-garde had nowhere to go but to post-modernism, an art of fragments, displacements, dissolves, flashbacks, accidents of quotation and collision.[91]

The curators of the New Museum of Contemporary Art in New York City mounted their show, "The End of the World: Contemporary Visions of the Apocalypse," in 1983, conscious that "Both the approach of the second [sic!] millennium and the year 1984 . . . have added fuel to a growing malaise and anxiety." There on the walls were James Poag's *Plants Marching on the City*, the *Exploding House* of Linda Burgess, Frank Gohlke's photographs of the aftermaths of tornadoes, Helen Oji's "Volcano" series, Roger Brown's "Disaster" series, the *End of the World with a Halo* by Marianne Stikas, a "Government Approved Home Fallout Shelter Snack Bar" constructed by Michael Smith and Alan Herman, a post-nuclear dialogue, "This Is Not a Test," installed by Beverly Naidus, a nuclear bomb aimed at the schematic have-a-nice-day "happy face" in Michael Cook's *Ashes*, maquettes for Revelation 13–18 by Robert Younger, and Rudolf Baranik's 24th-century references back to the apocalyptic fears at the end of the 20th century, *Finisterre: Dictionary and Manifesto*. There were also the cibachrome still lifes, *Apocalyptic Visions*, produced by Robert Richter, who had begun teaching the history of image-making to roaches and ants, "real survivors."[92]

This Is the Way the World Ends, wrote James Morrow in 1986, borrowing a title from T. S. Eliot, an epigraph from Nostradamus, then dividing his surreal novel into Book 1, "Those Who Favor Fire," and Book 2, "For Destruction Ice Is Also Great." John is selling Self-Contained Post-Attack Survival (SCOPAS) suits with built-in commode, dosimeter, and automatic pistol. For his sales pitch he uses an updated version of Aesop's fable, "The Grasshopper and the Cockroach," the moral of which is that the armored, self-contained cockroach (who else?) will survive nuclear war in much the same manner as someone in a SCOPAS suit. George Paxton, who works at the Gravestone Company and believes that war is imminent, buys a suit marked down to $6595 but, unable to make the payments, returns it. Visiting the MAD Hatter, Tailor of Thermonuclear Terror, Sartor of the Second Strike, George finds that he can obtain a free suit if only he signs a contract acknowledging his complicity in the nuclear arms race. The war comes: NORAD mistakes a flight of huge, ancient vultures for a Russian missile attack. Last refuge of the scoundrel human race is (where else?)

Antarctica, in Ice Limbo 414, Ice Limbo 37, Ice Limbo. . . . Morrow, for the morrow, prepares our epitaph:

IN LOVING MEMORY

OF

PEOPLE

4,500,000 B.C.–A.D. 1995

THEY WERE BETTER THAN THEY KNEW

THEY NEVER FOUND OUT

WHAT THEY WERE DOING HERE

So ends the "zero-sum" world.[93]

PHYSICS. A black hole is a dead star, for it will never become anything else. It just sits in space, dark and menacing, swallowing up any matter that comes too close. THE LEAP. During the 18th century, perhaps twenty species of living beings became extinct; during the 19th century, eighty-two; during the first part of this century, one species a year. Now one species becomes extinct about every five hours. In 1981 the official endangered species list stood at 230; now it stands at 35,000. By the end of the century, one species may become extinct every twenty minutes.[94]

None other than Imelda Marcos, hunter of ruby slippers, has told us that "Man [has become] the threatened species of our time." And in their 1982 *History of the End of the World*, Yuri Rubinsky and Ian Wiseman tell us that Nature has "no vested interest in keeping man alive, no more than it had in keeping dinosaurs alive." David M. Raup, a geophysicist and evolutionary biologist, tells us in *The Nemesis Affair* about a small star, Nemesis, whose orbit every twenty-six million years passes close enough to its companion, our sun, to wreak havoc upon the Earth; last pass it killed off the dinosaurs, and next pass it will kill us off. If human beings are still around. Delivering a presidential address to the American Academy of Religion, Gordon D. Kaufman in 1983 identified "perhaps the most momentous *change* in the human religious situation since symbolical frames of orientation were invented: the possibility that we humans, by ourselves, will utterly destroy not only ourselves but our species."[95]

Extinction, that menacing dead star at millennium's end, has as much now to do with suicide as with war or natural disaster. While our all too faithful friends the dolphins seem to be beaching themselves in desperation, we are finding that our own self-mutilation has become a widespread problem worthy of a new name, Deliberate Self-Harm Syndrome. Across the industrial and industrializing world, social scientists are alarmed at the increasing rates of suicide, especially among adolescents. The statistics mislead—our typically *fin de siècle* anxieties over individual mortality and collective futures prompt the more assiduous collection of data and the rearrangement of categories—but it is exactly our growing concern with suicide that can be documented. The first suicide prevention center opened in Los Angeles in 1958; by 1972 there were nearly two hundred suicide/crisis programs or centers in the United States. The *Bulletin of Suicidology* commenced in 1967, the *Journal of Life-Threatening Behavior* in 1970. Over the last twenty years suicide has become something of an international celebrity, with its own television specials, literary agents, authorized and unauthorized biographers, and public scandals (self-immolation as a form of protest during the 1970s; the mass suicide by the followers of Jim Jones in Guyana in 1978; deaths from starvation through anorexia nervosa in the 1980s). Private then publicly urgent requests for death from terminally ill or quadriplegic patients have become imbroglios for the courts, the churches, and the press. We smoke suicidally, drink suicidally, drive suicidally, and intimidate ourselves in the 1980s with a new Fimbulwinter, the "nuclear winter" of "a mutilated and moribund planet." Suicide: one for all and all for one.[96]

He who created Dr. Jekyll and Mr. Hyde published another story, "The Suicide Club," in 1896. The club provides the "last modern convenience"— "a decent, easy way to quit [life's] stage." The club is composed of "people in the prime of youth, with every show of intelligence and sensibility in their appearance, but with little promise of strength or the quality that makes success. Few were much above thirty, and not a few were still in their teens." Each evening, by a draw of the cards, one victim was selected, and one high priest appointed to carry out the fatal sentence. Robert Louis Stevenson meant his story as an attack upon *fin de siècle* decadence and neurasthenia, but "The Suicide Club" was also a thriller relying upon the semblance of real possibility and social consequence. This, I suspect, is how self-destruction at our century's end stands in relation to the extinction of species. Each individual act of suicide sustains a larger *fin de siècle* momentum, accumulates toward a dark and global conclusion.[97]

The first 1990 Plymouth Laser RS Turbo rolled out of the Chrysler-Mitsubishi plant in Normal, Illinois, in the fall of 1988. Our century's end was conceived in 1973 and brought forth no later than 1984; the 1990s began soon after. This chapter has been entirely circumspective: no need for the oracular when the (Nervous) Nineties are already here. Let the Countess Sophia Sabak prophesy that in 1992 Elvis Presley will reveal how he faked his own death to work as an auto mechanic in Georgia. Let the editors of the *Omni Future Almanac* establish the commercial success of the memory metal Nitinol in 1993 and the effective chemical treatment of schizophrenia in 1997. Let a computer predict that "On December 20, 1993, a mangled nuclear explosion will strike Cancun with wheezy animosity" and "On December 22, 1996, a pink tsunami will strike St. Peter's Cathedral with political supplies." Let psychic Francie Steiger foresee worldwide vegetarianism in 1995 and worldwide famine nonetheless in 1999. And let astrologer Edward J. Kluska, plotting Pluto in Scorpio, anticipate that "We will be forced to face the deepest, darkest, and ugliest part of ourselves and society" between 1984 and 1995. The affairs of this chapter have been less with augury than with recurrence. Those constellations I have been tracking are overhead now. In the next years they will become apparent even to the unaided eye.[98]

As we shall see, the black holes of the close of this millennium need be neither tragic nor final. They are the late Etruscan tombs of massive stars, ends of generations, but they may also be Augustan arches of exceptional dimensions. At century's turn there is always space, it seems, for another New Age.

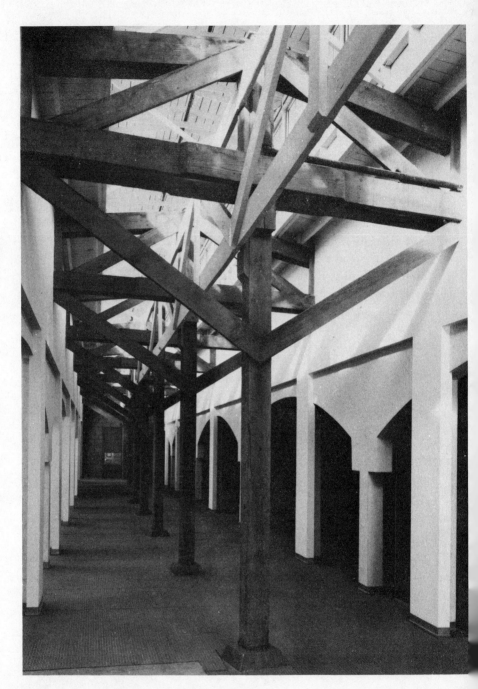

Central corridor through the building at 8522 National, Culver City, California, with cruciform trusses and clerestory remaining from the chaos of the odd set of previous warehouses, and two arched wall-systems added by the architects, Eric Owen Moss and Jay Vanos. Photo copyright © Tom Bonner 1988.

DOUBLE TIME

THE LEGEND

OF THE

YEAR 2000

—

FIRST THERE
WAS CHAOS

IT ALL STARTED WITH A SINGULARITY. WHERE THE SINGULARITY came from is a question for poets, prestidigitators, theologians, and philosophers, but our physicists tell us that the universe began with a black-hole absurdity of infinite mass and zero volume. Then, Space and Time erupted with a Big Bang: electrons, positrons, photons, neutrinos rushing posthaste apart from each other and from the few protons and neutrons of the primeval burst. After 226 seconds of collision and cooling, the stuff that stars are made of was all around. Later—about 700,000 years, 31 minutes later—stars were born. "The expansion of the universe is in many ways similar to the collapse of a star [into a black hole], except that the sense of time is reversed." Out of an impossibly dense void came pure energy and, in time, those impurities of gas, dust, stars, and planets known as galaxies. Ten billion years downstroke of the singularity, at the edge of a galaxy, life appeared on Earth. [1]

Or, as the Greeks thought and as Milton wrote in Book VIII of *Paradise Lost*, first there was Chaos,

> *the vast immeasurable abyss,*
> *Outrageous as a sea, dark, wasteful, wild,*
> *Up from the bottom turn'd by furious winds*
> *And surging waves, as Mountains to assault*
> *Heav'n's highth, and with the Centre mix the Pole.*

Chaos begat Nox (Night) and Erebus (Darkness), who between them begat Eros (Love), who begat Aether (Light) and Hemera (Day), who together awakened Gaia (Earth), whence life and, soon enough, us mortals.

Choose as we may between these two tall tales, between Hydrogen and Love, we have tradition and cause to believe, as physicist Stephen Hawking believes, that "Black holes ain't so black." Even now, ages past illimitable Chaos, billions of years beyond the initial singularity, a giant black hole

The ellipsoidal Board Room at 8522 National, with obelisk pilasters remaining from the chaos of the old construction. Photo copyright © Tom Bonner 1988.

may be powering the Milky Way, "driving billions of stars in giant orbits around the galactic center as it pulls in more and more mass." An outrageous black hole, "dark, wasteful, wild," may well be spinning at the heart of the universe itself, omega *and* alpha of space-time.[2]

A poetic leap would make of black holes the dynamos that generate New Ages out of Dark Ages, the *Aquarian Conspiracy* out of *Apocalypse Culture*. Black holes on our horizon can be taken for astrophysical machines by which to escape the images of monastic retreat and medieval closure so attractive at centuries' ends. Out of a "new monasticism," writes futurist Theodore Roszak, will arise "the capacity to synthesize qualities of life that have become fiercely polarized in our world"—the spiritual and the practical, the personal and the convivial. "The time is ripe," urges Roberto Vacca in *The Coming Dark Age*, "to begin thinking constructively about setting up independent operational units to conserve our civilized know-how, so that this knowledge might survive the coming era of darkness and bring a new era to birth." Through collapse and darkness into light.[3]

Not only do black holes assure us of the janiformity of the century's turn from senescence to youth; they also fit ideally at the center of *fin de siècle* fantasies of flight, transmigration, and fourth dimensions. Rotating black holes offer the mathematical possibility of a throat extending from the event horizon of the mouth of one black hole to the event horizon of another (or obverse) black hole. Were it physically possible to traverse this "wormhole" (or rabbit hole), Alice could indeed find herself in another or parallel universe, another or looking-glass time. A highly adept civilization alive with mathematicians of the ilk of Charles Lutwidge Dodgson (or Lewis Carroll) just might be able to construct and maintain wormholes as shortcuts through space-time from elsewhere to elsewhen.[4]

The shortcuts would likely be very short: instantaneous. Theories of black holes and wormholes appeal these days in the midst of a larger and millennial system of thought about how change comes about: abruptly. Evolutionary biologists, geologists, climatologists, biochemists, astrophysicists, and "social" scientists no longer expect transitions to be gradual. Things (and people) move from one phase to another in sudden jumps; there are historical and material discontinuities, mass extinctions, almost magical trapdoor exits and entrances. The French mathematician René Thom's topological analysis of equilibrium, known as catastrophe theory, has been applied in the past fifteen years to the behavior of the stock market, the buckling of an elastic beam, the binging and purging of a bulimarexic, the metamorphosis of a liquid into a gas, the shift of population from snowbelt to sunbelt, the conversion of young people to or from the Reverend Moon's Unification Church, the eventuality of landslips, the downpour of thunderstorms, the demand for works of art, the outbreak of prison riots, the abandonment of prehistoric sites, the disintegration of the empire of Alexander the Great, and the precipitous decline of Classic Mayan civilization. In each case, catastrophe theory has demonstrated that small, slow, steady, cumulative movements can result in an abrupt, tremendous cascade of events as ordinary as water boiling, as extraordinary as grasshoppers turning into locusts.[5]

We hardly require the mathematics of René Thom's sophisticated proofs to appreciate the congruence of catastrophe theory with our *fin de siècle* seriousness about sudden appearances (Creationism, UFOs, the Second Coming) and equally sudden disappearances (dinosaurs, Atlantis, the Rapture).[6] It seems reasonable at millennium's end that things and beings might fall (or rise) out of sight in the blink of an eye, that the wheel of fortune should accelerate to spin at a blinding speed. Cataclysm, once an event, has become an explanation, an epistemological model called "the paradigm shift." Thomas S. Kuhn, an historian of science studying the astronomical transit from the Ptolemaic to the Copernican theory of the universe, found that early modern Western scientists did not switch gradually and agreeably from one cosmological system to the next. The switch took place in the form of one of Thom's catastrophes, when the distance between theory and observation had reached, as it were, that historical cusp we now call the Scientific Revolution. Writing in 1962, Kuhn could know nothing of the folds, cusps, swallowtails, hyperbolic umbilics, elliptic umbilics, butterflies, and parabolic umbilics of Thom's book a decade later on *Structural Stability and Morphogenesis*. Kuhn wrote rather of "paradigms" in crisis, of anomalies mounting (suddenly) to "a reconstruction of the field from new fundamentals." The world of scientists, like the world that scientists investigate, proceeds ("progresses") not by ceaselessly regular ventures but from crisis to revolution, with long periods of relative equilibrium between shocks, such that each crisis must come as something of a cataclysm, each paradigm shift as something of a catastrophe.[7]

Updated and debated, revised and summarized, tested and digested, *The Structure of Scientific Revolutions* has itself become paradigmatic. Everyone who speaks of our times as times of (or in need of) fundamental changes in consciousness speaks in the original framework—although rarely the measured academic tones—of Kuhn, who has over the years muffled whatever might have been considered dynamic about his theory. Thus, directly, Marilyn Ferguson in *The Aquarian Conspiracy: Personal and Social Transformation in the 1980s*: "By naming a sharply recognizable phenomenon, Kuhn made us conscious of the ways of revolution and resistance. Now that we are beginning to understand the dynamics of revolutionary insights, we can learn to foster our own healthy change and we can cooperate to ease the collective change of mind without waiting for the fever of a crisis." Thus, proximately, the futurist Alvin Toffler in *The Third Wave*: "Humanity faces a quantum leap forward. It faces the deepest social upheaval and creative restructuring of all time. . . . We are the final generation of an old civilization and the first generation of a new one. . . . Whether we know it or not, most of us are already engaged in either resisting—or creating—the new civilization." Thus, indirectly, "Breakdown Is Breakthrough" for New Age avatar George Leonard as he goes *Walking on the Edge of the World*. Thus, facing "the basic issues of world politics at the end of the 20th century," Soviet General Secretary Mikhail Gorbachev proclaims, "We may be standing at the threshold of a uniquely interesting period in our history," one that demands *perestroika*, restructuring, and "a new outlook" on every subject.[8]

Talk these days of a threshold, a watershed, a decisive epoch, a hinge of history, a countdown stage, a critical transition, an evolutionary leap, a crossroads—of humankind at a cusp—is of course the old coin of apocalypse burnished for millennium's end, and it is still possible for fundamentalist Protestants to locate the Antichrist by the "birthmark" on Gorbachev's forehead. The cusps, swallowtails, and butterflies of Thom's catastrophe theory are this *fin de siècle*'s way of confirming the felt likelihood of instant, radical change; Kuhn's theory of the abrupt process of scientific revolution is itself a paradigm for the end of our 20th and sharply accelerating century. *Fin de siècle* vertigo makes it almost impossible for us to acknowledge anything but grand and thorough transformations. Being born on a cusp, according to the astrologer Hilarion, is the sign of change, of "breaking an incarnational pattern." Born or borne into the cusp of a century at the cusp of a millennium, we at this double time must stand ready for chaos and the new world that lies in its shadow. Writes Moira Timms as one of our contemporary Fates in *Everyone's Guide to the Coming Changes*: "There has never been a period in human history when the stakes were so high or the rewards so great. In cosmic history as in the affairs of humanity there comes a time for the consummation of the Age and the restitution of all things. Quite simply, this means that we're rapidly approaching a great era when the chaotic quality of life as we know it will cease to exist on the planet: a transmutation will have taken place."[9]

Already, Kuhn's paradigms and Thom's cusps are old news. The new news is fractal geometry, "the morphology of the amorphous," and chaos theory, "a new way of finding order in systems that appear to have no order at all." How timely it is that fractals, "geometric forms with irregular patterns that repeat themselves at different scales," should come to the cultural foreground as our social and political forms collapse toward century's end, and how timely that a science likely to illumine most of the complex problems in the physics of turbulence should come out of our laboratories onto the 1988 bestseller list "in a world nearing chaos."[10]

Around last century's end, William Butler Yeats, poet of the hermetic Order of the Golden Dawn, foresaw that during phases 26–28 of the Larger Wheels (1965–2000 A.D.) the West would be assailed by anarchic violence, but Yeats did not foresee the work of Benoit Mandelbrot at IBM or of the Dynamical Systems Collective (the Chaos Cabal) at the University of California, Santa Cruz. Had he been more of a mathematician and less of a magus, he might have had some inklings, for Mandelbrot's fractal geometry has its origins in late-19th-century encounters with a mathematical "gallery of monsters," continuous nondifferentiable functions and Peano (plane-filling) curves that avoid not only self-intersection but self-contact. The great French mathematician Charles Hermite in 1893 reported "turning away in fear and horror from this lamentable plague of functions with no derivatives," and by 1906 Jean Perrin had remarked the continuous irregularity of that most innocent of structures, the snowflake, whose irregularities endured no matter the degree of magnification. In 1907 Edmund Edward Fournier d'Albe, a mathematician and Spiritualist associated with Yeats's Pan-Celtic Movement, conceived of *Two New Worlds*, infra and supra; his Fournier universe had at its core what would turn out to be a fractal, just as it seems now that stars and galaxies form by a fractal cascade from a uniform gas.[11]

Lest this page read forbiddingly, imagine a walk on a beach, with or without Einstein. The coast is scenic, that is, irregular. You follow the shore barefoot with a romantic feeling for its ins and outs at water's edge. Now imagine an ant picking her path along that shore. Smaller and more perceptive (or more fearful of the slightest surf), the ant would follow a *longer* and *more complex* coastline, a coastline with many dangerous, dramatic ins and outs of which you could hardly have been aware. Your coastline is, in a manner of speaking, the first-order expression of a fractal; the ant's coastline is the second-order expression. A mite's coastline, longer and more irregular yet, would be a third-order expression. . . . And so on, each decreasing order of magnitude yielding a richer, interminable treasure of bays, coves, cliffs, peninsulas, river mouths. Fractal geometry is our *fin de siècle* means for appreciating the rules of transformation behind natural systems of increasing or unresolvable complexity. Chaos theorists make use of fractal geometry to discern the order behind apparently random phenomena, nonlinear sequences of events that never repeat in periodic ways: the formation of snowflakes, for example, or the irritating drip from a faucet, or the flapping of a banner in the wind.[12]

Psychologist David Loye and attorney Riane Eisler suggest that chaos theory may, "at a potentially chaotic juncture in human evolution, offer us a much clearer understanding of what happens, can happen, and can be made to happen in a time of mounting social, political, economic, and environmental crises." We might pursue chaos theory through pages of demographic analysis, organizational dynamics, quantitative economics, or Discordian philosophy from the Fifth Religious Erisian Disorganization of the Harpo Marx Cabal and its cockroach, St. Gulik, Messenger of the Goddess in Morristown, New Jersey. F.R.E.D., I should confess, is tempting—"the worship of **Eris**, the ancient Greek Goddess of joyous confusion, is not only MORE WEIRD and MORE FUN than any *other* major world religion, it's MORE TRUE, too!"—but the truth must not distract us from exploring what will be our most permanent, or mos visible, monument to chaos: architecture.[13]

Taking shape at century's end is an aesthetics of chaos. The strange attractors and irresistible attractions of fractal geometry have led to an impressive portfolio, *The Beauty of Fractals*, and to a new generation of computer graphics "revealing the richness and complexity that are hidden in even the most elementary equations." Fractal geometry has shown, wrote Mandelbrot, "that some of the most austerely formal chapters of mathematics had a hidden face: a world of pure plastic beauty unsuspected till now." In 1988 the influential Japanese architect Kisho Kurokawa began advocating "a rhizome world or 'chaosmos.' " Earlier, in 1986, he had articulated his own aesthetic as "an architecture of symbiosis," the mutually embracing relationship of part and whole. He had quoted fondly from Arthur Koestler's books on *Janus* and on *The Act of Creation*, in which Koestler explained "holarchy" (an open hierarchic system with self-transcending tendencies) and "bisociation" (the "merging on a new plane of two previously totally unrelated frames of awareness"). Kurokawa also referred to the comparable work of fractal geometer Mandelbrot and of physicist David Bohm, who had long been insisting that all movement of a whole is inherent within each part. Part and whole, concluded Kurokawa, are "joined like the two-faced God Janus." Then, in 1988, amidst debates about and misdefinitions of "Deconstructionist" architecture as practiced by Frank Gehry, Bernard Tschumi, Emilio Ambasz, Daniel Liebeskind, Peter Eisenman, Itsuko Hasegawa, Mark Wigley, and Elemér Zalotay, Kurokawa argued against the apocalyptic dichotomies of post-modernism. If there was "a renewed interest in the apparently accidental collision of forms" in Honold and Pöschl's Bogen 13 under the arches of Innsbruck, if Hasegawa's student hostel in Shizuoka was an almost *ad hoc* assemblage, a "deliberate participation in the anarchic chaos of the Japanese city," Kurokawa meant his Nagoya Municipal Museum of Modern Art as allusive fragments in an interlocking web (a rhizome, a "chaosmos," courtesy of the French critics Gilles Deleuze and Félix Guattari). Kurokawa's Memorial Hall for the Shirase Expeditionary Party to the South Pole would have a cone-shaped hall at the center of a white ring, the mediation of geometric opposites for adventurous human beings who should consider themselves, wrote Kurokawa, "animals possessed by chaos" yet very much alive and whole.[14]

The aesthetics of chaos has at its trembling point the principle that "order arises *because* of disorder." Listen to Eric Moss, recently twice blessed with prestigious national Honor Awards from the American Institute of Architects, talking in 1988 about one of his new buildings in Los Angeles: "At first you look at it and say, 'What the hell is going on here?' But if you dig long and hard enough you'll discover that there is a series of rules . . . a kind of unifying and rigorous series of visual rules that get lost, and then you find them, and then they get lost again. There is something at some level that ties the thing together." First there was chaos: five conjoined disjunct warehouses, sixty thousand square feet of plastics-factory partitions, catch-as-catch-can ceilings, bricked-in doorways, oddball walls, ducts, sprinklers, and crazyquilt floors dating from the '20s, the '30s, the '40s, the War, the Lost Horizon. "It was really incoherent as hell," really an epitome of the rest of the world according to Moss, which "isn't logical, linear, sequential, sensible. There are pieces of rationality that sit on something that is an accident and arational." But "Things which appear episodically may have connections you don't know about," says Moss's associate Jay Vanos, who has been reading James Gleick's *Chaos: Making a New Science*. Moss himself has long been impressed by the bold catastrophism of Immanuel Velikovsky's *Worlds in Collision*, an argument for the astronomical and geocosmic reality, early in the first millennium B.C., of the great floods and celestial battles between Mars and Venus recorded by myths worldwide. At 8522 National Boulevard, off center of a battle zone between rival teenage gangs, Moss and Vanos have remodeled a structural catastrophe in much the same fashion as the Chaos Cabal and fractal geometers have been remodeling our universe of ostensibly random or nonlinear phenomena—by exposing underlying systems (wooden cruciform trusses, archways, industrial clerestory) and by drawing from the site a chaosmos, a "mystery," a "religious idea" that "everything doesn't start or end with people." Whence an entryway whose cinder block ellipse has been arrested, as if abandoned at sudden notice to be resumed momentarily. Wherefore, at the other serif of the L of the now-conjunct building, a spacious ellipsoid with incurving walls of smooth golden birch plywood: a room that is itself an event; a *meeting* room ("things which appear episodically may have connections you don't know about"); a surprise; a fourth dimension.[15]

Order out of Chaos is the English title of a book by Ilya Prigogine, another speculative scientist with whom Kisho Kurokawa, Eric Moss, and Jay Vanos share a spiritual vision at this millennium's turn. Prigogine's theory of dissipative structures has led him to propose that the universal entropy mandated by the Second Law of Thermodynamics applies only to closed systems. More often paraphrased (therefore?) than directly quoted, Prigogine's work has been well digested by a Polish philosopher, Henryk Skolimowski: "When organisms and other open systems cannot take the evolutionary pressure any more, the result often is that, instead of collapsing and disintegrating, they actually reorganize in new wholes of a higher order." Such a vision, Prigogine himself has written, must lead beyond chaos to "the re-enchantment of the World."[16]

We are embarrassingly close, all of a sudden, to the New Age, whatever that is. "Does anyone really know what the New Age is?" asks Lazaris, a Spark of Light and Love channeled through Jach Pursel of Los Angeles. "Yes. It is an Age when people willingly and joyously accept personal responsibility for the world they are in and have created. . . . They create and co-create a new dawn, a new day, a New Age of Humanity. It is real. It is real." It is millennial. It is millennial. "Recorded prophecy . . . comes abruptly to a stop at the end of the 20th century and at the beginning of the 21st. Many point with a quaking finger claiming that this is proof of an End that is near. Yes. Yes, we would suggest that an end is near. An End to the Old Age and the beginning of a New Age." The New Age is post-industrial, post-economic, post-managerial, post-capitalist, post-socialist, post-political, post-modern, post-historical, and posthumous, unable quite "to define itself in terms of what it *is*, but only in terms of what it has *just-now-ceased-to-be*," and in desperate search of ADE, an Archetype of Death and Enlightenment. The New Age may be the trademark of the Freemasons and their long intrigue to control the world. It may be the password of a tightly knit occult group intent on melting down the nations into a single ball of wax for the Antichrist. It may be the astrological sign of the six planets conspiring toward an alignment under Aquarius, whereupon the Earth will be transformed. It may be the seismograph of a "psychotectonic shift" toward a peaceful, global consciousness. It may be guff. [17]

Whatever it is, it deserves notice. Attention must be paid. The coming New Age is to the coming Dark Age what the dawn of another century is to century's end, what 2000 and 2001 are to 1998 and 1999. The previous chapter, on the 1990s, was fretful and downcast; this chapter must be swept up (for a while) by the millennial premise of Russian novelist Aleksandr Solzhenitsyn: "If the world has not approached its end, it has reached a major watershed in history, equal in history to the turn from the Middle Ages to the Renaissance. It will demand from us a spiritual blaze. . . . This ascension is similar to climbing onto the next anthropological stage. No one on earth has any other way left but—upward." In the words of the non-physical entity Lazaris, "Now, when so many are so quick to tell you how terrible your world has become, is the easiest time of all to step into the New Dawn, the New Day, the New World, the New Age!" [18]

Welcome, then, to **Threshold Response**™—**The Next Step in Unlocking the Mind's Full Creative Powers**; to Auro Trading Company's *Alive Energy*™ health products for intelligence, ecstasy, spiritual awareness, and luminous spirit; to the New Life Spa and The Last Resort; to Green Magma nutrition powder, Trader Joe's Janus Spirulina, Mind Peak jade medicine, Super Blue Green Algae™ perfect food; to a videotaped "Evening with Dr. Bernie Siegel" on love, medicine, and miracles; to *Nada Brahma*, Joachim-Ernst Berendt's mystery tour of *Music and the Landscape of Consciousness*, available in the United States at 2500 New Age bookstores, which also carry cassettes of the soothing music of George Winston, a stride pianist suspicious of New Age "woo-woos" but "half woo-woo myself." [19]

The beaming, exorbitant confidences of New Age "woo-woos" are but the janiform complement of the extremes of despair at this century's close. The New Age counterposes thaumaturgical gifts of healing to the pathological *fin de siècle* fears of ageing, debility, exhaustion. Ambrosia herbal tablets from the Maharishi Ayurveda master physicians, Hawaiian-grown spirulina from Microlight Enterprises, the Bach Rescue Remedy, these must be to heroin, crack, and cocaine what rejuvenation is to decadence. Just now, thaumaturgy or wonderworking must appear not only more substantial but more necessary and more urgent. Magic, after all, is mainly redirection, and miracle what we take to be impossible *in so short a time*. If not hell then heaven: "Our highs can spring directly out of our lows, if we go through them to the end."[20] At the end of this millennium and the start of another, the highs (it would follow) should be higher than ever. Like it or not, there has always been something essentially woo-woo about the year 2000.

THEN CAME
THE PYRAMIDS

WAS THE SECOND KING OF THE FOURTH MEMPHITE DYNASTY OF the Old Kingdom counting the days to the 21st century? Was Khufu (Cheops) plotting the path toward the third millennium A.D. in concert with priests of the Egyptian sun god more than forty-five hundred years ago? Was his pyramid at Giza laid out on the grid of the world-week, its interior maze commencing at 4000 B.C. and winding through six thousand inch-years to the central chamber's 2000?[21]

No.

Did Maelmhaedhoc O'Morgair, while founding the first Cistercian monastery in Ireland, set down a prophetic list of 112 pontiffs from Celestine II (d. 1144) to the end of the papacy? Dying in the arms of St. Bernard of Clairvaux in 1148, did the blessed Maelmhaedhoc, soon St. Malachy, foresee a final pope for the year 2000?

No, and again no. The list spuriously attributed to Malachy appeared out of nowhere in 1595, published by a Benedictine monk. Each successive pope in *Prophetia de Futuris Pontificibus Romanis* is identified not by name but by an allusive epithet. Since the 17th century, fitting the popes to the epithets in the proper order has required exegetical virtuosity, and not until this century could it seem that the list was headed toward a 112th pope around the year 2000. If Paul VI (d. 1978) was the 108th pope, *Flors florum*, because his coat of arms had on it a fleur-de-lys, and if John Paul (1978, for 33 days) was the 109th pope, *De medietate lunae*, because he died in the middle of the lunar cycle, then John Paul II (1978–) must be the 110th and antepenultimate pope, *De labore solis*, "Of the work of the sun." His first encyclical, in 1979, concerned the work of the Son, *Redemptor Hominis (Redeemer of Man)*. It began with reference to "the close of the second millennium," and continued, "In fact, this time, in which God in his hidden design has entrusted to me . . . the universal service connected with the Chair of Saint Peter in Rome, is already very close to the year 2000." Born

The pyramid from Francesco Colonna's *Hypnerotomachia Poliphili* (Venice, 1499), based upon Pliny's description of the Mausoleum at Halicarnassus.

in 1920, John Paul II may have a pontificate that falls short of the year 2000, a year which he has mentioned often. There is still time for a 111th and penultimate pope, *De gloria olivae*, "From the glory of the olive," to cede the papacy in turn to the 112th pope, *Petrus Romanus*, "Peter of Rome," before "that year of a great Jubilee . . . which, without prejudice to all the correction imposed by chronological exactitude, will recall and reawaken in us in a special way our awareness of the key truth of faith."[22]

With an historian's prejudice for chronological exactitude, I return us not to Maelmhaedhoc O'Morgair's 12th century but to the 16th century, to Arnold Wion, the monk who published the "St. Malachy" list, and to Michel de Nostredame, whose millennial quatrain we have read once before:

> *The year 1999, seven months,*
> *From the sky will come a great King of terror,*
> *To resuscitate the great King of Angoulmois;*
> *Before, after, Mars will reign by good luck.*

Whoever may be the Kings of terror and Angoulmois, they do not necessarily enlist the forces of Armageddon. For Nostradamus, our world continues under astrological tergiversations through to 3797 and (vaguely) beyond. Nonetheless, over the centuries this quatrain and others have been translated and interpreted in the context of a darkly apocalyptic 1999 and a brightly millennial 2000. Such interpretations abound as we near this century's end. In 1987, for example, John Hogue took the quatrain to refer to "The Last Conflagration"—"the culmination of . . . twenty-seven years of war and the final destruction of the civilized world," followed (in 2026) by "one thousand years of peace in which a galactic community becomes a reality and man enters a period where science and religion merge into a higher consciousness."[23]

It would be pointless to dispute an interpretation so well aligned with the *fin de siècle* aesthetics of chaos and the New Age sense of imminent transformation. The point to make here is that the more significant the year 2000 seems to be, the more important it becomes to anchor anticipations of the year 2000 in the distant historical past. And, in fact, although neither Khufu's pyramid nor Arnold Wion's *Lignum Vitae* nor Nostradamus's centuries can be proved to have been inclined toward the majesty of the year 2000, others at mid-millennium did construct historico-prophetic charts that concluded with the end of the second millennium A.D. By 1700, Archbishop Ussher's oft-cited date for Creation, 4004 B.C., provided a most agreeable chronological symmetry. The world would last the traditional 6000 years of the world-week: 2000 from the Creation to Moses and the Old Testament, 2000 (with some arithmetickling) from Moses to Jesus and the New Testament, 2000 from Jesus to the Second Coming near the year 2000.[24]

Thenceforth, with ever greater frequency, the pendulum clock at the foot of the stairs of the Christian West would be wound up so as to demand rewinding by "the true key of faith" upon the New Year's chimes of Anno Domini 2000. This was the case in 18th-century Germany for the Protestant (pietist) theologian Johann Albrecht Bengel and the Catholic prophetess Anna Katharina Emmerich; in France for Jeanne Le Royer, an inspired lay sister in a Brittany convent, and Mlle. Le Normand, sibyl to Napoleon's Josephine; in Italy for the Chilean Jesuit Manuel Lacunza; in England for Thomas Newton, Bishop of Bristol, and the Reverend Samuel Madden whose memoirs of the future included an auction of the Ark of the Covenant on April 25, 1998; in America for the West Indian poet Charles Crawford, for Morgan Edwards, A.M., of Rhode Island College, and for the ministers Benjamin Gale and William F. Miller of Connecticut.[25]

From the 1860s on, John Taylor, Piazzi Smyth, Robert Menzies, and David Davidson inched their way through King Khufu's corridors until his Great Pyramid at Giza had become the providential monument to a growing legend of the year 2000 as the apex of history. By century's end, the year 2000 was the site of Edward Bellamy's cooperative utopia, William Morris's socialist revolution, Winnifred H. Cooley's feminist welfare state, Friedrich E. Bilz's universally deployed nature cure, and Edward Berwick's vegetarian farmers' paradise. New York inventor and proprietor John Jacob Astor was marveling at the technological prowess of the space travelers and the Terrestrial Axis Straightening Company of 2000 A.D.—a century ahead of his Astoria Hotel, which was spacious and comfortable but did not presume to provide a night's entertainment on dinosaurian Jupiter or to maintain an even temperature at each degree of earthly latitude. Jean Marc Coté, commissioned in 1899 to draw up a set of futuristic cigarette cards for turn-of-the-century festivities in France, painted the aero-cab stations and flying cops and robbers of the year 2000, schoolrooms with students in headphones, underwater croquet tournaments, submarine liners, and plush parlors heated by fireplaces glowing with radium.[26]

Coté also painted a dinner party with a dinner consisting entirely of pills and concentrates. Of all images of the year 2000 purveyed during the 1890s, this minimalist dinner most caught the public fancy. It had been conceived in 1897 by a French chemist concocting *The Year* 2000's achievements in chemistry, an organic and spiritual chemistry so evolved that the moral nature of humanity itself would be transformed. The sensible extrapolations of French sociologist Charles Richet's *Dans cent ans (In One Hundred Years)* and American forecaster David G. Croly's *Glimpses of the Future . . . To Be Read Now and Judged in the Year 2000* were put to shame by Marcellin Berthelot's chemical feast, which was not only more entertaining but more precisely emblematic of the year 2000. Satirists, exaggerating contemporary visions of the year 2000, could amuse with prognostications of golf clubs that keep score, department stores 2 miles long by 1½ miles wide by 1 mile high, wireless wire-haired terriers, Hyper-Super-Dreadnoughts, Ne Plus Ultra Pocket Phonographs of Everyday Phrases, and a compact necklace edition of the *Encyclopaedia Britannica*. Berthelot, however, had unwittingly chanced upon a perfect metonym for the millennial banquet of the legend of the year 2000. An almost insubstantial but nutritionally exact diet of essences is ideal to a year in which all that is good must be distilled from the dross of history and all those happy events that have yet to happen must come to pass in one short, powerfully condensed calendar period.[27]

On the verge of the 20th century, the historical compression of the year 2000 was already being felt. As early as 1873, Florence Nightingale had been asking, "What will be our religion in 1999?" She argued that the moral universe of 1999 depended upon the actions taken in 1873. It behooved every person to ask herself, "What in 1999 will have been the thing that we in 1999 should have wished to have done in 1873, to tell not only upon 1873, but upon 1899 and 1999?" Such back projections of remorse and regret have become unusually common during the 20th century, a century distinguished for its habit of bitter recrimination over lost opportunities and irreversible mistakes. Margins for error are impossibly narrow in these last days; anything we do has repercussions at millennium's end. For one hundred years and more, we have looked fearfully toward 1999 as the year of unappealable verdicts, then hopefully toward 2000 as the year of pardon and jubilee.[28]

Since World War II our "planners" have in practice been looking back over their shoulders at the 20th century from the legendary vantage point of the year 2000. In nearly every field, from glass manufacturing to training the mentally retarded to government management to primary education to the design of college entrance examinations to horsemanship to sports technology to gourmet cooking, and in nearly every part of the world, from Japan to Indonesia to India to Italy to Iowa and Illinois, from Pakistan to Poland to Portugal to Peru, from the Arabian Peninsula to Argentina, from

Egypt to England, from Hungary to Hawaii, from Fujian Province in China to the French magazine *L'Express*, from an international UNESCO roundtable in Paris to Liberia's Monrovia Symposium on the Future Development Prospects of Africa, from the Official Central National Long-Range Planning System of the Soviet Union to the American Academy of Arts and Sciences in the United States, the year 2000 has stood for the Future—the Inherent Future, that future by which our century has long been shaped.[29]

Social planners, technological forecasters, and "futurologists," ever squinting toward the terrible swift sword of change, have been the most forward scouts of historical compression. The future, they tell us, is not "a secretion of the past" but "the cause of the present." No longer stable, the future is "a moving target," it is "racing toward us." Read *How to Get to the Future Before It Gets to You*, and bear in mind that "To live well in the present, to live decently and humanely, *we must see into the future*." Moreover, "All living things act to anticipate the future; this is what chiefly distinguishes them from lifeless things. . . . Man is so constituted biologically that he *must* predict." In view of catastrophes immediately past and impending, to refrain from speculation about the future is "difficult if not impossible," and "given the fact that we are approaching a millennial symbol with the year 2000—the times [require] a more visionary statement." Our critical historical situation decrees, and our (20th-century) human nature demands, all the techniques of future-telling or "structural fabulation" that can be mustered: propaedeutic scenarios, cross-purpose matrices, brainstorming, nomothetics, ekistics, computer simulation, stochastic analysis, prevision, extrapolation, opinion polling, market research, Markov chains, prognoseology, envelope curves, and the Delphi Method for arriving at an objective consensus about what is possible and what is probable.[30]

We have had planners and forecasters since the late 19th century, "professors of the future" since the 1920s, futurists and futurologists since the 1940s, and many have seen themselves as the heroic soothseers of an alternative, expansive future beyond the threshold of the year 2000. "I go to Calcutta and Bombay and I see hell!" historian William Irwin Thompson told futurist Herman Kahn, who had just laid out *The Next 200 Years*. "You see marvelous things." But the net effect of futurological insistence upon the acceleration of change, the complexity of the world, and the scientificity of projections ahead has been to make the less statistically adept of us feel even more acutely the back projections of remorse and regret: every moment that we fail to respond to a Megatrend becomes an opportunity forever lost; every mistake is instantly compounded and surely irreversible. Futurists of socialist countries, believing that "Socialist society has a stronger organic bond with the future than any other society," have been especially careful to pass over "that magic date—the year 2000" so as to demonstrate their faith in their ability to make scientific forecasts: "Marx would say that if we were unable to predict the main tendencies of the future, we should also be unable to learn about the present and describe it adequately, since those future tendencies 'present themselves' in the present." Yet these days none of us, capitalist or socialist, seems able to describe the hugger-mugger present adequately, and that illusion of command which sustains the futurological endeavor also proves, by its very elusiveness, how foreshortened our time must be at the end of the 20th century.[31]

Desperate to escape the historical compression of this *fin de siècle*, eager to assume the aura and manna of a freer time, companies have begun naming themselves or their products into the millennial future. Tony Russo of 21st Century Publications (Tolland, Connecticut) explains: "The reason for our name is simply that we felt that as our human relations books always seemed to be light years ahead of the others, as have been our ideas, we should be associated with the future rather than the present or the sometimes (perhaps more often than not) 'yucky' past, e.g. the Holocaust, etc." Others may be neither so explicit nor so forthcoming, but they too imply at once an escape and an adventure when they name their businesses Twenty-First Century Books, Twenty-First Century Press, Twenty-First Century Media, Siglo XXI, 21st Century American Technology Development Corporation, 21st Century Envelope Company, 21st Century Genetics, 21st Century Robotics, 21st Century Paramount (for roofing compounds), and Century 21 Real Estate, or when they write *The 21st-Century Diet*, or advertise Twenty-First Century (Bulova) watches, 21st Century (Foot-Joy) shoes. Noblia watches and Maytag washers are warranted to the year 2001. There are 2000 Flushes to a toilet-bowl cleaner; there is a Pitman 2000 shorthand system, a Hero 2000 robot, a Twilight: 2000 computer game, an Impact 2000 voice stress analyzer, a Pontiac 2000 automobile, a 2000 Mile motor oil, 2000 High Tech sailboat hardware, Eyexam 2000, Furnishings 2000, and the fashionable European woman of the year 2000, *Due Millia*. Most blatantly, there are Millennium and Millenia *(sic)* watches, Millenium *(sic)* writing instruments, Millennium [Film] Productions, Millennium Records, Millennium Design Communications, a Millennium chamber music ensemble, and a *Theology for the Third Millennium*.[32]

Anyone or anything still locked into the 20th century must perforce be out of date, obsolete. (The life cycle for control engineering products is "down to four years and dropping. By the late 1990's, if not sooner, it will probably approach three years.") Fighting off the historical compression of these years and their own fears of obsolescence, politicians have begun staking boldly premature claims to the year 2000 and beyond. Young Senator Dan Quayle, accepting the Republican vice-presidential nomination in 1988, was confident that he could "lead us to the future and to the 21st Century." George Bush, accepting the Republican presidential nomination, spoke of the 20th century as the American Century, "because in it we were the dominant force for good in the world. . . . Now we are on the verge of a new century, and what country's name will it bear? I say it will be another American Century." Given the radiance of the American individual and the love of the American family, it should be so, "For it is the family that communicates to our children—to the 21st Century—our culture, our religious faith, our traditions and history." Governor Michael Dukakis, accepting the Democratic presidential nomination, spoke with surprising emotion of handing on a better America to the children and grandchildren who would be coming of age at the turn of a new century and, he pledged, a new era.[33]

Such statements of faith in the continuity of generations across the millennial divide are becoming more frequent and more impassioned as adults imagine themselves released from the anxieties of a *fin de siècle* by the blithe spirits of their young. Kindergarten teachers throughout the United States in the spring of 1988 held unusually public, festive rites of passage for those who will be the high school graduating class of the year 2000. During the 1980s educators, toymakers, and film producers began to relocate children in the 21st century and then beseech them to save the world. . . . It is the year 2005. In the year 2000, our galaxy established a parliament, the Galaxy Federation. Meanwhile, space pirates had gotten hold of Metroid, a vampirical life-form which can be used as a weapon to destroy civilization. The Galaxy Federation sends a cosmic warrior, Samus, to pirate headquarters inside the Fortress Planet Zebes, where he (you, my child) must destroy the Mother Brain with thirty continuous missile shots; otherwise all the energy of galactic life will be sucked away.—The 1987 Nintendo video game, METROID. . . . It is the year 2013. Six months ago, in October 2012, an accident at a nuclear reactor on the border of France and West Germany forced the evacuation of five million people. Sympathetic, the United States opens its doors to many of the evacuees by creating a new category, the "catastrophic immigrant," one who cannot return home due to disastrous circumstances expected to last more than five years. New Jamestown, a large planned city, receives 37,500 CIs. What problems will they face and how can we (you, my children) solve them?—The 1987 Fuzzy Situation for students at the State Bowls of the North American Future Problem Solving Program. . . . It is the year 2088. The Earth is overpopulated, polluted, fast-fooded; its air is almost unbreathable, its outer radiation belts are crackling. Aboard the last true starship, super-precocious super-good space cadets (that means you, dear spacelings) must navigate alone through the dangerous junk belt of satellites surrounding the Earth, elude or outwit outlaws from the Outlaw Technology Zone, and hypertravel toward Berenson's Star, 18.7 light-years away, to settle Demetur, a new, fertile planet for humankind.— The 1988 television movie, *Earth Star Voyager*.[34]

So, naming them Chris, Kris, Christine, Christophe, Christopher ("Christ-Bearer"), Noah, Jonah, Geneviève, Jennifer ("White Wave"), our children become, as literally as we can make them out to be, our future. Oh, perhaps we may find "expectancy waves" and "feed forward" mechanisms in the lobes of our brains, but along the ordinary run of this century's end we are waiting for our children to assume transcendent, millennial powers. If the majority of 600,000 primary and junior high school students surveyed in 1986 foresaw a grim global future (the future conditional of their elders), they were at the same time optimistic about their individual futures (the future perfect of their own generation). If Colorado children in 1984, writing essays on "Images of the Pikes Peak Region, 2001," more often than not began, "After the holocaust of World War III . . . ," still they went on to rebuild society in their own image under Plexiglas domes safe from the air pollution and radioactive waste of their parents and grandparents. Under those domes or up in orbiting colonies or inside huge floating pyramids lies the hope of the 21st century: *The Kids' Whole Future Catalog* in 1982 promised its readers, "If you keep this book and look through it 30 years from now, you may find that what really happened was even more fantastic than anyone imagined."[35]

Last chapter the children were missing and abused children, battered, terrorized, raped, dissociative, suicidal; this chapter they are the avant-garde, dodgers of asteroids, space explorers, masters of chaos and computer keyboards. Theirs is an *Education Without Frontiers* and the "altered state" of total, rapt concentration upon an interactive eternity, the video game screen. "Everyone knows that the game is going to end 'sometime,' but sometime is potentially infinite," notes Sherry Turkle, who has studied the intimate relations between children and computers. Jimmy says, "For me the game is to see how long I can be perfect. Every day I try to be perfect for ten minutes longer."[36]

Should this contrast between the ravaged children of the 1990s and the enraptured, self-perfecting children of the year 2000 seem too stark, that is just how it must be. At centuries' ends people are prone to live by the doctrine of the excluded middle, and never more so than at ours. Upon the approach of the year 2000 we have been turning A and not-A into A and V. Protest as some may against its "magical, sentimental *fin de siècle* quality" with its "overtures of superstition, of numerology, and astrology," the year 2000 does make for the most hyperbolic of centuries' ends. As early as 1892, a columnist for London's *Spectator* knew this would happen: "The fact that we are approaching the end of another century of our era, strongly affects the popular imagination. It is supposed that, in some undefined way, we must be better or worse merely because of this chronological fact. Were it the end, not of the nineteenth, but of the twentieth, we should be still more excited. Even now, the idea of that Annus Mirabilis, the Year of Grace 2000, begins to affect us. We feel that if we could live to witness its advent, we should witness an immense event. We should almost expect something to happen in the Cosmos, so that we might read the great date written on the skies."[37]

Why? The answer enjoins a synopsis of this book. Because, over the years, Western culture has become numerate and chronocratic, sensitive to calendar time and clock time. Because we have come to identify ourselves with our centuries and to plot history by even hundreds. Because we have come to use the ends of centuries as markers not only for history but for prophecy, and the year 2000 fits exceedingly well into the historico-prophetic symmetries of the world-week. Because as other anniversaries (saints' days, commemorative holidays, even birthdays) have lost much of their numen, their spiritual power, we have transferred our rituals of loss and resolve to years' and centuries' ends. Becauses we share Dennis the Diminutive's calendar and, in this century, all of us—Shiʿite or Sunni Muslim, Reform or Orthodox Jew, Protestant of whatever stripe, Roman Catholic or Greek Orthodox, agnostic or atheist, communist or libertarian, socialist or anarchist, parliamentarian or absolute dictator, democratic representative or tribal patriarch—all of us lead our public, secular lives by the terms of the Gregorian Reform, so that all of us will share a synchronous experience of this century's end. Because, now, we have evidence for, threats of, and momentum toward complete extinction, an End to centuries' ends. Because, as a result of the foregoing, the year 2000 has been the traditional terminus for prophecies, for "perpetual" calendars, for "long-range" forecasts, and it bears the cumulative emotional weight of thousands of deferred hopes and unfulfilled predictions. (Is government by the people possible? "Would that in the year 1999 or 2000 one could come back to earth, in order to hear the answer," wrote antiquarian Walter Besant in 1901.) No date, no bewitching number beyond the year 2000 has gathered about itself any extraordinary series of prophetic bets. Not 2020, 2099, 2100, 2101, 2222, 2345, 2468, 2999, 3000, 3003, 3333, 6666 . . . not even 2001.[38]

A few of these reasons have occurred to the directors of the Millennium Society who, assailed by calendrical prigs, must defend their intention to sponsor worldwide festivities the night of December 31, 1999. Some pessimists may already have booked seats on the fleet of blimps being assembled by Richard Kieninger in Adelphi, Texas,, to float in the skies while, down below, quakes, volcanoes, and tidal waves mark "a catastrophic shift in the Earth's axis" by (in) the year 2000, but the Millennium Society has reserved the Great Pyramid of Cheops for three thousand optimists congregating on the eve of the first day of January 2000. The *Queen Elizabeth II*, also reserved, will set sail from New York Harbor December 21, 1999, with a complement of the world's "most inspiring" people (the likes of—should they accept—Deng Xiaoping, Bruce Springsteen the singer, Pope John Paul II, George Burns the comedian, Bishop Desmond Tutu, Steven Spielberg the filmmaker, Dr. Masaki Nakajima of the Mitsubishi Research Institute, Ronald Reagan the performer, Corazon Aquino, Kathryn Sullivan the astronaut, and the Statue of Liberty). Mingling with Millennium Society members, mostly Young Republicans turned forty, the inspiring people will arrive at the Great Pyramid just as others in every time zone of the world, from Eden Crater, New Zealand, to the Great Wall of China to the Taj Mahal to Stonehenge, gather to toast the year 2000 and, if not the technical start of the new millennium, certainly the finale of the millennium. And then? Then, in the highest of spirits, the Millennium Society will begin planning festivities for the year 3000. Lawyer Edward E. McNally, one of the founders of the Society from the original "happy afternoon luncheon" of Yale seniors, Class of 1979, smiles over his brunch in 1987. "I'm convinced that we're going to have an extraordinary year 3000."[39]

All things being equal, and nothing being quite the same, the most inspirational people of that distant turning point will also meet at a great pyramid. Pyramids have become the fulcrums of centuries' ends, the symbolic structures by which we move from burial to rebirth, decay to wonder. In

Francesco Colonna's hermetic *Hypnerotomachia Poliphili* of 1499, the dreaming narrator arrived at a vermilion pyramid at the end of a valley, "And there in this so noble a piece of work, I found a proportioned substance to every shape and likeness that can be thought upon and called to remembrance, partly decayed, and some still whole remaining." A cube sat atop the pyramid, an obelisk atop the cube, and atop the obelisk, on a turning stand, stood an angelic nymph, left hand to her naked breast, right hand holding out a horn of plenty. Colonna's pyramid was at once mysterious antiquity and classical youth, a divinely inspired memory system for reconstructing the eternal solid geometry of the cosmos, and this was how pyramids made their way through early modern books of emblems to the emblems and seals of the Freemasons in the 18th century. Masonry, of course, had reached perfection in the Egyptian pyramid ("The squared stones joined together without any cement, and the pointed quadrangulate cornerstones straightly fitted and smoothly polished" so that the finest Spanish needle could not be hidden in any joint, wrote Colonna). Ancient masonic secrets by which to take full measure of the universe and achieve perfect joinery had not been lost. They had been passed along through the ages under the care of a secret brotherhood from Egyptian master builders to new and free masons. The 18th-century myth of an ancient, inspired "craft" perpetuated by enlightened men of science was, and is, attractive. By the end of the 18th century, buttressed by Egyptian revivals in the European styling of funerary architecture, theatrical sets, garden ruins, and tarot cards, pyramids had become the models of sublimity in mathematics and philosophy. Visionary French architects sketched massive pyramidal cenotaphs, stepped-pyramid cannon forges, a pharaonic Fountain of Regeneration, a bridge of pyramids and obelisks; the Comte de Volney urged the active construction of a new political pyramid, "a pyramid of the legislators." Pyramids were proposed as monuments to Archduchess Maria Christina of Sachsen-Teschen, Martin Luther, Frederick the Great, General François Marceau, and Napoleon Bonaparte, whose Egyptian campaign prompted a painstaking French survey of Khufu's pyramid to discover whether its basic unit of measurement was directly related to the circumference of the earth. Napoleon himself, on August 12, 1799, asked to be left alone in the King's Chamber to receive a presage of his destiny. In 1800 the U. S. House of Representatives approved a bill for a monument to the late George Washington. Plans called for a "mausoleum of American granite and marble, in pyramidal form, one hundred feet square at the base and of proportionate height." Washington, after all, had been the

POINT of that pyramid, whose solid base
Rests firmly founded on the nation's trust,
Which, while the gorgeous palace sinks in dust,
Shall stand sublime, and fill its ample space.

(The eventual obelisk, its cornerstone laid by a Masonic grand master in 1848, was crowned with a pyramidion in 1884, reaching a final height of five hundred feet, the height of the Great Pyramid.) Meanwhile, a truncated pyramid with a masonic, triangulated eye at its apex had been illuminating the obverse of the Great Seal of the United States, undergirded by the motto, NOVUS ORDO SECLORUM, New Order of the Ages.[40]

By the end of the 19th century, pyramidologists were out in full force with their prophetic inch-years. Friedrich Nietzsche, walking through the woods along an Alpine lake, had come to a "powerful pyramidal rock" and stopped, struck by "the idea of the eternal recurrence, this highest formula of affirmation that is at all attainable," and the source for his *Thus Spake Zarathustra*. If real estate tycoon James Lick of San Francisco had decided against erecting a gigantic marble pyramid to himself in favor of financing the world's largest telescope, Constant Désiré Despradelle in 1900 was designing a Beacon of Progress for Chicago, to be "the apotheosis of American civilization," an obelisk three times as high as the Washington Monument. English artist Fred T. Jane, painting scenes of Anno Domini 2000 for the *Pall Mall Magazine* in 1894–95, envisioned a half-Elizabethan, half-oriental world of stepped pyramids, pyramidal towers, pyramidal solar collectors, all under the aegis of *Janus Oedificator*, Janus the Builder. And Camille Flammarion, imagining the last couple during the last days of the planet around 2,200,000 A.D., sent Omegar and Eve to Egypt, to the Great Pyramid, "ruined, but still standing. . . . Its geometric stability had saved it. It was perhaps the only human idea that had attained its end."[41]

Now, pyramids are everywhere. In Japan, throughout the Yokohama Doll Museum; in Finland, at the "Crystal Pyramid" conservatory of Oulu University; in France, in the courtyard of the Louvre, I. M. Pei's four-story glass pyramid; in Florida, as the central form of the Dolphin Hotel at Walt Disney World, and at James Mount's pink beach house; in Wordsworth, Illinois, enclosing a five-bedroom house built by the owner of a construction company; in Los Angeles, presiding over the new Pacific Design Center as reconstrued by Cesar Pelli, and over Arata Isozaki's Museum of Contemporary Art. Smaller pyramids have become the architectural commonplace for designating entranceways, establishing light wells and skylights, and finishing off high-rise apartment buildings. We at this millennium's end have been building those pyramids which in the past were *fin de siècle* fictions. And where we cannot yet build, we see pyramids—ten miles southwest of the pharaonic, sphinxlike Face on Mars.[42]

"Some day a pyramid will be built for the public good, not for evil," a television commercial assures me, and no sooner said than done: Transamerica Corporation's pyramidal office tower in San Francisco is "a pyramid that will protect you from catastrophe and prepare you for the future." The Dow Corning Company, advertising its high-performance silicone scalants "for structures with monumental results," reminds us by way of the Great Pyramid of Giza that "The true test of greatness is the test of time." So far, American Appraisal Associates, Inc., of Milwaukee hasn't "been called on to determine the value of a pyramid. But we could." Pyramid Products of Vernon, California, already has: $50 for a basic pyramid of aluminum tubing (complete with compass for geocosmic alignment); $115 for a CHEOPS copper pyramid; $150 for the Lifetime Meditation Pyramid of "special plated steel tubing and polished hand-crafted connectors that have been engineered to the ultimate energy degree, $51° - 51' - 14.3''$." Prices are going up even as I write but, after all, the energy generated by pyramids is invaluable; Pyramid Energy may sharpen razor blades, restore the luster to tarnished jewelry, purify water, mummify and dehydrate meat and eggs, increase the growth rate of plants, improve the taste of coffee, speed meditation, deepen relaxation, heal wounds.[43]

Like New Age crystals to which they are related as one magical lattice of stone to another, pyramids have taken on the aspects of Janus. The Great Pyramid grounds us "at the exact center of land masses of the earth" and in the dark past of tyranny and forced labor, but it is also a monument to the future and immortality, to the "integration" of science, religion, art, and philosophy. That our media at century's end should engage us in illustrated debates over how the pyramids were constructed—by manic space brothers with levitating crystals or by weary Egyptian slaves with levers and ramps— is only further evidence for the present tension between extremes. The *fin de siècle* question is always this: Do we have the energy to go on, and if so, where will it come from? At the close of a millennium, we feel even greater fatigue and search for new sources of energy with even greater expectations. Does a new energy source appear at the end of each century, as political scientist Karl W. Deutsch has suggested? Are we on the verge of exhausting our "nonrenewable" energy supplies or does a new millennium promise us the secrets to "cold" nuclear fusion, room-temperature superconductivity, pyramid power, crystalline transmutations? "The Great Conjunction is the End of the World—or the Beginning," warns Aughra the witch in the 1982 puppet film, *Dark Crystal*. A thousand years ago the earth shook and the huge crystal cracked. The world since has gone downhill, to the Skeksis. Now, upon the approach of a millennial conjunction of stars, is the last chance to put things aright. Before the stars meet overhead, two Gelflings, last of their gentle and musical breed, must restore a remaining shard to the crystal and so restore the world. Raspy, greedy, ugly, shortsighted, murderous creatures (the Skeksis) must—and at the climax most assuredly do—unite with resonant, charitable, frail, wise, and mystical creatures (Ur Rus) to become a single extraterrestrial superbeing of shining ethereal white, while the Gelflings inherit a green, harmonious planet.[44]

"The only thing left to us [Gelflings?]," wrote Kurt Mendelssohn in *The Riddle of the Pyramids* in 1974, "is the creation of a new pattern of life which takes in all members of the species *homo sapiens*. . . . Together we must build a new pyramid." It's either that or decay: "The tombs of radioactive waste are becoming as elaborate and as expensive as those of the mummies of the Pharaohs." We will have global life or global death, and nothing in between except the pyramids, which are the sacred architecture of this millennium's end precisely because they are undeniably axial. They *are* aligned to the cardinal directions, equinoctial positions, or transits of Venus. They *are* stable and, of all the works of men, enduring. They *are* the keepers of still-sworn secrets and astronomical revelations. They *are*, in Mexico as in Egypt, models of joinery.[45]

And of Harmonic Convergence. José Argüelles first encountered the Pyramid of the Sun in 1953, when he was a child of fourteen in Mexico. At thirty-six, an older and wiser professor of art, he wrote *The Transformative Vision*, tracing the evolutionary path of human aesthetics during the Holocene Era (10,000 B.C. to 2000 A.D.) in correspondence with the Four Ages (Golden/Fire, Silver/Seed, Bronze/Sword, Iron/Machine) and Yeats's Twenty-Eight Phases of Western Civilization. At forty-seven he wrote something of a sequel, *The Mayan Factor*, which was published in 1987, the "Climax of matter, conclusion of the 16th sixty-year cycle of [the] Tibetan Kalachakra system" and Yeats's year of "The Multiple Man also called the Hunchback," a year of "Enforced disillusionment," of "technocratic collapse and dissolution of international world civilization." Argüelles explained, with impenetrable charts and incalculable arithmetic, that Mayan expertise in the telling of cosmic time, ostensibly derived from acute astronomical observations from atop their astonishing pyramids, was part of a greater scientific system "of holonomic resonance, as much of the future as it is of the past." In other words, the Mayan 5125-year calendar cycle, which had begun at 0 = 13.0.0.0.0. or August 6–13, 3113 B.C., was coming round to its beginning, 13.0.0.0.0. or December 21, 2012, and this meant another transformative vision. Those we call the Mayans were/are actually extragalactic powers who transmit themselves from one star system to another encoded in deoxyribonucleic acid (DNA). They had done their star planting of the Earth as it passed through a galactic beam, and a "great moment of transformation awaits us at beam's end in 2012." In 1987, wrote Argüelles, "we are at a point in time 26 years short of a major galactic synchronization. Either we shift gears right now or we miss the opportunity."[46]

August 16–17, 1987, would be the first Mayan reentry point before the Harmonic Convergence itself, that "point at which the counter-spin of history finally comes to a momentary halt, and the still imperceptible spin of post-history commences." In other words, "the exponential acceleration of the wave harmonic of history as it phases into a moment of unprecedented synchronization." In other words, "a major evolutionary upgrading of the light-life-radiogenetic process." We might perceive the Mayan presence during these next twenty-six years as "an inner light, or as feathered serpent rainbow wheels turning in the air." Then, oh yes then, "the past, the forgotten, and yes, even the 'what-is-to-come,' will become conscious," and "a new zeal will be born into that ill-fated creature, 'twentieth-century man.' "[47]

Appearing in the same year as *Communion*, José Argüelles's *Mayan Factor* was a New Age bestseller and New Age antidote to Whitley Strieber's tale of terror and missing time. The Harmonic Convergence would integrate and enliven, "like an awakening from cultural trance." It would bring each of us into warm contact with our "light body or etheric double, what Egyptians call KA." It would grant us "free energy" and perfect health, removing the "radical blockages in our collective bio-electromagnetic field." It would "make conscious at last the collective dream-time." UFOs were not alien surgical-scientific units but Unified Field Organizers, the "intelligent release of galactically programmed, psychically active, radiant energy simultaneously attracted to and emanated from Earth's resonant etheric body." In short, not abduction but transduction.[48]

Galactic synchronization crews would soon be taking their places at "all planetary light-body grid nodes." We too must prepare for the galactic synchronization. We must clean up our toxic wastes, divest the military of its power, establish "freely regulated" economies, advance the new "paradigm of a resonant unified field of planetary consciousness." We must, as the expression goes, get our act together, for, said Hopi spokesman Thomas Banyaca, "only those who are spiritually strong will survive the passing of the Fourth World [in 1987] and the coming of the Fifth."[49]

So, on Sunday morning, August 16, 1987, thousands of people gathered at geocosmic nodes ("earth acupuncture points") from Mount Fuji to Machu Picchu to the Grand Canyon to Mount Olympus to the Great Pyramid, for a Global Healing Event, a (preliminary) Celebration of Harmonic Convergence. "They say in the prophecies that 144,000 sun dancers, 144,000 filled with light, filled with the sun, will bring on the New Age," spake the leader of the group gathering on Mount Shasta in California. "Allow yourself to become one of the 144,000, one of the dancing suns." Those 144,000 (the sealed servants of God, 12,000 apiece from the twelve tribes of Israel, in Revelation 7.3–8, or the number of Hopi enlightened teachers, or Quetzalcoatl's numerological 9000 × the 4 seasons × the 4 directions) would provide the psychic linkage and critical mass "to support an evolutionary shift from separation to unity and from fear to love." According to Mesoamerican calendars converted to New Age agendas, August 15th would be the end of the ninth and last Hell; on August 16th, Texcatlipoca, god of death and destruction, would remove his jade mask to reveal himself as Quetzalcoatl, feathered serpent god of peace, who earlier had revitalized Uxmal and Chichén Itzá before leaving this world in, of all years, 999 A.D.[50]

The tenth anniversary commemoration of Elvis Presley's death (or disappearance) received more media coverage than the Harmonic Convergence. Graceland took precedence over Amazing Rays. But business quadrupled at my local crystal emporium, the Phoenix Phyre, and mellow Manhattan crowds practiced vibrational toning at 83rd and Central Park West. In her tent at the Eagle's Nest Camp in Pisgah Forest, North Carolina, Ruth Blackwell Rogers woke early on the first morning of the Harmonic Convergence, remembering a dream. "Quite distinctly I had dreamed I saw people 'blessing' the children, holding hands out toward kids for energy to flow into them, because they are the hope, the ones who will take this energy and run with it. Our generation is a bridge, but theirs is full fledged in the new age."[51]

It should be obvious—subtlety is never the trademark of a New Age—how completely the *Mayan Factor* and the Harmonic Convergence have reproduced all the motifs of the experience of centuries' ends. Let us tick them off:

a fearful, joyful insistence upon generational continuity in the midst of "unparalleled" turmoil;

deeply felt threats of mounting pollution, sudden disasters, eventual extinction;

a sense of omnipresent, accelerating change;

a widespread notion that this is the ultimate, critical moment, and that we are on the "event horizon";

appeals to calendrical numerology, astrological conjunctions, kabbalistic secrets;

desires for global reconciliation, global renewal, in lieu of global chaos;

battles against limits, personal, geographic, social, demographic, political, ideographic;

strong attractions to fourth dimensions, out-of-body travel, metempsychosis;

promises of new sources of energy in the light of an oppressive fatigue;

encounters with doubles of each kind;

alternate emphases on decay and purification, senescence and rejuvenation;

desperate needs for mythological and historical synchronicity;

allusions to the millennial year 1000;

strange stirrings of delight in the absolute fact that everything must be (on the verge of) falling apart for everything (at last) to come together.

If the focus of the Harmonic Convergers was not upon the year 2000, that was only an act of faith in the continuity of generations beyond the millennial divide. Make no mistake: those who assembled and chanted beneath Khufu's pyramid, or who held hands in the Black Hills of South Dakota, or who sat alone by the shore and meditated for World Peace on August 16 and 17, 1987, were rehearsing the century's turn and carrying forward the legend of the year 2000.

There will be other rehearsals. The legend will grow.

THE THIRD COMING

LATE THAT EVENING THEY SAW A LIGHT, "LIKE A WAX CANDLE that went up and down." Few but the Admiral believed the light to be a sign of land. The next morning they had reached the island of Guanahani.

Doonesbury

BY GARRY TRUDEA

Cartoon by Garry Trudeau, copyright © August 17, 1987. Universal Press Syndicate.

A message came from under the west stand of Stagg Field at the University of Chicago: "The Italian navigator has landed in the New World." The message meant that Enrico Fermi had succeeded in creating a controlled nuclear chain reaction.

"There will be a supercolossal hooperdooper of a celebration on October 12, 1992 (a Monday, if you want to make any week-end plans)," an American bibliophile assured readers of the *Nation's Business* shortly after the Second World War.

1492, 1942, 1992, new worlds all? The 1992 Olympics and World's Fair have been scheduled for Barcelona and Seville, the career of the Christ-bearing Dove must be rewritten for the quincentennial, but will signals come from Mars, or Soviet astronauts make it to the Red Planet, or a few of the surviving Martians, dwarfish, with leathery gray skins and bald heads, be on display in a World's Fair satellite fifty thousand miles above the Columbian Exposition? Will the United States swing back to liberalism ("concern for the wrongs of the many") from its cyclic romance with conservatism ("concern for the rights of the few"), or will the Greenhouse Effect baffle democratic politics as it turns the planet into a giant sauna, the people of the United States reacting to the crisis "the way a great people could be expected to react, with a mixture of bewilderment, name calling, catatonic aplomb within the conservative community, and in the high-tech community the morbid conceit of a haughty aristocrat about to blow his brains out with an heirloom dueling pistol"?[52]

Howsoever the attempt is made (and it will be made) to elevate 1992 to the status of an apocalyptic Millennium opening onto a New World, we shall have at best a half-millennial celebration, another practice run like the Harmonic Convergence of 1987, the Millennium Events of the Millennium Committee Commemorating 1000 Years of the Christianization of Rus' (988–1988), and the Earth Concert Project for World Harmony, December 31, 1989, hoping to bring two billion people into synchronous meditation.[53]

What we are practicing for is the globalism of the year 2000. The words themselves—"international," "global," "One World"—have arisen at centuries' ends amidst plans for world parliaments and ecumenical congresses, universal language schemes and designs for pentecostal evangelism. At this century's end, we are being exhorted from all sides to a global perspective. There is indeed a new universal language scheme, Lojban, a computer-compatible language that can be parsed by automated algorithms, has no syntactic ambiguity, no exceptions to rules of grammar and spelling, no cultural prejudices (its vocabulary drawn from the six most widely spoken languages: Chinese, English, Hindi, Russian, Spanish, Arabic), and yet allows for "poetically rich expressions that unleash the imagination and present new and different perspectives on reality." And while other computer diplomats work toward an Open Systems Interconnect, "a single worldwide standard networking protocol that will permit virtually any brand or size of computer using virtually any operating system to communicate and exchange information with any other," former American astronaut Jim Irwin flies around a planet that he has seen to be whole, speaking on behalf of Jesus and the High Flight Foundation, his cohorts searching for the real Ark of the Covenant and Noah's Ark, which we may need again.[54]

On the capitalist right, the corporate executives of the international Global One Hundred, acting "to combat a collectivist future" for a world that is "drifting toward financial chaos," advocate an open world market and a global organization for foreign investment. On the socialist left, dissecting earlier failures to arrive at "a viable concept of totality" and arguing for the need "to thwart nuclear totalization," Martin Jay in *Marxism and Totality* writes nonetheless that "it is both impossible and unwise to abandon [the discourse on totality] entirely," for "without acknowledging the complex interrelatedness of our planetary existence, no such solution [to the nuclear threat] is likely to be forthcoming." From the hierarchical orthodoxy of the Catholic Archdiocese of New Orleans comes "The Power of Faith/The Planet Is Alive," a videocassette biography of John Paul II, overlaying the globe on an image of the Pope and describing him as "one man for the whole world," the Slavic pontiff who will, according to a 19th-century Polish prophecy, "become the brother of all nations." From the anarchic heterodoxy of New Age San Francisco comes the audiocassette of a panel discussion on levels of consciousness for 2000 A.D., advising the cultivation of a spiritual immunity to apocalyptic pessimism "by coming away from a local polarity to a universal union." The American Geophysical Union seriously debates James Lovelock's Gaia hypothesis that the Earth is a single self-regulating system of living and nonliving matter; "mystic scientist" Peter Russell, after translating the Upanishads, writes *The Global Brain: Speculations on the Evolutionary Leap to Planetary Consciousness*. In the considered judgment of Saul Mendlovitz, director of the World Order Models Project in New York City, "there is no longer a question of whether or not there will be a world government by the year 2000. As I see it, the questions we should be addressing ourselves to are, how it will come into being—by cataclysm, drift, rational design—and whether it will be totalitarian, benign, or participatory (the probabilities being in that order)." In the considered prose of *The New Yorker*, "There was a time when the notion of a world order was thought to be a utopian vision. We can see now that, in many respects, it is a hellish necessity."[55]

Arrived at this final chapter, we have the privilege, and perhaps the obligation, to be skeptical of the *fin de siècle* rhetoric of hellish necessity and world order. This book, however, has not been an argument for utter skepticism or fatalism. We may now better appreciate the force of the recurrent cultural phenomena that (re)constitute our own century's end, but we cannot therefore disclaim them. Janus allows no such retirement from our times. And since we all lean at least a little into the future—a person with no future is in effect a corpse; a person with no past is mysterious but not terminal—we have the privilege *and* the obligation to deal astutely with the approach of the year 2000. "Tomorrow," as the Speidel (watchband) Corporation would have it, is "on every wrist."[56]

Invited to deliver the prestigious Charles Eliot Norton lectures at Harvard University, Italo Calvino late in 1984 settled on a subject and a scheme; from the first of January 1985, he devoted himself exclusively, obsessively, to his *Six Memos for the Next Millennium*. He had finished five of the lectures when he died, suddenly, on the eve of his departure for Harvard in September 1985. Had he not died, he would have begun his lectures with these words: "We are in 1985, and barely fifteen years stand between us and a new millennium. For the time being I don't think the approach of this date arouses any special emotion."[57]

He who had written *Cosmicomics*, who had traversed time-zero and considered the catastrophic end of the dinosaurs, who had crossed destinies with decks of tarot cards and compared the universe to the invisible city of Eudoxia with its "crooked streets, houses that crumble one upon the other amid clouds of dust, fires, screams in the darkness"—he should have known better. What, after all, was Calvino doing when he wrote of *barely* fifteen years standing between us and the new millennium?[58]

What he was doing, what he meant to do with his five completed memos on Lightness, Quickness, Exactitude, Visibility, Multiplicity, with a sixth (never found) on Consistency, a seventh (of which we know nothing), and an eighth "On the Beginning and the Ending (of novels?)," this is clear from the posthumously published work. He meant to defend the open-endedness of literature as an endeavor that takes us always beyond the limits we believe we have set for ourselves. He wrote in his fifth lecture that "we can no longer think in terms of a totality that is not potential, conjectural, and manifold." He was protesting against a simple future, and the scheme of his memos was the scheme of Genesis: Lightness, "Let there be light"; Quickness, the division of the waters from the waters; Exactitude, calling the dry land Earth and the waters Seas; Visibility, the sun and moon, day and night; Multiplicity, a world teeming with life; Consistency (never found), "Let us make man in our own image"; [absent], the Sabbath; On the Beginning and the Ending (a later, speculative addition), Genesis 2.5– 25, Paradise, the second account of Creation.[59]

Is it not a *fin de siècle* folly to be guided toward the next millennium by an interrupted set of unspoken lectures, incomplete but strikingly attentive to unresolvable ends? Italo Calvino, I suspect, would smile at the irony. And yet we should pay heed, should be wary of simple closures and simple futures. The Romance languages are presently losing their subjunctives, grammatically confusing volition, obligation, intention, imminence, like- lihood, doubt, and desire. The future auxiliary *go* ("we are *going* to live through the year 2000") may soon be seconded by the auxiliary *want*, further confusing propensity with prophecy. There are powerful accusations abroad that Western civilization as a whole is losing its capacity or its will to create inspiring, transcendent images of the future, which has become "a social problem." Brokers have been "trading in futures" and economists have been "discounting the future" since the 19th century. We think now of things around us changing very fast while we (our institutions, attitudes, ageing bodies) change very little. The future "comes upon" us out of the blue, time acts upon us, the 21st century "looms" on the horizon.[60]

We have the obligation, and perhaps the privilege, to take advantage of the cultural richness and historical weight of Anno Domini 2000. The millennial year may thunder in "with that portentous plop, that mildly derisory anti-climax which is the fated doom of the purely chrono- grammatical *jour de fête*." Wrinkled hermaphroditic Saturnians may rise from their seas of frozen ammonia to join us in a Festival of Earth. Or there may be authentic acts of mythopoeisis still available to us by which this century's end can become much more than a legend. I am not referring to the courtesies of Judith Martin's (Miss Manners) "The Proper Way to Turn a Century." Nor am I referring to the glister of "Transhumans—2000," futurist FM- 2030's panorama of a Super Festival in which the entire planet is lit for twenty-four hours by solar sats so that EVERYONE will be up at the same time celebrating "the upflow to whole new spectra of evolution" while reading unilang messages in the sky, "All Go on 21st Century," "We Will Storm the Universe." Nor to the Crapart of sculptor Sinbad Schwartz's exaltation of the plumbing of modern *angst*, his huge silver spindle with a huge silver disc on top, constructed at the end of 1999 and mistaken by True Seekers for a UFO beaming device. Nor to the kitsch of pink-robed, silver-crowned, clamshell-winged Ruth Norman in her Cosmic Cadillac and her UNARIUS (Universal, Articulate, Interdimensional Understanding of Science) disciples near San Diego who are preparing a power tower for a mass landing of extraterrestrials from thirty-two planets, Shunam, Vulna, Osnus, Emil, Po, Din, Severus, Delma, Basis, Zeton, Brundage. . . . Nor to the messianism of Dr. Joshua Christian's *Creed for the Third Millennium*, a millennium which (according to novelist Colleen McCullough) brought "Pain. Impotence. Anticlimax. Reality! A reality harder and crueler and more unendurable than any reality in the history of our planet since the Black Death"—a mini-Ice Age, the shrinking of land masses, and the state control of births. Nor to the bitterness of an ordinary person waking, "not particularly bright and not particularly early," on Saturday, January 1, 2000, in a small apartment in a forty-story building in a city where the only cats and dogs are in zoos, where food, water, clothes, fuel, and parenthood are rationed on a planet of seven billion other human beings. Nor to the utopianism of the earliest account of millennial festivities, John B. Clark's 1902 vision of trains of electric cars taking people to see a display of old 1901 military uniforms and rusty battleships, "insignificant in size but diabolical in their devastating power" and no longer of use to a pacific, democratic, technological society. Nor to the grimness of the most evocative of all projections of the turn of the century, Robert Silverberg's "Thomas the Proclaimer," a 1972 story about the sun standing still for one day in 1999 (from 6:00 A.M. on June 6th: 6/6/6) and the ensuing chaos as the world splits over the meaning of the millennial sign. "What do I see?" asks Thomas. "I see the rotting planet turning black inside and splitting open at the core. I see the cancer of doubt. I see the virus of confusion. I see His Sign misinterpreted on every hand, and its beauty trampled on and destroyed."[61]

What I am referring to, rather, is the construction of a tale that we shall tell ourselves at this century's end, and that our grandchildren will tell their grandchildren in the centuries ahead. It must be a twice-told tale, a tale of a third coming, a tale that takes at his words the fabulist Calvino.

Lightness. It should be a tale neither of grief nor grievance but of disembarrassment. Our lives are not engraved in stone. There are far better places to be at century's end than at Stonehenge or the Great Pyramid. "Were I to choose an auspicious image for the new millennium," wrote Calvino, "I would choose . . . the sudden agile leap of the poet-philosopher who raises himself above the weight of the world, showing that with all his gravity he has the secret of lightness." We should without advertisement divest ourselves of what we never needed in the first place, and conduct a giant potlatch, moving from house to hutch to hut to the millions of homeless. Thus, astride a flying empty bucket, wrote Calvino, "we shall face the new millennium, without hoping to find anything more in it than what we ourselves are able to bring to it."[62]

Quickness. It should be a tale of sharp epiphanies. The historical and the personal must come together to make sense all at once. "To articulate the past historically . . . means to seize hold of a memory as it flashes up at a moment of danger." The philosopher Walter Benjamin wrote this, not Calvino, and I have chosen here to quote from Benjamin rather than Calvino because I want to insist that the tale be a dangerous tale. In the year 2000 we should, consciously and conscientiously, put ourselves at risk. We can acknowledge the *fin de siècle* despair and millennial impatience by requiring of ourselves not total transformation but an experience of the *tremendum*, that which makes us tremble. We should commit ourselves individually to a week of living beyond our means—literally: uneasy, unaided, unprepared, uninsured, in surroundings that hint of those things we most fear. Then each of us should devote the year to acts of community and honesty that lay us further open than we ever cared to be. In his memo on quickness, Calvino wrote of planning a collection of tales consisting of one sentence only, but he had been unable to find any to match the one by the Guatemalan writer Augusto Monterroso: "When I woke up, the dinosaur was still there."[63]

Exactitude. The telling of the tale should last 368 days, from Friday, December 31, 1999, through the leap year 2000 and the first day, Monday, of 2001. The thought and passion that have gone into debates about the exact moment of the turn of a century must be redirected toward the entire year 2000 as an anniversary. Since the 1890s, people have anticipated a centurial debate over 1999/2000, and since the 1940s commentators have wondered how the years 2000 and beyond will be commonly spoken: "Two thousand? Twenty hundred? Twenty oh-oh? Twenty nought nought? Twenty cipher cipher? Twenty flat?" The favorite of a *New Yorker* columnist in 1963 was "Twenty oh-oh"—"a nervous name for what is sure to be a nervous year." Certainly the year will be a nervous year, for it comes down to us as a unique year, and the unique is another name for the unpredictable. Italo Calvino in his memo on Exactitude kept being drawn away from the limits of the unique toward endlessness and the problem (although he did not use the phrase) of fractal geometries. "The word," wrote Calvino, meaning the *exact* word and struggling for the exact words, "connects the visible trace with the invisible thing, the absent thing, the thing that is desired or feared, like a frail emergency bridge over an abyss." The year 2000, all 368 days of it, must be the anniversary of just such a bridge.[64]

Visibility. "The first point is to see people, of this and that kind . . . in all their variety of garments and gestures, some white and others black, some in peace and some at war, some weeping and others laughing, some healthy and others sick, some being born and others dying." This is Ignatius of Loyola's first spiritual exercise for the first day of the second week. Calvino considered it central to his memo on Visibility, by which he meant visual imagination, "the power of bringing visions into focus with our eyes shut." Exclusive of the Catholic, homiletic context, Loyola's exercise is clearly what we must demand of ourselves at this century's end. The tale we tell must be about people, not things, and about people in their disturbing complexity, neither gussied up for a Millennium Ball nor extravasated into specious psychic realms. I would like the millennial year to be dedicated to poverty work, that is, to ameliorating "the poverty of the modern human image," but any suggestion of the sort sounds, and is, pretentious. Rather, let each person dedicate New Year's Week, 1999/2000, to work with the infirm and the dying, and New Year's Week, 2000/2001, to work with infants and battered children, so that we are never tempted to deny the physicality, the visibility, of life. Such bodywork may heal us of the fatigue, invalidism, and powerlessness felt at centuries' ends.[65]

Multiplicity. The last half of the 20th century has overwhelmed us with the symbolism of numbers: six thousand symmetrical years; six million Jews murdered during World War II; the six-million-dollar man and woman; six billion people alive on Earth by 2000 A.D. The round numbers numb. They are the Claudian element of our century's end. Claudian rationality, regular, subdued, must be complemented in our millennial tale by the Etruscan emotional sense of a generation that has lived out its life to its furthest extent, and by the Augustan political and spiritual excitements of a new era. If, for many nations, the generations of the 20th century have been cut short, leaving us with a premature sense of survivorship, and if one "new era" has followed another like bees in a barrel, then the honor must devolve upon us in the year 2000 to welcome a polyphony of voices of all ages. So, yes, there must be carnival, wild carnival, and laughter, wild laughter. We must achieve by way of that carnival and that comedy a janiform feeling of permanent impermanence: *homo viator*, human being passing through.

Through to some greater prospect: "Think what it would be to have a work conceived from outside the *self*," wrote Italo Calvino on the last page of his memo on Multiplicity, "a work that would let us escape the limited perspective of the individual ego, not only to enter into selves like our own but to give speech to that which has no language."[66]

Consistency. What we make of the year 2000 we make, of course, in our own image, just as I at the conclusion of this book fall inevitable victim to the "Rhetorical Diseases" of centuries' ends—"inevitability," the "logic of history," the language of "must." It would be helpful to think of consistency (Calvino cannot help us here) as something like fortitude, and to enter the year 2000 as *Daybreak*, a journal edited by North American Indians, will enter the year 2000, dedicated to "the seventh generation yet unborn." The tale we tell ourselves at the millennium should remind us of the future. A peculiar construction, that: to remind us of the future. In the long run, however, it is the children who determine the legitimacy of their parents. We must be re-minded that our fortitude consists in the most precarious presumptions of continuity. Therefore, at the pivot of the millennial year, from daybreak to daybreak of the summer solstice, we should cease and desist. Silence. Fasting. Remembrance. Stillness.[67]

[   ]. At the stroke of midnight, January 1, 2000, a happy baby was born. Her name was Millenny, her first words were "Oh shit," and her next, "ambivalence," for she was often of two minds—and proud of it. "By 2000," wrote Letty Cottin Pogrebin in "Born Free: A Feminist Fable" of 1974, "society had evolved a mature, humane understanding that all children are our common future—and as such, we must care about them and use our collective resources and energies to nurture and enrich the life of every child." Maggie Gee wrote in *The Burning Book* (1983), "After the Alamogordo atomic test Churchill was handed this message: *Babies satisfactorily born.*" Science and technology have appeared in modern times as the true instruments of change; in fact they are caparisoned forms of couvade, the ritual (male) pantomime of pregnancy and parturition. If we are to avail ourselves of the millennium as a pregnant historical moment, we must do so (as futurists themselves tell me) naked, and we must be led (futurists do not tell me this) by women, who are as accustomed to griefwork as to childbirth. Editing *Woman in the Year 2000,* Maggie Tripp wrote, "*Relocate the future.* That is what women are about to do." It is time, then, to cast Janus out of his temple and, should we yet require a deity of different faces, acclaim perhaps Artemis/Diana, Lady of Wild Things, known in the sky as Selene/Luna/the

Moon, and in the lower world as Hecate, goddess of the crossways. An historian of goddesses, Christine Downing, would choose instead Sekhmet, "the Powerful One," Egyptian goddess of the scorching noonday sun, lion-headed daughter of Re the sun god. Sekhmet is also the Eye of Re, a creatrix with dominion over each of the 365 days of the year. She punishes the damned in the underworld. And she is a manifestation of Hathor, goddess of love, pleasure, beauty. "Deathbringing energy" is integral to her nature, but so too are blessing and weary compassion. "The myth about Sekhmet is a powerful reminder of the importance of coming to terms with destructive energy," Downing has written. "It is time now to acknowledge those energies as natural, not as evil or as satanic, but as part of a whole—as Sekhmet is an aspect of Hathor." The Egyptians knew that everything would eventually come to an end, "Yet they also loved ordinary daily life in this world so passionately that they did everything they could to extend it, even after death." One morning in the spring of 1985, Christine Downing had awakened with a fragment of a dream, the long title of a poem, "Love Song To This Doomed Self-Destroying But So Beautifully Creative Species Of Which I Am A Member." Reflecting upon the fragment, she had come to Sekhmet and to a sense of peace: "Accepting that we as a species may die means celebrating the beauty of our everyday life, living it as fully and creatively and gratefully as we are able." The closed, vacant brackets heading this, Italo Calvino's seventh (absent) memo, allude to annihilation and to possibility, sabbatical withdrawal and Sabbath joy. "To celebrate life, the Egyptians knew, means not holding on to the forms of it immediately given," Downing concluded. "I bless what I have learned from those who lived near the beginning that helps me to understand what it is like to live near what may be the ending."[68]

On the Beginning and the Ending. It is important here to be personal. In August 1988, I received a circular from a friend, a professor in Vermont, Dan Noel, who had earlier wandered and wondered in a Jungian way about the mythic significance of the Space Age. Now he was "Facing the Deep End"—that is, wondering what might be done to "foster a re-imagining of millennial and apocalyptic prospects" in the eleven years before the turn of the millennium. He had been in touch with those of the "post-Jungian" movement known as Archetypal Psychology, and he had attended a 1983 conference on "Facing Apocalypse." Organized by Jungian analyst Robert Bosnak on the premise that "the vision of a cataclysmic ending which has haunted the human imagination for the full 3000 years of recorded history is now no longer a symbolic and remote admonition but a literal menace and a source of present dread," the conference was stimulating but theoretical. Noel in his six-page letter called for "a process of collaborative myth- and ritual-making" through which to deepen the experience of the millennium, and he proposed that we should meet for those rituals at the southwesternmost tip of England, Cornwall's Land's End. Just beyond, under the sea, lies the land of Lyonesse, whose church bells can still, sometimes, be heard tolling. Tristan and Iseut foundered here, and twenty-eight miles to the west are the otherworldly Isles of Scilly (silly, from *saliq*, "blessed"), said to be mountain peaks at the frontier of Lyonesse. "One of the more tangled issues of modern mythography is whether individuals can presume to create what once would have functioned as an authentically communal myth or ritual," Noel wrote. "Probably not." And yet, Noel continued, "there is a vision and an event to be worked toward in behalf of 'the late great planet earth' between now and the turning of the Millennium." A funeral celebration, perhaps: "something which can align us, however briefly and imperfectly, with the subtlest necessities of the planet's or the race's prospective ending."[69]

If funeral it must be, then let us have a wake, from swerve of shore to bend of bay, agog and magog, with mistletropes and the shout-most shoviality, till thousendthee. It were best, however, to take the year 2000 not as a summing up but as a summons. We have come through many centuries' ends intact, raising the stakes each time since 1300, and always it seems that there can be no more to wager. We shuffle now between hearts and spades when we should be forgiving debts and paying our respects to Millenny. Divesting myself of that which I never did need, I will go, I think, to some Land's End on the eve of the year 2000 and again, on the eve of 2001, and I will presume with others of like mind to create a ritual. An invocation, maybe, to what we can see only with our eyes shut, or a dance to all that is, and must be, visible.

Finished at the age of forty,
Thursday noon, Candlemas,
27 Shevat 5749 2/2/1989
anniversary of the birth
of James Joyce

"To our next millennium together."

Cartoon by Henry R. Martin in his *Yak! Yak! Yak! Blah! Blah! Blah!* (1977). Courtesy of Henry R. Martin.

POSTFACE

I SHOULD SAY THAT THIS BOOK CAME TO ME IN A DREAM, ALL
of a piece, like many another *fin de siècle* work, but of course that is only
partly true. I have about a hundred people to thank for saving me from a
"whangdepootenawah" or (according to Ambrose Bierce's translation from
the Ojibwa) "disaster; an unexpected affliction that strikes hard."

For keeping me safe and warm while on the trail of many a century's
end: the Bolls in Boston, the Blumenthals in Washington, D.C., the Kellers
in Paris, the Kunzles in Los Angeles, and the Roskies family in Manhattan.

For keeping my chair warm at the Library of Congress: Renilde Loeckx,
who so generously offered her services as an enthusiastic research assistant.

For keeping my pursuits footloose, my bookshelves overflowing, and my
files fancy free: Paul Bresnick, Paul Encimer, Daria Flores, Mark Garofalo,
Walter Grossmann, Ruth Kavenoff, David Kunzle, Jane Laurent, Mary Ann
Montgomery, Michael Schudson, Rona Sebastian, and my parents, Harry
and Fritzie Schwartz.

For holding me true to my vision of time: Harold Boll, who spent hours
with me designing and executing the chart on Western Calendar Eras.

For holding me at a familiar arm's length in obsessive conversations or
long discussions: Larry Cruse, Bram Dijkstra, Peter John, Edward E.
McNally, Eric Moss, the Planetary Survival seminar group of the Society for
Values in Higher Education, Adam Schmidt, Leslie Smith, Linda Strauss,
Jay Vanos, László Vörös, Tim Willard, and members of the Committee for
Future Research of the Hungarian Academy of Science—Attila Ágh, Erzsébet
Gidai, Felix Karman, and Maria Kalas Köszegi.

For holding me true to my own words: Elise Hunt Avery, Sidney Blumenthal, Jonathan M. Butler, Jeanne M. Danch, Frank Fleck, Howard I.
Kushner, Yanna Liebes, Alden Mosshammer, Daniel C. Noel, Sheri Ritchlin,
David G. Roskies, Bobbi Sandberg, and Gene VanBrook, all of whom read
with care some part or draft of the manuscript.

For taking to heart the ideal of a corresponding community of scholars: Raja Ikram Azam, Thomas E. Bullard, Jerome Clark, Maqbool Elahi, Richard Landes, Michael Marien, Daniel S. Milo, and John Ohliger.

And for taking to heart the ideals of scholarship, the indefatigable reference librarians and archivists at, especially, the Beinecke Library (Yale), the Boston Public Library, the British Museum Library, the Library of Congress, the Library Company of Philadelphia, the New York Public Library, and the University of California at San Diego.

Those who have been following my acknowledgments from book to book should know that I still prepare the typescript myself, but now at an electronic typewriter, an Epson Elite 350 Plus.

Next time, perhaps, at a Series 2000.

Hillel Schwartz
Encinitas, CA

ENDNOTES

Second and subsequent citations within a chapter have been short-titled unless awkwardly distant from the initial reference. Many subtitles have been dropped. The original date of publication has been inset in brackets where a later edition was used and the chronological argument in the text demands precise dating of the first edition. New York City as the place of publication has been abbreviated: NY. Translations appearing in the text are mine unless otherwise indicated. Numerologists may make something of the number of these endnotes, but those who habitually start a book by thumbing through the notes should be cautioned that they are beginning at the wrong end.

FOREGONE CONCLUSIONS

1. I have fashioned this narrative from a variety of sources identified in the notes below. Quotes from Dorothy Whitelock, ed., *English Historical Documents, c. 500–1042*, 2nd ed. (London, 1979) 548, grant by King Athelstan, 934 A.D.; Edmond Pognon, ed. and trans., *L'An mille* (Paris, 1947) 87, from Book III of Raoul Glaber's History, c. 1030 A.D., Latin text in J.-P. Migne, ed., *Patriologiae Cursus Completus* (Paris, 1880) CXLII, 611–98.

2. William Robertson, "A view of the progress of society in Europe," preface to his *History of the Reign of the Emperor Charles the Fifth* (Boston, 1857 [1769]) I, 26; Charles Mackay, *Memoirs of Extraordinary Popular Delusions and the Madness of Crowds*, 2nd ed. (London, 1852 [1841]) 257–58; Frédéric V. Duval, *Les terreurs de l'an mille* (Paris, 1908) 18–19, Mordret; C. H. Fay, "Prophecies concerning the end of the world," *Universalist Quarterly* 14 (1857) 11; Richard Lewinsohn, *Science, Prophecy, and Prediction*, trans. Arnold J. Pomerans (NY, 1961) 78; Charles F. Berlitz, *Doomsday, 1999 AD* (NY, 1981) 9–12. Another uncritical popular work exploiting the motif of millennial panic has recently been published, and immediately excerpted in a popular magazine, with a prefatory review of end-of-the-world expectations. See Richard Erdoes, *AD 1000: Living on the Brink of Apocalypse* (San Francisco, 1988); Bill Lawren, "Apocalypse Now?" *Psychology Today* (May 1989) 38–44, with excerpt 44–45. The Erdoes book originally had as its subtitle, *A History of the Tenth Century for Those Who Hope to See the Year 2000.*

3. Surveys of the literature may be found in Bruno Barbatti, "Der heilige Adalbert von Prag und der Glaube an den Weltuntergang im Jahre 1000," *Archiv für Kulturgeschichte* 35 (1953)

123–41; George L. Burr, "The year 1000 and the antecedents of the Crusades," *American Historical Review* 6 (1901) 429–39; Henri Focillon, *The Year 1000*, trans. Fred D. Wieck (NY, 1969 [1952]); Daniel Le Blevec, *L'An mil* (Paris, 1976); A. Vasiliev, "Medieval ideas about the end of the world: East and West," *Byzantion* 16 (1942/43) 462–502. I have also used, here and below, Georges Duby, *L'An mil* (Paris, 1967); Duval, *Les terreurs*; Ferdinand Lot, "Le mythe des terreurs de l'an mille," *Recueil des travaux historiques de Ferdinand Lot* (Geneva, 1968) I, 398–414; Pietro Orsi, *Le paure del Finimondo nell'anno 1000* (Torino, 1891); François Plaine, "Les prétendues terreurs de l'an mille," *Revue des questions historiques* 13 (1873) 145–64; Pognon, *L'An mille*; Jules Roy, *L'An mille* (Paris, 1885).

4. This pedigree is outlined by Daniel Milo, "L'An Mil: un problème d'historiographie moderne," *History and Theory* 27 (1988) 261–81. For Jules Michelet, see his *Histoire de France*, new ed. (Paris, 1876 [1835]) II, livre 4, pp. 88–89.

5. See note 3 above and also, on Adso, Daniel Verhelst, "Adso van Montier-en-Der en de angst voor het jaar Duizend," *Tijdschrift voor Geschiedenis* 90 (1977) 1–10, which I have read in an unpublished translation kindly furnished by Richard Landes; Richard K. Emmerson, "Antichrist as anti-saint: the significance of Abbot Adso's *Libellus de Antichristo*," *American Benedictine Review* 30 (1979) 175–90. On comets and quakes, see V. Grumel, *La chronologie* (Paris, 1958) 472, 480. The story of Leutard, from Book II of Glaber's History, is given in French translation in Pognon, *L'An mille*, 78–79.

6. See, e.g., Frank E. Manuel and Fritzie P. Manuel, *Utopian Thought in the Western World* (Cambridge, MA, 1979) 59; G. J. Whitrow [first president of the International Society for the Study of Time], *Time in History* (Oxford, 1988) 80–81; George Steiner, "Killing time," *The New Yorker* (Dec. 12, 1983) 171; David Lowenthal, *The Past Is a Foreign Country* (Cambridge, 1985) 221; Raymond Williams, *The Year 2000* (NY, 1983) 3; A. Bartlett Giamatti, *A Free and Ordered Space* (NY, 1988) 295; Anthony Burgess, "Music at the millennium," *High Fidelity* 26 (May 1976) 46; Kenneth L. Woodward, "This way to Armageddon," *Newsweek* (July 5, 1982) 79; Jean Paul Simeray, *L'An 2000: apothéose ou apocalypse?* (Paris, 1980) 75; F. J. Ebling and G. W. Heath, eds., *The Future of Man* (London, 1972), from a symposium paper by H. S. Deighton warning of the care needed in the use of historical analogy yet comparing modern fears to the millennial fears of 1000 A.D.

7. Henri Pirenne, *Medieval Cities*, trans. Frank D. Halsey (NY, 1925 [from lectures, 1922]) 56.

8. Franz Borkenau, *End and Beginning: On the Generations of Culture and the Origins of the West*, ed. Richard Lowenthal (NY, 1981) but written 1947–57 and influenced by Oswald Spengler, who also used the year 1000 as an historical climacteric: *The Decline of the West*, trans. Charles F. Atkins (London, 1926 [from rev. ed., 1922]) esp. I, 15n.

9. Duby, *L'An mil*, 146.

10. Etienne Gilson, *The Terrors of the Year Two Thousand* (Toronto, 1984 [1949]) 1, 11; Daniel Cohen, *How the World Will End* (NY, 1973) 56.

11. Burr, "The year 1000," 435.

12. Julian Morgenstern, "Jubilee, year of," *Interpreter's Dictionary of the Bible* (Nashville, 1962) II, 1001–02 (sic!), and also on "Sabbath" and "Sabbatical year," IV, 135–44; Robert North, *Sociology of the Biblical Jubilee* (Rome, 1954) esp. 129–33; Eviatar Zerubavel, *The Seven Day Circle* (NY, 1985) ch. 1; Henry Chadwick, "Oracles of the end," in *Mémorial André-Jean Festugière*, eds. E. Lucchesi and H. D. Saffrey (Geneva, 1984) 125–29, on Augustine, as also Richard Landes, "Lest the Millennium be fulfilled," in *The Use and Abuse of Eschatology in the Middle Ages*, eds. W. Verbeke et al. (Louvain, 1988) 156ff.; Jonathan Z. Smith, "Ages of the world," *The Encyclopedia of Religion*, ed.-in-chief Mircea Eliade (NY, 1987) I, 128–33; Hillel Schwartz, "Millenarianism: an overview," *ibid.*, IX, 521–31. Throughout this book, "millennium" will be set in lower case when referring to calendar years, in upper case, as "Millennium," when referring to the notion of a thousand years of peace and plenty.

13. Roberto Vacca, *The Coming Dark Age*, trans. J. S. Whale (Garden City, NY, 1973 [1971]) 2; Grace Dalsell, *Prophecy and Politics: Militant Evangelists on the Road to Nuclear War* (Westport, CT, 1986) 46, Reagan.

14. Ralph A. Cram, *The Great Thousand Years* (Chicago, 1918) 55. Cram, gladly awaiting a new Middle Ages, looked back (p. 5) to the year 1000, "the beginnings of the great epoch of Mediaevalism," to get his bearings.

15. Thomas G. Gies, "A Golden Age—or doom?" *USA Today (NY)* 111 (Aug. 1982) 5.

16. Jacobus Gijsbertus de Beus, *Shall We Make the Year 2000? The Decisive Challenge to Western Civilization* (London, 1985 [1982]) 1.

17. Massimo Oldoni, "Gerberto e la sua storia," *Studi Medievali*, ser. 3, 18,2 (1977) 629–704, with sequels on the Sylvester legends in 21,2 (1980) 493–622, and 24,1 (1983) 167–245; Arturo Graf, "La leggenda di un Pontefici," in his *Miti, leggende e superstizioni del medio evo* (Bologna, 1965) II, 1–75; J. J. I. Döllinger, *Fables Respecting the Popes in the Middle Ages*, trans. A. Plummer, and H. R. Smith (NY, 1872) 267–69; William of Malmesbury, *Chronicle of the Kings of England*, trans. J. A. Giles (London, 1847) Book II, ch. 10; August Strindberg, "The close of the first millennium," in his *Historical Miniatures*, trans. Claud Field (London, 1913 [1905]) 201–19, quotes on 208 (Otto) and 218 (Sylvester); Spengler, *Decline of the West*, I, 15n., on the clock; *A Brief Description of the Future History of Europe from Anno 1650 to Anno 1710* (n.p., 1650) 6; Frank de Graaf, *Anno Domini 1000, Anno Domini 2000* (Kampen, 1977). Cf. Florence Trystram, *Le coq et la louve: Gerbert et l'an mille* (Paris, 1982); Focillon, *The Year 1000*, ch. 3. For less legendary perspectives on Sylvester II, see Pierre Riché, *Gerbert d'Aurillac, le pape de l'an mil* (Paris, 1987); Harriet P. Lattin, trans. and ed., *The Letters of Gerbert* (NY, 1971); *Gerberto: scienza, storia e mito. Atti del Gerberti Symposium* (Bobbio 25–27 luglio 1983), esp. Emmanuel Poulle's essay on Gerbert and astronomy, 597–617.

18. Gustav Gugitz, *Das Jahr und seine Feste im Volksbrauch österreichs* (Vienna, 1949) II, 327–32, which however identifies *Silvesternacht* with Sylvester I, although it seems clear that Sylvester II as legendary magus and pope of the millennium is the ruling presence over the celebration, datable no earlier than the 12th century. On Sylvester II as an original model for Faust, see E. M. Butler, *The Fortunes of Faust* (Cambridge, 1952) 11. On Sylvester's confession and entombment, see Walter Map, *De Nugis Curialium (Courtiers' Trifles)*, trans. F. Turner and M. B. Ogle (London, 1924) 227–29.

19. On anniversary reactions, see esp. Barney M. Dlin, "Psychobiology of anniversary reactions," *Psychosomatics* 26 (1985) 505–20; Stanley Brandes, *Forty: The Age and the Symbol* (Knoxville, 1985). On parallels between ends of centuries, see George Kubler, *The Shape of Time* (New Haven, 1962) 90–105; Martin Jay, *Fin-de-Siècle Socialism and Other Essays* (NY, 1988) 1–2, 11–12; *Annals of Scholarship* 5,4 (1989) issue on "The Revolutionary Eighties in the West."

20. Caesare Baronio, *Annales Ecclesiastici* (Venice, 1740) XI, 9–11; Pognon, *L'An mille*, xiii; Duval, *Les terreurs*, 17, and see Eugène Sue, *The Infant's Skull: or, The End of the World, A Tale of the Millennium*, trans. Daniel De Leon (NY, 1904), from the fifth volume of the series, *Les mystères du peuple* (1850–59), in which the translation (p. 39) gives the last day of the year 1000 as the end, then (p. 41) the last day of 999.

21. Richard Nixon, *1999: Victory Without War* (NY, 1988); Carl Sagan, *Contact* (NY, 1985) 127–28, 258–59, 316–17, where contact with extraterrestrial intelligences comes to its initial climax at "the end of the last month of nineteen hundred and anything." Cf. the exchange concerning 2000 and 2001 in Ben Bova, *Millennium: A Novel about People and Politics in the Year 1999* (NY, 1976) 218–19; Dina Fuller, "Turn of the century," *Psychology Today* (May 1989) letter to the editor.

22. On climatic cycles, see Brad Steiger, *A Roadmap of Time* (Englewood Cliffs, 1975), and contrast Nels Winkless III and Iben Browning, *Climate and the Affairs of Men* (NY, 1975).

23. There is one notable exception: Pierre Riché, "Le mythe des terreurs de l'An Mille," in *Les terreurs de l'An* 2000 (Paris, 1976) 28–29, from an international colloquium sponsored in 1975 by the Fondation Internationale des Sciences Humaines.

THE CENTURIES LAID END TO END

1. Raymond Bloch, "Etruscan religion," *Encyclopedia of Religion*, ed.-in-chief Mircea Eliade (NY, 1987) V, 182–85; John P. Brown, "The *Templum* and the *Saeculum*: sacred space and time in Israel and Etruria," *Zeitschrift für die altestamentliche Wissenschaft* 98 (1986) 415–33; C. Clemen, "Die etruskische Säkularrechnung," *Studi e materiali di storia delle religioni* 4 (1928) 235–42; Michael Grant, *The Etruscans* (NY, 1980); Christopher Hampton, *The Etruscan Survival* (Garden City, NY, 1970) quote on 1; Jacques Heurgon, *Daily Life of the Etruscans*, trans. James Kirkup (NY, 1964) 183–85; Otto-Wilhelm von Vacano, *The Etruscans in the Ancient World*, trans. Sheila A. Ogilvie (London, 1960) 13–21; Censorinus, *Le jour natal*, trans. and ed. Guillaume Rocca-Serva (Parts, 1980) v, 23–24; Massimo Pallottino, *The Etruscans*, ed. David Ridgway, trans. J. Cremona from 6th Italian ed. (Bloomington, 1975).

2. N. G. L. Hammond and H. H. Scullard, *Oxford Classical Dictionary*, 2nd ed. (Oxford, 1970) s.v. "Centumviri," "Centuria," "Centurio," 221–22, 272.

3. Lily Ross Taylor, "Secular Games," *ibid.*, 969–70; Gioacchino Mancini, "Ludi," *Enciclopedia Italiana* (Rome, 1949) XXI, 595; William Smith, ed., *Dictionary of Greek and Roman Antiquities*, 2nd ed. (London, 1853) 716–17; Hendrik Wagenvoort, "The origin of the *Ludi Saeculares*," in his *Studies in Roman Literature, Culture and Religion* (Leiden, 1956) 193–232; Kurt Latte, *Römische Religionsgeschichte* (Munich, 1960) 246–48, 298–300; Brown, "The

Templum and the *Saeculum*"; Edward Fraenkel, *Horace* (Oxford, 1957) 364–82; Horace, "Carmen Secular Cantatum pro Incolumitate Imperii Romani [The Secular Poem. Composed to be sung for the safety of the Roman Empire]," in his *Works*, trans. David Watson, new ed. (London, 1792) I, 458–63, quote on 460, and cf. translation by Joseph P. Clancy, *The Odes and Epodes of Horace* (Chicago, 1960) 188–90.

4. J.-A. Hild, "Saeculares ludi. Saeculum," *Dictionnaire des antiquités grecques et romaines*, eds. Ch. Daremberg and Edm. Saglio (Paris, 1887) IV, pt. 2, 986–92; Anthony Birley, *Septimius Severus the African Emperor* (London, 1971) ch. 15; Laura Breglia, *Roman Imperial Coins* (NY, 1968) 108–15.

The millennial celebrations of Philippus actually took place in the 1001st year after the legendary founding of Rome, and may have spawned attacks on Christians. Consider Marta Sordi, *The Christians and the Roman Empire*, trans. Annabel Bedini (London, 1983) 98–99.

5. Donald J. Wilcox, *The Measure of Times Past: Pre-Newtonian Chronologies and the Rhetoric of Relative Time* (Chicago, 1987) 88, 93–94; Arnaldo Momigliano, "Time in ancient historiography," *History and the Concept of Time* = *History and Theory*, Beiheft 6 (Middletown, CT, 1966) 4–8; William W. Hallo, "The concept of eras from Nabonassar to Seleucus," *Journal of the Ancient Near Eastern Society of Columbia University* 16–17 (1984–85) 143–51; Garry W. Trompf, *The Idea of Historical Recurrence in Western Thought from Antiquity to the Reformation* (Berkeley, 1979) ch. 1, explaining that Polybius used both a fixed cycle (a perfect political round) and a biological cycle (birth, maturity, death) in his theory of historical change.

6. V. Grumel, *La chronologie* (Paris, 1958) 3–8, 22; Alden A. Mosshammer, *The Chronicle of Eusebius and Greek Chronographic Tradition* (Lewisburg, ME, 1979) 146–57.

7. Olaf Pedersen, "The ecclesiastical calendar and the life of the Church," in *Gregorian Reform of the Calendar*, eds. G. V. Coyne et al. (Vatican City, 1983) 17–47; Mosshammer, *Chronicle of Eusebius*; Wilcox, *Measure of Times Past*, 105–07, 133; Jaroslav Pelikan, *The Finality of Jesus Christ in an Age of Universal History* (Richmond, VA, 1966); Richard Landes, "Lest the Millennium be fulfilled: apocalyptic expectations and the pattern of Western chronography, 100–800 CE," in *The Use and Abuse of Eschatology in the Middle Ages*, eds. W. Verbeke et al. (Louvain, 1988) esp. 149–56.

8. Grumel, *La chronologie*, 58, 86–89, 219–23; A. Vasiliev, "Medieval ideas of the end of the world: East and West," *Byzantion* 16 (1942–43) 467–68.

9. Pedersen, "The ecclesiastical calendar," 49–50; Elias J. Bickerman, *The Chronology of the Ancient World*, rev. ed. (London, 1980) 72.

10. Landes, "Lest the Millennium be fulfilled," 153–65; Paul J. Alexander, "Medieval apocalypses as historical sources," *American Historical Review* 73 (1968) 1002, noting that three apocalyptic texts did appear around the Byzantine year 6000 A.M. (c. 500 A.D.).

11. Gustav Teres, "Time computations and Dionysius Exiguus," *Journal for the History of Astronomy* 15 (1984) 177–88; J. Rambaud-Buhot, "Dionysius Exiguus," *New Catholic Encyclopedia* (NY, 1967) IV, 877–78; Grumel, *La chronologie*, 224; Pedersen, "The ecclesiastical calendar," 49–54; Charles W. Jones, "The Victorine and Dionysiac paschal tables in the West," *Speculum* 9 (1934) 408–22.

12. Landes, "Lest the Millennium be fulfilled," 165–205; Robert T. Hampson, *Medii Aevi Kalendarium* (London, 1841) I, 3–4, 44–47, 121–34; Grumel, *La chronologie*, 224, 227.

13. Grumel, *La chronologie*, 163–64; Jacques Le Goff, *Time, Work and Culture in the Middle Ages*, trans. Arthur Goldhammer (Chicago, 1980) 43–52; A. J. Gurevich, *Categories of Medieval Culture*, trans. G. L. Campbell (London, 1985) ch. 4. Don LePan, making an extreme case, argues that few people before 1600 shared a process of thought that could admit a sense of the future as rationally predictable, logically contingent, or probabilistic: *The Cognitive Revolution in Western Culture. I. The Birth of Expectation* (Houndmills, Basingstoke, Hamps., 1989).

14. For all that follows concerning Janus, see Gérard Capdeville, "Les épithètes cultuelles de Janus," *Mélanges de l'Ecole française de Rome. Antiquité* 85 (1973) 395–436; Jean Gagé, "Sur les origines du culte de Janus," *Revue de l'histoire des religions* 195 (1979) 3–33, 129–51; Louise A. Holland, *Janus and the Bridge* (Rome, 1962); John P. C. Kent, *Roman Coins* (London, 1978) 10–11, 33; L. A. MacKay, *Janus* (Berkeley, 1956); Robert Schilling, "Janus. Le dieu introducteur, le dieu des passages," *Mélanges d'archéologie et d'histoire* 72 (1960) 89–131; J. S. Speÿer, "Le dieu romain Janus," *Revue de l'histoire des religions* 26 (1892) 1–47; G. B. Townend, "Tacitus, Suetonius and the Temple of Janus," *Hermes* 108 (1980) 23–42; Robert Turcan, "Janus à l'époque impériale," in *Aufstieg und Niedergang der römischen Welt*, ed. Hildegard Temporini (Berlin, 1981) II, 374–402.

15. W. M. Flinders Petrie, *Janus in Modern Life* (London, 1907) vii, and cf. Benchara Branford, *Janus and Vesta: A Study of the World Crisis and After* (NY, 1916); William McDougall, *Janus: The Conquest of War* (NY, 1972 [1927]); Evelyn Anthony (= Eve Stephens), *The Janus Imperative* (NY, 1980), a novel playing with the idea that Adolf Hitler left an heir code-named Janus, actually twins, the boy now dead, the girl deposited in a nunnery but "wholly evil."

16. Arthur Koestler, *Janus: A Summing Up* (NY, 1978) 1, 2, 11, 34. Cf. *Janus: l'homme, son histoire et son avenir*, a short-lived journal published in Paris, 1964–68, with the intent of uniting history with the sciences; D. G. MacDonald Allen, *The Janus Sex: The Androgynous Challenge* (Hicksville, NY, 1975); Steven E. McDonald, *The Janus Syndrome* (Toronto, 1981).

17. Mircea Eliade, *Cosmos and History*, trans. Willard R. Trask, (NY, 1959) ch. 2; Vittorio Lanternari, *La grande festa: storia del Capodanno nella civiltà primitive* (Bari, 1959); V. G. Ardzinba, "The birth of the Hittite king and the new year," *Oikumene* 5 (1986) 91–101; Derek Wright, "Scapegoats and carriers: New Year festivals in history and literature," *Journal of African Studies* 14,4 (1986–88) 183–89; Jane M. Hatch, *American Book of Days*, 3rd ed. (NY, 1978) 1–4; Cora L. Daniels and C. M. Stevens, eds., *Encyclopedia of Superstitions* (Detroit, 1971 [1903]) 1562–71.

18. The historians—Christian Amalvi, Richard Landes, Daniel Verhelst—publish in French, English, and Dutch. Landes has in preparation an essay, "Millennium absconditus," dealing with the evidence for an apocalyptic era around the year 1000. See, in print, his entry on "Year 1000, the," *Dictionary of the Middle Ages*, ed.-in-chief Joseph Strayer (NY, 1989) XII, 722–23, and his dissertation, "The Making of a Medieval Historian: Adémar of Chabannes and Aquitaine at the Turn of the Millennium," Princeton, 1984, ch. 1.

19. Robert S. Lopez, *The Birth of Europe* (NY, 1967 [1962]) 108, 118; Henri Focillon, *The Year 1000*, trans. Fred D. Wieck (NY, 1969) 60, Thietmar quote, amended to refer to A.D. 1004 (not 1000, as typically mistranslated) after consultation with Richard Landes; Jerzy Gussowski et al., *L'An mille: Dieu, le monde en péril* (Paris, 1964) 13; Georges Duby, *L'An mil* (Paris, 1967) 175, 207; David Herlihy, ed., *Medieval Culture and Society* (NY, 1968) 154.

20. Constance E. Bouchard, *Sword, Miter, and Cloister: Nobility and the Church in Burgundy, 980–1189* (Ithaca, 1987) 102–24; Duby, *L'An mil*, 121–27, 175–76; Eleanor Duckett, *Death and Life in the Tenth Century* (Ann Arbor, 1967) esp. 130; Jean Musy, "Mouvements populaires et hérésies au XIᵉ siècle en France," *Revue historique* 253 (1975) 33–76.

21. On the Peace Movement, see L. E. Boyle, "Peace of God," *New Catholic Encyclopedia* (NY, 1967) XI, 45–46; H. E. J. Coudrey, "The Peace of God in the eleventh century," *Past & Present* 46 (1970) 42–67; Frédéric V. Duval, *De la Paix de Dieu à la Paix de Fer* (Paris, 1923); Thomas Head and Richard Landes, eds., "Essays on the Peace of God: the church and the people in eleventh-century France," *Historical Reflections* 14,3 (1987) 381–549, quote on 467; Hartmut Hoffmann, *Gottesfriede und Treuga Dei* (Stuttgart, 1964) esp. 11–44; Dolorosa Kennelly, "Medieval towns and the Peace of God," *Medievalia et Humanistica* 15 (1963) 35–53.

For other matters in this paragraph, see Duby, *L'An mil*, 29, on knights; Jeffrey B. Russell, *Lucifer: The Devil in the Middle Ages* (Ithaca, 1984) 160–61; Richard K. Emmerson, *Antichrist in the Middle Ages* (Seattle, 1981); John S. Martin, *Ragnarok* (Assen, 1972); Louis Grodecki et al., *Le siècle de l'an mille* (Paris, 1973) on apocalyptic art; William W. Heist, *The Fifteen Signs Before Doomsday* (East Lansing, 1952); Paul J. Alexander, *The Byzantine Apocalyptic Tradition*, ed. Dorothy deF. Abrahamse (Berkeley, 1985) on the Last World Emperor.

22. Boyle, "Peace of God," 45 for quote; Richard Landes, "The dynamics of heresy and reform," *Historical Reflections* 14,3 (1987) 492–93; Duby, *L'An mil*, 76, 93, 201ff.; Jacques Le Goff, *The Birth of Purgatory*, trans. Arthur Goldhammer (Chicago, 1984 [1981]) 125ff.; Patricia Ranft, "The maintenance and transformation of society through eschatology: Cluniac monasticism," *Journal of Religious History* 14 (1987) 248–49; Peter Brown, *Society and the Holy in Late Antiquity* (Berkeley, 1982) on holy men as points of contact between the living and the dead.

23. On Gallienus, who is occasionally but incorrectly identified with a last celebration of the Roman Secular Games, see Turcan, "Janus à l'époque impériale," 397; Elke W. Merten, *Zwei Herrscherfeste in der Historia Augusta* (Bonn, 1968) ch. 1.

24. Robert Folz, *The Coronation of Charlemagne 25 December 800*, trans. J. E. Anderson (London, 1974); Duckett, *Death and Life in the Tenth Century*, 106–30; Duby, *L'An mil*, 34, 187; Focillon, *The Year 1000*, 163–64; Pierre Riché, *Gerbert d'Aurillac* (Paris, 1987) 193, 217–18, 222.

25. The temptation is resisted by Elizabeth M. Hallam, *Capetian France 987–1328* (London, 1980). It is fought to a draw by Dorothy Bethurum, ed., *The Homilies of Wulfstan* (Oxford, 1957) 276–82, and by Milton M. C. Gatch, *Preaching and Theology in Anglo-Saxon England*

(Toronto, 1977) 60–116. Despite himself, it overcomes Charles Radding, *A World Made By Men: Cognition and Society, 400–1200* (Chapel Hill, 1985) ch. 6.

26. S. J. Crawford, trans. and ed., *Byrhtferth's Manual (A.D. 1011)* (London, 1966) 232–41, quotes on 235, 237, 239; George Turner, "Hundreds," *Encyclopaedia Britannica*, 11th ed. (London, 1910–11) XIII, 893; "Hundred," *Oxford English Dictionary*, V, 456. On the number 1000, see also Pierre Debord, "Chiliastys," *Revue des études anciennes* 86 (1984) 201–11, and cf. John Macqueen, *Numerology* (Edinburgh, 1985). On medieval arithmetic, see Alexander Murray, *Reason and Society in the Middle Ages* (Oxford, 1978) Part II, 141–63.

27. Edmond Pognon, ed. and trans., *L'An mille* (Paris, 1947) 79–80, 116, 127, quotations from Glaber (my English version from Pognon's French); Richard Landes, "Radulphus Glaber (Raoul Glaber)," *Dictionary of the Middle Ages*, X, 247; Amos Funkenstein, *Theology and the Scientific Imagination From the Middle Ages to the Seventeenth Century* (Princeton, 1986) 262; Focillon, *The Year 1000*, 67, on the famine; Adémar de Chabannes (= Ademarus Cabannensis), *Chronique*, ed. Jules Chavanon (Paris, 1897) 168–69; Daniel F. Callahan, "The Peace of God and the cult of the saints in Aquitaine in the tenth and eleventh centuries," *Historical Reflections* 14 (1987) 445–61; Duby, *L'An mil*, 106, 111; Bernhard Toepfer, *Volk und Kirche zur Zeit der beginnenden Gottesfriedensbewegung in Frankreich* (Berlin, 1957), esp. on the strength of the Peace Movement in the years leading up to 1033; Franz Kobler, ed. and trans., *Letters of Jews through the Ages*, 2nd ed. (NY, 1953) I, 131, on the quake.

28. Shlomo Eidelberg, ed. and trans., *The Jews and the Crusades: The Hebrew Chronicles of the First and Second Crusades* (Madison, WI, 1977) 21, quotations from the chronicle of Solomon bar Simson; David G. Roskies, *Against the Apocalypse: Responses to Catastrophe in Modern Jewish Culture* (Cambridge, MA, 1984) 41–44.

29. Eidelberg, *The Jews and the Crusades*, introduction; Yosef H. Yerushalmi, *Zakhor: Jewish History and Jewish Memory* (Seattle, 1982) 41–42; Michael Friedlander and Joseph Jacobs, "Era," *Jewish Encyclopedia* (NY, 1903) V, 198–99; Joseph Jacobs, "Chronology: Post-Biblical," *ibid.*, IV, 70–71; Benny Isaacson, "Chronology," *Encyclopaedia Judaica* (Jerusalem, 1971) XVI, 1261–66.

30. Abba Hillel Silver, *A History of Messianic Speculation in Israel From the First through the Seventeenth Centuries* (Boston, 1959 [1927]) ch. 1; Amos Funkenstein, "A schedule for the end of the world," in Saul Friedlander et al., eds., *Visions of Apocalypse: End or Rebirth?* (NY, 1985) 49–52; Jonathan Z. Smith, "Ages of the world," *Encyclopedia of Religion*, ed.-in-chief Mircea Eliade (NY, 1987) I, 130. On theory, see Gershom Scholem, *The Messianic Idea in Judaism*, trans. Michael A. Meyer and Hillel Halkin (NY, 1971) 1–36.

31. Silver, *History of Messianic Speculation*, ch. 2; Gerson D. Cohen, "Messianic postures of Ashkenazim and Sephardim (prior to Sabbatai Sevi)" in *Studies of the Leo Baeck Institute*, ed. Max Kreutzberger (NY, 1967) 117–56, on the lack of enthusiasm for messianic speculation among the Jews of Ashkenaz (northwestern, later also central and eastern Europe) as compared to the longstanding messianism among Sephardic Jews (of the Iberian Peninsula, southern Italy, the southern and eastern Mediterranean).

32. Silver, *History of Messianic Speculation*, ch. 3; Eidelberg, *The Jews and the Crusades*, 79. Muslims and Christians also took advantage of *gematria* for their own purposes.

33. Cohen, "Messianic postures," 127, on the fiction; Babylonian Talmud, 'Erubin 18a, on R. Jeremiah b. Eleazar's suggestion that Adam had two faces.

34. Léon Poliakov, *The History of Anti-Semitism from the Time of Christ to the Court Jews*, trans. Richard Howard (NY, 1974 [1965]) 32–36; Robert Chazan, *European Jewry and the First Crusade* (Berkeley, 1987) 34–35; Eidelberg, *Jews and the Crusades*, 28 for quote.

35. Alan Mintz, *Ḥurban: Responses to Catastrophe in Hebrew Literature* (NY, 1984) 88–89, and noting that the story of Masada as known to medieval Jews involved not ritual suicide but men going off to die in battle; Eidelberg, *Jews and the Crusades*, 22–23 for quotes from Solomon bar Simson.

36. Ivan G. Marcus, "From politics to martyrdom: shifting paradigms in the Hebrew narratives of the 1096 Crusade riots," *Prooftexts* 2 (1982) 40–52; Mintz, *Ḥurban*, 94ff.; H. H. Ben-Sasson, *Trial and Achievement: Currents in Jewish History* (Jerusalem, 1974) 209–16 on *Kiddush haShem*.

37. Eidelberg, *Jews and the Crusades*, 33, 41, 65 for quotes; Roskies, *Against the Apocalypse*, 44; Mintz, *Ḥurban*, 100.

38. Chazan, *European Jewry and the First Crusade*, 8, 62, 197–210; Roskies, *Against the Apocalypse*, esp. 82; Yerushalmi, *Zakhor*, 37, 49; Silver, *History of Messianic Speculation*, 76–78; Andrew Sharf, "An unknown messiah of 1096 and the Emperor Alexius," *Journal of Jewish Studies* 7 (1956) 59–70; Ben-Sasson, *Trial and Achievement*, 201; Eidelberg, *Jews and the Crusades*, 140n.; Mintz, *Ḥurban*, 99, on the turning point.

39. Jassim M. Hussain, *The Occultation of the Twelfth Imam* (London, 1982); Bernard Lewis, *The Arabs in History*, rev. ed., (NY, 1958) 64, 71–73, 107–08, 110; Abdulaziz A. Sachedina, *Islamic Messianism: The Idea of Mahdi in Twelver Shiʿism* (Albany, 1981); Samuel M. Stern, *Studies in Early Ismaʿilism* (Jerusalem, 1983) 213–15, 289–98.

40. Sachedina, *Islamic Messianism*; Josef van Ess, *Chiliastische Erwartungen und die Versuchung der Gottlichkeit: Der Kalif al–Hakim* (Heidelberg, 1977); Wadād al–Qāḍī, "Hakim bi–Amr Allāh, al–," *Dictionary of the Middle Ages*, VI, 73–74; David R. W. Bryer, "The origins of the Druze religion," *Der Islam* 52 (1975) 47–84, 239–62, and 53 (1976) 5–27; P. M. Holt, "Islamic millenarianism and the fulfillment of prophecy," in Ann Williams, ed., *Prophecy and Millenarianism: Essays in Honor of Marjorie Reeves* (Harlow, Essex, 1980) 335–47. The word for "century" in Arabic is *qarn*, meaning also an age or generation. Its root means "to join or connect."

41. Edward Burman, *The Assassins: Holy Killers of Islam* (London, 1987); Marshall G. S. Hodgson, *The Order of Assassins* (NY, 1980 [1955]); Bernard Lewis, *The Assassins: A Radical Sect in Islam* (London, 1967); Henry Corbin, *Cyclical Time and Ismaʿili Gnosis*, trans. Ralph Mannheim and James W. Morris (London, 1983) esp. 42–43. On Sunni mahdism in the Maghreb two decades later, see Roger Le Tourneau, *The Almohad Movement in North Africa in the Twelfth and Thirteenth Centuries* (Princeton, 1969).

42. T. S. R. Boase, *Death in the Middle Ages: Mortality, Judgment and Remembrance* (NY, 1972) 42 for quote; Jonathan Riley-Smith, *The First Crusade and the Idea of Crusading* (London, 1986) esp. 5–8, 17–18, 21–22, 27, 116; Hoffmann, *Gottesfriede und Treuga Dei*, 225; Pierre-

André Sigal, *L'Homme et le miracle dans la France médiévale (XIe–XIIe siècle)* (Paris, 1985) 259, 283; Jules A. Lair, *Etudes critiques sur divers textes des Xe et XIe siècles* (Paris, 1899) I, on the fraudulent bull.

43. Joshua Prawer, *The Latin Kingdom of Jerusalem: European Colonialism in the Middle Ages* (London, 1972) esp. 39; Louise Riley-Smith and Jonathan Riley-Smith, eds. and trans., *The Crusades, Idea and Reality 1095–1274* (London, 1981) 37–53, documents and letters on the preaching of the First Crusade; Ernest O. Blake and Colin Morris, "A hermit goes to war: Peter and the origins of the First Crusade," *Studies in Church History* 22 (1985) 79–107, with quotation from *Rosenfeld Annals* on p. 93; Norman Cohn, *The Pursuit of the Millennium*, rev. ed. (NY, 1970 [1957]) 61–68; Jean Chatillon, "The spiritual renaissance of the end of the eleventh century and the beginning of the twelfth," *American Benedictine Review* 36 (1985) 292–317.

44. Paul J. Alphandéry, *Notes sur le messianisme médiéval latin* (Paris, 1912) 7–20; Ann Wharton Epstein, "Frescoes of the Mavriotissa monastery near Kastoria: evidence of mille-narianism and anti-Semitism in the wake of the First Crusade," *Gesta* 21 (1982) 21–30; Cohn, *Pursuit of the Millennium*, 29–36; Jonathan Riley-Smith, "The First Crusade and the persecution of the Jews," *Studies in Church History* 21 (1984) 51–72.

45. Further special pleading would make note of the unusual weight given to the year 1100 in chronicles of events in countries as far apart as England and the Holy Land. When St. Anselm returned from Rome to the cliffs of Dover on September 23, 1100, wrote Eadmer in his *History of Recent Events in England* (trans. Geoffrey Bosanquet [Philadelphia, 1965]), "we found the whole country exultant with great joy at Anselm's arrival. For a hope, as it were of a resurrection to new life, was springing up in everyone's mind" (p. 124). Fulcher of Chartres in his *A History of the Expedition to Jerusalem* (ed. Harold S. Fink, trans. Frances Rita Ryan [Knoxville, 1969]), made the year 1100 the reference point for the success of the First Crusade:

> *In the year eleven hundred minus one*
> *From the Virgin Birth of the Illustrious Lord*
> *When Phoebus had illumined July fifteen times,*
> *The Franks in their might captured Jerusalem*
> *And soon made Godfrey prince of the fatherland.*

Then, "In the year eleven hundred of the Incarnation of our Lord, on the first day of the year, we all assumed the palm," emblem of pilgrimage to the Holy Land and of crusader victory (pp. 124, 133). Fulcher was chaplain to Baldwin, first crusader king in Jerusalem and another candidate for Last Emperor, as was Godfrey of Bouillon, who however declined the kingship and died of plague in July 1100.

46. M. Gaster, "The Letter of Toledo," *Folk-Lore* 13 (1902) 115–34; Robert E. Lerner, *The Powers of Prophecy: The Cedar of Lebanon Vision from the Mongol Onslaught to the Dawn of the Enlightenment* (Berkeley, 1983) 4–5, 190–91; Richard Lewinsohn, *Science, Prophecy, and Prediction*, trans. Arnold J. Pomerans (NY, 1961 [1958]) 81 for quote. The Toledo Letter was initially ascribed to a group of anonymous sages, only later to one or another John of Toledo.

47. J. D. North, "Medieval concepts of celestial influence," and Richard Lemay, "The true place of astrology in medieval science and philosophy," both in *Astrology, Science and Society: Historical Essays*, ed. Patrick Curry (Woodbridge, Suffolk, 1987) 5–17, 57–73; S. Jim Tester, *A History of Western Astrology* (Woodbridge, Suffolk, 1987) 145–203; E. S. Kennedy, "The world-year concept in Islamic astrology," in *Studies in the Islamic Exact Sciences*, eds. E. S. Kennedy et al. (Beirut, 1983) 351–71; Eugenio Garin, *Astrology in the Renaissance: The Zodiac of Life*, trans. Carolyn Jackson et al. (London, 1983 [1976]) ch. 1. As Tester notes (pp. 131–32), complex astrology was another of the dark innovations legendarily attributed to that millennial pope, Sylvester II.

48. R. W. Southern, *Robert Grosseteste: The Growth of an English Mind in Medieval Europe* (NY, 1986) 147–50; Matei Calinescu, *Faces of Modernity* (Bloomington, 1977) 14–15; Beryl Smalley, "Ecclesiastical attitudes to novelty c. 1100–c. 1250," *Studies in Church History* 12 (1975) 113–31; Benedicta Ward, *Miracles and the Medieval Mind: Theory, Record and Event, 1000–1215* (Philadelphia, 1982) esp. ch. 11; Le Goff, *Birth of Purgatory*, 135, 151, 157; Robert S. Lopez and Irving W. Raymond, trans. and eds., *Medieval Trade in the Mediterranean World* (NY, 1971 [1955]) 255–58; Florian Cajori, *A History of Mathematical Notation* (La Salle, 1928) 47–51; David Eugene Smith and Jekuthiel Ginsburg, "From numbers to numerals and from numerals to computation," in *The World of Mathematics*, ed. James R. Newman (NY, 1956) I, 442–64; Murray, *Reason and Society in the Middle Ages*, 167–82.

49. Southern, *Robert Grosseteste*, 125–29, 147–50; J. D. North, "The Western calendar— 'intolerabilis, horribilis, et derisibilis': four centuries of discontent," in *Gregorian Reform of the Calendar*, 75–113.

50. R. W. Southern, "Aspects of the European tradition of historical writing. 2. Hugh of St. Victor and the idea of historical development," *Transactions of the Royal Historical Association*, 5th ser., 21 (1971) 159–79; Gillian R. Evans, "Past, present, and future in the theology of the late eleventh and early twelfth centuries," *Studia Theologica* 32,2 (1978) 133–49; Marjorie Reeves, "History and prophecy in medieval thought," *Medievalia et Humanistica* n.s. 5 (1974) 51–75, and Amos Funkenstein, "Periodization and self-understanding in the Middle Ages and early modern times," in *ibid.*, 3–23; Barbara Nolan, *The Gothic Visionary Perspective* (Princeton, 1977) ch. 1; Hans-Werner Goetz, "Endzeiterwartung und Endzeitvorstellung in Rahmen des Geschichtsbildes des Fruheren 12. Jahrhunderts," in *Use and Abuse of Eschatology*, 306–32.

51. I rely here upon Bernard McGinn, *The Calabrian Abbot, Joachim of Fiore, in the History of Western Thought* (NY, 1985), which is also a fine bibliographic source for the recent outpouring of studies of Joachim; quote is from p. 21. See also E. Randolph Daniel, "Joachim of Fiore and medieval apocalypticism: some current research," *Medievalia et Humanistica* n.s. 14 (1986) 173–88; Delno C. West and Sandra Zimdars-Swartz, *Joachim of Fiore: A Study in Spiritual Perception and History* (Bloomington, 1983) esp. ch. 4.

52. McGinn, *The Calabrian Abbot*, 112–13; West and Zimdars-Swartz, *Joachim of Fiore*, 67; Marjorie Reeves and Beatrice Hirsch-Reich, *The Figurae of Joachim of Fiore* (Oxford, 1972).

53. Marjorie Reeves, *The Influence of Prophecy in the Later Middle Ages: A Study of Joachimism* (Oxford, 1969); Herbert Grundmann, "Die Papstprophetien des Mittelalters," *Archiv für Kulturgeschichte* 19 (1929) 77–138; Bernard McGinn, "Symbolism in the thought of Joachim

of Fiore," in Williams, *Prophecy and Millenarianism*, 143–64; Marjorie Reeves and Warwick Gould, *Joachim of Fiore and the Myth of the Eternal Evangel in the Nineteenth Century* (Oxford, 1987) 7–15 and throughout. Robert E. Lerner argues that Joachim himself did favor a millennial year 1260; see "Frederick II, alive, aloft, and allayed," in *Use and Abuse of Eschatology*, 363.

54. On the Cathars, see esp. Michel Roquebert, *L'Epopée cathare*, 3 vols. (Toulouse, 1970–86); R. I. Moore, *The Formation of a Persecuting Society: Power and Deviance in Western Europe, 950–1250* (Oxford, 1987); Emmanuel Le Roy Ladurie, *Montaillou: The Promised Land of Error*, trans. Barbara Bray (NY, 1978). Concerning the Spiritual Franciscans, who most strongly identified St. Francis as prototype of the Joachimite *viri spirituales*, see Reeves, *Influence of Prophecy*; E. Randolph Daniel, "A re-examination of the origins of Franciscan Joachitism," *Speculum* 43 (1968) 671–76. On Merlin and Camelot, see R. W. Southern, "Aspects of the European tradition of historical writing. 3. History as prophecy," *Transactions of the Royal Historical Association*, 5th ser., 22 (1972) 168–69; Paul Zumthor, *Merlin le prophète* (Geneva, 1973 [1943]); Valerie M. Lagorio, "The apocalyptic mode in the Vulgate cycle of the Arthurian romances," *Philological Quarterly* 57 (1958) 1–22; Roger of Wendover, *Flowers of History*, ed. and trans. J. A. Giles (NY, 1968 [1849]) II, 110 for quote.

55. Contrast Renato Poggioli, *The Theory of the Avant-Garde*, trans. Gerald Fitzgerald (Cambridge, MA, 1968 [1962]); John Weightman, *The Concept of the Avant-Garde: Explorations in Modernism* (LaSalle, IL, 1973) 13–37.

56. Dmitrij Tschizewskij, *Russian Intellectual History*, trans. John C. Osborne, ed. Martin P. Rice (Ann Arbor, 1978 [1959–61]) 57; John Godfrey, *1204 The Unholy Crusade* (Oxford, 1980); Cohn, *Pursuit of the Millennium*, 88–90; Allan Cutler, "Innocent III and the distinctive clothing of Jews and Muslims," *Studies in Medieval Culture*, ed. John R. Sommerfeldt, 3 (1970) 92–116; Moore, *Formation of a Persecuting Society*, 6–9, 29–43; Ben-Sasson, *Trial and Achievement*, 212, 245–46; Cohen, "Messianic postures," 129–31; Harry Bresslau, "Juden und Mongolen 1241," *Zeitschrift für die Geschichte der Juden im Deutschland* 1 (1887) 99–102; Julius Aronius, *Regesten zur Geschichte der Juden im fränkischen und deutschen Reiche bis zum Jahre 1273* (Hildesheim, 1970 [1902]) 227–30.

57. Lerner, *Powers of Prophecy*, ch. 1; Davide Bigalli, *I Tartari e l'Apocalisse* (Florence, 1971); Denis Sinor, "Le Mongol vu par l'Occident," in *1274: année charnière* (Paris, 1977) 55–72.

58. David S. Landes, *Revolution in Time: Clocks and the Making of the Modern World* (Cambridge, MA, 1983) 60–69; Crawford, *Byrhtferth's Manual*, 117.

59. Landes, *Revolution in Time*, 10, 53–56; Lynn White, Jr., *Medieval Technology and Social Change* (London, 1962) 119–24; Carlo Cipolla, *Clocks and Culture 1300–1700* (NY, 1967) 37–47.

60. Horace K. Mann, *The Lives of the Popes in the Middle Ages* (London, 1925–32) XVIII, 174–76, quote on 174; Giovanni Villani, *Villani's Chronicle*, trans. Rose E. Selfe, ed. Philip H. Wicksteed (London, 1906) 320–21; Herbert Thurston, *The Holy Year of Jubilee* (London, 1900) 13, 19; Don Louis Tosti, *History of Pope Boniface VIII and His Times*, trans. Eugene J. Donnelly (NY, 1911 [1848]) 521ff.

61. Arsenio Frugoni, "Il Giubileo di Bonifacio VIII," *Bullettino dell'Istituto Storico Italiano per il Medio Evo e Archivio Muratoriano* 62 (1950) esp. 5–13, 26–29; Piero Bargellini, *L'Anno santo* (Florence, 1974) 31–32. Thurston, *Holy Year*, 15, notes that a "jubilee" was not mentioned in Boniface's bull, but that the event was instantly understood as such. The closest thing to a Jubilee had been the northern Italian religious revival of 1233, known as The Alleluia, for which see George G. Coulton, *From St. Francis to Dante* (London, 1906) ch. 3, reference supplied by Richard Landes, and alluding perhaps to the 1200th year of the Passion.

62. T. S. R. Boase, *Boniface VIII* (London, 1933) 231 for quote; Philip Hughes, *A History of the Church* (NY, 1947) III, 738; Mann, *Lives of the Popes*, XVIII, 174.

63. Cohn, *Pursuit of the Millennium*, 128–31 on Flagellants, ch. 6 on the Fredericks; *1274: année charnière*, section IV on the year 1260; Stephen E. Wessley, "The thirteenth-century Guglielmites: salvation through women," in *Medieval Women*, ed. Derek Baker (Oxford, 1978) 289–303; Elise Boulding, *The Underside of History: A View of Women through Time* (Boulder, 1976) 451–52, relating the Guglielmites to other women's movements, for which see also Caroline W. Bynum, *Holy Feast and Holy Fast: The Religious Significance of Food to Medieval Women* (Berkeley, 1987) ch. 1; Hans Martin Schaller, "Endzeit-Erwartung und Antichrist-Vorstellungen in der Politik des 13. Jahrhunderts," in *Festschrift für Hermann Heimpel*, eds. Mitarbeitern des Max-Planck-Instituts für Geschichte (Göttingen, 1972) II, 924–47.

64. Bernard McGinn, "Angel Pope and Papal Antichrist," *Church History* 47 (1978) 155–73; Friedrich Baethgen, *Der Engelpapst* (Leipzig, 1943)—a curious Nazi work; David Burr, "Olivi's apocalyptic timetable," *Journal of Medieval and Renaissance Studies* 11 (1981) 237–60; idem, "Olivi, apocalyptic expectation, and visionary experience," *Traditio* 41 (1985) 273–88; Claude Carozzi and Huguette Taviani-Carozzi, eds. and trans., *La fin des temps: terreurs et prophéties au Moyen Age* (Paris, 1982) 153ff.; Marjorie Reeves, "Medieval attitudes," in *The Apocalypse in English Renaissance Thought and Literature*, eds. C. A. Patrides and Joseph Wittreich (Ithaca, 1984) 51–55; Robert E. Lerner, "An 'Angel of Philadelphia' in the reign of Philip the Fair: the case of Guiard of Cressonessart," in *Order and Innovation in the Middle Ages*, eds. William C. Jordan et al. (Princeton, 1976) 343–64.

65. Lionel Rothkrug, "Popular religion and holy shrines," in *Religion and the People, 800–1700*, ed. James Obelkevich (Chapel Hill, 1979) 23; Boase, *Boniface VIII*, 232.

66. Mann, *Lives of the Popes*, XVIII, 182; Frugoni, "Il Giubileo di Bonifacio VIII," 39, 121.

67. Lynn Thorndike, "Peter of Limoges on the comet of 1299," *Isis* 36 (1945) 3–5; Nicole Bériou, "Pierre de Limoges et la fin des temps," *Mélanges de l'Ecole française de Rome. Moyen Age, Temps Moderne* 98,1(1986) 65–107; Le Goff, *Birth of Purgatory*, 289, 330–31; Raffaello Morghen, *Bonifacio VIII e il Giubileo del 1300 nella storiografia moderna* (Rome, 1975) 36–37. Another notable comet, Halley's, appeared in 1301.

68. In the last half of the 13th century, Europeans like Roger Bacon were also becoming particularly concerned with the stages of life and the means by which to hold old age at bay. See Marie-Thérèse Lorcin, "Gérontologie et gériatrie au Moyen Age," in *Vieillesse et vieillissement au Moyen Age* (Aix-en-Provence, 1987) 202–03. Cf. J. A. Burrow, *The Ages of Man: A Study in Medieval Writing and Thought* (Oxford, 1986).

69. Villani, *Chronicle*, 320–21. Cf. the enthusiasm for 1300 in Antonia Gransden, ed. and trans., *The Chronicle of Bury St. Edmunds 1212–1301* (London, 1964) 154–55.

70. I am using Louis Biancolli's very clear translation (Dante, *The Divine Comedy* [NY, 1968]), checked against Giorgio Petrocchi's Italian edition, as edited and annotated by Charles Singleton, revising the work of C. H. Grandgent (Dante Alighieri, *La Divina Commedia* rev. ed. [Cambridge, MA, 1972]). Quotations here from the *Inferno*, canto 27, line 103, and the *Paradiso*, canto 24, lines 13–15. Dante may well have been to Rome during the Jubilee; Boniface himself was absent from Rome for fully half of the year: Boase, *Boniface VIII*, 234, 237.

71. Burrow, *Ages of Man*, 7, on Dante's schema; Ricardo J. Quinones, *The Renaissance Discovery of Time* (Cambridge, MA, 1972), 37, 72, on time in Purgatory. Quotations from *Inferno*, canto 1, lines 1 and 59–60; *Purgatorio*, canto 23, lines 4–6; *Paradiso*, canto 33, lines 142–45.

72. Ann G. Carmichael, *Plague and the Poor in Renaissance Florence* (Cambridge, 1986) 7.

73. *Ibid.*, 14–15, on the Black Death as a mix of many epidemics; Graham Twigg, *The Black Death: A Biological Reappraisal* (NY, 1985) on anthrax; John Gribbin and H. H. Lamb, "Climatic change in historical times," in *Climatic Change*, ed. Gribbin (Cambridge, 1978) 68–82; Thurston, *Holy Year*, 5.

74. Barbara W. Tuchman, *A Distant Mirror: The Calamitous 14th Century* (NY, 1978) 93, 96, 121–22, and 95 for quote from Agnolo; Philip Ziegler, *The Black Death* (NY, 1969) 190, 195 for Welsh quotes; Robert E. Lerner, "The Black Death and Western European eschatological mentalities," *American Historical Review* 86 (1981) 533–52.

75. Jean-Noël Biraben, *Les hommes et la peste en France et dans les pays européens et méditerranéens* (Paris, 1975) I, 125; Robert S. Gottfried, *The Black Death* (NY, 1983) 134–35; Ziegler, *Black Death*, 190, on the knob; Millard Meiss, *Painting in Florence and Siena After the Black Death* (NY, 1964 [1951]); Tuchman, *A Distant Mirror*, 317, on the Duc d'Anjou; Amy Turner Montague, "Introduction" to Hans Holbein, *The Dance of Death* (Boston, 1974); Hellmut Rosenfeld, *Der mittelalterliche Totentanz*, 2nd ed. (Köln, 1968); Ernst M. Manasse, "The dance motive of the Latin Dance of Death," *Medievalia et Humanistica* 4 (1946) 83–103.

76. Tuchman, *A Distant Mirror*, xiii, 581.

77. Thurston, *Holy Year*, 61–62. The uniqueness of the Jubilee indulgence had already been undermined by Clement VI, whose promotion of a Treasury of Merit in heaven soon led to the sale of indulgences.

78. Poliakov, *History of Anti-Semitism*, 101–69; Philippe Wolff, "The 1391 pogroms in Spain," *Past and Present* 50 (1971) 4–18; Tuchman, *A Distant Mirror*, 470–76, 513, 515, 538–63, 578–79; Margaret Harvey, *Solutions to the Schism: A Study of Some English Attitudes, 1378 to 1409* (St. Ottilien, 1983); Alec Glasfurd, *The Antipope (Peter de Luna, 1342–1423)* (NY, 1965); Philippe de Mézières, *Letter to King Richard II. A Plea Made in 1395 for Peace between England and France*, trans. and ed. G. W. Coopland (Liverpool, 1975); Hilary M. Carey, "Astrology at the English court in the later Middle Ages," in Curry, *Astrology, Science*

and Society, 43–46; John Froissart, *The Chronicles of England, France, Spain, Etc.*, trans. Thomas Johnes, condensed ed. (London, 1906 [1803–10]) first lines; Henry Kamen, *Inquisition and Society in Spain in the Sixteenth and Seventeenth Centuries* (Bloomington, 1985) 10–11 on Jews and Ferrer, for whose prophetic stance see Bernard Montagnes, "Saint Vincent Ferrier devant le Schisme," in *Genèse et débuts du Grande Schisme d'Occident* (Paris, 1980) 607–13, and Etienne Delaruelle, "L'Antéchrist chez S. Vincent Ferrier, S. Bernardin de Sienne et autour de Jeanne d'Arc," *La piété populaire au moyen âge* (Torino, 1975) 329–54. Since it was often thought that the Antichrist would be born among, harbored by, or exalted throughout the Jewish community, there was frequently an emotional and theological connection between Christian apocalypticism and Christian anti-Semitism.

79. Johan Huizinga, *The Waning of the Middle Ages*, 2nd ed. revised, trans. F. Hopman (Garden City, NY, 1954 [1921]) 33, which translation of Deschamps I have amended; Rodney Hilton, *Bond Men Made Free: Medieval Peasant Movements and the English Rising of 1381* (NY, 1973); Koenraad W. Swart, *The Sense of Decadence in Nineteenth-Century France* (The Hague, 1964) 13; Pierre Chaunu, *Histoire et décadence* (Paris, 1981) 70; Julien Freund, *La décadence* (Paris, 1984) 7; Tuchman, *A Distant Mirror*, 119; John Gower, *Confessio Amantis*, ed. Russell A. Peck (NY, 1968) Prologue, lines 26–31.

80. Cf. John R. Reed, *Decadent Style* (Athens, OH, 1985) esp. 10–11, 15–16, and contrast Norberto Bobbio, *The Philosophy of Decadentism*, trans. David Moore (Oxford, 1948).

81. John Swain, *The Pleasures of the Torture Chamber* (London, 1931) 47; Edward Peters, *Torture* (Oxford, 1985) ch. 2; Yitzhak Baer, *A History of the Jews in Christian Spain*, trans. Louis Schoffman (Philadelphia, 1961–66) II, 95–97; Meiss, *Painting in Florence and Siena*, 77–78; Roberto Salvini, *Medieval Sculpture*, trans. Peter Murray et al. (Greenwich, CT, 1969) 46–49, plates 325–26; Tuchman, *A Distant Mirror*, 507.

82. Kathleen Cohen, *Metamorphosis of a Death Symbol: The Transi Tomb in the Late Middle Ages and Renaissance* (Berkeley, 1974) esp. 12–14, 33–37, 77–83, and 13 for quotation, which I have revised; Tuchman, *A Distant Mirror*, 455–57, 502–03, 506; Françoise Autrand, *Charles VI. La folie du roi* (Paris, 1986) ch. 13; Huizinga, *Waning*, 249, 257–58, and cf. 167; Salvini, *Medieval Sculpture*, 46–49.

83. I rely here on Bynum, *Holy Feast and Holy Fast*. See W. Butler-Bowdon, *The Book of Margery Kempe* (London, 1954 [1936]) 116 for quote.

84. Claude Gaignebet and Jean-Dominique Lajoux, *Art profane et religion populaire au moyen âge* (Paris, 1985) 68–95, 120–27; Richard Bernheimer, *Wild Men in the Middle Ages* (Cambridge, MA, 1952); Hayden White, "The forms of wildness," in *The Wild Man Within: An Image in Western Thought from the Renaissance to Romanticism*, eds. Edward Dudley and Maximillian E. Novak (Pittsburgh, 1972) 3–38; Timothy Husband with Gloria Gilmore-House, *The Wild Man. Medieval Myth and Symbolism* (NY, 1980) and noting, p. 149, that Charles VI had also masqueraded as a wildman in 1389, before the onset of his madness; Pierre Gascar, *Charles VI: le bal des ardents* (Paris, 1977) ch. 5; Guillaume-Prosper, Baron de Barante, *Histoire des ducs de Bourgogne*, new ed. (Brussels, 1838), I, 138–39; Sir John Bourchier, Lord Berners, trans. *The Chronicle of Jean Froissart* (NY, 1967 [1523–25]) VI, 96–100 (= ch. 188); Tuchman, *A Distant Mirror*, 460, 503–05, 544; Huizinga, *Waning*, 74, 77–84, 193; Sandra L. Hindman, *Christine de Pizan's "Epistre Othea"* (Toronto, 1986); Christine de Pizan,

The Book of the City of Ladies, trans. Earl J. Richards (NY, 1982 [written c. 1405]) and note the special role of the Ten Sibyls, Part II, ch. 1; E. K. Chambers, *The Medieval Stage* (London, 1903), I, 292.

85. Gaignebet and Lajoux, *Art profane*, 190–219; Chambers, *Medieval Stage*, I, 294, 321, 325, 332, 393–95; Jacques Heers, *Fêtes des fous et carnavals* (Paris, 1983); Albert Hyma, *The Christian Renaissance: A History of the "Devotio Moderna,"* 2nd ed. (Hamden, CT, 1965 [1924]) esp. 543–81; Kees W. Bolle, "Structures of Renaissance mysticism," in *The Darker Vision of the Renaissance*, ed. Robert S. Kinsman (Berkeley, 1974) 133–35; Thomas à Kempis, *Of the Imitation of Christ*, trans. Anthony Hoskins (London, 1903) 19–20 for quotes; Huizinga, *Waning*, 196–97; R. K. Emmerson and R. B. Herzman, "The *Canterbury Tales* in eschatological perspective," in *Use and Abuse of Eschatology*, 404–24.

86. Alan C. Kors and Edward Peters, eds., *Witchcraft in Europe 1100–1700* (Philadelphia, 1972) 85–86 for Eymeric; Norman Cohn, *Europe's Inner Demons* (NY, 1975) 164–224, Stedelen on 204; Richard Kieckhefer, *European Witch Trials: Their Foundation in Popular and Learned Culture, 1300–1500* (Berkeley, 1976) 11, 18, 75–79, 117–18; Gaignebet and Lajoux, *Art profane*, 90–94, 130–41, 291–324; Jeffrey B. Russell, *A History of Witchcraft* (London, 1980) 77–78; William A. Christian, Jr., *Apparitions in Late Medieval and Renaissance Spain* (Princeton, 1981) 26–40; Iris Origo, *The Merchant of Prato* (London, 1957) 316–18; Daniel E. Bornstein, "The Bianchi of 1399," Ph.D. thesis, Univ. of Chicago, 1985, esp. p. 63 on expectations of peace with the new century; Arsenio Frugoni, "La devozione dei Bianchi del 1399," in *L'Attesa dell'età nuova nella spiritualità della fine del Medioevo* (Todi, 1962) 232–48; Roberto Rusconi, *L'Attesa della fine. Crisi della società, profezia ed apocalisse in Italia al tempo del grande scisma d'Occidente* (Rome, 1979) 204–18; Thurston, *Holy Year*, 63.

87. Morton W. Bloomfield, *Piers Plowman as a Fourteenth-Century Apocalypse* (New Brunswick, NJ, 1961); Elisabeth Lunz, "The Valley of Jehoshaphat in *Piers Plowman*," *Tulane Studies in English* 20 (1972) 1–10; Matthew Tobin, "Le 'Livre des révélations' de Marie Robine," *Mélanges de l'Ecole française de Rome—Moyen Age, Temps Moderne* 98,1 (1986) 229–64; Louise B. Pascoe, "Pierre d'Ailly: histoire, Schisme, et Antéchrist," in *Genèse et débuts*, 615–22; Eugenio Dupré Theseider, "L'attesa escatologica durante il periodo avignonese," in *L'Attesa dell'età nuova*, 67–126; Rusconi, *L'Attesa della fine*, esp. 71, 104; Manuel Calecas [Kalekas], *Correspondance*, ed. Raymond-J. Loenertz (Vatican City, 1950) 117–18; Robert E. Lerner, "Refreshment of the Saints: the time after Antichrist as a station for earthly progress in medieval thought," *Traditio* 32 (1976) 132, 136–38, and 141 on Frederick of Brunswick, who prophesied the defeat of Antichrist for 1400; Lopez and Raymond, *Medieval Trade*, with quote from Datini, 263, and cf. Gene Brucker, ed., *The Society of Renaissance Florence* (NY, 1971) 23; Cedric Jagger, *The World's Great Clocks & Watches* (London, 1977) 67–68; Coluccio Salutati, *Epistolario*, ed. Francesco Novati (Paris, 1896) III, 408, letter 23 on the two writers, Albertino Mussato and Geri d'Arezzo.

88. James H. Billington, *The Icon and the Axe* (NY, 1966) 72–74, 81–88, G. P. Fedotov, *The Russian Religious Mind* (Cambridge, MA, 1946–66) II, ch. 6; David M. Goldfrank, "Judaizers," *Modern Encyclopedia of Russian and Soviet History*, ed. Joseph L. Wieczynski (Gulf Breeze, FL, 1980) XV, 143–46; idem, "Pre-Enlightenment utopianism in Russian history," *Russian History* 11 (1984) 127–29; Poliakov, *History of Anti-Semitism*, 275–79; A. Vasiliev, "Medieval ideas of the end of the world: West and East," *Byzantion* 16 (1942–43) 497–

500; Constantine Zuckerman, "The 'psalter' of Feodor and the heresy of the 'Judaizers' in the last quarter of the fifteenth century," *Harvard Ukrainian Studies* 11 (1987) 77–99.

89. Henry Kamen, "The Mediterranean and the expulsion of Spanish Jews in 1492," *Past and Present* 119 (1988) 30–55; idem, *The Spanish Inquisition* (NY, 1965); Samuel Usque, *Consolation for the Tribulations of Israel* (1553), excerpted and translated by Michael A. Meyer, ed., *Ideas of Jewish History* (NY, 1974) 107 for quote; Silver, *History of Messianic Speculation*, 106, 109, 116–25; Cohen, "Messianic postures," 153; Stephen Sharot, "Jewish millenarianism: a comparison of medieval communities," *Comparative Studies in Society and History* 22 (1980) 394–415; Joseph R. Hacker, "Links between Spanish Jewry and Palestine, 1391–1492," in *Vision and Conflict in the Holy Land*, ed. Richard I. Cohen (Jersualem, 1985) 111–39; José C. Nieto, "Franciscan Alumbrados and the prophetic-apocalyptic tradition," *Sixteenth Century Journal* 8,3 (1977) 3–16; Angel Alcalá et al., *Inquisición española y mentalidad inquisitorial* (Barcelona, 1983) 373–460.

90. Jean Aubin, "La politique religieuse des Safavides," in *Le Shiʿisme imâmite* (Paris, 1970) 235–44; Said Amir Arjomand, *The Shadow of God and the Hidden Imam: Religion, Political Order and Societal Change in Shiʿite Iran from the Beginning to 1890* (Chicago, 1984) 80, 161; Irene Melikoff, "Le problème Ḳizilbaş," *Turcica* 6 (1975) 49–67.

91. Niccolò Machiavelli, *History of Florence and of the Affairs of Italy*, trans. M. Walter Dunne (NY, 1960 [written by 1525]) 407; Amnon Linder, "L'Expedition italienne de Charles VIII et les espérances messianiques des Juifs," *Revue des études juives* 137 (1978) 179–86; Donald Weinstein, *Savonarola and Florence* (Princeton, 1970) throughout, with quote on 143, and see esp. the discussion of Giovanni Nesi's *Oraculum de novo saeculo*, 192–99.

92. Weinstein, *Savonarola and Florence*, 88–97, 228–39; André Chastel, *Fables, formes, figures* (Paris, 1978) I, 167–97; Dietrich Kurze, *Johannes Lichtenberger. Eine Studie zür Geschichte der Prophetie und Astrologie* (Lübeck, 1960); Cesare Vasoli, "Temi mistici e profetici alla fine del Quattrocento," in his *Studi sulla cultura del Rinascimento* (Manduria, 1968) 180–240; Paola Zambelli, "Fine del mundo o inizio della propaganda?" in *Scienze, credenze occulte, livelli di cultura* (Florence, 1982) 291–368; Joseph Gantner, *Leonardos Visionen von der Sintflut und vom Untergang der Welt* (Bern, 1958) esp. ch. 3; Peter Glum, "Divine Judgment in Bosch's *Garden of Earthly Delights*," *Art Bulletin* 58 (1976) 45–54; Craig S. Harbison, *The Last Judgment in Sixteenth-Century Northern Europe* (NY, 1976) 64–82; Erwin Panofsky, *The Life and Art of Albrecht Dürer* (Princeton, 1955) 51–59; James B. Ross and Mary M. McLaughlin, eds., *Portable Renaissance Reader* (NY, 1968) 225–26 for Skelton.

93. Bernard Capp, *English Almanacs 1500–1800: Astrology and the Popular Press* (Ithaca, 1979) esp. 25–26; Jean Delumeau, *La peur en Occident, XIVᵉ–XVIIIᵉ siècles* (Paris, 1978) 213–15; Mary Catherine O'Connor, *The Art of Dying Well: The Development of the Ars Moriendi* (NY, 1942); Roger Chartier, "Les arts de mourir," *Annales: é. s. c.* 31 (1976) 51–75; Nancy Lee Beaty, *The Craft of Dying* (New Haven, 1970) 8, 19 for quotes from an early English version of the *Tractatus artis bene moriendi* (c. 1414–18).

94. Huizinga, *Waning*, 145–47; Suzanne F. Wemple and Denise A. Kaiser, "A death's dance of women," *Journal of Medieval History* 12 (1986) 333–43; Philippe Ariès, *Western Attitudes toward Death: From the Middle Ages to the Present*, trans. Patricia M. Ranum (Baltimore, 1974) 33–52; William H. McNeill, *Plagues and Peoples* (Garden City, 1976) 177–80, 221–

24, on syphilis as perhaps a new form of indigenous yaws, and on typhus, another new plague appearing in Europe in 1491; William W. Heist, *The Fifteen Signs Before Doomsday* (East Lansing, 1952); Lutz Malke, "Zur Ikonographie der 'Vier Letzten Dinge,' " *Deutscher Verein für Kunstwissenschaft Zeitschrift* 30 (1976) 44–66; Delumeau, *La peur*, 37.

95. Roberto Weiss, *The Renaissance Discovery of Classical Antiquity* (Oxford, 1969) 114–15, 119–20, 125–26, as also Esther G. Dotson, "Shapes of earth and time in European gardens," *Art Journal* 42,3 (1982) 210–16 on Nanni, and cf. Georges Dumézil, *Archaic Roman Religion*, trans. Philip Krapp (Chicago, 1970 [1966]) I, 327–33 on Janus; Giovanni Cipriani, *Il mito etrusco nel Rinascimento fiorentino* (Florence, 1980) esp. 33; Jean Seznec, *The Survival of the Pagan Gods*, trans. Barbara F. Sessions (NY, 1953) 116, 120; "Januskopf," *Lexikon der Kunst* (Leipzig, 1971) II, 451–52; Giorgio Vasari, *Lives of the Painters, Sculptors and Architects*, trans. A. B. Hinds, ed. William Gaunt (London, 1963 [1550]) III, 238–39 on the procession, designed by Pontormo.

96. Harry Levin, *The Myth of the Golden Age in the Renaissance* (Bloomington, 1969) 38 for pennant; Cesare Vasoli, "Il mito dell'età dell'oro nel Rinascimento," in *Giorgione e l'umanesimo veneziano*, ed. Rodolfo Pallucchini (Florence, 1981) I, 51–69; Language Department, School of Economic Science, London, trans., *The Letters of Marsilio Ficino* (London, 1975) I, 130; Marsilio Ficino, *Opera omnia* (Torino, 1962 [1576]) I, 944, translated in Ross and McLaughlin, *Portable Renaissance Reader*, 79–80.

97. Frances A. Yates, *Giordano Bruno and the Hermetic Tradition* (NY, 1964) esp. ch. 1; Eugenio Garin, *Astrology in the Renaissance*, trans. Carolyn Jackson et al. (London, 1983) 29–82, quote from Ficino on 76; D. P. Walker, *Spiritual and Demonic Magic from Ficino to Campanella* (London, 1958).

98. Daniel C. Matt, "Introduction," to his translation of the *Zohar: The Book of Enlightenment* (NY, 1983); Moshe Idel, *The Mystical Experience in Abraham Abulafia*, trans. Jonathan Chipman (Albany, 1988); Gershom Scholem, "The messianic idea in kabbalism," in his *The Messianic Idea in Judaism*, trans. Michael A. Meyer (NY, 1971) 37–48; Yates, *Giordano Bruno*, ch. 5; Garin, *Astrology in the Renaissance*, 56–82; Weinstein, *Savonarola and Florence*, 334–38 on Botticelli.

99. Pierre d'Ailly, *Ymago mundi*, with marginal notes by Columbus, trans. Edmond Buron, 3 vols. (Paris, 1930 [from Louvain edition, 1480–83]) I, 29, 91–92, and III, 213; Pauline M. Watts, "Prophecy and discovery: on the spiritual origins of Christopher Columbus's 'Enterprise of the Indies,' " *American Historical Review* 90 (1985) 73–102; Leonard I. Sweet, "Christopher Columbus and the millennial vision of the New World," *Catholic Historical Review* 72 (July 1986) 369–82. On active images, see Frances A. Yates, *The Art of Memory* (Chicago, 1966) ch. 4.

100. J. M. Cohen, ed. and trans., *The Four Voyages of Christopher Columbus* (Baltimore, 1969) 37, from the digest of the logbook made by Bartolomé de las Casas; John L. Phelan, *The Millennial Kingdom of the Franciscans in the New World*, 2nd ed. (Berkeley, 1970 [1956]) 17–28, starting point for Watts, "Prophecy and discovery," who cites also Alain Milhou, *Colón y su mentalidad mesiánica en el ambiente franciscanista español* (Valladolid, 1983), which is assessed by John Larner, "The certainty of Columbus," *History* 73 (1988) 19–21.

101. Watts, "Prophecy and discovery," 73, 96 for letters, as also Sweet, "Christopher Columbus," 379; Cohen, *The Four Voyages*, 221–89 *passim* for Paradise; Oliver Dunn and James E. Kelley, Jr., eds and trans., *The Diario of Christopher Columbus's First Voyage to America 1492–1493* (Norman, 1988) 67–69 for quote.

102. Frederick Turner, *Beyond Geography* (NY, 1980) 126; Cristóbal Colón, *Textos y documentos completos*, ed. Consuelo Varela, 2nd ed. (Madrid, 1984) 279–91 for his Libro de las Profecias, revealing also that Columbus was still using Roman numerals for adding up years; Cohen, *The Four Voyages*, 293; Sweet, "Christopher Columbus," 381.

103. Hugh Honour, *The New Golden Land: European Images of America from the Discoveries to the Present Time* (NY, 1975) 8, 10, 12, 18; J. H. Parry, *The Age of Reconnaissance* (NY, 1963) 155–58; Turner, *Beyond Geography*, 95 on mythic zones; Levin, *Myth of the Golden Age*, 59–60; Cohen, *The Four Voyages*, 31–32, 116, 119. The peoples of the Americas had their own golden age myths and their own prophetic calendars, whose coincidences with the Spanish "discoveries" were of great importance, see, e.g., David Carrasco, "Quetzalcóatl's revenge: primordium and application in Aztec religion," *History of Religions* 19 (1980) 296–320.

104. Thomas More, *Utopia*, trans. and ed. H. V. S. Ogden (NY, 1949) 28. For a fine discussion of More's Utopia, see James Holstun, *A Rational Millennium: Puritan Utopias of Seventeenth-Century England and America* (NY, 1987) 3–33, and cf. Frank E. Manuel and Fritzie P. Manuel, *Utopian Thought in the Western World* (Cambridge, MA, 1979) 117–49.

105. O. Zöckler, "Calendar, the Christian," *New Schaff-Herzog Religious Encyclopedia* (Grand Rapids, 1958) II, 344–45; Lopez and Raymond, *Medieval Trade*, 176; Lanes, *Revolution in Time*, 114; Jagger, *World's Great Clocks*, 65; Vincenzo Cioffari, "Fortune, fate, and chance," *Dictionary of the History of Ideas*, ed.-in-chief Philip P. Wiener (NY, 1973) II, 225–36; Erwin Panofsky, "Father Time," in his *Studies in Iconology* (NY, 1967 [1939]) 69–94; Niccolò Machiavelli, *The Prince and the Discourses*, trans. Luigi Ricci and E. R. P. Vincent (NY, 1950) 383, from ch. 29 of the Discourses, written by 1519, and cf. J. G. A. Pocock, *The Machiavellian Moment* (Princeton, 1975); Howard R. Patch, *The Tradition of the Goddess Fortuna in Medieval Philosophy and Literature* (Northampton, MA, 1922) 215, 229.

106. Machiavelli, *The Prince and the Discourses*, 383, 532–33; Francesco Guicciardini, *Selected Writings*, ed. Cecil Grayson, trans. Margaret Grayson (London, 1965) 11 from the Ricordi (no. 23), written 1512–30; Denys Hay, *Annalists and Historians* (London, 1977) 91; Erwin Panofsky, *Meaning in the Visual Arts* (Garden City, NY, 1955) 169–235; Samuel Kinser, "Ideas of temporal change and cultural process in France, 1470–1535," in *Renaissance Studies in Honor of Hans Baron*, eds. A. Molho and John A. Tedeschi (Florence, 1971) 703–56; Wilcox, *Measure of Times Past*, 181–85.

107. Ludwig Pastor, *The History of the Popes from the Close of the Middle Ages*, 5th ed. (London, 1950) VI, 147–48; Thurston, *Holy Year*, 5–6, 64–66, 76–77; Vespasiano, *Renaissance Princes, Popes, and Prelates*, trans. William George and Emily Waters (NY, 1963 [1926]) 48–49.

108. Pastor, *History of the Popes*, VI, 89–90, 150–54 (quote from Trithemius); Charles de Tolnay, *Michelangelo* (Princeton, 1947) I, 90–98.

109. Luca Landucci, *A Florentine Diary from 1450 to 1516*, trans. Alice de Rosen Jervis, ed. Iodoco del Badia (London, 1927) 170; Pastor, *History of the Popes*, VI, 151; Johannes Burchardus, *Pope Alexander VI and His Court*, ed. and trans. D.F. Glaser (NY, 1921) ch. 11; Elizabeth L. Eisenstein, *The Printing Press as an Agent of Change* (Cambridge, 1979) I, 375–77 on indulgences. Cf. Bernd Moeller, "Piety in Germany around 1500," trans. Joyce Irwin, in *The Reformation in Medieval Perspective*, ed. Steven E. Ozment (Chicago, 1971) 50–75.

110. A. C. Cawley, ed., *Everyman and Medieval Miracle Plays* (NY, 1959) 205, 207, 224 (*Everyman* quotes, lines 11–12, 608); Quinones, *Renaissance Discovery of Time*, 309; Claire L. Parkinson, *Breakthroughs: A Chronology of Great Achievements in Science and Mathematics* (Boston, 1985) for 1489 and 1491. See Karl W. Menninger, *Number Words and Number Symbols* (Cambridge, MA, 1969) 287 on the diverse numerals still in use at the turn of the 16th century.

111. C. M. Jacobs, trans., *Luther's Ninety-Five Theses*, rev. Harold J. Grimm (Philadelphia, 1957) thesis 30; Jaroslav Pelikan, ed., *Luther's Works* (St. Louis, 1967) XXX, 122, the Catholic Epistles, Sermon on the First Epistle of St. Peter, Chapter Four; Robin B. Barnes, *Prophecy and Gnosis: Apocalypticism in the Wake of the Lutheran Reformation* (Stanford, 1987) 40, 41, 51, 52, with quote on 41 from translation by Gerald Strauss, "The mental world of a Saxon pastor," in Peter N. Brooks, ed., *Reformation Principle and Practice* (London, 1980) 169.

112. Barnes, *Prophecy and Gnosis*, quote on 1 and see ch. 2; John Harvey, *A Discoursive Probleme concerning Prophesies* (London, 1588) 40, 93. Melanchthon figured the *terminus ad quem* of the Millennium for 2000 A.D. See G. J. R. Parry, *A Protestant Vision: William Harrison and the Reformation of Elizabethan England* (Cambridge, 1987) esp. 97, 125–37.

113. Of the enormous literature on Foxe, I have relied on the contrasting works by Richard Bauckham, *Tudor Apocalypse* (Oxford, 1978) and Katharine R. Firth, *The Apocalyptic Tradition in Reformation Britain, 1530–1645* (Oxford, 1979).

114. Johannes Burkhardt, *Die Entstehung der modernen Jahrhundertrechnung* (Göppingen, 1971) 11, 20, 29; Hay, *Annalists and Historians*, 123; Barnes, *Prophecy and Gnosis*, 76–77, 105–06, 190; Ernst Lewalter, "Das Jahrhundert als Epoche," *Romanische Forschungen* 49 (1935) 343–51 on Flacius's chiliasm.

115. Burkhardt, *Jahrhundertrechnung*, 5, 8, 29; *Oxford English Dictionary*, II, 227, s.v. "Centurial," "Century"; Paul J. G. Lehmann, "Einteilung und Datierung nach Jahrhunderten," in his *Erforschung des Mittelalters* (Stuttgart, 1959 [1941]) I, 118–19; Cyriac K. Pullapilly, *Caesar Baronius, Counter-Reformation Historian* (Notre Dame, 1975); Carlo Gasbarri, "Baronio, Cesare," *Bibliotheca Sanctorum* (Rome, 1962) II, 819–28; J. Wahl, "Baronius, Caesar," *New Catholic Encyclopedia* (NY, 1967) II, 105–06; Hay, *Annalists and Historians*, 125–27.

116. Pullapilly, *Caesar Baronius*, 85; John B. Peterson, "Baronius, Cesare," *Catholic Encyclopedia* (NY, 1907) II, 304–07.

117. Gordon Moyer, "The Gregorian calender," *Scientific American* 266 (May 1982) 144–52.

118. *Ibid.*, 144ff.; H. M. Nobis, "The reaction of astronomers to the Gregorian calendar," in *Gregorian Reform of the Calendar*, eds. G. V. Coyne et al. (Vatican City, 1983) 243–54; Anthony Grafton, "From *De die natali* to *De emendatione temporum*: the origins and setting of Scaliger's chronology," *Journal of the Warburg & Courtauld Institutes* 48 (1985) 100–43; Wilcox, *Measure of Times Past*, 197–200. Eastern Orthodox countries also stuck by the Old Style calendar, Russia until 1917.

119. Bruce T. Moran, "Princes, machines, and the valuation of precision in the sixteenth century," *Sudhoffs Archiv* 61 (1977) 209–28; Lansing Collins, "The Sultan's clock-organ, 1599," *History Today* 26 (Sept. 1976) 608–16; Louis L. Gallagher, trans., *China in the Sixteenth Century: The Journals of Matthew Ricci, 1583–1610* (NY, 1953) 369–75; Landes, *Revolution in Time*, 87, 104, 115; Thomas S. Kuhn, *The Copernican Revolution* (NY, 1959) 209–12.

120. Grafton, "Scaliger's chronology," quote on 115; Landes, *Revolution in Time*, 92–93, 103 on Calvinists and time-thrift; Benjamin Nelson, *The Idea of Usury*, 2nd ed. (Chicago, 1969); R. H. Tawney, "Introduction" to Thomas Wilson, *A Discourse Upon Usury*, ed. Tawney (London, 1965 [1572]); Fritz Saxl, "Veritas filia temporis," in *Philosophy and History: The Ernst Cassirer Festschrift* (Oxford, 1936) 197–222; Phoebe S. Spinrad, *The Summons of Death on the Medieval and Renaissance English Stage* (Columbus, OH, 1987) esp. 24; Edmund Spenser, *Books I and II of The Faerie Queene, The Mutability Cantos and Selections from the Minor Poetry*, eds. Robert Kellogg and Oliver Steele (Indianapolis, 1965) 267 (= Book II, canto iv of *The Faerie Queene*) and 407 (= canto vi, stanza 5 of *The Mutability Cantos*). Cf. LePan, *The Cognitive Revolution*, on time, probability, Shakespeare's dramatic plots, and (p. 91) cooking instructions.

121. ABC-TV, "World News Tonight," May 9, 1988; Beth Ann Krier and David Larsen, "Quaking with anticipation," *Los Angeles Times* (May 6, 1988) V,1, and see headlines in many papers on May 9, 1988, for the Reagans and astrology; Hadley Cantril, *The Invasion from Mars* (NY, 1966 [1940]).

122. Edgar Leoni, *Nostradamus: Life and Literature* (NY, 1961) reviews what is known about Nostradamus and supplies a full French text and decently literal English translations of the *Centuries*; see 22n. for the pills. On cosmetics and jelly, see James Laver, *Nostradamus* (Harmondsworth, 1952) 26–27.

123. John Hogue, *Nostradamus & The Millennium* (Garden City, NY, 1987) 18, following (as all must) biographical information given by Nostradamus's disciple, Jean Aimé de Chavigny. Quote about 3797 is from the preface to the first edition of the *Centuries*, as translated by Henry C. Roberts, *The Complete Prophecies of Nostradamus*, 3rd ed., rev. by Lee R. Amsterdam and Harvey Amsterdam (Oyster Bay, 1982) 6, which I prefer over Leoni's translation, *Nostradamus*, 126–27. See Capp, *English Almanacs*, 29, for quote on celebrity.

124. Roberts, *Complete Prophecies*, 7, and cf. Leoni, *Nostradamus*, 129; Frances A. Yates, "Oracle to the cock of France," in her *Ideas and Ideals in the North European Renaissance: Collected Essays* (London, 1984) III, 129–33, reviewing the book that best interprets Nostradamus in the context of his own century, Liberté E. LeVert, trans. and ed., *The Prophecies and Enigmas of Nostradamus* (Glen Rock, NJ, 1980); Roberts, *Complete Prophecies*, Century I, quatrain 22; Leoni, *Nostradamus*, 15–20 on Jewish background and on Scaliger; Frances A. Yates, *The*

Rosicrucian Enlightenment (London, 1972) 82–85 and throughout, on alchemy and Paracelsian thought; Franz Hartmann, *The Prophecies of Paracelsus* (Blauvelt, NY, 1973); Linda Fierz-David, *The Dream of Poliphilo*, trans. Mary Hottinger (NY, 1950)—a Jungian analysis (Jung saw Colonna's book as [p. xv] "Janus-headed, between two eras"); Laver, *Nostradamus*, 28–29 on Horapollo, as also Yates, *Giordano Bruno*, 163; Margery Corbett and R. W. Lightbown, *The Comely Frontispiece: The Emblematic Title-Page in England, 1550–1660* (London, 1979) 17.

125. Roberts, *Complete Prophecies*, Century I, quatrain 35 (which I have slightly amended); Laver, *Nostradamus*, 50–59, is best on the duel.

126. Leoni, *Nostradamus*, 30–38.

127. The exactly dated prophecies are listed by Leoni, *Nostradamus*, 547, although the first in his list, 1580, is actually "1580 more or less." The famous 1999 prophecy is in Century X, quatrain 72, which I have translated here as literally as possible from this French:

> *L'an mil neuf cent nonante sept mois,*
> *Du ciel viendra un grand Roi d'effrayeur;*
> *Ressusciter le grand Roi d'Angoulmois,*
> *Avant après Mars regner par bonheur.*

See also Jean Céard, "Jean Aimé de Chavigny: le premier commentateur de Nostradamus," in *Science, credenze occulte, livelli di cultura* (Florence, 1982) 427–42; Jean-Aimé de Chavigny, *La première face du Janus françois* (Lyon, 1594).

128. *Oxford English Dictionary*, VIII, 1261, s.v. "Predict," "Prediction," and cf. Richard H. Popkin, "Predicting, prophecying, divining and foretelling from Nostradamus to Hume," *History of European Ideas* 5 (1984) 117–36; Charles Augustus Ward, *Oracles of Nostradamus* (London, 1940 [1891]) 32 on Garancières, as also Leoni, *Nostradamus*, 63; Paul Imbs, ed., *Trésor de la langue française* (Paris, 1977) V, 397–98, s.v. "Centurie."

129. G. M. Artusi, *L'Artusi, ovvero, delle imperfezioni della moderna musica*, excerpted and translated in *Source Readings in Music History: The Baroque Era*, ed. Oliver Strunk (NY, 1965) 33, 34, 40, 42.

130. Claude V. Palisca, *Baroque Music* (Englewood Cliffs, 1968) 1–31; Alec Harman and Anthony Milner, *Man and His Music: Late Renaissance and Baroque Music* (NY, 1962) II, 128–35. To follow changing conceptions of time through music, see Rudolf Wendorff, *Zeit und Kultur* (Wiesbaden, 1980) 206–11, 256–66 *et passim*.

131. Palisca, *Baroque Music*, 31–37; Rinuccini's "Dedication" to *Euridice* translated in Strunk, *Baroque Era*, 7–9, quote on 8.

132. Gertrude Norman and Miriam L. Shrifte, eds., *Letters of Composers* (NY, 1946) 3–4 for Sweelinck's letter; Harman and Milner, *Late Renaissance and Baroque Music*, 295.

133. Kuhn, *Copernican Revolution*, 209–19, and 179–80 for quote; Yates, *Giordano Bruno*, 440–44. Cf. *Le soleil à la Renaissance, science et mythes. Colloque international tenu en avril 1963* (Brussels, 1965) esp. 33–54, 519–38.

134. Tommaso Campanella, *La Città del Sole: Dialogo Poetico / The City of the Sun: A Poetical Dialogue*, trans. Daniel J. Donno (Berkeley, 1981) 14, 31 for quote; Yates, *Ideas and Ideals*, III, 200.

135. Campanella, *La Città del Sole*, 93, 109, 118–19, 121, 123. The apsides are the apogee and perigee of an orbit; see Donno's commentary, 137–38.

136. *Ibid.*, Donno's introduction; Tommaso Campanella, *Lettere*, ed. Vincenzo Spampanato (Bari, 1927) 23; idem, *Articuli prophetales*, ed. Germana Ernst (Florence, 1977) 244; Manuel and Manuel, *Utopian Thought*, 261–88.

137. Pastor, *History of the Popes*, XXIV, 269–80; George T. Matthews, ed., *The Fugger Newsletters* (NY, 1959) 243; Pierre Victor Palma Cayet, *Chronologie septenaire de l'histoire de la paix . . .* (Paris, 1605) f. 194, printed as vol. 13 of *Nouvelle collection des mémoires relatifs à l'histoire de France* (Paris, 1857); N. E. McClure, ed., *The Letters of John Chamberlain* (Philadelphia, 1939) I, 92.

138. Yates, *Giordano Bruno*, with quote on 206; idem, *The Art of Memory* (Chicago, 1966) 199–319; Manuel and Manuel, *Utopian Thought*, ch. 8. Burnt at the stake in Italy in 1599 was a peasant counterpart to Bruno, the miller Domenico Scandella, whose heretical cosmogony drew upon images of chaos and putrefaction, and whose desires were for a new world of material comfort and universal salvation. See Carlo Ginzburg, *The Cheese and the Worms: The Cosmos of a Sixteenth Century Miller*, trans. John Tedeschi and Anne Tedeschi (Harmondsworth, 1982).

139. Yates, *Giordano Bruno*, ch. 19; Manuel and Manuel, *Utopian Thought*, 239 for quote.

140. Michael Kunze, *Highroad to the Stake*, trans. William E. Yuill (Chicago, 1987); H. R. Trevor-Roper, *The European Witch-Craze of the Sixteenth and Seventeenth Centuries and Other Essays* (NY, 1967) 90–192; Wolfgang Behringer, *Hexenverfolgung im Bayern* (Munich, 1987) on waves of witch-hunting 1586–1591, 1600–1630; Albert Van Helden, *The Invention of the Telescope* (Philadelphia, 1977); Richard S. Westfall, "Scientific patronage: Galileo and the telescope," *Isis* 76 (1985) 11–30; D. P. Walker, *Unclean Spirits: Possession and Exorcism in France and England in the Late Sixteenth and Early Seventeenth Centuries* (Philadelphia, 1981) 34–37, 49ff.; *Hamlet*, Act II, scene 2; R. W. Shirley, *The Mapping of the World: Early Printed World Maps 1472–1700* (London, 1983) xxxiv; Leo Bagrow, *History of Cartography*, trans. D. L. Paisey, 2nd ed., rev. by R. A. Skelton (Chicago, 1985) esp. 180; Frances A. Yates, *Theatre of the World* (Chicago, 1969); Giuseppe Sartori, "Decadenza, messianesimo e genio della nazione nella cultura spagnola del secolo XVII," *Acme* 22 (1969) 309–45; J. H. Elliott, "The decline of Spain," *Past & Present* 20 (1961) 59, 66; John Leddy Phelan, *The Millennial Kingdom of the Franciscans in the New World*, 2nd ed. (Berkeley, 1970) esp. ch. 12; Arthur B. Ferguson, *The Chivalric Tradition in Renaissance England* (Washington D.C., 1986) esp. 66–70; Margaret Aston, "English ruins and history: the Dissolution and the sense of the past," *Journal of the Warburg & Courtauld Institutes* 36 (1973) 231–55; Gad Freudenthal, "Theory of matter and cosmology in William Gilbert's *De magnete*," *Isis* 74 (1983) 22–37; Samuel Putnam, trans. and ed., *The Portable Cervantes* (NY, 1951) quote on 422 from *Don Quixote*, Part II, ch. 6.

141. Emmanuel Le Roy Ladurie, *Times of Feast, Times of Famine*, trans. Barbara Bray (Garden City, NY, 1971) 138–43; Jean M. Grove, *The Little Ice Age* (London, 1988) 137ff.; Richard J. Jaarsma with Edward L. Odenwald, "Nor heaven nor earth have been at peace: the contemporary foundations of Shakespeare's cataclysmic imagery," *Kronos* 5,4 (1980) 3–18 and 6,1 (1981) 12–24; *Midsummer Night's Dream*, Act II, scene 1, lines 111–14.

142. J. B. Bury, *The Idea of Progress* (London, 1920) 46–47 for Le Roy, discussed by Werner L. Gundersheimer, *The Life and Works of Louis Le Roy* (Geneva, 1966) 116, from f.113r; Maureen Perrie, " 'Popular Socio-Utopian Legends' in the Time of Troubles," *Slavonic and East European Review* 60 (1982) 221–43, critiquing the work of K. V. Chistov; Jean Lafond and Augustin Redondo, eds., *L'Image du monde renversé . . . de la fin du XVIe siècle au milieu du XVIIe: colloque international, Tours, 17–19 novembre 1977* (Paris, 1979) esp. essays by Yves-Marie Bercé on the Croquants and M. L. Launay on d'Acuto; David Kunzle, "World upside down: the iconography of a European broadsheet type," in *The Reversible World*, ed. Barbara Babcock (Ithaca, 1977) 39–94; Richard Gilman, *Decadence: The Strange Life of an Epithet* (NY, 1979) 74; Koenraad W. Swart, *The Sense of Decadence in Nineteenth-Century France* (The Hague, 1964) 25, quoting Cellorigo, and see also p. 31, quoting French lawyer Etienne Pasquier; Victor Harris, *All Coherence Gone* (Chicago, 1949) 115 for quote from Pont (p. 78). Cf. Bernard Lewis, "Ottoman observers of Ottoman decline," in his *Islam in History* (London, 1973) 199–213. The year 1591/1592 A.D. was the year 1000 A.H., but there was relatively little Islamic excitement except among the Nuqṭavīs; see Arjomand, *Shadow of God and the Hidden Imam*, 198.

143. Enrico De Mas, *L'Attesa del secolo aureo (1603–1625)* (Florence, 1982); Edward Topsell, *Time's Lamentation: or, an Exposition on the Prophet Joel* (London, 1599) Dedication, sig. A2, and 57. Cf. the internal debate in Peter Clark, ed., *The European Crisis of the 1590s* (London, 1985), esp. Clark's introduction, admitting that no 1590s crisis led to fundamental social changes but arguing anyhow (p. 18) that "one has a strong sense that the end of the sixteenth century saw the turning of a crucial page in European history, from an old world to the new." We in fact owe this sort of thinking to the late 16th century; see also the discussion of Sully in note 144 below. On the Fiery Trigon of 1583—or 1588—see Capp, *English Almanacs*, 166–67; R. J. W. Evans, *Rudolf II and His World* (Oxford, 1973) 278–80. On 7 + 9, see Manuel and Manuel, *Utopian Thought*, 286.

144. George B. Harrison, *The Elizabethan Journals* (Ann Arbor, 1955) III, 63; Maximilien de Béthune, duc de Sully, *Mémoires des sages et royales oeconomies d'estat de Henry Le Grand*, ed. Claude Bernard Petitot (Paris, 1820 [1638]) 21–24, published in *Collection des mémoires relatifs à l'histoire de France*, ser. 2, vol. 4. While the rainbow of the 1600 coin was an emblem of relief, the *jeton* for 1601 showed Hercules overthrowing a centaur, emblem of Opportunity. In the original edition, Sully left off the first volume of his history in 1598 after the Peace of Vervins and wrote at the start of the second volume (p. 5 of Petitot's edition), "nous avons estimé à propos de finir nostre premier livre et de commencer nos recueils du second, afin qu'il semble, que sortant d'un vieil et ténébreux monde tout remply de ruynes, dégats, meurtres, occisions, troubles, guerres, haines et combustions, nous venions à entrer dans un nouveau monde tout esclatant de belles lumières" (literally, "we have considered it fitting to conclude the first volume [with the Peace] and to commence the second so that it might seem that, on leaving behind an old and murky world overspread with ruins, ravages, murders,

killings, disturbances, wars, hatreds and conflagrations, we had just entered a new world shining with beautiful lights").

For an introduction to Jacob Boehme, see his *The Way to Christ*, trans. Peter Erb (NY, 1978). On the Holy Roman Emperor, see Evans, *Rudolf II and His World*, 47, 278, suggesting that in 1600 Rudolf (b. 1552) may have feared dying (like his father) before the age of fifty. On his "wonder rooms," see Yates, *The Rosicrucian Enlightenment*, 45. On the Jewish, kabbalist connections, see André Neher, *David Gans (1541–1613)* (Paris, 1974). Evans, Yates, and Neher all write explicitly of the *fin de siècle* atmosphere of the 1590s, the earliest century's end to be regularly attributed such an atmosphere by modern historians.

145. Peter J. French, *John Dee: The World of an Elizabethan Magus* (London, 1972); Firth, *Apocalyptic Tradition in Reformation Britain*, 132–49 on Napier; A. Kent Hieatt, *Short Time's Endless Monument* (NY, 1960) on the *Epithalamion*, and cf. Alastair Fowler, *Spenser and the Numbers of Time* (London, 1964), esp. 260–88; Yates, *Rosicrucian Enlightenment*, 22, 59, 74–75, and throughout.

146. Harvey, *A Discoursive Probleme*, 91; Manuel and Manuel, *Utopian Thought*, 243–60, 289–308; David A. Roberts, "Mystery to mathematics flown: time and reality in the Renaissance," *Centennial Review* 19,3 (1975) 136–56. Cf. Yates, *Rosicrucian Enlightenment*, 62–64.

147. *Post Boy* 895 (Dec. 31, 1700–Jan. 2, 1701).

148. *Le jubilé de l'an MDCC* (Amsterdam, 1701) 2–4, 120; Louis de Rouvroy, Duc de Saint-Simon, *Mémoires*, ed. A. De Boislisle (Paris, 1890) VII, 3–5, 446–52.

149. *Post Boy* 747 (Jan. 20–23, 1700); George Farquhar, *The Constant Couple, or A Trip to the Jubilee* in *The Works of George Farquhar*, ed. Charles Stonehill (NY, 1967) I, xviii, 100, 105, 118; *London Gazette* (Jan. 11–15, 1699/1700); Samuel Pepys, *Private Correspondence and Miscellaneous Papers*, ed. J. R. Tanner (NY, 1926) I, 303, letter from John Jackson, March 12/23, 1699/1700; *Le jubilé*, 17; Elisabeth Charlotte, Duchesse d'Orléans, *A Woman's Life in the Court of the Sun King. Letters of Liselotte von der Pfalz, 1652–1722*, trans. Elborg Forster (Baltimore, 1984) 119, with missing phrase inserted from Gertrude S. Stevenson, trans. and ed., *The Letters of Madame* (NY, 1924) I, 193–94.

150. Pepys, *Private Correspondence*, I, 260, 264, 285, 303, 304, 314, 324.

151. Gershom Scholem, *Sabbatai Ṣevi: The Mystical Messiah 1626–1676* (Princeton, 1975 [1957]), quote on 828.

152. Gershom Scholem, "The Crypto-Jewish sect of the Dönmeh (Sabbatians) in Turkey," in his *The Messianic Idea in Judaism* (NY, 1971) 142–66, and cf. Stephen Sharot, *Messianism, Mysticism, and Magic: A Sociological Analysis of Jewish Religious Movements* (Chapel Hill, 1982) 127–44; Robert O. Crummey, *The Old Believers & The World of Antichrist* (Madison, 1970); Jonathan P. Clark, " 'In der Hoffnung besserer Zeiten': Philipp Jakob Spener's reception of Quirinus Kuhlmann," *Pietismus und Neuzeit* 12 (1986) 54–69; Johannes Wallmann, *Philip Jakob Spener und die Anfang des Pietismus* (Tübingen, 1970) 283–330; George D. Henderson, *Mystics of the Northeast* (Aberdeen, 1934); George Balsama, "Madame Guyon, heterodox," *Church History* 42 (1973) 350–65; William Lamont, "The Muggletonians, 1652–1979," *Past & Present* 99 (1983) 22–40, and debate with Christopher Hill in 104 (1984) 153ff.;

Richard T. Vann, *The Social Development of English Quakerism, 1655–1755* (Cambridge, MA, 1969); Christopher Hill, "John Mason and the end of the world," in his *Puritanism and Revolution* (NY, 1969) 311–23; Julius F. Sachse, *The German Pietists of Provincial Pennsylvania 1694–1708* (Philadelphia, 1895), more accessible in a summary by Ernest Schell, "Hermit of the Wissahickon: Johannes Kelpius and the Chapter of Perfection," *American History Illustrated* 16 (Oct. 1981) 24–28, 48; Hillel Schwartz, *The French Prophets: The History of a Millenarian Group in Eighteenth-Century England* (Berkeley, 1980); Jean Seguy, "Millénarisme et 'ordres adventistes': Grignion de Montfort et les 'Apôtres des Derniers Temps,' " *Archives de sciences sociales des religions* 53 (1982) 23–48. Russian Old Believers did expect the end in 1699 and again in 1702, but in their Byzantine calendar, the century had turned in 1692 = 7400 A.M. See Dimitrij Tschizewskij, *Russian Intellectual History*, trans. John C. Osborne, ed. Martin P. Rice (Ann Arbor, 1978) 154–55.

153. Hillel Schwartz, *Knaves, Fools, Madmen, and That Subtile Effluvium* (Gainesville, 1978); J. G. A. Pocock, "Post-Puritan England and the problem of the Enlightenment," in *Culture & Politics from Puritanism to the Enlightenment*, ed. Perez Zagorin (Berkeley, 1980) 91–111; Michael Heyd, "The reaction to enthusiasm in the seventeenth century," *Journal of Modern History* 53 (1981) 258–80; Capp, *English Almanacs*, 176–79; Richard Kirby, *Vates Astrologicus or, England's Astrological Prophet* (London, 1683) quote on 45, nearly identical to John Holwell, *Catastrophe mundi* (London, 1682) 90; *A Brief Description of the Future History of Europe from Anno 1650, to Anno 1710* (London, 1659) 7–9; a Learned Pen, *Catastrophe Mundi* (London, 1683) 80, 113; *A Collection of Twenty-Three Prophecies and Predictions of the Famous Michael Nostradamus, the Learned Astrologer of France, As They Concern and Point at These Times* (London, 1690); [George Wither, comp.], *A Collection of Many Wonderful Prophesies Relating to the English Nation* (London, 1691) 27 for "Chronogrammistry"; *Annus Sophiae Jubilaeus, The Sophick Constitution* (London, 1700) on adepts; Henry J. Forman, *The Story of Prophecy* (London, 1936) 215–17, on the German invention in 1692 of prophecies put into the 13th-century mouth of Herman, Abbot of Lehnin; T.F., *Eclectical Chiliasm* (London, 1700).

154. Frank Parise, comp., *The Book of Calendars* (NY, 1982) 295–96 for convenient chart of dates of calendar conversions; Burkhardt, *Jahrhundertrechnung*, 117, on controversy. The new German Protestant calendar was not identical to the Gregorian—see O. Zöckler, "Calendar, the Christian," *The New Schaff-Herzog Religious Encyclopedia* (Grand Rapids, 1958) II, 345. Peter the Great decreed that, beginning in 1700 A.D., the Russian year would begin on January 1st, not September 1st, and he ordered all Muscovites to congratulate each other on the new New Year's Day, but he converted Russia from the Byzantine to the old Julian calendar, not to the Gregorian calendar. Eugene Schuyler, *Peter the Great, Emperor of Russia* (London, 1884) I, 419–21.

155. H. Bunker Wright and Monroe K. Spears, eds., *The Literary Works of Matthew Prior* (Oxford, 1959) I, 161–81, quotes from lines 19–22, 336–40, 482–87. Janus is the poem's supervening deity.

156. James Kinsley, ed., *The Poems of John Dryden* (Oxford, 1958) IV, 1758–1765.

157. John Locke, *Correspondence*, ed. E. S. De Beer (Oxford, 1982) VI, 745–46, and VII, 35, 37, 45, 206, 210, 213–25, quotes 206, 213–14.

158. *London Post* (Jan. 1–3, 1700/01); "Diary of Samuel Sewall, 1674–1729," *Massachusetts Historical Society Collections*, ser. 5, 6 (1879) 1, 27–28; Sacvan Bercovitch, "Horologicals to chronometricals: the rhetoric of the jeremiad," *Literary Monographs* 3 (1970) 1–124; idem, *The American Jeremiad* (Madison, WI, 1978). The English—and the New Englanders—called the first of January New Year's Day but held back the official (Julian calendar) year change to Annunciation or Lady Day, March 25th, whence both the day of the month *and* the year would differ from the Gregorian calendar in the period from January 1st through March 24th. See A. F. Pollard, "New Year's Day and leap year in English history," *English Historical Review* 55 (1940) 177–93.

159. Contrast, however, Paul Hazard, *The European Mind: The Critical Years (1680–1715)*, trans. J. Lewis May (New Haven, 1953).

160. Antoine Furetière, *Dictionnaire universel* (The Hague, 1690) s.v. "Siècle"; Abel Boyer, *The Royal Dictionary Abridged* (Menston, Yorks., 1971 [1700]) s.v. "Siècle" and "Age"; Burkhardt, *Jahrhundertrechnung*, 5, 8, 41, 45, 63; Lehmann, "Einteilung und Datierung nach Jahrhunderten"; W. Feldmann, "Jahrhundert und seine Sippe," *Zeitschrift für deutsche Wortforschung* 5 (1904) 229–37; Fritz Schalk, "Uber Epoche und Historie," in Fritz Schalk and Hans Diller, *Studien zur Periodisierung und Epochbegriff* (Mainz, 1972) 15–20; Klaus Arnold, "Das 'finstere' Mittelalter. Zur Genese und Phänomenologie eines Fehlurteils," *Saeculum* 32 (1981) 287–88; Johan Hendrik Van der Pot, *De Periodisering der Geschiedenis* ('sGravenhage, 1951); Ludwig Rohner, *Kalendargeschichte und Kalendar* (Wiesbaden, 1978) 28–30.

161. Agrippa d'Aubigné, *Les tragiques* (1616), Livre II, vers 77, in his *Oeuvres complètes*, eds. Réaume and de Caussade (Geneva, 1967 [1873]) IV, 73. D'Aubigné in 1616 wrote a world history whose contours were defined by the end of the 16th century: *Histoire universelle depuis 1550 jusqu'en 1601*. On nicknames, see Burkhardt, *Jahrhundertrechnung*, 45, 53, and ch. 10.

162. Jacques Barchilon and Peter Flinders, *Charles Perrault* (Boston, 1981) 43 for quote; Marc Soriano, *Les contes de Perrault: culture savante et traditions populaires* (Paris, 1968) ch. 6; Charles Perrault, *Hommes illustres qui ont paru en France pendant ce siècle*, 2 vols. (Paris, 1696–1700). Cf. Robert Darnton, *The Great Cat Massacre and Other Episodes in French Cultural History* (NY, 1984) 9–72. See Keith Thomas, *Religion and the Decline of Magic* (NY, 1971) 236–37, 613–14, on Goodwin Wharton, English Lord of the Admiralty, and his collaborations with fairyland in the 1690s; fairy tales at centuries' ends just might come true.

163. John Hayward, ed. and trans., *The Letters of Saint-Evremond* (NY, 1972) 355; "Diary of Samuel Sewall," January 15, 1699/1700; *Post-Angel* (Jan. 1701) 39. At this time also began the fascination with last words. See Karl S. Guthke, "Anthologies of last words," *Harvard Library Bulletin* 35 (1987) 311–46.

164. G. G. Coulton, comp., *Social Life in Britain from the Conquest to the Reformation* (NY, 1968 [1918]) 50–53; R. C. Fowler and M. T. Martin, "Legal proofs of age," *English Historical Review* 22 (1907) 101–03, 526–27; Ralph Linton and Adelia Linton, *The Lore of Birthdays* (NY, 1952) esp. 43, 47; Thomas, *Religion and the Decline of Magic*, 615–23; Nigel Thrift, "Owners' time and own time: the making of a capitalist time consciousness, 1300–1800," in *Space and Time in Geography*, ed. Allan Pred (Lund, 1981) 58–60; Landes, *Revolution in Time*, 125–28 and noting, 129–30, the introduction of the first (inaccurate) second hands on watches; Worthington C. Ford, ed., "Diary of Cotton Mather, 1681–1708," *Massachusetts*

Historical Society Collections ser. 7, 8 (1911) 335, 393–94. The rise of the birthday may also have been another manifestation of the early modern concern with pinpointing and acknowledging sources. See David Quint, *Origin and Originality in Renaissance Literature* (New Haven, 1983).

165. Peter Laslett, "The history of aging and the aged," in his *Family Life and Illicit Love in Earlier Generations* (Cambridge, 1977) 174–213; John Demos, *Past, Present, and Personal: The Family and the Life Course in American History* (NY, 1986) 128–29, 148–56; Gene Brucker, ed., *Two Memoirs of Renaissance Florence*, trans. Julia Martines (NY, 1967) 124; Robert Latham and William Matthews, eds., *The Diary of Samuel Pepys* (Berkeley, 1974) VIII, 423, for Sept. 6, 1667; Sacvan Bercovitch, *The Puritan Origins of the American Self* (New Haven, 1975) esp. ch. 2 on Mather and the millennium, as also David Levin, *Cotton Mather: The Young Life of the Lord's Remembrancer, 1663–1703* (Cambridge, MA, 1988) ch. 6, and Stephen J. Stein, "Transatlantic extensions: apocalyptic in early New England," in *The Apocalypse in English Renaissance Thought*, 266–98.

166. John Cotton, *Exposition upon the Thirteenth Chapter of the Revelation* (1655), reprinted in *The End of the World* (NY, 1982) 253 for quote on 666; Paolo Rossi, *Clavis Universalis* (Milan, 1960) ch. 7; Michel Foucault, *The Order of Things* (NY, 1970 [1966]); Mary M. Slaughter, *Universal Language and Scientific Taxonomy in the Seventeenth Century* (Cambridge, 1982).

167. Werner Hullen, "The paradigm of John Wilkins' thesaurus," in *The History of Lexicography*, ed. R. R. K. Hartmann (Amsterdam, 1986) 115–25; Tony Davies, "The ark in flames: science, language and education in seventeenth-century England," in *The Figural and the Literal*, eds. Andrew E. Benjamin et al. (Manchester, 1987) 83–102; James Knowlson, *Universal Language Schemes in England and France, 1600–1800* (Toronto, 1975); James Holstun, *A Rational Millennium: Puritan Utopias of Seventeenth-Century England and America* (NY, 1987) 137–42; Vivian Salmon, *The Study of Language in Seventeenth-Century England* (Amsterdam, 1979) 153 for quote from Cave Beck, *Universal Character* (London, 1657) sig. A7r; Barbara J. Shapiro, *John Wilkins 1614–72* (Berkeley, 1969); Robert L. Collison, *A History of Foreign-Language Dictionaries* (London, 1982). Note also the publication of R. A. Feuillet's *Chorégraphie* in 1700, providing a set of characters and rules for the notation of dance, parallel to those used in music.

168. Murray Cohen, *Sensible Words: Linguistic Practice in England, 1640–1785* (Baltimore, 1977) chs. 1–2; Hans Burkhardt, "The Leibnizian *Characteristica Universalis* as link between grammar and logic," in *Speculative Grammar, Universal Grammar and Philosophical Analysis of Language*, eds. Dino Buzzetti and Maurizio Ferriani (Amsterdam, 1987) 43–64.

169. Cohen, *Sensible Words*, 60–61; Barbara J. Shapiro, *Probability and Certainty in Seventeenth-Century England* (Princeton, 1983) 252–56; Stanley E. Fish, *Self-Consuming Artifacts* (Berkeley, 1972) 374–82 on "self-satisfied" prose.

170. Shapiro, *Probability and Certainty*, 257 for quote; Gale E. Christianson, *In the Presence of the Creator: Isaac Newton and His Times* (NY, 1984) esp. 203–36, 257–65; J. E. McGuire and P. M. Rattansi, "Newton and the 'Pipes of Pan,' " *Notes and Records of the Royal Society* 21 (1966) 108–43; Frank E. Manuel, *A Portrait of Isaac Newton* (Washington, 1979 [1968]) chs. 8, 17; Margaret C. Jacob, *The Newtonians and the English Revolution 1689–1720* (Ithaca, 1976) 116 on Newton and the year 2000.

171. Christianson, *In the Presence of the Creator*, 63, 429; Manuel, *A Portrait of Isaac Newton*, ch. 15; Woldemar Guerrier, ed., *Leibniz in seinen Beziehungen zu Russland und Peter dem Grossen* (Hildesheim, 1975) 48 for chronostichon; Gottfried Wilhelm Leibniz, *Philosophical Papers and Letters*, ed. and trans. Leroy E. Loemker (Chicago, 1956) II, 837, letter of March 24/ April 3, 1699, to Burcher de Volder.

172. G. W. Leibniz, *Annales Imperii Occidentis Brunsvicenses* in *Gesammelte Werke*, ed. G. H. Pertz, (Hildesheim, 1966) Section 1, vol. III, 746 for quote; idem, *Philosophical Papers*, II, 797; Ian Hacking, *The Emergence of Probability* (Cambridge, 1975) 184–85; Jacob, *The Newtonians*; and on globalism cf. David E. Mungello, *Curious Land: Jesuit Accommodation and the Origins of Sinology* (Wiesbaden, 1985) esp. 320.

173. E. P. Hutchinson, *The Population Debate: The Development of Conflicting Theories up to 1900* (NY, 1967) esp. 45–68, 110–15; James H. Cassedy, *Demography in Early America: Beginnings of the Statistical Mind, 1600–1800* (Cambridge, MA, 1969) 7–11, 68–69, 118–20; D. E. C. Eversley et al., *An Introduction to English Historical Demography* (NY, 1966) 174–77; Franklin L. Ford, *Strasbourg in Transition, 1648–1789* (NY, 1958) 115; Peter Burke, "Tradition and experience: the idea of decline from Bruni to Gibbon," *Daedalus* 105 (1975) 137–52.

174. R. Carlyle Buley, *The American Life Convention, 1906–1952: A Study in the History of Life Insurance* (NY, 1953) I, 16–20. Edmund Halley during this period constructed the first accurate table of the value of life annuities.

175. *Post-Angel* (Feb. 1701) 83–86; Albert Bayet, *Le suicide et la morale* (Paris, 1922) 581–82, citing a letter of July 2, 1699, from La Palatine on the great number of suicides, for which Bayet could find no legal or statistical evidence; Michael MacDonald, "The secularization of suicide in England 1660–1800," *Past & Present* 111 (1986) 50–97; John Adams, *An Essay concerning Self-Murther* (London, 1700) sig. A3v; and cf. Capp, *English Almanacs*, 129–30.

176. Marjorie Hope Nicolson, *Mountain Gloom and Mountain Glory* (NY, 1959) 184–270, quotes on 193n.–194n., 206, 223; Jacob, *The Newtonians*, 107–20.

177. Nicolson, *Mountain Gloom*, 257 for quote; David Kubrin, "Newton and the cyclical cosmos: providence and the mechanical philosophy," in *Science and Religious Belief*, ed. C. A. Russell (London, 1973) 147–69; Stephen Jay Gould, *Time's Arrow, Time's Cycle: Myth and Metaphor in the Discovery of Geological Time* (Cambridge, MA, 1987) 21–59; Simon Schaffer, "Newton's comets and the transformation of astrology," in *Astrology, Science and Society*, ed. Patrick Curry (Woodbridge, Suffolk, 1987) 219–43.

178. James E. Force, *William Whiston, Honest Newtonian* (Cambridge, 1985) ch. 2, and see 114–18 on dating the Millennium; John Ray, *Miscellaneous Discourses concerning the Dissolution and Changes of the World* (Hildesheim, 1968 [1692]) 39; Nicolson, *Mountain Gloom* 245–48, and see 189–90 on Burnet's *Sacred Theory* provoking yet another *fin de siècle* debate between Ancients and Moderns.

179. Charles Augustus Ward, *Oracles of Nostradamus* (London, 1940 [1891]) epigraph from Albumasar's *De Magnis Conjunctionibus*, Tract. II, Different. 8; Leoni, *Nostradamus*, 340–41;

Prophetic Conjectures on the French Revolution (Philadelphia, 1794) 21–22, 36, 41, and cf. Christopher Love, *Prophecies of the Reverend Christopher Love* (Boston, 1794) 7; Robert Fleming, *A Discourse on the Rise and Fall of Papacy* (Boston, 1794 [1701]) 47, 49. Cf. Jennifer Britnell and Derek Stubbs, "The *Mirabilis Liber*: its compilation and influence," *Journal of the Warburg & Courtauld Institutes* 49 (1986) 132–33, 137.

180. Clarke Garrett, *Respectable Folly: Millenarians and the French Revolution in France and England* (Baltimore, 1975) 45–46, 59, 168–72, 186–88, 205; [Joseph L. Towers, comp.], *Illustrations of Prophecy*, 2 vols. (London, 1796); *Characteristics in the Prophecies Applicable to, and Descriptive of, the Power and Duration of the French Republic* (NY, 1798); N. M. Dumaka (?), *Prophéties annoncées à tous les peuple de l'univers, par Nostradamus sur les événements les plus remarquables qui doivent arriver sur la terre pendant cette année* (Paris, 179–); *Réflexions et jugemens prophétiques, adressés aux patriotes français, par le prophète Nostradamus* (Paris, 1790); *Prophetic Conjectures*, quote on 78; Reinhart Koselleck, *Futures Past: On the Semantics of Historical Time*, trans. Keith Tribe (Cambridge, MA, 1985) 18, 39–54; Bernard Yack, *The Longing for Total Revolution* (Princeton, 1986); *Strange and wonderful . . .* (London, 1682) quote on 4.

181. Mme. du Hausset, *Mémoires*, ed. Crawfurd (Paris, 1824) xix; Thomas Robbins, *A Century Sermon* (Danbury, 1801) 9; Garrett, *Respectable Folly*, 153–54.

182. Georges Lefebvre, *The Great Fear of 1789*, trans. Joan White (NY, 1973 [1932]); Conrad L. Donakowski, *A Muse for the Masses: Ritual and Music in an Age of Democratic Revolution* (Chicago, 1977) 37–75; Mona Ozouf, *La fête révolutionnaire, 1789–1799* (Paris, 1976).

183. Christian Moreau, *Une mystique révolutionnaire: Suzette Labrousse* (Paris, 1886) iv; Garrett, *Respectable Folly*, 31–76, quote on 52. On prophecy and the phases of the Revolution, see esp. Hywel M. Davies, "Morgan John Rhys and James Bicheno: Anti-Christ and the French Revolution in England and Wales," *Bulletin of the Board of Celtic Studies* 29 (1980) 111–27.

184. Garrett, *Respectable Folly*, 118–19; *The Millennium; a Poem, in Three Cantos* (London, 1800) 13; Joanna Southcott, *The Strange Effects of Faith*, 2nd ed. (London, 1802) 5, 20, 24, 241. The word "ultimatum" was itself new to the English language in the 18th century.

185. Garrett, *Respectable Folly*, 176–77 *et passim*; Nathaniel Brassey Halhed, *Calculation on the Commencement of the Millennium* (London, 1795) 9; Thomas Williams, *The Age of Credulity* (Philadelphia, 1796) 34; Jacques Marx, "Problèmes d'Illuminisme," *Problèmes d'histoire du Christianisme* 5 (1974/75) 81–106; J. F. C. Harrison, *The Second Coming: Popular Millenarianism, 1780–1850* (New Brunswick, NJ, 1979); Anthony F. C. Wallace, *The Death and Rebirth of the Seneca* (NY, 1972) ch. 8; Robert Darnton, *Mesmerism and the End of the Enlightenment in France* (Cambridge, MA, 1968).

186. Ozouf, *La fête révolutionnaire*, ch. 7; *Gentleman's Magazine* 70 (April 1800) 381 on Lalande; Margaret M. O'Dwyer, *The Papacy in the Age of Napoleon and the Restoration* (Lanham, MD, 1985) 27–29; John Ashton, *Dawn of the Nineteenth Century in England* (Detroit, 1968 [1886]) 2 for Napoleon's letter, and Loren Reid, *Charles James Fox* (Columbia, MO, 1969) ch. 26 for ensuing English debate. The new metric system and the central zero of the new centigrade thermometer enhanced the decimal charm of 1800 as a starting point. In a

forthcoming paper, "Et la Révolution 'créa'—entre autres—le siècle," Daniel S. Milo argues that truly centurial thought became common only in consequence of the political drama of the French Revolution and the philosophical admiration for decimal clarity. He refers to Keith M. Baker, *Condorcet: From Natural to Social Mathematics* (Chicago, 1975) 109–28.

187. Mrs. Hester Lynch Thrale, *Thraliana*, 2nd ed. (Oxford, 1951) II, 1003, 1008; E. P. Thompson, *The Making of the English Working Class* (NY, 1963) 26–54, 161–62; Thomas R. Knox, "Thomas Spence: the trumpet of Jubilee," *Past & Present* 76 (1977) 75–98; Thomas Spence, *The Important Trial* (1803) letters 12 and 14, trans. Arthur W. Waters in *Spence and His Political Works* (Leamington Spa, 1917). The Dickens reference is of course to the opening of *Tale of Two Cities* (1859).

188. Joseph Slater, ed., *The Correspondence of Emerson and Carlyle* (NY, 1964) 501. See Ronald Paulson, *Representations of Revolution (1789–1820)* (New Haven, 1983) on the artistic problem of depicting the newness of the French Revolution, and Morton D. Paley on *The Apocalyptic Sublime* (New Haven, 1986) that arose at century's end.

189. Werner Krauss, "Der Jahrhundertbegriff im 18. Jahrhundert," in his *Studien zur deutschen und französischen Aufklärung* (Berlin, 1963) 25–26, with quotes from Juste van Effen (p. 14), Princess Luise Dorothea von Sachsen-Gotha-Meiningen (p. 15), the *Lorgnette philosophique* (p. 11), Beaumarchais (p. 17), and Poinsinct de Sivry (p. 23).

190. Burkhardt, *Jahrhundertrechnung*, 93; Koselleck, *Futures Past*, 246; John Stuart Mill, "The spirit of the age," (five essays of 1831) in his *Collected Works*, eds. Ann P. Robson and John M. Robson (Toronto, 1986) XXII, 227–29, and cf. Benjamin Constant's "Esquisse d'un essai sur la littérature du 18e siècle" (1807) in Roland Mortier, *Clartés et ombres du Siècle des Lumières* (Geneva, 1969) 154–56; Moriz Heyne et al., eds., *Deutsches Wörterbuch von Jacob Grimm und Wilhelm Grimm* (Leipzig, 1956) XV, 558, s.v. "Zeitgeist"; Amos Funkenstein, "Periodization and self-understanding in the Middle Ages and early modern times," *Medievalia et Humanistica* n.s. 5 (1974) 3–5, and cf. Isaiah Berlin, *Vico and Herder* (NY, 1976). See also Stephen Bann, *The Clothing of Clio* (Cambridge, 1984) ch. 4 on the ordering by centuries of the Parisian Musée des Petits-Augustins.

191. *London Chronicle* (Jan. 1–3, 1801) 11; T. Mot, "Letter," *Gentleman's Magazine* 70, 1 (Jan. 1800) 3; "On the NEW CENTURY," *Newburyport Herald*, reprinted in *Massachusetts Spy, or Worcester Gazette* (Jan. 7, 1801) 2; "Progress of Truth and Genius Thro' the Eighteenth Century," poem in the *American Mercury* (Jan. 2, 1800) 4; "The Enlightened Eighteenth Century," *Columbian Centinel* (Jan. 14, 1801) 1; Burkhardt, *Jahrhundertrechnung*, 121–22. On formal French retrospectives, see Roland Mortier, Le *"Tableau littéraire de la France au XVIIIe siècle"* (Brussels, 1972) esp. 13.

192. "Address to the public," *The Mercury and New-England Palladium* (Jan. 2, 1801) 1; Bury, *The Idea of Progress*; Robert A. Nisbet, *History of the Idea of Progress* (NY, 1980); John Evans, "Reflections on the commencement of the nineteenth century," *Monthly Visitor and Entertaining Pocket Companion* 12 (1801) 9, 12; David Ramsay, *A Review of the Improvements, Progress and State of Medicine in the XVIIIth Century* (Charleston, SC, 1801) 44; *New Haven Messenger* article reprinted in the *Political Repository* (Jan. 27, 1801) 1. It was in this context that Robert Burns's version of "Auld Lang Syne" was published in 1799.

193. Ignatius F. Clarke, *The Pattern of Expectation, 1644–2001* (NY, 1979) 27–28, 37; Louis Sebastien Mercier, *Memoirs of the Year Two Thousand Five Hundred*, trans. W. Hooper (Philadelphia, 1795 [London, 1772; Paris, 1770]) 16, 19, 20, 170–71, 236–37, 303; Manuel and Manuel, *Utopian Thought*, 458–59.

194. "History of our own times from the beginning of the current century," *Bell's Weekly Messenger* (Jan. 11, 1801) 1; *[Peter] Porcupine's Gazette*, a running battle, often reproducing Fenno's columns: (Oct. 31, 1798) 3; (Nov. 7, 1798) 3; (Nov. 9, 1798) 3, with Fenno quote; (Nov. 12, 1798) 2, with Cobbett quote; (Nov. 13, 1798) 3; (Nov. 14, 1798) 2–3; (Nov. 17, 1798) 3.

195. *[Peter] Porcupine's Gazette* (Nov. 9, 1798) 3; Henry D. Biddle, ed. *Extracts from the Journal of Elizabeth Drinker* (Philadelphia, 1889) 217, 336, 354–56, 366, 370.

196. "In what century is the year 1800?" *Kentucky Gazette* (Jan. 2, 1800) 2; Philomathes, "Letter to Mr. Printer," *Quebec Gazette*, Supplement (Jan. 2, 1800) 2; *Gentleman's Magazine*, Supplement, 69 (1799) 1176, and 70, 1 (1800) 132–34, 381; Burkhardt, *Jahrhundertrechnung*, 118 for German articles; William Holland, *Paupers and Pig-Killers: The Diary of William Holland, a Somerset Parson, 1799–1818* (Gloucester, 1984) 54. On the wagers, see F.H.B., "Letter to the editor," *London Times* (Jan. 1, 1900) 11:6; Alleyne Fitzherbert St. Helens, letter to Dr. Richard Pulteney, January 2, 1800, in Osborn Files, Beinecke Library, Yale University; Nowell C. Smith, ed., *Letters of Sydney Smith* (Oxford, 1953) I, 52–53; J.S.L., "When a century ends," *[Dawson's] Historical Magazine* 2 (1858) 12–13.

197. Henry James Pye, *Carmen Seculare for the Year 1800* (London, 1800) iii, 28; *London Review* 3 (1800) 353; *Gentleman's Magazine* 70 (Jan. 1800) 69; Samuel T. Coleridge, *Collected Letters*, ed. E. L. Griggs (Oxford, 1956) I, 557, 560; Charles Knight, *Passages of a Working Life during Half a Century* (London, 1864) I, 17–18, 28; A. Aspinall, ed., *The Later Correspondence of George III* (Cambridge, 1967) III, 309–10, 465, 468. West's windows, unshattered, were never completely installed; George objected to any "Bedlamite scene from the Revelation." See Allen Staley, "West's Death on the Pale Horse," *Detroit Institute of Arts Bulletin* 58,3 (1980) 137–49.

198. *Indépendance Belge* (Jan. 1, 1901) 3:1 on Napoleon in 1801; H. C. Robbins Landon, *Haydn: Chronicle and Works* (Bloomington, 1977) IV, 572–601, and V, 22.

199. Heinrich Düntzer, *Life of Goethe*, trans. T. W. Lyster (London, 1883) II, 180–81, 187 –88; Erwin Streitfeld and Viktor Žmegač, eds., *Schillers Briefe* (Königstein/Ts., 1983) 398 –99; Edgar A. Bowring, trans., *The Poems of Schiller*, 2nd ed. (NY, 1874?) 284–85; Johann Gottfried Herder, *Briefe*, ed. Wilhelm Dobbek and Günter Arnold (Weimar, 1984) VIII, 192; *Remains of the late Mrs. Richard Trench*, cited by A.G., "Letter to the editor," *London Times* (Jan. 6, 1900) 12:5; Asa Briggs, "Towards 1900: the nineteenth century faces the future," in his *Collected Essays* (Brighton, 1985) II, 292, on the Schlegel piece. Earlier, on *Silvesternacht*, 1799, Kotzebue's comedy *Das neue Jahrhundert* had had its premiere: a hypochondriac, believing he will die on the last day of the 18th century, fervently hopes that it does not end until 1801. See Doris Maurer, *August von Kotzebue* (Bonn, 1979) 152–57.

200. "Hundred years ago," *Washington Evening Star* (Dec. 29, 1900) 15:2, citing newspapers from 1801; Ephraim Bateman, "Journal," *Vineland Historical Magazine* 13 (1928) 111; Louisa

Adams Park, entry for "January 1801 1st Thursday" in her diary, 1800–1801, in Park Family Papers, American Antiquarian Society, Worcester, MA.

201. *Connecticut Courant* (Jan. 5, 1801), cited in F. G. Franklin, "Century once more," *Nation* 70 (Jan. 25, 1900) 71; W., "Letter to the editor," *Columbian Centinel* (Jan. 8, 1800) 1, on the ordinal/cardinal confusion; Herder, *Briefe*, VIII, 193, on the pretzel, and see his journal *Adrastea* for 1802 on "Säkularische Hoffnungen," in *Sämmtliche Werke*, ed. Bernhard Suphen (Hildesheim, 1967 [1885]) XXIII, 485–92.

202. Laurence Goldstein, *Ruins and Empire: The Evolution of a Theme in Augustan and Romantic Literature* (Pittsburgh, 1977) ch. 8 on Wordsworth at Grasmere; Carlos Baker, ed., *William Wordsworth's The Prelude with a Selection from the Shorter Poems, the Sonnets, The Recluse, and The Excursion* (NY, 1954) 201 for lines 804–19 of *Home in Grasmere*; William Wordsworth, *The Prelude: A Parallel Text*, ed. J. C. Maxwell (Harmondsworth, 1971) 36, edition of 1805–06, lines 36, 41; H. S. Harris, *Hegel's Development. II. Night Thoughts (Jena, 1801–1806)* (Oxford, 1983) xix; Hannah Arendt, *Rahel Varnhagen*, rev. ed., trans. Richard Winston and Clara Winston (NY, 1974 [1957]) ch. 3; Douglas Botting, *Humboldt and the Cosmos* (NY, 1973) 65, 76; L. Kellner, *Alexander von Humboldt* (London, 1963) 34, 44; Hanno Beck, *Alexander von Humboldt* (Wiesbaden, 1959) I, 152ff.

203. Entries for January 31 and December 31, 1800, from an extract of entries from John Pintard's diaries, January 1798 to June 1801, and entry for January 1, 1801, from his journal of studies, Box 2A and Box 2, Pintard Papers, New-York Historical Society. (Punctuation slightly amended for the sake of modern legibility.)

204. François René de Chateaubriand, *Mémoires d'Outre-Tombe*, eds. Maurice Levaillant and Georges Moulinier (Paris, 1951) 936, my translation; Ralph Straus, *Lloyd's: The Gentlemen at the Coffee-House* (NY, 1938) 132–36 on lifeboats; Ramsay, *Review of the Improvements*, 15 on rescue societies; Armand Hoog, "Who invented the *mal du siècle*?" *Yale French Studies* 13 (1954) 42–44.

205. R. B. McDowell, ed., *The Correspondence of Edmund Burke* (Cambridge, 1969) VIII, 363; K. F. Helleiner, "An essay on the rise of historical pessimism in the nineteenth century," *Canadian Journal of Economics and Political Science* 7 (1942) 514–36; E. de Selincourt, ed., *The Poetical Works of William Wordsworth*, 2nd ed. (Oxford, 1952) II, 264–65, "French Revolution as it appeared to enthusiasts at its commencement" (1804); John Aikin, *Letters from a Father to a Son. II. Written in the Years 1798 and 1799* (NY, 1971 [1800]) 3; Henri Brunschwig, *Enlightenment and Romanticism in Eighteenth-Century Prussia*, trans. Frank Jellinek (Chicago, 1974) chs. 9–11, and 163 for quote from Schlegel on "devouring need," 201 for quote from Ludwig Tieck's *William Lovell* (1795). At this time the word "oxymoron" began to be used in English literature.

206. *London Chronicle* (Jan. 1–3, 1801) 10c, and (Dec. 31, 1799–Jan. 2, 1800) Postscript, 7; Blake's "Milton" (1804–08) in David V. Erdman, ed., *The Poetry and Prose of William Blake* (Garden City, NY, 1965) 94–143, esp. 125–26; Ernst Benz, *Akzeleration der Zeit als geschichtliches und heilsgeschichtliches Problem* (Mainz, 1977) esp. 32ff., on Jung-Stilling as the "Prophet of Acceleration"; Alice Kuzniar, "Philosophic chiliasm: generating the future or delaying the end?" *Eighteenth-Century Studies* 19 (1985) 1–20; Meyer Abrams, *Natural Supernaturalism* (NY, 1971) esp. 30 (Hölderlin, late 1790s: "Let all be changed from its

Foundations!"), 325 (Hegel, 1807: "It surely is not difficult to see that our time is a time of birth and transition to a new period"), 329–34, 348–54; Lawrence Poston, "Millites and millenarians: the context of Carlyle's 'Signs of the Times,' " *Victorian Studies* 26 (1983) 385, Carlyle quoting Jean Paul, "Our present time is indeed a criticising and critical time, hovering between the wish and the inability to believe"; Koselleck, *Futures Past*, esp. 280–83, 252 for quote from E. M. Arndt, writing in 1807 on the *Geist der Zeit*.

207. Landes, *Revolution in Time*, 130–31; E. P. Thompson, "Time, work-discipline, and industrial capitalism," *Past & Present* 38 (1967) 56–97; Wilcox, *Measure of Times Past*, 7–8, 203, 207; Thomas Robert Malthus, *An Essay on the Principle of Population* (1798) eds. E. A. Wrigley and David Souden, in his *Works* (London, 1986) I, introduction and first lines of text; Hutchinson, *Population Debate*, 110–63, esp. 156; George Rudé, *Paris and London in the Eighteenth Century: Studies in Popular Protest* (NY, 1970); "TWO MEN BURNT ALIVE, In the United States, near the beginning of the nineteenth century!" *Otsego Herald* (Jan. 15, 1801) 2.

208. Stephen Toulmin and June Goodfield, *The Discovery of Time* (Harmondsworth, 1965) ch. 7, esp. 178 on Buffon's 93,000 years; Jean-Baptiste François-Xavier Cousin de Grainville, *The Last Man; or Omegarus and Syderia. A Romance in Futurity* (London, 1806 [1805])—and its numerous imitations, for which see Clarke, *Patterns of Expectation*, 44–45; Hoog, "Who invented the *mal du siècle?*" 43–44; Brunschwig, *Enlightenment and Romanticism*, 220–21 on suicides; Mary Shelley, *The Last Man* (London, 1985 [1826]) 192, 231, 337, 340. Another sort of last man was Faust; although Goethe's *Faust* did not appear until 1808, Faust was almost ubiquitous during the 1790s. See E. M. Butler, *The Fortunes of Faust* (Cambridge, 1952) 159–79; Frank Baron, *Faustus* (Munich, 1982) 107ff.

209. James Greig, ed., *The Farington Diary* (London, n.d.) I, 123, entry for December 16, 1795, on English sculptor John Flaxman's response to the ruins of Rome; Paul Zucker, *Fascination of Decay* (Ridgewood, NJ, 1968) 195–245; Goldstein, *Ruins and Empire*, frontispiece, 144, and throughout; Roland Mortier, *La poétique des ruines en France* (Geneva, 1974) 170 for Chateaubriand; Constantin François de Chasseboeuf, Comte de Volney, *The Ruins* (NY, 1926 [1791]) esp. ch. 13.

210. Edward Gibbon, *The History of the Decline and Fall of the Roman Empire*, ed. J. B. Bury (London, 1909 [1776–88]) IV, 180–81, and see entire issue of *Daedalus* 105 (1975). I draw "decay and uplift" from Gould, *Time's Arrow, Time's Cycle*, ch. 3, his discussion of James Hutton's *Theory of the Earth* (1795), who argued ahistorically for a world with "no vestige of a beginning,—no prospect of an end." On Condorcet's *Sketch* (trans. June Barraclough [NY, 1955] 4 for quote), see Manuel and Manuel, *Utopian Thought*, ch. 20.

211. Herbert Leventhal, *In the Shadow of the Enlightenment: Occultism and Renaissance Science in Eighteenth-Century America* (NY, 1976) 244–47 on planetary societies; Abraham Bradley, *New Theory of the Earth* (Wilkes-Barre, 1801) 9; Charles Sumner, *Prophetic Voices about America* (Boston, 1867) 277–81 on the popularity of Bp. George Berkeley's "Verses on the Prospect of Planting Arts and Learning in America" (1726), with its famous line, "Westward the course of empire takes its way"; William R. Hutchison, "New England's further errand: millennial belief and the beginnings of foreign missions," *Massachusetts Historical Society Proceedings* 94 (1982) 63 for Eamons. See also [Mathew Carey?], *Carmen pro Americani incol-*

umitate imperii aliquantulum more carminis secularis Horatiani (Philadelphia, 1800 or 1801); George A. Kelly, *Politics and Religious Consciousness in America* (New Brunswick, NJ, 1984) 125, 141.

212. *Massachusetts Spy* (Jan. 7, 1801) 2; William P. Cutler and Julius P. Cutler, eds., *Life, Journals and Correspondence of Rev. Manasseh Cutler* (Cincinnati, 1888) II, 10–15; Celadon, *The Golden Age; or, Future Glory of North-America Discovered by an Angel* (n.p., 1785) 12.

213. *The Messenger (New Haven)* (Jan. 1, 1800) 1, address in response to the President's speech of December 3, 1799, in which Adams had said much the same thing.

214. *Massachusetts Spy* (Jan. 7, 1801) 2; *Gazette of the United States* (Dec. 28, 1799) 3 and (Jan. 7, 1800) 3, Henry Lee's funeral oration to Congress; Mrs. Anne Ritson, *A Poetical Picture of America* (London, 1809) Part III, 49, on last words; George W. Corner, ed., *The Autobiography of Benjamin Rush* (Princeton, 1948) 248–49; *Massachusetts Mercury* (Dec. 26, 1800) 1 on the pyramid.

215. Seth Ames and W. B. Allen, eds., *Works of Fisher Ames* (Indianapolis, 1983 [1854]) II, 1404; *Spectator (New York)* (Jan. 3, 1801) 2; Lewis Beebe, entry for March 17, 1801, from vol. 3 of his diaries, 1799–1801, in Mss. Am .017, Historical Society of Pennsylvania; *American Citizen* (Jan. 1, 1801) 2.

216. *This Evening, January 1st, 1801. At Washington Hall, Part 1st. The celebrated Don Pedro Cloris, Will perform his Graceful and manly Feats of activity, on the slack Wire* (Salem, MA, 1801).

217. For examples of Etruscan themes, see *Two Discourses* (New Haven, 1801); Moses Welch, *A Century Sermon* (Hartford, 1801); Ruth Henshaw, entry for January 4, 1801, in her diary, 1789–1846, Ruth Henshaw Bascom Papers, American Antiquarian Society, Worcester, MA. For Claudian examples, see Timothy Dwight, *A Discourse on Some Events of the Last Century* (New Haven, 1801); Thomas Robbins, *A Century Sermon* (Danbury, 1801) and Increase N. Tarbox, ed., *Diary of Thomas Robbins, D.D.* (Boston, 1886) I, 127–29; Huntington Porter, *Divine Providences Noticed* (Portsmouth, NH, 1801); Elijah Waterman, *A Century Sermon* (Windham, 1801); Cyrus Gildersleeve, *A Century Sermon* (Savannah, 1797)—the earlier custom. For Augustan examples, see John Lathrop, *A Discourse* (Boston, 1801); Nathan Strong, *On the Universal Spread of the Gospel* (Hartford, 1801). For contemporary reviews of century sermons, see *American Review and Literary Journal* (1801–02) 77, 185, 189, 229, 353–57, 361. Quotes from Benjamin Trumbull, *A Century Sermon* (New Haven, 1801) 5, 27, 32–33. Of the many studies of millenarian ideas in 18th-century America, the most pertinent is Ruth H. Bloch's *Visionary Republic: Millennial Themes in American Thought, 1756–1800* (Cambridge, 1985) Part III, Eschatological Revival of the 1790s. On the Second Great Awakening that began in 1799, see esp. Miriam S. Houchens, "The Great Revival of 1800," *Register of the Kentucky Historical Society* 69 (1971) 216–34.

218. "One hundred planets," *Littell's Living Age* 99 (1868) 259–61, whose summary of Bode's Law was popular but imprecise; Constance A. Lubbock, *The Herschel Chronicle* (Cambridge, 1933) 268–71.

219. Henry James, *Letters*, ed. Leon Edel (Cambridge, MA, 1984) IV, 128; Albert B. Paine, ed., *Mark Twain's Notebook* (NY, 1935) 372; Howard A. Bridgman, "The Twentieth Century Club of Boston," *Review of Reviews* 24 (1901) 73–76.

220. Katherine A. Tingley, "Our objects," *The New Century* 1 (Sept. 30, 1897) 4; Hall Caine, "The old century and the new," *New Century Review* 8 (1900) 438; Enid Stacy, "A century of women's rights," in *Forecasts of the Coming Century*, ed. Edward Carpenter (London, 1897) 100; Henry B. Brown, "The twentieth century," *Forum* 19 (1895) 641–57; Wolfdietrich Rasch, "Fin de siècle als Ende und Neubeginn," in *Fin de siècle*, eds. Roger Bauer et al. (Frankfurt am Main, 1977) 45; Kenneth M. Roemer, *The Obsolete Necessity: America in Utopian Writings, 1888–1900* (Kent, OH, 1976) 7, citing *The Literary World* (July 19, 1890) 240; *The Dawn of the Twentieth Century, 1st January, 1901* (London, 1888) 150; Michael Paget Baxter, *The Great Crisis from 1890 to 1901*, enlarged ed. (London, 1887 [1866]) 1; John Cournos, ed., *A Book of Prophecy from the Egyptians to Hitler* (NY, 1942) 255, citing Mme. Blavatsky's *Lucifer*; Basil Mathews, *John R. Mott, World Citizen* (NY, 1934) 32, and cf. C. Howard Hopkins, *John R. Mott, 1865–1955* (Grand Rapids, 1979) 225–27.

221. Oliver W. Elsbree, "The rise of the missionary spirit in New England, 1790–1815," *New England Quarterly* 1 (1928) 299–305 on expectations for 1866, as also Joseph A. Seiss, *The Last Times*, 2nd ed. (Baltimore, 1859) 269, and A. Cleveland Coxe, *Prophecy and Our Own Times* (Buffalo, 1871) esp. 22; William H. Harrison, *Mother Shipton Investigated* (London, 1881); and cf. William Perrine, "When people thought the world would end," *Ladies' Home Journal* 22 (Sept. 1905) 14; Charles Rearick, *Pleasures of the Belle Epoque* (New Haven, 1985) 61–62 on the Incohérents; Huysmans quoted by Robert Baldick in the introduction to his translation of *A Rebours: Against Nature* (Harmondsworth, 1959) 7; Roger Shattuck, *The Banquet Years*, rev. ed. (NY, 1968) 4.

222. Alain Rey, ed., *Le Grand Robert de la langue française* (Paris, 1985) IV, 526; Fritz Schalk, "Fin de siècle," in Bauer, *Fin de siècle*, 3; H. Micard and François de Jouvenot, *Fin de siècle, pièce en quatre actes* (Paris, 1888) 39, 63 for quotes; Eugen Weber, *France, Fin de Siècle* (Cambridge, MA, 1986) 10; Jens Malte Fischer, *Fin de siècle: Kommentar zur einer epoche* (Munich, 1978) 86 for Arne Garborg's *Müde Seelen* and Dilthey's letter to Yorck von Wartenburg in 1892; Oscar Wilde, *The Picture of Dorian Gray* (Laurel edition, NY, 1968 [1891]), 181. Cf. Boyle Lawrence and Herbert Cadett, *Fin de Siècle Stories* (London, 1892) with their emphasis on suicide, murder, and necrophilia, and see Hans Hinterhäuser, *Fin de siècle: Gestalten und Mythen* (Munich, 1977).

223. "Fin de siècle," *Atlantic Monthly* 67 (1891) 859; "The twentieth century," *Century* 61 (Jan. 1901) 473; Weber, *France, Fin de Siècle*, 10; Rudolf Báron, *Fin de Siècle. (Doctor Faustina) Ballet in vier Bildern* (Budapest, 1897) with music by Karl Czobor; *A Század Végel/Fin de Siècle* (Budapest), 1892 newspaper edited by Jozsef Kahn; Archibald Humboldt, *Fin de Siècle Lincoln's Birthday Exercises for Schools, 1900* (Lebanon, OH, 1900); *Fun* 73 (Jan. 12, 1901) 22.

224. *Oxford English Dictionary* VII, 156, on the "Nineties" defined as such by 1894, and cf. Holbrook Jackson, *The Eighteen Nineties* (London, 1913) 14; William S. Walsh, "Century, end of," *Curiosities of Popular Customs* (Philadelphia, 1898) 203; "Fin de siècle," *Spectator (London)* 68 (Jan. 9, 1892) 52. On Queen Victoria's death as the end of an age, consider

Sara Norton and M. A. D. Howe, eds., *The Letters of Charles Eliot Norton* (Boston, 1913) II, 303, letter of January 20, 1901: "How impressive to the imagination is the passing from earth of the great figure of the Queen! She dies at the right moment, the end of the Century which will bear her name."

225. Katherine Arens, *Functionalism and Fin de Siècle: Fritz Mauthner's Critique of Language* (NY, 1984) 16–22, quote on 22.

226. Elhanan Winchester, *God the Glorious, Holy, Wonder-Working God, Worthy to be Feared and Praised! A Century Sermon, on the Glorious Revolution* (London, 1788); Charles, Count de Moüy, "The beginnings and endings of centuries," *Chautauquan* 15 (1893) 450–52, reprinted from *La nouvelle revue*. Consider also Antoine-Augustin Cournot, *Considérations sur la marche des idées et des événements dans les temps modernes* (1872) in his *Oeuvres complètes*, ed. André Robinet (Paris, 1973) IV, 87–90, suggesting epochs beginning 1492, 1592, 1692, 1792.

227. "At the turn of the century," *Chambers's Journal* 78 (Jan. 5, 1901) 84–86; "Fin-de-siècle," *Littell's Living Age* 228 (1901) 607, 613. reprinted from *Temple Bar*; Frank A. De Puy, *New Century Home Book* (NY, 1900) 329, 385–89, intermixed with W. T. Lynn, "The last year of the century," *Leisure Hour* 50 (1900–01) 152–53. During the 1890s public consciousness was also raised by a Century Atlas, Century Dictionary, Century Gallery, Century Rubber Company, and aloes that bloom at long intervals, first called "century plants" around 1850.

228. Cornelius B. Bradley, "Our annus mirabilis," *[California] University Chronicle* 4 (1901) 148, 163. Cf. Arthur J. Brown, "The opened world," *Review of Reviews* 30 (Oct. 1904) 460–63; Joseph N. Larned, "Retrospect and prospect," *Library Journal* 21 (1896) Supp., 5–12. A most eloquent defense of the notion of a centurial character or visage was earlier issued by Rev. James White, *The Eighteen Christian Centuries* (Edinburgh, 1882).

229. Rebecca West, *1900* (New York, 1982); Editorial, *Puck* 48 (Jan. 2, 1901) 7, and cf. Elizabeth Bisland, "The time-spirit of the twentieth century," *Atlantic Monthly* 87 (1901) 15–22; "Wins first century," *San Francisco Examiner* (Jan. 2, 1901) 10.

230. On the "modern," see Adolf Loos, *Spoken into the Void: Collected Essays, 1897–1900*, trans. Jane O. Newman and John H. Smith (Cambridge, MA, 1982) throughout, and looking often toward the 20th century; Malcolm Bradbury and James Mcfarlane, eds., *Modernism* (NY, 1976) 37–39; Steven Beller, "Modern owls fly by night [review article]," *Historical Journal* 31 (1988) 665–83. On the new, see Asa Briggs, "Towards 1900: the nineteenth century faces the future," in his *Collected Essays* (Brighton, 1985) II, 294; Rearick, *Pleasures of the Belle Epoque*, 165. The English Monotype Corporation in 1900 introduced a new typeface, Modern No. 1.

231. Alan Trachtenberg, *The Incorporation of America: Culture and Society in the Gilded Age* (NY, 1982) ch. 7; David F. Burg, *Chicago's White City of 1893* (Lexington, KY, 1976) 227–28, 264–65; Hezekiah Butterworth, *Zig-Zag Journeys in the White City* (Boston, 1894) 129, 131; Reid Badger, *The Great American Fair: The World's Columbian Exposition and American Culture* (Chicago, 1979) xiii; H. Arnold Barton, *Letters from the Promised Land: Swedes in America, 1840–1914* (Minneapolis, 1975) 221.

232. Richard D. Sonn, *Anarchism and Cultural Politics in Fin de Siècle France* (Lincoln, NE, 1989) esp. ch. 10; Richard D. Mandell, *Paris 1900: The Great World's Fair* (Toronto, 1967) xi, 4, 110, and throughout; Rearick, *Pleasures of the Belle Epoque*, 143; Weber, *France, Fin de Siècle*, 67, 71; Comtesse Pauline [de Broglie] de Pange, *Comment j'ai vu 1900* (Paris, 1962) I, 193–95; Paul Morand, *1900 A.D.*, trans. Mrs. Romilly Fedden (NY, 1931) 65; Robert A. Millikan, *Autobiography* (NY, 1950) 49; Edouard Bonnefous, *Avant l'oubli: la vie de 1900 à 1940* (Paris, 1985) 18, 25; J. Diane Radycki, trans., *Letters and Journals of Paula Modersohn-Becker* (Metuchen, 1980) 135.

233. Morand, *1900 A.D.*, 83; Mandell, *Paris 1900*, 80; President McKinley's "Fourth annual message to the Congress, December 3, 1900," in Fred M. Israel, ed., *The State of the Union Messages of the Presidents, 1790–1966* (NY, 1966) II, 1971–72; Arthur P. Greeley, "The age of invention," *Munsey's Magazine* 21 (1899) 706–09; Alonzo P. Connolly, ed., *The Nineteenth Century with Twentieth Century Appendix*, 6th ed. (Chicago, 1903) unpaginated; McCormick Harvesting Machine Company, *The End of the Century Witnesses the Triumph of the McCormick* (Chicago, 1899); Edward W. Byrn, *The Progress of Invention in the Nineteenth Century* (NY, 1900) 4; Frank B. Parsons, "Great movements of the nineteenth century. Part I," *Arena* 26 (1901) 3; George Torr, "Along many lines," [*Washington*] *Evening Star* (Dec. 29, 1900) 24. See "The Afro-American and the twentieth century," *The Colored American* (Jan. 5, 1901) 8 for a similar centurial comparison. A new journal for the history of science, appearing in Leiden in 1896, was entitled *Janus*.

234. Alfred Russel Wallace, *The Wonderful Century* (London, 1898) vii, and cf. the review by W. K. Brooks in *Popular Science Monthly* 56 (1899) 25; Jane de Forest Shelton, "The ends of the century: how they differ and how they blend," *Magazine of American History* 28 (Aug. 1982) 108; "The nineteenth century: a review, an interpretation, and a forecast," *Outlook (New York)* 66 (Dec. 29, 1900) 1019, 1024; James P. Boyd, *Triumphs and Wonders of the Nineteenth Century* (Philadelphia, 1899) i; Jerome H. Buckley, *The Triumph of Time: A Study of the Victorian Concepts of Time, History, Progress and Decadence* (Cambridge, MA, 1966) 9 for Harrison quote, and throughout; cf. P. B. M. Blaas, *Continuity and Anachronism* (The Hague, 1978).

235. Mandell, *Paris 1900*, 80; David J. Brewer, *Twentieth Century from Another Viewpoint* (NY, 1899) 33–34. See Peter J. Bowler, *The Eclipse of Darwinism* (Baltimore, 1983) on turn-of-the-century theories on spontaneous mutation and the acceleration of growth.

236. Reginald Pound and Geoffrey Harmsworth, *Northcliffe* (NY, 1959) 264–67; Editors of *American Heritage, The Nineties* (NY, 1967) 10; "The twentieth century," *Peking and Tientsin Times* (Jan. 5, 1900) 138; Stephen Kern, *The Culture of Time and Space, 1880–1918* (Cambridge, MA, 1983) 111, Kern's translation from German historian Karl Lamprecht, and see all of ch. 5; *San Francisco Examiner* (Jan. 1, 1901) 2:2.

237. Henry Adams, *The Education of Henry Adams* (Modern Library edition, NY, 1931 [1907]) 382, 457, 486–87, and see J. C. Levenson et al., eds., *The Letters of Henry Adams* (Cambridge, MA, 1988) V, 157, 169; Millikan, *Autobiography*, 31; W. R. Taylor, "Historical bifocals on the year 1800," *New England Quarterly* 23 (1950) 172–86; Jonathan Rose, *The Edwardian Temperament* (Athens, OH, 1986) 4–6 on Balfour.

238. Adams, *Education*, 494; Seth Low, *The Trend of the Century* (NY, 1899) 14; David Duncan, *Life and Letters of Herbert Spencer* (London, 1911) 448; Hall Caine, "The old century and the new," *New Century Review* 8 (1900) 436; Paul A. Carter, *The Spiritual Crisis of the Gilded Age* (De Kalb, IL, 1971) 217; Stephen Phillips, "Midnight—31st of December, 1900," *The Nineteenth Century and After* 49 (Jan. 1901) 2–6; "Prophecies of Stephen Phillips," *Independent (New York)* 53 (Jan. 24, 1901) 226. Cf. Kern, *Culture of Time and Space*, ch. 6.

239. Andrew Large, *The Artificial Language Movement* (Oxford, 1985) 59–78, 85; Oscar Browning, *Memories of Later Years* (London, 1923) 93–95.

240. Robert M. Anderson, *Vision of the Disinherited: The Making of American Pentecostalism* (NY, 1979) esp. 44 on expectations of a global revival for 1896–1901; Grant Wacker, "The Holy Spirit and the spirit of the age in American Protestantism, 1880–1910," *Journal of American History* 72 (1985) 45–62; George M. Marsden, *Fundamentalism and American Culture: The Shaping of Twentieth-Century Evangelicalism, 1870–1925* (NY, 1980) 38, 72.

241. Sarah F. Parham, *The Life of Charles F. Parham* (NY, 1985 [1930]); Anderson, *Vision of the Disinherited*, 46 ff.; Vinson Synan, *The Holiness-Pentecostal Movement in the United States* (Grand Rapids, 1974) ch. 5; Walter J. Hollenweger, *The Pentecostals*, trans. R. A. Wilson (London, 1972) 116–17.

242. Hollenweger, *The Pentecostals*, 117; Parham, *Life of Charles F. Parham*, esp. 52–54; Eric W. Gritsch, *Born Againism* (Philadelphia, 1982) 71–72; Anderson, *Vision of the Disinherited*, 57, and noting (pp. 34–35) earlier outbreaks of glossolalia at Holiness meetings in 1890 and 1896. Since *pentēkostē* refers literally to the 50th (or jubilee) day, the word and the experience were most congenial with a centurial "Watch Night," a religious tradition traceable to 18th-century Methodist prayer meetings on New Year's Eve.

243. Theodore M. Porter, *The Rise of Statistical Thinking 1820–1900* (Princeton, 1986) throughout, with quote on 29.

244. *Ibid.*, esp. 149, 310; Stephen M. Stigler, *The History of Statistics: The Measurement of Uncertainty before 1900* (Cambridge, MA, 1986) esp. 329, 354; D. W. Forest, *Francis Galton: The Life and Work of a Victorian Genius* (NY, 1974) 193–202, 238–39, 250–52 (quotes).

245. George C. Chase, "History of mechanical computing machinery," *Annals of the History of Computing* 2 (July 1980) 198–226; Marsden, *Fundamentalism and American Culture*, 56; Ernest R. Sandeen, *The Roots of Fundamentalism: British and American Millenarianism, 1800–1930* (Chicago, 1970) ch. 6; Klaus J. Hanson, *Quest for Empire: The Political Kingdom of God and the Council of Fifty in Mormon History* (East Lansing, 1967) 22–23; Richard W. Schwarz, "The perils of growth, 1886–1905," in *Adventism in America*, ed. Gary Land (Grand Rapids, 1986) 103–06, for the background of which see Ronald L. Numbers and Jonathan M. Butler, eds., *The Disappointed: Millerism and Millenarianism in the Nineteenth Century* (Bloomington, 1987); Ronald Matthews, *English Messiahs* (London, 1936) 186–87; Gaston Mery, *Le voyante de la rue du Paradis* (Paris, 1896) 33ff.; Baron de Novaye, *Demain . . . ? d'après les concordances frappantes de cent-vingt prophéties anciennes et modernes*, 6th ed. (Paris, 1905?) 319, 332–39; Béda Rigaux, "La redécouverte de la dimension eschatologique de l'Evangile," *Revue d'histoire et de philosophie religieuses* 56 (1976) 3–27, and see Frank C. Porter, *The Messages of the Apocalyptical Writers* (NY, 1905) 335ff. for an account of the many apocalyptic texts newly

published in the 1890s; Mario Vargas Llosa, *The War of the End of the World*, trans. Helen R. Lane (NY, 1984) on Conselheiro, a masterwork of historical fiction which should be supplemented by reference to the scholarly works of M. I. Pereira de Queiroz; Dikran Terzian, *Mathematics of Religion* (NY, 1898) 13–14; Akbar S. Ahmed, *Millennium and Charisma among the Pathans* (London, 1976); Sarat Chandra Roy, *The Mundas and Their Country* (London, 1970 [1912]) 187–200; Peter M. Holt, *The Mahdist State in the Sudan 1881–1898*, 2nd ed. (Oxford, 1970).

246. Edwin G. Boring, *Sensation and Perception of the History of Experimental Psychology* (NY, 1942) 246–52; Reba N. Soffer, *Ethics and Society in England: The Revolution in the Social Sciences, 1870–1914* (Berkeley, 1978) Parts II and V; Susanna Barrows, *Distorting Mirrors: Visions of the Crowd in Late Nineteenth-Century France* (New Haven, 1981) 114–36. One of the classics of sociology, Emile Durkheim's *Suicide*, appeared in 1897, and cf. Reginald A. Skelton, "Statistics of suicide," *Nineteenth Century* 48 (Sept. 1900) 465–95: "what connection, we ask ourselves, has the present abnormal extent of suicide with society and its actual institutions?" See also Olive Anderson, *Suicide in Victorian and Edwardian England* (Oxford, 1987) Part I.

247. Shelton, "The ends of the century," 102; A. Kh. Khrgian, *Meteorology: A Historical Survey* 2nd ed., rev. Kh.-P. Pogosyan, trans. Ron Hardin (Jerusalem, 1970) throughout, with spiders on 201; John M. Bacon, "The war of the winds: a commentary on weather forecasts," *National Review (London)* 34 (Dec. 1899) 727–33. Earthquake prediction advanced at the same time. See James W. Dewey and Perry Byerly, "The early history of seismometry," *Bulletin of the Seismological Society of America* 59 (1969) 183–277.

248. Samuel Benner, *Benner's Prophecies of Future Ups and Downs in Prices* (Cincinnati, 1876) quotes on 16–17, 131; Richard Lewinsohn, *Science, Prophecy, and Prediction*, trans. Arnold J. Pomerans (NY, 1961) 194–95 and ch. 10; Lewis H. Haney, *History of Economic Thought*, 4th ed. (NY, 1949) 667ff.; George W. Bishop, Jr., ed., *Charles H. Dow: Economist* (Princeton, 1967) 12, 42. Cf. Peter Hall, "The intellectual history of long waves," in *The Rhythms of Society*, eds. Michael Young and Tom Schuller (London, 1988) 37ff.

249. Jean-Pierre Vernant et al., *Divination et rationalité* (Paris, 1974) esp. 70–197; Peter Tompkins, *Secrets of the Great Pyramid* (NY, 1971) ch. 7; W.E.S.T., *The Great Pyramid and the Time of the End* (London, 1891); Benner, *Benner's Prophecies*, 27; Leonard R. N. Ashley, *The Wonderful World of Superstition, Prophecy, and Luck* (NY, 1984) 120.

250. Attila Ágh, "The future as history in a Marxist perspective," in *Future Research in Hungary*, eds. Ervin Bona et al. (Budapest, 1983) 70 for Engels; "In the sweet by-and-by," *Pick-Me-Up* 25 (Jan. 5, 1901) 237. See also Gotthart Wunberg, "Utopie und fin de siècle," *Deutsche Vierteljahrschrift für Literaturwissenschaft und Geistesgeschichte* 43 (1969) 685–706 on preoccupations with the future.

251. Frederic C. Jaher, *Doubters and Dissenters: Cataclysmic Thought in America, 1885–1918* (London, 1964); Roemer, *The Obsolete Necessity*, 6; Theodore E. Burton, *Financial Crises* (NY, 1902) 4 on contemporary "indiscriminate use" of the words "panic," "crisis," and "depression"; Arthur C. Young, ed., *The Letters of George Gissing to Edward Bertz* (New Brunswick, NJ, 1961) 284 on a smaller and sadder world; S. Charles Maurice and Charles W. Smithson, *The Doomsday Myth* (Stanford, 1984) 34–47 on the rubber and timber "crises" of the 1890s;

Max Wilhelm Meyer, *End of the World*, trans. M. Wagner (Chicago, 1905 [1902]) on varieties of planetary death; Gorton Carruth, *Encyclopedia of American Facts and Dates*, 8th ed. (NY, 1987) Casey Jones listing for April 30, 1900; President Theodore Roosevelt's "First annual message to the Congress, December 3, 1901," in Israel, ed., *State of the Union Messages*, II, 2018. In Thomas Hardy's novel, *Jude the Obscure* (1896), Jude's prematurely aged son "Father Time" murders his brothers then himself; the doctor says "it is the beginning of the coming universal wish not to live." Quoted by Geoffrey Harpham, "Time running out: the Edwardian sense of cultural degeneration," *Clio* 5 (1976) 283–301.

252. Peter C. Smith, *Hard Lying: The Birth of the Destroyer, 1893–1913* (Annapolis, 1971) 31; Arthur L. Wagner, in Boyd, *Triumphs and Wonders*, 300, 306; Louis Tracy, *The Final War* (NY, 1896) as one example of utopia through war, and Ignatius Donnelly, *Caesar's Column*, ed. Walter B. Rideout (Cambridge, MA, 1960 [1890]) on deadly war, as also Ingersoll Lockwood, *1900: or, the Last President* (NY, 1896); Richard Gid Powers, "Introduction" to Stanley Waterloo, *Armageddon* (Boston, 1976 [1898]); Cecil D. Eby, *The Road to Armageddon: The Martial Spirit in English Popular Literature, 1870–1914* (Durham, NC, 1988) esp. 11, counting more than sixty narrative fictions describing an invasion of Britain; Ignatius F. Clarke, *The Pattern of Expectation, 1644–2001* (NY, 1979) 183–87; George C. Griffith, *The Angel of the Revolution* (Westport, CT, 1974 [1893]) 33 for quote; H. Hamilton and Gayle Thornbrough, eds., *Indianapolis in the "Gay Nineties": High School Diaries of Claude G. Bowers* (Indianapolis, 1964) 189, and cf. John Higham, "The reorientation of American culture in the 1890s," in *Origins of Modern Consciousness*, ed. John H. Weiss (Detroit, 1965) 25–48.

253. Mark Sullivan, *Our Times: The United States 1900–1925. I. The Turn of the Century* (NY, 1927) 48–56 on American overseas expansion, 1898–1900; Walter LaFeber, *The New Empire: An Interpretation of American Expansion, 1860–1898* (Ithaca, 1963) 361–62, 410–17; Richard E. Welch, Jr., " 'The Philippine Insurrection' and the American press," *The Historian* 36 (1973) 34–51; David R. Sturtevant, *Popular Uprisings in the Philippines, 1840–1940* (Ithaca, 1976), which puts the "insurrection" into a Philippine and millenarian context; Joseph W. Esherick, *The Origins of the Boxer Uprising* (Berkeley, 1987), and cf. "The march of time," *Peking and Tientsin Times* (Jan. 6, 1900) 178, claiming that the Chinese in 1899 had "prognosticated for themselves a cycle of unprecedented disaster"; Arthur Conan Doyle, *The Great Boer War*, new ed. (London, 1901) esp. 195.

254. Sullivan, *The Turn of the Century*, 56–58 for Kaiser's speech; Eby, *Road to Armageddon*, ch. 7; Ellen Key, *The Century of the Child* (NY, 1972 [1909]) 1, and cf. *Le Figaro* (Dec. 31, 1900) 3, cartoon depicting the 19th century as an old man trying to restrain the 20th-century child from playing with the new armaments; Alfred Austin, "The Passing of the Century," *London Times* (Dec. 31, 1900) 10, and "The new century," same issue, 7, on Gore and Harrison; Jean Frollo, *Le petit parisien* (Dec. 29, 1900) 1; Jacinto López, "Nuevo siglo," *El Cojo Illustrado* 10 (1901) 5; Jeremiah Curtin, *Memoirs*, ed. Joseph Schafer (Madison, WI, 1940) 832; Briggs, "Towards 1900," 292, Twain quote. See also an editorial in the *United Irishman* (Jan. 5, 1901) 4:1, sending "The vilest of the nineteen centuries of the Christian reckoning" off to, "please God," eternal damnation.

255. Haguch, "A pseudo-millennium," *Westminster Review* 151 (Feb. 1899) 140–45, suspicious of the Czar's intentions; Arthur C. F. Beales, *The History of Peace* (NY, 1971 [1931])

175, 188, 215–18, 231ff.; Frederick W. Holls, *The Peace Conference at The Hague* (NY, 1900) 10 for quote.

256. Holls, *Peace Conference*, 37, 54, 94, 100, 111, 139–52, 350 for quote; Beales, *History of Peace*, 244.

257. Tony Gray, *Champions of Peace* (n.p., 1976) throughout, quotes on 13, 50, 83.

258. R. A. Proctor, "Lands and seas of another world," *Littell's Living Age* 99 (1868) 26–32, quote on 27, article reprinted from *Fraser's Magazine*; Roger L. Green, *Into Other Worlds: Space-Flight in Fiction, from Lucian to Lewis* (London, 1958) ch. 9; William G. Hoyt, *Lowell and Mars* (Tucson, 1976) throughout, 9 on signals; Percival Lowell, *Occult Japan or the way of the Gods* (Boston, 1895) esp. 14; idem, *Mars and Its Canals* (NY, 1906) dedication, 16–17, 177, 184, 363–64, 377, 382.

259. John G. Burke, *Cosmic Debris: Meteorites in History* (Berkeley, 1986) 104, and dating the first peak of scientific interest in meteors to the 1790s; George Locke, *Voyages in Space: A Bibliography of Interplanetary Fiction, 1801–1914* (London, 1975) 67–68; David C. Smith, *H. G. Wells, Desperately Mortal* (New Haven, 1986) 64–67; H. G. Wells, *The War of the Worlds* (London, 1898) quotes on 4, 41, 87, 173.

260. On the *fin de siècle* motifs of degeneration and decadence, see Max Nordau, *Entartung (Degeneration)* (1892), scorning and then defending the correlation between degeneracy and century's end; J. Edward Chamberlin and Sander L. Gilman, eds., *Degeneration: The Dark Side of Progress* (NY, 1985) esp. essays by Modris Eksteins and Eric T. Carlson; Barbara Charlesworth, *Dark Passages: The Decadent Consciousness in Victorian Literature* (Madison, WI, 1965); Richard Gilman, *Decadence: The Strange Life of an Epithet* (NY, 1979); Robert A. Nye, *Crime, Madness & Politics in Modern France: The Medical Concept of National Decline* (Princeton, 1984); and entire issue of *Journal of Contemporary History* 17,1 (Jan. 1982). On impotence, see Iwan Bloch, *The Sexual Life of Our Time in Its Relations to Modern Civilization*, trans. M. Eden Paul (NY, 1908 [1907]) 441–51; G. J. Barker-Benfield, *The Horrors of the Half-Known Life: Male Attitudes Toward Women and Sexuality in Nineteenth-Century America* (NY, 1976) esp. 175–88. On the three facets of exhaustion (the female equivalent of impotence, the more general malady of modern civilization, and the depletion of national or global resources), see Barbara Sicherman, "The uses of a diagnosis: doctors, patients, and neurasthenia," *Journal of the History of Medicine* 32 (1977) 33–54; Anson Rabinbach, "The body without fatigue: a nineteenth-century utopia," in *Political Symbolism in Modern Europe*, eds. Seymour Drescher et al. (New Brunswick, NJ, 1982) 42–62, and cf. 121–45; Robert McHenry with Charles Van Doren, eds., *A Documentary History of Conservation in America* (NY, 1972) 182–90, 287–99. On vampirism, see Bram Dijkstra, *Idols of Perversity: Fantasies of Feminine Evil in Fin-de-Siècle Culture* (NY, 1986) ch. 10, and note that Bram Stoker's *Dracula* was published in 1897.

261. H. G. Wells, *Anticipations of the Reaction of Mechanical and Scientific Progress Upon Human Life and Thought* (NY, 1902) 3n.–4n., 189–90, 250, 267, 325, and cf. his "Discovery of the future," *Nature* 65 (Feb. 6, 1902) 326–31.

262. Lowell wrote that the "value of Mars to man is the foresight it affords of the course earthly evolution is to pursue. On our own world we are able only to study our present and

our past; in Mars we are able to glimpse, in some sort, our future." *Mars and Its Canals*, 384. On the fictions, see Green, *Into Other Worlds*, 107, 112, 114; Thomas Blot (= William Simpson), *The Man from Mars* (San Francisco, 1891) 22–23, 141; Henry Olerich, *A Cityless and Countryless World* (NY, 1971 [1893]) 26, 436–38; Willis Mitchell, *The Inhabitants of Mars* (Malden, MA, 1895) 39, 58, 81; George Du Maurier, *The Martian* (NY, 1897) 360, 364, 406; Kurt Lasswitz, *Two Planets*, abridged by Erich Lasswitz, trans. Hans H. Rudnick (Carbondale, 1971 [1897]); Per Olof Sundman, *The Flight of the Eagle*, trans. Mary Sandbach (NY, 1970). Mars was also the site for the future emancipation of women; see Barbara C. Quissell, "The new world that Eve made: feminist utopias written by nineteenth-century women," in *America as Utopia*, ed. Kenneth M. Roemer (NY, 1981), 155–58.

263. Thomas Flournoy, *From India to the Planet Mars*, trans. Daniel B. Vermilye (New Hyde Park, 1963 [1900]) ch. 5; Edward Bellamy, *The Blindman's World* (Boston, 1898); Sylvia Bowman, *The Year 2000: A Critical Biography of Edward Bellamy* (NY, 1958) 58 and throughout; Sylvia Bowman et al., *Edward Bellamy Abroad* (NY, 1962); West, *1900*, 48; Victor Hicken, *The World Is Coming to an End! An Irreverent Look at Modern Doomsayers* (New Rochelle, 1975) 44, citing Dickens's *American Notes*; Peter Conrad, *Imagining America* (NY, 1980) and cf. Gerald E. Stearn, comp., *Broken Image: Foreign Critiques of America* (NY, 1972); *Letters from a Chinese Official* (Garden City, NY, 1928 [1903]) x–xi; Walter Besant, "The burden of the twentieth century," *North American Review* 173 (July 1901) 21; Martin J. Wiener, *English Culture and the Decline of the Industrial Spirit, 1850–1980* (Cambridge, 1981) 89; Frank L. Mott, "The magazine revolution and popular ideas in the 1890s," *American Antiquarian Society Proceedings* 64 (1954) 203 for Beveridge; Julia Hawthorne, "New Columbus," *Arena* 4 (June 1891) 2, speculating that Mars could be to Americans what America in 1492 had been to Europeans; Aleister Crowley, *Carmen Saeculare* (London, 1901) 14–15, 28 on a failed America; H. G. Wells, *The Future in America* (NY, 1906) 29.

264. Sam D. Cashman, *America in the Gilded Age* (NY, 1984) ch. 8; Paul O'Neil, *The Old West: The End and the Myth* (Alexandria, VA, 1979) esp. 26–27; Peter S. Onuf, "Liberty, development, and union: visions of the West in the 1780s," *William & Mary Quarterly*, ser. 3, 43 (1986) 179–213; Thomas Beer, *The Mauve Decade* (NY, 1926) ch. 2; Frederic L. Paxson, "A generation of the frontier hypothesis," *Pacific Historical Review* 2 (1933) 34–51; Charles J. Rooney, Jr., *Dreams and Visions: A Study of American Utopias, 1865–1917* (Westport, CT, 1985) 65–66 for Child; Higham, "Reorientation of American culture in the 1890s," 44 for Wright; Raymond J. DeMallie, "The Lakota Ghost Dance," *Pacific Historical Review* 51 (1982) 385–405; John Stands In Timber and Margot Liberty, *Cheyenne Memories* (New Haven, 1967) ch. 16; John G. Neihardt, *Black Elk Speaks* (Lincoln, 1961) ch. 21, quote on 237.

265. Jacques Vallée, *Passport to Magonia: From Folklore to Flying Saucers* (Chicago, 1969) 60, 179–81; Michael Hervey, *UFOs: The American Scene* (NY, 1976) 34–36; Thomas E. Bullard, "Newly discovered 'airship' waves over Poland," *Flying Saucer Review* 29,3 (1984) 12–14, and Bullard's notes from *New York Tribune* (March 31, 1892) 1, *New York Times* (March 26, 1892) 3, and *Neue Freie Presse* (March 18, 1892) 6, for which I am most grateful.

266. Daniel Cohen, *The Great Airship Mystery: A UFO of the 1890s* (NY, 1981) 27–28, 35–36, and throughout for hoaxes; Hervey, *UFOs*, 38; Ron Miller, "Jules Verne and the great airship scare," *International UFO Reporter* 12 (May/June 1987) 4–10.

267. *San Francisco Examiner* (Nov. 23, 1896) 12, and (Nov. 24, 1896) 12; Cohen, *Great Airship Mystery*, 19–22, 41, 63; Roger L. Welsch, "This mysterious light called an airship: Nebraska 'saucer' sightings, 1897," *Nebraska History* 60 (Spring 1979) 92–113; Vallée, *Passport to Magonia*, 141–43; David M. Jacobs, *The UFO Controversy in America* (Bloomington, 1975) ch. 1. I have also used, at the Library of Congress, the rare, privately printed book by Loren Gross, *The UFO Wave of 1896* (Fremont, CA, 1974).

268. Tom D. Crouch, *A Dream of Wings: Americans and the Airplane, 1875–1905* (NY, 1981); Marjorie Hope Nicolson, *Voyages to the Moon* (NY, 1948).

269. Timothy P. Weber, *Living in the Shadow of the Second Coming: American Premillennialism, 1875–1925* (NY, 1979) esp. 11, 21–22; Sandeen, *Roots of Fundamentalism*, 62–64, 87–89, 97–98, 139–41; *La fin du monde (le 11 avril 1901). De grandes guerres, en 1890 ou 1891. . . . L'Ascension de 144,000 chrétiens du ciel, sans qu'ils aient vu la mort, le jeudi 5 mars 1896* (Paris, 1889?) courtesy copy furnished me by the Sutro Library, San Francisco; Dijkstra, *Idols of Perversity*, 72–74, 258–72, 327–401. I draw upon W. R. Bion, *Experiences in Groups* (NY, 1961), for the paired opposition of fight and flight as a basic assumption in group behavior (especially pertinent at century's end, given the fears about closure).

270. Carlotta de Barsy, *The Gates of the Future thrown open* (Chicago, 1899) 81, 164—and to dream of an automaton meant that a great war would soon begin (p. 13); Ronald W. Clark, *Freud: The Man and the Cause* (NY, 1980) 180; S. R. F. Price, "The future of dreams: from Freud to Artemidorus," *Past & Present* 11 (1986) 3–37; Jeffrey M. Masson, trans. and ed., *The Complete Letters of Sigmund Freud to Wilhelm Fliess, 1887–1904* (Cambridge, MA, 1985) 251, 353, 361, 366, 368, 378, 379, 394, 398. I thank Beverly Schneider for bringing my attention to the still current legend about the publisher's intention in giving *Traumdeutung* a 1900 imprint, for which see Ernest Jones, *Life and Work of Sigmund Freud* (NY, 1953) I, 360.

271. Carl E. Schorske, *Fin-de-siècle Vienna: Politics and Culture* (NY, 1981) ch. 4 on Freud, fight/flight, and the trip to Rome; Masson, *Complete Letters*, 394.

272. Stefan Zweig, *The World of Yesterday* (NY, 1964 [1943]) 43, 92. The young poet Rainer Maria Rilke, twenty-three, wrote in 1899 of living in expectation of the century's turn and feeling the janiform "glance from a new face": Rasch, "Fin de siècle als Ende und Neubeginn," 30. On 19th-century generations, see the astute essay by Annie W. Allen, "Victorian hypocrisy," *Atlantic Monthly* 114 (Aug. 1914) 174–88.

273. Gerhard Masur, *Prophets of Yesterday: Studies in European Culture, 1890–1914* (NY, 1961) 131, 143, 184–87, on von Hofmannsthal, Barrès, and Weber; H. Stuart Hughes, *Consciousness and Society: The Reorientation of European Social Thought, 1890–1930* (NY, 1958) esp. 287–99 on Weber; Paul A. Schilpp, ed., *Albert Einstein: Philosopher-Scientist* (NY, 1957), Einstein's "Autobiographical Notes," 37, and see J. L. Heilbron, "Fin-de-siècle physics," in *Science, Technology and Society in the Time of Alfred Nobel*, eds., C. G. Bernhard et al. (Oxford, 1982) 51–73, and Katherine R. Sopka, *Physics for a New Century: Papers Presented at the 1904 St. Louis Congress* (n.p., 1986); Richard Pipes, *Struve: Liberal on the Left, 1870–1905* (Cambridge, MA, 1970) I, 263 for Lenin; Norman MacKenzie and Jeanne MacKenzie, eds., *The Diary of Beatrice Webb* (London, 1983) II, 203; John Maynard Keynes, "My early beliefs," in his *Two Memoirs* (NY, 1949) 82. Cf. Frank Kermode, *The Sense of an Ending* (London,

1967) 97–98. On the term "avant-garde" in the 1890s, see Robert Estivals et al., *"L'Avant-garde," étude historique et sociologique des publications ayant pour titre "Avant-garde"* (Paris, 1968); Donald D. Egbert, "The idea of 'avant-garde' in art and politics," *American Historical Review* 73 (1967) 339–66.

274. *New Century Leader* 1 (Jan. 1900) 25; Adams, *Education*, 379–80; Evangeline Adams, *The Bowl of Heaven* (NY, 1926) 31ff.; Brooks Adams, *The New Empire* (NY, 1902) xi.

275. R. Mallet, ed., *Correspondance d'André Gide et de Paul Valéry* (Paris, 1955) 379, Valéry to Gide, 31 décembre 1900; "At the turn of the century," *Chambers's Journal* 78 (1901) 85.

276. Arthur Hobhouse, "Battle of the centuries," *Contemporary Review* 77 (March 1900) 1107, citing H. W. S.-W., "Letter to the editor," *London Times* (Jan. 6, 1900) 12:5; J. H. Tingley, comp., *The Nineteenth Century Almanac* (Philadelphia, 1886) preface; "When the century begins," *New York Times* (Sept. 20, 1896) 20, and subsequent letters to the editor (Sept. 23rd) 4, (Sept. 27th) 12, (Sept. 29th) 4, (Sept. 30th) 4, (Oct. 1st) 4, (Oct. 2nd) 4, and then (Dec. 15, 1899) 6 for results of *Boston Herald* survey; Simeon E. Baldwin, "The date for the opening of the twentieth century," *Yale Law Journal* 9 (1900) 161–63; John Montgomery, *1900, The End of an Era* (London, 1968) 21 on Witt and Waddilove.

277. Max Halbe, *Jahrhundertwende* (Danzig, 1935) 290–92, and see Thomas E. Willey, "Thomas Mann's Munich," in *The Turn of the Century: German Literature and Art, 1890–1915*, eds. Gerald Chapple and Hans H. Schulte (Bonn, 1981) 482, 488–89, as well as editors' preface; *Die Fackel (Vienna)* 28 (Jan. 1900) 5–6, 29; *Frankfürter Zeitung* (Jan. 2, 1900) 1; Editorial, "The twentieth century," *Washington Post* (Jan. 1, 1901) 6; Montgomery, *1900*, 22; Oscar Blumenthal, "Säkular-Stimmen," *Berliner Tageblatt* (Dec. 27, 1899) 1. I have not seen Gustav Baumgärtel, *Warum könnte die Jahrhundertfrage nicht einheitlich gelöst werden?* (Dresden, 1901).

278. "The century," *Cape Argus* (Dec. 31, 1900) 4; Felix Buisán Cítores, *Nacimento del periodismo palentino a travers de "El Crepusculo" diario fin de siglo* (Palencia, 1983) 136; C. Brinsley Marlay, "Letter to the editor," *London Times* (Jan. 6, 1900) 12, citing *Le Temps* concerning the Bureau des Longitudes; Alfred Jarry, *Tout Ubu*, ed. Maurice Saillet (Paris, 1962) 401–12; William Jaffé, ed., *Correspondence of Léon Walras and Related Papers* (Amsterdam, 1965) III, 102, letter to Gustave Maugin, 31 décembre 1899; Silvanus P. Thompson, *The Life of William Thomson, Baron Kelvin of Largs* (London, 1910) II, 1150; *Levant Herald* (Jan. 2, 1901) 2:1; James, *Letters*, IV, 125, letter to Charles Eliot Norton, November 24–28, 1899, with postscript January 13, 1900; Hobhouse, "Battle of the centuries," 397, 403, 406; J. B. Dimbleby, "Letter to the editor," *London Times* (Jan. 1, 1900) 11:5. "A.G." wrote a poem satirizing the controversy: "The Only Way," *Littell's Living Age* 224 (March 24, 1900) 741–42.

279. "The Holy Year," *Panama Star and Herald* (Dec. 27, 1899) 4; "Buon anno e Anno Santo," *L'Osservatore romano (Vatican City)* (Jan. 3, 1900) 1 and (Jan. 1, 1901) 3 on new century; Joseph Rickaby, "The encyclical on the new century," *Month (London)* 97 (1901) 1.

280. Edward Alden, "Letter to the editor," *New York Times* (Sept. 27,1896) 12:7; Dionysus Minimus (= Mowbray Morris), "The twentieth century," *Macmillan's Magazine* 81 (Feb. 1900) 310–12; Hobhouse, "Battle of the centuries," 400, for E. J. Reed in the *London Times*

(Jan. 1, 1900); Courtenay Boyle, "Letter to the editor," *London Times* (Dec. 29, 1899) 10:5; K. B. Ferguson, "Letter to the editor," *London Times* (Jan. 2, 1900) 9:5; Neal H. Ewing, "When shall we greet the new era?" *New York Times* (July 22, 1899) 6. Cf. Robert Speaight, ed., *Letters from Hilaire Belloc* (London, 1958) 3, on 1900 as "a kind of Buffer Year."

281. Sullivan, *The Turn of the Century*, 12n.; Editorial, "The new century," *Christian Science Journal* 18 (Jan. 1901) 651–52.

282. John Ritchie, Jr., "When the new century will really begin," *Ladies' Home Journal* 17 (Jan. 1900) 7; *Spectator* (London) 86 (Jan. 5, 1901) 1 and *Manchester Guardian* (Jan. 2, 1901) 6 on Australia; Curtin, *Memoirs*, 832; "Suh-Hai put to death," *Washington Post* (Jan. 2, 1901) 1 on Peking (Beijing); "The New Year's Day" *The Hindu (Madras)* (Dec. 31, 1900) 3, and Editorial, "At the parting of the ways," 4; Wilfrid Scawen Blunt, *My Diaries* (NY, 1921) I, 376; *Journal de St. Petersbourg* (Dec. 18/31, 1900) 1; W. Miller, "The Prussian bicentenary," *Gentleman's Magazine* 290 (Jan. 1901) 17–20; Marcel Proust, *Correspondance*, ed. Philip Kolb (Paris, 1976) II, 415–16; "La fin du siècle," *L'Intrasigeant (Paris)* (Jan. 2, 1901) 2; Ralph D. Blumenfeld, *Diary, 1887–1914* (London, 1930) 81; "The new century," *London Times* (Jan. 1, 1901) 7; W., "Midnight, 1900–1901," *The Academy* 60 (1901) 17: *La Prensa (Buenos Aires)* (Jan. 1, 1901) 14 on Rio de Janeiro and also on Lima, Peru, with special supplementary pages on Argentina; Smoking, "La última noche del siglo," *El Mercurio (Valparaiso)* (Jan 1, 1901) 4; entry for December 31, 1900, in diary of Louise Merritt Parker, MS qAm 2293, Rare Book Room, Boston Public Library; "Twentieth century's triumphant entry," *New York Times* (Jan. 1, 1901) 1:7, and see Randolph Guggenheimer's resolution calling for a joint committee to arrange a celebration of the commencement of the 20th century, in "City Hall and century," *Evening Post (New York)* (Dec. 18, 1900) 2; "Old century passes," *Washington Post* (Jan. 1, 1901) 1 on Philadelphia; clipping attached to entry for January 1, 1901, in the diary of John L. Smith, Historical Society of Pennsylvania; Sullivan, *Turn of the Century*, 451 for Reed; Joe Lincoln, "Uncle Ezra's New Year Reverie," *The Recorder (Indianapolis)* (Dec. 29, 1900) 1; *Broad-Ax (Chicago)* (Jan. 5, 1901, misprinted as 1900) 1:1; *San Francisco Examiner* (Jan. 1, 1901) 4:3 on anarchist; "La despedida del siglo," *El Imparcial (Mexico City)* (Jan. 1, 1901) 1; entry for January 1, 1901, in diary of Brigham Young, Jr., in Rare Books and Manuscripts Division, New York Public Library, Astor, Lenox and Tilden Foundations; Lorenzo Snow, *Greeting to the World* (January 1, 1901), a short address, Amer M208 A1a #649, in Special Collections, Harold B. Lee Library, Brigham Young University, kindly provided by Chad J. Flake, Curator; *Los Angeles Daily Times* (Jan. 1, 1901); *San Francisco Examiner* (Jan. 1, 1901) 1:6–7, 2:2, and on the scheme for obtaining these greetings, "A new century idea staggers Mr. Higbee," *New York Times* (Dec. 21, 1900) 1, with follow-up, "New Year's Watch is off," (Dec. 25, 1900) 12; "Creek notes," *Yukon Sun and Klondike Pioneer* (Jan. 5, 1901) 6. A number of celebrations in the United States were reviewed by John T. Winterich, "Father Time's big night out," *Nation's Business* 37 (Jan. 1949) 46–48.

283. Bridgman, "The Twentieth Century Club of Boston," 76; "To greet the new century," *Evening Star (Washington, D.C.)* (Dec. 31, 1900) 1; entry for January 1, 1901, on the silencing of the centurial debate, in diary of John T. Trowbridge, MS qAm 1069 vol. 17, Rare Book Room, Boston Public Library, quoted here by courtesy of the Trustees; entry for January 1, 1901, under January 2nd, in Susan E. Parsons Brown Forbes Diaries, American Antiquarian Society, Worcester, MA; entry for December 31, 1900, p. 169 of Records for 1901 in diaries

of Robert Apthorp Boit, and entry for December 31, 1900, in Journal Jan. 1900 to June 1901, journals of Marian Lawrence (= Mrs. Harold) Peabody, Peabody MSS, both at Massachusetts Historical Society, Boston.

CONSTELLATIONS: THE 1990S

1. "Fin de siècle," *Atlantic Monthly* 67 (1891) 860; Edmund Verney, "The 1900 total eclipse of the sun," *Gentleman's Magazine* 289 (1900) 303–08; James M. Miller and John S. Durham, *The Martinique Horror and St. Vincent Calamity* (Philadelphia, 1901) subtitle; Ferdinand Lot, "Le mythe des terreurs de l'an mille," *Recueil des travaux historiques de Ferdinand Lot* (Geneva, 1968) I, 403, citing Pius X's encyclical, *E Supremi*; Leo Tolstoy, "The end of the age," *Littell's Living Age* 248 (1906) 323–35, 643–61, reprinted from *Fortnightly* 85 (1905). Virginia Woolf, of course, brought the age to an end in 1910 in her essay "Mr. Bennett and Mrs. Brown" (1924), and others now bring it to a close with World War I.

2. Vladimir Solov'ev, *Three Conversations on War, Progress and the End of World History* (1900) in *War and Christianity from the Russian Point of View* (London, 1915) 145; Charles Taze Russell, *Studies in the Scriptures* (Philadelphia, 1937) II, v, Foreword to 1916 edition, and see M. J. Penton, "The eschatology of Jehovah's Witnesses," in *Coming Kingdom: Essays in American Millennialism and Eschatology*, eds. M. Darrol Bryant and Donald W. Dayton (Barrytown, NY, 1984) 169–207; Christabel Pankhurst, *Pressing Problems of the Closing Age* (London, 1924) 2; Johan Huizinga, *In the Shadow of Tomorrow*, trans. J. H. Huizinga (NY, 1936) 15, 25–26; H. G. Wells, *The Shape of Things to Come* (NY, 1936 [1935]) 19.

3. Folke T. Kihlstedt, "Utopia realized: the world's fairs of the 1930s," in *Imagining Tomorrow*, ed. Joseph J. Corn (Cambridge, MA, 1986) quotes on 99, 104, 106; Joseph P. Cusker et al., *Dawn of a New Day: The New York World's Fair, 1939/40* (Flushing, NY, 1980); *The Book of Record of the Time Capsule of Cupaloy . . .* (NY, 1939; deposited Sept. 23, 1938) epigraph, 5, 46–49. In 1899, film negatives of Queen Victoria's 1897 Diamond Jubilee and of Gladstone's funeral in 1898 were sealed and deposited in the British Museum, precedent for the 1938 time capsule and "surely an advance on the primitive method of depositing an illustrated paper beneath a foundation stone!" H. V. Hopwood, *Living Pictures* (London, 1899) 230–32, quoted in *The Later Nineteenth Century, 1868–1969*, eds. Peter Teed and Michael Clark (London, 1969) 282.

4. Shimon Huberband, *Kiddush Hashem*, trans. David E. Fishman, eds. Jeffrey S. Gurock and Robert S. Hirt (Hoboken, 1987) 121–25, and cf. the response to the year 5600 A.M. in 1840, described by Arie Morgenstern, "Messianic concepts and settlement in the land of Israel," in *Vision and Conflict in the Holy Land*, ed. Richard I. Cohen (Jerusalem, 1985) 141–62, with commentary by Jacob Katz, 165–68.

5. The literature here is enormous. Begin with Jacob Katz, *Exclusiveness and Tolerance: Jewish-Gentile Relations in Medieval and Modern Times* (NY, 1961): Arthur Hertzberg, *The French Enlightenment and the Jews: The Origins of Modern Anti-Semitism* (NY, 1968); and Jean Paul Sartre, *Anti-Semite and Jew*, trans. George J. Becker (NY, 1965 [1946]). For a modern work exemplary of the bifrons perspective, see Ernest Van den Haag, *The Jewish Mystique* (NY,

1977). On the Russian pogroms, see esp. David G. Roskies, *Against the Apocalypse* (Cambridge, MA, 1984) 79–112; on the situation in France, Michael Marrus, *The Politics of Assimilation: A Study of the French Jewish Community at the Time of the Dreyfus Affair* (Oxford, 1971) 208–10, and Steven Wilson, "The antisemitic riots of 1898 in France," *Historical Journal* 16 (1973) 789–806; on Germany at century's turn, Fritz R. Stern, *The Politics of Cultural Despair* (Berkeley, 1961), and Thomas Flanagan, "The Third Reich: origins of a millenarian symbol," *History of European Ideas* 8,3 (1987) 283–95.

6. Paul Grunebaum-Ballin, "Grégoire convertisseur? ou la croyance au 'Retour d'Israel,' " *Revue des études juifs* 121 (1962) 383–98; James Parkes, "Lewis Way and his times," *Transactions of the Jewish Historical Society of England* 20 (1959–61) 189–201; George L. Berlin, "Joseph S. C. F. Frey, the Jews, and early nineteenth century millenarianism," *Journal of the Early Republic* 1 (1981) 27–49; Ruth Kark, "Millenarianism and agricultural settlement in the Holy Land in the nineteenth century," *Journal of Historical Geography* 9, 1 (1983) 47–62; Adoniram J. Gordon, *Ecce Venit: Behold He Cometh* (NY, 1889) 195 for quote; William E. Blackstone, *Palestine for the Jews. A Copy of the Memorial Presented to President Harrison, March 5, 1891* (Oak Park, IL, 1891); Beverly O. Kinnear, *Impending Judgments on the Earth* (London, 1892) employing the prophetic framework of the British Israelites, who believed that Anglo-Saxons in Britain and the United States were the true Jews of the Last Days. On Balfour and Allenby, see Blanche E. C. Dugdale, *Arthur James Balfour* (London, 1936) II, 216–17, 234; Walter Laqueur, *A History of Zionism* (NY, 1972) 188–89.

7. Steven E. Aschheim, "The East European Jew and German Jewish identity," *Studies in Contemporary Jewry* 1 (1984) 3–25, and entire volume; Todd M. Endelman, ed., *Jewish Apostasy in the Modern World* (NY, 1987); John M. Cuddihy, *The Ordeal of Civility: Freud, Marx, Levi-Strauss, and the Jewish Struggle with Modernity* (NY, 1974) esp. ch. 14 on Marx; Chaim Zhitlovsky, "The Jewish factor in my socialism," in *The Golden Tradition: Jewish Life and Thought in Eastern Europe*, ed. Lucy S. Dawidowicz (Boston, 1967) 420–22.

8. Carl E. Schorske, *Fin-de-siècle Vienna: Politics and Culture* (NY, 1981) 146; Marvin Lowenthal, ed. and trans., *The Diaries of Theodor Herzl* (NY, 1956) 3, and cf. the translation in Arthur Hertzberg, ed. and trans., *The Zionist Idea* (NY, 1975) 204.

9. Hertzberg, *The Zionist Idea*, 227–30, 240–41, for Herzl and Nordau; Nahum Sokolow, "Jan Bloch: the loyal convert," in *The Golden Tradition*, 344; Alex Bein, *Theodor Herzl*, trans. Maurice Samuel (NY, 1970) 231–32.

10. Yehuda Bauer, "On the place of the Holocaust in history," *Holocaust and Genocide Studies* 2 (1987) 209–20; Tim F. LaHaye, *The Beginning of the End* (Wheaton, IL, 1972) ch. 4; Hal Lindsey, *The Late Great Planet Earth* (Grand Rapids, 1970) ch. 4.

11. Larry Kickham, "The theology of nuclear war," in *Apocalypse Culture,* ed. Adam Parfrey (NY: Amok Press, 1987) 209–18, with the widely repeated quote from Reagan on 214; Edward B. Glick, *The Triangular Connection: America, Israel, and American Jews* (London, 1982); Sacvan Bercovitch, *The Puritan Origins of the American Self* (New Haven, 1975) esp. ch. 3; Ruth Mouly and Roland Robertson, "Zionism in American premillenarian fundamentalism," *American Journal of Theology and Philosophy* 4, 3 (1983) 97 for Falwell; Carl H. Voss and David A. Rausch, "American Christians and Israel, 1948–1988," *American Jewish Archives* 40 (1988) 41–81. Note, however, that like some other aggressively millenarian

Christians, Zionist Christians may also be deeply anti-Semitic. See Lloyd J. Averill, "Is the end near?" *Christian Century* (Jan. 19, 1983) 47; Ronald R. Stockton, "Christian Zionism: prophecy and public opinion," *Middle East Journal* 41 (1987) 242.

12. Fouad Ajami, *The Vanished Imam: Musa al Sadr and the Shia of Lebanon* (Ithaca, 1986); Nikki R. Keddie, "Shi'ism and revolution," in *Religion, Rebellion, Revolution*, ed. Bruce Lincoln (Basingstoke, 1985) 173; Said Amir Arjomand, *Shadow of God and the Hidden Imam: Religion, Political Order and Societal Change in Shi'ite Iran from the Beginning to 1890* (Chicago, 1884) 268–69 for prayer and speech.

13. Gideon Aran, "A mystic-messianic interpretation of modern Israeli history," *Studies in Contemporary Jewry* 4 (1988) 263–75; Gary S. Schiff, *Tradition and Politics: The Religious Parties of Israel* (Detroit, 1977); David K. Shipler, *Arab and Jew: Wounded Spirits in a Promised Land* (NY, 1986); Fouad Ajami et al., "Prophets of the Holy Land: Israel and the Arab world in 1994," *Harper's* (Dec. 1984) 33–48; Max Frankel and Judy Hoffman, "Jerusalem, my home: what it might be like in the year 2000," *I Live in Israel: A Text and Activity Book* (West Orange, 1979) 108–14.

14. William H. McNeill and Ruth S. Adams, eds., *Human Migration: Patterns and Policies* (Bloomington, 1978) on natives and aliens, esp. essays by McNeill, Patterson, Zolberg, and Shils; Raoelina Andriambololona, "Towards another development. Science, technology and South-South cooperation," *IFDA Dossier* 55 (Sept.–Oct., 1986) 29–40, an effort to resist the North-South polarization; George Allan, *The Importance of the Past: A Meditation on the Authority of Tradition* (Albany, 1986); Edmund Leach, "Two essays concerning the symbolic representation of time," *Rethinking Anthropology* (London, 1971) 125–36; Denis de Rougemont, *The Future Is Within Us*, trans. Anthony J. C. Kerr (Oxford, 1983) 3; John F. Laffey, "Cacophonic rites: modernism and postmodernism," *Historical Reflections* 14 (Spring 1987) 1–32 on the intelligibility of our times, and see the entire issue of *New German Critique* 33 (Fall, 1984), Daisaku Ikeda, "Toward the twenty-first century," in *A Lasting Peace* (NY, 1981) 124.

15. Schorske, *Fin-de-siècle Vienna*, 200; Jeffrey M. Masson, ed. and trans., *The Complete Letters of Sigmund Freud to Wilhelm Fliess, 1887–1904* (Cambridge, MA, 1985) 361; Raphael Patai, ed., *The Complete Diaries of Theodor Herzl*, trans. Harry Zohn (NY, 1960) III, 1017.

16. Robert L. Heilbroner, *An Inquiry into the Human Prospect, Updated and Reconsidered for the 1980s* (NY, 1980 [1974]) 176–77: Robert Bundy, ed., *Images of the Future: The Twenty-First Century and Beyond* (Buffalo, 1976) 46, statement by Drew Christiansen, S.J. The search for "a second naiveté" may also explain the currency of "revisionist" and anti-Semitic histories denying the reality or the intentionality of the Holocaust, as in the specious *Journal of Historical Review*.

17. For surveys, see N. Lukianowicz, "Autoscopic phenomena," *Archives of Neurology and Psychiatry* 80 (1958) 199–220, which notes the aborigine Double, and Carl F. Keppler, *Literature of the Second Self* (Tucson, 1972). On the archetypes, see Sigmund Freud, *Totem and Taboo*, trans. James Strachey (NY, 1950 [1913]) 88–90 on narcissism and animism, and Freud's *The Uncanny* (1919) in his *Collected Papers* (London, 1924–50) IV, 368ff.; Harry Redner, *In the Beginning Was the Deed: Reflections on the Passage of Faust* (Berkeley, 1982); Otto

Rank, *The Double: A Psychoanalytic Study,* trans. Harry Tucker, Jr. (Chapel Hill, 1971) esp. ch. 5.

18. Masao Miyoshi, *The Divided Self* (NY, 1969) 23 for quote from Godwin; André Parreaux, *The Publication of The Monk. A Literary Event, 1796–1798* (Paris, 1960) 71 for quote from Mrs. Thrale-Piozzi; Ralph Tymms, *Doubles in Literary Psychology* (Cambridge, 1949) 16, 30–33; Clifford Hallam, "The Double as incomplete self: toward a definition of Doppelgänger," in *Fearful Symmetry: Doubles and Doubling in Literature and Film,* ed. Eugene J. Crook (Tallahassee, 1981) 1–31.

19. Linda M. Strauss, "Automata: A Study in the Interface of Science, Technology, and Popular Culture, 1730–1885," Ph.D. thesis, University of California, San Diego, 1987, chs. 4 and 5; Allan Pinkerton, *A Double Life and the Detectives* (NY, 1985) v; Robert Louis Stevenson, *Strange Case of Dr. Jekyll and Mr. Hyde* (NY, 1909 [1886]) 373, 374, 386. Cf. Gaston Leroux, *The Double Life* (NY, 1909); Frank X. Braun, "Theodor Storm's *Doppelgänger* (1887)," *Germanic Review* 32 (1957) 267–72; Peter McKellar, *Mindsplit* (London, 1979) ch. 2.

20. Charles Brockden Brown, *Edgar Hartley; or, Memoirs of a Sleep-walker* (Port Washington, 1963 [1799]), which features the good Mrs. Lorimer and her evil twin brother Arthur Wiatte; Robert Darnton, *Mesmerism and the End of the Enlightenment in France* (Cambridge, MA, 1968) ch. 2; H. F. Ellenberger, *The Discovery of the Unconscious* (NY, 1970) 127; Eric T. Carlson et al., eds., *Benjamin Rush's Lectures on the Mind (1789–1813)* (Philadelphia, 1981) 669–70; Eric T. Carlson, "The history of multiple personality in the United States: Mary Reynolds and her subsequent reputation," *Bulletin of the History of Medicine* 58 (1984) 72–82; H. Dewar, "Report on a communication from Dr. Dyce of Aberdeen," *Transactions of the Royal Society of Edinburgh* 9 (1823) 365 on the terms; W. S. Taylor and Mabel F. Martin, "Multiple personality," *Journal of Abnormal and Social Psychology* 39 (1944) 281–300 for an historical review, and also M. Boor and P. M. A. Coons, "A comprehensive bibliography of literature pertaining to multiple personality," *Psychological Reports* 53 (1983) 295–310; Clair Rosenfield, "The shadow within: the conscious and unconscious use of the Double," in *Stories of the Double,* ed. Albert J. Guerard (Philadelphia, 1967) 318–19 on Dostoevsky.

21. Silas Weir Mitchell, "Mary Reynolds: a case of double consciousness," *Transactions of the College of Physicians of Philadelphia,* 3rd ser., 10 (1888) 366–89; Michael G. Kenny, *The Passion of Ansel Bourne: Multiple Personality in American Culture* (Washington, D.C., 1986) 28ff. on Reynolds; on Félida X. and other cases, see Hillel Schwartz, "The three-body problem and the end of the world," in *Fragments for a History of the Human Body. Part II. (= Zone, vol. 4),* eds. Michel Feher et al. (NY, 1989) 406–65.

22. *Oxford English Dictionary,* III, 846, s.v. "Double vision" and Supp. I, 847, s.v. "Double exposure"; James Coates, *Photographing the Invisible* (NY, 1973 [1911]); Irene Mawer, *The Art of Mime* (London, 1932) 71–74; A. J. L. Busst, "The image of the androgyne in the nineteenth century," in *Romantic Mythologies,* ed. Ian Fletcher (London, 1967) 57ff.; Hans Hinterhauser, *Fin de siècle: Gestalten und Mythen* (Munich, 1977) ch. 6 on centaurs, as also Georges Dumézil, *Le problème des centaures* (Paris, 1929), noting their close connection to New Year's festivities; Bram Dijkstra, *Idols of Perversity* (NY, 1986) 324–32 on sphinxes; D. W. Forrest, *Francis Galton* (NY, 1974) ch. 10 on twins; Anne Harrington, *Medicine, Mind, and*

the Double Brain: A Study in Nineteenth-Century Thought (Princeton, 1987); J. Miles Bramwell, "Hypnotic and posthypnotic appreciation of time: secondary and multiple personalities," *Brain* 23 (1900) 161–238; R. Osgood Mason, *Telepathy and the Subliminal Self,* 2nd ed. (NY, 1897 [1896]) 141; E. D. Mackerness, ed., *The Journals of George Sturt* (Cambridge, 1967) I, entries for 22 Nov. 1900 and 12 Jan. 1901.

23. R. Osgood Mason, "Duplex personality," *Journal of Nervous and Mental Disease* 18 (1893) 593–98 on Alma Z.; Morton Prince, "Some of the revelations of hypnotism," *Boston Medical and Surgical Journal* 122 (May 22, 1890) 493 on Janet's Léonie; Abram H. Dailey, *Mollie Fancher: the Brooklyn Enigma* (Brooklyn, 1894) 74–79; Morton Prince, *The Dissociation of a Personality*, 2nd ed. (NY, 1908 [1905]) 111, 142–43, 288–94, 461, 514.

24. " 'The Case of Becky': a remarkable play," *New York Times* (Oct. 2, 1912) 13:3; J. Hoenig, "The concept of schizophrenia," *British Journal of Psychiatry* 142 (1983) 551; Milton Rosenbaum, "The role of the term schizophrenia in the decline of diagnoses of multiple personality," *Archives of General Psychiatry* 37 (1980) 1383–85, his count of multiple personality cases amended; Corbett H. Thigpen and Hervey M. Cleckley, "On the incidence of multiple personality disorder," *International Journal of Clinical and Experimental Hypnosis* 32 (1984) 63–66; Danielle F. Turns, "Epidémiologie des schizophrénies," *Annales médico-psychologiques* 138 (1980) 637–46.

25. Bennett G. Braun, ed., *Treatment of Multiple Personality Disorder* (Washington, D.C., 1986) xvi; George B. Greaves, "Multiple personality: 165 years after Mary Reynolds," *Journal of Nervous and Mental Disease* 168 (1980) 577–97; Connie Zweig, "Messengers of the gods," *Omni* (Jan. 1986) 27; Judith Hooper and Dick Teresi, "Mind menagerie," *ibid.*, 76; Eugene L. Bliss, *Multiple Personality, Allied Disorders, and Hypnosis* (NY, 1986) 118.

26. Flora R. Schreiber, *Sybil* (NY, 1973); Daniel Keyes, *The Minds of Billy Milligan* (Toronto, 1982); Emily Peterson and Nancy Lynn Gooch, with Lucy Freeman, *Nightmare: Uncovering the 56 Strange Personalities of Nancy Lynn Gooch* (NY, 1987); Robert S. Mayer, *Through a Mind Divided: A Doctor's Exploration of Multiple Personality* (NY, 1988), prepublication typescript kindly provided by Paul Bresnick of Doubleday. Not "cured" by therapist Thigpen, Chris Sizemore (of *The Three Faces of Eve*) eventually displayed twenty-three personalities.

27. For critiques, see Stanley Abrams, "The multiple personality: a legal defense," *American Journal of Clinical Hypnosis* 25 (1983) 225–31; Pamela S. Ludolph, "How prevalent is multiple personality?" *American Journal of Psychiatry* 142 (1985) 1526–27; Nicholas P. Spanos et al., "Multiple personality: a social psychological perspective," *Journal of Abnormal Psychology* 94 (1985) 362–76. On media popularity of multiple personality and the First International Conference, see Mayer, *Through a Mind Divided.* The American Psychiatric Association's *DSM-III* recognizes multiple personality disorder but calls it "extremely rare." On the legal side, see Alan Ashby, "Ester Minor: multiple personalities in court," *Forum* 6,2 (1980) 5–8, 29–30; Martin T. Orne et al., "On the differential diagnosis of multiple personality in the forensic context," *International Journal of Clinical and Experimental Hypnosis* 32 (1984) 118–67; Ralph B. Allison, "The multiple personality defendant in court," *American Journal of Forensic Psychiatry* 3 (1982–83) 181–91; Alfred P. French and Bryan R. Schechmeister, "The multiple personality syndrome and criminal defense," *Bulletin of the American Academy of Psychiatry and the Law* 11 (1983) 17–25.

28. J. H. van den Berg, *Divided Existence and Complex Society* (Pittsburgh, 1974 [1963]); Gilles Deleuze and Felix Guattari, *Capitalisme et schizophrénie* (Paris, 1972–80); Henri M. Yaker, "The schizophrenic perception of time," in *The Future of Time*, ed. Yaker (NY, 1972) ch. 8; Schwartz, "The three-body problem and the end of the world," on the schizophrenic *Weltuntergangserlebnis*.

29. The confusion extends also to the neurophysiological laboratory. See H. Tristram Engelhardt, Jr., "Splitting the brain, dividing the soul, being of two minds: an editorial concerning mind-body quandaries in medicine," *Journal of Medicine and Philosophy* 2 (1977) 89–100; Clifton Perry, "Commissurotomy and multiple minds," *Ethics of Science and Medicine* 7 (1980) 171–77; David G. Benner and C. Stephen Evans, "Unity and multiplicity in hypnosis, commissurotomy, and multiple personality disorder," *Journal of Mind and Behavior* 5 (1984) 423–31; Norman I. Finkel and Steven R. Sabat, "Split-brain madness: an insanity defense waiting to happen," *Law and Human Behavior* 8 (1984) 225–52.

30. Carl G. Jung, "On the psychogenesis of schizophrenia" (1939) in *The Basic Writings of C. G. Jung*, ed. Violet Staub de Laszlo (NY, 1959) 382–86.

31. Van den Berg, *Divided Existence*, 50 on Goethe; Prince, "Some of the revelations," 464; *Brain/Mind Bulletin* 8 (Oct. 3, 1983) 4, statement by John Beahrs, and Brenda O'Regan of the Institute of Noetic Sciences says (p. 2), "Multiples may be *the* most important route to understanding and gaining access to the untapped skills and potential we all have." There had been a similar tendency to identify schizophrenia as "nothing less than the predicament of each one of us": David Cooper, *Psychiatry and Anti-Psychiatry* (London, 1967) 45, and R. D. Laing, *The Divided Self* (NY, 1969). Now that schizophrenia is being drawn into the circle of neurological genetic diseases (see Thomas H. Maugh, "Study ties schizophrenia to genetic flaw," *Los Angeles Times* [Nov. 10, 1988] 44), multiple personality has the more unrestricted metaphorical power—crucial, for example, to the innovative 1985–87 television series, "Max Headroom." Consider however the critique by Janice R. Stevens and Manuel F. Casanova, "Is there a neuropathology of schizophrenia?" *Biological Psychiatry* 24 (1988) 123–28.

32. Vicki Saltman and Robert S. Solomon, "Incest and the multiple personality," *Psychological Reports* 50 (1982) 1127–41, a seminal article; Mayer, *Through a Mind Divided*; Myron Boor, "The multiple personality epidemic," *Journal of Nervous and Mental Disease* 170 (1982) 302–04; National Center for Missing & Exploited Children, Washington, D.C., explanatory brochure (1988?); *Missing Children's Assistance Act, Hearings before the Subcommittee on Juvenile Justice of the Committee on the Judiciary, U. S. Senate, 98th Congress, 2d Session, on S. 2014 . . . February 7 and 21, March 8, 13, and 21, 1984* (Washington, D.C., 1984) 1, 11, 16. Contrast Neil Spitzer, "The children's crusade," *Atlantic* (June 1986) 18–22.

33. Keith Hawton, "Suicide in adolescents," in *Suicide*, ed. Alec Roy (Baltimore, 1986) 135–46; René F. W. Diekstra and Keith Hawton, eds., *Suicide in Adolescence* (Dordrecht, 1987); Howard I. Kushner, *Self-Destruction in the Promised Land: A Psychocultural Biology of American Suicide* (New Brunswick, NJ, 1989). On the equivalent concern in the 1890s with abandoned children, see K. D. Stoes, "The land of Shalam," *New Mexico Humanities Review* 33 (1958) 1–23, 103–27.

34. Christopher Lasch, *The Minimal Self: Psychic Survival in Troubled Times* (NY, 1984); Robert Jay Lifton, *The Broken Connection: On Death and the Continuity of Life* (NY, 1979) esp. ch. 16, and his *The Future of Immortality and Other Essays for a Nuclear Age* (NY, 1987) ch. 14; David Spiegel, "Multiple personality as a post-traumatic stress disorder," *Psychiatric Clinics of North America* 7,1 (1984) 101–10.

35. Annie Kriegel, "Generational difference: the history of an idea," in *Generations*, ed. Stephen R. Graubard (NY, 1979) 23–38; Michael Dorris and Louise Erdrich, "Bangs and whimpers: novelists at Armageddon," *New York Times Book Review* (March 13, 1988) 1, 24–25; Trudy Govier, "What should we do about future people?" *American Philosophical Quarterly* 16 (April 1979) 105–13.

36. Ronald M. Green, "Intergenerational distributive justice and environmental responsibility," in *Responsibilities to Future Generations: Environmental Ethics*, ed. Ernest Partridge (Buffalo, 1980) 91. See also John Rawls, *A Theory of Justice* (Cambridge, MA, 1971) 284–92, and Richard T. De George, "The environment, rights, and future generations," in *Ethics and Problems of the 21st Century*, eds. Kenneth E. Goodpaster and Kenneth M. Sayre (Notre Dame, 1979) 93–105.

37. Joanna Macy, *Despair and Personal Power in the Nuclear Age* (Philadelphia, 1983) xiii, 1, 2, and see also Susan Goldberg et al., "Thinking about the threat of nuclear war," *American Journal of Orthopsychiatry* 55 (Oct. 1985) 503–12, on children and despair. The goal of "fusion" was explicit as early as 1904 with Boris Sidis and Simon P. Goodhart, *Multiple Personality* (NY, 1905 [1904]) and Prince, *Dissociation of a Personality*, 403. Cf. J. G. Watkins and Helen H. Watkins, "Ego-state therapy," in *The Newer Therapies*, eds. L. E. Abt and I. R. Stuart (NY, 1982) 137–55, and Richard P. Kluft, "Treatment results in multiple personality," *Psychiatric Clinics of North America* 7 (1984) 9–29.

38. Mayer, *Through a Mind Divided*; Loompanics Unlimited, *1988 Main Catalog* (Port Townsend, WA, 1988); "Social security number for children disputed," *New York Times* (Aug. 21, 1988) 21; Edward Myers, *The Chosen Few: Surviving the Nuclear Holocaust* (South Bend, 1982); James Coates, *Armed and Dangerous: The Rise of the Survivalist Right* (NY, 1987); Bruce D. Clayton, *Life After Doomsday: A Survivalist Guide to Nuclear War and Other Major Disasters* (Boulder, 1980).

39. Howard J. Ruff, *How to Prosper during the Coming Bad Years* (NY, 1979) "Over Six Months on All National Bestseller Lists!"; Robert J. Ringer, *How You Can Find Happiness during the Collapse of Western Civilization* (NY, 1983); Myers, *Chosen Few*, 20–21.

40. Whitley Strieber and James W. Kunetka, *War Day and the Journey Onward* (NY, 1984) 3, 37.

41. Editors of *Flying Saucer Review, World Roundup of UFO Sightings and Events* (NY, 1958); David M. Jacobs, *The UFO Controversy in America* (Bloomington, 1975) esp. 110–16, 292–93; Ronald D. Story, ed., *The Encyclopedia of UFOs* (Garden City, NY, 1980) throughout; Leon Festinger et al., *When Prophecy Fails* (NY, 1956); Roy Wallis, "The Aetherius Society," in *Sectarianism*, ed. Wallis (NY, 1975) 17–34; Nada-Yolanda, *Visitors from Other Planets* (Miami, 1974); Timothy G. Beckley, *Psychic and UFO Revelations in the Last Days* (NY, 1980) esp. ch. 5; Brad Steiger, *Gods of Aquarius: UFOs and the Transformation of Man* (NY, 1976);

Ruth Montgomery, *Threshold to Tomorrow* (NY, 1983) on "Walk-ins" among us; Hayden Hewes and Brad Steiger, *UFO Missionaries Extraordinary* (NY, 1976) on Bo and Peep. For the genre identifying UFO aliens with satanic powers, see John A. Keel, *The Mothman Prophecies* (NY, 1975); John Weldon with Zola Leavitt, *UFO's: What on Earth Is Happening?* (Irvine, 1975). For critical analysis, see Ron Westrum et al., "Little green men and all that," *Society* 21 (Jan.–Feb., 1984) 37–44, and any issue of the *Skeptical Inquirer*. Cf. the emphasis on "fundamental mythology" in Jacques Vallée, *Dimensions: A Casebook of Alien Contact* (Chicago, 1988).

42. "Time," *Newsweek* (March 30, 1987) 65; Ragan Dunn, "Space aliens plot invasion of the earth!" *Weekly World News* (Oct. 18, 1988) 24–25; J. Allen Hynek et al., *Night Siege: The Hudson Valley UFO Sightings* (NY, 1987); Michael Winerip, "U.F.O. stakeout," *New York Times* (Oct. 17, 1987) B1; "Documents on '47 U.F.O. crash called false," *New York Times* (Aug. 26, 1987) 11; Edward Dolnick, "Closer encounters," *New Republic* (Aug. 10, 1987) 15 on "Cosmicgate"; Jean Sider, "Crashes d'OVNI: enfin des preuves," *Lumières dans la nuit* 30 (mai–juin 1987) 3–15; Robin James, "Cheeseburger kills space alien," *Weekly World News* (June 28, 1988) 2; Laura Mundo, "Sex and the UFO," mimeograph, May 1981, green sheet p. 2, mailed to me with *The Interplanetary News* (Feb. 25, 1988) by the Flying Saucer Information Center, 7803 Ruanne Ct., Pasadena, MD 21122.

43. Ragan Dunn, "Riddle from beyond the stars," *Weekly World News* (Oct. 25, 1988) 24–25; Jacobs, *UFO Controversy*, 296, citing a 1973 Gallup Poll; William Richman, "They came from inner space: UFO's. Is seeing believing?" *Mother Jones* (Dec. 1978) 33–34, 38–39, citing a 1978 Gallup Poll; James Oberg, "Astronaut 'UFO' sightings," *Skeptical Inquirer* 3 (Fall 1978) 39–46; Richard Gold, "UFO projects eye otherworldly B.O.," *Variety* (July 1, 1987) 5. Cf. the explanations for the popularity of UFOs in Richard F. Haines, ed., *UFO Phenomena and the Behavioral Scientist* (Metuchen, NJ, 1979).

44. Whitley Strieber, *Communion: A True Story* (NY, 1987) 22–30. See Thomas M. Disch, "The village alien," *Nation* (March 14, 1987) 328–36, on Strieber merging motifs of abduction with the "ritual protocols of bondage and domination."

45. Coral Lorenzen, " 'Little men' from UFOs," *Fate* 21 (May 1968) 55–64; Ted Bloecher, "Close encounters of the third kind," *Fate* 31 (Jan. 1978) 34–43; Clifford A. Wilson, *UFOs and Their Mission Impossible* (NY, 1975) 171–72 on number of contactees; D. Scott Rogo, *Alien Abductions* (NY, 1980); Budd Hopkins, *Missing Time: A Documented Study of UFO Abductions* (NY, 1981); Strieber, *Communion*, 83–85, 114–27, 216–20, 249.

46. Strieber, *Communion*, 15, 66, 253, 280, 295.

47. *Ibid.*, 69–71, 131–45, quotes on 70, 132; Bliss, *Multiple Personality*, 150; Walker Percy, *The Last Gentleman* (NY, 1966), his *The Second Coming* (NY, 1980) 3–12, and his *Lost in the Cosmos: The Last Self-Help Book* (NY, 1983) esp. 20–22; Michael Walsh, "The opera as science fiction," *Time* (Aug. 1, 1988) 58; National Public Radio, "All Things Considered," Sept. 26, 1988, review and interview with Philip Glass; Henry Weber, "Space traders from outer space!" *Weekly World News* (July 5, 1988) 31, and idem, "Elephants snatched by UFO," *ibid.* (July 26, 1988) 31. Almost as popular as Strieber's book on abductions has been the book by his friend Budd Hopkins, *Intruders* (NY, 1987).

48. Dolnick, "Closer encounters," 15, quoting Strieber. Note that reports of missing children are called "sightings," *Missing Children's Assistance Act. Hearings*, 73, 75. Present concerns with AIDS and immunology may also reflect anxieties about alien interference with our bodies; on this, see esp. Jean Hamburger, "Perspectives immunologiques et immunopathologiques de l'an 2000," in *Perspectives médicales de l'an 2000* (Liège, 1981?) 277–83.

49. F. S. Betten, "St. Boniface and the doctrine of the Antipodes," *American Catholic Quarterly Review* 43 (1918) 654–63; David Woodward, "Medieval *mappaemundi*," in *The History of Cartography*, eds. J. B. Harley and D. Woodward (Chicago, 1987) I, 300–05, 316, 319, 332–33; R. W. Shirley, *The Mapping of the World: Early Printed World Maps, 1472–1700* (London, 1983) xiii, xxv, 25; Leo Bagrow, *History of Cartography*, 2nd ed., trans. D. L. Paisey, rev. by R. A. Skelton (Chicago, 1985) 83, 126, 134; Pierre d'Ailly, *Ymago Mundi*, with marginal notes by Columbus, trans. Edmond Buron (Paris, 1930 [1410–14]) II, 529, note 488; James D. Tracy, ed. and trans., *True Ocean Found: Paludanus's Letters on Dutch Voyages to the Kara Sea, 1595–1596* (Minneapolis, 1980) 5ff. on black rock and islands around North Pole; Gabriel de Foigny, *A New Discovery of Terra Incognita Australis* (London, 1693 [1676]) esp. 63 on hermaphrodites; J. Enterline, "The southern continent and the false Strait of Magellan," *Imago Mundi* 26 (1972) 48–58; James De Mille, *A Strange Manuscript Found in a Copper Cylinder* (NY, 1888), an Egyptian South Pole; Frank Savile, *Beyond the Great South Wall: The Secret of the Antarctic* (NY, 1901), a Mayan South Pole.

50. Cyrus C. Adams, "New phases of polar research," *Review of Reviews* 24 (1901) 67, referring to the hollow-Earth theory of John Cleves Symmes (1780–1829) and to Henry W. Howgate's *Polar Colonization* (Washington, D.C., 1877). Cf. S. Byron Welcome, *From Earth's Centre: A Polar Gateway Message* (Chicago, 1894) and S. E. Chapman, *Dr. Jones' Picnic* (San Francisco, 1898), two of the many utopian fictions at century's end that took advantage of the "fevered" excitement as to the North Pole (described by Matthew Phipps Shiels in his survivor's tale, *The Purple Cloud* [London, 1901] 4), and see also Pierre Berton, *The Arctic Grail* (NY, 1988). On the South Pole, see F. T. Bullen, "The lonely Antarctic," *Leisure Hour* 49 (1900) 507–11; Jules Verne, *An Antarctic Mystery* (Philadelphia, 1899). On Peary, see "The coming era of dullness," *The Independent* (1912), quoted in "1984. If this is the future . . . ," *Science '84* (Jan.–Feb. 1984) 43. On the Russian expedition, see Dmitri Shparo, "In the polar night and across the drifting ice," *Soviet Life* (Oct. 1986) 10–15.

51. Alcestis Oberg, "Comradery," *Omni* (April 1986) 14, 114; Steven M. Rosen, *The Moebius Seed: A Visionary Novel of Planetary Transformation* (Walpole, NH, 1985) 278, suggesting that the poles are joined to make a "Klein bottle Earth"; Barbara Mitchell, "Undermining Antarctica," *Technology Review* (Feb.–March 1988) 48–57; Gunter Weller et al., "Laboratory Antarctica," *Science* 238 (Dec. 4, 1987) 1361–68; Lee Dye, "Arctic ozone loss a bigger threat due to pole's proximity," *Los Angeles Times* (Dec. 19, 1988) II,3:1–2; John W. White, *Pole Shift* (Garden City, NY, 1980); Charles W. Beale, *The Secret of the Earth* (London, 1899) 150; M. Lusson and D. Lusson, *The Beginning or the End* (Virginia Beach, 1975) 21–22, 66.

52. The Planetary Society (Pasadena), "The Mars Observer" fact sheet (1986?); Carl Sagan, *USA and USSR: Let's Go to Mars—TOGETHER* (Pasadena, 1985?) on Mars, Columbus, Lenin, and the Russians, whose November 7, 1987, parade celebrating the seventieth anniversary of the Bolshevik revolution featured a float promoting a joint venture to Mars; Lynton K. Caldwell, "1992: threshold of the postmodern world," in R. P. Warren et al.,

A Time to Hear and Answer (University, AL, 1977) 177, 212; Stackpole Books advertisement for Brian O'Leary's *Mars 1999* (Harrisburg, PA, 1988) in *Space World* (May 1988) 37, and see insert, "Space Advocate," for Backer letter; Harrison H. Schmitt, "A Millennium Project: Mars 2000," photocopied leaflet from the Planetary Society's *Planetary Report*; Young Astronaut Council advertisement in *Omni* (Jan. 1986) 99; Henry S. F. Cooper, Jr., "Letter from the Space Center," *The New Yorker* (June 8, 1987) 76–78, and 81 on the Titans. See also John Noble Wilford, *Mars: The Red Planet Beckons* (NY, 1989).

53. Sagan, *USA and USSR*, 3; Richard C. Hoagland, *The Monuments of Mars: A City on the Edge of Forever* (Berkeley, 1987) xviii, xxiv. See also Randolph R. Pazos, ed., *The Face on Mars: Evidence for a Lost Civilization?* (Chicago, 1986) reviewed in *Skeptical Inquirer* 11 (Spring 1987) 296–97.

54. John Noble Wilford, "Destination Mars," *New York Times Magazine* (Mar. 20, 1988) 39; Electric Blue Peggy Sue and the Revolutionions, "You Tell Me That's It's Revolution" (Gaga Goodies 45 RPM record, Helsinki, 1987?); Stewart Brand, ed., *Space Colonies* (Harmondsworth, 1978); K. C. Cole, "A theory of everything," *New York Times Magazine* (Oct. 18, 1987) 20ff. on Witten. Buckminster Fuller coined the term "Spaceship Earth" in 1951.

55. Edwin A. Abbott, *Flatland: A Romance of Many Dimensions*, 2nd ed. (NY, 1952 [1884]) quotes on 80–83; Edgar D. Mitchell, "Earth in a new light," *Cosmos* (Dec. 1973–Jan. 1974) 1; idem, introductory letter and brochure describing the work of the Institute of Noetic Sciences (Sausalito, n.d.), and cf. Daniel Noel, *Approaching Earth* (Amity, NY, 1986) for a critical analysis of this new perspective; Zweig, "Messengers of the gods," 27; Ian Wilson, *All in the Mind* (Garden City, NY, 1982).

56. Roger J. Woolger, *Other Lives, Other Selves: A Jungian Psychotherapist Discovers Past Lives* (Garden City, NY, 1987) ch. 9, quotes 219–21.

57. Francis Dobbs, *Millennium: A Poem* (London, 1787) xv, 38 and 38n., 39n., 40n.

58. Janet Oppenheim, *The Other World: Spiritualism and Psychical Research in England, 1850–1914* (Cambridge, 1985); Linda Dalrymple Henderson, *The Fourth Dimension and Non-Euclidean Geometry in Modern Art* (Princeton, 1983), extended in her essay, "Mysticism, romanticism, and the fourth dimension," in *The Spiritual in Art: Abstract Painting, 1890–1985* (NY, 1986, for the Los Angeles County Museum of Art), in which see also Sixten Ringbom, "Transcending the visible: the generation of the abstract pioneers," 131–54, quote on 134 from Annie Besant, *The Ancient Wisdom*, 2nd ed. (London, 1899) 146.

59. Shirley MacLaine, *Dancing in the Light* (Toronto, 1985) 28, 319 quoting Chris Griscom; Thea Alexander, *2150 A.D.* (NY, 1976) 30; George Gallup, Jr., with William Proctor, *Adventures in Immortality* (NY, 1982) 135–38, 192–93; Sylvia Cranston and Carey Williams, *Reincarnation: A New Horizon in Science, Religion and Society* (NY, 1984) 12, 304, and cf. Helen Wambach, *Reliving Past Lives* (NY, 1978) 122.

60. Richard Erdoes, A.D. *One Thousand: Living on the Brink of Apocalypse* (NY, 1988); John Brunner, *Total Eclipse* (Garden City, NY, 1974); James Hughes, *Ends: A Novel of Cessation* (NY, 1971); Raveendra N. Batra, *The Great Depression of 1990*, rev. ed. (NY, 1987 [1985])

on cycles of collapse; Charles Jencks, "Postmodern and late modern: the essential definitions," *Chicago Review* 35, 4 (1987) 31–58.

61. Carol G. Zaleski, *Otherworld Journeys: Accounts of Near-Death Experiences in Medieval and Modern Times* (NY, 1987); Gallup, *Adventures in Immortality*, ch. 4; Robert A. Monroe, *Far Journeys* (Garden City, NY, 1987); Karlis Osis and Erlendur Haraldsson, *At the Hour of Death* (NY, 1977).

62. John R. Audette, "Historical perspectives on near-death episodes and experiences," in *A Collection of Near-Death Research Readings*, comp. Craig R. Lundahl (Chicago, 1982) 21–43; Albert Heim, "Remarks on fatal falls," trans. Russell Noyes and Roy Kletti for *Omega* 3 (1972) 45–52; Ronald K. Siegel, "The psychology of life after death," *American Psychologist* 35 (1980) 911–31; Raymond A. Moody, Jr., *Life After Life* (Harrisburg, PA, 1976) esp. 23–24; Ian Stevenson, "Interview," *Omni* (Jan. 1988) 77ff.; Philip José Farmer, *The Dark Design* (NY, 1977) back cover; Sheldon Ruderman, "A personal encounter with death and some consequences," in *Between Life and Death*, ed. Robert Kastenbaum (NY, 1979) 12; Kenneth Ring, *Heading Toward Omega* (NY, 1984) 258–59.

63. Joyce Dell'Acqua, "The search for extraterrestrial intelligence," *The Futurist* (May–June 1988) 16–18; Richard P. Marsh, "Kneeling to the axe," *American Cryonics* 5 (June 1988) 7 for quote; John Day and David S. Pizer, "Letter to the editor," *ibid.*, 11–13 on Venturists, and cf. *The Immortalist*, a journal published in Oak Park, MI; Harvey J. Irwin, *Flight of Mind: A Psychological Study of the Out-of-Body Experience* (Metuchen, 1985); Ry Redd, "Afterlife traditions and psychical research: introducing a messianic geocosmic model," *Psychical Research and Spirit*, ed. Mary Carman Rose (Bloomfield, CT, 1987) 22–42; Herbert B. Greenhouse, *The Astral Journey* (NY, 1974); letter, June 9, 1987, from Phillel (= Philip J. Jacobs) of Mark-Age Inform-Nations, Healing Haven, and University of Light, Fort Lauderdale, FL, on the years between 1960 and 2000 as the Age of Marks or the Mark Age.

64. Richard Schulz and Janet Schlarb, "Two decades of research on dying," *Omega* 18,4 (1987–88) 299–317; Elisabeth Kübler-Ross, *On Death and Dying* (NY, 1969); idem, *Death, The Final Stage of Growth* (Englewood Cliffs, 1975); idem, "Foreword" to Ring, *Heading Toward Omega*; Kenneth Ring, *Life at Death* (NY, 1980) 256–57.

65. Camille Flammarion, "Last days of the earth," *Contemporary Review* 59 (1891) 558–69; James S. Trefil, "How the universe will end," *Smithsonian* (June 1983) 73–83; Steven Weinberg, *The First Three Minutes* (Toronto, 1984 [1977]) 144.

66. Iris Macfarlane, *The Black Hole, or The Making of a Legend* (London, 1975) 25, 219, 230.

67. Pierre-Simon Laplace, *Exposition du système du monde* (Paris, 1796) II, 305, page reproduced in Charles W. Misner et al., *Gravitation* (San Francisco, 1973) 623. Laplace's mathematical proof, published in 1799, is printed in modern translation in Appendix A of S. W. Hawking and G. F. R. Ellis, *The Large-Scale Structure of Space-Time* (Cambridge, 1973) 365–68. See Eric Sheldon, "A champion to the rescue of Laplace," *Observatory* 99 (1979) 91–93, contending that Laplace did indeed anticipate the physics of black holes even though he did not conceive of an immediate event horizon; for Laplace, light would be so slowed by the gravitational pull of a massive body that at *a large but finite remove* its light would come to a standstill and the body no longer be visible.

68. Ambrose Bierce, "Charles Ashmore's Trail," *Can Such Things Be?* (1893) in *Collected Works* (NY, 1910) III, 421; Simon Newcomb, "The end of the world," *McClure's Magazine* 21 (May 1903) 3ff., quotes on 10. Cf. Robert M. Adams, *Nil: Episodes in the Literary Conquest of Void during the Nineteenth Century* (NY, 1966).

69. Joseph Conrad, "Heart of Darkness" (1902) in *Modern Short Stories*, 4th ed., ed. Arthur Mizener (NY, 1979) 5–92, quotes on 11, 79–80, 82–83, 87.

70. Harry L. Shipman, *Black Holes, Quasars, & the Universe* (Boston, 1976) 65, 83, 97–105; Paul Murdin and David Allen, *Catalogue of the Universe* (NY, 1979) 86–87; Phil Hardy, *Encyclopedia of Science Fiction Movies* (Minneapolis, 1986) 346.

71. Shipman, *Black Holes*, 14; Frederick R. Karl, *Modern and Modernism: The Sovereignty of the Artist, 1885–1925* (NY, 1985) 4, 19; John Boslough, *Stephen Hawking's Universe* (NY, 1985) 66–67.

72. Shipman, *Black Holes*, 15.

73. *Ibid.*, 69; James McMillan, *The Way We Were 1900–1914* (London, 1978) 134 on the horses; Werner Fallaw, "Atomic apocalypse," *Christian Century* 63 (Sept. 25, 1946) 1146; Romano Guardini, *End of the Modern World*, trans. Joseph Theman and Herbert Burke, ed. F. D. Wilhelmsen (NY, 1956) 113, 130; John L. Stipp et al., *The Rise and Development of Western Civilization* (NY, 1967) 683, citing Sartre's play at the conclusion of their book; Kenneth Boulding, *The Meaning of the Twentieth Century: The Great Transition* (NY, 1964) 2, 180; Michael Harrington, *The Accidental Century* (NY, 1966) 13 for quote.

74. Daniel Bell, *Toward the Year 2000* (Boston, 1968) 1; Jean Christoph Bailly and Serge Sautreau, "Editorial preface," *Fin de siècle* 1 (1974) 5; Centre national d'art et de culture Georges Pompidou, *Fin de siècle Daniel Pommereulle* (Paris, 1975).

75. Omar V. Garrison, *Encyclopedia of Prophecy* (Secaucus, 1978) 2; Charles Krauthammer, "The end of the world," *New Republic* (March 28, 1983) 12–15, quoting Flora Lewis; *Turn-of-the-Century Women* 1,1 (1984) inside cover; "Politique fin de siècle," *Traverses* 33–34 (1985) 8–16 for Baudrillard's "L'an 2000 ne passera pas"; Tom Wolfe, "A eulogy for the 20th century," *Utne Reader* (March–April 1988) 32–35, reprinted from *American Spectator* (Dec. 1987). In the fall of 1988, *People* magazine and the New York Public Library sponsored a lecture series on science, economics, AIDS, art, and historic preservation at the "Turn of the Century," their promotional brochure stating, "A hundred years ago, people looked forward to the turn of the century with eagerness and hope. Now, fewer than a dozen years remain before the arrival of the twenty-first century." Steve Goodman's song "The Twentieth Century Is Almost Over" had already appeared in 1977, on his album *Say It In Private*.
    On the year and mythography of 1984, see Daphne Patai, *The Orwell Mystique: A Study in Male Ideology* (Amherst, 1984). Then cf. Russell Baker, "The year that was," *New York Times Magazine* (Dec. 30, 1984) 10, an ordinary year; Paul Chilton and Crispin Aubrey, eds., *Nineteen Eighty-Four in 1984* (London, 1983), dystopia ahead; "Do Jehovah's Witnesses still hold to their 1984 doomsday deadline?" *Christianity Today* (Sept. 21, 1984) 66–67, no, they do not; Tilden H. Edwards, *Living with Apocalypse* (San Francisco, 1984), despondent staff of the World Bank; George Gallup, Jr., *Gallup Report* (Princeton, 1984) 36–57; Annie Gottlieb, "Is 1984 really here?" *McCalls* (Jan. 1984) 20ff., mostly no; A. Bartlett Giamatti,

A Free and Ordered Space (NY, 1988) 293ff. for his 1980 and 1984 addresses to the Yale Class of '84, against the Apocalyptic Style; Irving Howe, *1984 Revisited* (NY, 1983), political enigmas; Ejner Jensen et al., *The Future of Nineteen Eighty-Four* (Ann Arbor, 1984), still viable; Rob Kroes, ed., *Nineteen Eighty-Four and the Apocalyptic Imagination in America* (Amsterdam, 1984), esp. valuable for Doeko Bosscher's analysis of response to the 1983 television special on nuclear catastrophe, "The Day After"; Everett Mendelsohn and Helga Nowotny, eds., *Nineteen Eighty-Four: Science between Utopia and Dystopia* (Dordrecht, 1984), problems, problems; Norman Podhoretz, "1984 is here. Where is Big Brother?" *Reader's Digest* (Jan. 1984) 33–38, nowhere to be seen; George Steiner, "Killing time," *The New Yorker* (Dec. 12, 1983) 168–88, the true Orwell; Abigail Trafford et al., "Orwell's 1984—coming true?" *U.S. News and World Report* (Dec. 26, 1983–Jan. 2, 1984) 86–95, and 24–25, "A Watershed Year" even though it looks sunny; Warren W. Wagar, "Looking back on '1984,' " *Consumers Digest* (Jan.–Feb. 1984) 17–20, H. G. Wells was more accurate; "Orwell's world: how close," *Atlas World Press Review* 30 (Dec. 1983) 33–40, newspeak and doublethink everywhere.

76. Shipman, *Black Holes*, 24; László Vörös, M.D., and Balint Suranyi, interview, Budapest, July 31, 1987; Paul A. Carter, *The Creation of Tomorrow: Fifty Years of Magazine Science Fiction* (NY, 1977) 227 on context for Anderson's novel; Donald G. Bloesch, *Crumbling Foundations* (Grand Rapids, 1985); Alvin Toffler, *The Eco-Spasm Report* (NY, 1975); Paul Ehrlich, *The End of Affluence* (NY, 1974); Batra, *Great Depression*; Ruff, *How to Prosper*; William Lareau, *Millennium Management* (Piscataway, 1986) produced, *n.b.*, by New Century Publications; Walter R. Mead, *Mortal Splendor* (Boston, 1987); Daniel Yankelovich, *New Rules* (NY, 1981); Paul Kennedy, *The Rise and Fall of the Great Powers* (NY, 1988). Mike Gunderloy describes *Darknerve* and *Zero Hour* in his *Factsheet Five* (Troy, NY).

77. James H. Charlesworth, *The Old Testament Pseudepigrapha* (Garden City, NY, 1983–85) I, ix, xiii, xxii, and idem, with James R. Mueller, *The New Testament Apocrypha and Pseudepigrapha* (Metuchen, 1987) I for quote. On doom, Victor Canning, *Doomsday Carrier* (London, 1976); Elizabeth S. Benoit, *Doomsday Clock* (San Antonio, 1975); Tony Williamson, *Doomsday Contract* (London, 1977); John Lofland, *Doomsday Cult* (NY, 1977 [1966]), a sociological study; Kin Platt, *Doomsday Gang* (NY, 1978); Boyd Upchurch, *Doomsday Gene* (NY, 1973); Mary Lupton, *Doomsday Ghost* (NY, 1984); Dean B. Peskin, *Doomsday Job* (NY, 1973) on economics; Dom Gober, *Doomsday Squad* (Los Angeles, 1975); John R. Maddox, *Doomsday Syndrome* (NY, 1972), among many others, including Fred Warshofsky, *Doomsday: The Science of Catastrophe* (NY, 1977). On apocalypse as aphrodisiac, see Hans Magnus Enzensberger, "Two notes on the end of the world," trans. David Fernbach for *New Left Review* 110 (July 1978) 74–80, quotes on 74, 75, and Arthur Kopit, *End of the World: A Play in 3 Acts* (NY, 1984) esp. 32. On films, see Christopher B. Sharrett, "Apocalypticism in the Contemporary Horror Film," Ph.D. thesis, New York University, 1983, quote from abstract, *Dissertation Abstracts International* 44/12A, p. 3523. On population, see Donella H. Meadows et al., *The Limits to Growth* (NY, 1972); H. S. D. Cole et al., *Models of Doom* (NY, 1973); Mihajlo D. Mesarovic, *Mankind at the Turning Point* (NY, 1974); William H. McNeill's "historical overview" in *Human Migration: Patterns and Policies*, eds. McNeill and Ruth S. Adams (Bloomington, 1978) 3–19. On fatigue, see Martin K. Chen, "The epidemiology of self-perceived fatigue among adults," *Preventive Medicine* 15 (1986) 74–81; Dedra Buchwald et al., "Frequency of 'Chronic Active Epstein-Barr Virus Infection' in a general medical practice," *Journal of the American Medical Association* 257 (May 1, 1987) 2303–07, and other studies in same

issue. CEBV is being tranformed into Chronic Fatigue Syndrome: C. Vaughan, "New name and identity for mysterious Epstein-Barr syndrome," *Science News* 133 (March 12, 1988) 167. On panic, see Thomas W. Uhde et al., "Phenomenology and neurobiology of panic disorder," in *Anxiety and the Anxiety Disorders,* eds. A. Hussain Tuma and Jack Maser (Hillsdale, NJ, 1985) 557–76. A new journal, *Anxiety Research,* appeared in 1988.

78. W. Jackson Davis, *The Seventh Year: Industrial Civilization in Transition* (NY, 1979) xv; Barbara Tuchman, interviewed by Rushworth M. Kidder, *An Agenda for the 21st Century* (Cambridge, MA, 1987) 48; Alasdair MacIntyre, *After Virtue* (Notre Dame, 1981) quote from book jacket, and see pp. 235–36, and 245 on the new dark ages; Joel Colton, "Foreword" to *Progress and Its Discontents,* eds. Gabriel A. Almond et al. (Berkeley, 1982) xi; Giscard d'Estaing quoted by David Webber and N. W. Hutchings, *Is This the Last Century?* (Nashville, 1979) 141; Warren Wagar, *Terminal Visions: The Literature of Last Things* (Bloomington, 1982) xi–xiii; Hal Lindsey, *The 1980s: Countdown to Armageddon* (NY, 1981); *Oxford English Dictionary,* Supp. I, 655, dating "countdown" to 1953, but there was a countdown in the 1928 science fiction film, *Die Frau im Mond.*

79. Shipman, *Black Holes,* 24; Global Awareness in Action, "Some Facts about the Environment Compiled from official sources," factsheet (Anse St.-Jean, Quebec, 1988) and their Earth Concert brochure, p. 4, "The Planetary ecological clock Compiled from official sources." Cf., most recently, the entire issue of *Time* (Jan. 2, 1989) devoted to the "Planet of the Year: Endangered Earth." In 1987 *Third World Affairs (London)* initiated an annual "Disaster Monitor," which ran to sixty pages that first year.

80. Shipman, *Black Holes,* 70; Felix G. Rohatyn, *The Twenty-Year Century* (NY, 1983) 7 on margins; *Insight on the News* (May 23, 1988) cover; "The thriller is back," *Time* (Nov. 16, 1987) cover story, 72–79; *Oxford English Dictionary,* Supp. III, 1295, s.v. "risk"; Allan Mazur, "Societal and scientific causes of the historical development of risk assessment," in *Society, Technology, and Risk Assessment* (NY, 1980) 151–57; William D. Rowe, *An Anatomy of Risk* (NY, 1977); Kenneth R. MacCrimmon et al., *Taking Risks: The Management of Uncertainty* (NY, 1986); Niels C. Lind, "Is risk analysis an emerging profession?" *Risk Abstracts* 4 (Oct. 1987) 167–69; Timothy O'Riordan, "The cognitive and political dimensions of risk analyses," *Journal of Environmental Psychology* 3 (1983) 345–54; Paul Slovic, "Perception of risk," *Science* 236 (April 17, 1987) 280–85 and citing the seminal article on risk-benefit analysis by Chauncey Starr in the same journal in 1969, p. 1232; A. Jan Jouhar, ed., *Risk in Society* (London, 1984), which consists of the proceedings of the First International Risk Seminar, March 14–15, 1983, London; Charles Perrow, *Normal Accidents: Living with High-Risk Technologies* (NY, 1984) 12 on shamans; John Taylor, "Nervous about the Nineties," *New York* (June 20, 1988) 28–35; Mary Douglas and Aaron Wildavsky, *Risk and Culture* (Berkeley, 1982) 16 for quote.

81. Perrow, *Normal Accidents,* 11, 21; Slovic, "Perception of risk," quoting "Talk of the town," *The New Yorker* (Feb. 18, 1985) 29. See also Sheila Jasanoff, *Risk Management and Political Culture* (NY, 1986); Shlomo Breznitz, *Cry Wolf: The Psychology of False Alarms* (Hillsdale, NJ, 1984) esp. xiii.

82. Hermann Bondi, "Risk in perspective," in *Risk: Man-Made Hazards to Men,* ed. M. G. Cooper (Oxford, 1985) 11; Jouhar, *Risk in Society,* 67–68; for Giovacchini's examples; John

Urquhart and Klaus Heilman, *Risk Watch: The Odds of Life* (NY, 1984) xvi–xvii; Chester R. Richmond et al., eds., *Health Risk Analysis* (Philadelphia, 1981) 39 on 1980 OSHA court decision. Note also how completely AIDS was associated with "risk" and "risky behavior" in the U.S. Surgeon General's national circular, *Understanding AIDS* (Rockville, MD, 1988).

83. W. Kip Viscusi, *Risk by Choice: Regulating Health and Safety in the Workplace* (Cambridge, MA, 1983) 98–105, 111; Jouhar, *Risk in Society*, 3, comments of William W. Lowrance; Federal Emergency Management Agency, *Shelter Systems Officer Training Course Instruction Guide* (Washington, D.C., 1982) scenario exercises, 3–35; idem, *Behavior Attitudes under Crisis Conditions* (Washington, D.C., 1984) 14–15 for rhetoric; idem, *Radiological Defense Manual. Student Manual* (Washington, D.C., 1981) 1. On sanctity and sanctuary, consider James F. Short, Jr., "The social fabric at risk: toward the social transformation of risk analysis," *American Sociological Review* 49 (1984) 711–25, a presidential address to the American Sociological Association; Douglas and Wildavsky, *Risk and Culture*.

84. Aaron Wildavsky, "No risk is the highest risk of all," *American Scientist* 67 (Jan.–Feb. 1979) 32; Heilbroner, *Inquiry*, 44, citing Richard Falk's *This Endangered Planet* (NY, 1971); Gerard Piel, *The Acceleration of History* (NY, 1972) 30.

85. Charles R. Walker, *Technology, Industry and Man: The Age of Acceleration* (NY, 1968); Alvin Toffler, *Future Shock* (NY, 1970) ch. 2; John Platt, "What we must do," *Science* 166 (Nov. 28, 1969) 1115–21; G. R. Urban, ed., *Can We Survive Our Future?* (London, 1971) 20; Roderic Gorney, *The Human Agenda* (NY, 1972) 570; Jeremy Rifkin, *Time Wars* (NY, 1987) 4; Michael Young, *The Metronomic Society: Natural Rhythms and Human Timetables* (Cambridge, MA, 1988) 218–20, 229, 261. Also contributing to the sense of unprecedented acceleration are the many charts showing industrial civilization as a sliver at the end of the very long finger of geologic (even astrophysical) time; e.g., Nigel Calder, *Timescale: An Atlas of the Fourth Dimension* (NY, 1983) 190–91 on "1976 to 1984, Earthlings Discovered Their Place In Cosmic Time / Never Before Were the Contrasts of Hope and Danger So Stark."

86. Piotr Sztompka, "The global crisis and the reflexiveness of the social system," in *The Global Crisis*, ed. Edward A. Tiryakian (Leiden, 1984) 45, and also Johan Galtung, "On the dialectic between crisis and crisis perception," 4–32; Henri Guitton, *Le sens de la durée* (Paris, 1985) 41–42 on permanent crisis; R. J. Zwi Werblowsky, "Crisis consciousness and the future," *Diogenes* 113 (1981) 55–69; Elizabeth L. Eisenstein, "Clio and Chronos: an essay on the making and breaking of history-book time," in *History and the Concept of Time* (Middletown, CT, 1966) 36–64; Freeman Dyson, interviewed by Kidder, *Agenda*, 117.

87. Shipman, *Black Holes*, 80; Beverly Raphael, *When Disaster Strikes* (NY, 1986); Robert Jay Lifton, "The image of 'the end of the world': a psychohistorical view," in *Visions of Apocalypse: End or Rebirth?*, eds. Saul Friedlander et al. (NY, 1985) 151–67; Andrew Buckwalter, paraphrasing the position of Wolf-Dieter Narr, in "Translator's Introduction" to *Observations on [Karl Jaspers's] "The Spiritual Situation of the Age": Contemporary German Perspectives*, ed. Jürgen Habermas, trans. Buckwalter (Cambridge, MA, 1984) xxvi, and see the comments of Habermas on the millenarian import of this 1000th volume of Edition Suhrkamp, 1–2; Norman Macrae, *The 2025 Report: A Concise History of the Future, 1975–2025* (NY, 1985) 176 on termites; Betty Adcock, "Digression on the Nuclear Age," reprinted by permission of Louisiana State University from *Beholdings*, copyright © 1988 by Betty Adcock,

and first published in *Triquarterly* 71 (Winter 1988) 117; quote on world after nuclear war from a fanzine produced by Black Dazzle in Davis, CA, *Nuclear Bull Crust* 7 (1987) Peace Club insert; Frances Ferguson, "The nuclear sublime," *Diacritics* 14 (Summer 1984) 5; Alfred Fabre-Luce, *Men or Insects? A Study of Population Problems*, trans. Robert Baldick (London, 1964), originally entitled *Six milliards d'insectes: L'homme de l'an 2000* (Paris, 1962), 147, citing Marcel Sire; Paul MacTyre, *Doomsday, 1999* (NY, 1962) on midges.

88. Vincent B. Wigglesworth, *Insects and the Life of Man* (London, 1976) 7 on insects as our chief competitors; Ray F. Smith et al., eds., *History of Entomology* (Palo Alto, 1973) essays by Max Beier and S. L. Tuxen; E. O. Essig, *A History of Entomology* (NY, 1965 [1931]); Mark R. Hillegas, *The Future as Nightmare: H. G. Wells and the Antiutopians* (Carbondale, 1974) 22; Matthew 12.24 in *The New Testament of the Jerusalem Bible* (Garden City, NY, 1966) 35, note *f* on Beelzebub; George M. Sternberg, "Malaria," *Popular Science Monthly* 58 (1901) 360–71.

89. E. H. Sellards, "Geological history of cockroaches," *Popular Science Monthly* 68 (March 1906) 244; J. Raloff, "Roach hormone clue to human ancestry," *Science News* (Nov. 8, 1986) 295; Franz Kafka, "The metamorphosis," in *The Penal Colony*, trans. Willa and Edwin Muir (NY, 1961 [1915]) 65–132; Don Marquis, *archy and mehitabel* (NY, 1927) the first in a series, all in lower case, since archy cannot manage the typewriter shift; Ian Pearson, "Cockroach Trilogy [review]," *Maclean's* (Jan. 25, 1982) 58. The *Time* issue devoted to the Endangered Earth (Jan. 2, 1989) also quotes (p. 28) archy on ants, centipedes, and scorpions as the last survivors of a desert planet.

90. Shipman, *Black Holes*, 79; Jacques Derrida, "No apocalypse not now," trans. Catherine Porter and Philip Lewis for *Diacritics* 14 (Summer 1984) 20–32, quote on 30.

91. Daniel Bell, *The Coming of Post-Industrial Society* (NY, 1973) 383; Peter Schjeldahl, "The hydrogen jukebox: terror, narcissism . . . and art," *Journal: The L. A. Institute for Contemporary Art* 20 (Oct.–Nov. 1978) 44; Malcolm Bradbury and James McFarlane, "The name and nature of modernism," in *Modernism, 1890–1930*, eds. Bradbury and McFarlane (NY, 1976) 19 for quote; Richard Kostelanetz, "What is avant-garde?" in *The Avant-Garde Tradition in Literature*, ed. Kostelanetz (Buffalo, 1982) 3–6; Xavier Rubert de Ventos, *Heresies of Modern Art*, trans. J. S. Bernstein (NY, 1980 [1974]) ch. 5.

92. Lynn Gumpert, *The End of the World: Contemporary Visions of the Apocalypse* (NY, 1983, for the New Museum of Contemporary Art) throughout, quotes on 11, 63. Cf. Nancy Marmer, "Death in black and white," *Art in America* 71 (March 1983) 128–33 on the "catastrophic sublime" of the work of another artist, Robert Morris.

93. James Morrow, *This Is the Way the World Ends* (NY, 1986) with epitaph on 311, quoted by permission of Henry Holt & Co., and cf. Andrew Taylor, *Waiting for the End of the World: A Novel of Suspense* (NY, 1984); *Oxford English Dictionary*, Supp. IV, s.v. "Zero-sum," quoting the *Listener* (Dec. 15, 1983) 31, "We live in a Zero-sum world"; Adams, *Nil*, 3.

94. Shipman, *Black Holes*, 25; Warshofsky, *Doomsday*, 226; Global Awareness in Action, "Some Facts about the Environment" and "Planetary Clock."

95. *Realizing the Vision of a New Society: National Multi-Year Human Settlements Plan, 1978 to 2000* (Makati, Manila, 1978) 1; Yuri Rubinsky and Ian Wiseman, *A History of the End of*

the World (NY, 1982) 146; David M. Raup, *The Nemesis Affair* (NY, 1986) esp. 141, Stephen Jay Gould arguing against the name "Nemesis" and proposing Siva, goddess of destruction, instead; Gordon D. Kaufman, "Nuclear eschatology and the study of religion," *Journal of the American Academy of Religion* 51 (March 1983) 5. See also Walter M. Miller's introduction to *Beyond Armageddon: Twenty-One Sermons to the Dead*, eds. Miller and Martin H. Greenberg (NY, 1985).

96. Josh Getlin, "Scientists race the clock to solve dolphin deaths," *Los Angeles Times* (Aug. 17, 1987) 1, 22; Armando Favazza with Barbara Favazza, *Bodies Under Siege: Self-Mutilation in Culture and Society* (Baltimore, 1987); Fakir Musafar, interview and "Body play," in *Apocalypse Culture*, ed. Adam Parfrey (NY, 1987) 101–14 on mutilation as an art form; Nagasada Miyawaki, "Direction of the civilized societies of today viewed on the basis of anomie indexes," in *Problems of Advanced Economies*, ed. Miyawaki (Berlin, 1984) 17; Lee A. Headley, ed., *Suicide in Asia and the Near East* (Berkeley, 1983) throughout; Peter O'Neill, *Health Crisis 2000* (London, 1982) 36–37; Diekstra and Hawton, *Suicide in Adolescence*; Kushner, *Self-Destruction in the Promised Land*, ch. 4, for a critique of the statistics; Richard K. McGee, *Crisis Intervention in the Community* (Baltimore, 1974) 3–17; A. Alvarez, *The Savage God* (NY, 1972) agent; Eli Robins, *The Final Months: A Study of the Lives of 134 Persons Who Committed Suicide* (NY, 1981) authorized biographer; Claude Grillion, *Suicide, mode d'emploi* (Paris, 1982) unauthorized; Marshall Kilduff and Ron Javers, *The Suicide Cult* (NY, 1978) on Jim Jones and the Peoples Temple; Joan J. Brumberg, *Fasting Girls: The Emergence of Anorexia Nervosa as a Modern Disease* (Cambridge, MA, 1988) first and last chapters; Jacques Pohier et al., eds., *Suicide and the Right to Die* (Edinburgh, 1985); Derek Humphry, *Let Me Die Before I Wake* (Los Angeles, 1982); Kenneth B. Cohen, *Hospice, Prescription for Terminal Care* (Germantown, MD, 1979); Marv Miller, *Suicide After Sixty* (NY, 1979); Yevgeni Velikhov, ed., *The Night After*, trans. A. Rosenzweig and Y. Taube (Moscow, 1985) on nuclear winter, as also Lester Grinspoon, ed., *The Long Darkness: Psychological and Moral Perspectives on Nuclear Winter* (New Haven, 1986).

97. Robert Louis Stevenson, *The Suicide Club* (NY, 1896) quote on 21.

98. Marshall Schuon, "Laser that turns eyes and ears," *New York Times* (Nov. 20, 1988) Y:30; Sophia Sabak, "Predictions through the year 2001," *Weekly World News* (Sept. 6, 1988) 46–47; Robert Weil, ed., *Omni Future Almanac* (NY, 1982) 277; Thomas A. Easton, "Psychics, computers, and psychic computers," *Skeptical Inquirer* 11 (Summer 1987) 383, 387; David Wallechinsky et al., *The Book of Predictions* (NY, 1980) 288–89; Edward J. Kluska, *Astrological Megatrends 1996* (Cincinnati, 1986) 34.

DOUBLE TIME: THE LEGEND OF THE YEAR 2000

1. S. W. Hawking and G. F. R. Ellis, *The Large Scale Structure of Space-Time* (Cambridge, 1973) 348; Steven Weinberg, *The First Three Minutes* (NY, 1984 [1977]) 2–5, 94–105; Victor Weisskopf, "How the universe began," *New York Review of Books* (Feb. 16, 1989) 10–15.

2. Stephen W. Hawking, *A Brief History of Time* (Toronto, 1988), ch. 7; Lee Dye, "Ribbon of gas may be clue to power of galaxy," *Los Angeles Times* (Jan. 11, 1989) 1, 19.

3. Marilyn Ferguson, *The Aquarian Conspiracy: Personal and Social Transformation in the 1980s* (Los Angeles, 1980); Adam Parfrey, ed., *Apocalypse Culture* (NY, 1987); Theodore Roszak, *Person/Planet: The Great Disintegration of Industrial Society* (Garden City, NY, 1978) 288–89; Roberto Vacca, *The Coming Dark Age* (Garden City, NY, 1973 [1971]) 17. See also Leften S. Stavrianos, *The Promise of the Coming Dark Age* (San Francisco, 1976); Umberto Eco, *Travels in Hyperreality*, trans. William Weaver (San Diego, 1986) 73–85; Walter M. Miller, Jr., *A Canticle for Leibowitz* (Philadelphia, 1959), adapted for National Public Radio in the 1980s; Richard E. Sullivan, "The Middle Ages in the Western tradition," in *Essays on Medieval Civilization*, eds. B. K. Lackner and K. R. Philip (Austin, 1978) 3–31. For the medievalism of other centuries' ends, see esp. Arthur B. Ferguson, *The Chivalric Tradition in Renaissance England* (Washington, D.C., 1986); T. J. Jackson Lears, *No Place of Grace* (NY, 1981).

4. Frank Durham and Robert D. Purrington, *The Frame of the Universe: A History of Physical Cosmology* (NY, 1983) 230; Michael S. Morris et al., "Wormholes, time machines, and the weak energy condition," *Physical Review Letters* (Sept. 26, 1988), reported in *Physical Review Abstracts* 19 (Oct. 1, 1988), 42.

5. David S. Weaver, "Catastrophe theory and human evolution," *Journal of Anthropological Research* 36 (1980) 403–10; Niles Eldredge and Ian Tattersall, *Myths of Human Evolution* (NY, 1982) 3–8; W. A. Berggren and John A. Van Couvering, eds., *Catastrophes and Earth History: The New Uniformitarianism* (Princeton, 1984)—"a revised gradualism"; Robert Gilmore, *Catastrophe Theory for Scientists and Engineers* (NY, 1981) ch. 16 on climate; Michael Hutchison, *Megabrain* (NY, 1986) 71 on neurochemistry; Harry L. Shipman, *Black Holes, Quasars, & the Universe* (Boston, 1976) ch. 1; Alexander Woodcock and Monte Davis, *Catastrophe Theory* (NY, 1978), a good popular introduction; E. C. Zeeman, *Catastrophe Theory* (London, 1977) on stock market, beams, bulimarexia, liquids; Emilio Casetti, "Catastrophe model of regional dynamics," *Annals of the Association of American Geographers* 71 (1981) 572–79; Flo Conway and Jim Siegelman, *Snapping: America's Epidemic of Sudden Personality Change* (Philadelphia, 1978) esp. ch. 12; Michael Day and Jacqueline Tivers, "Catastrophe theory and geography: a Marxist critique," *Area* 11 (1979) 54–58; C. R. de Freitas and E. Woolmington, "Catastrophe theory and catastasis," *Area* 12 (1980) 191–94; Roger A. McCain, "Cultivation of taste, catastrophe theory, and demand for works of art," *American Economic Review* 71 (1981) 332–34; Tom Poston and Ian N. Stewart, *Catastrophe Theory and Its Applications* (London, 1978), esp. 417, reviewing Zeeman et al. on prison riots; A. Colin Renfrew and Tim Poston, "Discontinuities in the endogenous change of settlement pattern," in *Transformations*, eds. Renfrew and K. L. Cooke (NY, 1978) 437–61; John W. G. Lowe, *The Dynamics of Apocalypse: A Systems Simulation of the Classic Maya Collapse* (Albuquerque, 1985). For René Thom's positions and speculations, see esp. his discussions with Giulo Giorello and Simona Morini in *Parables et catastrophes* (Paris, 1983).

6. On the dinosaurs, see David M. Raup, *The Nemesis Affair* (NY, 1986); on Atlantis, currently being revived, see the late 19th-century source, Ignatius Donnelly, *Atlantis: The Antediluvian World* (NY, 1882). Creationism is not simply Bible literalism; it is also apocalyptic, in three senses: 1) in the belief that sudden change is possible, and has happened before as part of the moral economy of history; 2) in the faith that divine authority is not coterminous with natural laws and is manifested separately on earth and in time; 3) in the set of calculations that restore both the nearness of an abrupt Creation *and* the nearness of

an abrupt finale. It is the apocalyptic tenor of Creationism, rather than its Biblical literalism, which makes for the present intensity of the controversy. Cf. Francis B. Harrold and Raymond A. Eve, "Noah's Ark and ancient astronauts," *Skeptical Inquirer* II (Fall 1986) 61–75, polling for these connections.

7. Thomas S. Kuhn, *The Structure of Scientific Revolutions*, Phoenix[!] ed. (Chicago, 1964) 84, and contrast his "Second thoughts on paradigms," in *The Essential Tension* (Chicago, 1977); Gilmore, *Catastrophe Theory*, prefatory scientific chronology; E. C. Zeeman, "Catastrophe theory," *Scientific American* 234,4 (1976) 65–83, the seven basic catastrophes.

8. Gary Gutting, ed., *Paradigms and Revolutions: Appraisals and Applications of Thomas Kuhn's Philosophy of Science* (Notre Dame, 1980); Ferguson, *Aquarian Conspiracy*, 28; Alvin Toffler, *The Third Wave* (NY, 1980) 22, 26, 28; George Leonard, *Walking on the Edge of the World* (Boston, 1988) Part III; Mikhail S. Gorbachev, *At the Summit* (NY, 188) 8, 25, 197, and note his frequent centurial allusions, pp. 9, 60, 101, 244.

9. David M. Culver, CEO, Alcan Aluminium Ltd., in *Toward the Year 2000*, ed. Ruth Karen (NY, 1985) 16, watershed; S. Takdir Alisjahbana, "A dynamic anthropology in a decisive epoch of history," *Art and the Future (Manila)* 13–14 (1978) 93–106; Ed Naha, "After future shock [Toffler interview]," *Future (NY)* 1 (Aug. 1978) 60, hinge; Kiplinger Washington Letter, *The New American Boom* (Washington, D.C., 1986) 5, countdown; Harvey Brooks, "Technology-related catastrophes," in *Visions of Apocalypse: End or Rebirth?*, eds. Saul Friedlander et al. (NY, 1985) 109, critical period; John Platt, "The greatest evolutionary jump in history," in *Through the 80's: Thinking Globally, Acting Locally*, ed. Frank Feather (Washington, D.C., 1980) 12–15; József Bognár, *End-Century Crossroads of Development and Cooperation* (Budapest, 1980) I, 9, cusp; Art Levine, "The devil in Gorbachev," *Washington Post* (June 5, 1988) C1, C4; Hilarion, *Answers from the Pages of Lightline* (Toronto, 1983) 102–03; Moira Timms, *Prophecies & Predictions: Everyone's Guide to the Coming Changes* (Santa Cruz, CA, 1980) 8.

10. Benoit B. Mandelbrot, *The Fractal Geometry of Nature* (San Francisco, 1982) 1; James Gleick, "New images of chaos that are stirring a scientific revolution," *Smithsonian* (Dec. 1987) 122, and see his *Chaos: Making a New Science* (NY, 1987); "Unmashing chaos," *Scientific American* (Feb. 1987) 61; Jules H. Masserman, "The riots and therapy of violence in a world nearing chaos," *American Journal of Social Psychiatry* 4, 3 (1984) 5–8; Alvin M. Saperstein, "Chaos—a model for the outbreak of war," *Nature* 309 (1984) 303–05.

11. W. H. G. Armytage, *Yesterday's Tomorrows* (Toronto, 1968) 110 on Yeats; Mandelbrot, *Fractal Geometry*, 3, 4, 35, 58, 62, 77ff., 396. See Gary Taubes, "The mathematics of chaos," *Discover* (Sept. 1984) 30–39, for an account of early "chaotic" equations, and Henri Guitton, *Le sens de la durée* (Paris, 1985) 181ff. on applications of models of turbulence to economics since the 1890s.

12. Gleick, *Chaos*, esp. 83–118, 215–40 on fractals; WGBH-TV, Boston, "NOVA: The Strange New Science of Chaos," aired January 31, 1989, emphasizing that "most of Nature is composed of turbulent [chaotic] phenomena." Another way to explain chaotic phenomena is to discuss (in truly Augustan, centurial language) their "sensitive dependence on initial conditions, such that very small changes in initial conditions will yield very different results.

13. David Loye and Riane Eisler, "Chaos and transformation," *Behavioral Science* 32 (1987) 53; Karl E. Weick, "Cosmos vs. chaos," *Organizational Dynamics* 14, 2 (1985) 51–64; François Melese and William Transue, "Unscrambling chaos through thick and thin," *Quarterly Journal of Economics* 101 (1986) 419–23; Discordian pamphlets c/o F.R.E.D., 36 Erskine Dr., Morristown, NJ 07960.

14. Heinz-Otto Peitgen and P. H. Richter, *The Beauty of Fractals* (Berlin, 1986); Bruce Schechter, "Fractal fairy tales," *Omni* (Oct. 1988) 86–91, quote on 91; Mandelbrot, *Fractal Geometry*, 4; Kisho Kurokawa, "An architecture of symbiosis: the two-faced god Janus," *Japan Architecture* 61 (Oct. 1986) 40–43; idem, "Toward a rhizome world or 'chaosmos,' " *The Japan Architect* (Aug. 1988) 8–23; David Bohm, *Wholeness and the Implicate Order* (London, 1980); Charles Jencks, editor (?), "Deconstruction in architecture," *Architectural Design* 58,3/4 (1988) entire issue; Jeremiah Sheehan, "Deconstruction: crystallising an attitude," *Contemporary Architecture* 58, 7–8 (1988) 20–23; E. M. Farrelly, "The new spirit," *Architectural Review* 180 (Aug. 1986) 6–12, quote on 11.

15. Hutchison, *Megabrain*, 63; Marie Moneysmith, "Postmodern polyglot," *L.A. Style* (Nov. 1988) 209–12, a misleading title concerning the work of Moss and Vanos; Jay Vanos, telephone interview, January 13, 1989; Eric Moss and Jay Vanos, discussion, Del Mar, CA, January 21, 1989. On Velikovsky, see Alfred De Grazia, ed., *The Velikovsky Affair* (New Hyde Park, 1966); Editors of *Pensée, Velikovsky Reconsidered* (Garden City, NY, 1976); Lewis M. Greenberg and Warner B. Sizemore, *Velikovsky and Establishment Science* (Glassboro, NJ, 1977); *Catastrophism and Ancient History*, a Los Angeles journal devoted since 1979 to exploring Velikovsky's theories.

16. Ilya Prigogine and Isabelle Stengers, *Order out of Chaos* (NY, 1984 [1979]) last chapter; Henryk Skolimowski, "Evolutionary illuminations," in *The Desire to Be Human*, eds. L. Zonneveld and R. Muller (Wassenaar, 1983) 61. Prigogine, a Russian-Belgian physical chemist, was awarded the 1977 Nobel Prize in Chemistry. See his *From Being to Becoming* (San Francisco, 1980) for close correlations to catastrophe and chaos theory.

17. Lazaris [through Jach Pursel], *The Sacred Journey: You and Your Higher Self* (Beverly Hills, CA, 1987) 23; Daniel Bell, *The Coming of Post-Industrial Society* (NY, 1973); Hazel Henderson, *Creating Alternative Futures: The End of Economics* (NY, 1978); Steven C. Brandt, *Entrepreneuring in Established Companies: Managing toward the Year 2000* (Homewood, IL, 1986) vii, 19; William L. Luttrell, *Post-Capitalist Industrialization: Planning Economic Independence in Tanzania* (NY, 1986); Attila Ágh, Erzsébet Gidai, Maria Kalas Köszegi, and Felix Karman, discussion on futurology and "post-socialist" thought, Budapest, July 31, 1987; Manfred Stanley, "Beyond progress: three post-political futures," in *Images of the Future*, ed. Robert Bundy (Buffalo, 1976) esp. 118; Charles Jencks, "Postmodern and late modern: the essential definitions," *Chicago Review* 35,4 (1987) 31–58; Roderick Seidenberg, *Posthistoric Man* (Chapel Hill, 1950); Stephen Toulmin, *The Return to Cosmology: Postmodern Science and the Theology of Nature* (Berkeley, 1982) 254 quoting Frederick Ferré on the posthumous; Michael Grosso, *The Final Choice* (Walpole, NH, 1985) 181 on ADE; *New Age (Washington, D.C.)*, founded in 1904 by Scottish Rite Freemasons; Texe Marrs, *Dark Secrets of the New Age* (Westchester, IL, 1988), "Number One Nonfiction Christian Bestseller" as of April 3, 1988; Randy Frame, "Is the antichrist in the world today?" *Christianity Today* 27 (Sept. 2, 1983) 55ff.; Timms, *Prophecies & Predictions*, 183, and see Vincent Lopez, *What's Ahead? A Musician's Prophecies of*

World Events (Philadelphia, 1944) 54 for one of the earliest anticipations of the Aquarian Age; David Hoffman, "Chasing our shadow," *New Age Journal* (Jan.–Feb., 1986) 28; Jonathan Adolph, "What is New Age?" in the *New Age Journal 1988 Guide to New Age Living* (Winter 1988) 4ff. Cf. Claude Combet, "L'avenir d'astres est sur minitel," *Livres hebdo* (Dec. 14, 1987) 71–72.

18. Capitol Memorial Church, *New Age or Nuclear Winter?* (Washington, D.C., 1988) invitational brochure to five-part seminar; Raymond Ouellette, *1998, the Year of Destiny* (Fall River, MA, 1978) I, 134–41, casting out nines to show that 1998 = 0; Geoffrey P. Dennis, *The End of the World* (NY, 1930) 120, for 1998 as 3 × 666 (the Number of the Beast), and Jesus being crucified in the 1998th week of his life; "Michael Jackson has weird fear of year 1998," *Weekly World News* (Jan. 17, 1989) 13; Ronald Berman, ed., *Solzhenitsyn at Harvard* (Washington, D.C., 1980) 20; Lazaris, *Sacred Journey*, 25.

19. *New Age Journal 1988 Guide*, 13, 16, 24, 27, 31–33, 54–55, 86.

20. *Ibid.*, 106, 115, 119, and 58 for Colin Wilson on highs and lows; Otto Friedrich et al., "New Age harmonies," *Time* (Dec. 7, 1987) 62ff.; Bryan R. Wilson, *Magic and the Millennium* (NY, 1973) ch. 4 on thaumaturgy.

21. Georges Barbarin, *Le secret de la Grande Pyramide ou la fin du monde adamique* (Paris, 1936) 98; Henry J. Forman, *The Story of Prophecy* (London, 1936) 53–54; Pierre Lemesurier, *The Great Pyramid Decoded* (NY, 1977).

22. Peter Bander, *The Prophecies of St. Malachy and St. Columbkille*, 3rd ed. (Gerrards Cross, 1974 [1969]); Martin Lings, "St. Malachy's prophecy of the popes," *Studies in Comparative Religion* 16 (1984) 148–53; Joe Fisher, *Predictions* (NY, 1980) 38; Juan Antonio Cabezas, *El fin del mundo o el segundo milenario* (Madrid, 1967) ch. 21; Omar V. Garrison, *Encyclopedia of Prophecy* (Secaucus, 1978) 158–64 prints the entire list with identifications, and see Felix Bodin, *Le roman de l'avenir* (Paris, 1834) 402, a very early connection of Malachy's prophecy to the end of the 20th century. For Pope John Paul II, see his *Encyclical Redemptor Hominis/Redeemer of Man* (Washington, D.C., 1979), 3, 4, 50, 87, and also the symposium, *From Rerum Novarum to Laborem Exercens: Towards the Year 2000. Rome 3–5/IV 1982.* (Vatican City, 1982) 6, 44, 132.

23. John Hogue, *Nostradamus & The Millennium* (Garden City, NY, 1987) 204–05, and cf. Jean Charles de Fontbrune, *Nostradamus 2: Into the Twenty-First Century*, trans. Alexis Lykiard (London, 1984) 33, 133–34; Rene Noorbergen, *A.D. 2000* (Indianapolis, 1984) 42–44; *Nostradamus no Daiyogen = Prophecies of Nostradamus = Catastrophe 1999* (Toho Film, 1974) directed by Toshio Masuda and described by Phil Hardy, *Encyclopedia of Science Fiction Movies* (Minneapolis, 1986) 320; The Bollock Brothers, "The Prophecies of Nostradamus" (S. P. V. Records, Bellmore, NY, 1987).

24. John W. Montgomery, *Cross and Crucible* (The Hague, 1973) I, 128n.–129n.; Douglas Bush, "English poetry: time and man," in his *Prefaces to Renaissance Literature* (NY, 1965) 67, quoting John Donne on the three historical sets of 2000 years; R. Buick Knox, *James Ussher, Archbishop of Armagh* (Cardiff, 1967) 105–06, 157–59; a Learned Pen, *Catastrophe Mundi* (London, 1683) 71–72; Robert Fleming, *A Discourse on the Rise and Fall of Papacy*

(Boston, 1794 [1701]) 18–19. Ussher was also fascinated with the year 1000, esp. in his *Gravissimae Quaestionis . . .* (London, 1613) chs. 3–4.

25. André-Clément Decouflé, *L'An 2000: une anti-histoire de la fin du monde* (Paris, 1975) 174 on Bengel; Garrison, *Encyclopedia of Prophecy*, 109, on Emmerich (or Emmerick, as in her entry in the *Neue Deutsche Biographie* [Berlin, 1959] IV, 473–84—her prophecies not known before the 19th century), and see also *Höchste merkwürdige Prophezeiungen eines alten Mönches in Polen, welche vom Jahre 1790 bis zum Ende der Welt im Jahre 2000 in Erfüllung gehen sollen*, 6th ed. (Leipzig, 1848); Caterina Kolosimo, *Sopravviveremo al 1982?* (Milan, 1979) 134 on Le Royer; Mlle. Le Normand, *Souvenirs prophétiques d'une sibylle* (Paris, 1814) 324; Manuel Lacunza, *La venida del Mesiàs en gloria y majestad*, ed. Maria Góngora (Santiago, 1969); Thomas Newton, *Dissertations on the Prophecies*, 8th ed. (Elizabethtown, 1787 [1754–58]) II, 382; Samuel Madden, *Memoirs of the Twentieth Century* (NY, 1972 [1733]) 102–03; Charles Crawford, *Observations upon the Fall of Antichrist* (Philadelphia, 1786) 10; Morgan Edwards, *Two Academical Exercises on Subjects Bearing the Following Titles: Millennium, Last-Novelties* (Philadelphia, 1788) 34; Benjamin Gale, *A Brief Essay, or, An Attempt to Prove . . . What Period of Prophecy the Church of God is Now Under* (New Haven, 1788) 55; Ruth Bloch, *Visionary Republic: Millennial Themes in American Thought, 1756–1800* (Cambridge, 1985) 217 on Miller.

26. Peter Tompkins, *Secrets of the Great Pyramid* (NY, 1971) ch. 7; Sylvia Bowman, *The Year 2000: A Critical Biography of Edward Bellamy* (NY, 1958); William Morris, *News from Nowhere (1890)* in *Three Works by William Morris* (NY, 1968) 187, 317; Winnifred H. Cooley, "A dream of the twenty-first century," *Arena* 28 (1902) 511–16; Friedrich E. Bilz, *Der Zukunftsstaat: Staatseinrichtung im Jahre 2000* (Leipzig, 1904); Edward Berwick, "Farming in the year 2000, A.D.," *Overland Monthly*, ser. 2, 15 (June 1890) 569–73; John Jacob Astor, *A Journey in Other Worlds*, 6th ed. (NY, 1894)—this Astor was nephew to the famous millionaire; Isaac Asimov, *Futuredays: A Nineteenth-Century Vision of the Year 2000* (NY, 1986) on Coté, whose cards were never distributed because the toy company sponsoring them went into bankruptcy.

27. Theodore Zeldin, *France 1848–1945. Volume Four: Taste and Corruption* (Oxford, 1980) 236 on Berthelot; Charles Richet, *Dans cent ans*, 2nd ed. (Paris, 1892); David G. Croly, *Glimpses of the Future* (NY, 1888), and see also John E. Watkins, Jr., "What may happen in the next hundred years," *Futurist* 16 (Oct. 1982) 8–13, reprinting forecasts from *Ladies' Home Journal* (Dec. 1900); J.A.C.K., *Golf in the Year 2000 or, What We Are Coming To* (London, 1892) 69; Walter Emanuel, *One Hundred Years Hence: Being Some Extracts from the Hourly Mail of A.D. 2000* (London, 1911) 26, 33, 46, 72. Cf. Alvarado M. Fuller, A.D. 2000 (NY, 1971 [1890]) ch. 15.

28. Florence Nightingale, "A sub-'note of interrogation.' I. What will be our religion in 1999?" *Fraser's Magazine* n.s. 8 (July 1873) 25–36, quote on 31. Poets should also see John Cooper Powys, *Autobiography* (Hamilton, NY, 1968 [1934]) 300, on watching the turn of the centuries and the prospect of his son reaching the year 2000.

29. Fields: William B. Hall, "Raw material outlook for 2000," *Glass Industry* 62 (Dec. 1981) 20–27, adequate; Stanley C. Plog and Miles B. Santamour, eds., *The Year 2000 and Mental Retardation* (NY, 1980) evolution by prosthesis; Elmer B. Staats, "The government manager in 2000 A.D.," *Wilson Library Bulletin* 42 (March 1968) 701–10, more problems

and an "optimistic fatalism"; Harold G. Shane and M. Bernardine Tabler, *Educating for a New Millennium* (Bloomington, 1981) interdisciplinary, and anticipatory of a crisis of crises; College Entrance Exam Board, *An Agenda for the Year 2000* (NY, 1985) more of the same; Michel Jussiaux, *Le cheval à la fin du XXᵉ siècle* (Paris, 1968) horsefeathers; Frank Deford, "Gridiron 2000," *Sports Illustrated* (Sept. 3, 1979) 42–49, more techno-logic and less violence—contrast Richard Starnes, "My safari into darkest atrophy," *Field & Stream* (Aug. 1966) 14ff., squandered heritage; Doris Tobias, "What we'll be eating in the year 2000," *W* [*Women's Wear Daily*] (June 27, 1975) 10, duck.

Places: Long-term Outlook Committee, *Japan in the Year 2000* (Tokyo, 1983) a major turning point; S. Salamah P. of the Center for Futures Studies, Universitas Nasional, Jakarta, letter, December 12, 1988, "three weeks ago there was a large conference on 'Indonesia facing the year 2000' "; National Committee on Science and Technology, *An Outlook to India's Future, 2000 A.D.* (New Delhi, 1978), population as a resource; Ugo Apollonio, *L'Uomo nel 2000* (Milan, 1968) no problem; Clement Bezold, ed., *Anticipatory Democracy: People in the Politics of the Future* (NY, 1978) 3–8, state futures projects; Ikram Azam, Director, Pakistan Futuristics Foundation and Institute, Islamabad, letter, August 8, 1987, concerning a recent PFI seminar, "Pakistan: 2000 A.D.," a critical period; Andrezej Wierzbicki, Secretary, Committee for Future Studies of National Development "Polska 2000 [Poland 2000]," Polish Academy of Sciences, Warsaw, letter, October 1, 1987, and excellent bulletins such as *Indicators of Development: Early Identification of Imminent Dangers in Social Life* (1985), need for warning systems; Jaime Nogueiro Pinto, ed., *Portugal no ano 2.000* (Braga, 1980) new international economic order; Gonzalo H. Garland, Associate Researcher, Grupo de Análisis para el Desarrollo (GRADE), Lima, letter, December 1, 1987, on the President of Peru in December 1986 asking for a "National Project that would lead us to the change of a century in a preestablished way, instead of arriving to year 2000 by accident and with no clear directions"; O. A. El-Kholy, Senior Adviser, Kuwait Institute for Scientific Research, Safat, letter, September 7, 1987, on active speculation about life in the year 2000 now that the "easy-going atmosphere of the 70's has come to an end"; *Futurable (Buenos Aires)* 1 (1979–) published by the Fundación Argentina Año 2000; Ismail-Sabri Abdalla et al., *Images of the Arab Future*, trans. Maissa Talaat (NY, 1983) 207, on the series of studies, "Egypt in the Year 2000"; Andrew Kopkind, "The future-planners," *American Psychologist* 22 (Nov. 1967) 1036 on "Mankind 2000" conference in 1966 in London, and see Brian McConnell, *Britain in the Year 2000* (London, 1970) cover blurb, "from pollution and over-population to the final apocalypse of social breakdown"; Geza Kovács, "On the history of Hungarian future research (1965–1980)," in *Future Research in Hungary*, eds. Ervin Bona et al. (Budapest, 1983) 15, on 1979 request by Hungarian National Planning Board for a long-term plan 1981–2000; George Chaplin and Glenn D. Paige, eds., *Hawaii 2000* (Honolulu, 1973), the first such state report; Huang Qing, "Chinese scholars take a look at the future," *China Daily* (Dec. 3, 1986), prospects for Fujian in 2000, and Zheng Guanglin, "The China 2000 study: a personal view," *Futures Research Quarterly* 1 (Spring 1985) 7–12, and Annie Batlle, *Les travailleurs du futur* (Paris, 1986) 286, on the 1983 conference at Huang Mountain on "China in the Year 2000"; "Spécial 2000," *L'Express (Paris)* (Jan. 5, 1980) 31–53, satire; Amadou-Mahtar M'Bow et al., *Suicide or Survival: The Challenge of the Year 2000* (Paris, 1978), UNESCO roundtable; Organisation of African Unity, *What Kind of Africa by the Year 2000? Final Report of the Monrovia Symposium* (Addis Ababa, 1979) esp. 6, Edern Kodjo: "in our own hearts we dream that we can get out of our predicament alone"; I. Bestuzhev-Lada, undated handwritten note, 1987, inside cover of his *Essai de futurologie* (Moscow, 1985), translated into German, Danish, Polish, etc., as *The World in the Year 2000*, optimistic, and cf. V. V. Kosolapov, *Mankind and the Year 2000* (Moscow, 1976); Council on Environmental Quality of the Department of State, *The Global 2000 Report to the President*, director Gerald O. Barney (Washington, D.C., 1980), bleak.

30. André Cournand, "A futurologist considers the past," in *Future Life*, ed. Michel Salomon, trans. Guy Daniels (NY, 1983) 3; Armytage, *Yesterday's Tomorrows*, 202, quoting Wendell E. Moore's 1966 presidential address to the American Sociological Association, "The future is the cause of the present in substantial degree"; Pierre Wack, "Scenarios: uncharted waters ahead," *Harvard Business Review* 63 (Sept.–Oct. 1985) 73; Howard Zimmerman, editorial introduction to first issue of *Future* 1 (April 1978) 4; Shepherd Mead, *How to Get to the Future Before It Gets to You* (NY, 1974); Robert Scholes, *Structural Fabulation: An Essay on Fiction of the Future* (Notre Dame, 1975) 75; Ferdinand Lundberg, *The Coming World Transformation* (Garden City, NY, 1963) 38, quoting Jacob Bronowski on "All living things"; Richard H. Popkin, "Predicting, prophecying, divining and foretelling from Nostradamus to Hume," *History of European Ideas* 5 (1984) 130, and cf. Benjamin Akzin, "On conjecture in political science," *Political Studies* 14 (1966) 1–14; Daniel Bell, ed., *Toward the Year 2000: Work in Progress* (Boston, 1968) 22; Bruce Mazlish, "Promise them anything but give them a propaedeutic scenario," in "The future isn't what it used to be," *Horizon* 16 (Summer 1974) 39–40; Stuart A. Sandow, *The Pedagogical Structure of Methods for Thinking about the Future* (Syracuse, 1970) on cross-purpose matrices; Gian Paolo Tozzolli, *La tentazione profetica: Analisi storica e filosofica previsionale* (Bologna, 1978) 173–219, listing futurological methods; François Hetman, *Le langage de la prévision* (Paris, 1969) esp. 201 on "prognoseology"; W. L. Swager, "Technological forecasting in R & R," *Chemical Engineering Progress* 65 (Dec. 1969) 39 on envelope curves; Olaf Helmer, *The Delphi Method* (Los Angeles, 1966), and see RAND Corporation, *Delphi and Long-Range Forecasting* (Santa Monica, 1988) a bibliography.

31. Ignatius F. Clarke, *The Pattern of Expectation, 1644–2001* (NY, 1979) 167ff. on the late 19th century, as also H. G. Wells, "Discovery of the future," *Nature* 65 (Feb. 6, 1902) 326–31; Philippe Girardet, *Le professeur d'avenir* (Paris, 1928); Archibald M. Low, *The Future* (NY, 1925); Richard Lewinsohn, *Science, Prophecy, and Prediction*, trans. Arnold J. Pomerans (NY, 1961) 111 on the advent of horoscopes in newspapers in the 1920s and see Fritz Lang's 1925 film, *Metropolis*, set in the year 2000; Roger W. Babson, *Looking Ahead Fifty Years* (NY, 1942) esp. 44 on his first forecasting in 1900; Ossip Flechtheim, "Warum Futurologie?" *Futurum* 1 (1968) 3–22, concise history of futurology from the invention of the word itself in 1946, and cf. Flechtheim's *History and Futurology* (Meisenheim am Glan, 1966) written 1941–51; *CIBA Symposium on the Future as an Academic Discipline* (Amsterdam, 1975) 5–7, 35–36; Batlle, *Les travailleurs du futur*; Bernard Cazes, *Histoire des futurs* (Paris, 1986) ch. 9; Stanislaw Lem, *The Futurological Congress*, trans. Michael Kandel (NY, 1974 [1971]) 146 on "soothseers"; John H. Goldthorpe, "Theories of industrial society: reflections on the recrudescence of historicism and the future of futurology," *Archives européennes de sociologie* 12 (1971) 263–88; Kevin Sanders, moderator, "Margaret Mead, Herman Kahn, and Bill Thompson look toward the year 2000," *Politicks, & Other Human Interests* 1 (April 11, 1978) 4; Herman Kahn et al., *The Next 200 Years* (NY, 1976); John Naisbitt, *Megatrends* (NY, 1982); S. Kotlobye and L. Tetskaya, eds., *The Year 2017, Past, Present, and Future*, trans. A. Shkarovsky (Moscow, 1968) 7, 9; Murad Saifulin, ed., *The Future of Society: A Critique of Modern Bourgeois*

Philosophical and Socio-Political Conceptions (Moscow, 1973) esp. 10–13, 313, 343; Valentina V. Ivasheva, *On the Threshold of the Twenty-First Century*, trans. Doris Bradbury and Natalie Ward (Moscow, 1978) 27; Attila Ágh, "The future as history in a Marxist perspective," in Bona, ed., *Future Research in Hungary*, 64 for quote. On the illusion of command, see Helga Nowotny, "Science and utopia: on the social ordering of the future," in *Nineteen Eighty-Four: Science Between Utopia and Dystopia*, eds. Everett Mendelsohn and Nowotny (Dordrecht, 1984) 3–18; Bell, *Toward the Year 2000*, 143, 253. For critiques of futurology, see esp. Eberhard Klumpp, *Verführung in die Zukunft: Von Irrweg der Futurologie* (Köln, 1970); Georges Elgozy, *Le bluff du futur* (Paris, 1974); J. Scott Armstrong, "The seer-sucker theory: the value of experts in forecasting," *Technology Review* 82 (June/July 1980) 18–24, and cf. his *Long-Range Forecasting: From Crystal Ball to Computer* (NY, 1978) with 88 pages of bibliography. A useful self-critique is F. G. Withington's "Backcast," *Datamation* 31 (July 1, 1985) 124–34. For the future of futurology, see Michael Marien, "Toward a new futures research," *Futures Research Quarterly* 1 (Spring 1985) introductory essay. For a splendid satire of futurism (and futurology) in art, see Ronald A. Knox, *Memories of the Future* (NY, 1923?) 202–03.

32. Tony Russo, letter, May 12, 1988; Hans Küng, *Theology for the Third Millennium*, trans. Peter Heinegg (NY, 1988). Magazine publishers have also begun to appreciate the titular magic of the year (or number) 2000: the Korean 2000-*yŏn* (Seoul), the Arabic 2000/*Alfān* (London), the Belgian *Gestion 2000* (Liège), the English 2000 A.D. (London) and *Millennium: Journal of International Studies* (London School of Economics). Contrast the title of a new and less sanguine German periodical, inaugurated in 1988 and oriented toward critical social history, 1999: *Zeitschrift für Sozialgeschichte des 20. und 21. Jahrhunderts* (Hamburg). "We are not interested in futurology," Dr. Angelika Ebbinghaus, the editor, assured me in a letter of April 27, 1988.

33. Byron K. Ledgerwood, "Short product life cycle problems," *Control Engineering* (April 1988) 162; "Bush text: 'Stakes are high and choice is crucial,' " *Los Angeles Times* (Aug. 19, 1988) 6; Quayle and Dukakis quotations from television coverage of, respectively, the Republican National Convention, August 8, 1988, and the Democratic National Convention, July 20, 1988. As President, Bush on June 12, 1989, held out the promise of clean air for the year 2000.

34. C. Bobbi Hansen, "The Class of 2000," *Person-Centered Review* 3, 1 (Feb. 1988) 7–8; Nintendo of America, *Official Nintendo Player's Guide* (1987) 52; Future Problem Solving Program newsletter, *Footnotes (Laurinburg, NC)* 9 (May 1987) 4; "Earth Star Voyager (Disney Sunday Movie)," *Variety* (Jan. 27, 1988) 76, aired January 10th.

35. The present popularity of names traditionally related to apocalyptic motifs of deluge and redemption is my personal impression. Barbara Kay Turner, *Name That Baby* (NY, 1988) 14, gives the name frequency for NY babies born 1986—Michael (1st), Christopher (2nd), David (4th), Daniel (5th), Joshua (6th) among males, and Jessica (1st), Jennifer (4th), Christina (14th) among females; on Jonah, see also John Berger's screenplay of a film directed by Alain Tanner, *Jonah Who Will be 25 in the Year 2000*, trans. Michael Palmer (Berkeley, 1983). On neurology, see David Loye, "The brain and the future," *Futurist* (Oct. 1982) 15–19, and cf. Maurice Maeterlinck, "The foretelling of the future," *Fortnightly Review* 78 (1902) 241. On children's attitudes to the future, see Anne B. Crabbe, ed., *Thinking Ahead: Teaching for the Future* (Laurinburg, NC, 1987) 3–5, 8–16; Paul Vieille, "Les enfants et l'an

2000," *Revue 2000* (Dec. 1968–June 1969) reported in Decouflé, *L'An 2000*, 178–81; Thomas Kutsch, *Die Welt im Jahr 2000* (Kronberg Ts., 1974); H. Ornauer et al., eds., *Images of the World in the Year 2000: A Comparative Ten Nation Study* (Atlantic Highlands, NJ, 1976). On future promise, see Paula Taylor, *The Kids' Whole Future Catalog* (NY, 1982) 7, 44 *et passim*, and "Happy holidays: the year 2000," *Senior Scholastic* (Dec. 16, 1975) 3–6.

36. Gabriel Fragnière, ed., *Education Without Frontiers: A Study of the Future of Education from the European Cultural Foundation's "Plan Europe 2000"* (London, 1976); Sherry Turkle, *The Second Self: Computers and the Human Spirit* (NY, 1984) 87–88.

37. Cullen Murphy, introduction to *Change Magazine*'s *The Third Century* (n.p., 1977) 6— and even so, most of the contributors to the anthology focused on the year 2000; John Strong, *The Doomsday Globe*, 2nd ed. (Kensington, New South Wales, 1977 [1973]) 110, and cf. Morris Ernst, *Utopia 1976* (NY, 1955) 11, a book "first aimed to hit the target year 2000"; "Fin de siècle," *Spectator* 68 (Jan. 9, 1892) 52.

38. Searching serial data bases 1984–87 at the University of Wisconsin, the director of Basic Choices, Inc. (1023 Drake St., Madison, WI 53715-1609) found more than five thousand articles relating to the year 2000 or the Millennium; a computer search for books 1977–87 yielded six hundred titles. John Ohliger, letters, June 19, July 9, and July 10, 1988, with appended computer printouts, and annotated bibliography, "Millennia: the past, the present issues, and the future of adult education." My own highly conservative estimate of the number of articles worldwide since 1950 explicitly devoted to concerns about the year 2000 would be around fifteen thousand, and the number of books around two thousand.

On "perpetual" calendars, see Sherrard B. Burnaby, *Elements of the Jewish and Muhammadan Calendars* (London, 1901) vi. On "long-range" planning, Ikram Azam, an adult student in the Studies of the Future program at the University of Houston, Clear Lake, tells me in a letter, January 12, 1988, that the "foreseeable future" is there taken to be 2–3 years for "short term," 5–7 years for "medium term," and 10–15 years for "long term." Quotation from Walter Besant, *Autobiography*, ed. S. S. Sprigge (NY, 1902) 21. For other explanations of the present significance of the year 2000, see Michael Barkun, "Divided apocalypse: thinking about the end in contemporary America," *Soundings* 66 (1983) 257–80; Engbert G. Vander Werff, *Utopia or Doom: A Study in Locating the Millennium* (London, Ontario, 1978) iii, 68–78.

39. Ann Hagedorn, "To mark the year 2000, some events will be out of this world," *Wall Street Journal* (June 27, 1988) 1:4, 4:4; Richard W. Noone, *5/5/2000. Ice: The Ultimate Disaster* (NY, 1986 [1982]); Millennium Society, promotional brochure accompanying invitation to the Millennium Ball, New York City, New Year's Eve, 1988 (a Society tradition since 1984, proceeds going to scholarships to promote world peace); Mark Hensen, interview, Washington, D.C., October 15, 1987; Edward E. McNally, interview, New York City, October 24, 1987. The first call for a big celebration of the year 2000 may have come from the World Millennial Association or World Association for Celebrating Year 2000, founded in 1963 (and prematurely defunct?), and directed from London by Gerry Carter, who has not answered my inquiries; cf. David Kucharsky, "The Bimillennial—a great year coming," *Christianity Today* (Jan. 3, 1975) 4–6.

40. Erik Iversen, *The Myth of Egypt and Its Hieroglyphs in European Tradition* (Copenhagen, 1971) esp. 67–71, 116–18; Francesco Colonna, *Hypnerotomachia Poliphili* (Venice, 1499), translated (by Robert Dallyngton?) as *The Strife of Love in a Dream*, new ed., Andrew Lang (London, 1890 [1592]) 15 for quotes, spelling modernized; Frances A. Yates, *The Rosicrucian Enlightenment* (London, 1975) ch. 15; David Stevenson, *The Origins of Freemasonry* (Cambridge, 1988) esp. 79–85; James S. Curl, *The Egyptian Revival* (London, 1982); Richard C. Carrott, *The Egyptian Revival* (Berkeley, 1978) 8, 11, 30, 52–53; Hillel Schwartz, "On reading the tarot," *Brick* 34 (Fall 1988) 55–60; Musée d'art et d'histoire, Geneva, *Les architectes visionnaires de la fin du XVIIIᵉ siècle* (Geneva, 1965); Mona Ozouf, *La fête révolutionnaire, 1789–1799* (Paris, 1976) plate 5; Laurence Goldstein, *Ruins and Empire* (Pittsburgh, 1977) 144, Volney quote; Tompkins, *Secrets of the Great Pyramid*, 44–50 on Napoleon; Frederick L. Harvey, *A History of the Washington National Monument* (Washington, D.C., 1903) 15 for quote; Dr. Aiken [= John Aikin], "To his Excellency George Washington," *The American Ladies Pocket Book for the Year 1801* (Philadelphia, 1800) 103; Mark C. Taylor, "Archetexture of pyramids," *Assemblage* 5 (1988) 17–28.

41. Bourchier Wrey Savile, *Prophecies and Speculations Respecting the End of the World*, 2nd ed. (London, 1883) preface on pyramidology; Tompkins, *Secrets of the Great Pyramid*, 70ff.; Georges Bataille, *Visions of Excess*, ed. and trans. A. Stoekl et al. (Minneapolis, 1985) 213–22, Nietzsche on 219, from his *Ecce Homo*, for which see the translation by Walter Kaufmann (NY, 1967) 295; Helen Wright, *James Lick's Monument* (NY, 1987); Curl, *Egyptian Revival*, 194; Fred T. Jane, "Guesses at futurity," *Pall Mall Magazine* 4 (1894) 289, and 5 (1895) 161, 342, and 6 (1895) 97 for Janus; Camille Flammarion, "Last days of the earth," *Contemporary Review* 59 (April 1891) 558–69.

42. Sakakura Associates, "Yokohama Doll Museum," *Japan Architecture* 61 (Oct. 1986) 44–48; "Kristallpyramiden," *Connaissance des Arts* (Dec. 1985) 39; François Chaslin, "Eaux baptismales," *L'Architecture d'aujourd'hui* 258 (Sept. 1988) 33, I. M. Pei's pyramid; Michael Graves, "Dolphin and Swan Hotels," *Contemporary Architecture* 58, 7–8 (1988) 61–62; Stevens Anderson, "Solid geometry and deconstruction," *Architecture* (July 1988) 88–89, Mount's house; "Mummy, mummy, what's that?" *Life* 9 (Oct. 1986) 6, Wordsworth pyramid; Richard C. Hoagland, *The Monuments of Mars* (Berkeley, 1987); "Pacific Design Center expansion," *Progressive Architecture* 68 (Jan. 1987) 92–93; P. Failing, "L.A. gets a new temple of art," *Art News* (Nov. 1986) 88–94. Cf. Ulrich Kowalski's *Wohnpyramide* in *Terrassenturm und Sonnenhugel: Internationale Experimente für die Stadt 2000*, eds. Robert Jungk and Werner Filmer (Düsseldorf, 1970) 18.

43. Transamerica television commercial aired December 1987; Dow Corning ad in *Architectural Record* 176 (Oct. 1988) 48; American Appraisal ad in *Harvard Business Review* 63 (Sept.–Oct. 1985) 67; Pyramid Products, *Catalog* (March 1986). See also the pyramids of General Products Headquarters, c. 2100 A.D., in David Stableford and David Langford, *The Third Millennium: A History of the World* A.D. 2000–3000 (NY, 1985) 27.

44. On crystals, see esp. Joy Gardner, "Healing with obsidian," *The New Times (Seattle)* (Oct. 1987) 32, from her book, *The Magik of Crystals*; Randall N. Baer and Vicki W. Baer, *Windows of Light: Using Quartz Crystals as Tools for Self-Transformation* (San Francisco, 1984). On the pyramid debate, see Pyramid Products, *Catalog*, front page, quote; Erich von Däniken, *Chariots of the Gods?*, trans. Michael Heron (NY, 1969) ch. 7; Martin Isler, "On pyramid

building," *Journal of the American Research Center in Egypt* 22 (1985) 129–42. On energy, see Lawrence Badash, "Radium, radioactivity, and the popularity of scientific discovery," *American Philosophical Society Proceedings* 122, 3 (1978) 145–54; Bell, *Toward the Year 2000*, 24 for Deutsch; Heinz Knoepfel, *Energy 2000* (NY, 1986) esp. vii, 10; James W. Carey and John J. Quirk, "The mythos of the electronic revolution," *American Scholar* 39 (1970) 219–41, 395–424.

45. Kurt Mendelssohn, *The Riddle of the Pyramids* (NY, 1974) 198; Ritchie Calder, *After the Seventh Day* (NY, 1961) 297 on radioactive waste; Jamake Highwater, "Spirit dwellings," *Omni* (May 1988) 64ff. John Shirley's *A Splendid Chaos* (NY, 1988) fuses all the themes of this chapter: for the sake of drama, beings from 31 planets have been abducted and placed on Fool's Hope by the Meta, floating Masonic pyramids with floating apical eyes. The Meta tell Zero, the human hero, that Chaos Theory is close to describing how God operates within the universe.

46. José Argüelles, *The Transformative Vision* (Boulder, 1975) Appendices A, B; idem, *The Mayan Factor* (Santa Fe, 1987) 9, 16, 25, 41, 59, 114. On the Mayan calendar, see esp. Nancy M. Farriss, "Remembering the future, anticipating the past: history, time and cosmology among the Maya of Yucatan," *Comparative Studies in Society and History* 29 (1987) 566–93.

47. Argüelles, *Mayan Factor*, 158, 173, 178, 182, 192.

48. *Ibid.*, 131, 159, 169, 170–71.

49. *Ibid.*, 33, 135, 193–94.

50. Jonathan Weisman, "New Age dawning on fewer than expected," *Los Angeles Times* (Aug. 16, 1987) I, 38, with follow-up, "New Age believers greet a new day" (Aug. 17, 1987) V, 1; Karen Cos, "Harmonic Convergence: the prophecies," in Healing Our World leaflet, "Harmonic Convergence, World Harmony Days, August 16–17, 1987" (Palo Alto, 1987); Bob Mendel, "The Harmonic Convergence," *Master of Life* (1987 promotional paper for New Age entrepreneur Dick Sutphen) 14; Argüelles, *Mayan Factor*, 42. Cf. Daniel C. Noel, "Ironic convergence: nuclear numbing and New Age scientism," *Artifex* 7, 4 (Winter 1988) 29–34.

51. Bill Barol and Pamela Abramson, "The end of the world (again)," *Newsweek* (Aug. 17, 1987) 70–71; Ruth Blackwell Rogers, letter, Sept. 1987, in brochure for Eagle's Nest Camp (Pisgah Forest, NC, 1988).

52. J. M. Cohen, ed. and trans., *The Four Voyages of Christopher Columbus* (Harmondsworth, 1969) 52–53; Paul Loeb, *Nuclear Culture* (Philadelphia, 1986 [1982]) 189; John T. Winterich, "Father Time's big night out," *Nation's Business* 37 (Jan. 1949) 50; John Larner, "The certainty of Columbus," *History* 73 (Feb. 1988) 5; Byron A. Brooks, *Earth Revisited [in 1992]* (Boston, 1893) 95–96 on lights from Mars; Robert Silverberg, *World's Fair, 1992* (Chicago, 1970), and note that Ray Bradbury's famous *Martian Chronicles* (1950) begin in January 1999; Arthur M. Schlesinger, Jr., *The Cycles of American History* (Boston, 1986) 24, 47; Dakota James, *Greenhouse: It Will Happen in 1997* (NY, 1984) 10, for 1992.

53. The truly millennial event of 1992 may be the (scheduled) full integration of the European (Economic) Community.

54. *Oxford English Dictionary*, V, 409, s.v. "International," and Supp. I., 1240, s.v. "Global"; W. Warren Wagar, *The City of Man: Prophecies of a World Civilization in Twentieth-Century Thought* (Boston, 1963) esp. 52; Logical Language Group, Inc., leaflet "Announcing Lojban" (Fairfax, VA, 1988?), and see "Loglan GPA has begun," *Ju'i Lobypli* 4 (Feb. 1988); Special Issue on "Future computing: problems and solutions in the '90s," *Computer Design* 25 (July 1986) 49–137, quote on 113; James B. Irwin, letter, May 25, 1988. Note that Dr. John Lilly, in another sort of universal language project, used the acronym JANUS, Joint Analog Numerical Understanding System, for his work toward reliable human-dolphin communication.

55. Karen, *Toward the Year* 2000, 35, 38, 47, and see Business International Corporation, *Toward an Unlimited Future: A Report of the Global One Hundred* (NY, 1983); Martin Jay, *Marxism and Totality* (Berkeley, 1984) 536; Robert Evans, "The Power of Faith/The Planet Is Alive" videocassette (New Orleans, 1987), kindly provided me by Mark Hensen, and cf. Pierre Teilhard de Chardin, *The Future of Man*, trans. Norman Denny (NY, 1964), transitional to Alexander Everett et al., "2000 A.D.: Future Perspective. Panel Discussion I," audiocassette (San Francisco, Feb. 28, 1976) quote from David Spangler; James Lovelock, *Gaia* (Oxford, 1982); Richard A. Kerr, "No longer willful, Gaia becomes respectable," *Science* 240 (April 22, 1988) 393–95; Rex Wyler, "The global brain," *New Age (Allston, MA)* 8 (June 1983) 48–53; Richard A. Falk, *A Study of Future Worlds* (NY, 1975) xxvi, preface by Saul Mendlovitz, and 2, quoting from *The New Yorker* (Dec. 10, 1973) 38. See also *Interaction*, newsletter of the Global Tomorrow Coalition (Washington, D.C.), and Theodore H. Von Laue, "Responsibility over mindset," *Perspectives* 26 (Jan. 1988) 15, urging the American Historical Association that "Sensible history must be global history."

56. Arnold J. Toynbee wrote in *Janus at Seventy-Five* (NY, 1964) 1, "Every human being is a Janus. 'We look before and after.' " There are nonetheless wide cultural differnces in the personal experience of time and the sense of past and future. I am fully aware that the scope of my book has led to blanket statements that might well be reconsidered from more regional or more rigidly socioeconomic perspectives. The most apt cautionary studies are Thomas J. Cottle and Stephen L. Klineberg, *The Present of Things Future: Explorations of Time in Human Experience* (NY, 1974) esp. ch. 8 on working-class experience; Magoroh Maruyama and Arthur M. Harkins, eds., *Cultures of the Future* (The Hague, 1978) esp. essay by James Gifford on Mayan concepts of the future; Dale F. Eickelmann, "Time in a complex society: a Moroccan example," *Ethnology* 16 (1977) 39–56; Clifford Geertz, *Person, Time and Conduct in Bali* (New Haven, 1966); Derek Wright, "Flux and form: the geography of time in 'The Beautiful Ones Are Not Yet Born,' " *Ariel* 17, 2 (1986) 63–77; John S. Mbiti, "The concept of time as a key to the understanding and interpretation of African religions and philosophy," in his *African Religions and Philosophy* (London, 1969) 15–28, an exposition still under debate; James A. Mau, *Social Change and Images of the Future: A Study of the Pursuit of Progress in Jamaica* (Cambridge, MA, 1987).

These studies, however, must themselves be subjected to the critiques of Johannes Fabian, who argues (in *Time and the Other: How Anthropology Makes Its Object* [New York, 1983]) that assertions or assumptions of temporal distance between peoples are imperial denials of the fundamental coevalness—the shared time—necessary to all communication. Anthropologists' "allochronic discourse" makes anthropology too often "a science of other men in another Time." This, claims Fabian, is a scandal, for "Anthropology's Other is, ultimately, other people who are our contemporaries" (p. 143). It is probably true, for example, that people in different environments, or with different religious or political commitments, or of different classes of society have differently mixed emotions about the approach of the year 2000, but I *am* presuming (as perhaps I could not have presumed at any other *fin de siècle*) a fundamental coevalness in the anticipation of this coming calendrical millennium.

57. Italo Calvino, *Six Memos for the Next Millennium*, trans. Patrick Creagh (Cambridge, MA, 1988) Esther Calvino's "A note on the text" and p. 1, quoted with the permission of Harvard University Press.

58. Italo Calvino, *Cosmicomics*, trans. William Weaver (NY, 1968 [1965]) esp. 97–112 on dinosaurs; idem, *Castle of Crossed Destinies*, trans. William Weaver (NY, 1977 [1969]); idem, *Invisible Cities*, trans. William Weaver (NY, 1974 [1972]) quote about Eudoxia on 97; idem, *Six Memos*, 1. Calvino is quoted on the front cover of the paperback edition (Toronto, 1984) of Ilya Prigogine's *Order Out of Chaos*, which Calvino evidently called "A passionate meditation on Man and Universe."

59. Calvino, *Six Memos*, 106, 116.

60. Suzanne Fleischman, *The Future in Thought and Language* (Cambridge, 1982) 129, 140–44; Frederik L. Polak, *The Image of the Future* (Leiden, 1967) 43, 49, and throughout; Harold S. Irwin, *Evolution of Futures Trading* (Madison, WI, 1954); Thomas H. Thompson, "Are we obligated to future others?" in *Responsibilities to Future Generations*, ed. Ernest Partridge (Buffalo, 1980) 197; Ronald Fernandez, ed., *The Future as a Social Problem* (Santa Monica, 1977).

61. [British Royal Society of Arts], "Life in the year 2,000," *New York Times Magazine* (Dec. 26, 1954) 8, the plop; Charles E. Maine, *Crisis 2000* (London, 1958 [1955]) on Saturnians; Judith Martin, "The Proper Way to Turn a Century," talk given to the Friends of the Schlesinger Library, Cronkite Graduate Center, Radcliffe College, Cambridge, MA, May 7, 1987; F. M. Esfandiary, "Transhumans—2000," in *Woman in the Year 2000*, ed. Maggie Tripp (NY, 1974) 332–35, and on his name change to FM-2030, see Connie Koenen, "Are you ready?" *Los Angeles Times* (Jan. 11, 1989) V, 1; Russell M. Griffin, *Century's End* (NY, 1981) 43 on Sinbad Schwartz; Ruth Norman, *Preview for the Spacefleet Landing on Earth in 2001 A.D.* (El Cajon, 1987) 15, 83ff., and ABC-TV report on UNARIUS in segment of "A Current Affair," aired January 28, 1988; Colleen McCullough, *A Creed for the Third Millennium* (NY, 1985) 25; W. P. Jeffery, Jr., *Unless* (NY, 1975) 15–16, 21; John B. Clark, "Recollections of the twentieth century," *Atlantic Monthly* 89 (Jan. 1902) 4–5; Robert Silverberg, "Thomas the Proclaimer," in his *Born with the Dead* (NY, 1974) 99–181. We do "know" that by the year 2000, according to standing treaties, Hong Kong will be under Chinese control (1997) and the Panama Canal under Panamanian control (2000). Are these also millennial fictions?

62. Calvino, *Six Memos*, 12, 29.

63. Walter Benjamin, "Theses on the philosophy of history," in his *Illuminations*, ed. Hannah Arendt, trans. Harry Zohn (NY, 1955) 257; Calvino, *Six Memos*, 51.

64. Arthur Hobhouse, "Battle of the centuries," *Contemporary Review* 77 (March 1900) 410; Winterich, "Father Time's big night out," 50; Hayes B. Jacobs, "Warning: new century ahead," *The New Yorker* 39 (April 27, 1963) 142; Calvino, *Six Memos*, 77. Cf. Arthur C. Clarke in *Hawaii* 2000, eds. Chaplin and Paige, 82, suggesting that we declare "the whole of 2000 a holiday. If we make it to there, we'll be fully justified." See also George H. Pollock, "On time and anniversaries," in *The Unconscious Today*, ed. Mark Kanzer (NY, 1971) 233–57; Ira Mintz, "The anniversary reaction," *Journal of the American Psychoanalytic Association* 19 (1971) 720–35.

65. Calvino, *Six Memos*, 84–85; Sheldon R. Isenberg and Gene R. Thursby, "Esoteric anthropology: 'devolutionary' and 'evolutionary' orientations in perennial philosophy," *Religious Traditions* 7–9 (1981–86) 177–225 on the modern human image.

66. Mikhail Bakhtin, *Rabelais and His World*, trans. Helene Iswolsky (Cambridge, MA, 1968) on the role of carnival; cited by Calvino, *Six Memos*, 117, and quote on 124. Cf., on generations, John J. McDermott, "Do not bequeath a shamble: the child in the twenty-first century—innocent hostage to mindless oppression; or, children as messengers to the world," in his *Streams of Experience* (Amherst, 1986) 169–79.

67. Doris Lessing, *Documents Relating to the Sentimental Agents in the Volyen Empire* (NY, 1983) 8, 23 on Rhetorical Diseases; Oren Lyons, "The seventh generation yet unborn," *Futurist* (March–April 1988) 60.

68. Letty Cottin Pogrebin, "Born free: a feminist fable," in Tripp, *Woman in the Year* 2000, 31, 35, 42, and quote from Tripp herself, 26. Cf. Virginia Kidd, ed., *Millennial Women* (NY, 1978); Kathy Keeton, *Woman of Tomorrow* (NY, 1985); Zoë Fairbanks, *Benefits* (London, 1979), grimmest but most politically sophisticated book about women in the future.

For the rest of this paragraph, Maggie Gee, *The Burning Book* (NY, 1983) 67; Yana Friedman, interview, Paris, July 20, 1987; Michel Godet, interview, Paris, July 21, 1987; Edith Hamilton, *Mythology* (NY, 1942) 31–32, and see Whitley Strieber, *Communion* (NY, 1987) 285, using Hecate to the same purpose; Christine Downing, *What Use Are Poets in a Time of Need? Fourth Annual Memorial Lecture of the Society for Values in Higher Education*, delivered at St. Mary's College, Notre Dame, IN, 1985, and printed in *Soundings* (1986) 301–17, quotes from 315–17.

69. Daniel C. Noel, RR1, Box 43, Brattleboro, VT 05301, "Lyonesse Letter #1," August 11, 1988; idem, *Approaching Earth: A Search for the Mythic Significance of the Space Age* (Amity, NY, 1986); Carl Oglesby, "Life at the end of the road: Jungians at the Apocalypse," *New Age (Brookline, MA)* 9 (Sept. 1983) 42–47ff., quote on 44. For models and theories of celebration, see Victor Turner, ed., *Celebration: Studies in Festivity and Ritual* (Washington, D.C., 1982).

A SNAPSHOT IN A.D. 3000.

Illustration by Henry Hewitt to *What's the World Coming To?* by Archibald
M. Low (London, 1951). By permission of Burke Publishing Co., Ltd.

INDEX
or, Cast of Thousands

Due to the exigencies of the End, names of places, titles of literary works, and passing references to planets have generally been excluded from this Index. However, because calendars themselves have in this book taken on a supernal significance, the Index has as prelude a list of references to centurial, prophetic, and millennial numbers and years.

Lifton, Robert Jay, 219
Lincoln, Abraham, 171
Lindsey, Hal, 206
Little Ice Age, 108
Livy (Titus Livius), 23
Locke, John, 119, 121, 125, 138
logarithms, 110
Lojban, 285–86
Lollards, 92
Loompanics Unlimited, 220
Lopez, Jacinto, 179
Lorenzo the Magnificent, 77–78, 81
Louis I of Anjou, 64
Louis XIV of France, 113–14, 121
Louis XV of France, 134
Love, Christopher, 132
Lovelock, James, 286
Low, Seth, 169
Lowell, Amy, 181
Lowell, Percival, 181, 229
Loye, David, 262
Lucius II, Pope, 52
Ludi Saeculares. See Secular Games
Lusson twins, 228
lustra, 26
Luther, Martin, 90, 92, 277
Lutherans, 90
Lyonesse, 294

M, the number, 36
Maccabees, the, 10, 23
McCullough, Colleen, 289
Machiavelli, Niccolò, 87–88
Mackay, Charles, 5
MacKaye, Steele, 164
McKinley, William, 163
MacLaine, Shirley, 232
McNally, Edward E., 276
Macy, Joanna, 220, 225
Madden, Samuel, 269
Magdeburg Centuries, 93–94
magic, 82–83, 104, 106; ritual, 72; spiritual, 89
magnetism, 108, 183
Mahdi, the, 45–46, 77
mahdism, 45–46, 77, 173, 207, 208

mal du siècle, 148–50, 152
Malachy, St., 266, 268
Malthus, Thomas, 149
Mandelbrot, Benoit, 261, 262
Mann, Heinrich, 158
Mann, Thomas, 158, 203
Marceau, François, 277
Marconi, Guglielmo, 163, 180
Marcus Aurelius, Emperor, 24
Maria Christina of Sachsen-Teschen, 277
Marlowe, Christopher, 105
Maroons, revolt of, 108
Marquis, Don, 249
Marranos, 75
Mars, 156, 172, 180–84, 195, 228–30, 237, 248, 263, 268, 285, 340n.262, 353n.52; as America, 185; face on, 229–30, 279; the god, 118
"Marseillaise, La," 134
Martians, 97, 180–82
Martin, Judith, 288
Marx, Karl, 204, 233, 272
Marxists, 15
Masada, 208, 307n.35
Maskelyne, John Nevil, 213
Mason, John, 116
Mason, R. Osgood, 214
masonry. *See* Freemasonry
mathematics, 13, 75, 230, 261; as the language of truth, 111, 126–27
Mather, Cotton, 123, 124
Mauthner, Fritz, 161, 162
"Max Headroom," 350n.31
Mayan Factor, The, 280–82
Mayans, 226, 259, 280
Mayfreda di Piravano, 59–60
Medici, Catherine de', 97, 99
Medici, Maria de', 102
medievalism, 258
Medway, Lord, 192
Melanchthon, Philipp, 90, 92, 318n.112
Melusine, 73
memory, 105; loss of, 218, 224–25
Mendelssohn, Kurt, 280
Mendelssohn, Moses, 204
Mendlovitz, Saul, 286

FINISH LINE

In such a period as the present, when the state of society is so disturbed, when the minds of men are so generally set afloat, and when so many ancient landmarks, so many standards of opinion and practice, are thrown down; when ambition, avarice, and sensuality deliberate and decree, and violence and cruelty are charged with the execution, throughout a great part of the civilized world, a contemplative and serious mind cannot but ask, *What shall the end of these things be?*

Timothy Dwight,
A Discourse on Some Events of the Last Century (1801)

BOOK MARK

The text of this book was set in the typeface Garamond
No. 3 with display in Bernhard Bold Condensed by PennSet,
Inc., Bloomsburg, Pennsylvania.

It was printed on 50 lb. Heritagebook Antique
and bound by R. R. Donnelley, Harrisonburg, Virginia.

Designed by Bonni Leon